Engraved by F. Halpin. From a Painting by J. Comerford of Dublin.

The Right Hon.

JOHN PHILPOT CURRAN.

Master of the Rolls in Ireland.

J. P. Curran

THE LIFE OF

THE RIGHT HONORABLE

JOHN PHILPOT CURRAN

LATE MASTER OF THE ROLLS IN IRELAND

BY HIS SON

WILLIAM HENRY CURRAN

WITH ADDITIONS AND NOTES

BY R. SHELTON MACKENZIE, D.C.L.

NEW YORK:
W. J. WIDDLETON, PUBLISHER.

EDITOR'S PREFACE.

JOHN PHILPOT CURRAN, one of the truest patriots and greatest men ever native of Irish soil, was the centre of the sparkling wits, the renowned orators, the brilliant advocates, and the honored statesmen who flashed upon the darkness of his country's latest hours of freedom, and vainly endeavored to maintain the national independence which they had achieved for her. His life is identified with the latest years of Ireland's nationality. He manifested an independence as advocate for the accused, during the State Trials, which endeared him to the people from whose ranks he sprung. To use the words of Thomas Davis (who resembled him in many things), he was "a companion unrivalled in sympathy and wit; an orator, whose thoughts went forth like ministers of nature, with robes of light and swords in their hands; a patriot, who battled best when the flag was trampled down; and a genuine earnest man, breathing of his climate, his country, and his time."

He has been fortunate in his biographers. The life by his Son (who is yet living), contains materials which were inaccessible to other writers. Also came a volume of Recollections by Charles Phillips, who knew him well in his later years—a work which, greatly enlarged, was republished a few years ago, with all the charm of novelty. Later still appeared the Memoir, by Thomas Davis, prefixed to his edition of Curran's Speeches—a brilliant but brief tribute by one honest and gifted man to the worth and memory of another. Anterior to all these is the Memoir, by William O'Regan (the friend and contemporary of Curran, and often engaged with him in the same causes), written during Curran's lifetime, with his knowledge, if not with his direct sanction, and published within six weeks after his death—a book little known, but full of interesting personal details, and abounding with anecdotal and other illustrations of Curran's wit.

It appeared to me that there was sufficient in the career and character of Curran to interest not only the members of his own profession but a large number of general readers in this country. I have therefore taken the life by his Son, and without alterations or omissions, have introduced a large quantity of new matter, principally relating to his legislative and personal life. These additions will be found between brackets, and, with the notes which I have occasionally found it requisite to add, have made the Memoir more full of interest than any yet presented.

In the Appendix I have placed a few specimens of the wit with which Curran and his friends were wont "to set the table in a roar."

The portrait which embellishes this work is a characteristic likeness, by Comerford, of Dublin, now for the first time engraved in this country, and little known even in Ireland.

R. Shelton Mackenzie.

New York, September 20, 1855.

CONTENTS.

CHAPTER I.

CHAPTER II.

CHAPTER III.

CHAPTER IV.

CHAPTER V.

CHAPTER VI.

CHAPTER VII.

CHAPTER VIII.

CHAPTER IX.

CHAPTER X.

CHAPTER XI.

CHAPTER XII.

CHAPTER XIII.

CHAPTER XIV.

CHAPTER XV.

CHAPTER XVI.

CHAPTER XVII.

CHAPTER XVIII.

CHAPTER XIX.

APPENDIX.

LIFE OF

THE

RIGHT HON. JOHN PHILPOT CURRAN.

CHAPTER I.

Mr. Curran's origin—His parents—Early education—Originally intended for the Church—Enters Trinity College—His ardour for the classics—Letter to Mr. Stack—Anecdote of his Mother—Her Epitaph—While in College fixes on the Bar—Anecdote connected with the change of Profession—His character in College—Addicted to Metaphysics—Anecdote on the subject—Verses to Apjohn.

John Philpot Curran was born on the 24th day of July, 1750, at Newmarket, an obscure town of the county of Cork, in Ireland.* In several accounts that have been published of his origin and advancement, it has, by a general consent, been asserted that the one was very low and the other unassisted; that he was the sole architect of his own fortune, and the sole collector of the materials which were to raise it; and lovers of the marvellous implicitly believed and repeated the assertion. Let not, however, the admirers of what is rare, be offended at being told, that, no matter how much praise may be due to his personal merit (and the allowance unquestionably should not be scanty), a portion must still be given to the institutions of his country, and to those relatives and friends whose industry and protection placed him in a condition of sharing their advantages. It is of far more importance to the intellectual interests of men to diffuse a rational confidence in the

* **Newmarket is eight miles distant from the dismantled castle of Kilcolman, where Spencer is said to have composed his "Faery Queen."—M.**

efficacy of instruction, than idly to excite their wonder, and perhaps their despair, by insinuating that there are persons who, by nature, are above it. It is not by hearing that the subject of the following pages was a heaven-taught, unaided genius, that others can be encouraged to emulate his mental excellencies, but by learning the real, and to him no less creditable fact, how he studied and struggled—what models he selected—what deficiencies he corrected—by what steps he ascended; to tell this is the duty of his biographer, and not to amaze his readers by uninstructive panegyric.

The lowness* of his origin has been much exaggerated. His father, James Curran, who has been represented as an unlettered peasant, was Seneschal of a manor court at Newmarket.† It is confidently asserted, by those who knew him, that he possessed a mind and acquirements above his station; that he was familiar with the Greek and Roman classics, which he often cited in con-

* When Mr. Curran had risen to eminence, many tables of his pedigree were sent him, all of them varying, and the most of them, he conceived, too flattering to be authentic. Among his papers is the latest of these, tendered to him while he was Master of the Rolls, and made out by a resident of his native place. In the paternal line it ascends no higher than his grandfather, who is stated to have been "a north-countryman, of the county Derry, from which, having met with disappointments, he came and settled in the county Cork:" it adds, that "his only son, Mr. Curran's father, was educated at a school in Newmarket, then kept by the Rev. Mr. Dallis, and afterwards by the Rev. Mr. Morduck, by whom he was considered the best Greek and Latin scholar in their school." In the maternal line, it presents a long list of ancestors, among whom are judges, bishops, and noblemen; but Mr. Curran has marked his incredulity or his indifference by indorsing this paper with "Stemmata quid faciunt." Some other pedigrees derived his descent from the English family of Curwen in Cumberland.—C. [O'Regan, who was Curran's contemporary, and long on the most intimate terms with him, says that the family was "of an English stock, transplanted from one of the northern counties, and encouraged to settle in that part of Ireland, under the protection of the highly respectable family of the Allworth's, who retain considerable landed estates there to the present time, acquired after the fall of the Desmonds." Phillips says, that the paternal ancestor of the Curran family came over to Ireland one of Cromwell's soldiers, "and the most ardent patriot she ever had owed his origin to her most merciless and cruel plunderer!"—M.]

† The emoluments of the office were very small. The Aldworth estates at Newmarket (formerly belonging to the Irish family or clan of the McAuliffes) consisted of 32,000 acres. As Seneschal, James Curran had jurisdiction to the value of forty shillings, and thus was—a Judge!—M.

versation; that he delighted in disputation, and excelled in it; and, among his other favorite subjects of discussion, it is still remembered, that, after his son's return from college, the old man was frequently to be found in ardent contention with him upon the metaphysical doctrines of Locke.*

His mother, whose maiden name was Philpot, belonged to a family well known and respected, and of which the descendants continue in the class of gentry. She was a woman of a strong original understanding, and of admitted superiority, in the circles where she moved.† In her latter years, the celebrity of her son rendered her an object of additional attention and scrutiny; and the favorers of the opinion that talent is hereditary, thought they could discover, in the bursts of irregular eloquence that escaped her, the first visible gushings of the stream, which, expanding as it descended, at length attained a force and grandeur that incited the admirer to explore its source. This persuasion Mr. Curran himself always fondly cherished—"The only inheritance," he used to say, "that I could boast of from my poor father, was the very scanty one of an unattractive face and person like his own; and if the world has ever attributed to me something more valuable than face or person, or than earthly wealth, it was that another and a dearer parent gave her child a portion from the treasure of her mind." He attributed much of his subsequent fortune to the early influence of such a mother; and to his latest hour would dwell with grateful recollection upon the wise counsel, upon the lessons of honourable ambition, and of sober, masculine piety,

* Phillips says, "old James Curran's education was pretty much in the ratio of his income." Thomas Davis says that Curran's father had learned reading, writing, cyphering, and, it is said, some Greek and Latin.—M.

† "She was of gentle blood, and what is more to our purpose, she had a deep, fresh, womanly, irregular mind; it was like the clear river [the Avendala] of her town, that came gushing and flashing and discoursing from the lonely mountains—from the outlaw's and the fairy's home—down to the village. She had, under an exalted piety, a waste of passions and traditions lying grand and gloomy in her soul, and thence, a bright, human love of her son, came pouring out on him, and making him grow green at her feet."—Davis.

which she enforced upon the minds of her children. She was not without her reward, she lived to see the dearest of them surpassing every presage, and accumulating public honors upon a name, which she, in her station, had adorned by her virtues.

John Philpot, the eldest of their sons,* having given very early indications of an excellent capacity, the Rev. Nathaniel Boyse, the resident clergyman at Newmarket, pleased with the boy, and moved by regard for his parents, received him into his house, and by his own personal tuition initiated him in the rudiments of classical learning. This, his first acquired friend and instructor, had also the satisfaction of seeing all his care repaid by the rapidity with which its object ascended to distinction, and still more by the unceasing gratitude with which he ever after remembered the patron of his childhood. Many of this gentleman's letters to him, written at a subsequent period, remain; and it is not unpleasing to observe in them the striking revolution that a few years had effected in the fortunes of his pupil. In some of them the little villager, whom he had adopted, is seen exalted into a senator, and is solicited by his former protector to procure the enactment of a statute that might relieve himself and all of the clergy from the vexations of the tythe-laws.

The rapid progress that he made under the instructions of Mr. Boyse, and the fond predictions of his parents, determined them to give their son, what has always been a prevailing object of parental ambition in Ireland, a learned education. It was also their wish, which he did not oppose at the time, that he should eventually enter the church. With this view he was soon transferred to the free-school of Middleton, upon which occasion his generous friend insisted upon resigning a particular ecclesiastical emolument (in value 10*l.* a year) for the purpose of partly defraying the expenses of his young favorite's studies.† He remained

* Mr. Curran had three brothers and a sister, all of whom he survived.

† O'Regan says that he was "transplanted" to the school of Middleton, by Mrs.

at this school until he had attained the preparatory knowledge of the Greek and Latin languages, which should capacitate him to become a student of Trinity College, Dublin. It may not be unworthy of remark, that the same seminary had, a few years before, sent up to the capital the late Lord Avonmore, then commencing *his* career in circumstances, and with a success so resembling those of his future friend.*

The early history of eminent persons so generally contains some presaging tokens of the fortune that awaits them, that something of the kind may be expected here, yet Mr. Curran's childhood, if tradition can be credited, was not marked by much prophetic originality.† At the first little school in the town of Newmarket to which he resorted, previous to his reception into Mr. Boyse's family, he used to say that he was noted for his simplicity, and was incessantly selected as the dupe and butt of his play-fellows. This, however, it would appear that he soon laid aside, for

Aldworth. In mature life, speaking of this lady, Curran said, "It is not to be wondered at, that she does not do all that is expected of her. To be enabled so to do, nature should have supplied her with three hands. It is impossible that, stintedly furnished as she is, she could accomplish the great purposes of her heart; she is not prepared for so enlarged a charity. Such in truth is her benevolence, that she would have occasion for the constant employment of three hands; but having only two, and these always engaged, one in holding the petition of the poor, the other in wiping away the tears which flow for their distresses; and not having a third to put into her pocket for their relief, she is thus rendered incapable of administering to their wants; but still she is excellent, and her heart is bountiful."—M.

* Another of Curran's schoolfellows at Middleton, was Jeremiah Keller, subsequently well known as the witty and sardonic senior of the Munster bar. He presided, says Sheil, at their mess, "and ruled in all the autocracy of wit." Yelverton, afterwards Viscount Avonmore, and, for more than twenty-one years, Lord Chief Baron of the Exchequer, in Ireland, was fourteen years older than Curran—which leads me to doubt their having been at school together, though, no doubt, both had been educated by the same master, Mr. Carey. Robert Day, afterwards one of the Irish Judges, and a friend of Grattan's, is also said to have been Curran's schoolfellow.—M.

† Thomas Davis, who was himself from that part of Ireland, honored by Curran's birth and pupilage, gathered up many recollections of his childood, which had floated down to these later times, on the current of tradition. He reports, from there, that Curran, at school, was "a vehement boy, fonder of fun than books." He describes him as being among the hills and the streams, his father's court, the fairs, markets, and merry-makings, and his mother's lap. He learned much passion and sharpness, and some vices, too.—M.

a puppet-show having arrived in Newmarket, and Punch's prompter being taken suddenly ill, he, then a very little boy, volunteered to perform the sick man's duty, and seizing the opportunity, mercilessly satirized the reigning vices of the neighbours. This is almost the only exploit of his childhood that has been related.

He entered Trinity College as a sizer, in 1769, being then nineteen years old, an age at which the students of the present day have, for the most part, nearly completed their college course.* Here he studied the classical writings of antiquity with great ardour, and with eminent success. Nor did his enthusiastic admiration of them ever after subside. Amidst all the distractions of business and ambition, he was all his life returning with fresh delight to their perusal; and in the last journey that he ever took, Horace and Virgil were his travelling companions. He obtained a scholarship, and that his general scholastic attainments were not inconsiderable, may be inferred from his having commenced a course of reading for a fellowship,† but, deterred by the labor, or diverted by accident, he soon gave up the project.

When we reflect upon the lustre of his future career, it becomes a matter of natural curiosity to inquire how far his mind now began to indicate those qualities, by which it was to be subsequently so distinguished; and upon this interesting subject there happened to be preserved some documents, principally a portion of his early correspondence and his first poetical attempts, from which a few occasional extracts shall be offered, for the purpose of giving some idea of the writer's juvenile habits and capacity. Whatever may be considered to be their intrinsic merit, several

* Curran entered Trinity College, Dublin, on the 16th June, 1769. The examination is a severe one, but Curran's answering must have been very good, as he obtained the second place at entrance. His Sizarship entitled him to free rooms and commons, at College.—M.

‡ O'Regan states that besides acquiring an intimate acquaintance with the Classics, Curran had made considerable advance in science, particularly in metaphysics and morality, while the purest modern classics in the English and French literature, became equally familiar to him. With the Bible he was familiar, and once said, "It would be a reproach not to examine the merits of a work in which all mankind are so much engaged, and have taken so deep an interest."—M.

of them were at least written with considerable care, and may therefore be introduced as no unfair specimens of the progress of his intellectual strength. To the student of eloquence their defects will not be without instruction, if they inspire him with a reliance upon that labor and cultivation, which alone conduct to excellence.

One of the most intimate friends of Mr. Curran's youth, and of his riper years, was the late Rev. Richard Stack, his contemporary at Trinity College, and since a fellow of that University.* The following is a formal letter of consolation to that gentleman upon the death of a brother. The writer had just completed his 20th year, and appears to have been so pleased with his performance, that no less than three transcripts of it remain in his own handwriting.

"Dublin, *August* 20, 1770.

"Dear Dick.

"I am sorry to find by your letter (which I have just now received), that you judge my silence for some time past with so much more severity than it deserves. Can my friend suspect me of being unconcerned at his sorrows? I would have wrote to you on hearing from Vincent of his late misfortune, but that I was unwilling to press a subject upon your thoughts which you should take every means of avoiding. To offer consolation to a man of sense, upon the first stroke of affliction, is perhaps one of the most cruel offices that friendship can be betrayed into. All the fine things that can be addressed to the fancy will have but small effect in removing a distemper fixed in the heart. Time and reflection only can cure that; and happy is it for us that in this chequered scene, where everything feels perpetual decay, and seems created only for dissolution, our sorrows cannot boast of exemption from the common fate. Time, though he sometimes tears up our happiness by the roots, yet, to make amends for that,

* Mr. Stack wrote a Treatise on Optics, long a College Text-book.—M.

kindly holds out a remedy for our afflictions; and though he violently breaks our dearest connexions, yet he is continually teaching us to be prepared for the blow. 'Tis true, nature on these occasions will weep, but, my dear Dick, reason and reflection should wipe away these tears. A few years may see us numbered with those whom we now regret, or will give us cause to congratulate those whose happy lot it was, by an early retreat from this scene of misery and disappointment, to escape those troubles which their survivors are reserved to suffer. 'Tis true, the inattention of youth will leave the great account more unsettled than might be wished; but at this age, we have everything to plead for that defect—the violence of passions, want of reason to moderate them. Faults, no doubt we have, but they are the faults of youth, of inexperience; not a course of wickedness riveted by habit, and aggravated by obdurate perseverance, which (heaven help us) in a length of years they may become; but, above all, that Being who is pleased to call us so suddenly from hence, has mercy and compassion to make allowance for these involuntary omissions. But I find I have fallen unawares upon a theme which I had no intention to pursue so far, as I was persuaded your own good sense would suggest much stronger reasons for your consolation than I could.

"J. P. C."

At the date of this letter, the writer, if he looked forward to fame, expected to find it in the pulpit; but this, and a short religious discourse, are all that remain of his early compositions, which, from the style, would appear to be written with a view to his first destination. Mr. Stack, however, entertained so very high an opinion of his talents for the solemn eloquence of the church, that being appointed a few years after (1775) to preach before the judges of assize at Cork, and being anxious that his matter should be worthy of his auditors, he entreated of his young friend, who was then upon the spot, and going his first circuit, to compose a sermon for the occasion. Mr. Curran complied; and his production excited such general admiration, that his mother, in answer to the congratulations of the neighbourhood upon so flattering a proof of her son's abilities, could not avoid tempering her maternal exultation with Christian regret, and exclaiming—"Oh, yes, it was very fine; but it breaks my heart to think what a noble preacher was lost to the church when John disappointed us all, and insisted on becoming a lawyer." All his subsequent success and celebrity at the bar could never completely reconcile her to the change; and in her latter years, when her friends, to gratify and console her, used to remind her that she had lived to see her favorite child one of the judges of the land, she would still reply—"Don't speak to me of *judges*—John was fit for anything; and had he but followed our advice, it might hereafter be written upon my tomb, that I had died the mother of a bishop."

This excellent and pious woman died about the year 1783, at the advanced age of eighty. It is not written upon her tomb that she died the mother of a bishop or of a judge; but there is to be seen upon it an attestation to her worth from the son who was her pride, which, as long as virtue and filial gratitude are preferred to the glare of worldly dignities, will be considered as an epitaph no less honorable both to the parent and the child.*

It was during the second year of his college studies that he fixed on the profession of the law. In his original intention of taking orders he had been influenced by the wishes of his friends,

* Her remains lie in the churchyard of Newmarket; over them is the following epitaph, written by Mr. Curran:

HERE LIES THE BODY OF
SARAH CURRAN.
She was marked by
Many Years,
Many Talents,
Many Virtues,
Few Failings,
No Crime.
This frail memorial was placed here by a
Son
Whom she loved.

and by the promise of a small living in the gift of a distant relative, and probably still more strongly by a habitual preference for the calling to which his early patron belonged; but his ambition soon overruled all these motives, and he selected the bar as more suited to his temperament and talents. According to his own account, it was the following incident that suggested the first idea of a change in his destination.

He had committed some breach of the college regulations, for which he was sentenced by the Censor, Dr. Patrick Duigenan, either to pay a fine of five shillings, or translate into Latin a number of the *Spectator.* He found it more convenient to accept the latter alternative; but, on the appointed day, the exercise was not ready, and some unsatisfactory excuse was assigned. Against the second offence a heavier penalty was denounced—he was condemned to pronounce a Latin oration *in laudem decori* from the pulpit in the college chapel. He no longer thought of evading his sentence, and accordingly prepared the panegyric; but when he came to recite it, he had not proceeded far before it was found to contain a mock model of ideal perfection, which the Doctor instantly recognized to be a glaring satire upon himself. As soon, therefore, as the young orator had concluded, and descended from his station, he was summoned before the Provost and Fellows to account for his behaviour. Doctor Duigenan was not very popular, and the Provost was secretly not displeased at any circumstance that could mortify him. He, therefore, merely went through the form of calling upon the offender for an explanation, and listening with indulgence to the ingenuity with which he attempted to soften down the libel, dismissed him with a slight reproof. When Mr. Curran returned among his companions, they surrounded him to hear the particulars of his acquittal. He reported to them all that he had said, "and all that he had not said, but that he might have said;" and impressed them with so high an idea of his legal dexterity that they declared, by common acclamation, that the bar, and the bar alone, was the proper profession for one who possessed the talents of which he had that day given such a striking proof. He accepted the omen, and never after repented of his decision.

In College he distinguished himself by his social powers. He had such a fund of high spirits and of popular anecdote; his ordinary conversation was so full of "wit, and fun, and fire," that in the convivial meetings of his fellow-students he was never omitted. His general reputation among them was that of being very clever and very wild. He often joined in those schemes of extravagant frolic so prevalent in that University, and after one of the nocturnal broils to which they usually led, was left wounded and insensible from loss of blood to pass the remainder of the night on the pavement of Dublin.

He was at this time supported partly from the funds appropriated to the sizers, and partly by scanty remittances from Newmarket. But he was frequently without a shilling; for he was incorrigibly improvident, and would often squander, in entertaining his companions, what should have been meted out to answer the demands of the coming quarter. Yet, whatever his privations were, he bore them with singular good humor, and when he had no longer money to treat his friends, he never failed to divert them with ludicrous representations of his distresses and expedients.

One of his sayings while he was in College has been preserved, and is a favorable instance of the felicitous use that he made of his classical knowledge in the production of comical effect.* A fellow-student in reciting a Latin theme assigned a false quantity

* Another classical application shews his readiness, if not his wit. A gentleman of very ordinary countenance, whose forehead was so prominent on the one side that it rose like a rugged hill, while on the other it was depressed like a valley, being charged by one of his friends with an affair of gallantry, blushed exceedingly, and defended himself from the imputation by good humoredly offering his deformity as a proof of his innocence; on which Curran observed: "On the *first blush* I should think you ought to be acquitted, but the maxim is still strong against you—*Fronti nulla fides, nimium ne crede colori.*"—M.

to the syllable *mi* in the word *nimirum*. A buzz of disapprobation succeeded; Mr. Curran, to relieve his friend's confusion observed, "that it was by no means surprising that an Irish student should be ignorant of what was known by only one man in Rome, according to the following testimony of Horace—

"Septimius, Claudi, nimirum intelligit unus."

He was at this early period remarkable for his disposition to subtle disputation and metaphysical inquiries, connected with which a circumstance may be mentioned that strikingly illustrates the speculative propensities of his young and ardent mind. A frequent topic of conversation with one of his companions was the investigation of the nature of death and eternity, and the immortality of the soul; but finding that the farther they followed the bewildering light of reason, the more they were "in, wandering mazes lost," they came to the romantic agreement, that whoever of them might first receive the summons to another state, should, if permitted, for once revisit the survivor, and relieve his doubts by revealing, whatever could be revealed to him, of the eternal secret. A very few years after, the summons came to Mr. Curran's friend, who, finding his end approach, caused a letter to be addressed to his former fellow-student, apprising him of the impending event, and of his intention to perform his promise (if it should be allowed) on a particular night. The letter did not reach its destination till after the expiration of the appointed hour; but it was the first, and the only intimation, that arrived of the writer's decease.

Something of the same turn of mind may be observed in a little poem that Mr. Curran wrote the year before he left Trinity College. One of his contemporaries there, was a young gentleman, named Apjohn, with whom he became intimately connected by a community of taste and pursuits, and who claims a passing mention as a friend from whose example and encouragement he derived the most important advantages at this trying period of his career, when hope and ardour were the most precious benefits that a friend could bestow.

During a temporary absence of Apjohn from college, a report reached his companions that he had died suddenly at his native place, Killaloe. It was soon discovered to have been unfounded, upon which occasion, while the others congratulated him in prose, his more ambitious friend addressed him in the following verses:

TO W. APJOHN.

PEACE! whining slut, dismiss those sighs,
Those epitaphs and elegies;
And throwing off those weeds of sorrow,
Go laughing bid my friend good morrow!
Go bid him welcome here again,
From Charon's bark and Pluto's reign!

The doleful tale around was spread:
"Hast heard the news? Poor Apjohn's dead!"—
"Impossible!"—"Indeed it's true—
He's dead—and so is Casey too—
In Limerick this, and that Killaloe.
As St. Paul says, 'we all must die!'
I'm sorry for 't."—"Faith so 'm I—
Extremely so—But tell me, pray,
If you were on the ice to-day?
There was great skating there, they say—"
"I could n't go for want of shoes—
In truth I'm sorry for the news—
And yet I knew and always said,
When he had got into his head
That strange abstemious resolution,
'Twould quite destroy his constitution.'
Thus careless, tearless sorrow spoke,
And heaved the sigh, or told the joke,
Yet, must I own, there were a few
Who gave your memory its due;

And while they dropt a friendly tear
Said things that——but you must n't hear.
And now, methought, a wandering ghost,
You whizz'd along the Stygian coast;
And if, perchance, you gained the wherry,
And tugg'd an oar across the ferry,
That, sitting on the further shore,
You watch'd each boatful wafted o'er,
While with impatience you attend
Th' arrival of your quondam friend;
To tell his wonder where you 've been,
And what surprising things you 've seen;
And, from experience wise, relate
The various politics of fate;
And show where hoary sages stray,
And where they chance to keep their way;
Then laugh to think, how light as air,
Our blind dogmatic guesses were;
When, fancy throned and placed on high
We sat in judgment o'er the sky.
There envy too began to rise,
To think that you were grown so wise;
That bursting from this shell of clay,
You now enjoy'd eternal day;
While I was left perplex'd and blind,
In anxious ignorance behind;
Doom'd this insipid part to play
In life's dull farce another day,
That, bent with sorrows and with age,
I late might totter off the stage:
But yet my Muse, I cried, will pay,
The tribute of a weeping lay:
And though the flowers strewn o'er his tomb
May boast, perhaps, a longer bloom,
The short-liv'd verse he 'll still receive,
Since that is all a Muse can give.
The Muse, contented, took her place—
I solemnly composed my face,
And took the pen, prepared to write
What she sat ready to indite,

When Rumor, lo! with deaf'ning sound,
More gladsome tidings blows around,
And bids her thousand tongues to tell,
That Apjohn is alive and well!
And louder now the torrent grows,
Gathering new murmurs as it flows,
When the poor Muse, in sad affright,
Swift to Parnassus wings her flight;
But promised, ere away she fled,
That when you should indeed be dead,
She 'd call again, and write a verse,
To please your friend, and grace your hearse;
Unless that I myself ere then
Should grow fatigued and quit the scene.
And yet how short a time can live
Those honors that the Muses give—
Soon fades the monument away,
And sculptured marbles soon decay;
And every title, now defaced,
Mix with the dust which once they graced:
But if we wish a deathless name,
Let Virtue hand us down to Fame.
Our honors then may Time defy,
Since we will have, whene'er we die,
For epitaph—a life well spent,
And mankind for a monument.
What matter then for you and me,
Though none upon our graves should see
A W. A. or J. P. C.

William Apjohn is a name of which the world has heard nothing. He died prematurely, and "without his fame;" but had his days been lengthened, he would probably have acted a distinguished part in the history of his country. Like his friend, he had chosen the bar as the most honorable road to fortune and celebrity, and had already given a promise of such talents for public life, that his success was looked to as undoubted. Mr. Curran never spoke of his capacity but in terms of the most respectful admiration. "Apjohn's mind," he used to say, "was, beyond exception, the most accomplished that I ever met: his abilities and attainments were so many and so rare, that if they could have been distributed among a dozen ordinary persons, the share of each would have promoted him to the rank of a man of talents."

CHAPTER II.

Mr. Curran leaves College—Enters the Middle Temple—Letter to Mr. Weston—Letter to Mr. Keller—His first attempts in Oratory fail—His own account of the failure, and of his first success—A regular attendant at Debating Clubs—Anecdotes—His Poem on Friendship—Dr. Creagh's character of him—Mr. Hudson's predictions and friendship—His early manners and habits—Subject to constitutional melancholy—Letters from London—His society in London—Anecdote of his interview with Macklin—His early application and attainments—Favorite authors—Early attachment to the Irish peasantry—His marriage—Remarks upon the English Law.

Mr. Curran completed his college studies in the early part of the year 1773, having qualified himself to a Master's degree, and passed over to London, where he became a student of law in the Society of the Middle Temple.* During his residence in England he wrote regularly, and at considerable length to his friends in Ireland. A collection of these letters has been preserved, and as several of them contain a more striking picture of his circumstances, and of many traits of individual character, than any description by another could convey, he shall in this stage of his life be occasionally made his own biographer.

The following was written immediately after his arrival in the British capital. The gentleman to whom it is addressed was a resident of Newmarket, and one of the most attached of Mr. Curran's early friends.

* It is indispensable that every person who seeks admission to the *Irish* bar, shall have "studied" (*i. e.*, eaten a certain number of dinners during two years) at one of the Inns of the Court, in London, as well as at the Queen's Inn of law, in Dublin!—M.

"LONDON, 31 Chandos-street, July 10, 1773.

"THE REV. HENRY WESTON,

NEWMARKET, CO. CORK.

"I would have taken a last farewell of my dear Harry from Dublin, if I had not written so shortly before I left it; and, indeed, I was not sorry for being exempt from a task for which a thousand causes conspired to make me, at that juncture, unqualified. It was not without regret that I could leave a country, which my birth, education, and connections had rendered dear to me, and venture alone, almost a child of fortune, into a land of strangers. In such moments of despondence, when fancy plays the self-tormentor, she commonly acquits herself to a miracle, and will not fail to collect in a single group the most hideous forms of anticipated misfortune. I considered myself, besides, as resigning for ever the little indulgences that youth and inexperience may claim for their errors, and passing a period of life in which the best can scarce escape the rigid severity of censure; nor could the little trivial vanity of taking the reins of my own conduct alleviate the pain of so dear-bought a transition from dependence to liberty. Full of these reflections as I passed the gate, I could not but turn and take a last lingering look of poor Alma-mater; it was the scene of many a boyish folly, and of many a happy hour. I should have felt more confusion at a part of the retrospect, had I not been relieved by a recollection of the valuable friendship I had formed there. Though I am far from thinking such a circumstance can justify a passed misconduct, yet I cannot call that time totally a blank, in which one has acquired the greatest blessing of humanity. It was with a melancholy kind of exultation I counted over the number of those I loved there, while my heart gave a sigh to each name in the catalogue; nay, even the *fellows*, whom I never loved, I forgave at that moment; the parting tear blotted out every injury, and I gave them as hearty a benediction as if they had deserved it: as for my general acquaintance (for I could not but go the round). I packed their respective little sighs into one great sigh, as I turned round on my heel. My old friend and handmaid Betty, perceiving me in motion, got her hip under the *strong box* with my seven shirts, which she had rested against the rails during the delay, and screwed up her face into a most rueful caricature, that might provoke a laugh at another time; while her young son Denny, grasping his waistband in one hand, and a basket of sea-provision in the other, took the lead in the procession; and so we journeyed on to George's Quay,* where the ship was just ready to sail. When I entered, I found my fellow-passengers seated round a large table in the cabin: we were fourteen in number. A young Highland lord had taken the head of the table and the conversation, and, with a modesty peculiar to himself, gave a history of his travels, and his intimate connections with the princes of the empire. An old debauched officer was complaining of the gout, while a woman, who sat next to him (good heaven! what a tongue), gave a long detail of what her father suffered from that disorder. To do them all justice, they exerted themselves most zealously for the common entertainment. As for my part, I had nothing to say; nor, if I had, was any one at leisure to listen to me; so I took possession of what the captain called a bed, wondering with Partridge, 'how they could play so many different tunes at the same time without putting each other out.' I was expecting that the sea-sickness would soon give those restless mouths different employment, but in that I was disappointed; the sea was so calm that one only was sick during the passage, and it was not my good fortune that the lot should fall on that devil who never ceased chattering. There was no cure but patience; accordingly, I never stirred from my tabernacle (unless to visit my basket) till we arrived at Parkgate.† Here, after the usual pillage at the custom-house, I laid my box down

* In Cork.—M.

† Parkgate, in Cheshire, was the usual port of debarcation, for Irish voyagers to England, in the last century.—M.

on the beach, seated myself upon it, and, casting my eyes westward over the Welsh mountains towards Ireland, I began to reflect on the impossibility of getting back without the precarious assistance of others. Poor Jack! thought I, thou wert never till now so far from home but thou mightest return on thine own legs. Here now must thou remain, for where here canst thou expect the assistance of a friend? Whimsical as the idea was, it had power to affect me; until, at length, I was awakened from this reverie by a figure which approached me with the utmost affability; methought his looks seemed to say, 'Why is thy spirit troubled?' He pressed me to go into his house, and to 'eat of his bread,' and to 'drink of his drink.' There was so much good-natured solicitude in the invitation, 't was irresistible. I arose, therefore, and followed him, ashamed of my uncharitable despondence. Surely, thought I, 'there is still humanity left among us,' as I raised my eyes to the golden letters over his door, that offered entertainment and repose to the wearied traveller. Here I resolved to stay for the night, and agreed for a place in his coach, next morning, to Chester; but, finding my loquacious fellow-passenger had agreed for one in the same vehicle, I retracted my bargain, and agreed for my box only. I perceived, however, when I arose next morning, that my box was not sent, though the coach was gone. I was thinking how I should remedy this unlucky disappointment, when my friendly host told me that he could furnish me with a chaise! Confusion light upon him! what a stroke was this! It was not the few paltry shillings that vexed me, but to have my philanthropy till that moment running cheerily through my veins, and to have the current turned back suddenly by the detection of his knavery! Verily, Yorick, even thy gentle spirit, so meekly accustomed to bear and forbear, would have been roused on such an occasion. I paid hastily for my entertainment, and, shaking the dust from my feet at his gate, I marched with my box on my shoulder to a waggoner's at the other end of the town, where I entered it for London, and sallied forth towards Chester on foot.

I was so nettled at being the dupe of my own credulity, that I was almost tempted to pass an excommunication on all mankind, and resolved never more to trust my own skill in physiognomy. Wrapt up in my speculations, I never perceived at what a rate I was striding away, till I found myself in the suburbs of Chester, quite out of breath, and completely covered with dust and dirt. From Chester, I set out that evening in the stage: I slept about four hours next day at Coventry, and the following evening, at five o'clock, was in view of near a hundred and twenty spires, that are scattered from one side of the horizon to the other, and seem almost bewildered in the mist that perpetually covers this prodigious capital. 'T would be impossible for description to give any idea of the various objects that fill a stranger, on his first arrival, with surprise and astonishment. The magnificence of the churches, hospitals, and other public building, which everywhere present themselves, would alone be ample subject of admiration to a spectator, though he were not distracted by the gaudy display of wealth and dissipation continually shifting before his eyes in the most extravagant forms of pride and ostentation, or by a hurry of business that might make you think this the source from which life and motion are conveyed to the world beside. There are many places here not unworthy of particular inspection; but as my illness prevented me from seeing them on my first arrival, I shall suspend my curiosity till some future time, as I am determined to apply to reading this vacation with the utmost diligence, in order to attend the Courts next winter with more advantage. If I should happen to visit Ireland next summer, I shall spend a week, before I go, in seeing the curiosities here (the king and queen, and the lions); and, if I continue in my present mood, you will see a strange alteration in your poor friend. That cursed fever ever brought me down so much, and my spirits are so reduced, that, faith, I don't remember to have laughed these six weeks. Indeed, I never thought solitude could lean so heavily on me as I find it does: I rise, most commonly, in the morning between five and six, and read as much as my eyes will permit me till dinner-time; I then go out and dine, and from that till bed-time, I mope about between my lodgings and the Park. For heaven's sake, send me some news or other (for, surely, Newmarket cannot be barren in such things) that will teach me once more to laugh. I never received a single line from any one since I came here! Tell me if you know anything about Keller; I wrote twice to that gentleman without being favored with any answer. You will give my best respects to Mrs. Aldworth and her family; to Doctor Creagh's; and don't forget my good friends Peter and Will Connel.

"Yours sincerely,

"J. P. C.

"P.S.—I will cover this blank edge with intreating you to write closer than you commonly do when you sit down to answer this, and don't make me pay tenpence for a halfpenny-worth of white paper."

[Curran's correspondence with Mr. Weston was collected and published in 1819, but is only slightly known. It extends over only a year and a half (1773–4), when Curran was yet very young, but contains some passages too characteristic not to be added to this life of him. Here is a lively bit of description:

"No doubt Keller has informed you of Schoole's exploit in the matrimonial way, with the daughter of the widow Craigan in Limerick. It seems the whole posse comitatus was hunting the fugitives for three or four days; but Schoole made a valiant running fight of it, and has the dear creature here in London. I have the honor of being introduced as a particular friend of Mr. Schoole's, though I fancy the desire of showing me the prize was the chief ground of the particularity. She is a curious little puppet, smart and chattering, and looks upon her good man as an oracle of taste and erudition. By her means I have got acquainted with a Miss Hume, who is also an original in her way. She is a relation of the celebrated David Hume; and, I suppose, on the strength of the kindred, sets up for a politician as well as a sceptic; she has heard his

Essays recommended, and shews her own discernment by pronouncing them unanswerable; and talks of the famous Burke, by the familiar appellation of Ned. Then she is so romantic and so sentimental—nothing for her but grots, and purling streams, and piping shepherds; and to crown all, it sings like a nightingale. As I have not the best command of my muscles, I always propose putting out the candles, before the song begins, for the greater romanticality of the thing. This is an expedient I used to have recourse to in the college, when I had the honor of teaching Nixon to sing. 'T is a miserable thing when a poor girl is so mistaken in her qualifications, as to display only her absurdities, and studiously conceal everything that she ought not to be ashamed of. Even this being wants not common sense, if she would but use it. But what have you or I to do with the text or comment?"

Here, after an unfavorable character of the English *boor*, is Curran's panegyric on his own countrymen:

"Their fondness for genealogy, so much despised here, and not without reason, yet gives them an advantage they could derive from no other source. When each poor individual is supposed to contain in his own person the accumulated honors of many generations, they are led to treat each other with a politeness and respect proportioned to this imaginary merit, and to cultivate a friendly intercourse that contributes not a little to reclaim, and even to refine the sentiments of the illiterate; and I have often thought, their manner of lamenting over their dead, co-operates strongly to preserve and improve this untutored sort of politeness, by keeping alive something like a taste for composition in a language, that wants neither expression nor extent, and by preventing that language from a decay, into which it must otherwise have fallen: and to these you add the severe political grievances, and the still more cruel miserable inducement to a strict association, the community of affliction and wretchedness, more than can be found in either France or Germany. and yet fostered in the bosom of a constitution boasted to be free. You will smile, no doubt, at these observations as being unseasonable as well as exaggerated. To the first I must plead guilty: but for the latter, there certainly is some truth in it; would to Heaven there was not so much!"

There is life, spirit and vivacity in this account of his visit to

Hampton Court, one of the Royal Palaces near London, to which the public at large, as its true proprietors, have free admission now:

"The servant who showed us the apartments, which were very splendid, gave us a circumstantial detail of the pictures, and the judgments passed upon them by different connoisseurs: he seemed to be a good deal pleased with his manner of explaining a suite of tapestry, representing the Persian war of Alexander: though a simple fellow, he had his lesson well by rote, and ran over the battles of Issus and Arbela, &c., with a surprising flippancy. 'But where is Alexander?' cries Apjohn. 'There sir, at the door of Darius's tent, with the ladies at his feet.' 'Surely,' said I, 'that must be Hephestion, for he was mistaken by the Queen for Alexander.' 'Pardon me, sir: I hope I know Alexander better than that;' and he shook his head in confirmation of his opinion, while I paid myself the same compliment. 'But which of the two do you really think the greater man?' 'Greater! Bless your soul, sir, they are both dead this hundred years.' O Harry! what a comment on human vanity! By my soul, there was the marrow of a thousand folios in the answer. I could not help thinking, at the instant, what a puzzle that mighty man would be in, should he appear before a committee from the Temple of Fame, to claim those laurels he thought so much of, and be opposed in his demand, though his competitors were Thersites, or the fellow who rubbed Bucephalus's heels. How would his identity be ascertained? Chærilus, stand forth; but should Mævius contest the bays with Chærilus, would a million of critics decide the difference? What then must be the sentence? Why, since the conqueror cannot be distinguished from the slave, let the chaplet be divided between them, et curru servus portetur eodem. Thus, in a few years, may my dear Harry be a Tillotson, and his friend as much Cicero as Cicero himself."

The following extract shows how Curran spent his time in London. What a happy kind of life, what a blessed flashing of mirth and meditation—sport and study—fun and philosophy—purl and politics—shaded, as it must have been, with the constitutional melancholy which pressed on him through life, and at length wrapped his mind in the darkest folds of despondency and hopelessness, such a way of living must have had charms for one who liked variety, and could accommodate himself to all phases of society.

"I happened at first to be rather unlucky in my lodgings; I was not aware of their being situated exactly under the bells of St. Martin, and that I was to be eternally stunned with the noise of praying bells, rejoining bells, and passing bells. I had the additional inconvenience of being exposed to the conversation of a man, no ways agreeable to me, a dull, good-natured, generous, unexperienced, opinionated, deep-read, unlearned, disputative sort of a character, still more offensive to me than my other neighbour, the steeple; for I had learned to endure unpleasing sounds, but I never had an opportunity of learning to bear with a troublesome companion. So I changed my tabernacle not a little to my satisfaction Besides being disengaged from the nuisances that infected me before, I have procured much better accommodations, on more reasonable terms. For the future, you will direct to me, No. 9 Orange Street, Leicester Fields.

" Notwithstanding a fit of illness, which somewhat retarded my application in the beginning, I have exerted a degree of assiduity, of which I once thought myself incapable. For the first five months I was almost totally a recluse, indeed, too much so. When we seclude ourselves entirely from all intercourse with the world, our affections will soon grow impatient of the restraint, and strongly convince us that much of our happiness must be drawn from society; and if we exert too much rigour, however philosophical it may appear at the time, to suppress these struggles, the temper is apt to fall into a gloomy kind of apathy. This I found to be my case, and I accordingly resolved to soften the severity of the discipline I had over-zealously adopted, and to that end made some additions to my wardrobe, and purchased a fiddle, which I had till then denied myself. Do not think, however, from my mentioning those indulgences, that I have diminished my hours of reading; all I have done by the change is, employing the time that must otherwise be vacant, in amusement instead of solitude. I still continue to read ten hours every day, seven at law, and three at history, or the general principles of politics; and that I may have time enough, I rise at half after four. I have contrived a machine after the manner of an hour-glass, which, perhaps, you may be curious to know, which wakens me regularly at that hour. Exactly over my head I have suspended two vessels of tin, one above the other; when I go to bed, which is always at ten, I pour a bottle of water into the upper vessel, in the bottom of which is a hole of such a size, as to let the water pass through, so as to make the inferior reservoir overflow in six hours and a half. I have had no small trouble in proportioning those vessels; and I was still more puzzled for a while how to confine my head, so as to receive the drop, but I have at length succeeded.

* * * * * * * * *

"You will, perhaps, be at some loss to guess what kind of amusement I allow myself, why, I'll tell you. I spend a couple of hours every night at a coffee-house where I am not a little entertained with a group of old politicians, who meet in order to debate on the reports of the day, or to invent some for the next, with the other business of the nation. Though I don't know that sociability is the characteristic of this people, yet politics is a certain introduction to the closest intimacy of coffee-house acquaintance. One meets with a great deal of amusement from this sort of conversation, and I think it can scarcely be devoid of improvement. Six or seven old fellows who have spent the early part of their lives in a variety of adventures, and are united at last by no other principle than a common vacancy, which makes it necessary for them to fill up their time by meddling in other people's business, since they have none of their own, is certainly a miscellany not unworthy a perusal; it gives a facility at least of discerning characters, and what is no less useful, enures us to a toleration that must make our passage through life more easy. I also visit a variety of ordinaries and eating-houses, and they are equally fertile in game for a character-hunter. I think I have found out the cellar where Roderick Random ate shin of beef for three-pence, and actually drank out of the identical quart, which the drummer squeezed together when poor Strap spilt the broth on his legs."

From the last letter in this collection I quote a passage, a little too formal, perhaps, for the off-hand style of friendly letters, but showing vigour of thought, feeling and expression:

"My not writing to you since I came to England, proceeding wholly from a scarcity of any thing worth communicating, I might justify a continuance of silence from the same cause. But yet I know not well how it happens, there is something in the first day of the new year that seems peculiarly to demand the tribute of remembrance: I could not let it pass without apprizing you that I am still in the land of the living: "*vivo equidem.*" These anniversary days serve as light-houses on the great ocean of time, by which we direct and compute our courses. They alarm us to a momentary recollection of the tempests we have weathered, the quicksands we have escaped, or the fortunate gales we have enjoyed. If any of the stars of heaven have shone with propitious influence, we adore them for their benevolent regards, and endeavour to engage their superintendence for the remainder of our voyage.

"As Young says—

'We take no heed of time but by its loss;'

the moments slide unperceived away, we think it still in our possession, still in being, till the knell of our departed hours startles us into a perception of its decease. These returning periods are not then without their advantage. They admonish us, at least, to dedicate one day in the year to a little reflection. The incidents of our life crowd in upon our thoughts, the pleasures we have found, the anxious moments we have spent—and Reason, elated with the temporary submission of her authority, makes a merit of passing an impartial sentence, and of changing, for an instant, from the venal advocate to the upright judge of our passions or our follies. Then, too, the heart counts over its attachments; and if Fate has blotted out any name of the catalogue, we fix our expectation with a more anxious solicitude on the survivors. When any of our fortresses against the outrages of fortune have sunk into ruin, we are doubly bound to attend to the preservation of those that remain, lest we should be found totally defenceless in the day of danger.

"Thus have I in some sort accounted for my troubling you with a letter at this particular time, as well as for the melancholy mood in which I sit down to write: in truth I do not remember to have been much more dejected. To you, my dear Harry, I hope this merry season has been more favourable. And yet, situated as you are, you can scarcely avoid sometimes feeling the heaviness of time, especially now when Newmarket has lost so many who might contribute to enliven it. As for my part, you can neither envy nor congratulate my situation with half the reason that I may yours. I once thought that solitude amidst thousands was no better than a paradox; but now I find it effectually verified. It is, indeed, the most dreary of all solitudes to walk abroad amongst millions, to read the most legible of all characters, those written by fortune or affliction, in every face you meet; to feel your heart elated or depressed by every story, and with the most disinterested solicitude, acknowledging the object for its fellow-creature; to have all these exquisitely respondent sympathies for which nature has so finely formed the bosoms of her children, unobserved and unavailing. * * * *]

In a letter of nearly the same date, to another friend,* he says:

"By the time you receive this I shall have relapsed into the same monastic life that I led before. I do not expect, however, that it will lean so heavily on me, as I am now tolerably recovered, and shall continue to read with unabated application; indeed, that is the only means of making solitude supportable; yet, it must be owned, a man of speculative turn will find ample matter in that way without stirring from his window. It is here that every vice and folly climb to their meridian, and that mortality seems properly to understand her business. If you cast your eyes on the thousand gilded chariots that are dancing the hayes in an eternal round of foppery, you would think the world assembled to play the fool in London, unless you believe the report of the passing bells and hearses, which would seem to intimate that they all made a point of dying here. It is amazing, that even custom should make death a matter of so much unconcern as you will here find it. Even in the house where I lodge, there has been a being dead these two days. I did not hear a word of it till this evening, though he is divided from me only by a partition. They visit him once a day, and so lock him up till the next (for they seldom bury till the seventh day), and there he lies without the smallest attention paid to him, except a dirge each night on the Jew's-harp, which I shall not omit while he continues to be my neighbour."

It was during his attendance at the Temple that Mr. Curran made the first trial of his rhetorical powers. He frequented a debating society that was composed of his fellow-students. His first attempt was unsuccessful, and for the moment quite disheartened him. He had had from his boyhood a considerable precipitation and confusion of utterance, from which he was denominated by his school-fellows "stuttering Jack Curran." This defect he had labored to remove, but the cure was not yet

* Jeremiah Keller, Esq., a member of the Irish bar.—C.

complete. From the agitation of a first effort he was unable to pronounce a syllable; and so little promise did there appear of his shining as a speaker, that his friend Apjohn said to him, "I have a high opinion of your capacity; confine yourself to the study of law, and you will, to a certainty, become an eminent chamber counsel; but, depend upon it, nature never intended you for an orator." Fortunately for his fame, this advice was disregarded: he continued to attend the above and other debating clubs, at one of which, during a discussion, some personal and irritating expressions having been levelled at him, his indignation, and along with it his talent, was roused. Forgetting all his timidity and hesitation, he rose against his assailants, and, for the first time, revealed to his hearers and to himself that style of original and impetuous oratory, which he afterwards improved into such perfection, and which now bids fair to preserve his name. He used often to entertain his friends by detailing this event of his mind's having "burst the shell." The following was the manner in which he once related it; for one of the great charms of his colloquial powers was the novelty that he could give to the same facts upon every repetition: he adorned a favorite anecdote, as a skilful musician would a favorite air, by an endless variety of unpremeditated *ad libitum* graces.

One day after dinner, an acquaintance, in speaking of his eloquence, happened to observe that it must have been born with him. "Indeed, my dear sir," replied Mr. Curran, "it was not; it was born three and twenty years and some months after me; and, if you are satisfied to listen to a dull historian, you shall have the history of its nativity.

"When I was at the Temple, a few of us formed a little debating club—poor Apjohn, and Duhigg,* and the rest of them! they have all disappeared from the stage; but my own busy hour will soon be fretted through. and then we may meet again behind the scenes. Poor fellows! they are now at rest; but I still can

* The late B. T. Duhigg, Esq., of the Irish Bar.—C.

see them, and the glow of honest bustle on their looks, as they arranged their little plan of honourable association (or, as Pope would say, 'gave their little senate laws'), where all the great questions in ethics and politics (there were no gagging-bills in those days) were to be discussed and irrevocably settled. Upon the first night of our assembling, I attended, my foolish heart throbbing with the anticipated honour of being styled 'the learned member that opened the debate,' or 'the *very* eloquent gentleman who has just sat down.' All day the coming scene had been flitting before my fancy, and cajoling it; my ear already caught the glorious melody of 'hear him, hear him!' Already I was practising how to steal a cunning side-long glance at the tear of generous approbation bubbling in the eyes of my little auditory; never suspecting, alas! that a modern eye may have so little affinity with moisture that the finest gunpowder may be dried upon it. I stood up—the question was Catholic claims or the slave trade, I protest I now forget which, but the difference, you know, was never very obvious—my mind was stored with about a folio volume of matter, but I wanted a preface, and for want of a preface the volume was never published. I stood up, trembling through every fibre; but remembering that in this I was but imitating Tully, I took courage, and had actually proceeded almost as far as 'Mr. Chairman,' when to my astonishment and terror, I perceived that every eye was riveted upon me. There were only six or seven present, and the little room could not have contained as many more; yet was it, to my panic-struck imagination, as if I were the central object in nature, and assembled millions were gazing upon me in breathless expectation. I became dismayed and dumb; my friends cried 'hear him!' but there was nothing to hear. My lips, indeed, went through the pantomime of articulation, but I was like the unfortunate fiddler at the fair, who, upon coming to strike up the solo that was to ravish every ear, discovered that an enemy had maliciously soaped his bow; or rather like poor Punch as I once saw him (and how many like him have I seen in our old House of Commons! but it is dead, and let us not disturb its ashes) grimacing a soliloquy, of which his prompter behind had most indiscreetly neglected to administer the words. So you see, sir, it was not born with me. However, though my friends, even Apjohn, the most sanguine of them, despaired of me, the *cacoethes loquendi* was not to be subdued without a struggle. I was for the present silenced, but I still attended our meetings with the most laudable regularity, and even ventured to accompany the others to a more ambitious theatre, 'the Devils of Temple Bar;' where truly may I say, that many a time the Devil's own work was going forward. Here, warned by fatal experience that a man's powers may be overstrained, I at first confined myself to a simple 'ay or no,' and by dint of practice and encouragement, brought my tongue to recite these magical elements of parliamentary eloquence with 'such sound emphasis and good discretion,' that in a fortnight's time I had completed my education for the Irish senate.

"Such was my state, the popular throb just beginning to revisit my heart, when a long expected remittance arrived from Newmarket; Apjohn dined with me that day, and when the leg of mutton, or rather the bone, was removed, we offered up the libation of an additional glass of punch for the health and length of days (and heaven heard the prayer) of the kind mother that had remembered the necessities of her absent child. In the evening we had repaired to 'the Devils.' One of them was upon his legs; a fellow of whom it was impossible to decide, whether he was most distinguished by the filth of his person or by the flippancy of his tongue; just such another as Harry Flood would have called 'the highly gifted gentleman with the dirty cravat and greasy pantaloons.'* I found this learned personage

* Mr. Curran here alluded to the celebrated Mr. Flood's custom of distinguishing the speakers at the London Debating Societies by such ludicrous descriptions of their dress, as "the eloquent friend to reform in the threadbare coat," "the able supporter of the present ministry with the new pair of boots," &c.—C.

in the act of calumniating chronology by the most preposterous anachronisms (and as I believe, I shortly after told him) traducing the illustrious dead by affecting a confidential intercourse with them, as he would with some nobleman, *his very dear friend*, behind his back, who, if present, would indignantly repel the imputation of so insulting an intimacy. He descanted upon Demosthenius, the glory of the Roman forum; spoke of Tully as the famous cotemporary and rival of Cicero; and in the short space of one half hour, transported the straits of Marathon three several times to the plains of Thermopylæ. Thinking that I had a right to know something of these matters, I looked at him with surprise; and whether it was the money in my pocket, or my classical chivalry, or most probably the supplemental tumbler of punch, that gave my face a smirk of saucy confidence, when our eyes met, there was something like wager of battle in mine; upon which the erudite gentleman instantly changed his invectives against antiquity into an invective against me, and concluded by a few words of friendly counsel (*horresco referens*) to 'Orator Mum,' who he doubted not possessed wonderful talents for eloquence, although he would recommend him to show it in future by some more popular method than his silence. I followed his advice, and I believe not entirely without effect; for when sitting down, I whispered my friend, that I hoped he did not think that my dirty antagonist had come 'quite clean off?' 'On the contrary, my dear fellow,' said he, 'every one around me is declaring that it is the first time they ever saw him so well dressed.' So, sir, you see that to try the bird, the spur must touch his blood. Yet, after all, if it had not been for the inspiration of the punch, I might have continued a mute to this hour; so for the honor of the art, let us have another glass."

The speech which Mr. Curran made upon this occasion was immediately followed by a more substantial reward than the applauses of his hearers; the debate was no sooner closed than the *president* of the society dispatched his *secretary* to the eloquent stranger, to solicit the honor of his company to partake of a *cold collation*, which proved to consist of bread and cheese and porter; but the public motives of the invitation rendered it to the guest the most delicious supper that he had ever tasted.

From this time till his final departure from London, he was a regular attendant and speaker at debating clubs; an exercise which he always strongly recommended to every student of eloquence, and to which he attributed much of his own skill and facility in extemporaneous debate. He never adopted or approved of the practice of committing to memory intended speeches, but he was in the habit of assisting his mind with ample notes of the leading topics, and trusted to the occasion for expression.

The society that he latterly most frequented was the well-known Robin Hood. He also sometimes attended a meeting for the discussion of religious questions, which was held on Sunday evenings at the Brown Bear in the Strand, and resorted to by persons of every persuasion, and by many who were honorary members of all faiths. Whenever the claims of the Roman Catholics were the subject of debate, he uniformly supported them. From his zeal in their cause, and from his dress (a brown surtout over black), he was supposed by strangers to be a young priest of that Order, and was known in the club by the name of "the little Jesuit from St. Omers."*

Among Mr. Curran's juvenile productions was a poem of some length, written while he was at the Temple; it is entitled, "On Friendship," and addressed to Mr. Weston, of Newmarket. When we consider the character of Mr. Curran's oratory, to which an

* The same zeal for the emancipation of the Roman Catholics which distinguished him for the rest of his life, produced similar mistakes among strangers upon the subject of his religion. When he was at Paris, in 1814, he accompanied some friends to see Cardinal Fesch's gallery of paintings. The Frenchman in attendance there was a good deal struck by Mr. Curran's observations, and, upon the latter's retiring before the others, asked, with some curiosity, who he was. As soon as he heard his name, "Ah!" said he, with great surprise, "je voyois bien qu'il avoit beaucoup d'esprit, mais, mon Dieu! je n'aurois jamais soupçonne que ce petit monsieur fut *le grand Catholique Irlandois*."—C.

excess of fervor and imagination has been by some imputed as its imperfection, we should naturally expect to see those qualities predominating when he found himself engaged in subjects to which they so peculiarly belong; but this is not the case. From his youth to his old age, he was fond of writing poetry, and produced a considerable quantity; but in little of it do we meet with that sustained ardour, with those fearless conceptions, and that diction teeming with imagery, which distinguish his other productions. When he occupied himself with poetry, he appears to have considered it rather as a recreation to soothe himself, than as a means of exciting others. With the exception of a very few instances (which, however, prove his poetic capacity, had he anxiously cultivated it), his verses are, in general, placid, familiar, and unaspiring, seldom venturing beyond expressions of established form, and, for the most part, contented with those sentiments of obvious tenderness to which no mind of any sensibility is a stranger. The opening of the poem on Friendship is here inserted, for the sake of the concluding image, which the late Mr. Fox (among others) particularly admired.

Here, on these banks, where many a bard has sung,
While Thames, in listening silence, flow'd along,
Where friendship's flame inspir'd the glowing verse,
To hail the triumph, or to mourn the hearse;
On the same spot where weeping Thompson paid
The last sad tribute to his Talbot's shade,
A humbler muse, by fond remembrance led,
Bewails the absent, where he mourned the dead.
Nor differ much the subjects of the strain,
Whether of death or distance we complain;
Whether we're sundered by the final scene,
Or envious seas disjoining roll between;
Absence, the dire effect, is still the same,
And death and distance differ but in name:
Yet sure they're different, if the peaceful grave
From haunting thoughts the low-laid tenant save,

While in this breathing death reflection lives,
And o'er the wreck of happiness survives.
Alas! my friend, were Providence inclined
(In unrelenting wrath to human kind)
To take back every blessing that she gave,
From the wide ruin, she would memory save,
Else would severest ills be soon o'erpast,
Or kind oblivion bury them at last:
But Memory, with more than Egypt's art,
Embalming every grief that wounds the heart,
Sits at the altar she hath rais'd to Wo,
And feeds the source whence tears for ever flow.

In the course of this poem, allusions are made to the writer's future career in public life; and those who have not yet learned to sneer at the mention of political integrity, will be gratified to observe how completely, in the present instance, the visions of the poet were realized by the subsequent conduct of the man.

But in his country's cause, if patriot zeal
Excite him, ardent for the public weal,
With generous warmth to stem corruption's rage,
And prop the fall of an abandon'd age,
Bold in the senate, he confronts the band
Of willing slaves that sell their native land;
And, when the mitred hireling would persuade
That chains for man by Heaven's high will were made,
Or hoary jurist, in perversion wise,
Would sap the laws, and on their ruin rise,
While the mute 'squire and star-enamour'd beau
Are base in all they can—an "ay" or "no!"
With equal scorn he views the venal train,
And sordid bribe that such a tribe can gain.

And a little further on:

But if oppression lord it o'er the land,
And force alone can lawless force withstand,

Fearless he follows where his country calls,
And lives with freedom, or with glory falls;
He gives that shackle he disdains to wear,
For endless fame, nor thinks the purchase dear.

This may not be very good poetry, but it evinces, what is more honorable to the writer, and what was in those days of more value to Ireland than good poetry, an indignant sense of her condition, and an impatience to redress it. It will hereafter appear how far he fulfilled the engagements of his youth.

From the above and similar productions,* and from the indications of talent that his ordinary conversation afforded, great hopes were now entertained of him. According to all the accounts of those who knew him at this time, his colloquial powers were even then of a very high order. Having no hereditary fortune or powerful connections on which to depend, and having embraced an ambitious and hazardous profession, where, without the reputation of superior ability, there was little prospect of success, he appears to have habitually exerted himself upon every occasion to substantiate his claims, and justify his choice. The following judgment was passed upon him, at this period, by his future father-in-law, Dr. Richard Creagh, of Newmarket, a scholar and a man of cultivated taste, whose prediction, in the present instance, has been so completely verified. After mentioning, in one of his letters, the future ornament of the Irish bar, as "a young man of this town, one Jack Curran," he proceeds, "take his character from me. He possesses a good understanding; is an excellent scholar; has some taste, and, for his years, I think, a tolerable judgment; has uncommon abilities; is a proficient in music; has received an university education; is now preparing for the bar, for

* During the two years that preceded his admission to the bar, he wrote, besides the poem of "Friendship," "Lines upon visiting the Cave of Pope," and "Lines upon the poisoning a stream at Frenchay" (where he had been driven by foul winds, in one of his passages from England to Ireland), which he composed for the purpose of expressing his gratitude to a family of that place, who had given him a very hospitable reception.—C.

which profession he possesses extraordinary talents, and will disappoint all his friends if he does not distinguish himself there. As far as I can observe, he seems to be extremely cheerful and good-natured, and is remarkable pleasant in conversation."*

In a letter of about the same date from one of Mr. Curran's earliest friends, Mr. Hudson,† we find similar expectations prevail; alluding to the melancholy that ran through a letter he had just received from the other, he says—"Consider, now and then, Jack, what you are destined for; and never, even in your distresses, draw consolation from so mean a thought, as that your abilities may one day render your circumstances easy or affluent; but that you may one day have it in your power to do justice to the wronged, to wipe the tear from the widow or orphan, will afford the satisfaction that is worthy of a man."

It would be injustice to suppress another passage. Having a little before chided his friend for neglecting to inform him of the state of his finances, Mr. Hudson goes on, "I think I shall be a man of no small fame to-morrow or next day, and though 'tis but

* Doctor Creagh was a physician, and a member of a very respectable family of that name in the county of Cork. Much of the earlier part of his life had been passed on the Continent, where he had mixed in the society of the most celebrated men of talent; but he used often to declare that, neither abroad nor at home, had he ever met so delightful a companion as "young Jack Curran;" yet, the conversation of the latter was not, at this time, what it subsequently became. It was full of vivacity and of anecdotes, to which he could give an extraordinary degree of dramatic effect; but it had not, as at a later period, those incessant and magical transitions from the most comic trains of thought to the deepest pathos, which were for ever bringing a tear to the eye, before the smile was off the lip; nor that surprising control over all the mysteries of language, which he acquired by his subsequent habits of extemporaneous speaking. Dr. Creagh was a determined Whig, and had, no doubt, an influence in confirming the political inclinations of his son-in-law. It was also from Dr. Creagh, who had spent several years in France, and was an excellent French scholar, that Mr. Curran derived much of his early taste for the language and literature of that country.—C.

† Mr. Edward Hudson, for a long course of years the most eminent dentist in Ireland.—C. He built a beautiful mansion near Dublin, and asked Curran what order of architecture he should adopt. Gaily smiling at the dentist, the wit replied, "The *Tusk*-an, of course." In allusion to this, Hudson was commonly spoken of, familiarly, as The Grand Duke of Tusk-any;" and when his nephew entered the military service of a foreign country, Curran said that the young man's first engagement would naturally be the Battle of Pul-tusk.—M.

the fame of a dentist, yet if that of an honest man is added to it, I shall not be unhappy. Write speedily to me, and if you are in want, think I shall not be satisfied with my fortunes—believe me I shall never think I make a better use of my possessions than when such a friend as Jack can assist me in their uses." The amiable and respectable writer of the above still lives [1819], and if the union of the two characters, to which, in his youth, he aspired, could confer happiness, he has been completely happy.

Many other proofs might be added (were it necessary) to show that Mr. Curran was, even at this period, considered as much more than an ordinary man; that he had already obtained a very high degree of estimation in the opinions of every person of discernment who knew him. To be regarded as an object of admiration and of hope by the immediate circle of his friends, is, indeed, no more than happens to every young man of any intellectual pretensions; but to Mr. Curran's honour it should not be overlooked, that the friends who entertained such sentiments towards him were, all of them, those whose zeal and approbation he had won for himself by his own character and talents; nor was a mere general respect for the latter the only feeling that united them with him—they all appear to have been animated by the most anxious and affectionate attachment to his person. Their letters to him abound with expressions of more than usual endearment, with offers of pecuniary supplies, and many other unequivocal demonstrations of the extreme value in which they held him. At this period of life he used to pass considerable intervals of time at his native village, where he always entered, with the most good-natured vivacity, into all the little parties and interests of the place. He, whose lofty and independent spirit was a few years after to bring upon him the charge of "lecturing the Privy Council,"* was in his social intercourse so little fastidious or assuming, that he could find abundant amusement among the harmless wits and politicians of an obscure little town. Nor were these mere

* An expression of Lord Clare's. The whole scene is given hereafter.—C.

temporary feelings, adopted for convenience, and as evanescent as the occasions that excited them—all his impulses were intensely social, and, whether present or absent, his heart was still in the midst of the friends and companions that he loved. His letters from the Temple abound with proofs of these amiable propensities; in none of them is the Newmarket circle omitted; he dedicates a portion of every day to thinking of them, and of every letter to inquiries after their health and fortunes. This unpretending facility of manners, showing how little natural the alliance between superiority of intellect and austereness of demeanour, continued ever after prominent in his character; and from the event we may learn that such cheerful, conciliating, and sympathising habits are the surest road to lasting friendships. Of these, few persons ever enjoyed more—the greater number have gone where he has followed—still a few, and among them some of his earliest friends, survive; and it is no less honourable to their constancy than to his memory, that the same men, who, more than forty years ago, were cheering his efforts, and admitting him to their affections, are, at this day, with unabated ardour, mourning his loss and cherishing his fame.

The despondency which Mr. Curran's generous correspondent has just been seen so anxious to alleviate was not merely casual. Notwithstanding the liveliness of his conversation, from which a stranger would have supposed that his spirits never knew depression, he was all his life subject to visitations of constitutional melancholy, which the most ordinary accidents excited and embittered; even at this early time it may be observed constantly breaking out in his communications to his friends. After having passed the long vacation of 1774 with his family in Ireland, he thus writes to one of them upon his return to London:

"Apjohn and I arrived in London about eight o'clock on Thursday. When I was set down, and threw myself into a box in the next coffee-house to me, I think I never felt so strangely in my life. The struggle it cost me to leave Ireland, and the pain of leaving it as I did, had been hurried into a sort of numbness by the exertion of such an effort, and a certain exclusion of thought, which is often the consequence of a strong agitation of mind: the hurry also of the journey might in some measure have contributed to soothe for a moment these uneasy sensations. But the exertion was now over, the hurry was past; the barriers between me and reflection now gave way, and left me to be overwhelmed in the torrent; all the difficulties I had encountered, the happy moments I had lately passed, all now rushed in upon my mind, in melancholy succession, and engrossed the pang in their turn.

> Revolving in his alter'd soul
> The various turns of chance below,
> And now and then a sigh he stole,
> And tears began to flow.

"At length I roused myself from this mournful reverie, and, after writing a few words to Newmarket, set out in search of some of my old acquaintance. I sought them sorrowing, but there was not even one to be found; they had either changed their abodes or were in the country. How trivial a vexation can wound a mind that is once depressed! Even this little disappointment, though it was of no consequence, though it could not surprise me, yet had the power to afflict me, at least to add to my other mortifications. I could not help being grieved at considering how much more important changes may happen even in a shorter time; how the dearest hopes and most favorite projects of the heart may flourish, and flatter us with gaudy expectations for a moment, and then, suddenly disappearing, leave us to lament over our wretchedness and our credulity. Pleased with the novelty of the word, we fasten eagerly on the bauble, till satiated with enjoyment, or disgusted with disappointment, we resign it with contempt. The world, in general, follows our example, and we are soon thrown aside, like baubles, in our turn. And yet, dreary as the prospect is, it is no small consolation to be attached to, and to be assured of the attachment of some worthy affectionate souls, where we may find a friendly refuge from the rigours of our destiny; to have even one congenial bosom on which the poor afflicted spirit may repose, which will feelingly participate our joys or our sorrows, and with equal readiness catch pleasure from our successes, or strive to alleviate the anguish of disappointment."

In another letter, written a few weeks after, the same unfortunate sensibility is more strikingly exemplified, and more vigorously expressed. In one passage we clearly recognise the peculiarities of his subsequent style.

"I this day left my lodgings; the people were so very unruly that I could stay no longer; I am now at No. 4, in St. Martin's Street, Leicester Fields, not far from my former residence. You will perhaps smile at the weakness, yet I must confess it; never did I feel myself so spiritless, so woe-begone, as when I was preparing for the removal. I had settled myself with an expectation of remaining till I should finally depart for Ireland; I was now leaving it before that period, and my spirits sunk into a mixture of peevishness and despondence at the disappointment. I had emptied the desk belonging to the lodgings of my few moveables, which I collected in a heap on the floor, and prepared to dispose of in my little trunk. Good heavens! in how many various parts, and by how many various ways may the poor human heart be wounded! Is it that even Philosophy cannot so completely plunge her children in the waters of wisdom, that an heel, at least, will not be left vulnerable, and exposed to the danger of an arrow? Is the fable equally applicable to the mind as to the body? And is all our firmness and intrepidity founded ultimately on our weakness and our foibles? May all our giant fortitude be so lulled into slumber, as, ere it awakes, to be chained to the ground by a few Lilliputian grievances, and held immoveably by such slender fetters? Why else shall we be unaccountably depressed? To leave the friends of my heart, to tear myself from their last affecting farewell, to turn my face to a distant region, separated from them by mountains, and oceans, and tempests; to endure all this with something like calmness, and yet to feel pain at changing from one street to another! Strange inconsistence! and yet so it was. I proceeded very slowly to fill the trunk. I could not please myself in the packing. Some letters now presented themselves; I could not put them in without reading. At length I made an end to the work, and fell into another reverie; I called to mind my first acquaintance with my little trunk; I industriously hunted my memory for every thing that any way related to it, and gave my recollection a great deal of credit for being so successful in making me miserable. At length I got it behind Tom Gess, and saw poor Tom edging forward to avoid its jolting, and longing to be relieved from his durance. I saw it embark: over how many billows was it wafted, from Cork to Bristol, over how many miles from Bristol to London! And how small a portion of that distance must it measure back to-day! And must I be equally slow in my return? With such sensations I left Mr. Turner's, perhaps as completely miserable as any man in London."

Of some of his occupations, he gives the following account:

"As to my amusements, they are very few. Since I wrote last, I went to one play. I commonly spend even more time at home, than I can employ in reading of an improving and amusing kind.* As I live near the Park, I walk there some time every day. I sometimes find entertainment in visiting the diversity of eating-places with which this town abounds. Here every coal-porter is a politician, and vends his maxims in public with all the importance of a man who thinks he is exerting himself for the public service: he claims the privilege of looking as wise as possible, and

* Mr. Curran's cotemporaries at the Temple have confirmed his own account of his habits at that period. He rose very early, studied till he was exhausted, and then went out in search of his fellow students, with whom he passed the interval till the evening, when they all generally repaired to any debating society that was open. During his second year at the Temple, he spent a considerable portion of his time in the courts of law —C.

of talking as loud, of damning the ministry, and abusing the king, with less reserve than he would his own equal. Yet, little as these poor people understand of the liberty they contend so warmly for, or of the measures they rail against, it reconciles one to their absurdity, by considering that they are happy at so small an expense as being ridiculous; and they certainly receive more pleasure from the power of abusing, than they would from the reformation of what they condemn. I take the more satisfaction in this kind of company, as, while it diverts me, it has the additional recommendation of reconciling economy with amusement.

"Another portion of time I have set apart every day for thinking of my absent friends. Though this is a duty that does not give much trouble to many, I have been obliged to confine it, or endeavour to confine it, within proper bounds: I have, therefore, made a resolution to avoid any reflections of this sort, except in their allotted season, that is, immediately after dinner. I am then in a tranquil, happy humour, and I increase that happiness by presenting to my fancy those I love in the most advantageous point of view: so that however severely I treat them when they intrude in the morning, I make them ample amends in the evening; I then assure myself that they are twice as agreeable, and as wise and as good as they really are."

The conclusion of this letter shall be given, if not for the sake of the incidents, at least to show the writer's sensibility to any pathetic occurrence that fell in his way.

"I have lately made two acquaintances; one a Frenchman, Dr. Du Garreau; the other is a German, Mr. Skell, for whom I am indebted to the doctor. With this latter I am not yet much acquainted; the former is really a man of understanding, and, I believe, of worth: he is the son of an advocate in Paris, and practised there himself, as a physician, for some time. He had conceived an affection for a young lady with whom the difference of their religion prevented his union at home; but, alas! I believe love is of no particular sect; at least so the lady seemed to think, for she quitted France with him, and took his honour as the security for his adhering to a ceremony performed between them in Holland. After three or four years' residence in Amsterdam, where I suppose his practice was not considerable, he brought his wife and child to England, last November. She survived the journey but a few weeks, and left the poor man surrounded by every distress. His friends have pressed him to return; but he is determined, at all events, to remain in England, rather than carry his daughter to a country where she would not be considered as legitimate. Rouelle had hinted to me that there was something singular in his fortune, but I did not know the particulars till a few days since, that I breakfasted with him. He had taken his little child on his knee, and, after trifling with her for a few moments, burst into tears. Such an emotion could not but excite, as well as justify, some share of curiosity. The poor doctor looked as if he were conscious I felt for him, and his heart was too full to conceal his affliction. He kissed his little orphan, as he called her, and then endeavoured to acquaint me with the lamentable detail. It was the hardest story in the world to be told by a man of delicacy. He felt all the difficulties of it; he had many things to palliate, some that wanted to be justified; he seemed fully sensible of this, yet checked himself when he slided into anything like defence. I could perceive the conflict shifting the colours on his cheek, and I could not but pity him and admire him for such an embarrassment. Yet, notwithstanding all his distresses, he sometimes assumes all the gaiety of a Frenchman, and is a very entertaining fellow. These are the occasions on which we are almost justified in repining at the want of affluence; to relieve such an heart from part of its affliction, surely, for such a purpose, it is not ambitious to wish for riches."

One more of his letters, in this year, shall be introduced, as characteristic of his mind. The person to whom it is addressed, a gentleman of the most amiable and respected character, has survived the writer, but his name is, at his own request, reluctantly omitted. The friendship of which the commencement of this letter contains a proof, continued without diminution to the day of Mr. Curran's death.

"MY DEAR DICK:—

"Your packet was one of the most seasonable, on every account. As I think I mentioned to you when I should repay this kindness, in my last, I need not repeat it here. I hope you do n't expect any news from me; if you did, I would be under a necessity of disappointing you. Unfortunately, I have no gratification in seeing high houses or tall steeples, no ear to be ravished by barrel-organs, no public anxiety or private importance by which vanity might lay hold on me, no fine clothes, no abundance of money, to recommend me to the deity of pleasure. What, then, can a poor devil like me either see or hear that is worth communicating to a friend? In truth, I think I am nearly the same man I ever was; affecting to look wise, and to talk wise, and exhausting most lavishly on looking and talking, the wisdom that a better economist would reserve for acting. And yet, Dick, perhaps this is natural; perhaps we are mistaken when we wonder at finding frugality, or even avarice, on such good terms with affluence, and extravagance inseparable from poverty. In both cases, they are effects that flow naturally from their causes. They are the genuine issue of their respective parents; who, to own the truth, cherish and preserve their offspring with a care truly parental, and unfailingly successful. 'Tis just so in wisdom, and, on the same principle, the man who has but a very small share of wisdom (like him whose purse is equally shallow) squanders it away on every silly occasion; he thinks it too trifling to be worth hoarding against emergencies of moment: but a very wise man, or a very rich man, acts in a manner diametrically opposite to this. When the one has ranged his sentiments and marshalled his maxims, and the other computed his tens of thousands, the symmetry of their labours would be destroyed should a single dogma escape to the banners of unwiseness, or a single guinea take its flight to supply an extravagance. Each atom of the aggregate is held fast by its gravitation to the whole mass; hence the fool is prodigal of his little wisdom, and the sixpence departs in peace from the pocket where it is not troubled with the ceremony of bidding adieu to another. If any chance should make me master of some enormous treasure, I would not despair of finding out its value; and if experience, and the industry of my own folly, shall reap a harvest of prudence, I will make you wonder at my care in drying it for use. I will regale myself in my old age with the spirit of it, and dispense the small tea to those who may have occasion for it."

During Mr. Curran's attendance at the Temple, the society in which he mixed was almost exclusively that of his Irish fellow-students. He was at that time too unknown to have access to the circle of literature or fashion, and it was perhaps fortunate for him that his obscurity saved him from those scenes where he might have contracted the dangerous ambition of soaring when he should have been learning to fly. Of the celebrated persons then in London, he used to mention that he had seen Goldsmith once at a coffee-house, Garrick (whom he recollected with enthusiasm) two or three times upon the stage, and Lord Mansfield, whose dignified appearance made a very solemn impression upon him, upon the bench. The only man of any eminence that he came into personal contact with vas Macklin, the actor, and the origin of their acquaintance was rather singular.

After Mr. Curran had concluded his terms, he was detained for some time in London in expectation of a remittance from Ireland, without which he could neither discharge his arrears at his lodgings, nor return to his own country. At length, just as his purse had attained "the last stage of inanition," he received a bill of exchange upon a banking-house in Lombard-street: without stopping to examine the bill minutely, he flew to present it; but the banker soon discovered that a necessary indorsement was omitted, and of course refused to pay it. Of the scene upon this occasion, as it took place across the counter, his own consternation at the dreadful tidings, and the banker's insensibility to his distress, his solemn and repeated protestations that the bill came from the *most* respectable merchant in the butter trade at Cork, and the wary citizen's marked distrust of all that was Irish, Mr. Curran used to give a most dramatic and luxurious description. Having left the banker's, and being without a shilling in his pocket, he strolled into St. James' Park, where he remained during his usual dinner hour, considering the means of relieving himself from his present necessity; but after long reflection, he could only come to one certain conclusion, that the misfortune could never have happened more inopportunely, every one of his Irish friends, to whom alone he could have applied, having quitted London, leaving him behind, awaiting this remittance.

As he sat upon one of the benches, exhausted with devising expedients, he began to whistle a melancholy old Irish air; an old gentleman seated at the other end (it was Macklin) started at the well-known sounds.

"Pray, sir," said the stranger, "may I venture to ask where you learned that tune?"

"Indeed, sir," replied the whistler, in the meek and courteous tone of a spirit which affliction had softened, "indeed you may, sir; I learned it in my native country, in Ireland."

"But how comes it, sir, that at this hour, while other people are dining, you continue here, whistling old Irish airs?"

"Alas! sir, I too have been in the habit of dining of late, but to-day, my money being all gone, and my credit not yet arrived, I am even forced to come and dine upon a whistle in the park."

Struck by the mingled despondence and playfulness of this confession, the benevolent veteran exclaimed, "Courage, young man! I think I can see that you deserve better fare; come along with me, and you shall have it."

About ten years after this interview Macklin came to Dublin:

Mr. Curran, who in the interval had risen to eminence, was invited one evening to a party where the actor was one of the company; they were presented to each other, but Macklin failed to recognize in the now celebrated advocate and orator, the distressed student in St. James' Park. Mr. Curran, perceiving this, abstained for the moment from claiming any acquaintance; but he contrived in a little time to introduce a conversation upon the acts of kindness and hospitality which Irishmen so generally receive abroad from such of their countrymen as they may chance to meet; as a proof of which, he began to relate what had happened to himself, and proceeded to give a vivid picture of the scene, and (suppressing the name) of the generous old man who had befriended him in a land of strangers. A glow of recollection was soon observed upon the player's countenance; he started, and fixing his eyes upon the speaker, "If my memory fails me not, sir," said he, "we have met before?" "Yes, Mr. Macklin," replied Mr. Curran, taking his hand, "indeed we have met; and though upon that occasion you were only performing upon a private theatre, let me assure you, that (to adopt the words of a high judicial personage, which you have heard before) *you never acted better.*"*

Before dismissing this period of Mr. Curran's history, a few words may be added upon the subject of the studies, and intellectual habits of his early days; for, in consequence of his not having devoted much time in his latter years to books, and still more from the great predominance of imagination over learning, to be observed in all the productions of his mind, an opinion has generally prevailed that his reading was extremely circumscribed, and that he was, from taste or by constitution, intolerant of any regular application. If such were the fact, notwithstanding the dan-

* These words were addressed from the bench by Lord Mansfield to Mr. Macklin, to mark his approbation of the liberal conduct of the latter in a cause to which he was a party, and which was tried before his lordship in 1774. The proceedings in that interesting case are given at length in Kirkman's life of Macklin.—C.

ger of the example, it still would not be denied; the indolent should have all the benefit or all the mischief of such a precedent; but, in truth, Mr. Curran never was a mere gifted idler. He might not, indeed, have been always found with a book before him, he might not have been nominally a severe student, but for the course of forty years he kept his faculties in perpetual exercise; and if all that he created in public, or in the society of his friends, had been composed in the retirement of the closet, it would have scarcely been asserted that idleness was the habit of his mind.

In his youth he was a formal student, to a greater extent than is generally supposed. Before he had attained the age of twenty-five, when he was called to the bar, independent of his classical acquirements, which have never been doubted, his acquaintance with general literature was far from inconsiderable; he was perfectly familiar with all the most popular of the English poets, historians, and speculative writers. He had, at the same age, with little assistance but that of books, acquired more than a common knowledge of the French language. If he did not pursue a long consecutive course of legal reading, he was yet perpetually making a vigorous plunge, from which he seldom returned without some proof that he had reached the bottom. For several years after his admission to the bar, he devoted more of his mornings and evenings to the study of his profession than his most intimate friends at the time could have believed to be compatible with his convivial habits and public avocations. His frame was never robust, but it was extremely patient of fatigue; and no matter how great the exhaustion of the day, or the evening, a very few hours sleep completely restored it; this natural felicity of constitution he confirmed by early rising, constant exercise, the daily practice of cold bathing, and similar methods of invigorating the system.

Indeed, when it is recollected that Mr. Curran, at the period of his life at present under consideration, was looking to the bar alone for the means of future subsistence, and for the gratification of his ambition, it is utterly incredible that he should have neglected the ordinary arts by which success was to be attained. According to the concurring accounts given by himself and his cotemporaries, he neglected none of them. Eloquence was at that time not only the most popular, but one of the shortest roads to eminence at the Irish bar; and from the moment of the discovery of his powers as a speaker, he began, and continued, to cultivate them with the utmost assiduity. His enunciation (as has been already observed) was naturally impeded, his voice shrill, and his accent strongly provincial, or (to use his own expression) "in a state of nature;" to remove these defects, he adopted the practice of daily reading aloud, slowly and distinctly, and of most studiously observing and imitating the tones and manner of more skilful speakers. The success of this exercise and study was so complete, that among his most unrivalled excellencies as an orator, were the clearness of his articulation, and a peculiar, uninterrupted, graduated intonation; which whatever was the subject, whether tender or impassioned, melodised every period. His person wa without dignity or grace—short, slender, and inelegantly propor tioned. To attain an action, that might conceal as much as pos sible these deficiencies, he recited perpetually before a mirror, and selected the gesticulation that he thought best adapted to his imperfect stature. To habituate his mind to extemporaneous fluency, he not only regularly attended the debating clubs of London, but, both before and after his admission to the bar, resorted to a system of solitary exercise, of which the irksomeness cannot be well appreciated by those who have never practised it. He either extracted a case from his books, or proposed to himself some original question; and this he used to debate alone, with the same anxious attention to argument and to diction, as if he were discussing it in open court. There is nothing in all this to excite any won der; but certainly the person who early submitted to these modes of labour, and frequently resumed them, cannot be considered as careless or incapable of application.

It may be a matter of curiosity with some, to know the writers, that, having been Mr. Curran's early favourites, may be supposed to have had an influence in forming his style. Some of his letters, already given, discover in different passages a preference for the manner of Sterne; a similar resemblance appears more frequently, and more strongly, in several others of about the same date, which have not been introduced. It was from the "Letters of Junius," that he generally declaimed before a glass.* Junius and Lord Bolingbroke, were the English prose writers, whom he at that time studied as the most perfect models of the declamatory style. Among the English poets, he was passionately fond of "Thomson's Seasons." He often selected exercises of delivery from "Paradise Lost," which he then admired, but subsequently (and it is hoped that few will attempt to justify the change) his sensibility to the beauties of that noble poem greatly subsided.† In this list, the sacred writings must not be omitted; independent of their more solemn titles to his respect, Mr. Curran was from his childhood exquisitely alive to their mere literary excellencies; and in his maturer years seldom failed to resort to them, as to a source of the most splendid and awful topics of persuasion.‡

* The single exercise that he most frequently repeated for the purpose of improving his action and intonation, was the speech of Antony over Cæsar's body, from Shakspeare's Julius Cæsar. This he considered to be a master-piece of eloquence, comprising in itself, and involving in its delivery, the whole compass of the art. He studied it incessantly, and pronounced it with great skill, but though he delighted his auditors, he never entirely satisfied himself; he uniformly recommended it as a lesson to his *young friends at the bar*.—C.

† In criticising Milton, Mr. Curran always dwelt upon what others have considered among the most splendid and attractive parts of his work, the scenes in Paradise; in objecting to which, he contended that the human characters introduced are detached and solitary beings, whose peculiar situation precluded them from displaying the various social feelings and passions, which are the proper subjects of poetic emotion. For a vigorous and eloquent answer to this objection, see Hazlitt's observations on Paradise Lost, in his Lectures upon the English Poets.—C.

‡ Of all the profane writers, Virgil, whom he considered "the prince of sensitive poets,"

Before quitting the subject of Mr. Curran's youthful habits, it is proper to mention the pleasure that he took in occasionally mingling in the society of the lower orders of his countrymen: he was a frequent attendant at the weddings and wakes of his neighbourhood. Being from his infancy familiar with the native Irish language, he lost nothing of whatever interest such meetings could afford. They appear to have had considerable influence on his mind; he used to say himself, that he derived his first notions of poetry and eloquence from the compositions of the hired mourner over the dead.* It was probably amidst those scenes that he acquired the rudiments of that thorough knowledge of the Irish character, of which he afterwards made so amusing an use in enlivening a company, and so important a one in confounding a perjured witness. It may have been too in this humble intercourse that some even of his finer tastes and feelings originated or were confirmed. Out of Ireland the genius of its natives is, in general, but partly known. They are, for the most part, represented as comical and impetuous, qualities which, lying upon the surface, strike the stranger and superficial observer; but with these they unite the deepest sensibility. It is the latter that prevails; and if their pathetic sayings had been as sedulously

was his favourite. For a considerable part of his life, he made it a rule to read Homer once a year; but the more congenial tenderness of Virgil attracted him every day.—C.

* It may be necessary to inform some English readers, that the practice of formal lamentations over the dead is one of the ancient customs of the Irish, which is continued among the lower orders to the present day. In the last century, it was not usual upon the death of persons of the highest condition. The ceremony is generally performed by women, who receive a remuneration for composing and reciting a "Coronach" at the wake of the departed. In some parts of Ireland, these women used formerly to go about the country, to "look in" upon such elderly persons as might soon require their attendance; and to remind them, that whenever the hour might arrive, a noble Coronach should be ready. Mr. Curran's father-in-law, Dr. Creagh, was so molested by one of these dispiriting visitors, and had such an aversion to the usage, that in the first will he ever made, he thus begins, after the usual preamble, "requesting it as a favour of my executors, that, neither at my wake nor at my funeral, they will suffer any of the savage howlings, and insincere lamentations, that are usually practised upon these serious and melancholy occasions, but to see the whole of my burial conducted with silence and Christian decency."—C.

recorded as their lively sallies, it would be seen that they can be as eloquent in their lamentations as they are original in their humour. Of these almost national peculiarities, so opposite, yet to constantly associated. Mr. Curran's mind strongly partook; and in his, as in his country's character, melancholy predominated. In his earliest, as well as his latest speculations, he declined to take a desponding view of human affairs—he appeared, indeed, more frequently in smiles to relax his mind, or to entertain his companions; but when left entirely to his original propensities, he seems to have ever wept from choice.

[If Mr. O'Regan's account can be relied on, Curran's predisposition for eloquence may be traced to an event which occurred while he was a child, at a wake, in his native Newmarket. The story runs thus:

"At one of those national carnivals, where the common excitements of snuff, tobacco, and whiskey, and the fruits of plundered orchards, are abundantly supplied, Mr. Curran felt the first dawn, the new-born light, and favourite transport which almost instantly seized upon his imagination, and determined his mind to the cultivation and pursuit of oratory. It was produced by the speech of a tall, finely-shaped woman, with long black hair flowing loosely down her shoulders; her stature and eye commanding; her air and manner austere and majestic. On such occasions, nothing is prepared: all arises out of the emotion excited by the surrounding circumstances and objects.

"Some of the kindred of the deceased had made funeral orations on his merits: they measured their eulogies by his bounties; he was wealthy; his last will had distributed among his relations his fortune and effects; but to this woman, who married without his consent, to her, his favourite niece, a widow, and with many children, he carried his resentment to the grave, and left her poor and totally unprovided for. She sat long in silence, and at length, slowly, and with a measured pace, approaching the dead body from a distant quarter of the room, with the serenest calm of meditation, laying her hand on his forehead, she paused; and, whilst all present expected a passionate and stormy expression of her anger and disappointment, she addressed these few words to him: 'Those of my kindred who have uttered praises, and poured them forth with their tears, to the memory of the deceased, did that which, by force of obligation, they were bound to do. They have been benefited; they have, in their different degrees, profited by that bounty which he could no longer withhold. He forgot, in his life, the exercise of that generosity by which his memory might now be held regarded and embalmed in the hearts of a disinterested affection. Such consolation, however, as these purchased praises could impart to his spirit, I would not, by any impiety, tear from him. Cold in death is this head, not colder than that heart while living, through which no thrill of nature did ever vibrate. This has thrown the errors of my youth, and of an impulse too obedient to that affection which I still cherish, into poverty and sorrow, heightened beyond hope by the loss of him who is now in heaven, and still more by the tender pledges he has left after him on earth. But I shall not add to these reflections the bitter remorse of inflicting even a merited calumny; and because my blood coursed through his veins, I shall not have his memory scored or tortured by the expression of my disappointment, or of the desolation which sweeps through my heart. It, therefore, best becomes me to say, his faith and honor, in the other relations of life, were just and exact; and that these may have imposed a severity on his principles and manners. The tears which now swell my eyes are those I cannot check; but they rise like bubbles on a mountain-stream—they burst never more to appear."]

One conjecture more shall be hazarded, and so pleasing a one, that few can wish it to be unfounded. It was probably from this early intercourse with the peasantry of his country, and from the consequent conviction of their unmerited degradation, that sprang that unaffected soul-felt sympathy for their condition, so conspicuous in Mr. Curran's political career. Upon this subject, it was evident that his heart was deeply involved. From them, notwithstanding much temptation and many dangers, his affections never wavered for an instant. From the first dawn of political obligation upon his mind to his latest hour (an interval of more than half a century), he never thought or spoke of them but with tenderness, and pity. At the bar, in the senate,* on the bench,

* Upon one occasion, alluding in parliament to the general apathy of the ministry to the condition of the great body of the Irish people, he observed: "I am sorry to see that the rays of the honourable member's panegyric were not vertical; like the beams of the morning, they courted the mountain-tops, and left the valleys unilluminated—they fell only upon the great, while the miserable poor were left in the shade."—*Debates in Irish House of Commons*, 1787.—C.

amidst his family and friends, or in the society of the most illustrious personages of the empire, the sufferings of the Irish peasant were remembered, and their cause pleaded with an energy and reality that proved how well he knew, and how deeply he felt for, that class whose calamities he deplored. "At any time of my life," said he, "I might, to a certain degree, as well as others, have tied up my countrymen in bundles, and sold them at the filthy market of corruption, and have raised myself to wealth and station, and remorse—to the envy of the foolish, and the contempt of the wise; but I thought it more becoming to remain below among them, to mourn over and console them; or, where my duty called upon me, to reprimand and rebuke them, when they were acting against themselves."

In some of the published accounts of Mr. Curran's life, it has been stated that, when at the Temple, and afterwards while struggling into notice at the bar, he derived part of his subsistence from contributions to literary works; but for this there is no foundation. During the first year of his residence in London, his means were supplied partly by his relatives in Ireland, and partly by some of his more affluent companions, who considered his talents a sufficient security for their advances. In the second year, he married a daughter of the Dr. Creagh already mentioned; her portion was not considerable, but it was so carefully managed, and his success at the bar was so rapid, that he was ever after a stranger to pecuniary difficulties.

It may, too, be here observed that, had he been originally more favoured by fortune, his prospect of distinguished success in his profession might not have been so great. There is, perhaps, fully as much truth as humour in the assertion of an English judge, that a barrister's first requisite for attaining eminence is "*not to be worth a shilling*."* The attractions of the bar, when viewed from

* The learned judge alluded to, upon being asked "What conduced most to a barrister's success?" is said to have replied, "that barristers succeeded by many methods; some by great talents, some by high connections, some by a miracle, but the *majority by commencing without a shilling*."—C.

a distance, will dazzle and seduce for a while. To a young and generous spirit, it seems, no doubt, a proud thing to mix in a scene where merit and talent alone are honoured, where he can emulate the example, and perhaps reach the distinctions of our Hales, and Holts, and Mansfields. But all this fancied loveliness of the prospect vanishes, the moment you approach and attempt to ascend. As a calling, the bar is perhaps the most difficult, and, after the first glow of enthusiasm has gone by, the most repelling. To say nothing of the violence of the competition, which alone renders it the most hazardous of professions, the intellectual labour, and the unintellectual drudgery that it involves, are such as few have the capacity, or, without the strongest incitements, the patience to endure. To an active and philosophic mind, the mere art of reasoning, the simple perception of relations, whatever the subject matter may be, is an exercise in which a mind so constituted may delight; but, to such a one, the study of the law has but little to offer. If the body of English law be a scientific system, it is a long time a secret to the student: it has few immutable truths, few master-maxims, few regular series of necessary and nicely adapted inferences. In vain will the student look for a few general principles, to whose friendly guidance he may trust, to conduct him unerringly to his object: to him, it is all perplexity, caprice, and contradiction*—arbitrary and mysterious rules, of which to trace and comprehend the reasons is the work of years—forced constructions, to which no equity of intention can reconcile—logical evasions, from which the mind's pride indignantly revolts—of all these, the young lawyer meets abundance in his books; and to encounter and tolerate them, he must have

* This was, at least, what Mr. Curran found it. In his poem on "Friendship," already mentioned, he says:

"Oft, when condemn'd 'midst Gothic tomes to pour,
And, dubious, con th' embarras'd sentence o'er,
While meteor meaning sheds a sickly ray
Through the thick gloom, then vanishes away,
With the dull toil tired out, th' indignant mind
Bursts from the yoke, and wanders unconfined."—C.

some stronger inducement than a mere literal ambition of learning or of fame. We consequently find that there is no other profession supplying so many members who never advance a single step; no other which so many abandon, disgusted and disheartened by the sacrifices that it exacts.

To these fearful pursuits, Mr. Curran brought every requisite of mind and character, and education, besides the above and grand requisite of want of fortune. Instead of being surprised at his eminent success, the wonder would have been if such a man had failed. Having acquirements and hopes, and a station, above his circumstances, to hold his ground, he could not allow his powers to slumber for a moment. His poverty, his pride, a secret consciousness of his value, and innate superstitious dread of obscurity, "that last infirmity of noble minds," kept him forever in motion, and impatient to realize his own expectations, and the predictions of those friends by whom his efforts were applauded and assisted.

It appears, in a passage of one of his letters from the Temple, that he had, for a while, an idea of trying his fortune at the American bar. "Mrs. W.," says he, "concluded her letter with mentioning her purpose of revisiting America, and repeating her former advice to me on that subject. As for my part, I am totally undetermined. I may well say, with Sir Roger de Coverly, that 'much may be said on both sides.' The scheme might be attended with advantage; yet I fear my mother, especially, would not be easily reconciled to such a step." But he soon abandoned the idea; for, in a letter dated a few weeks after, he says: "As to the American project, I presume it is unnecessary to tell you that the motives are now no more, and that the design has expired of consequence. I have been urged to be called to that bar, and my chief inducement was my friendship for Mrs. W., to whom I might be useful in that way; but there is so little likelihood of her going, that I shall scarcely have an opportunity of sacrificing that motive to my attachment for Ireland."

CHAPTER III.

Mr. Curran called to the Irish Bar—Dissimilarities between that and the English Bar—Causes of the Difference.

Mr. Curran was called in Michaelmas term, 1775, to the Irish bar, which was to occupy so distinguished a portion of his future life; but as the genius and habits of that bar, during the whole of his career, differed in many particulars essentially from that of England, it will be necessary to make a passing allusion to those distinctions, without which English readers might find it difficult to reconcile the specimens of his eloquence that occur in the following pages, with their previous ideas of forensic oratory.

No person who has attended to the course of forensic proceedings in the two countries can have failed to have observed, that while in England they are (with a very few exceptions) carried on with cold and rigorous formality, in Ireland they have not unfrequently been marked by the utmost vivacity and eloquence. The English barrister, even in cases of the deepest interest, where powerful emotions are to be excited, seldom ventures to exercise his imagination, if, indeed, long habits of restraint have left him the capacity to do so: yet in the Irish courts, not only are such subjects discussed in a style of the most impassioned oratory, but many examples might be produced, where questions more strictly technical, and apparently the most inappropriate themes of eloquence, have still been made the occasion of very fervid appeals to the feelings or the fancy. This latitude of ornament and digression, once so usual at the Irish bar, has been never known, and would never have been tolerated in Westminster Hall. It would be there accounted no less new than extravagant to hear a counsel pathetically reminding the presiding judge of the convivial meetings of their early days,* or enlivening his arguments on a grave question of law by humorous illustration.† Yet was all this listened to in Ireland with favor and admiration. It had, indeed, little influence upon the decisions of the bench. The advocate might have excited the smiles or tears of his hearers, but no legal concessions followed. The Judges who showed the most indulgence and sensibility to these episodes of fancy were ever the most conscientious in preserving the sacred stability of law. Into the Counsel's mirth or tenderness, no matter how digressive, they entered for the moment more pleased than otherwise with irregularities that gratified their taste and relieved their labour; but with them the triumph of eloquence was but evanescent—the oration over, they resumed their gravity and firmness, and proved by their ultimate decision, that if they relaxed for an instant, it was from urbanity, and not from any oblivion of the paramount duties of their station. The effects, however, which such appeals to the passions produced (as they still continue to do) upon juries, was very different; and when the advocate transferred the same style into his addresses to the bench, it was not that his judgment had selected it as the most appropriate, but

* See Mr. Curran's apostrophe to Lord Avonmore, chap. iv.—C.

† Of these examples without number might be produced from Mr. Curran's law arguments. His published speech in the Court of Exchequer, on Mr. Justice Johnson's case, is full of them. Equally striking instances occur in his argument on the same question before the Court of King's Bench. "The minister going to the House of Commons might be arrested upon the information of an Irish chairman, and the warrant of a trading justice. Mr. Pitt might be brought over here *in vinculis*. What to do? to see whether he can be bailed or not. I remember Mr. Fox was once here—during the lifetime of this country—so might he be brought over. It may facilitate the intercourse between the countries, for any man may travel at the public expense; as, suppose I gave an Irishman in London a small assault in trust, when the vacation comes, he knocks at the door of a trading justice, and tells him he wants a warrant against the counsellor. What counsellor? Oh, sure every body knows the counsellor. Well, friend, and what is your name? Thady O'Flannigan, please your honour. What countryman are you? An Englishman, *by construction*. Very well, I'll draw upon my correspondent in Ireland for the body of the counsellor."—C.

because he found it impossible to avoid relapsing into those modes of influencing the mind, which he had been long habituated to employ with so much success in another quarter.

In accounting for this adoption at the Irish bar, of a style of eloquence so much more fervid and poetical than the severer notions of the English Courts would approve, something must be attributed to the influence of the national character. From whatever cause it has arisen, the Irish are by temperament confessedly more warm and impetuous than their neighbours: their passions lying nearer the surface, their actions are more governed by impulse, and their diction more adorned by imagination, than it would be reasonable to expect in a colder, more advanced, and philosophic people. In addressing persons so constituted, the methods most likely to prevail are sufficiently obvious. The orator, who knows anything of his art, must be aware that frigid demonstration alone is not the best adapted to men who take a kind of pride in regulating their decisions by their emotions, and that a far more certain artifice of persuasion must be to fill their minds with those glowing topics by which they habitually persuade themselves.

It may be observed, too, that although the habits of mind which must be cultivated, in order to succeed in such a style of eloquence, are altogether different from those involved in the study of the law; yet in Ireland they have never been deemed incompatible with legal occupations. The preparation for the bar there has never been so entirely technical as it usually is in England: a very general taste for polite literature and popular acquirements has been united with the more stern and laborious attainments of professional knowledge, and it is to this combination of pursuits, that invigorate the understanding with those which exercise the imagination and improve the taste, that must be attributed that mass of varied and effective talent, which has so long existed among the members of the Irish bar.

But the immediate cause of that animated style of eloquence

that has of late years prevailed there, appears to have been the influence of the Irish House of Commons.

It was principally in the productions of the eminent leaders in that house, that originated the modern school of Irish oratory. In Ireland this popular style made its way from the senate to the bar; though at first view such a transition may not seem either necessary or natural. In England it has not taken place. At the time that the first Mr. Pitt, the pride of the English senate, was exalting and delighting his auditors by the majesty of his conceptions and the intrepid originality of his diction, Westminster Hall remained inaccessible to any contagious inspiration. At a later period, upon the memorable trial of Warren Hastings, the contrast is brought more palpably to view. While the celebrated prosecutors in that cause were soaring as high as imagination could find language to sustain it, while they were "shaking the walls that surrounded them with those anathemas of super-human eloquence,"* which remain among the recorded models of British oratory, the lawyers, who conducted the defence, were in general content to retaliate with tranquil argument and uninspired refutation. Introduction, therefore, of the parliamentary manner into the courts of Ireland, is to be accounted for by some circumstances peculiar to the country.

During that period when eloquence flourished most in the Irish Parliament, that is, for the last forty years of its existence, the number of barristers in the House of Commons bore a much

* Erskine's defence of Stockdale. This celebrated advocate may be adduced in refutation of some of the above opinions, and it must be admitted that in some degree he forms an exception; yet, without inquiring now, whether his was a style of eloquence peculiar to the individual, or characteristic to the English bar, it may be observed, that it differed essentially from that which prevailed at this time in the British parliament, and to a still greater extent in the Irish senate and at the Irish bar. If he had produced many such passages as that of the American savage, it would have been otherwise; but his general strength did not lie in the fervour of his imagination; it was by the vigour of his ethics and his logic, enforced by illustrations rather felicitous than impassioned, that he brought over the judgment to his side. It is not intended by these remarks to assign a superiority to either style—it is to be supposed that the eminent advocates of the two bars adopted the manner that was best suited to their respective countries.—C.

greater proportion to the whole than has been at any time usual in England. In those days the policy by which Ireland was governed being in the utmost degree unpopular, the whole patronage of the Irish administration was necessarily expended in alluring supporters of the measures against which the nation exclaimed. A majority of *numbers* in the House of Commons could then be easily procured, and for a long time such a majority had been sufficient for every purpose of the government; but at that period in question, the increasing influence and talent of the minority rendered it necessary to adopt every method of opposing them (if possible) with a predominance of intellect. The means of doing this, it would appear, were not to be found in that body which ruled the country, and recourse was had to the expedient of enlisting the rising men of the bar in the service of the Administration.* Accordingly, every barrister who had popular abilities enough to render his support of any moment, found a ready admission into Parliament, upon the condition of his declaring for the Viceroy; and in the event of his displaying sufficient talent and constancy, was certain of being rewarded with the highest honours of his profession.

But independent of those who were thus introduced to the senate, the bar was the profession most generally resorted to by the members or dependents of the highest families; as one in

* Such was the commencement of (among others) the late Lord Clonmel's fortune. "The Marquis of Townshend had expressed his wishes to Lord Chancellor Lifford, for the assistance of some young gentleman of the bar, on whose talent and fidelity he might rely, in the severe parliamentary campaigns then (1769) likely to take place. Lord Lifford, recommended Mr. Scott, who was accordingly returned to parliament, to oppose the party led on by the celebrated Flood."—*Hardy's Life of Lord Charlemont.* The necessity of calling in such aid gives us but a poor idea of the education and talents of the Irish aristocracy of the time. Mr Grattan, in 1797, thus mentions the great improvement in the intellect of his country that he had witnessed. "The progress of the human mind in the course of the last twenty-five years has been prodigious in Ireland; I remember when there scarcely appeared a publication in a newspaper of any degree of merit, which has not been traced to some person of note, on the part of government or the opposition; but now a multitude of very powerful publications appear, from authors entirely unknown, of profound and spirited investigation."—*Letter to the citizens of Dublin*—C.

which, without any claim of merit, they could, through the influence of their patrons, obtain situations of professional emolument, and where, if they possessed such a claim, the road was so open to legal preferment and to political distinction; and consequently all of the latter description, recommended by their talents, and supported by the power of their connexions, found access to the House of Commons, long before that period of standing and of professional reputation, at which the successful English barrister is accustomed or deems it prudent to become a senator.

These circumstances alone would in a great degree account for the number of lawyers in the Irish Parliament; but it should be farther observed, that it was not any particular class that looked to or obtained a seat in that assembly: the ambition of appearing there was very general at the Irish bar; it was the grand object upon which every enterprising barrister fixed his eye and his heart. This was the age of political speculation; it was "Ireland's lifetime." Great original questions were daily in her Parliament: the struggle between popular claims and ancient prerogatives was a scene where much seemed likely to be gained —by the venal for themselves, by the honest for their country; but whether considered as a post of honour or of profit, it was one to which men of colder temperaments than the Irish might be easily moved to aspire.

The consequence of this intermixture of political with legal pursuits was, that the talents most suited to advance the former were much cultivated and constantly exercised; and from this difference in the objects and habits of the bars of the two countries appear to have principally resulted the different styles of oratory displayed by the members of each, both in their parliamentary and forensic exertions. The English barrister, long disciplined to technical observances, having passed the vigour of his intellect in submissive reverence to rules and authorities, brings into the House of Commons the same subtle propensities, and the same dread of expanded investigation and of rhetorical ornament that his professional duties imposed; but in Ireland the leading counsel were also from an early age distinguished members of the senate. If in the morning their horizon was bounded by their briefs, in a few hours their minds were free to rise, and extend it as far as the statesman's eye could reach; they had the daily excitation and tumult of popular debate to clear away any momentary stagnations of fancy or enterprize; the lawyer became enlarged into the legislator, and instead of introducing into the efforts of the latter the coldness and constraint of his professional manner, he rather delighted to carry back with him to the forum, all the fervour, and pomp, and copiousness of the deliberative style.

The Parliament of Ireland, the nurse of the genius and ambition of its bar, is now extinct; but the impulse that it gave is not yet spent; the old have not yet forgotten the inspiration of the scene where they beheld so many accomplished orators pass their most glorious hours; the young cannot hear without a throb of emulation the many wonderous things of that proud work of their fathers, which was levelled for having towered too high; nor is the general regret of the bar for its fall unincreased by their possession and daily admiration of two noble and still perfect relics, attesting the magnificence of the structure they have survived.*

Another peculiarity of the Irish bar that is now passing away, but which prevailed to a great extent during Mr. Curran's forensic career, was the frequency of collision between the bar and the bench. It was often his fate to be involved in them, and many are the instances of the promptness of repartee, and of the indignant intrepidity with which, on all such occasions, he defended the

* Messrs. Bushe and Plunkett, two of the members of the Irish House of Commons, the most distinguished for eloquence, continue at the Irish bar.—C. [This was written in 1818. Bushe became Lord Chief Justice of Ireland in 1822, and died in 1843. Plunkett, twice Irish Lord Chancellor, died 1854, a British Peer.—M.]

privileges of the advocate. It will be presently seen that he had scarcely appeared at the bar, when he showed how he could encounter and triumph over all the taunts and menaces of a hostile judge. The same spirit of resistance and retaliation will be found in his contests with Lord Clare; and at a much subsequent period, when he was exerting himself in a cause with his characteristic firmness, the presiding judge having called the sheriff to be ready to take into custody any one who should disturb the decorum of his court, "Do, Mr. Sheriff," replied Mr. Curran, "go and get ready my dungeon; prepare a bed of straw for me; and upon that bed I shall to-night repose with more tranquillity than I should enjoy were I sitting upon that bench with a consciousness that I disgraced it."

The same political causes that have been already alluded to as influencing the oratory of the Irish bar, will, in a great measure, account for these conflicts in the courts, and for that tone of sarcasm and defiance assumed by the barrister on such occasions.

It was one of the public calamities of the period when such scenes were most frequent, that, in the selection of persons to fill the judicial seat, more attention was often paid to family interest and political services than to the claims of merit, or the benefit of the community. No doubt, it sometimes happened that this important office was bestowed upon men, to whom the appointment to situations of honour and of trust was less a gift, than the payment of the justest debt. What dignity could be too exalted for the learned and accomplished Lord Avonmore? What trust too sacred for Lord Kilwarden, the most conscientious, and pacific, and merciful of men?* But if Ireland beheld such persons

* Arthur Wolfe, son of a country gentleman in Kildare, was born in 1739, became a barrister, and soon after, a member of the Irish parliament. In this latter capacity, siding with the government, he contended with Flood and Grattan. He was appointed Solicitor-General in 1787, Attorney-General in 1789, and Chief Justice of Ireland in 1798, being then created Lord Kilwarden; in 1800 was raised to the rank of Viscount, and in 1802 was made Vice-Chancellor of the University of Dublin. On the evening of July 28, 1803 (when Emmett's insurrection prematurely broke out), Lord Kilwarden was met by a band of armed men, in Thomas street, Dublin, who killed him and his nephew by stab-

adorning their station, she had the anguish and humiliation to see others degrading it by their political fury, or by the more indecent gratification of their particular animosities. Influenced by such unworthy feelings of party or of private hostility, the judges, in those days, were too prone to consider it a branch of their official duty to discountenance any symptoms of independence in their court; and though at times they may have succeeded, yet, at others, indignant and exemplary was the retaliation to which such a departure from their dignity exposed them: for it was not unusual that the persons who made these experiments upon the spirit of the bar, and whose politics and connections had raised them to a place of nominal superiority, were, in public consideration, and in every intellectual respect, the inferiors of the men that they undertook to chide. It sometimes happened, too, that the parties, whose powers might be less unequal, had been old parliamentary antagonists; and when the imputed crimes of the oppositionist came to be visited upon the advocate, it is not surprising that he should have retorted with pride, and acrimony, and contempt. Hence arose in the Irish Courts those scenes of personal contention, which the different character of the bench in later times precludes, and which (whatever side gain the victory) must be ever deprecated as ruinous to the client, and disgraceful to that spot, within whose precincts faction and passion should never be permitted to intrude.

But though the solemnity of judicial proceedings in Ireland might have been often disturbed by the preceding causes, they have been more frequently enlivened by others of a less unamiable description. Notwithstanding the existence there of that religious and political bigotry which tends to check every cheerful impulse, and, in their place, to substitute general distrust and gloom, these baneful effects have been powerfully counteracted by the more

bing them with pikes. It was supposed that his administration of the Criminal Law, in 1795, had created enmity to him. Lord Kilwarden, who supported the Union, was an eloquent speaker, in the Senate as well as at the bar, and a very eminent lawyer.—M.

prevailing influence of the national character. The honest kindly affections of nature, though impeded, have still kept on their course. In spite of all the sufferings and convulsions of the last century, the social vivacity of the Irish was proverbial. It subsisted, as it still subsists, in an eminent degree, in their private intercourse; it may be also seen constantly breaking forth in their public discussions. At the bar, where the occasions of jocularity so frequently occur, it is, as might be expected, most strikingly displayed. The Irish judges have not disdained to resign themselves to the favourite propensity of their country. The humorous sally or classical allusion, which would have pleased at the table, has not been frowned upon from the bench; their habits of social intimacy with the bar, and their own tastes as scholars and companions, have rather prepared them to tolerate, and even join in those lively irregularities which the more severe decorum of Westminster Hall might condemn. This urbanity and indulgence still remains; and scarcely a term passes over without many additions, either from the bar or the bench, to the large fund of Irish forensic humour.*

A more frequent and less dignified description of mirth, of which so much may be observed in the legal proceedings of Ireland, is that which originates in the particular character of the lower orders of that country. They abound in sagacity and repartee—qualities to which, when appearing as unwilling witnesses, or when struggling under the difficulties of a cross-examination, they seldom fail to fly to shelter. Their answers, on such occasions, are singularly adroit and evasive,† and the advocate is conseqently obliged to adopt every artifice of humour and ridicule, as more effectual than seriousness or menace, to extract the truth and expose their equivocations. The necessity of employing

* It is worth noting that the jokes which now amuse judges, counsel, clients, and witnesses, in Courts of Law, are notoriously poor ones. Real forensic fun and wit appear to have disappeared. This holds good on both sides of the Atlantic.—M.

† See Mr. Curran's cross-examination of O'Brien, inserted hereafter.—C.

such methods of confounding the knavish ingenuity of a witness, perpetually occasions the most striking contrasts between the solemnity of the subjects, and the levity of the language in which they are investigated. It is particularly in the Irish criminal courts that scenes of this complicated interest most constantly occur. In the front appear the counsel and the evidence in a dramatic contest, at which the auditors cannot refrain from bursts of laughter, and at a little distance behind, the prisoner under trial, gazing upon them with agonized attention, and catching at a presage of his fate in the alternating dexterity or fortune of the combatants.

This intrusion of levity into proceedings that should be marked by pomp and dignity may be indecent, but it is inevitable. Without this latitude of examination, no right would be secure, and, when exerted, no gravity can resist its influence; even the felon's visage is often roused from its expression of torpid despair by the sallies that accompany the disclosure of his crimes. As long, therefore as the Irish populace retain their present character of vivacity and acuteness, the Irish advocate must cultivate and display his powers of humour, often, perhaps, to a greater extent than his own better taste would desire; and the courts, aware of the necessity of such an instrument for eliciting the truth, will not consider it incumbent on them to interfere with its use.

CHAPTER IV.

Mr. Curran's early success at the bar—His contest with Judge Robinson—His defence of a Roman Catholic priest—His duel with Mr. St. Leger—Receives the dying benediction of the priest—Lord Avonmore's friendship—His character of Lord Avonmore—Monks of St. Patrick, and list of the original members—Anecdotes of Lord Avonmore—Mr. Curran's entrance into Parliament.

Mr. Curran has been frequently alluded to as one of the many examples in the history of the bar, of the highest talents remaining for a long time unknown and unrewarded. This, however, was not the fact: so general was the reputation of his abilities, and so numerous his personal friends, that he became employed immediately, and to an extent that is very unusual with those, who, like him, have solely depended upon their own exertions and upon accidental support.*

The failure of Mr. Curran's first attempt at speaking has been mentioned: a more singular instance of that nervousness which so frequently accompanies the highest capacity, occurred to him upon his debut in the courts. The first brief that he held was in the Court of Chancery; he had only to read a short sentence from his instructions, but he did it so precipitately and inaudibly, that the chancellor, Lord Lifford, requested of him to repeat the words, and to raise his voice: upon this his agitation became so extreme that he was unable to articulate a syllable; the *brief dropped from his hands*, and a friend who sat beside him was obliged to take it up and read the necessary passage.†

* The fact of his early practice appears from his own fee-book, in which the receipts commence from the day after he was called to the bar. The first year produced eighty-two guineas, the second between one and two hundred, and so on, in a regularly increasing proportion.—C.

† Lord Erskine, on his debut at the English bar, is said to have been equally nervous,

This diffidence, however, totally vanished whenever he had to repel what he conceived an unwarrantable attack. It was by giving proofs of the proud and indignant spirit with which he could chastise aggression, that he first distinguished himself at the bar:* of this his contest with Judge Robinson is recorded as a very early and memorable instance. Mr. Curran having observed in some case before that judge, "That he had never met the law as laid down by his lordship, in any book in *his* library," "That may be, sir," said the judge, in an acrid, contemptuous tone; "but I suspect that *your* library is very small." His lordship, who, like too many of that time, was a party zealot, was known to be the author of several anonymous political pamphlets, which were chiefly conspicuous for their despotic principles and excessive violence. The young barrister, roused by the sneer at his circumstances, replied that true it was that his library might be small, but he thanked heaven that, among his books, there were none of the wretched productions of the frantic pamphleteers of the day. "I find it more instructive, my lord, to study good works than to compose bad ones; my books may be few, but the title-pages give me the writers' names: my shelf is not disgraced by any of such rank absurdity that their very authors are ashamed to own them."

He was here interrupted by the judge, who said, "Sir, you are forgetting the respect which you owe to the dignity of the judicial character." "Dignity!" exclaimed Mr. Curran; "my lord, upon that point I shall cite you a case from a book of some authority, with which you are perhaps not unacquainted. A poor

until (to use his own words) "I thought I felt my hungry little ones pulling my gown, and that gave me courage to speak."—M.

* His first occasion of displaying that high spirit which was afterwards so prominent in his character, was at the election of Tallagh, where he was engaged as counsel, a few months after his admission to the bar. One of the candidates, presuming upon his own rank, and upon the young advocate's unostentatious appearance, indulged in some rude language towards him; but was instantly silenced by a burst of impetuous and eloquent invective, which it at that time required an insult to awaken.—C.

Scotchman,* upon his arrival in London, thinking himself insulted by a stranger, and imagining that he was the stronger man, resolved to resent the affront, and taking off his coat, delivered it to a bystander to hold; but having lost the battle, he turned to resume his garment, when he discovered that he had unfortunately lost that also, that the trustee of his habiliments had decamped during the affray. So, my lord, when the person who is invested with the dignity of the judgment-seat lays it aside, for a moment, to enter into a disgraceful personal contest, it is vain, when he has been worsted in the encounter, that he seeks to resume it—it is in vain that he endeavours to shelter himself from behind an authority which he has abandoned."

Judge Robinson—If you say another word, sir, I'll commit you.

Mr. Curran—Then, my lord, it will be the best thing you'll have committed this term.

The judge did not commit him; but he was understood to have solicited the bench to interfere, and make an example of the advocate by depriving him of his gown, and to have received so little encouragement, that he thought it most prudent to proceed no further in the affair.†

From this, and many other specimens of spirit and ability, Mr. Curran's reputation rapidly increased; but it was not till he had been four or five years at the bar that his powers as an advocate became fully known. His first opportunity of displaying them was in a cause at the Cork Assizes, in which a Roman Catholic priest, the Rev. Mr. Neale, brought an action against a nobleman of that county (Lord Doneraile), for an assault and battery.

* Perhaps it is unnecessary to remind most readers, that the Scotchman alluded to is Strap, in Smollett's Roderic Random.—C. [Mr. O'Regan relates this reply to Judge Robinson as having been made, not by Curran, but by Mr. Hoare, his friend and cotemporary.—M.]

† As a companion to this anecdote, let me mention that, once upon a time, when a gigantic and ignorant barrister who had been wounded by some of the shafts of Curran's wit, half seriously threatened to put him in his pocket—Curran being of stunted stature and size—the quick retort was, "Do! and then you'll have more law in your pocket than you ever had in your head!"—M.

The circumstances attending this case mark the melancholy condition of the times. They afford a single, but a very striking example of those scenes of local despotism and individual suffering, of which, at this degraded period, Ireland was daily the witness and the victim.

The nobleman in question had contracted an intimacy with a young woman, whose family resided in the parish of which the plaintiff in this action was the priest. This woman's brother having committed some offence against religion, for which the Roman Catholic Bishop of the diocese had directed that the censures of the church should be passed upon him, she solicited Lord Doneraile to interfere, and to exert his influence and authority for the remission of the offender's sentence. His lordship, without hesitation, undertook to interpose his authority. For this purpose he proceeded, accompanied by one of his relatives, to the house, or rather cabin, of the priest. As soon as he arrived there, disdaining to dismount from his horse, he called in a loud and imperious tone, upon the inhabitant to come forth. The latter happened at that moment to be in the act of prayer; but, hearing the voice, which it would have been perilous to disregard, he discontinued his devotions to attend upon the peer. The minister of religion appeared before him (an affecting spectacle, to a feeling mind, of infirmity and humility), bending under years, his head uncovered, and holding in his hand the book which was now his only source of hope and consolation. His lordship ordered him to take off the sentence lately passed upon his favourite's brother. The priest, struggling between his temporal fears and the solemn obligations of his church, could only reply, with respect and humbleness, that he would gladly comply with any injunction of his lordship, but that to do so in the present instance was beyond his power; that he was only a parish priest, and, as such, had no authority to remit an ecclesiastical penalty imposed by his superior; that the Bishop alone could do it. To a second and more angry mandate, a similar answer was returned, upon which the nobleman, forgetting what he owed to his own dignity, the pity and forbearance due to age, and the reverence due to religion, raised his hand against the unoffending old man, who could only escape the blows directed against his person by tottering back into his habitation, and securing its door against his merciless assailant.

For this disgraceful outrage, to which the sufferer was exposed, because he would not violate the sanctity of his own character, and the ordinances of his church, for the gratification of a profligate woman, who chanced to be the mistress of a peer, he for some time despaired of obtaining redress. So great was the provincial power of this nobleman, and such the political degradation of the Roman Catholic clergy, that the injured priest found a difficulty in procuring an advocate to plead his cause. At length, several to whom he applied having (according to the general report) declined to be concerned for so unpopular a client,* Mr. Curran justly conceiving that it would be a stain upon his profession if such scenes of lawless violence were allowed to pass without investigation, took a step which many considered as most romantic and imprudent, and only calculated to baffle all his prospects upon his circuit; he tendered his services to the unfriended plaintiff, and, the unexpected offer being gratefully accepted, laid the story of his unmerited wrongs before a jury of his country.

No printed report of this trial has been preserved, but all the accounts of it agree that the plaintiff's counsel acquitted himself with eminent ability. And it is only by adverting to the state of those times that we can appreciate the ability that could obtain success. This was not, as an ordinary case, between man and man, where each may be certain of an equitable hearing. The advocate had to address a class of men who were full of furious

* In 1735, a Catholic nobleman (Lord Clancarty) brought an ejectment to recover his family estates that had been confiscated, but by a resolution of the Irish House of Commons, all barristers, solicitors, attorneys or proctors, that should be concerned for him, were voted public enemies (*O'Connor's History of the Irish Catholics*, p. 218 :) and in Ireland the prejudices, which had dictated so iniquitous a measure, were not extinct in 1780.—C.

and inveterate prejudices against his client. The very appearance of a Roman Catholic clergyman, obtruding his wrongs upon a court of justice, was regarded as a presumptuous novelty. To the minds of the bigoted jurors of that day, his demand of redress was an act of rebellion against the Protestant ascendency—a daring effort to restore a deposed religion to its throne. The cause had also, from the characters of the parties, excited the greatest public interest, and the sympathy of the public, as is always the case when no epidemic passions intervene, was upon the side of the oppressed; but the general expression of such a feeling was rather detrimental to its object. The crowds that filled and surrounded the court, upon the day of trial, were Roman Catholics, and were supposed, by a very obvious construction, to have assembled, not so much to witness a triumph of justice, as to share in a triumph of their religion. Upon such an occasion, the advocate had not merely to state the fact and apply the law; before he could convince or persuade, he had to pacify—to allure his hearers into a patient attention, and into a reversal of the hostile verdict, which, before they were sworn, they had tacitly pronounced. These were the difficulties against which Mr. Curran had to contend, and which he overcame. The jury granted a verdict to his client, with thirty guineas damages. So small a sum would now be deemed a very paltry remuneration for such an injury; but in Ireland, about seventy years ago, to have wrung even so much from a Protestant jury, in favour of a Catholic priest, against a Protestant nobleman, was held to be such a triumph of forensic eloquence, and to be in itself so extraordinary a circumstance, that the verdict was received by the people at large as an important political event.

In a part of his address to the jury in this case, the plaintiff's counsel animadverted, with the utmost severity of invective, upon the unworthy conduct of the defendant's relative (Mr. St. Leger). who had been present, and countenancing the outrage upon the priest.* At length, his zeal and indignation hurrying him beyond his instructions, he proceeded to describe that gentleman (who had lately left a regiment that had been ordered on actual service), as "a renegado soldier, a drummed-out dragoon, who wanted the courage to meet the enemies of his country in battle, but had the heroism to redeem the ignominy of his flight from danger, by raising his arm against an aged and unoffending minister of religion, who had just risen from putting up before the throne of God a prayer of general intercession, in which his heartless insulter was included.

As soon as the trial was over, he was summoned to make a public apology for those expressions, or to meet Mr. St. Leger in the field. He was fully sensible that his language had not been strictly warrantable, and that a barrister had no right to take shelter under his gown from the resentment of those whose feelings and character he might have unjustifiably attacked; but perceiving that an apology would, in the eyes of his countrymen, have tarnished the lustre of his recent victory, and that it might have the effect of inviting future challenges whenever he should perform his duty with the necessary boldness, he deemed it more eligible to risk his life than his reputation.† A duel

* There was another circumstance during this trial which had given equal offence, and which, whatever judgment may be passed upon it now, was well calculated to influence the jury. Mr. Curran knew that Mr. St. Leger was to be produced as one of the defendant's witnesses, and it was in order to diminish the weight of his testimony, that he had described him as above. He had, however, mentioned no name, but merely apprised the jury that such a character might be brought to impose upon them. When Mr. St. Leger came upon the table, and took the Testament in his hand, the plaintiff's counsel, in a tone of affected respect, addressed him saying, "Oh, Mr. St. Leger, the jury will, I am sure, believe you without the ceremony of swearing you; you are a man of honour, and of high moral principle; your character will justify us from insisting on your oath." The witness, deceived by this mild and complimentary language, replied with mingled surprise and irritation, "I am happy, sir, to see you have changed the opinion you entertained of me when you were describing me awhile ago." "What, sir! then you confess it was a description of yourself! Gentlemen, act as you please, but I leave it to you to say whether a thousand oaths could bind the conscience of such a man as I have just described."

† When each had taken his ground, Mr. St. Leger called out to his adversary to fire;

accordingly followed; upon which occasion Mr. Curran not only established for himself a character for personal intrepidity (an acquisition of no small moment in a country where the point of honour has always been so sacredly observed), but afforded infinite entertainment to the bystanders, by a series of those sportive sallies, which, when the impulse was on him, no time or place could repress. He declined returning Mr. St. Leger's fire; so that the affair, after a single shot, was terminated.

A more solemn and interesting scene soon followed. The poor priest was shortly after called away to another world. When he found that the hour of death was at hand, he earnestly requested that his counsel, to whom he had something of importance to communicate, might be brought into his presence. Mr. Curran complied, and was conducted to the bed-side of his expiring client. The humble servant of God had neither gold nor silver to bestow; but what he had, and what with him was above all price, he gave—the blessing of a dying Christian upon him who had employed his talents, and risked his life, in redressing the wrongs of the minister of a proscribed religion. He caused himself to be raised, for the last time, from his pillow, and, placing his hands on the head of his young advocate, pronounced over him the formal benediction of the Roman Catholic Church, as the reward of his eloquence and intrepidity. Mr. Curran had also the satisfaction of being assured by the lower orders of his countrymen, that he might *now* fight as many duels as he pleased, without apprehending any danger to his person—an assurance which subsequently became a prophecy, as far as the event could render it one.

Shortly after this trial, the successful orator was given to understand that his late triumph should cost him dear. As he was

"No, sir," replied he, "I am here by your invitation, and you must open the ball." A little after, Mr. Curran, observing the other's pistol to be aimed wide of its mark, called out in a loud voice, "Fire!" St. Leger, who was a nervous man, started, and fired: and having died not long after, was reputed in Munster to have been killed by the report of his own pistol.—C.

standing amidst a circle of his friends in one of the public streets of Cork, he was called aside by a person who brought him an intimation from Lord Doneraile, that in consequence of his late unprecedented conduct, he might expect never to be employed in future in any cause where his lordship, or his extensive connections, should have the power to exclude him. The young barrister answered, with contemptuous playfulness, and in a voice to be overheard by every one: "My good sir, you may tell his lordship that it is vain for him to be proposing terms of accommodation; for, after what has happened, I protest I think, while I live, I shall never hold a brief for him or one of his family." The introduction of these particulars may almost demand an apology; yet it is often by little things that the characters of times and individuals are best displayed, as (according to an eminent English writer) "throwing up little straws best shows which way the wind lies."

Previous to this trial, Mr. Curran's fame and practice had been unusual for his standing; but after his display of eloquence and conduct upon this occasion, they increased with unprecedented rapidity.* It was probably, too, with this event that originated his great popularity among the lower orders of the Irish—a feeling which a little time matured into an abounded veneration for his capacity, combined with a most devoted attachment to his person. Their enthusiasm in this instance can be scarcely conceived by such as have only witnessed the common marks of

* The motto to the first carriage he set up on the strength of his fees was, "PER VARIOS CASUS," on which some person observed that he prudently omitted the latter part of the sentence, "*per tot discrimina rerum*," which gave him, he said, a better opinion of his judgment than he was otherwise inclined to entertain. It being remarked to him that he might have still something more appropriate; he answered, "Why, yes, to be sure, '*Ore tenus*.' but the herald painter dissuaded me; he did not like the brevity of wit; and being then engaged about discovering, amidst the bones of the crusaders, armorial bearings suitable to the motto, I left to him the profit of two syllables, and he counted out the letters—a course since, very wisely, I assure you, adopted in Chancery: nay, I rather think also by the common law courts; and thus you perceive, my friend, from what small sources great rivers begin to flow. God knows they sometimes do inundate without fertilizing; but things being so, who can force back those noxious streams?"—M.

respect paid to ordinary favourites of the people. So much of his life, and so many of its proudest moments were passed in their presence, in the courts of Dublin, and on the circuit towns, his manners were so unaffectedly familiar and accessible, his genius and habits were so purely national, that the humblest of his countrymen, forgetting the difference of rank in their many common sympathies, fondly considered him *as one of themselves*, and cherished his reputation not more as a debt of gratitude to him than as a kind of peculiar triumph of their own. These sentiments, which he never descended to any artifices to cultivate, continued unimpaired to his death, and will probably survive him many years.

In relating the steps by which Mr. Curran advanced to professional distinction, it would be an injustice to omit the support which he found in the friendship of the late learned and respected Lord Avonmore, then Mr. Yelverton, a leading counsel at the Irish bar. This excellent and rarely gifted man had himself risen from an humble station, and knowing, by experience, "how hard it is to climb," was ever most prompt in encouraging and assisting those whom he saw imitating his own honorable example. His friendship for Mr. Curran commenced in 1775 (through the father-in-law of the latter, Dr. Creagh, between whom and Mr. Yelverton an old and tender intimacy had subsisted;) and, with the exception of a few intervals of temporary alienation from political differences, continued unimpaired to his death.*

* Mr. O'Regan says, "Barry Yelverton, afterwards Lord Avonmore, probably possessed more of the vehemence of masculine intellect than most others of his countrymen. Comprehensive and luminous, of a copious wit and extensive erudition, he was among the order of talent which Mr. Curran was to succeed. Lord Clonmel had a coarse jocularity, which was received as an useful talent. Mr. Burgh had the majesty of Virgil, and Duquery the elegance of Addison. Temple Emmett possessed the vigour of a great and original mind; he was certainly a person of singular natural and acquired endowments; a man who read Coke on Littleton in his bed, as others do Tom Jones or the Persian Tales. Of the chaste, accomplished and classic Duquery, it is related on his own authority, that he read Robertson on the day before his best displays, to catch his unrivalled style, and to harmonize his composition by that of the master of historic eloquence. He had also to contend with the wit of Mr. Keller, and the unbending stubbornness of Hoare.

In one of Mr. Curran's latest efforts at the bar,* we find him fondly turning aside for a moment to indulge his respect for the judge and the scholar, and his gratitude to the friend of his younger years. The following is the character that he has drawn of Lord Avonmore. To strangers it may appear overwrought, but those who were familiar with the simple antique grandeur of mind that dignified the original, recognise the fidelity of the likeness.

"I am not ignorant that this extraordinary construction has received the sanction of another court, nor of the surprise and dismay with which it smote upon the general heart of the bar. I am aware that I may have the mortification of being told in another country of that unhappy decision, and I foresee in what confusion I shall hang down my head when I am told it. But I cherish, too, the consolatory hope, that I shall be able to tell them, that I had an old and learned friend, whom I would put above all the sweepings of their Hall, who was of a different opinion—who had derived his ideas of civil liberty from the purest fountains of Athens and of Rome—who had fed the youthful vigour of his studious mind with the theoretic knowledge of their wisest philosophers and statesmen—and who had refined that theory into the quick and exquisite sensibility of moral instinct, by contemplating the practice of their most illustrious examples—by dwelling on the sweet-souled piety of Cimon—on the anticipated Christianity of Socrates—on the gallant and pathetic patriotism of Epaminondas—on that pure austerity of Fabricius, whom to move

John Fitzgibbon, afterwards Lord Clare, and Lord High Chancellor of Ireland, was a competitor whose ardent and energetic decision of character, whose precision of mind and legal capacity, rendered him a formidable rival. They did not uniformly run the same course of competition; Mr. Curran was not early qualified to start for the hunter's plate, nor had he ever much taste for the Olympics of a Castle chase; for such, he said, he was short by the head. Yet Mr Curran often repeated, that had not the father of Mr. Fitzgibbon pre-occupied the ground for his son, by one stage, he never should or could have gone beyond him. But whenever these high-mettled racers started fairly, and on an equal plain, Mr. Curran was always first at the winning-post."—M.

* Speech in the case of Mr. Justice Johnson, in the Court of Exchequer, where Lord Avonmore presided.—C. [The date was February 4 1805.]—M.

from his integrity would have been more difficult than to have pushed the sun from his course. I would add, that if he had seemed to hesitate, it was but for a moment—that his hesitation was like the passing cloud that floats across the morning sun, and hides it from the view, and does so for a moment hide it, by involving the spectator without even approaching the face of the luminary."

Lord Avonmore was the person under whose auspices was formed, in the year 1779, a patriotic and convivial society—"The Monks of the Order of St. Patrick,"* which was in those days

* Of this society, so interesting as connected with the most splendid era of Ireland's history, Mr. Hudson has kindly supplied the following notice and list of the original members:

This celebrated society was partly political and partly convivial; it consisted of two parts, professed and lay brothers. As the latter had no privileges, except that of commons in the refectory, they are unnoticed here. The professed (by the constitution) consisted of members of either house of parliament, and barristers, with the addition from the other learned professions of any number not exceeding one-third of the whole. They assembled every Saturday in Convent, during term-time; and commonly held a chapter before commons, at which the abbot presided, or in his (very rare) absence, the prior, or senior of the officers present. Upon such occasions, all the members appeared in the habit of the order, a black tabinet domino. Temperance and sobriety always prevailed. A short Latin grace, "Benedictus benedicat," and "Benedicto benedicatur" (since adopted as the grace of the King's Inns Society, in Dublin) was regularly and gravely pronounced by the præcentor or chaplain, before and after commons.

It will be seen by the following list, that there were many learned men and men of genius in their number, and I may venture to say, that few productions (either in pamphlets or periodical publications) of any celebrity, during the arduous struggle for Irish emancipation, appeared, which did not proceed from the pen of one of the brethren. Nor did they forego their labours, till, by their prayers and exertions, they attained emancipation for their country. The sad change which has taken place since their dispersion need not be related.

THE

MONKS OF THE ORDER OF ST. PATRICK.

COMMONLY CALLED

THE MONKS OF THE SCREW.

Assembled at their Convent in St. Kevin Street, Dublin, on and after September the 3d, 1779.

Members' Names.

1. *Founder.*—Barry Yelverton, barrister, M.P., since Lord Viscount Avonmore, Lord Chief Baron.

2. *Abbot.*—William Doyle, barrister, Master in Chancery.

sufficiently celebrated, and composed of men such as Ireland could not easily assemble now. It was a collection of the wit, the

3. *Prior.*—John Philpot Curran, barrister, since M.P., Privy Counsellor and Master of the Rolls.
4. *Præcentor.*—Rev. Wm. Day, S. F. T. C. D.
5. *Bursar.*—Edward Hudson, M.D.*
6. *Sacristan.*—Robert Johnson, barr. M.P., and since a Judge.*
7. Arran, the Earl of.
8. Barry, James (painter), elected an honorary member, never joined.
9. Brown, Arthur, barr. M.P., and F. T. C. D.
10. Burgh, Walter Hussey, barr., Rt. Hon. and M.P., and since Chief Baron
11. Burston, Beresford, barr., and K. C.*
12. Carhampton, Earl of.
13. Caldbeck, William, barr., and K. C.
14. Chamberlayne, W. Tankerville, barr. M.P., and since a Judge.
15. Charlemont, Earl of.
16. Corry, Rt. Hon. Isaac, M.P., and since Chancellor of the Exchequer.
17. Daly, Rt. Hon. Denis, M.P.
18. Day, Robert, barr. M.P., and since a Judge.*
19. Dodds, Robert, barr.
20. Doyle, John, M.P., and since a General in the army, and Bart.*
21. Dunkin, James, barr.
22. Duquery, Henry, barr., and M.P.
23. Emmett, Temple, barr.
24. Finucane, Matthew, barr., and since a Judge.
25. Fitton, Richard, barr.
26. Forbes, John, barr., M.P.
27. Frankland, Richard, barr., and K.C.
28. Grattan, Rt. Hon. Henry, barr., and M.P.
29. Hacket, Thomas, barr.
30. Hardy, Francis, barr., and M.P. (Lord Charlemont's biographer.)
31. Harstonge, Sir Henry, Bart. and M.P.
32. Herbert, Richard, barr., and M.P.
33. Hunt, John, barr.
34. Hussey, Dudley, barr., M.P., and Recorder of Dublin.
35. Jebb, Frederic, M.D.
36. Kingsborough, Lord Viscount, M.P. [afterwards Earl of Kingston]
37. Mocawen, ——, barr.
38. Martin, Richard, barr., and M.P.
39. Metge, Peter, barr., M.P., and since a Judge.
40. Mornington, Earl of [the late Marquis Wellesley.]
41. Muloch, Thomas, barr.
42. Newenham, Sir Edward, M.P.
43. Ogle, Rt. Hon. George, M.P.

* Surviving.—C. [In 1819].—M

genius, and public virtue of the country; and though the name of the society itself is not embodied in any of the national records,

44. O'Leary, Rev. Arthur, honorary.
45. O'Neal, Charles, barr., K.C., and M.P.
46. Palliser, the Rev. Doctor, chaplain.
47. Pollock Joseph, barr.
48. Ponsonby, Rt. Hon. George, barr., M.P., and since Chancellor of Ireland.
49. Preston, William, barr.
50. Ross, Lieut. Col. M.P.
51. Sheridan, Charles Francis, barr., M.P., and Secretary at War.
52. Smith, Sir Michael, Bart. barr., M.P., and since Master of the Rolls.
53. Stawel, William, barr.
54. Stack, Rev. Richard, F.T.C.D.
55. Townshend, Marquis of.*
56. Woolfe, Arthur, barr., M.P., and since Lord Viscount Kilwarden, Chief Justice King's Bench.

The society dwindled away towards the end of the year 1795.

Shortly after the formation of this club, Mr. Curran, having been one evening called upon for a song, gave one of his own composition, which was immediately adopted as the charter song of the order. The following are all the verses of it that have been recollected.

When St. Patrick this order established,
He called us the "Monks of the Screw;"
Good rules he revealed to our Abbot
To guide us in what we should do.
But first he replenished our fountain
With liquor, the best in the sky;
And he swore, on the word of a saint,
That the fountain should never run dry.

Each year, when your octaves approach,
In full chapter convened let me find you;
And, when to the convent you come,
Leave your favorite temptation behind you.
And be not a glass in your convent,
Unless on a festival, found;
And, this rule to enforce, I ordain it
One festival all the year round.

My brethren, be chaste, till you're tempted;
Whilst sober, be grave and discreet;
And humble your bodies with fasting,
As oft as you've nothing to eat.

* Elected, professed, and joined on his visit to Dublin, after his vice-royalty.

the names of many of its members are to be found in every page, and will be remembered, while Ireland has a memory, with gratitude and pride. The primary object of their association was to give her a Constitution, and to nourish and diffuse among her people the spirit and intelligence which should render them worthy of the gift; and when the day arrived, as it shortly did, when the rights to which they aspired were not to be gained without a struggle, the leading members of the "Order of St. Patrick" may be seen conspicuous in the post of honour and of danger. Mr. Curran always bore a distinguished part in their meetings; it was to them, and to the many happy and instructive hours he had passed there, that he so pathetically alluded in the fine burst of social enthusiasm which immediately follows the passage above cited. "And this soothing hope I draw from the dearest and tenderest recollections of my life—from the remembrance of those Attic nights, and those refections of the gods, which we have spent with those admired, and respected, and beloved companions, who have gone before us; over whose ashes the most precious tears of Ireland have been shed. [Here Lord Avonmore could not refrain from bursting into tears.] Yes, my good Lord, I see you do not forget them. I see their sacred forms passing in sad review before your memory. I see your pained and softened fancy recalling those happy meetings, where the innocent enjoyment of social

Yet, in honour of fasting, one lean face
  Among you I'll always require;
If the Abbot should please, he may wear it,
  If not, let it come to the Prior.*

* * * * * *

Come, let each take his chalice, my brethren,
  And with due devotion prepare,
With hands and with voices uplifted
  Our hymn to conclude with a prayer.
May this chapter oft joyously meet,
  And this gladsome libation renew,
To the Saint, and the Founder, and Abbot,
  And Prior, and Monks of the Screw!

* Mr. Doyle, the Abbot, had a remarkably large full face; Mr. Curran's was th

mirth became expanded into the nobler warmth of social virtue, and the horizon of the board became enlarged into the horizon of man—where the swelling heart conceived and communicated the pure and generous purpose—where my slenderer and younger taper imbibed its borrowed light from the more matured and redundant fountain of yours. Yes, my Lord, we can remember those nights without any other regret than that they can never more return, for

"We spent them not in toys, or lusts, or wine,
But search of deep philosophy,
Wit, eloquence, and poesy,
Arts which I loved, for they, my friend, were thine."*

COWLEY.

Lord Avonmore was one of those men in whom a rare intellect and vast acquirements are found united with the most artless unsuspecting innocency of nature. Whatever the person in whom he confided asserted, he considered to be as undoubted as if he had uttered it himself. His younger friend, aware of this amiable imperfection, used often to trifle with it, and, in moments of playful relaxation, to practice harmless impositions upon his lordship's credulity. His ordinary artifice was to touch his sensibility, and thus excite his attention by relating in his presence some affecting incident, and, then pretending to be unconscious that his lordship was listening, to proceed with a detail of many strange and improbable particulars, until he should be interrupted, as he regularly was, by the good judge's exclaiming, "Gracious heavens! sir, is it posssible? I have overheard all those most truly amazing circumstances, which I could never have

* Lord Avonmore, in whose breast political resentment was easily subdued, by the same noble tenderness of feeling which distinguished the late Mr. Fox upon a more celebrated occasion, could not withstand this appeal to his heart. At this period (1805) there was a suspension of intercourse between him and Mr. Curran; but the moment the court rose, his Lordship sent for his friend, and threw himself into his arms, declaring that unworthy artifices had been used to separate them, and that they should never succeed in future.—C.

believed, if they did not come from such good authority." His lordship at length discovered the deception, and passing into the opposite extreme, became (often ludicrously) wary and incredulous as to every thing that Mr. Curran stated. Still, however, the latter persisted, and, quickening his invention as the difficulties increased, continued from year to year to gain many a humour ous triumph over all the defensive caution of his friend. Even upon the bench, Lord Avonmore evinced the same superstitious apprehension of the advocate's ingenuity, whom he would frequently interrupt, sometimes in a tone of endearment, sometimes of impatience, saying, "Mr. Curran, I know your cleverness; but it's quite in vain for you to go on. I see the drift of it all, and you are only giving yourself and me unnecessary trouble." Upon one of these occasions, the judge having frequently interposed to prevent the counsel's putting forward some topic that was really relative and necessary to his case, declaring, as often as it was attempted, that the tendency of his argument was quite obvious, and that he was totally straying from the question, Mr. Curran addressed him thus: "Perhaps, my lord, I am straying; but you must impute it to the extreme agitation of my mind. I have just witnessed so dreadful a circumstance, that my imagination has not yet recovered from the shock." His lordship was now all attention. "On my way to court, my lord, as I passed by one of the markets, I observed a butcher proceeding to slaughter a calf. Just as his hand was raised, a lovely little child approached him unperceived, and, terrible to relate—I still see the life-blood gushing out, the poor child's bosom was under his hand, when he plunged his knife into—into"——"Into the bosom of the child!" cried out the judge, with much emotion—"into the *neck of the calf*, my lord; but your lordship sometimes anticipates."*

There are no reports of Mr. Curran's early speeches at the bar; but the celerity of his ascent to distinction in his profession, and in the public estimation, may be inferred from the date of his

* Phillips also tells this story, but has worked it up too dramatically.—M.

entrance into Parliament. He had been only seven years at the bar, when Mr. Longfield (afterwards Lord Longueville) had him returned for a borough in his disposal.* At this time boroughs were the subject of notorious traffic, and it seldom happened that the members returned for them did not bind themselves to remunerate the patrons in money or in services. There was no such stipulation in the present instance; the seat was given to Mr. Curran upon the express condition of perfect freedom on his part; but having soon differed from Mr. Longfield on political subjects, and there being then no way of vacating, he insisted upon purchasing a seat, to be filled by any person whom that gentleman might appoint; an arrangement against which, it is but justice to add, that Mr. Longfield anxiously endeavoured to dissuade him.†

* The borough of Kilbeggan, for which the other member was the celebrated Mr. Flood. It was also about this period that Mr. Curran obtained a silk gown.—C.

† In the succeeding parliament Mr. Curran also came in, at his own expense, for the borough of Rathcormack.—C.

CHAPTER V.

The Irish House of Commons, in 1783—Sketch of the previous history of Ireland—Effects of the revolution of 1688—Catholic penal code—System of governing Ireland—Described by Mr. Curran—Intolerance and degradation of the Irish parliament—Change of system—Octennial bill—American Revolution—Its effects upon Ireland—The Irish volunteers—Described by Mr. Curran—Their numbers, and influence upon public measures—Irish revolution of 1782—Mr. Grattan's public services—Observations upon the subsequent conduct of the Irish Parliament.

It was at the eventful era of 1783 that Mr. Curran became a member of the Irish House of Commons*—an assembly at that day thronged with groups of original historic characters,† the

* The manner in which Curran got a seat in Parliament has been thus related, as "well authenticated:" Lord Longueville, an Irish peer, with vast property, and large borough-interest, wishing to avail himself of Curran's talents, offered him a seat in Parliament Curran replied that his politics were opposed to the party to which Lord L. belonged. He was reminded, with a laugh, that patriotism was unprofitable, and that, with a young family, his good sense would tell him so. Some time after, one of Curran's friends asked him for a frank, and informed him that he was gazetted as member for one of Lord Longueville's boroughs. He took his seat, and voted against Lord L.'s friend, the minister. In explanation, he said that he entered Parliament independent and unshackled, and that so he would remain. At that time, he had saved only five hundred pounds. This money, and about twice as much more, which he borrowed from his friends, he sent to Lord Longueville, in payment for his seat.—M.

† Of some of these, Mr. Grattan (in his answer to Lord Clare's pamphlet, 1801) has given the following masterly sketches, over which he has, perhaps, unconsciously distributed the noble traits which, if collected, would form the portrait of himself.

"I follow the author through the graves of these honourable dead men, for most of them are so; and I beg to raise up their tombstones as he throws them down; I feel it more instructive to converse with their ashes than with his compositions.

"Mr. Malone, one of the characters of 1753, was a man of the finest intellect that any country ever produced. 'The three ablest men I ever heard were Mr. Pitt (the father), Mr. Murray, and Mr. Malone. For a popular assembly, I would choose Mr. Pitt; for a privy council, Murray; for twelve wise men, Malone.' This was the opinion which Lord Sackville, the secretary of 1753, gave to a gentleman from whom I heard it. He is a great sea in the calm,' said Mr. Gerrard Hamilton, another great judge of men and talents; 'Ay,' it was replied, 'but had you seen him when he was young, you would have

vigorous product of unsettled times: great public benefactors, great public delinquents, but both of rare capacity and enterprise,

said he was a great sea in a storm.' And like the sea, whether in calm or storm, *he was a great production of nature.*

"Lord Pery.—He is not yet canonized by death; but he, like the rest, has been canonized by slander. He was more or less a party in all those measures which the pamphlet condemns, and indeed in every great statute and measure that took place in Ireland for the last fifty years. A man of the most legislative capacity I ever knew, and the most comprehensive reach of understanding I ever saw; with a deep-engraven impression of public care, accompanied by a temper which was adamant. In his train is every private virtue that can adorn human nature.

"Mr. Brownlow—Sir William Osborne.—I wish we had more of these criminals. The former seconded the address of 1782, and in the latter, and in both, there was a station of mind that would have become the proudest senate in Europe.

"Mr. Flood, my rival, as the pamphlet calls him: and I should be unworthy the character of his rival, if in the grave I did not do him justice.—He had his faults; but he had great powers, great public effect; he persuaded the old, he inspired the young; the Castle vanished before him. On a small subject, he was miserable: put into his hand a distaff, and, like Hercules, he made sad work of it: but give him the thunderbolt, and he had the arm of a Jupiter. He misjudged when he transferred himself to the English Parliament; he forgot that he was a tree of the forest, too old and too great to be transplanted at fifty; and his fate in the British Parliament is a caution to the friends of union to stay at home, and make the country of their birth the seat of their action.

"Mr. Daly, my beloved friend.—He, in a great measure, drew the address of 1779, in favour of our trade, that 'ungracious measure;' and he saw, read, and approved of the address of 1782, in favour of our constitution, that 'address of separation.' He visited me in my illness, at that moment, and I had communication on those subjects with that man whose powers of oratory were next to perfection, and whose powers of understanding, I might say, from what has lately happened, bordered on the spirit of prophecy.

"Mr. Forbes—a name I shall ever regard, and a death I shall ever deplore.—Enlightened, sensible, laborious, and useful; proud in poverty, and patriotic; he preferred exile to apostacy, and met his death. I speak of the dead—I say nothing of the living; but that I attribute to this constellation of great men, in a great measure, the privileges of your country; and I attribute such a generation of men to the residence of your Parliament.

"Mr. Burgh: another great person in those scenes which it is not in the little quill of this author to depreciate.—He was a man singularly gifted, with great talent, great variety—wit, oratory, and logic. He, too, had his weakness; but he had the pride of genius, also, and strove to raise his country along with himself, and never sought to build his elevation on the degradation of Ireland. I moved an amendment for a free export; he moved a better amendment, and he lost his place. I moved a declaration of rights: 'With my last breath will I support the right of the Irish Parliament,' was his note to me, when I applied to him for his support; he lost the chance of recovering his place and his way to the seals, for which he might have bartered. The gates of promotion were shut on him, as those of glory opened."—C.

Walter Hussey Burgh, thus eulogized by Grattan, merits more particular notice. Called

and exhibiting in their virtues or their crimes all the turbulent energy of the storms that were agitating their country. The Irish revolution of 1782, with the memorable acts and deliberations of which period the political history of Ireland commences, had just taken place; and, although it preceded by a little time Mr. Curran's entrance into Parliament, it still cannot but be adverted to as an event which had a powerful influence upon the fortune and conduct of his future life. He was of too ardent a temper not to be deeply moved by the circumstances which accompanied that measure: he was the familiar friend of the eminent Parliamentary leaders who had been so instrumental in achieving it; he had witnessed the virtuous struggles and the scenes of civic heroism displayed by them, and by the nation, at this arduous crisis; and the impression that they made upon his imagination and his conviction was never after effaced. In order, therefore, fully to comprehend the feelings with which he entered upon his duties as an Irish senator, it will be necessary to make a few observations upon the condition in which he found his country, and upon that from which she had recently emerged. The fervour of his political opinions, and his devoted adherence to the popular cause, exposed him, at different periods of his life, to no little calumny and

to the Irish bar, in 1769, he had previously obtained a seat and won distinction in the Irish Parliament. In 1772, at the early age of thirty-five, he was placed at the head of the Irish bar, as Prime Serjeant, in which he continued for two years, when, siding with Grattan against the government, on the question of Ireland's right to a free export trade, he resigned his lucrative office. It was restored to him in 1782, in which year he was made Chief Baron of the Irish Exchequer, declining a proffered peerage. He died the following year, before he had completed the age of forty. Ireland might well be proud of such a man, whose persuasive eloquence made an æra at the Irish bar and in the senate, equally distinguished for the grace and harmony of his style, and the sweetness and fulness of his voice: of him it may be said, as of the Greek orator, *he was the Bee.* Burgh and Yelverton being both engaged on opposite sides in some great and important cause, all the powers of their talents were called forth, as well by the interest the case excited, as by a competition for fame. In speaking of the effect of Burgh's oration, Yelverton observed to a friend, that he would have been satisfied that he had obtained the victory; "But," said he, "when I perceived an old *case-hardened attorney* sitting in a distant corner of the court, and saw the tears silently coursing down his iron cheeks, and these wrung from him by the touching eloquence of Mr. Burgh, I confess," said Yelverton, "I felt myself vanquished."—M.

reproach; but those who impartially consider the past and cotemporary history of Ireland will find, in every page of it, his excuse, if not his most ample justification.

For centuries Ireland had been in a state of miserable bondage; her history is but the disgusting catalogue of her sufferings, exciting to unprofitable retaliation, from which she regularly sunk, subdued but untranquilized, into a condition of more embittered wretchedness,* with the penalties of rebellion superadded to the calamities of oppression. From the period of her annexation to England in the 12th century, down to the close of the 17th, she had thus continued, barbarous and restless; too feeble and disunited to succeed, too strong, and proud, and irritated to despair; alternating in dreary succession between wild exertions of delirious strength and the troubled sleep of exhausted fury. It would be foreign to the present purpose to enter into the merits of these melancholy conflicts; to grope amidst uninteresting records to ascertain whether Ireland as an unruly province deserved her fate, or whether her condition was attributable to an inveterate spirit of vindictive domination in the English governments. But as we approach more modern times, all obscurity on the subject ceases: we find the ruling country adopted a formal avowed design of humiliation, which, however applauded (as it still continues to be by some) under the imposing phrase of the "wisdom of our ancestors," was, in reality, founded in much injustice, and, if effects be any test, in as much folly; and after agitating and afflicting the kingdom for the last century, seems likely to visit in its consequences the next.

It was immediately after the revolution of 1688, that era of glory and freedom to England, that Ireland became the victim of this systematic plan of debasement. Her adhe-

*"The slave, that struggles without breaking his chain, provokes the tyrant to double it, and gives him the plea of self-defence for extinguishing what at first he only intended to subdue."—*Mr. Curran's speech in Howison's case.* C.

rence to the deposed monarch and its result are familiar to all. James's party having been crushed, Ireland was treated as a conquered country, that merited nothing but chastisement and scorn. This was not the policy of the English king; it was that of the English whigs,* the framers of the Bill of Rights, the boasted champions of liberty at home. By these men, and by their successors (who, of whatever political denomination, agreed with them in their intolerance), was Ireland, without shame or pity, dismantled of her most precious rights. Laws were made to bind her, without consulting the Irish parliament, which, when it remonstrated, was charged with riot and sedition.† Ireland's commerce was openly discouraged: a code more furious than bigotry had hitherto penned was levelled against the mass of the nation, the Roman Catholics.‡ They were successively excluded from the right to sit in Parliament, to acquire land, to hold any employment under the crown, to vote in elections of members of Parliament, to intermarry with Protestants, to exercise religious worship; in short,

* "I am sorry to reflect that since the late revolution in these kingdoms, when the subjects of England have more strenuously than ever asserted their own rights and the liberty of Parliaments, it has pleased them to bear harder on their poor neighbours than has ever yet been done in many ages foregoing."—*Molyneux's Cause of Ireland.* This little volume, written throughout with a modesty and ability worthy of the friend of Locke, was formally censured by the English House of Commons., A circumstance that preceded its publication is not without interest. The author, apprehensive of any unconscious bias upon his mind, wrote to his friend for his opinion of some of the arguments; Locke replied by inviting him to pass over to England, and confer with him in person upon the subject. Molyneux complied, and after spending, as the account states, and as may be well believed, the five most delightful weeks of his life in the society of his illustrious friend, returned to Dublin, and published his work.—C.

† When the Irish Commons, in 1792, claimed the right of originating money bills, they were told by the viceroy, Lord Sydney, that "They might go to England and beg their majesties' pardon for their riotous and seditious assemblies."—C.

‡ "You abhorred it, as I did, for its vicious perfection; for I must do it justice, it was a complete system, full of coherence and consistency, well digested and well composed in all its parts. It was a machine of wise and elaborate contrivance, and as well fitted for the oppression, impoverishment, and degradation of a people, and the debasement in them of human nature itself, as ever proceeded from the perverted ingenuity of man."—*Burke's Letter to Sir H. Langrishe.*

by a kind of constructive annihilation, "the laws did not presume a papist to exist in the kingdom, nor could they breathe without the connivance of government."*

This state of national humiliation lasted almost a century. Viceroy succeeded viceroy with no other rule of government than to continue the system as he found it. A race of subordinate ministers sprang up within the land, of no public virtue, no expanded thought, utterly unconscious that man can be improved; exhibiting in their heartless measures that practical ferocity for which jailors or keepers would be selected, rather than those mild and sanative qualities that might have soothed the distempers of the times. "Hence it is," said Mr. Curran, speaking of this period, "that the administration of Ireland so often presents to the reader of her history, not the view of legitimate government, but rather of an encampment in the country of a barbarous enemy, where the object of an invader is not government but conquest; where he is of course obliged to resort to the corrupting of clans, or of single individuals, pointed out to his notice by public abhorrence, and recommended to his confidence only by a treachery so rank and consummate as precludes all possibility of their return to private virtue or to public reliance, and therefore only put into authority over a wretched country, condemned to the torture of all that petulant unfeeling asperity with which a narrow and malignant mind will bristle in unmerited elevation; condemned to be betrayed, and disgraced, and exhausted by the little traitors that have been suffered to nestle and grow within it; who make it at once the source of their grandeur and the victim of their vices; reducing it to the melancholy necessity of supporting their consequence and of sinking under their crimes, like the lion perishing by the poison of a reptile that finds shelter in the mane of the noble animal, while it is stinging him to death."†

Ireland was in those times, in as strange and disastrous a situa-

* Such was the declaration from the bench of the Irish chancellor in 1759.—C.

† Mr. Curran's speech in Howison's case.—C.

tion as can well be imagined; her own legislature hating and trampling upon her people, and the English government suspecting and despising both. There may have been sufficient intricacy in the minor details of the policy of the time, but the leading maxims appear in all the clearness of despotic simplicity. They were to awe the real or imputed disaffection of the natives by means of a harsh domestic administration, and to check any more general exercise of power assumed by that administration as an intrusion upon the legislative supremacy of England. As far as respected internal concerns, the Irish Lords and Commons were a triumphant faction, despoiling and insulting the remains of a fallen enemy: in their relation with England, they were miserable instruments, without confidence or dignity; armed by their employers with the fullest authority to molest or to crush, but instantly and contemptuously reminded of their own degradation, if ever they evinced any presumptuous desire to redress.

Against so unnatural a system, it is no wonder that the discountenanced claims of freedom should have no avail. If a transient scream was heard among the people, it excited immediate alarm at home, as ominous of an approaching storm;* if her voice issued, as it sometimes did, from the Irish Commons, it was considered a daring invasion of the rights of a higher power.† If the spirit of that House became too unruly for provincial purposes, the patriotic murmur was quickly hushed by lengthening the pension list; a given number of oppressors was required, and while a venal heart was to be had in the market, no matter how high the price, the price was paid, and the nation called on (in addition to its other burdens) to defray the expenses of its own wrongs.

* Upon the trial of the printer of Swift's celebrated "Letters of a Drapier," the lord chief-justice, Whitshed, declared that the author's intention was to bring in the Pretender.—*Plowden's History of Ireland*, vol. ii., p. 81. Dr. Lucas, who ventured, in his writings, to vindicate the rights of the Irish Commons, was declared by that House an enemy to his country, and obliged to seek for safety in exile, 1747.—C.

† Vide question of the appropriation of the surplus, in 1753.—

Thus it continued for many years: with all the miseries of despotism without its repose; commerce extinguished, the public spirit broken, public honour and private confidence banished, and bigotry and faction alone triumphant.

Sentiments of wisdom and pity at length occurred to the English Cabinet: it began to doubt if the Irish people were so incurably furious as their tormentors had represented; it resolved to inquire, and if necessary, to redress. A very little investigation proved that never was some merciful interposition more opportune; it was like a visit to some secret cell to rescue the victims of imputed frenzy from their inhuman immurers, who had chained their persons and traduced their intellects, that they might prey upon their inheritance.

The subject of the first healing measure was the Parliament. There was no representation of the people in Ireland; there was a House of Commons, which, having no limits to its duration, had become a banditti of perpetual dictators.* The octennial bill was passed, and the hardened veterans disbanded.† This was not for the purpose of making even a nominal appeal to the sense of the nation; it was to give the Crown an opportunity of dispersing that provincial oligarchy whose maxims had been so ruinous to their country, and of substituting in their place a class of more pliant dependants, who might readily accord with the purposed lenity of the new system. As a right, or a security for a right, which nothing can give a people if they give it not themselves, this act effected little. As a diminution of calamity, as a transfer from the barbarous dominion of their domestic tyrants to the more considerate and enlightened control of the English ministry, it had its value. It was received by the nation, who have been ever as precipitate in their gratitude as in their resentments, with transports of enthusiastic and unaccustomed joy; a

* And four-fifths of the people were excluded from the elective franchise by the 1st Geo II. c. 9.—C.

† 1767, under the administration of Lord Townshend.—C.

signal proof, if such were wanting, of their loyalty and their debasement.

The Irish House of Commons, however, began now to wear in some degree the appearance of a constitutional assembly; notwithstanding the political ignominy into which the nation had fallen, there still existed in that house a small band of able and upright men, who entertained more manly and charitable notions of a people's claims than their ungenerous opponents; and who, though they might not possess the power of redressing the immediate wrongs, were still ever at hand to refute the baneful doctrines that would have sanctioned their continuance. In the British senate too (it should be gratefully remembered) Ireland had her advocates; whose expanded minds, superior to the paltry ambition of domination, would have made the noblest use of their own privileges, that of liberally imparting them. The consequence of these better opinions occasionally appeared; the Viceroy was defeated upon some constitutional questions;* the Commons were reprimanded and prorogued; measures full of honour to them, and of hope to their country.

But these were only transitory visitations of spirit; the effects rather of the negligence than the weakness of the viceroy. The ranks of the opposition were soon thinned by the never-failing expedient, and whatever relief was meditated for the Irish, was to come in the form of a gift, and not a concession. Relief was certainly in the contemplation of the English minister (Lord North), to what extent it is now immaterial to inquire; he was anticipated by events that were above his control.

Ireland was now upon the eve of "a great original transaction." The American colonies had revolted; the Irish linen trade with those provinces, which had been the principal of Ireland's few sources of commercial wealth, instantly vanished; to this was

* Among other instances of the increasing spirit of the House of Commons, was their repeated rejections of the money bills, *because they did not take their rise in that house.* 1769—C.

added a general embargo upon the exportation of provisions, lest they might circuitously reach the insurgents. Universal distress ensued. The Commons, for the first time, assumed the attitude of representatives of the nation: they addressed the viceroy upon the public emergencies with dignity and firmness, and were dissolved in 1777. Strenuous measures were taken by the government to secure a majority in the Parliament that followed; but the crisis soon arrived when the destinies of the country were transferred to other hands.

The internal wretchedness of Ireland had been great; it was now aggravated by the danger of war: the regular forces in the kingdom exceeded not 5,000 men, the remainder having been called off to recruit the army in America. The enemy's fleets, superior to that of Great Britain, were careering in triumph through the channel, and daily expected upon Ireland's unprotected coasts. In this emergency, the town of Belfast, having applied to Government for a military reinforcement, and its requisition having been answered by an offer of supply that cannot be related with gravity,* had the honour of first raising that warning voice, which, hushing every baser murmur, awoke the nation to confidence and strength. She called upon the citizens to arm in their defence. A corps of Volunteers was immediately established. The noble example was ardently followed by the country at large, and Ireland soon beheld starting up with a scenic rapidity, a self-collected, self-disciplined body of forty thousand Volunteers. "You cannot but remember," said Mr. Curran, describing the scene, of which he had been a witness, "that at a time when we had scarcely a regular soldier for our defence, when the old and young were alarmed and terrified with apprehensions of descent upon our coasts, that Providence seemed to have worked a sort of miracle in our favour. You saw a band of armed men come forth at the great call of nature, of honour,

* The answer of the government was, that all the assistance it could afford was half a troop : dismounted horse, and half a company of invalids.—C.

and their country. You saw men of the greatest wealth and rank; you saw every class of the community give up its members, and send them armed into the field, to protect the public and private tranquillity of Ireland. It is impossible for any man to turn back to that period, without reviving those sentiments of tenderness and gratitude which then beat in the public bosom; to recollect amidst what applause, what tears, what prayers, what benedictions, they walked forth amongst spectators agitated by the mingled sensations of terror and reliance, of danger and of protection, imploring the blessings of heaven upon their heads, and its conquest upon their swords. That illustrious, and adored and abused body of men stood forward and assumed the title which I trust the ingratitude of their country will never blot from its history, 'The Volunteers of Ireland.'"*

The original object of these associations had been to defend the country from foreign invasion. The administration, forgetting the loyalty of the proceeding in their affright at so unexpected an exhibition of strength and enterprise, beheld an enemy already in possession of the land, but affecting to countenance what they could not control, they supplied the Volunteers with several thousand stands of arms, and looked to the return of more tranquil and servile times, to disarm and defame them.

The Volunteers soon swelled into an army of 80,000 men. In their ranks appeared the most admired characters in the kingdom, animating them with the enthusiasm, and tempering the general ardour by all the courtesy, and the high moral discipline, that the presence of so many noblemen, and senators, and gentlemen, could inspire. They had armed to protect the crown—no invader appeared; another and more precious object of protection now remained. Ireland was at their disposal, and they unanimously determined that, to consummate their work, they should continue under arms until they saw

† Speech in Hamilton Rowan's case.—C.

her free. They resolved "to show, that if man descends, it is not in his own proper motion; that it is with labour and with pain, and that he can continue to sink only until, by the force and pressure of the descent, the spring of his immortal faculties acquires that *recuperative* energy and effort, that hurries him as many miles aloft."*

The demands of the Volunteers were altogether unlike a mere sudden ebullition of popular discontent. They were the result of deep convictions, the splendid signs of the improved opinions of the age. The example of America was before them, and the cry for redress in Ireland was but the echo of that "voice which shouted for liberty"† there. The mode of their constitution, too, was peculiarly fortunate and authoritative. They were not a regular military force, mutinously dictating measures to the state; they were not a band of insurgents, illegal in their origin and objects. The circumstances of the times had invested the Volunteers with a constitutional character. The Government had recognized them, and aided their formation; the House of Commons voted them a formal declaration of thanks for their public services; the people looked up to them with admiration and respect, as a brave, united, and zealous body, combining the intelligence and moderation of loyal citizens with the influence and resources of a powerful army.

The effects of the firmness and wisdom of their proceedings were soon apparent. The demand of the nation for a free trade, and the memorable declaration in parliament, "*that no power on earth, save the King, Lords, and Commons of Ireland, had a right to make laws for Ireland*,"‡ were no longer disregarded. The case of America had just shown how a struggle for principle might terminate. "British supremacy had fallen there like a spent thunderbolt."§ The bigotry, and servility,

* Mr. Curran's speech in Finnerty's case.—C. † An expression of Mr. Flood's.—C.
‡ The words of Mr. Grattan's motion, April 19, 1780.—C.
§ Mr. Grattan's speech, Nov. 13, 1781.—C.

and disunion, which had so long supported it in Ireland, had for the moment disappeared. Ireland declared, and England felt, that no other policy remained, " but to do justice to a people who were otherwise determined to do justice to themselves."* The British ministry, whose infatuated counsels had lost America, and whose tardiness and insincerity with respect to Ireland had been encouraging the spirit of resistance there, were removed, and successors appointed with instructions to make such honourable concessions as were due to the services, the strength, and the just pretensions of the Irish people. The principal restrictions upon the trade of Ireland had been previously taken off. Under the Marquis of Rockingham's administration, the great leading grievance, that included in its principle so many more, was redressed. England resigned her legislative pretensions, and recognized Ireland to be a *free nation.*†

This signal event, so justly denominated by Mr. Burke the Irish revolution, was the work of the Irish Volunteers. Their efforts were powerfully aided by the momentary spirit which they infused into the Irish House of Commons. In many of its members, the enthusiasm vanished with the occasion; but there remained a few, whose better natures, superior to the control of accident, continued to struggle for the public good with a constancy, ability, and zeal, which sprang from within themselves. Their merits have been long since recorded: the preeminent merits of their illustrious leader, now associated with the proudest recollections of his country, require new attestation. For Mr. Grattan's most splendid panegyric, for the only one truly worthy of him, we are to look in what he has himself pronounced. His public exertions, the monuments of his genius and his worth, are preserved; his historian will have but to col-

* Mr. Grattan's speech, April 19, 1780.—C.

† 1782.—Several important constitutional acts were passed in Ireland during this short administration. A habeas corpus act, the repeal of the perpetual mutiny bill, the act for the independence of the judges, an act in favour of the Dissenting Protestants. A slight relaxation of the penal code had taken place in 1778.—C.

lect and refer to them, justly confiding, that as long as eloquence, patriotism, intrepidity, and uncompromising honour are valued in public men, the example of Mr. Grattan will remain the subject of lasting gratitude and praise.*

The triumph which Ireland gained in the declaration of independence was the triumph of a principle, which, however glorious it might have been to those who achieved it, failed to confer upon the nation the benefit and repose that the political philanthropist fondly anticipated. The spirit of the Parliament was exhausted in the single effort—they had emancipated themselves from the control of another legislature; but no sooner was the victory obtained, than it became evident that very few of its fruits were to be shared among the people. Great domestic abuses still prevailed; the corrupt state of the legislature;† its consequence, an enormous and increasing Pension List; and,

* Mr. Grattan, like other men of original genius and character, has been many times in the course of his memorable career misrepresented and reviled. The following spirited defence of him against such attacks was made in the Irish House of Commons, by his friend, Mr. Peter Burroughs, a gentleman long distinguished for his eloquence in the senate and at the bar, and for the unsuspected purity of his public and private life:—"I cannot repress my indignation, at the audacious boldness of the calumny, which would asperse one of the most exalted characters which any nation ever produced; and that in a country which owes its liberty and its greatness to the energy of his exertions, and in the very house which has so often been the theatre of his glorious labours and splendid achievements. I remember that man the theme of universal panegyric—the wonder and the boast of Ireland, for his genius and his virtue. His name silenced the sceptic, upon the reality of genuine patriotism. To doubt the purity of his motives was a heresy which no tongue dared to utter. Envy was lost in admiration; and even those whose crimes he scourged, blended extorted conpraises with the murmurs of resentment. He covered our (*then*) unfledged constitution with the ample wings of his talents, as an eagle covers her young; like her he soared, and like her could behold the rays, whether of royal favour or royal anger, with undazzled, unintimidated eye. If, according to Demosthenes, to grow with the growth, and decay with the decline of our country, be the true criterion of a good citizen, how infinitely did this man, even in the moment of his lowest depression, surpass those upstart patriots who only become visible when their country vanishes!"—C.

† According to a table of the state of the representation of Ireland, published in 1783, out of the 300 members of the House of Commons (viz, for 32 counties, 64 knights; for seven cities, 14 citizens; for one university, two representatives; for 110 boroughs, 220 burgesses), the people returned 81, including the 64 for counties, and the patrons the remaining 219.—C.

above all, the exclusion of the Roman Catholics from the most valuable privileges of the constitution. There were many others of subordinate importance. From Mr. Curran's entrance into Parliament, he joined those whose opinion it was that these abuses should be corrected. The result of the exertions of himself and the party with which for the fourteen years that he was a senator, he acted, is shortly told. They almost uniformly failed in every measure that they brought forward or opposed. It would far exceed the limits and the objects of this work to discuss at any length the merits of these several measures, some of which continue to this day the subject of anxious controversy upon another and a greater theatre. Yet it may be observed, that the acts of the Irish legislature during the period in question afford matter, if not of a very attractive kind, at least of very solemn and important instruction. Whoever takes the pains to examine them will find how transitory, and almost valueless to a nation the glory of asserting nominal rights, if there be not diffused throughout its various classes that fund of conservative virtue and spirit, which alone can give dignity and stability to its independence, by operating as a perpetual renewal of its claims. He will find one practical and terrible example (illustrated by continued discontents and disturbances, and finally by a rebellion) of the folly of expecting that human beings, in whom the political passions have been once awakened, can be attached, or even reconciled, to the most admired form of government, by any other means, than by a real and conscientious communication of those privileges, for which they would deem it dishonorable not to thirst. For the last eighteen years of her separate existence, Ireland was in the theoretic enjoyment of the same constitution which has long made Great Britain the wonder of other nations; but in Ireland, however boasted the acquisition, it soon appeared to be but a lifeless copy, minutely exact in external form, but wanting all the vigour, and warmth, and imparting spirit of the glorious original. The

Irish legislature, seduced by their fatal ardour for monopoly, would not see that their own emancipation had sent abroad a general taste for freedom, which it was most perilous to disappoint. Unwisely and ungenerously separating their interests and pride from those of their country, they preferred taking a weak and hostile position upon the narrow ground of exclusive privilege, instead of taking their stand, where there was ample space for the parliament and people, and for all, upon the base of the British constitution.* They affected to think that the time had not arrived when the Catholic could be trusted; as if the enjoyment of rights and confidence for a single year would not prove a more instructive school of fidelity than centuries of suspicion and exclusion. But in reality it does not appear from the transactions of those times, that the minds of the excluded Catholics were less matured for all the responsibilities of independence than those of the Irish aristocracy, upon whom alone the recent revolution had confered it. The 80,000 Volunteers, who had been the instruments of that independence, were not a Protestant association. The depreciated Catholic was in their ranks, adding the authority of his strength, his zeal, and his moderation, to the cause of the Irish Parliament, and not unreasonably confiding, that in the hour of victory his services would be remembered. These services and claims were, however, forgotten; and here it is that the Irish legislature will be found utterly unworthy of that controlling power which they had lately acquired over the destinies of their country—in abandoning, as they did, a proud, irritated, and robust population, to all the contingent suggestions and resources of their indigna-

* "I have read," said Mr. Curran, speaking of these unpopular maxims of the Irish Parliament, "I have read the history of other nations. I have read the history of yours. I have seen how happily you emerged from insignificance and obtained a constitution. But when you washed this constitution with the waters which were to render it invulnerable, you forgot that the part by which you held it was untouched by the immersion; it was benumbed and not rendered invulnerable, and should therefore attract your nicest care."—*Irish Par. Deb.* 1787.

tion—in not having "interposed the Constitution," to save the State.

But the point of view, in which a regular history of the latter conduct and character of the Irish House of Commons would supply matter of no ordinary interest to a lover of the British Constitution, is in the example which it would afford, of an assembly, founded upon the model of that constitution, exhibiting itself in its stage of final deterioration. In Ireland the prediction of Montesquieu* has been verified—not in all its dismal extent, for Irish independence has found an *euthanasia* peculiar and accidental; but still the spectacle of legislative immorality, and its instructive warnings, are the same. The corrupted Commons of Ireland surrendered all that was demanded—all that a few years before they had gloried in having acquired; and if a valuable portion of their country's rights and hopes was not included in the sale, the praise of having respected them is due to the wisdom and mercy of the purchasers, and not to any honourable reluctance on the side of the mercenary sellers. In whatever light the Act of Union be viewed, in its ultimate consequences to the empire, the assembly which perpetrated it must be considered as having reached the farthest limits of degeneracy; because the terms on which they insisted have stamped upon them a character of political dishonour that disdained every control of compunction or of pride. For if the surrender to which they consented was regarded by them as a sacrifice of Ireland's rights, how enormous and unmitigated the delinquency!—or if, on the other hand, they imagined it to be essential to the welfare of the empire, how vile and fallen that spirit which could degrade a necessary act of state into a sordid contract! The Parliament that could do this had no longer any morals to lose—and therefore it is, that the constitutional Englishman, who is labouring to procrastinate the fulfilment of the prophecy that impends over his own hitherto more fortunate country,

* "That the British Constitution would not survive the event of the legislative power becoming more corrupt than the executive."—*Spirit of Laws.*

is referred for abundant illustrations of the apprehended crisis to the decline and fall of the Irish Legislature. In contemplating that scene, he will have an opportunity of observing the great leading symptoms, and (which may equally deserve his attention) of discerning the minute, but no less unerring signs which portend that the spirit which gives it life is about to depart from the representative body; and should it ever be his calamity to witness, what he will find Ireland was condemned to see, the members of that body betraying, by their conduct and language, that they held their station as a portion of their private property, rather than as a temporary, public trust—should he observe a general and insatiate appetite for power, for the sake of its emoluments and not its honours—should he see, as Ireland did, grave and authenticated charges of public delinquency answered by personal menaces, or by most indecent ridicule—skilful duellists and jesters held in peculiar honour—public virtue systematically discountenanced, by imputing its profession to a factious disappointed spirit—should he see, within the walls of the Commons' assembly, a standing brigade of mercenaries, recognising no duty beyond fidelity to their employers, the Swiss defenders of any minister or any principle—should he, lastly, observe a marked predilection for penal restraints, an unseemly propensity to tamper with the Constitution, by experimental suspensions of its established usages—should Englishmen ever find all, or many of these to be the characteristics of the depositories of their rights, let them remember the prediction of the philosopher, and the fate of Ireland, and be assured that their boasted securities are becoming but a name.

But to record at length the progress of that fate, to dwell in any detail upon the various characters, and the various inducements (whether of hope, terror, avarice, ambition, or public duty) of the men who accelerated, and of those who would have averted the catastrophe, might well be the subject of a separate and a very considerable work. It will be sufficient for the purposes of Mr. Curran's history to have made these cursory allusions to the spirit of the times in which he acted, leaving more ample developments of it to himself, in the specimens of his eloquence that will be found in the following pages.

Mr. Curran's Parliamentary speeches have been always, and justly, considered as inferior to his displays at the Bar. To this deficiency many circumstances contributed. Depending solely upon his profession for support, he was not only seldom able to give an undivided attention to the questions that were brought before the senate, but he perpetually came to the discussion of them, exhausted by the professional labours of the day. The greater number of the important questions that emanated from the Opposition were naturally introduced by the older leaders of that party; while he, whose talents were most powerful in reply, was reserved to combat the arguments of the other side. The debates, upon these occasions, were in general protracted to a very late hour, so that it often happened, when Mr. Curran rose to speak, that the note-takers were sleeping over their task, or had actually quitted the gallery. But, most of all, the same carelessness of fame, which has left his speeches at the Bar in their present uncorrected state, has irretrievably injured his Parliamentary reputation. While other members sat up whole nights retouching their speeches for publication, he almost invariably abandoned his to their fate, satisfied with having made the exertion that his sense of duty dictated; and deeming it of little moment that what had failed of success within the house should circulate and be applauded without.*

Notwithstanding these disadvantages, however, his career in Parliament supplies much that is in the highest degree honourable to his talents, spirit, and public integrity; of which the leading examples shall be adverted to as they occur in the order of time.

* Another circumstance contributed greatly to the inaccuracy of the reported speeches of such opposition members as would not take the pains of correcting them. The most skilful note-takers, of whom the number was very small, were in the service of the Government, and considered it a part of their duty to suppress whatever it might not be agreeable to the Administration to see published.—C.

CHAPTER VI.

Mr. Flood's plan of Parliamentary Reform—Mr. Curran's contest and duel with Mr. Fitzgibbon (afterwards Lord Clare)—Speech on Pensions—His professional success—Mode of life—Occasional verses—Visits France—Letters from Dieppe and Rouen—Anecdote—Letters from Paris—Anecdote—Letter from Mr. Boyse—Anecdote of Mr. Boyse—Letters from Holland.

The first occasion upon which Mr. Curran's name appears in the Parliamentary register, is in the tempestuous debate of November 29, 1783, upon Mr. Flood's proposition for a Reform in Parliament.* The Convention of Volunteers, by whom Mr. Flood's plan had been approved, was still sitting in Dublin. About four o'clock in the afternoon of the 29th of November, that gentleman rose in the Convention, and proposed that he, accompanied by such members of Parliament as were then present, should immediately go down to the House of Commons, and move for leave to bring in a bill exactly corresponding with the plan of reform approved of by them, and that the Convention should not adjourn till the fate of his motion was ascertained. Lord Charlemont's biographer, who, apparently with much reason, condemns the violence of this proceeding, describes the scene in the House of Commons as terrific: several of the minority, and all the delegates from the Convention, appeared in their military uniforms. As to the debate, "it was uproar, it was clamour, violent menace, and furious recrimination."† In the little that Mr. Curran said, he supported Mr. Flood's motion.‡

* This is an error. Curran's name first appears in the Parliamentary Debates on November 12, 1783, when he briefly objected to the issue of a new writ for Enniscarthy. Again, on November 18, he casually recommended immediate attention to the claims of some distressed manufacturers. Mr. Curran, as member for the borough of Kilbeggan, was then colleague of Henry Flood.—M.

† *Hardy's Life of Lord Charlemont*, page 270, where the particulars of this interesting scene are very strikingly detailed.—C.

‡ Barry Yelverton, then Attorney-General, had made a damaging speech against

In the following month he spoke more at length in prefacing a motion on the right of the House of Commons to originate money bills; but as neither this, nor any of his parliamentary speeches during the session of 1783 and 1784, contain much that is remarkable, it would be unnecessarily swelling these pages to dwell upon them in detail.

[Some notice of Curran's early parliamentary career may not be quite uninteresting. On December 16, 1783, on moving "that it is the sole and undoubted privilege of the Commons of Ireland to originate all bills of supply and grants of public money, in such manner, and with such clauses as they shall think proper," Curran spoke at some length, declaring that he was no party man, and entering into a history of the right of the Commons to originate and frame money-bills. He said, "I lament that a learned and honourable member, with whom I once had the pleasure of living on terms of friendship, is now absent; because I think I might rely upon his supporting the resolution I intend to propose; that support would, perhaps, renew the intercourse of our friendship, which has been lately interrupted. And I must beg the indulgence of the House to say, that that friendship was upon the footing of perfect equality, not imposed by obligation on the one side, or bound by gratitude by the other; for I thank God, when that friendship commenced, I was above receiving obligations from any man, and therefore, our friendship, as it was more pure and disinterested, as it depended on a sympathy of minds, and congeniality of sentiments, I trusted would have endured the longer. I think myself bound to make this public declaration, as it has gone forth from this House, that I am a man of ingratitude, and to declare, that for any difference

Flood's proposition; Langrishe, George Ponsonby, Fitzgibbon, Burke, and Hutchinson also opposed it. Then weakly but pertly, Hardy (afterwards Lord Charlemont's biographer) spoke in opposition, and Curran's speech, in which he cautioned the House not to make a public declaration against the Volunteers, was in reply to Hardy. Leave to bring in the bill was refused by a large majority; a counter resolution against interference by the Volunteers was then carried: and, soon after, the Convention dissolved.—M.

of opinion with my learned and right honorable friend, I cannot be taxed with ingratitude; for that I never received any obligation from him, but lived on a footing of perfect equality, save only so far as his great talents and erudition outwent mine."

Leonard MacNally's copy of Curran's speeches, a present from Curran himself, contains a note in which it is stated that the person thus referred to was Barry Yelverton—but their coolness was of a much later date. Besides, their friendship commenced in youth, when neither was in independent circumstances.

On February 14th, 1785, Curran supported an unsuccessful motion of Flood's, that the immediate and effectual retrenchment of the national expenses was necessary. On the same day, Curran delivered a panegyric on the Volunteers, and personally attacked Mr. Luke Gardiner, whom he called "the little advocate," for voting ministerially, in the hope of being rewarded by being raised to a higher rank. (In fact, he was created Lord Mountjoy at the Union.) This led to a wordy wrangle with Gardiner, whose defence was undertaken by Fitzgibbon, afterwards Earl of Clare, who, assailing Curran as champion of the Volunteers, said, "As I feel myself in a very different situation from that honourable member, I shall ever entrust the defence of the country to gentlemen, with the King's commission in their pockets, rather than to his friends, the beggars in the streets."]

In the year 1785 took place his quarrel with the late Lord Clare, then Mr. Fitzgibbon, the Attorney-General* an event which deeply affected his future fortunes. During Mr. Curran's first years at the bar they had been on terms of polite and even familiar intercourse;† but the dissimilarity of their public characters, the high aristocratic arrogance of the one, and the

* John Fitzgibbon was made Solicitor-General on November 9th, 1783, and on December 20th, 1783, succeeded Yelverton as Attorney-General. This latter office he retained until he was made Lord Chancellor, on August 12th, 1789, his place as leading law officer to the Crown, being then taken by Arthur Wolfe, afterwards Lord Kilwarden.—M.

† The first bag that Mr. Curran ever carried was presented to him by Mr. Fitzgibbon, *for good luck's sake.*—C.

popular tenets of the other, soon separated them; even their private tastes and habits would have forbidden a lasting friendship. Lord Clare despised literature, in which Mr. Curran so delighted. The one in private as in public, disdained all the arts of winning; he was sullen or overbearing, and when he condescended to be jocular was generally offensive. The other was in all companies the reverse; playful, communicative, and conciliating. Mr. Curran never, like his more haughty rival, regulated his urbanity by the rank of his companions; or if he did, it was by a diametrically opposite rule; the more humble the person, the more cautiously did he abstain from inflicting pain. For all those lighter talents of wit and fancy which Mr. Curran was incessantly and almost involuntarily displaying, Lord Clare had a real or an affected contempt, and would fain persuade himself that they were incompatible with those higher powers which he considered could alone raise the possessor to an equality with himself. Mr. Curran was perhaps equally hasty in underrating the abilities of his antagonist. Detesting his arbitrary principles, and disgusted with his unpopular manners, he would see nothing in him but the petty despot, ascending to a bad eminence by obvious and unworthy methods, and therefore meriting his unqualified hatred and invective.

With such elements of personal dislike and political hostility, it is not surprising that when they met they should clash, and that the conflict should be violent and lasting. The very destinies of the two men seemed to have placed them where their contrasted qualities and peculiar force might be most strikingly displayed. Lord Clare was fitted by nature to attain power and to abuse it. Many men of inferior capacity might have attained as much; but without his resources and perseverance, few could have continued so long to abuse it with impunity. Mr. Curran was either ignorant of, or despised the arts which led to station; his talent lay not in defending doubtful measures or selecting political expedients, but in exposing violated trust; in braving and denouncing public delinquents, in pathetic or indignant appeals to those natural elementary principles of human rights, against which political expedients are too frequently directed. He could never, like Lord Clare, have managed a venal, restless aristocracy, so as to command their concurrence in a long system of unpopular encroachments; nor like him have continued for years to face the public reprobation of such conduct: as little could the latter, had he sided with the people, have brought to their cause such varied stories of wit and ridicule, and persuasive eloquence, as the harangues of his more gifted rival display.

In a debate on the Abuse of Attachments by the King's Bench, in the Irish House of Commons (February 24, 1785), as Mr. Curran rose to speak against them, perceiving that Mr. Fitzgibbon had fallen asleep on his seat, he thus commenced: "I hope I may say a few words on this great subject without disturbing the sleep of any right honourable member, and yet, perhaps, I ought rather to envy than blame the tranquillity of the right honourable gentleman. I do not feel myself so happily tempered as to be lulled to repose by the storms that shake the land. If they invite rest to any, that rest ought not to be lavished on the guilty spirit."* Provoked by these expressions, and by the general tenor of the observations that followed, Mr. Fitzgibbon replied to Mr. Curran with much personality, and among other things denominated him a *puny babbler*. The latter retorted by the following description of his opponent: "I am not a man whose respect in person and character depends upon the importance of his office; I am not a young man who thrusts himself into the foreground of a picture, which ought to be occupied by a better figure; I am not one who replies with invective when sinking under the weight of argument;

* Although Mr. Curran appears here to have commenced hostilities, it should be mentioned, that he was apprised of Mr. Fitzgibbon's having given out in the ministerial circles that he should take an opportunity, during this debate, in which he knew that Mr. Curran would take a part, *of putting down the young patriot*. The Duchess of Rutland and all the ladies of the Castle were present in the gallery to witness what Mr. Curran called, in the course of the debate, "this exhibition by command."—C.

I am not a man who denies the necessity of a parliamentary reform at the time that he proves its expediency by reviling his own constituents, the parish-clerk, the sexton, and grave-digger; and if there be any man who can apply what I am not to himself, I leave him to think of it in the committee, and to contemplate upon it when he goes home." The result of this night's debate was a duel between Mr. Curran and Mr. Fitzgibbon; after exchanging shots they separated, only confirmed in their feelings of mutual aversion, of which some of the consequences will appear hereafter.*

[The first of Curran's speeches displaying remarkable ability (Davis says) is a short one made on Orde's Commercial Propositions. Orde,† who was Chief Secretary of Ireland, had proposed several resolutions by which Reciprocity would be nominally granted to Ireland in trade, commerce, and manufactures, as regarded England. In reality, their design was to draw large sums from Ireland for "general defence" (of England), in return for which the poorer country would be allowed to compete with the wealthier and stronger. Curran spoke briefly on the subject on June 30, 1785, and, at much greater length, on July 23. He spoke again on the 11th and 12th of August—his last speech not having commenced until six in the morning, when he declared, exhausted as he was, that his zeal had renewed his strength, and hoped that his then state of mind and body might not be ominous of the condition to which Ireland would be reduced, if the bill should become a law. He prophetically said that if England were allowed the right of taxing Ireland as she pleased, "we must either

* When the parties were placed on the ground they were left to fire when they pleased. Curran had the first shot, without effect. Fitzgibbon then took aim for nearly half a minute, and on his fire being ineffectual, Curran exclaimed, "It was not your fault, Mr. Attorney; *you were deliberate enough*."—M.

† Mr. Thomas Orde had married the natural daughter of the fifth Duke of Bolton, on whom her father had entailed the principal part of his large estates, of failure of male heirs to his brother Henry, sixth Duke. In 1794, the Dukedom became extinct, by the death of the sixth Duke, and, in 1797, Mr. Orde was created Baron Bolton, of Bolton Castle, County of York He died in 1807.—M.

sink into utter slavery, or the people must wade to a re-assumption of their rights through blood, *or be obliged to take refuge in a Union, which would be the annihilation of Ireland, and what, I suspect, the Ministry is driving at.*" Three days after this, Orde withdrew his bill—but, from that hour, Pitt determined to carry the Union.

On March 11, 1786, Curran spoke on the Portugal Trade, and glanced at Toler's (afterwards Lord Norbury) unfortunate "knack of turning matters of the most serious nature into ridicule." Toler was then at once the *buffo* and bravo of Ministers.]

One of the public grievances, which the Irish Opposition frequently, but vainly, attempted to redress, was the enormity of the Pension List. On the 13th of May, in this year (1786), Mr. Forbes brought forward a motion upon the subject, which, as usual, failed.* A part of Mr. Curran's speech upon that occasion may be given as a specimen of the lighter mode of attack to which he sometimes resorted where he saw that gravity would have been unavailing; and it may be observed that this, like many more of the same kind, are historical documents, which are, perhaps, the most descriptive of the times. The very absence of serious remonstrance shows that serious remonstrance had been exhausted, and that nothing remained but that ridicule should take its vengeance upon those whom argument could not reform.†

"I am surprised that gentlemen have taken up such a foolish opinion as that our constitution is maintained by its different component parts, mutually checking and controlling each other. They seem to think, with Hobbes, that a state of nature is a state of warfare, and that, like Mahomet's coffin, the constitution is sus-

* The debate took place, not in *May*, but in March. Mr. Forbes's motion was leave to bring in a bill to limit the amount of pensions. Sir Hercules Langrishe moved the adjournment of the question until August (equivalent to *sine die*), and it was adjourned, but again brought on in the following year.—M.

† Upon this occasion, Mr. Grattan caused the Pension List to be read aloud by the clerk, and concluded his speech by saying, "If I should vote that pensions are not a grievance, I should vote an impudent, an insolent, and a public lie."—C.

pended by the attraction of different powers. My friends seem to think that the Crown should be restrained from doing wrong by a physical necessity, forgetting that if you take away from a man all power to do wrong, you at the same time take away from him all merit of doing right; and by making it impossible for men to run into slavery, you enslave them most effectually. But if, instead of the three different parts of our constitution drawing forcibly in right lines at opposite directions, they were to unite their power, and draw all one way, in one right line, how great would be the effect of their force—how happy the direction of their union! The present system is not only contrary to mathematical rectitude, but to public harmony: but if, instead of Privilege setting up his back to oppose Prerogative, he was to saddle his back and invite Prerogative to ride, how comfortably might they both jog along; and, therefore, it delights me to hear the advocates for the royal bounty flowing freely and spontaneously, and abundantly as Holywell, in Wales.* If the Crown grants double the amount of the revenue in pensions, they approve of their royal master, for he is the breath of their nostrils.

"But we will find that this complaisance—this gentleness between the Crown and its true servants—is not confined at home; it extends its influence to foreign powers. Our merchants have been insulted in Portugal, our commerce interdicted. What did the British lion do? Did he whet his tusks? Did he bristle up and shake his mane? Did he roar? No, no such thing; the gentle creature wagged his tail for six months at the court of Lisbon; and now we hear from the Delphic oracle on the treasury bench, that he is wagging his tail in London to Chevalier Pinto, who, he hopes soon to be able to tell us, will allow his lady to entertain him as a lap-dog; and when she does, no doubt the British factory will furnish some of their softest woollens to make

* Sir Boyle Roche, who was a Ministerialist and placeman, had opposed the motion, saying: "I would not stop the fountain of royal favour, but let it flow freely, spontaneously, and abundantly, as Holywell, in Wales, that turns so many mills. Indeed, some of the best men have drank of this fountain, which gives honour as well as vigour."—M.

a cushion for him to lie upon. But though the gentle beast has continued so long fawning and couching, I believe his vengeance will be great as it is slow, and that that posterity, whose ancestors are yet unborn, will be surprised at the vengeance he will take.

"This polyglot of wealth—this museum of curiosities—the Pension List, embraces every link in the human chain, every description of men, women, and children, from the exalted excellence of a Hawke or a Rodney, to the debased situation of a lady who humbleth herself that she may be exalted. But the lessons it inculcates form its greatest perfection. It teacheth that sloth and vice may eat that bread which virtue and honesty may starve for, after they have earned it; it teaches the idle and dissolute to look up for that support which they are too proud to stoop and earn; it directs the minds of men to an entire reliance upon the ruling power of the State, who feeds the ravens of the royal aviary that cry continually for food; it teaches them to imitate those saints on the Pension List that are like the lilies of the field—they toil not, neither do they spin, and yet are arrayed like Solomon in his glory: in fine, it teaches a lesson, which, indeed, they might have learned from Epictetus, that it is sometimes good not to be over-virtuous; it shows that, in proportion as our distresses increase, the munificence of the Crown increases also—in proportion as our clothes are rent, the royal mantle is extended over us.

"Notwithstanding the Pension List, like charity, covers a multitude of sins, give me leave to consider it as coming home to the members of this house; give me leave to say, that the Crown, in extending its charity, its liberality, its profusion, is laying a foundation for the independence of Parliament; for, hereafter, instead of orators or patriots accounting for their conduct to such mean and unworthy persons as freeholders, they will learn to despise them, and look to the first man in the State; and they will by so doing have this security for their independence, that while any man in the kingdom has a shilling they will not want one.

"Suppose at any future period of time the boroughs of Ireland should decline from their present flourishing and prosperous state; suppose they should fall into the hands of men who wish to drive a profitable commerce by having members of parliament to hire or let; in such case a secretary would find a great difficulty, if the proprietors of members should enter into a combination to form a monopoly. To prevent which in time, the wisest way is to purchase up the raw material, young members of parliament just rough from the grass; and when they are a little bitted, and he has got a pretty stud, perhaps of seventy, he may laugh at the slave merchant. Some of them he may teach to sound through the nose like a barrel organ: some in the course of a few months might be taught to cry, Hear! hear! some, Chair! chair! upon occasion; though these latter might create a little confusion if they were to forget whether they were calling inside or outside of these doors. Again, he might have some so trained, that he need only pull a string, and up gets a repeating member; and if they were so dull that they could neither speak nor make orations (for they are different things) he might have been taught to dance, *pedibus ire in sententiam.* This improvement might be extended; he might have them dressed in coats and shirts all of one colour, and of a Sunday he might march them to church, two and two, to the great edification of the people, and the honour of the Christian religion; afterwards, like the ancient Spartans, or the fraternity at Kilmainham, they might dine altogether in a large hall. Good heaven! what a sight to see them feeding in public, on public viands, and talking of public subjects, for the benefit of the public! It is a pity they are not immortal; but I hope they will flourish as a corporation, and that pensioners will beget pensioners to the end of the chapter."

Mr. Curran was now (1786) in full practice at the bar. It may be acceptable to hear the manner he spoke himself of his increasing celebrity. The following is an extract from one of his private letters of this period.

"Patterson, chief justice of the common pleas, has been given over many days, but still holds out. My good friend Carleton succeeds him. Had he got this promotion some time ago, it might have been of use to me; for I know he has a friendship for me; but at present his partiality can add little to whatever advantage I can derive from his leaving about four thousand a year at the bar.

"I understand they have been puffing me off to you from this (Dublin). I have been indeed very much employed this term, and I find I have the merit imputed to me of changing a determination which the Chancellor [Lord Lifford] had formed against Burroughs,* a few days ago. He has really been uncommonly kind and polite to me. This, I believe, is the first time I ever became my own panegyrist, therefore excuse it: I should scarcely mention it for any vanity of mine, if it were not of some little value to others; tot it up, therefore, on the table of pence, not on the scale of vain glory."

His life at this time was passed in a uniform succession of the same occupations, his professional and parliamentary duties. The intervals of business he generally spent at Newmarket, where he had taken a few acres of land, and built a house, to which he gave the name of the Priory, as the residence of the Prior of the Order of St. Patrick. In Dublin the reputation of his talents and his convivial powers introduced him to every circle to which he could desire to have access; in the country he entered into all the sports and manners of his less polished neighbours, with as much ardour as if it was with them alone that he had passed and was to pass his days. The ordinary routine of his profession, took him twice every year to Mun-

* Sir William Burroughs, Bart., afterwards one of the Judges of the supreme court of Judicature at Calcutta. The cause to which Mr. Curran's letter alludes was that of Newberg and Burroughs; by his exertions in which he had acquired a considerable accession to fame.—C.

ster;* and among the many attractions of that Circuit, he always considered, as one of the greatest, the frequent opportunities it gave him of visiting and spending some happy hours with two of his oldest and dearest friends (once his college fellow-students), the Rev. Thomas Crawford, of Lismore, and the Rev. Richard Cary, of Clonmel; both of them persons unknown to fame, but both so estimable, as men, and scholars, and companions, that his taste and affections were perpetually recalling him to the charms of their society.

It may not be a very dignified circumstance in his history, yet it must be mentioned that his arrival at Newmarket was always considered there as a most important event. Gibbon somewhere observes that one of the liveliest pleasures which the pride of man can enjoy, is to reappear in a more splendid condition among those who had known him in his obscurity. If Mr. Curran had

* Upon one of these journeys, and about this period, as Mr. Curran was travelling upon an unfrequented road, he perceived a man in a soldier's dress, sitting by the roadside, and apparently much exhausted by fatigue and agitation. He invited him to take a seat in his chaise, and soon discovered that he was a deserter. Having stopped at a small inn for refreshment, Mr. Curran observed to the soldier, that he had committed an offence of which the penalty was death, and that his chance of escaping it was but small: "Tell me then," continued he, "whether you feel disposed to pass the little remnant of life that is left you in penitence and fasting, or whether you would prefer to drown your sorrow in a merry glass?" The following is the deserter's answer, which Mr. Curran, in composing it, adapted to a plaintive Irish air:

If sadly thinking, with spirits sinking,
Could more than drinking my cares compose,
A cure for sorrow from sighs I 'd borrow,
And hope to-morrow would end my woes.
But as in wailing there 's naught availing,
And Death unfailing will strike the blow,
Then for that reason, and for a season,
Let us be merry before we go!

To joy a stranger, a way-worn ranger,
In every danger my course I 've run;
Now hope all ending, and Death befriending,
His last aid lending, my cares are done:
No more a rover, or hapless lover,
My griefs are over, and my glass runs low;
Then for that reason, and for a season,
Let us be merry before we go!

been proud, he might have enjoyed this pleasure to the full. Upon the occasion of every return to the scene of childhood, visits and congratulations upon his increasing fame poured in upon "the counsellor" from every side. "His visitors" (according to his own description) "were of each sex and of every rank, and their greetings were of as many kinds. Some were delivered in English, and some in Irish, and some in a language that was a sort of a compromise between the two—some were communicated verbally—some by letter or by deputy, the absentees being just at that moment 'in trouble,' which generally meant, having been lately committed for some 'unintentional' misdemeanour, from the consequences of which, who could extricate them so successfully as 'the counsellor?' some came in prose—some in all the pomp of verse; for Mr. O'Connor, the roving bard (of whom Mr. Curran used to say, that if his imagination could have carried him as far as his legs did, he would have been the most astonishing poet of the age), was never absent; at whatever stage of their poetical circuit he and his itinerant muse might be, the moment certain intelligence reached them that the master of the Priory had arrived, they instantly took a short cut across the country, and laid their periodical offering at the feet of him whose high fortune they had of course been the first to predict."

All these petty honours gratified his heart, if not his pride, and he never fastidiously rejected them. Those who came from the mere ambition of a personal interview, he sent away glorying in their reception, and delighted with his condescension and urbanity; to those who seemed inclined "to carry away anything rather than an appetite," he gave a dinner. The village disturber of the peace had once more a promise that his rescue should be effected at the ensuing assizes, while the needy laureat seldom failed to receive the "*crown*," which he had "long preferred to the freshest laurels."*

* The poetry of the roving bard has by some accident perished; but his name is preserved in a short and unambitious specimen of his favourite art. His muse at one time became so importunate, that Mr. Curran found it necessary to discourage her addresses;

[During the Session of 1787, Mr. Curran constantly attended to his parliamentary duties. At the commencement of the

instead therefore of rewarding one of her effusions with the expected donation, he sent the bard the following impromptu:

A collier once in days of yore,
From famed Newcastle's mines, a store
Of coals had rais'd and with the load
He straightway took Whitehaven road;
When thither come, he look'd around,
And soon a ready chap he found;
But after all his toil and pain,
He measured out his coals in vain,
For he got naught but coals again.
Thus Curran takes O'Connor's lays,
And with a verse the verse repays;
Not *verse* indeed as good as thine,
Nor rais'd from such a genuine mine;
But were it better, 't were in vain
To emulate O'Connor's strain.
Then take, my friend—and freely take,
The verses for the poet's sake:
Yet one advice from me receive,
'T will many vain vexations save;
Should, by strange chance, your muse grow poor,
Bid her ne'er seek a poet's door.

The disappointed bard retorted: and his concluding verse,

If you 're paid such coin for your law,
You 'll ne'er be worth a single straw,

was felt to contain so important and undeniable a truth, that his solicitations could be no longer resisted. These are trifles; but the subject of these pages gladly sought relief in them, when satiated with more splendid cares.

Mr. Curran composed two other little poems, of a different description. about this time. The first of the following has been praised, as possessing peculiar delicacy of thought, by the most admired poet that Ireland has ever produced.

ON RETURNING A RING TO A LADY.

Thou emblem of faith—thou sweet pledge of a passion,
By heaven reserved for a happier than me—
On the hand of my fair go resume thy loved station,
Go back in the beam that is lavish'd on thee!
And if, some past scene thy remembrance recalling,
Her bosom shall rise to the tear that is falling,
With the transport of love may no anguish combine,
But be *hers* all the bliss—and the sufferings all *mine*.

Session of 1786, and again in 1787, the Viceroy's speech alluded to the disturbances in the South of Ireland. On the latter occasion, a vehement debate arose on the address in reply to the viceregal missive, and Curran delivered a speech which Davis calls "one of his best in parliament." The government party

Yet say (to thy mistress ere yet I restore thee),
  Oh say why thy charm so indifferent to me?
To her thou art dear—then should I not adore thee?
  Can the heart that is hers be regardless of thee?
But the eyes of a lover, a friend, or a brother,
Can see naught in thee, but the flame of another;
On me then thou 'rt lost; as thou never couldst prove
The emblem of faith or the token of love.

But, ah! had the ringlet thou lov'st to surround—
  Had it e'er kiss'd the rose on the cheek of my dear,
What ransom to buy thee could ever be found,
  Or what force from my heart thy possession could tear?
A mourner, a suff'rer, a wanderer, a stranger—
In sickness, in sadness, in pain, and in danger,
Next my heart thou shouldst dwell till its last gasp were o'er—
Then *together* we 'd sink—and I 'd part thee no more.

ON MRS. BILLINGTON'S BIRTH-DAY.

The wreath of love and friendship twine,
  And deck it round with flow'rets gay—
Tip the lip with rosy wine,
  'T is fair Eliza's natal day!

Old Time restrains his ruthless hand,
  And learns one favourite form to spare;
Light o'er her tread, by his command,
  The Hours, nor print one footstep there.

In amorous sport the purple Spring
  Salutes her lips, in roses drest;
And Winter laughs, and loves to fling
  A flake of snow upon her breast.

So may thy days, in happiest pace,
  Divine Eliza, glide along!
Unclouded as thy angel face,
  And sweet as thy celestial song.

declared that the disturbance almost exclusively consisted of resistance to the clergy (*i. e.*, to tithes), and accused the landlords of grinding the people and abetting the disturbances, and demanded fresh powers. Fitzgibbon, then Attorney-General, speaking of his general knowledge of the Province of Munster, said, "I know it is *impossible* for human wretchedness *to exceed that of the miserable peasantry in that province. I know that the unhappy tenants are ground to powder by relentless landlords.*" The Address was an echo of the viceregal speech, and Curran moved an amendment to it, to the effect that the ordinary powers of the law were fully adequate, if duly exerted, to punish and restrain the excesses complained of, and also, that it was necessary to reduce the burthens of the people by every honorable mode of retrenchment. In proposing this, Curran entered fully into the causes of the general distress which had produced partial disturbances. "Unbound to the sovereign by any proof his affection, unbound to government by any instance of its protection, unbound to the country, or to the soil, by being destitute of any property in it, 't is no wonder that the peasantry should be up for rebellion and revolt; so far from being matter of surprise, it must naturally have been expected." Another passage is very good:—"I have read the history of other nations, and I have read the history of yours. I have seen how happily you emerged from insignificance, and obtained your Constitution. But when you washed this Constitution with the waters which were to render it invulnerable, like the mother of Achilles, you forgot that the part by which you held it was untouched on the immersion; it was benumbed, and not rendered invulnerable, and therefore it should attract your nicest care."

On January 23d, 1787, again alluding to the disturbances, Mr. Curran said, "The low and contemptible state of your magistracy is the cause of much evil, particularly in the Kingdom of Kerry. I say Kingdom, for it seems absolutely not a part of the same county."

In what was called the Right Boy Oath, there was a clause authorizing magistrates to pull down Roman Catholic Churches at which combinations should be formed, or unlawful oaths administered. On February 19th, 1787, on the motion for the committal of the bill, this clause was objected to, and, though not insisted on, was strongly defended by the Attorney-General, Fitzgibbon. Mr. Curran declared that such an act would be a proclamation of a religious war in Ireland.

On the following day, on the motion that the application of the bill be limited to Cork, Kerry, Limerick and Tipperary, Mr. Curran supported the limitation—which was lost by a large majority.

On March the 12th, 1787, on the renewal of the lost bill for limiting pensions, Mr. Curran again supported it; on the following day he spoke in favour of a resolution moved by Mr. Grattan, that, if tranquillity were restored at the next opening of the Session, the House would consider the tithe question. Speaking of the Protestant clergy, he said, "I will never hear of any attempt to injure their legal rights. I love their religion; there is only one religion under Heaven which I love more than the Protestant, but I confess there is one—the Christian religion." Grattan's motion was lost, without a division.

It was sought to introduce into Ireland, the English Navigation Law, originated by Cromwell, in 1650, and carried out by 12th Charles II., c. 18. The Dublin merchants petitioned against it. Fitzgibbon insulted their petition, Grattan moved an amended clause (not carried) that the act should bind Ireland, only while the benefits and restraints of it were equal in the two countries. He was supported by Mr. Curran, who said that the Navigation Act was founded on principles of imperial monopoly—to depress the rivals of Great Britain, and to advance the power of the navy. To accept it would be to deprive Ireland of a great commercial right.]

In the year 1787 Mr. Curran visited France, a country for whose literature and manners he had had a very early predilection. The following letters give an account of its first impression on him; and, however carelessly written, their insertion will be at least some relief to the harsher scenes of political contention, which occupy so much of his future history.

DIEPPE, Friday, August 31st, 1787.

"My last from Brighton told you I was setting sail—I did so about eight o'clock yesterday evening, and after a pleasant voyage, landed here this day at twelve. To-morrow I set out for Rouen, where I shall probably remain two or three days.

"I cannot say the first view of France has made a very favourable impression on me. I am now writing in the best lodging-room in the best inn of Dieppe, l'hôtel de la Ville de Londres. Monsieur de la Rue, the host, danced up to me on board the packet, did everything I wanted, and offered a thousand services that I had no occasion for. I mounted to my present apartment by a flight of very awkward stairs; the steps, some of brick, some of wood, but most of both. The room contains two old fantastical chests of drawers; a table, on which I now write; four chairs, with cane backs and bottoms; and a bed, five feet from the bricks that compose the floor (the first floor); the walls half covered with lime and half with a miserable tapestry. I dined very well, however, on a small fish like a trout, a beefsteak, and a bottle of Burgundy, which the maid that attended me would not admit to be 'chevalier.'

"I then walked out to see the town, and, God knows, a sad sight it is: it seems to have been once better, but it is now strength fallen into ruin, and finery sunk into decay. It smote me with a natural sentiment of the mortality of all human things; and I was led by an easy transition to inquire for the churches. I inquired of a decent-looking man, who sat at a door, knitting stockings, and he, with great civility, stopped his needles, and directed me to the church of St. Jacques, having first told me how fine it was, and how many years it was built. It has a profusion of sculpture in it, and, I suspect, not of the best kind; however, the solemnity of the whole made amends, and indeed, I think, well might, for that deficiency, to me who am so little a connoisseur in the matter. I could not but respect the disinterestedness and piety of our ancestors, who laboured so much to teach posterity the mortality of man; and yet, on turning the idea a little, I could not but suspect that the vain-glory of the builders of pyramids and temples was no small incentive to their labours; why else engrave the lessons of mortality in characters intended to endure for ever, and thus become an exception to the rule they would establish? But I am turning preacher instead of traveller.

"I reserved the view of the inhabitants for the last. Every nation, 't is said, has a peculiar feature. I trust poor France shall not be judged of, in that point, by Dieppe. I had expected to see something odd on my arrival, but I own I was unprepared for what I met; the day was warm, and, perhaps, the better sort of people were all within. Many hundreds were busy on the quays and streets, but any thing so squalid, so dirty, and so ugly, I really never saw. At some little distance, I mistook the women for sailors, with long boddices, and petticoats not completely covering their knees, which I really took for trousers; however, on a nearer view, I saw their heads covered with linen caps, their beards unshaved, and perceived they wore slippers with rather high heels; by which, notwithstanding the robust shape of their legs, and their unusual strut, I ascertained their sex sufficiently for a traveller.

"I may say, truly, I did not see a being this day between the ages of fifteen and fifty. I own I was therefore surprised to find that there were children; for such I found to be a parcel of strange little figures; the female ones with velvet hoods, and the male with their little curled heads covered with woollen nightcaps, regardless of the example of their hardy old fathers, if they were not their grandsires, who carried about heads without a hair or a hat to protect them.

"In truth, I am at a loss to reconcile so many contradictions as

I have met with here even in a few hours. Even though I should not mention the height of their beds, nor the unwieldiness of their carriages, as if the benefit of rest was reserved for vaulters and rope-dancers, and the indolent and helpless only were intended to change their place; but perhaps those impressions are only the first and the mistaken views of a traveller, that ought to see more and reflect more before he forms his opinions. I believe so, too; and, if I change or correct them, the French nation shall have the benefit of my change of opinion. If not, I hope my mistake will not do much injury to the power, or riches, or vanity of his most Christian Majesty.

"Yours ever,

"J. P. C."

A few days after, in a letter from Rouen, he says: "I still find myself confirmed every day in a preference for my own poor country. The social turn of these people certainly has the advantage; their manners are wonderfully open and pleasant; but still, in everything I have yet seen, I have observed a strange medley of squalid finery and beggarly ostentation, with a want of finishing in every article of building or manufacture, that marks them at least a century behind us. Yet have they their pleasant points: gay, courteous, temperate, ill-clothed, and ill-accommodated, they seem to have been negligent only in what regarded themselves, and generously to have laboured in what may render them agreeable to their visitors."

As Mr. Curran travelled on towards Paris, he received a mark of public attention, for which he was, in a great measure, indebted to his eloquent defence of the Roman Catholic priest already mentioned. His friend, the Reverend Arthur O'Leary (more generally called Father O'Leary*), knowing that he was to pass

* Arthur O'Leary, born at Cork, and educated in France, was a Capuchin friar of the order of St. Francis. He was a true and tried patriot, a wit as well as a humourist, and a clear-headed, powerful writer. In despair for his country, he retired to England, and

through a particular town, wrote to the superior of a convent in the neighbourhood, describing the traveller that was shortly to arrive there, and requesting that so ardent a friend of their religion should be welcomed and entertained with all courtesy and honour. Mr. Curran no sooner reached the place, than he received a pressing invitation to take up his abode at the convent. He accordingly proceeded thither, and was met at the gates by the abbot and his brethren in procession. The keys of the convent were presented to him, and his arrival hailed in a Latin oration, setting forth his praises and their gratitude for his noble protection of a suffering brother of their church.

Their Latin was so bad, that the stranger, without hesitation, replied in the same language. After expressing his general acknowledgments for their hospitality, he assured them that nothing could be more truly gratifying to him than to reside for a few days among them; that he should feel himself perfectly at home in their society; for that he was by no means a stranger to the habits of a monastic life, being himself no less than a Prior of an Order in his own country—the Order of St. Patrick, or the Monks of the Screw. Their fame, he added, might never have reached the Abbot's ears, but he would undertake to assert for them, that, though the brethren of other Orders might be more celebrated for learning how to die, the "Monks of the Screw" were, as yet, unequalled for knowing how to live. As, however, humility was their great tenet and uniform practice, he would give an example of it upon the present occasion, and, instead of accepting all the keys which the Abbot had so liberally offered, would merely take charge, while he stayed, of the key of the wine-cellar.

This little playful sally was accepted in the same spirit of good

for many years was officiating clergyman in the Roman Catholic chapel in Soho Square, London. He died in 1802. He was an eminently social man. One of his retorts has been preserved. To a person endeavouring to draw him into a discussion about Purgatory, he answered, "You may go farther, and fare worse."—M.

humour with which it was offered; and the traveller, after passing two or three days with the Abbot, and pleasing every one by his vivacity and conciliating manners, proceeded on his journey, not without a most pressing invitation to take advantage of any future occasion of revisiting his friends at the convent.

The following is extracted from one of his letters from Paris:

"PARIS, September 15, 1787.

"I have been all about the world with the Carletons,* visiting churches, libraries, pictures, operas, &c. Yesterday, we went to Versailles, and, though a week-day, had the good luck to see his Majesty† at chapel, after which we went out hunting; after which we viewed the palace, the gardens, statues, &c.; bought two pair of garters at a pedlar's stall in an ante-chamber adjoining the great gallery, and so returned to town. All that could be seen, even on a Sunday, besides, would be the Queen, who would probably take very little notice of her visitors; so I shall probably, I think, go no more to Versailles. Mr. Boyse‡ is perfectly well. I have written to him this day. My health, thank God, has been perfectly good since I came here, to which, I suppose, the temperance of this country has contributed not a little. I am early as usual; read, write, dine, go to the coffee-house, the play, as usual; one day now seems to be the former, and I begin to be vexed at its being the model of the next. Perhaps upon earth there cannot be found in one city such a variety of amusements: if you walk the Boulevards in the evening, you see at least ten thousand persons employed in picking the pockets of as many millions, reckoning players, rope-dancers, jugglers, buffoons, bird-sellers, bear-dances, learned beasts, &c. Yet, I begin to grow satiated, and often wish for a more tranquil habitation."

Among the traits of French manners, which Mr. Curran, upon

* The family of the late Lord Carleton, an Irish judge.—M.

† Louis XVI.—M.

‡ The benevolent clergyman to whom he chiefly owed his education.—M.

his return, related as having greatly entertained him, was the following little incident, which will be also found to be perfectly characteristic of his own.

He was one evening sitting in a box, at the French Opera, between an Irish noblewoman, whom he had accompanied there, and a very young Parisian female. Both the ladies were peculiarly interesting in their appearance, and very soon discovered a strong inclination to converse, but, unluckily, each was ignorant of the other's language. To relieve their anxiety, Mr. Curran volunteered to be their interpreter, or, in his own words, "to be the carrier of their thoughts, and accountable for their safe delivery." They accepted the offer with delight, and immediately commenced a vigorous course of observations and inquiries upon dress and fashion, and such commonplace subjects; but their interpreter, betraying his trust, changed and interpolated so much, that the dialogue soon became purely his own invention. He managed it, however, with so much dexterity, transmitting between the parties so many finely-turned compliments, and elegant repartees, that the unsuspecting ladies became fascinated with each other. The Parisian *demoiselle* was in raptures with the wit and colloquial eloquence of *milady*, whom she declared to be *parfaitement aimable ;* while the latter protested that she now, for the first time, felt the full charm of French vivacity. At length, when their mutual admiration was raised to its most ecstatic height, the wily interpreter, in conveying some very innocent question from his countrywoman, converted it into an anxious demand, if she might be favoured with a kiss. "Mais oui, mon Dieu, oui !" cried out the animated girl, "j'allois le proposer moi-même;" and, springing across Mr. Curran, imprinted an emphatic salutation, according to the custom of her country, upon each cheek of his fair companion; and then turning to him, added, "vraiment, monsieur, madame votre amie est un veritable ange." The latter never discovered the deception; but, after her return to Ireland, used often to remind Mr. Curran of the circumstance, and ask "what in the world the young lady could have meant by such strange conduct?" to which he would only archly reply: "Come, come, your ladyship must know that there is but one thing in the world that it *could* have meant, and the meaning of that is so literal, that it does not require a commentator."

The name of Mr. Boyse occurred in his last letter; the friend of his childhood, between whom and Mr. Curran the most cordial intercourse continued, until death dissolved it.* The delicacy of that gentleman's health had obliged him to reside, for several years past, upon the Continent, from which he regularly corresponded with his former pupil. One of his letters, written in this year, shall be inserted, as an example of the kind and confidential feeling that pervades them all.

"TO J. P. CURRAN, ESQ.—ELY PLACE, DUBLIN.

"BRUXELLES, Feb. 7, 1787.

"DEAR JACK,

"I hope my friend's affairs are going well, and flourishing as when I left him: mine, I suppose, are in the last stage of consumption, so that I almost dread to make inquiry about them. My health has been so good this winter, that I came from Aix here to escort a Mr. Low and family, my relations, who are on their road to England and Ireland. To-morrow, I return to Aix-la-Chapelle, for the remainder of the winter. I hope you were paid the money I drew on you for, as I must soon draw on you again for £60. If I have no funds at Newmarket, I shall write to Dick Boyse to pay you, and shall always take care that you shall be no sufferer by me.

"Let me hear how you go on, and what chance you have of the bench. I wish you had realized seven or eight hundred a year for your family. Is your health good, and your life regular? I saw Grattan and Fitzgibbon at Spa; the former friendly and agreeable, the latter disagreeable to every one. I dined with

* Mr. Boyse died a few years after the date of this letter.—C.

him and Mr. Orde, at a club where we are members, but he was solemn and displeasing to us all. My compliments to Grattan and his wife, and ask him for her on my part; she is very amiable. What is to become of us with the White Boys? If I am not an absolute beggar, I will go home the latter end of the summer. How go on all your children? An account of yourself and them will give me pleasure. With best wishes to you all,

"I am, dear Jack, yours, sincerely,

"NAT. BOYSE."

Mr. Boyse came over to Ireland in the following year. Upon the morning of his arrival in Dublin, as he was on his way to Ely Place, he was met by his friend, who was proceeding in great haste to the Courts, and had only time to welcome him, and bid him defer his visit till the hour of dinner. Mr. Curran invited a number of the eminent men at the bar to meet Mr. Boyse; and on returning home at a late hour from court, with some of his guests, found the clergyman, still in his travelling dress, seated in a familiar posture at the fire, with a foot resting upon each side of the grate. "Well, Jack," said he turning round his head, but never altering his position, "here have I been for this hour past, admiring all the fine things that I see around me, and wondering where you could have got them all." "You would not dare," returned Mr. Curran, deeply affected by the recollections which the observation called up, "to assume such an attitude, or use so little ceremony, if you were not conscious that every thing you see is your own. Yes, my first and best of friends, it is to you that I am indebted for it all. The little boy whose mind you formed, and whose hopes you animated, profiting by your instructions, has risen to eminence and affluence; but the work is yours; what you see is but the paltry stucco upon the building of which *you* laid the foundation."*

* Mr. Phillips has worked up this incident into a very dramatic scene—but without

[In 1788, the Parliamentary Reports only gave one speech by Mr. Curran. It was on contraband trade, and bears date February 19, 1788. It is not without a touch of wit and quaintness. After saying that high duties were a premium to the contraband trader, he continued, "The conduct of the gentlemen who conduct the revenue department reminds me of a circumstance which happened in our University some time ago. The lads had got a custom of breaking the lamps. For a long time there could be found no remedy for this grievance, but mending them when broken, till at length a very sagacious member of the Board of Fellows hit upon a very extraordinary expedient. 'The lamps,' said he, 'cannot be well broken in the daytime without immediate detection, wherefore if they were taken down at nightfall every evening, and put up every morning, the mischief might be prevented!' The learned doctor's argument has been adopted by the gentlemen of the revenue: they find that smuggling has risen to a great height, they then shut up the ports, thereby making them of no use."]

This year (1788) Mr. Curran visited Holland, from which he writes as follows:

"HELVOETSLUYS, August 1, 1788.

"Just landed, after a voyage of forty-two hours, having left Harwich, Wednesday, at six in the evening. We are just setting out in a treckscuit for Rotterdam.

"I can say little, even if I had time, of the first impression that Holland makes on a traveller. The country seems as if it were swimming for its life, so miserably low does it appear; and from the little I have seen of its inhabitants, I should not feel myself much interested in the event of a struggle. We were obliged to put up an orange cockade on our entrance. We have just dined, and I am so disturbed by the settling the

improving it. Even as related here there is much coarseness in Curran's telling the old clergyman, his benefactor, that he would not *dare* to assume such an attitude, &c.—M.

bill, and the disputes about guilders and stivers, &c., that I must conclude.

"Yours ever,

"J. P. C."

"AMSTERDAM, August 5, 1788.

"You can't expect to find much entertainment in any letter from Holland. The subject must naturally be as flat as the country, in which, literally, there is not a single eminence three inches above the level of the water, the greater part lying much below it. We met Mr. Hannay, a Scotchman, on the passage, who had set out on a similar errand. We joined accordingly. A few moments after my letter from Helvoetsluys was written, we set out in a treckscuit for Rotterdam, where, after a voyage of twenty-four hours easy sail, we arrived without any accident, notwithstanding some struggle between an adverse wind and the horse that drew us. We staid there only one day, and next day set out for the Hague, a most beautiful village, the seat of the Prince of Orange, and the residence of most of the principal Dutch. Yesterday we left it, and on going aboard found four inhabitants of Rouen, and acquaintances of my old friend Du Pont. We were extremely amused with one of them, a little thing about four feet long, and for the first time in his life a traveller. He admired the abundance of the waters, the beauty of the windmills, and the great opulence of Holland, which he thought easy to be accounted for, considering that strangers paid a penny a mile for travelling, which was double what a French gentleman was obliged to pay at home; nor could it otherwise be possible for so many individuals to indulge in the splendor of so many country villas as we saw ranged along the banks of the canals, almost every one of which had a garden and menagerie annexed. The idea of the menagerie he caught at the instant from a large poultry coop, which he spied at the front of one of those little boxes, and which contained half a dozen turkeys and as many hens.

"The evening, yesterday, brought us to Amsterdam. We had an interpreter who spoke no language. We knew not, under heaven, where to go; spoke in vain to every fellow-passenger, but got nothing in return but Dutch; among the rest to a person in whom, notwithstanding the smoke, I thought I saw something of English. At length he came up to me, and said he could hold out no longer. He directed us to an inn; said he sometimes amused himself with concealing his country, and that once at Rotterdam he carried on the joke for five days, to the great annoyance of some unfortunate Englishmen, who knew nobody, and dined every day at the table d'hôte he frequented. Last night we saw a French comedy and opera tolerably performed. This day we spent in viewing the port, stad-house, &c., and shall depart to-morrow for Rotterdam or Utrecht, on our way to Antwerp.

"You cannot expect much observation from a visitor of a day: the impression, however, of a stranger, cannot be favourable to the people. They have a strange appearance of the cleanliness, for which they are famous, and of the dirt that makes it necessary: their outsides only have I seen, and I am satisfied abundantly with that. Never shall I wish to return to a country that is at best dreary and unhealthy, and is no longer the seat of freedom; yet of its arbitrariness I have felt nothing more than the necessity of wearing an orange riband in my hat. My next will be from Spa, where I hope to be in six or seven days; till then farewell.

"Yours ever,

"J. P. C."

CHAPTER VII.

His Majesty's illness—Communicated to the House of Commons—Mr Curran's speech upon the Address—Regency question—Formation of the Irish Whig opposition—Mr. Curran's speech and motion upon the division of the boards of stamps and accounts—Answered by Sir Boyle Roche—Mr. Curran's reply—Correspondence and duel with Major Hobart—Effects of Lord Clare's enmity—Alderman Howison's case.

THE year 1789 was in many respects one of the most interesting and important in Mr. Curran's life. From his entrance into Parliament he had hitherto been chiefly engaged in an occasional desultory resistance to the Irish administration, rather acting with, than belonging to the party in opposition; but in this year a momentous question arose, in the progress and consequence of which, there was such a development of the system by which Ireland was in future to be governed, that he did not hesitate to fix his political destiny for ever, by irrevocably connecting himself with those whose efforts alone he thought could save their country. His late Majesty's most afflicting indisposition had taken place towards the close of the year 1788. It is known to all that upon the announcement of that melancholy event, the British parliament proceeded to nominate His Royal Highness the Prince of Wales regent, under particular limitations and restrictions; a mode of proceeding which the Irish ministry were peculiarly anxious that the Irish parliament should studiously imitate. For this purpose great exertions were now made to secure a majority. To Mr. Curran it was communicated that his support of the government would be rewarded with a judge's place, and with the eventual prospect of a peerage; but he was among those who considered it essential to the dignity of the parliament, and the interests of Ireland, that the Heir Apparent should be invited by address to assume the full and unrestricted exercise of the regal functions; and fortunately for his fame, he had too much respect for his duties and his character, to sacrifice them to any considerations of personal advancement.

The Irish administration had been anxious to defer the meeting of the legislature until the whole proceedings respecting the regency should be completed in England, in the hope that the conduct pursued by the British parliament might be followed as a precedent in Ireland; but the urgencies of the public business not admitting so long a delay, the session was opened on the 5th of February, 1789, by the viceroy (the Marquis of Buckingham), when the King's illness was for the first time announced to the country.* On the following day, in the debate on the address of thanks, his Excellency's late conduct was made the subject of much severe animadversion. Upon that occasion Mr. Curran spoke as follows:

"I oppose the address,† as an address of delay. I deeply lament the public calamity of the King's indisposition: it is not so welcome a tale to me as to call for any thanks to the messenger

* Early in 1764, (the year in which George III. suggested to Lord Granville the taxation of America, as a grand financial measure for relieving the mother country from the heavy war expenses, which had chiefly been incurred for the security of the Colonies), George III. was attacked by an indisposition of six weeks' duration, which is suspected to have been similar in its nature to, though less in its degree than, the malady which assailed him in 1788-'9, and completely clouded the last ten years of his life. It is a well-known fact, that the Royal Family of England have a predisposition to insanity, attributed to their in-and-in breeding system, caused by their marriages with other than royal and Protestant houses being prohibited by law, which has led to their union with cousins and such near relations. It has been sharply said, "that the Guelphs are divided into only two classes,—those who are bad, and those who are mad."—M.

† One of the paragraphs of the address upon which the debate arose was the following: "We return your excellency sincere thanks (however we must lament the necessity of such a circumstance) for ordering the communication of such documents as you have received respecting his majesty's health, as well as for your intention of laying before us such further information as may assist our deliberations upon that melancholy event."—C.

[In 1782-'3, Earl Temple (subsequently created Marquis of Buckingham) was Lord Lieutenant of Ireland. In December, 1787, he was again appointed and held the office for two years.]—M.

that brings it. Instead of thanks for communicating it now, it should be resented as an outrage upon us that he did not communicate it before.* As to thanks for the wishes of Ireland, it is a strange time for the noble Marquis to call for it. I do not wish that an untimely vote of approbation should mix with the voice of a people's lamentation: it is a picture of general mourning, in which no man's vanity ought to be thrust in as a figure. But if it is pressed, what are its pretensions? One gentleman (Mr. Boyd) has lost hundreds a year by his arts, and defends him on that ground; another (Mr. Corry) praises his economy for increasing salaries in the ordnance—the economy of the noble lord is then to be proved only by public or by private losses. Another right honourable gentleman (the Attorney-General) has painted him as

* George III. had a bilious fever in October, 1788. On the 24th of that month, however, he attended a levee, but, immediately after, exhibited symptoms of insanity. For some time before, he had complained of weight or pressure on the brain, and anticipated how it would end. At a private concert, one evening, he said to Dr. Ayrton, "I fear, sir, I shall not be able long to hear music; it seems to affect my head, and it is with some difficulty I bear it. Alas! the best of us are but frail mortals." The King's illness was publicly known in November. Dr. Warren, the regular physician to the Royal Household, had no hope of his recovery. Dr. Willis, famous for his success in the treatment of mad people, declared that the malady would be of short duration. Charles Fox and the Opposition held on by Warren's prognostication. William Pitt, and the ministerial party confided in the opinion of Willis. It was generally admitted that a Regency was indispensable, and that the Prince of Wales (afterwards George IV.) was the proper person, as his heir-apparent, to be appointed. Then came the dispute as to the degree of power which, as the King's representative, the Regent should exercise. Fox contended that he should have the royal authority in as much plenitude as the Sovereign himself. Pitt advocated the necessity and legality of imposing various restrictions upon his authority. Pitt's proposition was carried, and the bill had reached its last stage, in the English Parliament, when the King suddenly recovered—in consequence, it is said, of Dr. Willis having calmed him by sleep, brought on by the use of a pillow stuffed with hops. Meanwhile, the Irish Parliament had hastily carried a measure giving an unrestricted Regency to the Prince of Wales. The Viceroy, having refused to transmit their resolutions to London, a deputation from the Irish Lords and Commons was despatched with them, and made such good speed as to arrive in London a week *after* the king's convalescence was announced! In one of the stages of the King's malady, it was announced in one of the bulletins of health, that his Majesty had been so far recovered, as to be able to take the air on horseback. "Then," said Curran, "all this work about appointing a Regent is gone for nothing. What happiness will be diffused among his Majesty's subjects, when they learn that he is now able *to take the reins*."—M.

a man of uncouth manners, much addicted to vulgar arithmetic, and therefore entitled to praise. But what have his calculations done? They have discovered that a dismounted trooper may be stript of his boots, as a public saving, or that a mutilated veteran might be plundered of half the pittance of his coals, as a stoppage for that wooden leg, which perhaps the humane marquis might consider as the most proper fuel to keep others warm.

"But a learned gentleman (Mr. Wolfe)* has defended the paragraph, as in fact meaning nothing at all. I confess I find the appeal to the compassion of the puplic stronger than that to their justice. I feel for the reverses of human fate. I remember this very supplicant for a compliment, to which he pretends only because it is no compliment, drawn into this city by the people, harnessed to his chariot, through streets blazing with illumination; and now, after more than a year's labour at computation, he has hazarded on a paragraph stating no one act of private or of public good; supported by no man that says he loves him; defended, not by an assertion of his merit, but by an extenuation of his delinquency.

"For my part I am but little averse to accede to the sentment of an honourable friend who observed, that he was soon to leave us, and that it was harsh to refuse him even a smaller civility than every predecessor for a century had got. As for me, I do not oppose his being borne away from us in a common hearse of his political ancestors; I do not wish to pluck a single faded plume from the canopy, nor a single rag of velvet that might flutter on the pall. Let us excuse his manners, if he could not help them; let us pass by a little peculation, since, as an honourable member says, it was for his brother; and let us rejoice that his kindred were not more numerous. But I cannot agree with my learned friend who defends the conduct of the noble lord, on the present occasion. The Viceroy here, under a party that had taken a peculiar line in Great Britain, should not have availed himself of his trust to forward any of their measures: he should have considered

* Mr. Pitt was the party thus referred to.—M.

himself bound by duty and by delicacy to give the people the earliest notice of their situation, and to have religiously abstained from any act that could add to the power of his party, or embarrass any administration that might succeed him. Instead of that, he abused his trust by proroguing the two Houses, and has disposed of every office that became vacant in the interval, besides reviving others that had been dormant for years. Yet the honourable member says he acted the part of a faithful steward. I know not what the honourable member's idea of a good steward is; I will tell mine. A good steward, if his master was visited by infirmity or by death, would secure every article of his effects for his heir; he would enter into no conspiracy with his tenants; he would remember his benefactor, and not forget his interest. I will also tell my idea of a faithless, unprincipled steward. He would avail himself of the moment of family distraction; while the filial piety of the son was attending the sick bed of the father, or mourning over his grave, the faithless steward would turn the melancholy interval to his private profit; he would remember his own interest, and forget his benefactor, he would endeavour to obliterate or conceal the title deeds; to promote cabals among the tenants of the estate, he would load it with fictitious incumbrances; he would reduce it to a wreck, in order to leave the plundered heir no resource from beggary except continuing him in a trust which he had been vile enough to betray. I shall not appropriate either of these portraits to any man: I hope most earnestly that no man may be found in the community, whose conscience would acknowledge the resemblance of the latter.*

"I do not think the pitiful compliment in the address worthy a debate or a division; if any gentleman has a mind to stigmatize the object of it by a poor, hereditary, unmeaning, unmerited panegyric, let it pass; but I cannot consent to a delay at once so dangerous and so disgraceful."

The opposition proved upon this occasion the stronger party;

* Afterwards Lord Kilwarden.—M.

Mr. Grattan's proposal that the 11th of February should be fixed for taking into consideration the state of the nation was carried, against the exertions of the ministry to postpone that important discussion to a more distant day. On the 11th accordingly both Houses met; when, upon the motion of Mr. Grattan in the one, and of Lord Charlemont in the other, the address to the Prince of Wales, requesting his royal highness to take upon himself the government of Ireland, with the style and title of Prince Regent, and in the name and behalf of his majesty, to exercise all regal functions during his majesty's indisposition, was carried by large majorities in both houses.*

The particulars of the debate in the House of Commons upon this interesting subject, in which Mr. Curran bore a distinguished part, it would be superfluous to detail in this place, as the legislative union has for ever prevented the recurrence of such a question; it will be sufficient merely to observe, that the Whig majority who planned and carried the measure of an address were influenced by two leading considerations.† In the first place it seemed to them that the proceeding by an address was the only one which would not compromise the independence of the Irish Parliament. They conceived the present situation of Ireland as similar in many respects to that of England at the period of the revolution: the throne, indeed, was not actually vacant, but an efficient executive was wanting; and upon the

* Pitt's plan was that the Prince Regent should not have the power of making peers, of granting offices or pensions, save during *royal* pleasure, or of making leases, or of having the care of the King's person, or of administering, save in the King's name. Protesting against them, the Prince of Wales had accepted them from the *English* Parliament. In Ireland, the legislative resolution was that the Regent should exercise and administer "*all* regal powers, jurisdiction, and prerogatives" belonging to the Crown. In 1811, when the Prince of Wales really became Regent, it was under the restrictions of 1789—which, however, were to cease at the end of twelve months.—M.

† The resolution (giving unrestricted power to the Regent) was moved by Mr. Thomas Conolly, supported by C. F. Sheridan, Lord Henry Fitzgerald, Sir Henry Cavendish, Curran, Bushe, and Grattan, opposed by Hobart, Corry, and Attorney-General Fitzgibbon (afterwards Lord Clare), and carried without a division.—M.

same principle that the two houses in England had, of their own authority, proceeded to supply the vacancy by the form of an address to the Prince of Orange, so it appeared should those of Ireland (an equally independent legislature) provide for the deficiency of their third estate in the present instance. This line of conduct was strenuously opposed by the Attorney-General (Mr. Fitzgibbon); but the strongest of his arguments were rather startling than convincing, and made but little impression upon the majority, who justly felt that a great constitutional proceeding upon an unforeseen emergency should not be impeded by any narrow technical objections, even though they had been more unanswerable than those adduced upon this occasion.*

Next to supporting the dignity of the Irish Parliament, the Whig leaders of 1789 were actuated by the prospects of advantage to Ireland which they anticipated from the change of administration and of system that were expected to follow their exertions. They were anxious to invest the Heir Apparent with the most unrestrained regal authority, in the fullest con-

* The following was one of Mr. Fitzgibbon's arguments: "Let me now for a moment suppose, that we, in the dignity of our independence, appoint a Regent for Ireland, being a different person from the Regent of England, a case not utterly impossible, if the gentlemen insist upon our appointing the Prince of Wales before it shall be known whether he will accept the regency of England; and suppose we should go farther, and desire him to give the royal assent to bills, he would say, 'My good people of Ireland, you have, by your own law, made the great seal of England absolutely and essentially necessary to be affixed to each bill before it passes in Ireland; that seal is in the hands of the Chancellor of England, who is a very sturdy fellow; that Chancellor is an officer under the Regent of England; I have no manner of authority over him; and so, my very good people of Ireland, you had better apply to the Regent of England, and request that he will order the Chancellor of England to affix the great seal of England to your bills; otherwise, my very good people of Ireland, I cannot pass them.'"

"This," said Mr. Curran, in his observations upon this argument, "is taking seals for crowns, and baubles for sceptres; it is worshipping wafers and wax in the place of a King; it is substituting the mechanical quibble of a practising lawyer for the sound deduction of a philosopher standing on the vantage ground of science; it is more like the language of an Attorney particular than an Attorney-General; it is that kind of silly fatuity that on any other subject I should leave to be answered by silence and contempt; but when blasphemy is uttered against the constitution, it shall not pass under its insignificance, because the essence should be reprehended, though the doctrine cannot make a proselyte."—M.

fidence that the benefits on which they calculated would be commensurate with the power to confer them. How far these sanguine hopes would have been realized, how far the measures of a ministry listening to the counsel of Mr. Fox could have healed the existing discontents, or have prevented the calamities that succeeded, must now be matter of controversial speculation, his Majesty's health having been fortunately restored before the arrangements regarding the Regency were yet concluded.

Although the conduct of the Irish House of Commons at this important crisis has been generally adduced as a proof of the dangerous spirit of independence that pervaded that assembly, and therefore insisted on as an argument for a legislative union; yet, were it now worth while to examine the subject, it would not be difficult to show that the crowd who on that occasion so zealously volunteered their support of the opposition were influenced by far other motives than a lofty sense of their own country's dignity; and that, however the English government might, at some rare conjuncture, be embarrassed by their versatility, it had nothing to apprehend from their patriotic virtue. No sooner was it ascertained that the cause which they had lately espoused was to be unattended with emolument, than they returned in repentance to their tenets; and incontestably did they prove in their subsequent life the extent and the sincerity of their contrition.

There were a few, however, who would upon no terms continue their support of the Irish Administration: they lost their places, which they might have retained, and, joining the opposition, adhered to it with undeviating and "desperate fidelity," as long as the Irish Parliament continued to exist.*

* Among these were Mr. George Ponsonby, and his brother, Lord Ponsonby; and in the upper house, the Duke of Leinster. In a letter to Mr. Grattan, Mr. Curran thus alludes to the formation of the last Opposition in the Irish Parliament: "You well remember the state of Ireland in 1789, and the necessity under which we found ourselves of forming some bond of honourable connexion, by which the co-operation of even a small number might be secured, in making some effort to stem that torrent which was carrying every thing before it. For that purpose our little party was then formed; it

[On April 21, 1789, Curran supported the bill for preventing excise officers from voting at parliamentary elections—a measure then defeated by a majority of 148 to 93, but since adopted all through the United Kingdom. Four days later he supported Sir H. Cavendish's resolutions condemnatory of the waste and useless patronage with which the Dublin police system was attended.]

It has been seen in the preceding pages, that the zeal with which Mr. Curran performed his public duties had already twice endangered his life: in the beginning of the year 1790, it was again exposed to a similar risk. If his duel with the Irish Secretary, Major Hobart (now alluded to), had been the consequence of accidental intemperance of language or conduct on either side, the account of it should be hastily dismissed; but such was not its character. The circumstances that preceded it are peculiarly illustrative of the condition of the times, of the state of the Irish House of Commons, of the manner in which that state rendered it incumbent upon an honest senator to address it, and of the dangers that attended him who had the boldness to perform his duty.

In the month of February, 1790, Mr. Curran made the following speech in that House:* independent of the other reasons for which it is here introduced, it may be offered as among the most favourable examples of his parliamentary oratory.

consisted of yourself, the late Duke of Leinster, that excellent Irishman, the late Lord Ponsonby, Mr. George Ponsonby, Mr. Daly, Mr. Forbes, and some very few others. It may not be for us to pronounce encomiums upon it, but we are entitled to say, that had it been as successful as it was honest, we might now look back to it with some degree of satisfaction."—C. [The Ministerial deserters in Ireland were cashiered in all direction. It was said that the Minister thus made more patriots in one day than patriotism had ever made in a year. Sheridan's younger brother, Charles, the Irish Secretary-at-War, was among the ejected—but he fared well, for Pitt gave him a pension of £1,200 a year, with a reversion of £800 to his wife.]—M.

* This speech was delivered on February 4, 1790, on the question of stamp officers' salaries. At that time the Earl of Westmoreland was Viceroy (he succeeded the Marquis of Buckingham on January 5, 1790), and Major Hobart was his Chief Secretary—a position not to be confounded with that of Secretary of State for Ireland, abolished at the Union.—M.

"I rise with that deep concern and melancholy hesitation, which a man must feel who does not know whether he is addressing an independent Parliament, the representatives of the people of Ireland, or whether he is addressing the representatives of corruption: I rise to make the experiment; and I approach the question with all those awful feelings of a man who finds a dear friend prostrate and wounded on the ground, and who dreads lest the means he should use to recover him may only serve to show that he is dead and gone for ever. I rise to make an experiment upon the representatives of the people, whether they have abdicated their trust, and have become the paltry representatives of Castle influence: it is to make an experiment on the feelings and probity of gentlemen, as was done on a great personage, when it was said, 'thou art the man.' It is not a question respecting a paltry Viceroy; no, it is a question between the body of the country and the administration; it is a charge against the government for opening the batteries of corruption against the liberties of the people. The grand inquest of the nation are called on to decide this charge; they are called on to declare whether they would appear as the prosecutors of the accomplices of corruption: for though the question relative to the division of the Boards of Stamps and Accounts is in itself of little importance, yet will it develop a system of corruption tending to the utter destruction of Irish liberty, and to the separation of the connexion with England.

"Sir, I bring forward an act of the meanest administration that ever disgraced this country. I bring forward as one of the threads by which, united with others of similar texture, the vermin of the meanest kind have been able to tie down a body of strength and importance. Let me not be supposed to rest here; when the murderer left the mark of his bloody hand upon the wall, it was not the trace of one finger, but the whole impression which convicted him.*

* The allusion here is probably to a little story popular among children in Ireland.

"The Board of Accounts was instituted in Lord Townshend's administration,* it came forward in a manner rather inauspicious; it was questioned in Parliament, and decided by the majority f the five members who had received places under it. Born in corruption, it could only succeed by venality. It continued an useless board until the granting of the stamp duties in Lord Harcourt's time:† the management of the stamps was then committed to it, and a solemn compact was made that the taxes should not be jobbed, but that both departments should be executed by one board. So it continued till it was thought necessary to increase the salaries of the commissioners in the Marquis of Buckingham's famous administration; but then nothing was held sacred: the increase of the Revenue Board, the increase of the Ordnance, thirteen thousand pounds a year added to the infamous Pension List, these were not sufficient, but a compact, which should have been held sacred, was violated, in order to make places for members of parliament. How indecent! two county members prying into stamps! What could have provoked this insult? I will tell you: you remember when the sceptre was trembling in the hand of an almost expiring monarch; when a factious and desperate English minister attempted to grasp it, you stood up against the profanation of the English, and the insult offered to the Irish crown; and had you not done it, the union of the empire would have been dissolved. You remember this; remember then yourselves—remember your triumph: it was that triumph which exposed you to submit to the resentment of the Viceroy: it was that triumph which exposed you to disgrace and flagellation. In proportion as you rose by the union, your tyrant became appalled; but when

which states that the murderer, intending to cover the whole mark with dust, left that of one finger unconcealed; but that he continued firmly to protest his innocence, until the removal of the dust convicted him, by displaying an impression corresponding exactly with the size of his hand. A similar circumstance is introduced in an old Spanish play.—C.

* From 1767 to 1772.—M.

† Lord Harcourt succeeded Lord Townshend as Viceroy.—M.

he divided, he sunk you, and you became debased. How this has happened, no man could imagine; no man could have suspected that a minister without talents could have worked your ruin. There is a pride in a great nation that fears not its destruction from a reptile; yet is there more than fable in what we are told of the Romans, that they guarded the Palladium, rather against the subtlety of a thief, than the force of an invader.

"I bring forward this motion, not as a question of finance, not as a question of regulation, but as a penal inquiry; and the people will now see whether they are to hope for help within these walls, or turning their eyes towards heaven, they are to depend on God and their own virtue. I rise in an assembly of three hundred persons, one hundred of whom have places or pensions; I rise in an assembly, one third of whom have their ears sealed against the complaints of the people, and their eyes intently turned to their own interest: I rise before the whisperers of the Treasury, the bargainers and runners of the Castle; I address an audience before whom was held forth the doctrine, that the Crown ought to use its influence on this house. It has been known that a master has been condemned by the confession of his slave, drawn from him by torment; but here the case is plain: this confession was not made from constraint; it came from a country gentleman deservedly high in the confidence of Administration, for he gave up other confidence to obtain theirs.

"I know I am speaking too plain; but which is the more honest physician, he who lulls his patient into a fatal security, or he who points out the danger and the remedy of the disease?

"I should not be surprised if bad men of great talents should endeavour to enslave a people; but, when I see folly uniting with vice, corruption with imbecility, men without talents attempting to overthrow our liberty, my indignation rises at the presumption and audacity of the attempt. That such men should creep into power, is a fatal symptom to the constitution; the political, like the material body, when near its dissolution, often bursts out in swarms of vermin.

"In this administration, a place may be found for every bad man, whether it be to distribute the wealth of the Treasury, to vote in the House, to whisper and to bargain, to stand at the door and note the exits and entrances of your members, to mark whether they earn their wages—whether it be for the hireling who comes for his hire, or for the drunken aid-de-camp who swaggers in a brothel; nay, some of them find their way to the treasury-bench, the political-musicians, or hurdygurdy-men, to pipe the praises of the viceroy.

"Yet notwithstanding the profusion of Government, I ask, what defence have they made for the country, in case it should be invaded by a foreign foe? They have not a single ship on the coast. Is it then the smug aid-de-camp, or the banditti of the Pension List, or the infantine statesmen, who play in the sunshine of the Castle, that are to defend the country? No, it is the stigmatised citizens. We are now sitting in a country of four millions of people, and our boast is, that they are governed by laws to which themselves consent; but are not more than three millions of the people excluded from any participation in making those laws? In a neighboring country,* twenty-four millions of people were governed by laws to which their consent was never asked; but we have seen them struggle for freedom—in this struggle they have burst their chains, and on the altar, erected by despotism to public slavery, they have enthroned the image of public liberty.

"But are our people merely excluded? No, they are denied redress. Next to the adoration which is due to God, I bend in reverence to the institutions of that religion, which teaches me to know his divine goodness! but what advantage does the peasant of the South receive from the institutions of religion?

* France.—M.

Does he experience the blessing? No, he never hears the voice of the shepherd, nor feels the pastoral crook, but when it is entering his flesh, and goading his very soul.

"In this country, sir, our King is not a resident; the beam of royalty is often reflected through a medium, which sheds but a kind of disastrous twilight, serving only to assist robbers and plunderers. We have no security in the talents, or responsibility of an Irish ministry; injuries which the English constitution would easily repel may here be fatal. I therefore call upon you to exert yourselves, to heave off the vile incumbrances that have been laid upon you. I call you not as to a measure of finance or regulation, but to a criminal accusation, which you may follow with punishment. I, therefore, sir, most humbly move:

"That an humble address be presented to his Majesty, praying that he will order to be laid before this house the particulars of the causes, consideration, and representations, in consequence of which the Boards of Stamps and Accounts have been divided with an increase of salary to the officers; also that he will be graciously pleased to communicate to this house the names of the persons who recommended that measure."

To this speech, containing charges so grave and direct, and so demanding an equally solemn refutation if they were refutable, it is curious to observe the style of answer that was made. When appeals of this nature are received with contumely and mockery, it is, perhaps, among the most certain signs, that the legislature which can tolerate such a practice has completely survived its virtue.

Sir B. Roche.—"Though I am in point of consequence the smallest man amongst the respectable majority of this house, yet I cannot help feeling the heavy shower of the honourable gentleman's illiberal and unfounded abuse.

"If I had the advantage of being bred to the learned profession of the law, I should be the better enabled to follow the honourable gentleman through the long windings of his declamation; by such means I should be blessed with '*the gift of the gab*,' and could declaim for an hour or two upon the turning of a straw, and yet say nothing to the purpose; then I could stamp and stare, and rend, and tear, and look up to the gods and goddesses for approbation. Then in the violence of such declamation, I should suppose myself standing at the head of my shop (at the bar of the King's bench), dealing out my scurrility by the yard to the highest bidder; my shop being well stored with all sorts of masquerade dresses to suit all descriptions of persons. The Newgate criminal (if I was well paid for it) I would dress up in the flowing robes of innocence. The innocent man (being also well paid for it) I could cover up in a cloak of infamy, that should stick as close to him as his regimentals.

"I am sorry to find that the military character does not seem to meet with the honourable gentleman's approbation. I profess myself to have had the honour to be bred a soldier, and if there is any thing amiable or praiseworthy in my character, I am entirely indebted to that school for it. If indeed I was bred a pettifogger, or a Newgate solicitor, I should be better enabled to follow the learned gentleman through the variety of matter which he has introduced to the house. My right honourable friend,* upon the floor, is animadverted on and abused, because he is a soldier; but let me tell the honourable gentleman below me, that the high ground of his honour and character places him above the reach of his envenomed shafts, bearded with envy, hatred and malice.

* * * * * * * * * * * * *

The Viceroy of this country is surrounded by military gentlemen of the first families in both kingdoms; they are supposed to be out of the line of all politics, yet the indecent and disrespectful manner in which they are, on this occasion, held out in this house,

* Major Hobart.—C.

does, in my apprehension, deserve the severest censure. I would, however, recommend it to the honourable gentleman to stop a little in his career of general abuse of men, who cannot be here to answer for themselves; lest those gentlemen, (who never offended him) *might speak to him on the subject in another place.* Oh, shame! shame! shame and reprobation on such behaviour!"

After a long debate, Mr. Curran replied, and concluded with the following observations upon Sir Boyle Roche's language:

"We have been told this night in express words, that the man who dares to do his duty to his country in this house may expect to be attacked without those walls by the military gentlemen of the Castle. If the army had been directly or indirectly mentioned in the course of the debate, this extraordinary declaration might be attributable to the confusion of a mistaken charge, or an absurd vindication; but without connexion with the subject, or pretence of connexion with the subject, a new principle of government is advanced, and that is the bayonet; and this is stated in the fullest house, and the most crowded audience I ever saw. We are to be silenced by corruption within, or quelled by force of arms without. Nor is it necessary that those avowed principles of bribery and arms should come from any high personal authority; they have been delivered by the known retailers of administration, in the face of that bench, and heard even without a murmur of dissent, or disapprobation. As to my part, I do not know how it may be my destiny to fall; it may be by chance, or malady, or violence, but should it be my fate to perish the victim of a bold and honest discharge of my duty, I will not shun it. I will do that duty, and if it should expose me to sink under the blow of the assassin, and become a victim to the public cause, the most sensible of my regrets would be, that on such an altar there should not be immolated a more illustrious sacrifice. As to myself, while I live, I shall despise the peril. I feel, in my own spirit, the safety of my honour, and in my own and the spirit of the people, do I feel strength enough to hold that Administration, which can give a sanction to menaces like these, *responsible for their consequences to the nation and the individual.*

Mr. Curran had soon occasion to act upon this last declaration. In a few days subsequent to the preceding debate, he was openly insulted by a person belonging to one of those classes, upon which he had accused the Administration of squandering the public money. He accordingly deputed one of his friends, Mr. Egan,* to acquaint the Secretary with the outrage that had been committed on him, in consequence of what he had asserted in the House of Commons, and to express his expectation, "that Major Hobart would mark his sense of such an indignity offered to a Member of Parliament by one of his official servants, in the dismissal of the man from his service." To this application Major Hobart replied, that "he had no power to dismiss any man from the service of government," and after referring Mr. Curran to the House of Commons, as the tribunal, before which he should complain of any breach of his privileges, expressed his surprise "that any application should have been made to him upon the occasion of an outrage committed by a person who was as much a stranger to him as he could be to Mr. Curran." Upon this, the following respondence ensued:

"TO THE RIGHT HON. MAJOR HOBART.

"March 28, 1790.

"SIR:—

"A man of the name of ——, a conductor of your press, a writer for your government, your notorious agent in the city,

* Notwithstanding their friendship, Curran and Egan fought a duel. Curran was small in stature and very slight. Egan was a giant. When the seconds were measuring the ground Egan said, "Curran, my boy, this is not fair, I might as well fire at a lamp post as you, so small are you. Look at me (striking his enormous bulk), you cannot help hitting me." Curran answered, "Very true, my good fellow. Suppose that we chalk my size upon your person, and every bullet outside the outline shall count for nothing!" They both smiled at the ludicrous idea, harmlessly exchanged shots, went and breakfasted together, and never again met in a hostile manner.—M.

your note-taker in the House of Commons, in consequence of some observation that fell from me in that House on your prodigality, in rewarding such a man with the public money for such services, had the audacity to come within a few paces of me, in the most frequented part of this metropolis, and shake his stick at me in a manner which, notwithstanding his silence, was too plain to be misunderstood. I applied to you to dismiss him, because he is your retainer, for whom you ought to be responsible. You have had recourse to the stale artifice of office, and have set up incapacity and irresponsibility against doing an act which, as a minister, you were able, and which, as a man of honour, you should have been ready to do. As to your being a stranger to the man, you knew when you wrote it that it was a pitiful evasion; I did not apply to the Secretary to discard a companion, but to dismiss the runner of his administration. As to your attempt to shelter yourself under the Lord Lieutenant, who, during the continuance of his government, cannot be responsible for such outrages, you should have felt that to be equally unworthy of you. If such subterfuges were tolerated, every member of Parliament, every gentleman of the country, who might become obnoxious to the Castle, would be exposed to personal violence from the ruffians of your administration. I should give up the cause of both, if I did not endeavour to check this practice, not in the person of the instrument, but of his abettor. I knew perfectly well, the resentments I had excited by my public conduct, and the sentiments and declarations I have expressed concerning your administration. I knew I might possibly become the victim of such declarations, particularly when I saw that an attempt at personal intimidation was part of the plan of government; but I was too deeply impressed with their truth to be restrained by any consideration of that sort from making them in public, or asserting them with my latest breath.

"Sir, I am aware that you could not be convicted of having actually commissioned this last outrage upon me; but that you have protected and approved it. I own I am very sorry that you have suffered so unjustifiable a sanction of one of your creatures to commit you and me personally. However, as you are pleased to disclaim the offender, and the power of punishing him, I feel I must acquiesce, whatever may be my opinion on the subject, and though you have forced upon me a conviction that you have sacrificed the principles of a man of honour to an official expediency. This sentiment I should have conveyed through my friend, but that it might possibly become necessary that our communication on this business should be public.

"I have the honour to be, sir,

"Your obedient servant,

"JOHN P. CURRAN."

"TO JOHN PHILPOT CURRAN, ESQ.

"DUBLIN CASTLE, March 29, 1790.

"SIR:—

"Your original application to me, through Mr. Egan, was, that Mr. —— should be dismissed from the service of Government, for the insult which he had offered to you; or that Government should co-operate with you in preferring a complaint to the House of Commons against him for a breach of their privileges. This application was, on the face of it, official; and, in answer to it, I pointed out to you, by direction of his Excellency, the Lord Lieutenant, the only mode by which you could have the redress you had sought for the outrage of which you had complained. You have now thought fit to desert the mode of official proceeding, and to couple a personal attack against me with an appeal to the public.

"Whatever are your hopes and motives in such conduct, be assured that the attempt of making your cause the cause of the public will never succeed. The public will never believe that I could have directly or indirectly instigated any man to insult you. They will see that the regular mode of redress was open to you, even the redress you at first affected to seek. You will never fasten a belief on the public that any man was mad enough to insult a member of Parliament, merely for his having accused the Government of prodigality in rewarding him: nor will all your ingenuity serve to entangle me in that transaction, merely because you are pleased to style Mr. —— my retainer; or to create a persuasion that I am personally responsible for the resentment of a servant of the Government, who was placed in the situation which he now fills many years before I came into office. The public will view this matter in its true light; and they will clearly perceive, what no man can ever justify, that you have transferred to me the quarrel which another has provoked, for no one reason, but because you think it politic so to do.

"Your parade of the resentments which you boast to have excited by your public conduct, and your insinuation that an attempt at personal intimidation was part of the plan of Government, I cannot condescend to notice. The public will never be the dupes of such a paltry affectation, to give a popular complexion to your quarrel.

"As to your charge of my having sacrificed the principles of a man of honour to political expediency, the motive of the accusation is too evident to demand a reply. I trust to my own character for its refutation.

"I pity the condition of any man who feels himself reduced to the desperate expedient of endeavouring to wipe off the affronts and insults he has submitted to from others, by forcing a quarrel upon a man who never injured him in the remotest degree; and I am at a loss to conceive how such a conduct can be reconciled to the principles or feelings of a gentleman or a man of honour.

"Perhaps a man in a public situation, and who has given no offence, might be well justified in appealing to the laws, if he should be personally called upon. I do not mean, sir, to avail myself of your example. You say, sir, that it may be necessary that the communication on this subject should be public: had you not said so, my answer to you would have been short, indeed. I have the honour to be

"Your obedient, humble servant,

"R. HOBART.

"P. S.—Having put you in possession of my sentiments, I shall consider it unnecessary to answer any more letters."

"TO THE RIGHT HON. MAJOR HOBART.*

March 30, 1790.

"SIR,

"As I wish to stand justified to the public and to you for having had recourse to you on the present extraordinary occasion, I beg leave once more to trouble you with a few lines, to which no answer can be necessary. They will be addressed to you in that temper which the general purport of the last letter I had the honour to receive entitles you to expect.

"An unparalleled outrage was offered to me—the person was beneath my resentment. In this very difficult situation to whom could I resort but his masters? and if to them, to whom but the first?

"I never charged you, sir, with instigating that man to such an act; but am sorry that I cannot add, that such a part has been taken to punish him as was necessary to acquit *all* your administration. I know perfectly well you found him in office, and also in certain lower confidential departments, which are more easily understood than expressed; and my complaint was, that, after such gross misconduct, he continued there.

"I beg leave to remind you, that I did not say that any man was mad enough to insult a Member of Parliament, merely for accusing Government of prodigality in rewarding him; but I

* Major Hobart was son of and successor to the third Earl of Buckinghamshire, and died in 1816.—M.

did say, and must repeat, that the insult upon me was made in consequence of my having arraigned the prodigality of rewarding *such* a man for *such* services. Permit me to add, that you cannot but have reason to believe this to be the fact. Some of your Court have talked freely upon the subject; and the man, by his own application of the word, has acknowledged his vocation and his connexion.

"I must still continue to think, that what you are pleased to call a quarrel is nothing but the result of my public conduct. Sure I am that I should have escaped the attacks that have been made upon my person and character, and this last among others, if that conduct had been less zealous and decided.

"As to your charge of my forcing a quarrel upon a man—"who never in the remotest degree injured you"—there is something in the expression which, I acknowledge, excites in my mind a very lively concern. And it is an aggravation of the outrage upon me, that it left me no resort, save one painful to my feelings, but necessary to my situation.

"As to the insinuation which accompanies your expression of regret, I am sorry it should have escaped from Major Hobart. He cannot seriously mean that I should squander my person upon every ruffian who may make an attempt upon my life. In the discharge of political and professional duties, every man must expect to excite enemies. I cannot hope to be more fortunate; but I shall commit myself only with such as cannot disgrace me. A farther answer may be necessary to this part of your letter; but that, as it cannot be so properly conveyed in writing, my friend, Mr. Egan, will have the honour to explain.

"I have the honour to be, sir,

"Your obedient servant,

"J. P. CURRAN."

A duel immediately followed, in which neither party received any injury.

In reviewing this transaction, it would not be difficult for any one, who should feel so disposed, to produce many arguments in support of the conclusion, that Mr. Curran's demand of personal satisfaction from the Irish minister was a departure from the usages of public life. Such a person would, however, leave out of his consideration the circumstances that provoked and that could justify such a proceeding—the inflamed state of the times—the previous debate in parliament—the minister's tacit sanction of the menaces of his adherents—and Mr. Curran's remonstrance upon the occasion not having produced an observation that could deter the future insulter. The latter was the view which convinced himself and his friends that it was only by some such decisive measure as that which he adopted that the privileges and persons of his party could be secured from farther violence. The particulars of the affair, however, are given here, not as a subject of controversy, but as a striking public fact, and an event in Mr. Curran's political life.

Mr. Curran's dispute and frequent collisions in Parliament with Mr. Fitzgibbon have been already adverted to; and, in what has been hitherto related, the conduct of neither party has appeared marked by any peculiar aggravations; but the latter having now become Chancellor of Ireland,* Lord Clare remembered the resentments of Mr. Fitzgibbon, and avenged the wounds he had received in the senate by excluding Mr. Curran from all practice in his court.† Such a mode of reprisals has been generally

* He was appointed in June, 1789, and was then called to the House of Lords as Baron Fitzgibbon, of Lower Connello, county of Limerick. In 1793, he was created Viscount Fitzgibbon, and in 1795, Earl of Clare, all in the Peerage of Ireland. In 1799, he was made a Baron in the Peerage of Great Britain, and died in 1802.—M.

† This was effected by letting the public see that Mr. Curran had not (in the technical phrase) *the ear of the court*—and in this Lord Clare so entirely succeeded, that in a very little time no client would venture to entrust a Chancery cause of any importance to the discountenanced advocate. Mr. Curran's loss of professional income was extreme.

reprehended as merely unmanly and ungenerous, but it was a great deal more. The misconduct of persons in elevated stations is seldom canvassed with the rigour necessary to their perfect reprobation. So much does Power impose upon the understandings of men, that, almost trembling to scrutinize the offences that should be most exposed, they are rather satisfied to consider the enjoyment of high trust as a kind of apology for its violation. A judge setting his face against a particular advocate does not commit a simple act of unkindness or indecorum; he offers as criminal an outrage as can be imagined to the most sacred privileges of the community. The claim of the subject to be heard with impartiality is not derived from the favour of the judge; it is a right, as independent of persons, and as sanctioned by law, as that which entitles the judge to sit upon the bench: it is the bounden duty of the latter to afford an honest, unbiassed attention to every suitor in his court, or (what is equivalent) to such counsel as the suitor appoints to represent himself: when the judge, therefore, from motives of private or political dislike, refuses, on hearing of a cause, the fullest indulgence that legal proceedings admit, he not only unworthily marks out an obnoxious individual as the victim of his own angry passions, diminishing his credit, and thereby, perhaps, depriving him of his bread; but as far as in him lies, he directly tends to defraud the unoffending subject of his property, or his reputation, or his life; he does the same indirectly, by compelling the advocate, if he has a spark of the spirit befitting his station, to exhaust in resistance to such unseemly partiality a portion of that time and vigour which should be exclusively appropriated to the service of his client. These scenes of indecent strife too inevitably strip the seats of law of their character and influence; for who can look up with confidence or respect to a tribunal, where he sees faction

There was an immediate diminution of £1,000 a year, which the Court of Chancery alone had produced; and this an increasing income. The aggregate of his loss he always estimated at £30 000.—C.

domineering over equity, and the minister of justice degraded into a partizan?

This flagrant abuse of the judicial functions by Lord Clare has never incurred, in Ireland, all the odium that it merited—with his admirers it was a speck upon the sun, and his enemies had deeper crimes to execrate. The widely different deportment of his successors has also removed all present apprehensions of a repetition of such scenes; still the vicious model may find its imitators—the tramplers upon human rights are not peculiar to any generation; and wherever they do appear, their exposure should be insisted on as a future protection to the public; the characters of such men should be rendered an antidote to their example.

For this deadly injury inflicted on him by the highest law-officer in the kingdom, Mr. Curran was not tardy in taking signal vengeance. He saw that his enemy had advanced too far to recede—he disdained to conciliate him by submission or by mild expostulation. To have acted with forbearance, or even with temper, (however amiable and prudent, had it been a private case) would have been in the present one, as he considered it, a desertion of what was to him above every personal consideration, of a great constitutional principle, involving the rights and securities of the client, and the honour and independence of the Irish bar. He was not insensible (it could hardly be expected that he should) to such an invasion of his feelings and his income; but in resisting it as he did, with scorn and exposure, he felt that he was assuming the proud attitude of a public man, contending against a noxious system of "frantic encroachments," of which he was the accidental victim; and that the result, however unproductive to his private interests, would, at least, show that the advocate was not to be scared from the performance of his duty by the terrors of contumely or pecuniary loss; and that though the judge might be for the moment victorious in the contest, his victory should cost him dear.

The opportunities of hurling direct defiance at Lord Clare

might have now been rare. They could no longer meet in the House of Commons; and the Chancellor provided against a frequent intercourse in his court;* but an extraordinary occasion soon presented itself, and enabled the injured advocate to execute his objects of retaliation, in the dignified character of a public avenger, before an audience where every blow was more public and more humiliating.

The Lord Mayor of the city of Dublin is chosen by the Board of Aldermen, whose choice is confirmed, or disapproved, by the Common Council. In the year 1790 [April 16th,] the board elected a person (Alderman James) whom the Commons, without assigning the reasons of their disapprobation, successively rejected.† Their real motive was a determination to continue rejecting the names returned to them, until the election of the Aldermen should fall upon a person attached to the popular cause. The Board perceiving this, and denying that the Common Council had such a right of capricious rejection, returned no more, and broke up without having duly elected a Lord Mayor. Upon this the Sheriffs and Commons (according to the law that provided for such an event) proceeded to elect one, and fixed upon a popular candidate, Alderman Howison.‡

* The occasional style of their warfare in the Court of Chancery, for the little time that Mr. Curran continued to be employed there, may be collected from the following instance. Lord Clare had a favourite dog that sometimes followed him to the bench. One day, during an argument of Mr. Curran's, the Chancellor, in the spirit of habitual petulance which distinguished him, instead of attending to the argument, turned his head aside and began to fondle the dog. The counsel stopped suddenly in the middle of a sentence—the judge started. "I beg pardon," said Mr. Curran, "I thought your Lordships had been in consultation; but as you have been pleased to resume your attention, allow me to impress upon your excellent understandings, that"—&c.—C.

† The fact is, the burgesses of Dublin in their guilds had pledged themselves not to return any one as Lord Mayor or Member of Parliament for the city, who held place or pension from the government. Alderman James was doubly obnoxious—first as a placeholder and next from the nature of his place,—Commissionership of Police.—M.

‡ Howison was elected by 81 votes to 8. Napper Tandy led the popular party—Gifford headed the Opposition in the Common Council. The Aldermen again elected Alderman James. This led to the appeal to the Privy Council, on petition from James, who contended that the Commons could not *legally* reject without *assigning* a cause.—M.

This contest between the Board of Aldermen and the Commons, after having undergone much violent discussion, and excited the utmost agitation in the metropolis, was now brought before the Lord Lieutenant and Privy Council (at which Lord Clare presided as Lord Chancellor) for their final decision. The Council Chamber was thrown open as a public court. The concourse of spectators, among whom were the most opulent and respectable citizens of Dublin, was immense. The question before the Court was to be the mere legal construction of an act of parliament,* but the Chancellor and the Ministry notoriously favored the pretensions of the Board of Aldermen, so that the question before the public was whether the rights of the city were to be treated with constitutional respect, or to be crushed by the despotic power of the Castle.†

Upon this solemn and vital question, Mr. Curran appeared as one of the leading counsel for the Commons and the object of their choice, Alderman Howison. He had not proceeded far in his argument before he showed that he did not mean to confine it to the literal and technical interpretation of a statute; but that, looking at the question as the public did, he should raise it from a cold legal discussion into a great constitutional struggle between the privileges of the subject and the influence of the Irish Ministry. But he could not have taken a more infallible method of soon reducing it from a question of law, or of principle, into a personal contest between himself and the aristocratic Chancellor. Accord-

* The 33d of George II., c. 16.—M.

† Grattan, Lord Charlemont, Lord Perry, Lord Carhampton, the Viceroy, and others attended. Fitzgibbon presided as Lord Chancellor. Evidence was heard for both sides. The Privy Council decided for a new election. The Aldermen re-elected James, and the Common Council again elected Howison. Two new petitions were sent in. On June 7th, 1790, counsel were heard by the Privy Council for James and Howison, respectively. The former decision was repeated,—the election went as before. On July 10th, when the case came before the Privy Council for the third time, Curran made the speech, given in the text, in which he attacked the Lord Chancellor. Eventually, the Privy Council gave a decision in favour of James, who resigned, and both parties then agreed on electing Howison, the popular man, whom the Privy Council were compelled to approve of, his character and claims being unexceptionable.—M.

ingly, their hostility immediately burst forth in the interruptions of the judge, and the contemptuous indifference with which they were treated by the advocate. At length, the latter (by way of allusion to the unconstitutional conduct of a former chancellor, Sir Constantine Phipps, upon a similar occasion) proceeded to draw the following picture of his irritated enemy, in his own presence, and in that of the assembled community.*

"On grounds like these, for I can conceive no other, do I suppose the rights of the city were defended in the time to which I have alluded; for it appears, by the records which I have read, that the city was then heard by her counsel; she was not denied the form of defence, though she was denied the benefit of the law. In this very chamber did the Chancellor and Judges sit, with all the gravity and affected attention to arguments in favour of that liberty and those rights which they had conspired to destroy. But to what end, my lords, offer argument to such men? A little and a peevish mind may be exasperated, but how shall it be corrected by refutation? How fruitless would it have been to represent to that wretched Chancellor that he was betraying those rights which he was sworn to maintain; that he was involving a government in disgrace, and a kingdom in panic and consternation; that he was violating every sacred duty, and every solemn

* The person who was the most zealous in exciting a spirit of opposition in the Common Council was Mr. Tandy, a member of the Whig Club. Mr. Grattan, one of the most distinguished members of the same association, speaks thus of the above transaction:—"An attack was made on the rights of the city. A doctrine was promulgated, that the Common Council had no right to put a negative on the Lord Mayor chosen by the Board of Aldermen, except the board itself should assent to the negative put on its own choice. This doctrine was advanced by the court, to secure the election of the mayor to itself. In the course of the contest, the Minister involved himself in a personal altercation with the citizens; with Mr. Tandy he had carried on a long war, and with various success. In the compass of his wrath, he paid his compliments to the Whig Club, and that club advanced the shield of a free people over the rights of the city, and humbled the minister, in the presence of those citizens, whose privileges he had invaded, and whose persons he had calumniated."—*Answer to Lord Clare's Pamphlet.*

Alderman Howison's counsel, Mr. Curran, and the late Mr. George Ponsonby (afterwards Chancellor) were members of the Whig Club, and refused to accept any remuneration for their exertions upon this occasion.—C.

engagement that bound him to himself, his country, his sovereign, and his God! Alas! my lords, by what arguments could any man hope to reclaim or to dissuade a mean, illiberal, and unprincipled minion of authority, induced by his profligacy to undertake, and bound by his avarice and vanity to persevere? He would probably have replied to the most unanswerable arguments by some curt, contumelious, and unmeaning apothegm, delivered with the fretful smile or irritated self-sufficiency and disconcerted arrogance: or even if he could be dragged by his fears to a consideration of the question, by what miracle could the pigmy capacity of a stunted pedant be enlarged to a reception of the subject? The endeavour to approach it would have only removed him to a greater distance than he was before, as a little hand that strives to grasp a mighty globe is thrown back by the reaction of its own efforts to comprehend. It may be given to an Hale or an Hardwicke to discover and retract a mistake: the errors of such men are only specks that arise for a moment upon the surface of a splendid luminary: consumed by its heat, or irradiated by its light, they soon purge and disappear; but the perversenesses of a mean and narrow intellect are like the excrescences that grow upon a body naturally cold and dark;—no fire to waste them, and no ray to enlighten, they assimilate and coalesce with those qualities so congenial to their nature, and acquire an incorrigible permanency in the union with kindred frost and kindred opacity. Nor, indeed, my lords, except where the interest of millions can be affected by the folly or the vice of an individual, need it be much regretted, that to things not worthy of being made better, it hath not pleased Providence to afford the privilege of improvement."

Lord Clare.*—"Surely, Mr. Curran, a gentleman of your eminence in your profession must see that the conduct of former Privy Councils has nothing to do with the question before us.

* He was only Baron Fitzgibbon at the time, not being created Earl of Clare until 1795.—M.

The question lies in the narrowest compass; it is merely whether the Commons have a right of arbitrary and capricious rejection, or are obliged to assign a reasonable cause for their disapprobation. To that point you have a right to be heard, but I hope you do not mean to lecture the Council."

Mr. Curran.—"I mean, my lords, to speak to the case of my clients, and to avail myself of every topic of defence which I conceive applicable to that case. I am not speaking to a dry point of law, to a single judge, and on a mere forensic subject; I am addressing a very large auditory, consisting of co-ordinate members, of whom the far greater number is not versed in law. Were I to address such an audience on the interests and rights of a great city, and address them in the hackneyed style of a pleader, I should make a very idle display of profession, with very little information to those I address, or benefit to those on whose behalf I have the honour to be heard. I am aware, my lords, that truth is to be sought only by slow and painful progress: I know also that error is in its nature *flippant and compendious; it hops with airy and fastidious levity over proofs and arguments, and perches upon assertion, which it calls conclusion.*"

Here Mr. Curran's triumph over his proud enemy was complete. The sarcastic felicity of this description of the unfavourable side of Lord Clare's mind and manner was felt by the whole audience. The Chancellor immediately moved to have the chamber cleared, and during the exclusion of strangers was understood to have ineffectually endeavoured to prevail upon the Council to restrain the advocate from proceeding any further in that mode of argument which had given him so much offence.

From this period till the year 1794, Mr. Curran's public history consists principally of his Parliamentary exertions. The Opposition "persisted to combat the project to govern Ireland by corruption:" for this purpose they brought forward a series of popular measures;* in the support of all of which Mr. Curran

* The most important of these were Mr. Forbes's motion for a place bill, Mr. Grattan's

took a leading part.* Lord Charlemont's biographer, who heard him upon all those occasions, says of him, "That he animated

for an inquiry into the sale of Peerages, the Catholic question, Parliamentary Reform. The inquiry regarding the sale of Peerages was twice moved; by Mr. Grattan, in 1790, and by Mr. Curran in the following year: both motions failed, although the fullest evidence of the fact was offered. "I have proof," said Mr. Curran, "and I stake my character on producing such evidence to a committee, as shall fully and incontrovertibly establish the fact, that a contract has been entered into with the present ministers to raise to the peerage certain persons, on condition of their purchasing a certain number of seats in this house." Upon this last occasion Mr. Curran was loudly called to order, for having reminded the house, "that they should be cautious in their decision on this question for they were *in the hearing of a great number of the people of Ireland*." Mr. Grattan defended the expression, and thought the doctrine of censure passed upon it inconsistent with the nature of a popular assembly such as a House of Commons: in support of this opinion he quoted an expression of Lord Chatham, who in the house of peers, where such language was certainly less proper than in a house of commons, addressed the peers, "My Lords, I speak not to your lordships; I speak to the public and to the constitution." "The words," added Grattan, "were at first received with some murmurs, but the good sense of the house and the *genius of the constitution* justified him." Mr. Curran, on resuming, repeated the expression, and was again interrupted by violent cries to order, which, however, he silenced by observing, "I do not allude to any strangers in your gallery, but I allude to the *constructive* presence of four millions of people, whom a serjeant at arms cannot keep unacquainted with your proceedings."—*Irish Parl. Deb.*, 1791.

During the debate upon the same subject in the preceding year, Mr. Grattan produced a paper, and read as follows: "We charge them (the Ministers) publicly, in the face of their country, with making corrupt agreements for the sale of peerages: for doing which, we say that they are impeachable. We charge them with corrupt agreements for the disposal of the money arising from the sale, to purchase for the servants of the Castle seats in the Assembly of the People; for which we say that they are impeachable. We charge them with committing these offences, not in one, nor in two, but in many instances; for which complication of offences we say that they are impeachable; guilty of a systematic endeavour to undermine the Constitution, in violation of the laws of the land. We pledge ourselves to convict them; we dare them to go into an inquiry; we do not affect to treat them as other than public malefactors; we speak to them in a style of the most mortifying and humiliating defiance; we pronounce them to be public criminals. Will they dare to deny the charge? I call upon and dare the ostensible member to rise in his place and say, on his honour, that he does not believe such corrupt agreements

* The debates in which, during this period (1791–4), Curran took a leading part were on February 12, 1791, when he made a long and powerful attack on the corruption of the Irish Government, and being reproved for alluding to strangers in the House, said, "I do not allude to strangers in the gallery, but to the constructive presence of the people of Ireland;" on February 18, 1792, when he argued in favour of the removal of Roman Catholic disabilities; on January 11, 1793, on the approaching war with France; on February 9, 1793, in favor of Parliamentary Reform.—M.

every debate with all his powers; that he was copious, splendid, full of wit, and life, and ardour." Of the justice of this praise sufficient proofs might be given, even from the loose reports of his speeches upon those questions; but it will be necessary in the following pages to offer so many examples of his forensic oratory, upon which his reputation so mainly depends, that his efforts in Parliament become, as far as his eloquence is concerned, of secondary moment, and claim a passing attention, rather with reference to his history and conduct, than as necessary to his literary fame.

have taken place. I wait for a specific answer." Major Hobart avoided a specific answer. Six days after, Mr. Grattan, alluding to these charges, observed, "Sir, I have been told it was said that I should have been stopped, should have been expelled the Commons, should have been delivered up to the bar of the Lords for the expressions delivered that day. I will repeat what I said that day." After reciting the charges *seriatim* in the same words, he thus concluded, "I repeat these charges now, and if any thing more severe was on a former occasion expressed, I beg to be reminded of it, and I will again repeat it. Why do you not expel me now? Why not send me to the bar of the Lords? Where is your adviser? Going out of the House, I shall repeat my sentiments, that his Majesty's Ministers are guilty of impeachable offences, and advancing to the bar of the Lords, I shall repeat these sentiments; and if the Tower is to be my habitation, I will there meditate the impeachment of these Ministers, and return not to capitulate, but to punish. Sir, I think I know myself well enough to say, that if called forth to suffer in a public cause, I will go further than my prosecutors both in virtue and in danger."—C.

CHAPTER VIII.

State of parties—Trial of Hamilton Rowan—Mr. Curran's fidelity to his party—Rev. William Jackson's Trial, Conviction, and Death—Remarks upon that Trial—Irish Informers—Irish Juries—The influence of the times upon Mr. Curran's style of Oratory.

THE period was now approaching which afforded to Mr. Curran's forensic talents their most melancholy, but most splendid occasions of exertion. With this year (1794) commences the series of those historical trials which originated in the distracted condition of his country, and to the political interest of which his eloquence has now imparted an additional attraction.

From the year 1789 the discontents of Ireland had been rapidly increasing; the efforts of the Opposition in Parliament having failed to procure a reform of the abuses and grievances of which the nation complained, an opinion soon prevailed throughout the community that the Irish Administration had entered into a formal design to degrade the country, and virtually to annul its lately acquired independence, by transferring the absolute dominion over it from the English Parliament, which had previously governed it, to the English Cabinet, which was to be its future ruler. Without inquiring now into the truth of this opinion, it will be sufficient to observe, that, in the agitation of the many irritating questions that it involved, it soon appeared that Ireland had little hope of seeing them terminated by the gentle methods of argument or persuasion. The adherents of the Administration, and their opponents, were agreed upon the fact of the universal discontent, and upon the dangers that it threatened; but they differed widely upon the measures that should be adopted for the restoration of repose.

The first were determined to use coercion. They seemed to think that popular excesses are almost solely the people's own creation—that they are naturally prone to disaffection—that complaints of grievances are resorted to as a mere pretext to gratify this propensity; and, consequently, that a provident government should vigourously resist every movement of discontent as the fearful tokens of projected revolution. In conformity with these opinions it appeared to them that terror alone could tranquilize Ireland; and, therefore, that every method of impressing upon the public mind the power of the State, no matter how unpopular their nature, or how adverse to the established securities of the subject, should be adopted and applauded as measures of salutary restraint.

The truth and expediency of these doctrines were as firmly denied by others, who maintained that conciliation alone could appease the popular ferment. They deplored the general tendency to disaffection as notorious and undeniable; but they considered that there would have been more wisdom in preventing than in punishing it; that a very little wisdom would have been sufficient to prevent it; and that in punishing it now, the Ministry were "combating, not causes, but effects." They denied that the great mass of the Irish, or of any community, were naturally prone to disaffection. "Their natural impulses (they observed, in replying to the advocates of coercion) are all the other way." Look into history; for one revolution, or attempt at revolution, of how many long and uninterrupted despotisms do we read; and, whenever such attempts occur, it is easy to assign the cause. There is one, and only one, way of measuring the excellence of any Government—by considering the condition of the governed. No well governed people will desire to exchange real and present blessings for the danger and uncertainty of remote and fantastic speculations: and if ever they are found to commit their lives and fortunes to such desperate experiments, it is the most conclusive evidence that they are badly governed, and that their sufferings have impelled them "to rise up in vengeance, to rend their chains upon the heads of their oppressors." Look to the neighbouring example of France, and see what abominations an infuriated populace may be brought to practise upon their rulers and upon themselves. Let Ireland be saved from the possibility of such a crisis. The majority of its people are in a state of odious exclusion, visiting them in its daily consequences with endless insults and privations, which, being minute and individual, are only the more intolerable. Would it not be wise then, to listen to their claim of equal privileges, which, if granted, would give you the strongest security for their loyalty? There are other grievances—the notorious corruption of the legislature—the enormity of the Pension List—and many more—of these the nation complains, and seems determined to be heard.* The times are peculiar; and, if the popular cry be not the voice of wisdom, it should at least be that of warning. The mind of all Europe is greatly agitated: a general distrust of Governments has gone abroad; let that of Ireland exhibit such an example of virtue and moderation, as may entitle it to the confidence of the people. The people seem inclined to turbulence; but treat it as a disease

* Every session the Opposition, again and again, pressed upon the Ministers the dangers to which their system was exposing the State. Thus Mr. Grattan observed, early in 1793, "They (the Ministers) attempted to put down the Constitution; but now they have put down the Government. We told them so—we admonished them—we told them their driving would not do. Do not they remember how in 1790 we warned them? They said we were severe—I am sure we were prophetic. In 1791 we repeated our admonition—told them that a Government of clerks would not do—that the Government of the Treasury would not do—that Ireland would not long be governed by the trade of Parliament; we told them that a nation, which had rescued her liberty from the giant of Old England, would not long bear to be trodden on by the violence of a few pigmies, whom the caprice of a Court had appointed Ministers." Mr. Curran's language was equally emphatic—"Ireland thinks, that, without an immediate reform, her liberty is gone—I think so too. While a single guard of British freedom, either internal or external, is wanting, Ireland is in bondage. She looks to us for her emancipation. She expects not impossibilities from us—but she expects honesty and plain dealing; and, if she finds them not, remember what I predict—she will abominate her Parliament, and look for a reform to herself."—*Parl. Deb.*, 1793. C.

rather than avenge it as a crime. Between a State and its subjects there should be no silly punctilio; their errors can never justify yours: you may coerce—you may pass intemperate laws, and unheard-of tribunals, to punish what you should have averted—you may go on to decimate, but you will never tranquilize."

These were in substance the views and arguments of the minority in the Irish House of Commons, and of the more reflecting and unprejudiced of the Irish community; but such mild doctrines had little influence with that assembly, or with the nation. By the Parliament the few that advanced them were regarded as the advocates of the existing disorders, because they ventured to explain their origin, and to recommend the only cure; while the people were industriously taught to withdraw their confidence from public men, who, instead of justifying the popular resentments by more unequivocal co-operation, were looking forward to the impending crisis as an object of apprehension, and not of hope.

Such was the condition of the public mind—the Government depending upon force—the People familiarising themselves to projects of resistance—and several speculative and ambitious men of the middle classes watching, with yet unsettled views, over the fermenting elements of revolution, until it should appear how far they could work themselves into union and consistency, when Mr. Archibald Hamilton Rowan* published an adress to the Volunteers of Ireland, setting forth the dangers with which the country was threatened from foreign and domestic foes, and inviting them to resume their arms for the preservation of the general tranquillity. This publication was prosecuted by the state as a sedi-

* Mr. Rowan was secretary to the Society of United Irishmen in Dublin. It is proper to observe here, that this was one of the original societies of that denomination, whose views did not extend beyond a constitutional reform. They have been sometimes confounded with the subsequent associations, which, under the same popular appellation, aimed at a revolution.—C.

tious libel, and Mr. Curran was selected by Mr. Rowan to conduct his defence.

The speech in defence of Hamilton Rowan has been generally considered as one of Mr. Curran's ablest efforts at the bar. It is one of the few that has been correctly reported; and to that circumstance is, in some degree, to be attributed its apparent superiority. Notwithstanding the enthusiastic applause which its delivery excited, he never gave it any peculiar preference himself.

The opening of it has some striking points of resemblance to the exordium of Cicero's defence of Milo. If an imitation was intended by the Irish advocate, it was very naturally suggested by the coincidence of the leading topics in the two cases—the public interest excited—the unusual military array in the court—the great popularity of the clients—and the factious clamours which preceded their trials.*

"When I consider the period at which this prosecution is brought forward—when I behold the extraordinary safeguard of armed soldiers resorted to, no doubt, for the preservation of peace and order—when I catch, as I cannot but do, the throb of public anxiety, that beats from one end to the other of this hall—when I reflect on what may be the fate of a man of the most beloved personal character, of one of the most respected families of our country, himself the only individual of that family, I may almost say of that country—who can look to that possible fate with unconcern? Feeling, as I do, all these impressions, it is in the honest simplicity of my heart I speak, when I say that I never rose in a court of justice with so much embarrassment as on this occasion.

* Nam illa præsidia, quæ pro templis omnibus cernitis, etsi contra vim collocata sunt, nobis afferunt tamen horroris aliquid: neque eorum quisquam, quos undique intuentes cernitis, unde aliqua pars fori adspici potest, et hujus exitum judicii expectantes, non cum virtuti Milonis favet, tum de se, de liberis suis, de patria, de fortunis hodierno die decertari putat.

Unum genus est adversum infestumque nobis eorum, quos P. Clodii furor rapinis et incendiis et omnibus exitiis publicis pavit; qui hesterna etiam concione incitati sunt, ut vobis voce præirent, quid judicaretis.—C.

"If, gentlemen, I could entertain a hope of finding refuge for the disconcertion of my own mind in the perfect composure of yours; if I could suppose that those awful vicissitudes of human events that have been stated or alluded to, could leave your judgments undisturbed or your hearts at ease, I know I should form a most erroneous opinion of your character. I entertain no such chimerical hope- I form no such unworthy opinion—I expect not that your hearts can be more at ease than my own—I have no right to expect it; but I have a right to call upon you in the name of your country, in the name of the living God, of whose eternal justice you are now administering that portion which dwells with us on this side of the grave, to discharge your breasts, as far as you are able, of every bias of prejudice or passion—that, if my client be guilty of the offence charged upon him, you may give tranquillity to the public by a firm verdict of conviction; or, if he be innocent, by as firm a verdict of acquittal; and that you will do this in defiance of the paltry artifices and senseless clamours that have been resorted to, in order to bring him to his trial with anticipated conviction. And, gentlemen, I feel an additional necessity of thus conjuring you to be upon your guard, from the able and imposing statement which you have just heard on the part of the prosecution. I know well the virtues and talents of the excellent person who conducts that prosecution.* I know how much he would disdain to impose on you by the trappings of office; but I also know how easily we mistake the lodgment which character and eloquence can make upon our feelings, for those impressions that reason, and fact, and proof only ought to work upon our understandings."

When Mr. Curran came to observe upon that part of the publication under trial, which proposed complete Emancipation to persons of every religious persuasion, he expressed himself as follows:

"Do you think it wise or humane, at this moment, to insult

* The Attorney-General, Mr. Wolfe, afterwards Lord Kilwarden.—C.

them (the Catholics) by sticking up in the pillory the man who dared to stand forth as their advocate? I put it to your oaths; do you think that a blessing of that kind, that a victory obtained by justice over bigotry and oppression, should have a stigma cast upon it by an ignominious sentence upon men bold and honest enough to propose that measure?—to propose the redeeming of religion from the abuses of the church, the reclaiming of three millions of men from bondage, and giving liberty to all who had a right to demand it?—Giving, I say, in the so much censured words of this paper—giving 'Universal Emancipation?'

"I speak in the spirit of the British law, which makes Liberty commensurate with, and inseparable from, British soil; which proclaims even to the stranger and the sojourner, the moment he sets his foot upon British earth, that the ground on which he treads is holy, and consecrated by the genius of Universal Emancipation. No matter in what language his doom may have been pronounced—no matter in what complexion incompatible with freedom, an Indian or an African sun may have burnt upon him—no matter in what disastrous battle his liberty may have been cloven down—no matter with what solemnities he may have been devoted upon the altar of slavery—the first moment he touches the sacred soil of Britain, the altar and the god sink together in the dust; his soul walks abroad in her own majesty; his body swells beyond the measure of his chains that burst from around him; and he stands redeemed, regenerated and disenthralled, by the irresistible genius of Universal Emancipation."

There is, farther on, a passage on the freedom of the press, too glowing and characteristic to be omitted:

"If the people say, let us not create tumult, but meet in delegation, they cannot do it; if they are anxious to promote parliamentary reform in that way, they cannot do it; the law of the last session has, for the first time, declared such meetings to be a crime. What then remains?—The liberty of the press *only*—that sacred palladium which no influence, no power, no minister, no government, which nothing but the depravity, or folly, or corruption of a jury can ever destroy. And what calamities are the people saved from, by having public communication left open to them? I will tell you what they are saved from, and what the government is saved from. I will tell you also to what both are exposed, by shutting up that communication. In one case sedition speaks aloud, and walks abroad; the demagogue goes forth—the public eye is upon him—he frets his busy hour upon the stage; but soon either weariness, or bribe, or punishment, or disappointment, bear him down, or drive him off, and he appears no more. In the other case, how does the work of sedition go forward? Night after night the muffled rebel steals forth in the dark, and casts another and another brand upon the pile, to which, when the hour of fatal maturity shall arrive, he will apply the flame. If you doubt of the horrid consequences of suppressing the effusion even of individual discontent, look to those enslaved countries, where the protection of despotism is supposed to be secured by such restraints. Even the person of the despot there is never in safety. Neither the fears of the despot, nor the machinations of the slave, have any slumber; the one anticipating the moment of peril, the other watching the opportunity of aggression. The fatal crisis is equally a surprise upon both; the decisive instant is precipitated without warning, by folly on the one side, or by phrensy on the other; and there is no notice of the treason till the traitor acts. But if you wish for a nearer and more interesting example, you have it in the history of your own Revolution; you have it at that memorable period when the monarch found a servile acquiescence in the ministers of his folly—when the liberty of the press was trodden under foot—when venal sheriffs returned packed juries, to carry into effect those fatal conspiracies of the few against the many—when the devoted benches of public justice were filled by some of those foundlings of fortune, who, overwhelmed in the torrent of corruption at an early period, lay at the bottom like drowned bodies, while soundness or sanity remained in them; but, at length, becoming buoyant by putrefaction, they rose as they rotted, and floated to the surface of the polluted stream, where they were drifted along, the objects of terror, and contagion, and abomination.*

"In that awful moment of the nation's travail—of the last gasp of tyranny and the first breath of freedom, how pregnant is the example? The Press extinguished, the People enslaved, and the Prince undone. As the advocate of society, therefore, of peace, of domestic liberty, and the lasting union of the two countries, I conjure you to guard the Liberty of the Press, that great sentinel of the State, that grand detector of public imposture—guard it—because when it sinks there sinks with it, in one common grave, the liberty of the subject, and the security of the Crown."

The concluding passage of this speech (of which the preceding extracts are inserted merely as examples of its style) contains one of those fine Scriptural allusions, of which Mr. Curran made such frequent and successful use:

"I will not relinquish the confidence that this day will be the period of his sufferings; and however mercilessly he has been hitherto pursued, that your verdict will send him home to the arms of his family and the wishes of his country. But if (which Heaven forbid) it hath still been unfortunately determined that, because he has not bent to power and authority, because he would not bow down before the golden calf and worship it, he is to be bound and cast into the furnace; I do trust in God, that there is a redeeming spirit in the Constitu-

* Although it has been doubted by some who have observed upon this passage, whether its vigour could atone for the images that it presents, it may not be ungratifying to hear the manner in which it was suggested to the speaker's mind. A day or two before Mr. Rowan's trial, one of Mr. Curran's friends showed him a letter that he had just received from Bengal, in which the writer, after mentioning the Hindoo custom of throwing the dead into the Ganges, added, that he was then upon the banks of that river, and that, as he wrote, he could see several bodies floating down its stream. The orator, shortly after, while describing a corrupted bench, recollected this fact, and applied it as above.—C.

tion, which will be seen to walk with the sufferer through the flames, and to preserve him unhurt by the conflagration."

If the expression of excited emotions by the auditors be the test of eloquence, this was the most eloquent of Mr. Curran's forensic productions. To applaud in a court of justice, is at all times irregular, and was then very rare; but both during the delivery and after the conclusion of this speech, the by-standers could not refrain from testifying their admiration by loud and repeated bursts of applause: when the advocate retired from the court, they took the horses from his carriage, which they drew to his own house; yet notwithstanding this public homage to his talents, the most grateful reward of his exertions was wanting—the jury, of whose purity very general suspicions were entertained, found a verdict against his client.*

[In the autumn of 1792, the Government issued a Proclamation against the Irish Volunteers, who replied to it, in an address, written by Dr. Drennan, and signed by Archibald Hamilton Rowan, as Secretary. Both were prosecuted. Rowan, as here related, was defended by Curran. It is stated by Thomas Davis that he had seen the back of Curran's brief, on which were written the catch-words of his speech in this case, viz., "To Arms—

* Mr. Rowan was sentenced to fine and imprisonment. In the month of June, 1794, Dr. William Drennan was prosecuted for the publication of the same libel. He was defended by Mr. Curran, and acquitted; not, however, on the merits of the imputed libel, but on failure of proof that Dr. Drennan had published it. On the first of the preceding May, Mr. Rowan effected his escape from prison, and fled to France. After a long exile, and many wanderings, he was permitted, a few years ago, to return to his country.—C.

[The reason why Hamilton Rowan escaped from prison was simply this. After he was incarcerated, in pursuance to his sentence, the Rev. William Jackson, an emissary from the Committee of *Salut Publique* of Paris, accompanied by one Cockayne (a London pettifogging attorney, acting as incendiary and spy for William Pitt, the English Prime Minister), visited him in prison, and engaged him rather deeply, and most unsuspectingly, in the schemes of obtaining French aid for Ireland, in which Jackson was interested. On Jackson's arrest, on a charge of high treason, Rowan dreaded the vengeance of the Government, and escaped to France. Thence he went to America, returned to Europe in 1800, received the King's pardon in 1802, and died in 1834, at the age of eighty-four.—M.]

2nd, Reform—3rd, Catholic Emancipation—4th, Convention—now unlawful—Consequence of Conviction—Trial before Revolution—Lambert—Muir—Character of R.—Furnace, &c.—Rebellion Smothered Stalks—Redeeming Spirit."

The trial commenced on January 29th, 1794, Wolfe (Attorney-General, and afterwards Chief Justice) stated the case. Witnesses were examined to show Rowan's connexion with the document charged as a seditious libel. Curran's speech (one of the best he ever made) then followed, and on its conclusion, a shout of admiration and sympathy arose in the crowded Court, which the Judge (Lord Clonmel) with difficulty stopped. When Curran quitted the Court-house that day, the populace, who waited for him, took the horses from his carriage, and drew him home. The Attorney-General replied to Curran, vindicating himself from the charge of having unnecessarily and oppressively endeavored to delay the trial. The Prime Sergeant (James Fitzgerald, father of O'Connell's vanquished opponent at Clare election in 1828) replied *seriatim* to Curran. Lord Clonmel charged, not only strongly but violently, against Rowan. The jury convicted, after only ten minutes' deliberation. Rowan waived his right of taking four days to decide whether he would move for an arrest of judgment, but Lord Clonmel declined passing sentence until the four days had expired, and committed Rowan to prison during the interval.

On February 4, 1794, however, Rowan's counsel applied to set aside the verdict, on several grounds, viz., that one of the jurors, before the trial, had made a hostile declaration against the prisoner; that one of the High Sheriffs, who struck the jury panel, was partial and hostile; that the principal witness had committed perjury; and that the Judge (Lord Clonmel) had misdirected the jury. The case was argued at great length, by Curran, and responded to by the Crown lawyers. On February 7, the Judges (Clonmel and Boyd) decided against the application for a new trial. Before sentence was passed, Rowan himself addressed the Court, stating that from his position and large stake in the country, he was the last man who could wish for an insurrection. The sentence was a fine of £2,000, two year's imprisonment, and to find security (himself in £2,000, and two others in £1,000 each) for his good behaviour for seven years. It had been suggested to, and discussed by the Government, whether, to make the punishment as exemplary as possible, Rowan should not also be put in the *pillory*. It was feared that this would array the gentry against the Crown (the pillory being a punishment for criminal and not *political* offences), and that the populace would not permit it. So the idea was abandoned—if ever seriously entertained.

In April, 1794, Mr. Curran appeared at Drogheda Assizes for Patrick Kenna and six others, in a respectable sphere of life (commonly called "The Drogheda Defenders"), for seditiously conspiring to raise a levy war and insurrection against the King. They were acquitted, whereupon the Crown withdrew their indictments against other persons.

In May, 1794, when the proprietors of the *Northern Star* (a Belfast liberal paper) were prosecuted for publishing "wicked and seditious libels," as many as seven informations were filed, but only one brought to trial. Curran, for the defence, raised the point that there was no evidence that twelve of them were guilty of a deed not done by themselves. The sole printer (John Rabb) was convicted; all the rest, by direction of the court, were acquitted. The defence of Rabb was that the publication was no libel. The mere cost of the license (£10 in each case) for Mr. Curran, the King's Counsel, to plead against the Crown, on the seven informations, was £70.

In June, 1794, Doctor William Drennan, who, as Chairman of the meeting of Volunteers, had signed the Counter-proclamation, for issuing which (as Secretary) Rowan had been tried, convicted, fined and imprisoned, was put on his trial for having published that document, which was declared to be "a seditious libel." Lord Clonmel, Mr. Justice (afterwards Lord) Downes and Mr. Justice Chamberlain were the judges. Sir John Trail, was objected o by Mr. Curran—on the ground that he had formed an opin on on the subject of the prosecution. The Crown-Lawyer not allowing him to be sworn to ascertain the truth of this, from his own lips, the Knight was sworn on the jury and became its foreman. The evidence was inconclusive, weak, and insufficient. Curran addressed the jury at considerable length. The Prime Sergeant replied angrily. The judges charged hostilely. The jury returned a verdict of "Not guilty," and when this was received with applause, Trail (the foreman), called the spectators "an unruly and seditious rabble," adding the regret of the jury "at seeing a criminal they cannot reach — and guilt which they cannot punish."]*

In the beginning of the year 1795, Lord Fitzwilliam having become Viceroy of Ireland, Mr. Curran was upon the point of being raised to the situation of Solicitor-General; but the sudden recall of that nobleman defeated this, as well as many other projected changes.

It should be mentioned here, that from the year 1789, frequent attempts were made by the adherents of the Administration to detach Mr. Curran from the party which he had formally joined, at that period. Every motive of personal ambition was held out to allure him, and all the influence of private solicitations exerted, but in vain. About this time, when the general panic was daily thinning the ranks of the Opposition, his most intimate and attached friend, the late Lord Kilwarden (then the Attorney-General) frequently urged him to separate himself from a hopeless cause, and to accept the rewards and honours that were so open

* Dr. Drennan, the accused, was the author of "Letters of Orellana, an Irish Helot," in a Belfast paper, in which he strenuously urged the necessity of Parliamentary Reform. He was one of the earliest and most zealous promoters of the Society of United Irishmen, and author of the well-known test of their confederacy. He wrote some admirable Letters to Pitt and Fox against the Union. In the song of "Erin to her own tune?" he first spoke of Ireland as "the Emerald Isle." Who has not heard his "When Erin first rose." He died in 1820.—M.

to him. Upon one occasion, when Mr. Curran was confined by illness to his bed, that gentleman visited him, and renewing the subject, with tears in his eyes, implored him to consult his interest and his safety: "I tell you (said Mr. Wolfe) that you have attached yourself to a desperate faction, that will abandon you at last; with whom you have nothing to expect but danger and disappointment. With us, how different would be your condition—I ask for no painful stipulations on your part, only say that you would accept of office—*my* situation will probably soon be vacant for you, and after that, the road would be clear before you." This proof of private affection caused Mr. Curran to weep, but he was unshaken. He replied, "that he knew, better than his friend could do, the men with whom he was associated; that they were *not* a desperate faction; that their cause was that of Ireland, and that even though it should eventually be branded with the indelible stigma of failure, he should never regret that it was with such men, and such a cause, that he had linked his final destinies."

TRIAL OF THE REV. W. JACKSON.

The next state trial of importance in which Mr. Curran was engaged, was that of Mr. William Jackson, a case of which some of the attending circumstances were so singular, that they cannot be omitted here.

Mr. Jackson was a clergyman of the established church; he was a native of Ireland, but had for several years resided out of that country. A part of his life was spent in the family of the noted Duchess of Kingston, and he is said to have been the person who conducted that lady's controversy with the celebrated Foote.* At the period of the French Revolution, he passed over Paris, where he formed political connections with the ruling

* Foote, at the close of his letter to her Grace, observes: "pray, madam, is not J——n

powers there: from France he returned to London in 1794, for the purpose of procuring information as to the practicability of an invasion of England, and was thence to proceed to Ireland on a similar mission. Upon his arrival in London, he renewed an intimacy with a person named Cockayne, who had formerly been his friend and confidential attorney. The extent of his communications, in the first instance, to Cockayne did not exactly appear; the latter, however, was prevailed upon to write the directions of several of Jackson's letters, containing treasonable matters, to his correspondents abroad; but in a little time, either suspecting or repenting that he had been furnishing evidence of treason against himself, he revealed to the British minister, Mr. Pitt, all that he knew or conjectured relative to Jackson's objects. By the desire of Mr. Pitt, Cockayne accompanied Jackson to Ireland, to watch and defeat his designs, and as soon as the evidence of his treason was mature, announced himself as a witness for the Crown. Mr. Jackson was accordingly arrested, and committed to stand his trial for high treason.

It did not appear that he had been previously connected with any of the political fraternities then so prevalent in Ireland, but some of them took so deep an interest in his fate, that the night before his trial, four persons of inferior condition, members of those societies, formed a plan (which, however, proved abortive) to seize and carry off Cockayne, and perhaps to dispatch him, in order to deprive the Government of the benefit of his testimony.*

Mr. Jackson was committed to prison in April, 1794, but his

the name of your female confidential secretary?" and afterwards, "that you may never want the *benefit of clergy* in every emergency, is the wish of Yours, &c."—C.

* Trial of John Leary for high treason, Dec. 28th, 1795. This fact came out on the cross examination of Lawler, an informer, and the witness against the prisoner in this case. Lawler was one of the party that was to have seized Cockayne: he did not actually admit that he was to have been assassinated; but he allowed that the objection to such a measure was, "that if Cockayne were put to death, and the court should know it, the informations he had given could be read in evidence against Jackson." From the character of Lawler, however, it was generally suspected that assassination was intended.—C.

trial was delayed, by successive adjournments, till the same month in the following year. In the interval, he wrote and published a refutation of Paine's Age of Reason, probably in the hope that it might be accepted as an atonement.*

[The trial took place on April 23, 1795. The judges were Lord Clonmel, Mr. Justice Downes, Mr. Justice Chamberlain. The principal witness was Cockayne, the spy. Curran, who defended Jackson, principally relied on the fact that no conviction for high treason could take place in *England* with TWO witnesses to the facts, whereas it was thus attempted, in *Ireland*, to convict on the evidence of ONE. The anomaly was not removed until 1854, when the law was made the same in both countries.

The trial lasted until four in the morning, when Jackson was

* Examples of honourable conduct, no matter by whom displayed, are heard with pleasure by every friend to human nature. Of such, a very rare instance was given by this gentleman during his imprisonment. For the whole of that period he was treated with every possible indulgence, a fact which is so creditable to the Irish Government, that it would be unjust to suppress it. Among the other acts of lenity extended to him, was a permission to enjoy the society of his friends. A short time before his trial, one of these remained with him to a very late hour of the night: when he was about to depart, Mr. Jackson accompanied him as far as the place where the gaoler usually waited on such occasions, until all his prisoner's visitors should have retired. They found the gaoler in a profound sleep, and the keys of the prison lying beside him. "Poor fellow!" said Mr. Jackson, taking up the keys, "let us not disturb him; I have already been too troublesome to him in this way." He accordingly proceeded with his friend to the outer door of the prison, which he opened. Here the facility of escaping naturally struck him—he became deeply agitated; but after a moment's pause, "*I could do it*," said he, "but what would be the consequence to you, and to the poor fellow within, who has been so kind to me? No! let me rather meet my fate." He said no more, but locking the prison door again, returned to his apartment. It should be added that the gentleman, out of consideration for whom such an opportunity was sacrificed, gave a proof upon this occasion that he deserved it. He was fully aware of the legal consequences of aiding in the escape of a prisoner committed under a charge of high treason, and felt that in the present instance, it would have been utterly impossible for him to disprove the circumstantial evidence that would have appeared against him; yet he never uttered a syllable to dissuade his unfortunate friend. He, however, considered the temptation to be so irresistable that, expecting to find the prisoner, upon further reflection, availing himself of it, he remained all night outside the prison door, with the intention, if Mr. Jackson should escape, of instantly flying from Ireland.—C.

convicted. He was brought up for judgment on the 30th April, 1795.*]

It is at this stage of the proceedings that the case of Jackson becomes terribly peculiar. Never, perhaps, did a British court of justice exhibit a spectacle of such appalling interest as was witnessed by the King's Bench of Ireland, upon the day that this unfortunate gentleman was summoned to hear his fate pronounced. He had a day or two before made some allusions to the subject of suicide. In a conversation with his counsel in the prison, he had observed to them that his food was always cut in pieces before it was brought to him, the gaoler not venturing to trust him with a knife or fork. This precaution he ridiculed, and observed, "that the man who feared not death, could never want the means of dying, and that as long as his head was within reach of the prison-wall, he could prevent his body's being suspended to scare the community." At the moment, they regarded this as a mere casual ebullition, and did not give it much attention.

On the morning of the 30th of April, as one of these gentlemen was proceeding to Court, he met in the streets a person warmly attached to the Government of the day; the circumstance is trivial, but it marks the party spirit that prevailed, and the manner in which it was sometimes expressed: "I have (said he) just seen your client, Jackson, pass by on his way to the King's Bench to receive sentence of death. I always said he was a coward, and I find I was not mistaken; his fears have made him sick—as the coach drove by, I observed him with his head out of the window, vomiting violently." The other hurried on to the Court, where he found his client supporting himself against the dock; his frame was in a state of violent perturbation, but his mind was still col-

* The report of Mr. Curran's defence of Jackson will be found in the lately published volume of Howell's State Trials. It was (as he observed himself) "a narrow case," and afforded few materials for the display of eloquence. The principal points which he urged were the necessity of two witnesses (as in England) and the impeached character of the single witness, Cockayne.—C.

lected. He beckoned to his counsel to approach him, and making an effort to squeeze him with his damp and nerveless hand, uttered in a whisper, and with a smile of mournful triumph, the dying words of Pierre:

"We have deceived the senate."*

The prisoner's counsel having detected what they conceived to be a legal informality in the proceedings, intended to make a motion in arrest of his judgment; but it would have been irregular to do so until the counsel for the Crown, who had not yet appeared, should first pray the judgment of the court upon him. During the interval, the violence of the prisoner's indisposition momentarily increased, and the Chief Justice, Lord Clonmel, was speaking of remanding him, when the Attorney General came in, and called upon the court to pronounce judgment upon him. Accordingly, "the Reverend William Jackson was set forward," and presented a spectacle equally shocking and affecting. His body was in a state of profuse perspiration; when his hat was removed, a dense steam was seen to ascend from his head and temples; minute and irregular movements of convulsions were passing to and fro upon his countenance; his eyes were nearly closed, and when at intervals they opened, discovered by the glare of death upon them, that the hour of dissolution was at hand. When called on to stand up before the Court, he collected the remnant of his force to hold himself erect; but the attempt was tottering and imperfect; he stood rocking from side to side, with his arms in the attitude of firmness, crossed over his breast, and his countenance strained by a last proud effort into an expression of elaborate composure. In this condition he faced all the anger of the offended law, and the more confounding gazes of the assembled crowd. The Clerk of the Crown now ordered him to hold up his right hand; the dying man disentangled it from the other, and held it up, but it instantly dropped again! Such was his state, when in the solemn simplicity of the language of the law, he was asked, "What he

* Otway's Venice Preserved.

had now to say why judgment of death and execution thereon, should not be awarded against him according to law?" Upon this Mr. Curran rose, and addressed some arguments to the Court in arrest of judgment. A legal discussion of considerable length ensued. The condition of Mr. Jackson was all this while becoming worse. Mr. Curran proposed that he should be remanded, as he was in a state of body that rendered any communication between him and his counsel impracticable. Lord Clonmel thought it lenity to the prisoner to dispose of the question as speedily as possible. The windows of the Court were thrown open to relieve him, and the discussion was renewed; but the fatal group of death tokens were now collecting fast around him; he was evidently in the final agony. At length, while Mr. Ponsonby, who followed Mr. Curran, was urging further reasons for arresting the judgment, their client *sunk in the dock.**

The conclusion of the scene is given as follows in the reported trial.

Lord Clonmel—"If the prisoner is in a state of insensibility, it is impossible that I can pronounce the judgment of the Court upon him."

Mr. Thomas Kinsley, who was in the jury box, said he would go down to him; he accordingly went into the dock, and in a short time informed the Court that the prisoner was certainly dying.

By order of the court, Mr. Kinsley was sworn.

* As soon as the cause of Mr. Jackson's death was ascertained, a report prevailed that his counsel had been previously in the secret, and that their motion in arrest of judgment was made for the sole purpose of giving their client time to expire before sentence could be passed upon him: but for the assertion of this fact, which, if true, would have placed them in as strange and awful a situation as can well be imagined, there was no foundation. So little prepared were they for such an event, that neither of his assigned counsel (Messrs. Curran and Ponsonby) appeared in court until a considerable time after the prisoner had been brought up. It was Mr. M'Nally, who had been one of his assistant counsel upon the trial, and who found him in the condition above described, that first became acquainted with the fact of his having taken poison; and he, at the request of the unfortunate prisoner, rose as *amicus curiæ*, for the purpose of occupying the court till the others should arrive and make their intended motion. It was probably from this circumstance that the report originated.—C.

Lord Clonmel—"Are you in any profession?"

Mr. Kinsley—"I am an apothecary."

Lord Clonmel—"Can you speak with certainty of the state of the prisoner?"

Mr. Kinsley—"I can; I think him verging to eternity."

Lord Clonmel—"Do you think him capable of hearing his judgment?"

Mr. Kinsley—"I do not think he can."

Lord Clonmel—"Then he must be taken away; take care that in sending him away no mischief be done. Let him be remanded until further orders; and I believe it as much for his advantage as for all yours to adjourn."

The Sheriff informed the Court that the prisoner was *dead.*

Lord Clonmel—"Let an inquisition, and a respectable one, be held on the body. You should carefully inquire by what means he died."

The Court then adjourned, and the body of the deceased remained in the dock, unmoved from the position in which he had expired, until the following day, when an inquest was held. A large quantity of metallic poison was found in his stomach. The preceding day, a little before he was brought up to Court, the gaoler having visited his room, found him with his wife, much agitated, and vomiting violently; he had just taken, he said, some tea, which disagreed with him; so that there remained no doubt that the unfortunate prisoner, to save himself and his family the shame of an ignominious execution, had anticipated the punishment of the laws by taking poison.

The following sentences, in his own handwriting, were found in his pocket.

"Turn thee unto me, and have mercy upon me, for I am desolate and afflicted."

"The troubles of my heart are enlarged; oh, bring thou me out of my distresses."

"Look upon my affliction and my pain, and forgive all my sins."

"Oh! keep my soul and deliver me. Let me not be ashamed, for I put my trust in thee."

Independent of this awful scene, the trial of Jackson was a memorable event. It was the first trial for high treason which had occurred in that Court for upwards of a century. As a matter of legal and of constitutional interest, it established a precedent of the most vital (Englishmen would say, of the most fatal) importance to a community having any pretension to freedom. Against the authority of Coke, and the reasoning of Blackstone, and against the positive reprobation of the principle by the English legislature, it was solemnly decided in Jackson's case, that in Ireland one witness was sufficient to convict a prisoner upon a charge of high treason—"that the breath which cannot even taint the character of a man in England, shall in Ireland blow him from the earth."* This decision has ever since been recognised and acted upon, to the admiration of that class of politicians (and they have abounded in Ireland) who contend that in every malady of the State, blood should be plentifully drawn; and to the honest indignation of men of equal capacity and integrity, who consider that, without reason or necessity, it establishes an odious distinction, involving in it a disdain of what Englishmen boast as a precious privilege, alluring accusations upon the subject, and conferring security and omnipotence upon the informer.

It is a little singular to observe, in the State Trials that followed, the effects of such a law, and to what a class of witnesses it familiarized the Irish Courts of Justice. From the event it would appear, that there was as much prophecy, as of constitutional zeal, in Mr. Curran's efforts to prevent its establishment, and afterwards to produce its repeal.† To say nothing but

* Mr. Curran's defence of Jackson.—C.

† Two days after Jackson's conviction, Mr. Curran moved in the House of Commons for leave to bring in a bill for amending the law of Ireland in cases of high treason, and assimilating it with that of England.

The Attorney-General earnestly intreated of the mover to postpone the introduction of a few of those cases in which he acted as counsel, the facts of Jackson, Weldon, M'Cann, Byrne, Bond, the Sheareses, Finney, rested almost entirely upon the credibility of a single witness. All of these, except the last, were convicted; and that they were involved in the projects, for which they were tried and suffered, is now a matter of historical notoriety. Few, it is hoped, will maintain the dangerous principle, that the subject should have the inducement of impunity to conspire against

of this bill, lest it might throw a character of illegality upon Jackson's conviction. He believed that the present difference in the law of the two countries (as to the number of witnesses required) did not arise from casual omission, but from serious deliberation; it was (he thought) rather necessary to strengthen the Crown against the popular crime, than to strengthen the criminal against the Crown.

Mr. Curran differed, and considered the rock on which criminal law generally split was its excessive severity. For the reason first assigned, however, he agreed to postpone the bill; but foreseeing its inevitable failure, he never brought it forward again.

In England, by different statutes regulating trials for high treason, two witnesses are required. (Algernon Sydney's attainder, as is well known, was reversed, because, among other reasons, there had been but one legal witness to any act of treason.) When those statutes were enacted in Ireland, the clauses requiring two witnesses were omitted. Upon Jackson's trial, therefore, the question was, what had been the old common law of England. Lord Coke lays it down, that by that law one witness was never sufficient. Judge Foster, differing from him, gives it as his, and as the general opinion, that two were not required by the common law. Of the same opinion is Sergeant Hawkins. These (according to the report of Jackson's trial) were the only authorities referred to by Lord Clonmel in deciding the point. For the contrariety of opinions upon this subject, see the proceedings in Sir J. Fenwick's case, State Trials.

It cannot be too much lamented, that in such an important particular the law of the two countries should thus differ. The principle cannot be right in both. Inferior regulations may vary, but the laws that provide for the safety of the State and the security of the subject are not local ordinances; they are general laws, and should be founded on the principles which are to be derived from an experience of the operation of human passions, and of the value of human testimony. In Ireland, it has been said, that from the state of society, the Crown demanded additional security; but the same argument applies as strongly the other way; for if any community is in such a state of demoralization that its members are found violating their oaths, and indulging their passions by frequent acts of treason, is it not equally clear that they will not refrain from doing the same by frequent acts of perjured evidence? Whoever will submit to the "penance" of reading the English or Irish State Trials, will soon perceive that treason and perjury are always cotemporary crimes, and that the dangers of the Crown and of the subject are at every period are reciprocal and commensurate. Certainly, as the laws at present stand, either the English subject enjoys too many privileges, or the Irish too few; but that the former is not the case long experience has now incontestably established.—C.

the State—such a doctrine would bring instant ruin upon any society; but every friend to constitutional law will distinguish between the evidence that precedes a conviction and that which follows; he will remember that the forms of trial, and the legality of evidence, have not been established for the solitary purpose of punishing the guilty; that their most precious use is for the security of innocence; and that if, forejudging the real offender, we too hastily deprive him of a single privilege of defence, we establish a perilous rule that survives the occasion and extends beyond it, and of which those who never offended may hereafter be the victims. If the trials of the individuals just named be considered with reference to this view, they will be found to contain matter of important reflection. We may not feel justified in lamenting their personal fate—in giving to their memories "the traitorous humanity and the rebel tear," yet we cannot but be shocked at the characters of the persons by whose evidence they were carried off. These were all of them men of blighted reputation. It was not merely that they had been accomplices in the crimes which they came to denounce; and that, finding the speculation dangerous and unprofitable, they endeavoured to retrieve their credit and circumstances, by setting up as "loyal apostates." Deeper far was, if not their legal offence, their moral depravity. Dreadful were the confessions of guilt, of dishonour, and irreligion extorted from these wretches. If their direct examination produced a list of the prisoners' crimes, as regularly did their cross-examination elicit a darker catalogue of their own. In the progress of their career, from participation to discovery, all the tender charities of life were abused—every sacred tie rent asunder. The agent, by the semblance of fidelity, extracted the secret of his client and his friend, and betrayed him!* The spy resorted to the habitation of his victim, and, while sharing his hospitality,

* Jackson's Trial.

and fondling his children, was meditating his ruin.* Here was to be seen the wild Atheist, who had gloried in his incredulity, enjoying a lucid interval of faith, to stamp a legal value on his oath†—there the dishonest dealer, the acknowledged perjurer, the future murderer.‡

It has been often a matter of surprise that juries had not the firmness to spurn altogether the testimony of such delinquents. In England, upon a recent occasion,§ a jury did so; but in Ireland there raged, at this time, an epidemic panic. In the delirious fever of the moment, even though the juror might not have thirsted for the blood of the accused, he yet trembled for his own—affrighted by actual danger, or by the phantoms of his disturbed imagination, he became blind or indifferent to the horrors of the immediate scene. The question was often not whether the witness was a man he could believe, but whether his verdict dare assert the contrary. Perhaps the more flagitious the witness, the more absolutely was he the tyrant of the juror's conscience. Any movements of humanity or indignation in the breast of the latter must have instantly been quelled by the recollection, that to yield

* Jackson's Trial and the Trial of the Sheareses. A few days before Cockayne had openly announced himself as an informer, he was invited to accompany Jackson to dine with a friend of the latter. After dinner, as soon as the wine had sufficiently circulated, Jackson, according to a previous suggestion from Cockayne, began to sound the political dispositions of the company, and particularly addressed himself to a gentleman of rank who sat beside him, and who, there was subsequent reason to believe, was deeply involved in the politics of the time. During the conversation, Cockayne appeared to have fallen asleep; but, in the midst of it, the master of the house was called out by his servant, who informed him, that he had observed something very singular in Mr. Jackson's friend—"he has his hand," said the servant, "over his face, and pretends to be asleep, but when I was in the room just now I could perceive the glistening of his eye through his fingers." The gentleman returned to his guests; and whispering to him who was conversing with Jackson to be cautious of his language, probably prevented some avowal which might eventually have cost him his life. Upon such trivial accidents do the fates of men depend in agitated times!—C.

† Trial of the Sheareses.—C.

‡ Finney's Trial; and the other State Trials of 1798.—C.

§ Trial of Watson and others for high treason.—C.

to them might be to point out himself as an object of suspicion, and as the next experiment for an adventurous and irritated informer.

It is in the same circumstances that we are to look for an excuse (if excuse be necessary) for those impassioned appeals, for that tone of high and solemn obtestation, by which Mr. Curran's professional efforts at this period are distinguished. In more tranquil times or in a more tranquil country, such enthusiasm may appear extravagant and unnatural; but it should be remembered, that, from the nature of the cases, and the character of his audience, his address often became rather a religious exhortation than a mere forensic harangue.* His situation was very different from that of the English advocate, who, presupposing in his hearers a respect for the great fundamental principles of law and of ethics, securely appeals to them, in the conviction, that, if his client deserves it, he shall have all their benefit. In Ireland, the client was not certain of all their benefit. In Ireland, during those distracted days, every furious passion was abroad. The Irish advocate knew

* Of this, examples will occur, in the following pages. Upon inferior occasions we find him impressing the most obvious political truths, by a simplicity of illustration, which shows the description of men among whom he was thrown. When he wished to explain to a jury, "that their country could never be prosperous, or happy, without a general participation of happiness to all its people," he thus proceeds:—"A privileged order in a state may, in some sort, be compared to a solitary individual separated from the society, and unaided by the reciprocal converse, affections, or support of his fellow men. It is like a tree standing singly on a high hill, and exposed to the rude concussions of every varying blast, devoid of fruit or foliage. If you plant trees around it, to shade it from the inclemency of the blighting tempest, and secure to it its adequate supply of sun and moisture, it quickly assumes all the luxuriance of vegetation, and proudly rears its head aloft, fortified against the noxious gales which agitate and wither the unprotected brambles lying without the verge of the plantation. Upon this principle acted the dying man, whose family had been disturbed by domestic contentions. Upon his death-bed he calls his children around him; he orders a bundle of twigs to be brought; he has them untied; he gives to each of them a single twig; he orders them to be broken, and it is done with facility; he next orders the twigs to be united in a bundle, and directs each of them to try his strength upon it. They shrink from the task as impossible. 'Thus, my children, (continued the old man) it is union alone that can render you secure against the attempts of your enemies, and preserve you in that state of happiness which I wish you to enjoy.'" —*Speech in Defence of Bird, Hamil and others, tried at Drogheda*, 1794.—C.

that the juries with whom he had to deal were often composed of men whose feelings of humanity and religion were kept under by their political prejudices—that they had already foredoomed his client to the grave—that, bringing with them the accumulated animosities of past centuries, they came less to try the prisoner than to justify themselves, and make their verdict a vote of approbation upon the politics of their party.* To make an impression upon such men, he had to awaken their dormant sympathies by reiterated statements of the first principles of morals and religion: he addressed himself to their eternal fears, his object being frequently, not so much to direct their minds to the evidence or the

* The following observations of Mr. Curran will give some idea of the juries of those days: he is addresing a jury impannelled to try the validity of a challenge:—

"This is no common period in the history of the world—they are no ordinary transactions that are now passing before us. All Europe is shaken to its centre; we feel its force, and are likely to be involved in its consequences. There is no man who has sense enough to be conscious of his own existence, who can hold himself disengaged and unconcerned amidst the present scenes; and, to hear a man say that he is unbiassed and unprejudiced, is the surest proof that he is both. Prejudice is the cobweb that catches vulgar minds; but the prejudices of the present day float in the upper regions—they entangle the lofty heads—they are bowing them down—you see them as they flutter, and hear them as they buzz. Mr. —— has become a very public and a very active man; he has his mind, I doubt not, stored with the most useful and extensive erudition—he is clothed with the sacred office of a minister of the Gospel—he is a magistrate of the county—he is employed as agent to some large properties—he is reputably connected, and universally esteemed, and therefore is a man of no small weight and consideration in this country. He has more than once positively sworn that he has applied to the high sheriff—that he struck off no names but those that wanted freeholds; but to-day, he finds that freeholders were struck off by his own pen—he tells you, my lords, and gentlemen triers, with equal modesty and ingenuity, that he has made a mistake—he returns eighty-one names to the sheriff—he receives blank summonses, fills what he deems convenient, &c. Gracious heaven! what are the courts of justice? what is trial by jury? what is the country brought to? Were it told in the courts above—were it told in other countries—were it told in Westminster Hall, that such a man was permitted to return nearly one half of the grand panel of the county from one particular district,—a district under severe distress,—to which he is agent and on which, with the authority he possesses, he is able to bring great calamity! He ascends the pulpit with the Gospel of benignity and peace—he endeavours to impress himself and others with its meek and holy spirit:—he descends—throws off the purple—seizes the insurrection act in the one hand, and the whip in the other—flies by night and by day after his game; and, with his heart panting, his breath exhausted, and his belly on the ground in the chase, he turns round, and tells you that his mind is unprejudiced—that his breast is full of softness and humanity."—*Down Assizes*, 1795.—C.

law, as to remind them of the Christian duties; and even in those cases, where both law and fact were upon his side, and where, under other circumstances, he might have boldly demanded an acquittal, he was in reality labouring to extort a pardon.

It was with the same view that he so often made the most impassioned appeals, even to the Bench, when he saw that its political feelings were hostile to the interests of his client. Thus, upon the trial of Hamilton Rowan, the principal witness for the Crown, having deposed that he had seen Mr. Rowan at a meeting of United Irishmen, consisting of one hundred and fifty persons, and his evidence upon this most material fact having been impeached, the Chief Justice (Lord Clonmel), in his charge to the jury, observed, "One hundred and fifty Volunteers, or United Irishmen, and not one comes forward! Many of them would have been proud to assist him (the traverser). *Their silence speaks a thousand times more strongly than any cavilling upon this man's credit —the silence of such a number is a volume of evidence in support of the prosecution.*" * Upon a motion for a new trial, Mr. Cur-

* This passage of Lord Clonmel's charge was omitted, and, no doubt, designedly, in the original edition of Hamilton Rowan's trial, published in Dublin.—C.

Lord Clonmel, for many years Chief Justice of the King's Bench in Ireland, was a man whose mind and form were very coarse. He had risen from a low origin to great wealth and high station, but never looked like a gentleman. His manners were coarse. His appearance was peculiar—his face was the color of the scarlet robe which he wore, as Judge, and literally "flared up" (so rubicund was it) when he got into a passion, which was about once in every twenty minutes. He and Curran did not agree. At the bar, when both were young, they had had several wordy contests, in which Curran succeeded. This was never forgotten by his opponent when a Judge. It is related that on one occasion the noble lord was so pressed both by the argument, the eloquence, and the wit of Mr. Curran, that he lost temper, and called on the sheriffs to be ready to take any one into arrest who would be found so contemptuously presuming to fly into the face of the court. Mr. Curran, perceiving the twittering of a swallow actively in pursuit of flies, in his turn called on the sheriffs to take that swallow into arrest, for it was guilty of contempt, as it had contemptuously presumed *to fly in the face of the court.* The ridicule of this, and the peals of laughter which ensued, closed the scene. On some contested argument in the Court of King's Bench, Lord Clonmel, who was said to have a stronger dash of the overbearing than of the brave, stood out against Mr. Curran with a brow-beating vehemence, and showed a determination to have things entirely in his own way. He made repeated but ineffectual efforts to reduce Mr. Curran, or (as the phrase is used) to put him down. He, however, withstood all the violence of those attempts, and the

ran, in commenting upon those expressions, could not refrain from exclaiming, "I never before heard an intimation from any judge to a jury, that bad evidence, liable to any and every exception, ought to receive a sanction from the silence of the party. With anxiety for the honour and religion of the law, I demand it of you, must not the jury have understood that this silence was evidence to go to them? Is the meaning contained in the expression 'a volume of evidence' only an insinuation? I do not know where any man could be safe—I do not know what any man could do to screen himself from prosecution—I know not how he could be secure, even when he was at prayers before the throne of Heaven, that he was not passing that moment of his life, in which he was to be charged with the commission of some crime to be expiated to society, by the loss of his liberty or of his life—I do not know what shall become of the subject, if the jury are to be told that the silence of a man charged is 'a volume of evidence that he is guilty of the crime.' Where is it written? I know there is a place where vulgar phrensy cries out that the public instrument must be drenched in blood—where defence is gagged, and the devoted wretch must perish. But even there the victim of such tyranny is not made to fill, by voluntary silence, the defects of his accusation; for his tongue is tied, and therefore no advantage is taken of him by construction: it cannot be there said that his not speaking is 'a volume of evidence' to prove his guilt." After some farther observations, he thus concluded his arguments: "You are standing on a narrow isthmus, that divides the great ocean of duration—on the one side of the past, on the other of the

encounter was upheld with all that passion could supply, or courage hope to extinguish. Mr. Curran looked, and lighted up all the fire of his mighty eye, surveyed his adversary with the most intense and indignant scowl, such as would have pierced through all impediments; while the red and inflamed countenance of the Judge, with the menace and attitude of an overwhelming passion, kindled into a burning blaze. With a firm, calm, and measured tone, Mr. Curran addressed him, and whilst he did so, he seemed armed with the bolt of heaven, ready to hurl destruction on his victim. After some prelude, he concluded his address in these words: "Does your lordship think I am that silly dog to bay *that* moon—to bay *that* moon—which I am not able to extinguish?"—M.

future—a ground that, while you yet hear me, is washed from beneath your feet. Let me remind you, my lords, while your determination is yet in your power—*dum versatur adhuc intra penetralia Vestæ*—that on the ocean of the future you must set your judgment afloat; and future ages will assume the same authority which you have assumed; posterity will feel the same emotions which you have felt, when your little hearts have beaten, and your infant eyes have overflowed at reading the sad story of the sufferings of a Russel or a Sydney."

All this has been represented as very strange, and even absurd, by those who would not reflect upon the state of the times, and the necessity which it imposed upon the advocate of addressing the passions which he knew to be actuating his hearers, no matter to what order of the community they might belong.

CHAPTER IX.

Catholic Emancipation—Mr. Curran moves an address to the Throne for an inquiry into the state of the poor—Other Parliamentary questions—Mr. Ponsonby's plan of Reform rejected—Secession of Mr. Curran and his friends—Orr's trial—Finnerty's trial—Finney's Trial—The informer, James O'Brien.

[ON May 4, 1795, a sharp debate took place in the Irish Commons, on the second reading of a Catholic Emancipation Bill, which had been introduced, during the preceding January, under the liberal auspices of Lord Fitzwilliam, the new and liberal Viceroy. But George III. was determined not to admit his Roman Catholic subjects to the enjoyment of civil rights, and the too liberal Viceroy was recalled. The Irish Commons, on the strength of the Emancipation Bill being a fact, had liberally voted large supplies for carrying on the war then raging between France and England. The money received, the Irish Government threw over the Catholics, and the second reading of the Emancipation Bill was lost—there being 155 votes against and 84 for it. Mr. Curran supported the measure, and defended the character and conduct of Lord Fitzwilliam.]

In May, 1795, Mr. Curran moved an address to the throne upon the distresses of Ireland, the recall of Lord Fitzwilliam, and the misconduct of his Majesty's ministers in their government of Ireland. It was not expected, by the opposition, that this motion would be carried: their object in bringing it forward was merely to leave a record of their opinions upon the subjects contained in the address.* Mr. Curran prefaced his motion by a long speech,

* This address, after a few prefatory clauses stating the attachment of the Commons to his Majesty's person, and the monarchical form of government, and their late extraordinary supplies for carrying on the present most eventful war, proceeds—

That we were the more induced to this, from a zeal for his Majesty's service, and an

in the course of which he emphatically warned the House of the dangers that impended over the public tranquillity; but upon this, as upon many former occasions, his predictions were disregarded. "I know," said he, "that this is not a time when the passions of the public ought to be inflamed; nor do I mean to inflame them (*murmurs from the other side of the House*). Yes, I speak not to inflame; but I address you in order to allay the fever of the public mind. If I had power to warn you, I would exert that power in order to diminish the public ferment—in order to show the

attachment to Great Britain; but accompanied with an expectation that our extraordinary grants would be justified to our constituents by a reform, under a patriot viceroy, of the various and manifold abuses that had taken place in the administration of the Irish Government; a reformation which we conceived, in the present times, and under such an increase of debt and taxes, indispensable, and which we do, therefore, most humbly persist to implore and expect.

That, after the supply was granted and the force voted, and whilst the chief governor, possessing the entire confidence of both Houses of Parliament, and the approbation of all the people, was reforming abuses, and putting the country in a state of defence, he was suddenly and prematurely recalled, and our unparalleled efforts for the support of his Majesty answered by the strongest marks of the resentment of his ministers.

That, in consequence of such a proceeding, the business of Government was interrupted, the defence of the country suspended, the unanimity which had under the then Lord Lieutenant existed converted into just complaint and remonstrance, and the energy, confidence, and zeal of the nation, so loudly called for by his Majesty's ministers, were, by the conduct of those very ministers themselves, materially affected.

That these, their late proceedings, aggravated their past system; in complaining of which, we particularly refer to the notorious traffic of honours—to the removal of the troops contrary to the law, and in total disregard of the solemn compact with the nation and safety of the realm—to the criminal conduct of Government respecting the Irish army—to the disbursements of sums of money, without account or authority—to the improvident grant of reversions, at the expense of his Majesty's interest, sacrificed, for the emolument of his servants, to the conduct of his Majesty's ministers in both countries, towards his Protestant and Catholic subjects of Ireland, alternately practising on their passions, exciting their hopes, and procuring their disappointment.

That, convinced by the benefits which we have received under his Majesty's reign that the grievances of which we complain are as unknown to his Majesty as abhorrent from his paternal and royal disposition.

We, his Commons of Ireland, beg leave to lay ourselves at his feet, and, with all humility to his Majesty, to prefer, on our part, and on the part of our constituents, this our just and necessary remonstrance against the conduct of his ministers; and to implore his Majesty that he may be graciously pleased to lay his commands upon his minister to second the zeal of his Irish Parliament in his Majesty's services, by manifesting in future to the people of Ireland due regard and attention.

people that they have more security in your warmth than they can have in their own heat—that the ardour of your honest zeal may be a salutary ventilator to the ferment of your country—in order that you may take the people out of their own hands, and bring them within your guidance. Trust me, at this momentous crisis, a firm and tempered sensibility of injury would be equally honourable to yourselves and beneficial to the nation: trust me, if, at a time when every little stream is swollen into a torrent, we alone should be found to exhibit a smooth, and listless, and frozen surface, the folly of the people may be tempted to walk across us; and, whether they should suppose they were only walking upon ice, or treading upon corruption, the rashness of the experiment might be fatal to us all."

[He said that the abuses and grievances which afflicted Ireland were "the sale of the honours of the peerage; the open and avowed sale, for money, of the peerage, to any man rich and shameless enough to be a purchaser." Such a course, he said, depraved the Commons, profaned the sanctity of the Lords, poisoned the sources of legislation and the fountains of justice, and annihilated the very idea of public honour and public integrity—but all this had been done by the government of Lord Westmorland. Next was the depriving Ireland of troops, when the enemy was at the gate, and the breach of the compact to maintain 12,000 soldiers in Ireland, might have been the loss of the island. Then came the wasteful expenditure of public money. There was the abuse of patronage—every office of value, of which a reversion could be granted, having been so disposed of for years and years to come. There was the injustice of neglecting, refusing, delaying relief to the Roman Catholics. Lastly, there were the restraints upon Irish Commerce.

This was a full budget. Curran moved the address, Grattan seconded, and Ponsonby supported it. The Government moved and carried the adjournment of the House, and thus the address was not even put to the vote.]

In the beginning of the following year, Mr. Curran moved "that a committee should be appointed to inquire into the state of the lower orders of the people," to whose wretchedness he attributed the prevailing discontents; but his motion was, as usual, "suffocated by the question of adjournment." He also distinguished himself by his support of Mr. Grattan's amendments to the addresses in this year, by his exertions on the question of Catholic emancipation, and by his opposition to the suspension of the habeas corpus act.

[In December, 1795, Mr. Curran appeared in the Court at Dublin, as counsel for James Weldon, charged with high treason. His client had been one of the "Dublin Defenders," and was charged not only with associating with traitors unknown, to assist the French, the public enemies of the Crown, but with associating with the Defenders to subvert the Protestant religion, and with corrupting one William Lawler to become a Defender. The chief evidence for the Crown was this Lawler, whose testimony Mr. Curran cut up into tatters, besides giving proof that he was not credible. Weldon was convicted and hanged; though Leary, another prisoner, was acquitted, under precisely similar facts!

Some more particular notice of Mr. Curran's last year of Parliamentary life appears required here. In February, 1796, in the debate on the Indemnity Bill, he supported Grattan's unsuccessful motion that Justice Chamberlain and Baron Smith, the judges who had gone circuit in the disturbed districts, should first be examined, to open the state of the country and the general conduct of the magistrates. In the same month, he spoke in favour of free trade between England and Ireland, and strongly opposed the Insurrection Act, which gave magistrates the arbitrary power of transportation, describing it as "a bill *for* the *rich* and *against* the poor," constituting poverty a crime, and leaving it to the discretion of wealth to apportion the punishment.

In October, 1796, when the French were preparing Hoche's expedition for the invasion of Ireland, and the Irish Government recommended union as a means of strength, Grattan moved that unanimity could best be obtained by enacting such laws as would secure to all of the King's subjects "the blessings and privileges of the Constitution, without distinction of religion." Mr. Curran was among those who supported this liberal view. His speech on this occasion contained many truths, well put. "Believe me, Sir," he said, "an invader can look for nothing but certain destruction when he is opposed by the wishes and passions of the people. It is not garrisons, it is not generals, nor armies, upon which we can repose in safety. It is on the union and zeal of the general inhabitants, removing provisions, discovering designs, marring the projects, and hanging on the retreats of an enemy, that baffles and defeats him more than any regular force can do." In all probability, this was suggested by the orator's recollection of the manner in which, during the American War of Independence, the troops of Great Britain were discomfited. Mr. Curran was fond of historic studies, and had warmly sympathised with the Americans in their arduous contest for national independence.

Another passage is worthy of quotation, as illustrative of Mr. Curran's figurative style. Answering the remark that the Irish Catholics had got much, and ought to be content, he said: "Why have they got much? is it from the Minister? is it from the Parliament which threw its petition over its bar? No, they got it by the great revolution of human affairs, by the astonishing march of the human mind; a march that has collected too much moment on its advance to be now stopped in its progress. The bark is still afloat, it is freighted with the hopes and liberties of men; she is already under weigh—the rower may faint, or the wind may sleep, but rely upon it, she has already acquired an energy of advancement that will support her course, and bring her to her destination; rely upon it, whether much or little remains, it is now vain to withhold it; rely upon it, you may as well stamp your foot upon the earth, in order to prevent its revolution. You cannot stop it! you will only remain a silly gnomon upon its surface to measure the rapidity of rotation, until you are forced round and buried in the shade of that body, whose irresistible course you would endeavour to oppose."

The Attorney-General moved that leave be given to bring in a Bill similar to what had been enacted when England was threatened with invasion, authorizing the Irish Executive to take up and detain all persons suspected of treasonable practices. Leave was given, the bill was forthwith presented, read a first and second time that night (Oct. 13, 1796), and ordered to pass into committee the next day. On the motion that it be committed, a small opposition party, headed by Mr. George Ponsonby, resisted the measure. Mr. Curran, commenting on the haste with which it had progressed, said: "At two o'clock in the morning, the House was moved for leave to bring in a Bill to suspend the Habeas Corpus Act; at five minutes past two in the morning, the bill was read a first time, and, after *grave* and *mature* deliberation, the bill was ordered to be read, and was accordingly read a second time at ten minutes past two in the morning. Its principle was then *fully considered* and approved of; and at fifteen minutes after two in the morning, it was laid before a Committee of the whole House!" The division was 137 to 7, and the Habeas Corpus act was suspended accordingly.

On October 17th, 1796, in a debate on Grattan's motion in favour of the admission to seats in Parliament (seconded by George Ponsonby, and strenuously opposed by the Government), Dr. Duigenan, a polemical and political intolerant of the first (mud-and-) water, used violent and offensive language against the Catholics, in whose communion he had participated in his youth. Mr. Curran replied to him, and said, "He has abused the Catholics, he has abused their ancestors, he has abused the merchants of Ireland, he has abused Mr. Burke, he has abused those who voted for the order of the day." Mr. Curran then described his manner and matter of speaking—"that confusion of history and divinity, and civil law and canon law—that rollicking mixture of politics and theology, and antiquity, with which he has overwhelmed the debate; for the havoc and carnage he has made of the population of the last age, and the fury with which he seemed determined to exterminate, and even to devour, the population of this; and which urged him, after tearing and gnawing the characters of the Catholics, to spend the last efforts of his rage, with the most unrelenting ferocity, in actually gnawing the names.* In truth, sir, I felt some surprise, and some regret, when I heard him describe the sceptre of lath, and the tiara of straw, and mimic his bedlamite Emperor and Pope with such refined and happy gesticulation, that he could be prevailed on to quit so congenial a company." Alluding to the declaration that the Catholics must not have Emancipation, because they demanded it with insolence, Mr. Curran said, "Suppose that assertion, false as it is in fact, to be true, is it any argument with a public assembly that any incivility of demand can cover the injustice of refusal? How low must that assembly be fallen, which can suggest as an apology for the refusal of an incontestible right, the answer which a bankrupt buck might give to the demand of his tailor—he will not pay the bill, because 'the rascal had dared to threaten his honour.'" The motion in favour of Catholic Emancipation was lost by 143 to 19.

On January 6, 1797, Mr. Curran strongly joined in the animadversions of the Opposition on the inactivity of the British navy, when invasion was anticipated, whereby Hoche's expedition was within an ace of success. When the French fleet were in Bantry Bay, not a British line-of-battle ship was on the whole course of the kingdom of Ireland. A few weeks later (February 24th 1797), Curran supported an address for the increase of the domestic army of Ireland, especially the yeomanry corps. The Ministerial

* Dr. Duigenan, who used excessive gesticulation, and sometimes lashed himself into such a rage as to foam at the mouth, had such a peculiar way of barking out the name of Mr. Keogh, one of the Catholic leaders, that Mr. Curran said it was a sort of pronunciatory defamation.—M.

party resisted the proposition, which was based on the increasing power of France, the inability or inactivity of England for the defence of Ireland, and the danger of Ireland herself. Mr. Curran mentioned, as a fact, that when the French fleet arrived in Bantry, there were not, in that quarter of the country, including Cork (the second city of Ireland), one thousand men to meet the enemy!

In February, 1797, Mr. Curran also spoke on Ponsonby's motion of censure on the Irish Ministry, and on Vandeleur's motion for an Absentee Tax. In March of the same year, he went rather freely, and very forcibly, into the motion of censure for disarming the inhabitants of Ulster, on the pretext that "daring and horrid outrages" had been perpetrated in that province. This, in effect, was declaring the inhabitants generally to be guilty of high treason. The Government had obtained a great majority in the Commons, and the motion was defeated. In truth, by this time, they had so distributed places, pensions, peerages, and promises, that they could carry or defeat any and every motion in both Houses of Parliament.]

His last parliamentary effort was in the debate on Mr. William Brabazon Ponsonby's plan of parliamentary reform,* which included Catholic Emancipation, and was brought forward by the Opposition as a final experiment to save Ireland from the horrors of the impending rebellion. By the late report of the secret committee, it had appeared that extensive associations for treasonable objects existed throughout the country: the Administration considered that force alone should be resorted to—the Opposition were as decided that conciliation, and conciliation alone, would restore tranquillity. The ostensible objects of the conspiracy were reform and Catholic Emancipation: the Administration admitted that these were merely pretexts, and that revolution was the real though covert design; but they argued "that the House ought to make a stand, and say that *rebellion must be*

* May 15th, 1797.—C.

put down, before the grievances that were made its pretext should be even discussed." To this it was answered by Mr. Curran, "if Reform be only a pretence, and separation be the real objects of the leaders of the conspiracy, confound the leaders by destroying the pretext, and take the followers to yourselves. You say they are one hundred thousand; I firmly believe they are three times the number; so much the better for you. If these seducers can attach so many followers to rebellion, by the hope of reform through blood, how much more readily will you engage them, not by the promise, but the possession, and without blood." "Reform (he continued) is a necessary change of mildness for coercion: the latter has been tried, and what is its success? The Convention Bill was passed to punish the meetings at Dungannon and those of the Catholics: the Government considered the Catholic concessions as defeats that called for vengeance—and cruelly have they avenged them; but did that act, or those which followed, put down those meetings? the contrary was the fact; it most foolishly concealed them. When popular discontents are abroad, a wise Government should put them in an hive of glass; you hid them. The associations at first were small—the earth seemed to drink it as a rivulet; but it only disappeared for a season: a thousand streams, through the secret windings of the earth, found their way to one source, and swelled its waters; until at last, too mighty to be contained, it burst out a great river, fertilizing by its exundations, or terrifying by its cataracts. This was the effect of your penal code—it swelled sedition into rebellion. What else could be hoped from a system of terrorism? Fear is the most transient of all the passions—it is the warning that nature gives for self-preservation; but when safety is unattainable, the warning must be useless, and nature does not therefore give it. The Administration mistook the quality of penal laws: they were sent out to abolish conventicles; but they did not pass the threshold, they stood sentinels at the gates. You thought that penal laws, like great dogs, would wag their tails to their masters, and bark only at their enemies: you were mistaken; they turn and devour those they were meant to protect, and were harmless where they were intended to destroy. Gentlemen, I see, laugh—I see they affect to be still very ignorant of the nature of fear: this cannot last; neither, while it does, can it be concealed: the feeble glimmering of a forced smile is a light that makes the cheek look paler. Trust me, the times are too humanized for such systems of government—humanity will not execute them; but humanity will abhor them, and those who wished to rule by such means. We hoped much, and, I doubt not, meant well by those laws; but they have miserably failed us: it is time to try milder methods. You have tried to force the people: but the rage of your penal laws was a storm that only drove them in groups to shelter. Before it is too late, therefore, try the better force of reason, and conciliate them by justice and humanity. Neither let us talk of innovation—the progress of nature is no innovation—the increase of people, the growth of the mind, is no innovation, unless the growth of *our* mind lag behind. If we think otherwise, and consider it an innovation to depart from the folly of our infancy, we should come here in our swaddling clothes; we should not innovate upon the dress more than the understanding of the cradle.

"As to the system of peace now proposed, you must take it on its principles; they are simply two—the abolition of religious disabilities, and the representation of the people. I am confident the effects would be every thing to be wished; the present alarming discontent will vanish, the good will be separated from the ill-intentioned; the friends of mixed government in Ireland are many—every sensible man must see that it gives all the enjoyment of rational liberty, if the people have their due place in the state. This system would make us invincible against a foreign or domestic enemy; it would make the empire strong at this important crisis; it would restore to us liberty, industry, and peace, which I am satisfied can never by any other means be restored."

The counsels of peace and conciliation which Mr. Curran and his friends now proposed to the Parliament were the last which they had to offer; and finding that they were to be rejected, they resolved to take no farther part in deliberations where their interference was so unavailing. "I agree (said Mr. Curran, in conclusion) that unanimity at this time is indispensable; the house seems pretty unanimous for force; I am sorry for it, for I bode the worst from it: I shall retire from a scene where I can do no good, and where I certainly should disturb that unanimity; I cannot, however, go without a parting entreaty, that men would reflect upon the awful responsibility in which they stand to their country and their conscience, before they set an example to the people of abandoning the constitution and the law, and resorting to the terrible expedient of force."

Mr. Grattan, who followed Mr. Curran, concluded his speech by announcing the same intention:—"Your system is perilous indeed. I speak without asperity; I speak without resentment; I speak, perhaps, my delusion, but it is my heartfelt conviction; I speak my apprehension for the immediate state of our liberty, and for the ultimate state of the empire; I see, or imagine I see, in this system, every thing which is dangerous to both; I hope I am mistaken—at least, I hope I exaggerate; possibly I may: if so, I shall acknowledge my error with more satisfaction than is usual in the acknowledgment of error. I cannot, however, banish from my memory the lesson of the American war, and yet at that time the English Government was at the head of Europe, and was possessed of resources comparatively unbroken. If that lesson has no effect on ministers, surely I can suggest nothing that will. We have offered you our measure—you will reject it: we deprecate yours—you will persevere; having no hopes left to persuade or to dissuade, and having discharged our duty, we shall trouble you no more, and *after this day shall not attend the House of Commons.*"

[The Opposition ceased to attend, and after a few more sittings

Parliament was adjourned on July 3, 1797. In England, about the same time, Charles James Fox, leader of "His Majesty's Opposition," finding his party invariably in a minority, declared his intention to forbear prosecuting an useless attendance in Parliament. In 1800, however, Fox resumed his seat, and used his most strenuous opposition as a friend of Ireland, to the Union. In 1799, Mr. Grattan returned to the Irish Parliament for a short time, to oppose the Union. Mr. Curran's senatorial life closed with his secession in 1797.]

A few weeks after the secession of the Opposition, Mr. Grattan addressed a letter to the citizens of Dublin upon the part of himself and the other members of the minority, to explain their motives in taking that step. This letter, besides being a splendid monument of the writer's genius, is an important historical document, and when confronted with the reports of secret committees and similar official statements, will show what an imperfect idea they convey of the real condition of the times.

TRIAL OF MR. PETER FINNERTY.

Mr. Curran's next great professional exertion was in the defence of Mr. Finnerty, who was tried in December, 1797, for a libel on the Government and person of the Viceroy (Lord Camden). The subject of the libel was the trial and execution of a person named William Orr, which had taken place a little before. Orr, who had been committed on a charge of high treason, was arraigned on an indictment framed under the Insurrection Act, for administering unlawful oaths, and convicted. A motion in arrest of judgment was made, in the argument upon which Mr. Curran, who was his leading counsel, is said to have displayed as much legal ability and affecting eloquence as upon any occasion of his life. This argument is so imperfectly reported as to be unworthy of insertion. It contains, however, one striking example of that peculiar idiom in which he discussed the most technical questions; in contending that the act under which his client was tried had expired, he observes: "The mind of the judge is the repository of the law that *does exist*, not of the law that *did exist;* nor does the mercy and justice of our law recognize so disgraceful an office as that of a judge becoming a sort of *administrator to a dead statute*, and *collecting the debts of blood that were due to it in its lifetime*."

Another of his arguments for arresting the judgment was, "that the state had no right to wage a piratical war against the subject under false colours:"—that Orr's offence (supposing the informer who gave evidence against him to have sworn truly) amounted to high treason, and that he should therefore have been indicted under the constitutional statute relating to that crime, from which the accused derive so many privileges of defence. It may be necessary to inform some readers, that when acts of high treason are made merely *felony* by a particular statute, the persons under trial lose, among other advantages, the benefit of their counsel's address to the jury, to which, had they been indicted for high treason, they would have been entitled.* Upon such occasions, when Mr. Curran, in addressing the Court upon questions of law, happened to let fall any observations upon the general merits of the case, he had to sustain the reproach of "attempting to *insinuate* a speech to the jury."

But all his efforts were unavailing; his legal objections were overruled by the Bench; and in answer to what he had addressed to the feelings of the Court, the presiding judge, Lord Yelverton, from whose mind classical associations were never absent, adverted to a passage in the history of the Roman commonwealth, where, after the expulsion of the Tarquins, it was attempted by the Patricians to restore royalty; and the argument made use of was, "that a government by laws was stern and cruel, inasmuch as laws had neither hearts to feel, nor ears to hear; whereas government by kings was merciful, inasmuch as the sources of humanity and

* The law and practice have been altered since this was written.—M.

tenderness were open to entreaty."* "For my part," added his Lordship, "I am acting under a government by laws, and am bound to speak the voice of the law, which has neither feeling nor passions."

But this excellent and feeling judge soon showed how little of legal insensibility belonged to his own nature. When he came to pronounce sentence of death upon the prisoner, he was so affected as to be scarcely audible, and the fatal words were no sooner concluded than he burst into tears, and, sinking his head between his hands, continued for many minutes in that attitude of honourable emotion.

The prisoner was recommended to the jury for mercy, but, after receiving no less than three respites, was finally executed.† He died protesting his innocence; and though such a declaration be very doubtful evidence of the fact (for who, about to suffer for a political crime, would not prefer to be remembered as a martyr?), still there were, in the case of Orr, some corroborating circumstances which render it a matter of surprise and regret that they should have been disregarded. His previous life and character had been irreproachable: subsequent to his trial, it appeared that the informer, upon whose evidence he had been convicted, had, according to his own confession, perjured himself on a former

* Regem hominem esse, a quo impetres ubi jus, ubi injuria opus sit—esse gratiæ locum, esse beneficio, et irasci et ignoscere posse—inter amicum atque inimicum discrimen nosse. Leges rem surdam, inexorabilem esse, salubriorem melioremque inopi, quam potenti—nihil laxamenti nec veniæ habere, si modum excesseris.—*Tit. Liv. lib.* 2.—Lord Yelverton was considered as one of the most accomplished classical scholars of his time. An unfinished translation of Livy (his favourite historian) remains among his papers.—C.

[A lawyer pleading before Lord Avonmore, having to oppose some principles urged against him on the authority of Judge Blackstone, treated the works of that great commentator in terms of disrespect; at which Lord Avonmore was so provoked that he instantly burst forth into the following beautiful compliment to that eminent writer: "He first gave to the law the air of science; he found it a skeleton, and clothed it with flesh, colour, and complexion; he embraced the cold statue, and by his touch it grew into life, sense, and beauty. His great works survive the vagaries which pass through the crude minds of each giddy innovator, and which every packet imports in the form of a blue paper report."—M.]

† On October 14, 1797.—M.

occasion, and had been, in other particulars, a person of infamous conduct and reputation; but above all, the circumstances under which the verdict was found against Orr pointed him out, if not as an object constitutionally entitled to mercy, at least as one to whom it would have been an act of salutary mildness to have extended it. The jury had continued from seven o'clock in the evening till six on the following morning considering their verdict; in the interval, spirituous liquor had been introduced into the jury-room, and intimidation used to such as hesitated to concur with the majority. To these latter facts two of the jury made a solemn affidavit in open court, before the judge who tried the cause.

Upon these proceedings, a very severe letter of remonstrance to the Viceroy appeared in the "Press" newspaper, of which Mr. Finnerty was the publisher; and the letter being deemed a libel, the publisher was brought to immediate trial.

Mr. Curran's address to the jury in this case must be considered, if not the finest, at least the most surprising specimen of his oratorical powers. He had had no time for preparation; it was not till a few minutes before the cause commenced that his brief was handed to him. During the progress of the trial he had occasion to speak at unusual length to questions of law that arose upon the evidence; so that his speech to the jury could necessarily be no other than a sudden extemporaneous exertion: and it was, perhaps, a secret and not unjustifiable feeling of pride at having so acquitted himself upon such an emergency that inclined his own mind to prefer this to any of his other efforts.

The following is his description of the scenes which attended and followed the trial of William Orr:

"Let me beg of you for a moment to suppose that any one of you had been the writer of this strong and severe animadversion upon the Lord Lieutenant, and that you had been the witness of that lamentable and never-to-be-forgotten catastrophe; let me suppose that you had known the charge upon which Mr. Orr was apprehended—the charge of objuring that bigotry which had torn and disgraced his country, of pledging himself to restore the people to their place in the Constitution, and of binding himself never to be the betrayer of his fellow-laborers in that enterprise; that you had seen him upon that charge torn from his industry and confined in a gaol; that, through the slow and lingering progress of twelve tedious months, you had seen him confined in a dungeon, shut out from the common use of air and of his own limbs; that, day after day, you had marked the unhappy captive, cheered by no sound but the cries of his family or the clanking of his chains; that you had seen him at last brought to his trial; that you had seen the vile and perjured informer deposing against his life; that you had seen the drunken, and worn out, and terrified jury give in a verdict of death; that you had seen the same jury, when their returning sobriety had brought back their reason, prostrate themselves before the humanity of the Bench, and pray that the mercy of the Crown might save their characters from the reproach of an involuntary crime, their consciences from the torture of eternal self-condemnation, and their souls from the indelible stain of innocent blood. Let me suppose that you had seen the respite given, and the contrite and honest recommendation transmitted to that seat where mercy was presumed to dwell: that new and before unheard-of crimes are discovered against the informer; that the royal mercy seems to relent; that a new respite is sent to the prisoner; that time is taken to see 'whether mercy could be extended or not;' that after that period of lingering deliberation had passed, a third respite is transmitted; that the unhappy captive himself feels the cheering hope of being restored to a family that he had adored, to a character that he had never stained, and to a country that he had ever loved; that you had seen his wife and his children upon their knees, giving those tears to gratitude which their locked and frozen hearts had refused to anguish and despair, and imploring the blessings of eternal Providence upon his head who had graciously spared the father and restored him to his children:

> 'Alas!
> Nor wife, nor children, no more shall he behold,
> Nor friends, nor sacred home!'

"Often did the weary dove return to the window of his little ark; but the olive leaf was to him no sign that the waters had subsided. No seraph Mercy unbars his dungeon, and leads him forth to light and life; but the minister of Death hurries him to the scene of suffering and of shame: where, unmoved by the hostile array of artillery and armed men collected together to secure or to insult, or to disturb him, he dies with a solemn declaration of his innocence, and utters his last breath in a prayer for the liberty of his country.

"Let me now ask you, if any of you had addressed the public ear upon so foul and monstrous a subject, in what language would you have conveyed the feelings of horror and indignation? Would you have stooped to the meanness of qualified complaint? Would you have checked your feelings to search for courtly and gaudy language? Would you have been mean enough—but I entreat your pardon: I have already told you I do not think meanly of you. Had I thought so meanly of you, I could not suffer my mind to commune with you as it has done: had I thought you that base and servile instrument, attuned by hope and fear into discord and falsehood, from whose vulgar string no groan of suffering could vibrate, no voice of integrity or honour could speak, let me honestly tell you I should have scorned to fling my hand across it; I should have left it to a fitter minstrel; if I do not, therefore, grossly err in my opinion of you, you could invent no language upon such a subject as this, that must not lag behind the rapidity of your feelings, and that must not disgrace those feelings if it attempted to describe them."

The distracted condition of Ireland at this unfortunate period, may be collected from the following description. To the general reader of Mr. Curran's speeches, the frequent recurrence of so painful a theme must diminish their attractions; but it was too intimately connected with his subjects to be omitted; and as has been previously remarked, the scenes which he daily witnessed had so sensible an influence upon the style of his addresses to juries, that some advertence to them here becomes indispensable.

"The learned counsel has asserted that the paper which he prosecutes is only part of a system formed to misrepresent the state of Ireland and the conduct of its government. Do you not therefore discover that his object is to procure a verdict to sanction the parliaments of both countries in refusing an inquiry into your grievances? Let me ask you then, are you prepared to say, upon your oath, that those measures of coercion which are daily practised, are absolutely necessary, and ought to be continued? It is not upon Finnerty you are sitting in judgment; but you are sitting in judgment upon the lives and liberties of the inhabitants of more than half of Ireland. You are to say that it is a foul proceeding to condemn the Government of Ireland; that is a foul act, founded in foul motives, and originating in falsehood and sedition; that it is an attack upon a government under which the people are prosperous and happy; that justice is administered with mercy; that the statements made in Great Britain are false—are the effusions of party or of discontent; that all is mildness and tranquillity; that there are no burnings—no transportations; that you never travel by the light of conflagrations; that the jails are not crowded month after month, from which prisoners are taken out, not for trial, but for embarkation! These are the questions upon which, I say, you must virtually decide. It is vain that the counsel for the Crown may tell you that I am misrepresenting the case; that I am endeavouring to raise false fears, and to take advantage of your passions; that the question is, whether this paper be a libel or not, and that the circumstances of the country have nothing to do with it. Such assertions must be in vain; the statement of the counsel for the Crown has forced the introduction of those important topics; and I appeal to your own hearts whether the country is misrepresented, and whether the Government is misrepresented. I tell you therefore, gentlemen of the jury, it is not with respect to Mr. Orr or Mr. Finnerty that your verdict is now sought; you are called upon, on your oaths, to say that the Government is wise and merciful; the people prosperous and happy; that military law ought to be continued; that the Constitution could not with safety be restored to Ireland; and that the statements of a contrary import by your advocates in either country are libellous and false. I tell you, these are the questions; and I ask you, if you can have the front to give the expected answer in the face of a community who know the country as well as you do. Let me ask you how you could reconcile with such a verdict, the gaols, the tenders, the gibbets, the conflagrations, the murders, the proclamations, that we hear of every day in the streets, and see every day in the country? What are the processions of the learned counsel himself, circuit after circuit? Merciful God! what is the state of Ireland, and where shall you find the wretched inhabitant of this land? You may find him perhaps in gaol, the only place of security, I had almost said of ordinary habitation! If you do not find him there, you may see him flying with his family from the flames of his own dwelling—lighted to his dungeon by the conflagration of his hovel; or you may find his bones bleaching on the green fields of his country; or you may find him tossing on the surface of the ocean, and mingling his groans with those tempests, less savage than his prosecutors, that drift him to a returnless distance from his family and his home, without charge, or trial or sentence. Is this a foul misrepresentation? Or can you, with these facts ringing in your ears, and staring in your face, say, upon your oaths, they do not exist? You are called upon, in defiance of shame, of truth, of honour, to deny the sufferings under which you groan, and to flatter the prosecution that tramples you under foot. Gentlemen, I am not accustomed to speak of circumstances of this kind, and though familiarized as I have been to them, when I come to speak of them, my power fails me, my voice dies within me; I am not able to call upon you: it is now I ought to have strength; it is now I ought to have energy and voice, but I have none; I am like the unfortunate state of the country, perhaps like you. This is the time in which I ought to speak, if I can, or be dumb forever; in which, if you do not speak as *you* ought—*you* ought to be dumb forever."

When Mr. Curran came to comment upon that part of the publication under trial, which stated that informers were brought forward by the hopes of remuneration—"Is that," said he, "a foul assertion? or will you, upon your oaths, say to the sister country, that there are no such abominable instruments of destruction as informers used in the state prosecutions in Ireland? Let me honestly ask you, what do you feel when in my hearing—when, in the face of this audience, you are called upon to give a verdict that every man of us, and every man of you, know, by the testimony of your own eyes, to be utterly and absolutely false? I speak not now of the public proclamations for informers with a promise of secrecy and extravagant reward. I speak not of those unfortunate wretches, who have been so often transferred from the table to the dock, and from the dock to the pillory—I speak of what your own eyes have seen, day after day, during the course of this commission, while you attended this court—the number of horrid miscreants who acknowledged, upon their oaths, that they had come from the seat of government—from the very chambers of the Castle (where they had been worked upon, by the fear of death and the hopes of compensation, to give evidence against their fellows) that the mild, the wholesome, and merciful councils of this Government are holden over those catacombs of living death, where the wretch, that is burried a *man*, lies till his heart has time to fester and dissolve, and is then dug up a *witness*. Is this a picture created by an hag-ridden fancy, or is it fact? Have you not seen hin, after his resurrection from that tomb, make his appearance upon your table, the living image of life and death, and the supreme arbiter of both? Have you not marked, when he entered, how the stormy wave of the multitude retired at his approach? Have you not seen how the human heart bowed to the awful supremacy of his power, in the undissembled homage of deferential horror? How his glance, like the lightning of Heaven, seemed to rive the body of the accused, and mark it for the grave, while his voice warned the devoted wretch of woe and death—a death which no innocence can escape, no art elude, no force resist, no antidote prevent? There was an antidote—a juror's oath! But even that adamantine chain, which bound the integrity of man to the throne of eternal justice, is solved and molten in the breath which issues from the mouth of the informer. Con science swings from her moorings; the appalled and affrighted juror speaks what his soul abhors, and consults his own safety in the surrender of the victim—

——et quæ sibi quisque timebat
Unius in miseri exitium conversa tulere.

Informers are worshipped in the temple of justice, even as the devil has been worshipped by Pagans and savages—even so in this wicked country, is the informer an object of judicial idolatry—even so is he soothed by the music of human groans—even sc is he placated and incensed by the fumes and by the blood of human sacrifices."

It is some relief to turn from these descriptions (the truth of which any who may doubt it, will find authenticated by the historian), to the attestation which the advocate bore (and which he was always ready to bear) to the honourable and dignified demeanour of a presiding judge.* "You are upon a great forward

* The Hon. William Downes.—C. [Downes was a dull and prosy man of great bulk, with an immense face terminating in a great double chin, like a gigantic dewlap,—Curran said.

ground, with the people at your back, and the Government in your front. You have neither the disadvantages nor the excuses of juries a century ago. No, thank God! never was there a stronger characteristic distinction between those times, upon which no man can reflect without horror, and the present. You have seen this trial conducted with mildness and patience by the court. We have now no Jefferies, with scurvy and vulgar conceits, to browbeat the prisoner and perplex his counsel. Such has been the improvement of manners, and so calm the confidence of integrity, that during the defence of accused persons, the judges sit quietly, and show themselves worthy of their situation, by bearing, with a mild and merciful patience, the little extravagancies of the bar, as you should bear with the little extravagancies of the press. Let me then turn your eyes to that pattern of mildness in the bench. The press is your advocate; bear with its excess, bear with everything but its bad intention. If it comes as a villanous slanderer, treat it as such; but if it endeavour to to raise the honour and glory of your country, remember that you reduce its power to a nonentity, if you stop its animadversions upon public measures. You should not check the efforts of genius, nor damp the ardour of patriotism. In vain will you desire the bird to soar, if you meanly or madly steal from it its plumage. Beware lest, under the pretence of bearing down the licentiousness of the press, you extinguish it altogether. Beware how you rival the venal ferocity of those miscreants, who rob a printer of the means of bread, and claim from deluded royalty the reward of integrity and allegiance."*

"The most appropriate reply I ever made in my life was to Bushe. It is rather long and somewhat laboured, but if you will bear with me, I will repeat it all in less than half an hour, by a stop watch. 'My Lord chief justice Downes,' says Bushe to me one day, with that large plausible eye, glittering in that kind of light which reveals to a shrewd observer that he is quite sure *he has you*, 'my Lord chief justice Downes is beyond all comparison, the wittiest companion I have ever known or heard of.' I looked into B.'s eye, and said *hum! It required all his own oil to keep smooth the surface of that face.*"—M.

* The jury found a verdict against the traverser. The above extracts are taken from

TRIAL OF PATRICK FINNEY.

Mr. Curran's defence of Patrick Finney (who was brought to trial on January 16th, 1798, on a charge of high treason), if not the most eloquent, was at least the most successful of his efforts at the bar. This may be also considered as the most important cause that he ever conducted, as far as the number of his clients could render it so; for in addition to the prisoner at the bar, he was virtually defending fifteen others, against whom there existed the same charge, and the same proof, and whose fates would have immediately followed had the evidence against Finney prevailed. The principal witness for the Crown in this case was an informer, named James O'Brien, a person whom his testimony upon this trial, and his subsequent crimes, have rendered notorious in Ireland. The infamy of this man's previous life and morals, and improbability and inconsistencies of his story, were so satisfactorily proved to the jury, that, making an effort of firmness and humanity very unusual in those days, they acquitted Finney; and, at the next sitting of the court, the fifteen other prisoners were in consequence discharged from their indictments. [On taking the oath of allegiance, and filing recognizances for good behaviour.]

In speaking of Finney's acquittal, it would be an act of injustice to attribute it to the ability of Mr. Curran alone. He was assisted, as he was upon so many other occasions of emergency, by Mr. M'Nally,* a gentleman in whom the client has always found a

a fuller report of Mr. Curran's speech upon this occasion than that which is to be found in the published collection.—C.

[Finnerty was sentenced to two years' imprisonment, to stand in the pillory for an hour, to pay a fine of £20, and to give security for his future good behaviour. He finally became a member of the newspaper press in London, and suffered imprisonment, in that capacity, for the publication of seditious libels.]—M.

* Leonard M'Nally, Esq., for many years an eminent Irish barrister, and long since known to the English public as the author of Robin Hood, and other successful dramatic pieces, the productions of his earlier days. Among many endearing traits in this gentleman's private character, his devoted attachment to Mr. Curran's person and fame, and, since his death, to the interests of his memory, has been conspicuous. The writer of this cannot advert to the ardour and tenderness with which he cherishes the latter, without emotions of the most lively and respectful gratitude. To Mr. M'Nally he has to express

zealous, intrepid advocate, and in whom Mr. Curran, from his youth to his latest hour, possessed a most affectionate, unshaken, and disinterested friend. An instance of Mr. Curran's confidence in the talents of his colleague occurred upon this trial; the circumstance, too, may not be without interest, as an example of the accidents which influence the most important questions.

The only mode of saving their client was by impeaching the credit of O'Brien. It appeared in their instructions that they had some, though not unexceptionable, evidence of his having extorted money, by assuming the character of a revenue officer.

Some extracts from the cross-examination of this witness shall be inserted as too singular, on many accounts, to be omitted. It should be observed that Mr. Curran, upon this occasion, departed in some measure from his ordinary method of confounding the perjurer. Instead of resorting to menace or ridicule, he began by affecting a tone of respect, and even submission; and, by thus encouraging O'Brien's insolence, threw him off his guard, and led him on more completely to develope his own character to the jury:—

James O'Brien cross-examined by Mr. Curran

Q. Pray, Mr. O'Brien, whence came you?
A. Speak in a way I will understand you.
Q. Do you not understand me?
A. Whence? I am here. Do you mean the place I came from?
Q. By your oath, do you not understand it?

many obligations for the zeal with which he has assisted in procuring and supplying materials for the present work. The introduction of these private feelings is not entirely out of place—it can never be out of place to record an example of stedfastness in friendship. For three and forty years Mr. M'Nally was the friend of the subject of these pages; and during that long period, uninfluenced by any obligation, more than once, at his own personal risk in repelling the public calamities which Mr. Curran's political conduct had provoked, he performed the duties of the relation with the most uncompromising and romantic fidelity. To state this is a debt of justice to the dead: the survivor has an ampler reward than any passing tribute of this sort can confer, in the recollection that during their long intercourse not even an unkind look ever passed between them.—C.

Leonard M'Nally died on the 15th of February, 1820.—M.

A. I partly *censure* it now.

Q. Now that you partly *censure* the question, answer it. Where did you come from?

A. From the Castle.

Q. Do you live there?

A. I do while I am there.

Q. You are welcome, sir, to practice your wit upon me. Where did you live before you came to Dublin?

A. In the Queen's county.

Q. What way of life were you engaged in before you came to Dublin?

A. I had a farm of land which my father left me; and I let it, and afterwards sold it, and came to Dublin to follow business I learned before my father's death. I served four years to Mr. Latouche of Marley.

Q. To what business?

A. A gardener.

Q. Were you an excise officer?

A. No.

Q. Nor ever acted as one?

A. I don't doubt but I may have gone of messages for one

Q. Who was that?

A. A man of the name of Fitzpatrick.

Q. He is an excise officer?

A. So I understand.

Q. What messages did you go for him?

A. For money when he was lying on a sick bed.

Q. To whom?

A. To several of the people in his walk.

Q. But you never pretended to be an officer yourself?

A. As I have been walking with him, and had clean clothes on me, he might have said to the persons he met that I was an excise officer.

Q. But did you never pretend to be an officer?

A. I never did pretend to be an officer.

Q. Did you ever pass yourself for a revenue officer?

A. I answered that before.

Q. I do not want to give you any unnecessary trouble, sir; treat me with the same respect I shall treat you. I ask you again, did you ever pass yourself for a revenue officer?

A. Never, barring when I was in drink, and the like.

Q. Then, when you have been drunk, you have passed as a revenue officer?

A. I do not know what I have done when I was drunk.

Q. Did you at any time, drunk or sober, pass yourself as a revenue officer?

A. Never, when sober.

Q. Did you, drunk or sober?

A. I cannot say what I did when I was drunk.

Q. Can you form a belief—I ask you upon your oath—you are upon a solemn occasion—Did you pass yourself for a revenue officer?

A. I cannot say what happened to me when I was drunk.

Q. What! Do you say you might have done it when you were drunk?

A. I cannot recollect what passed in my drink.

Q. Are you in the habit of being drunk?

A. Not now; but some time back I was.

Q. Very fond of drink?

A. Very fond of drink.

Q. Do you remember to whom you passed yourself for a revenue officer?

A. I do not.

Q. Do you know the man who keeps the Red Cow, of the name of Cavanagh?

A. Where does he live?

Q. Do you not know yourself?

A. There is one Red Cow above the Fox and Geese.

Q. Did you ever pass yourself as a revenue officer there?

A. I never was there but with Fitzpatrick; and one day there had been a scuffle, and he abused Fitzpatrick and threatened him; I drank some whiskey there, and paid for it, and went to Fitzpatrick and told him, and I summoned Cavanagh.

Q. For selling spirits without licence?

A. I did, and compromised the business.

Q. By taking money and not prosecuting him?

A. Yes.

Q. Did you put money in your own pocket by that?

A. I did.

Q. But you swear you never passed yourself for a revenue officer?

A. Barring when I was drunk.

Q. Were you drunk when you summoned Cavanagh?

A. No.

Q. When you did not prosecute him?

A. No.

Q. When you put his money into your pocket?

A. No.

Q. Do you know a man of the name of Patrick Lamb?

A. I do not; but if you brighten my memory, I may recollect.

Q. Did you ever tell any man you were a supernumerary, and that your walk was Rathfarnham and Tallaght?

A. I never did, except when I was drunk; but I never did anything but what was honest when I was sober.

Q. Do you believe you did say it?

A. I do not know what I might have said when I was drunk. You know when a man is walking with an exciseman, he gets a glass at every house.

Mr. Curran.—I know no such thing, never having walked with an exciseman.

Witness.—Then, you may know it.

Q. Do you know any man passing by the name, or called Patrick Lamb?

A. Not that I recollect, *upon my word.*

Q. Upon your oath?

A. I do not recollect: I mean to tell everything against myself as against any other.

Q. Do you know a person of the name of Margaret Moore?

A. Where does she live? Is she married?

Q. She lives near Stradbally. Do you know her?

A. I know her well—I thought it might be another. I was courting a woman of that name before my marriage.

Q. Did you come to Dublin before her or after?

A. I was in Dublin before I knew her.

Q. Did you get a decree against her?

A. I did get a summons for money she owed me.

Q. Were you taken to the Court of Conscience by her?

A. No. (Contradicted by the evidence on the defence.)

* * * * * *

Q. When you met Hyland, were you an United Irishman?

A. Always united to every honest man.

Q. Were you an United Irishman?

A. Never sworn.

Q. Were you in any manner an United Irishman before that day?

A. Never sworn in before that day.

Q. Were you in any manner?

A. Don't I tell you that I was united to every honest man?

Q. Do you believe you are answering my question?

A. I do.

Q. Were you ever in any society of United Irishmen before that day?

A. I do not at all know but I may, but without my knowledge: they might be in the next box to me, or in the end of the seat with me, and I not know them.

Q. Were you ever in a society of United Irishmen but that day?

A. I was since.

Q. Were you ever of their meetings, or did you know anything of their business before that day?

A. No; but I have heard of the Defenders' business.

Q. Were you of their society?

A. No; but when they came to my father's house, I went to Admiral Cosby's and kept guard there, and threatened to shoot any of them that would come; one Connelly told me I was to be murdered for this expression.

Q. Hyland made signs to you in the street?

A. He did.

Q. Did you answer them?

A. No.

Q. Why did you not?

A. Because I did not know how.

Q. Then, is your evidence this—that you went into the house in order to save your life?

A. I was told that I might lose my life before I went half a street, if I did not.

Q. Then, it was from the fear of being murdered before you should go half a street, that you went in to be an United Irishman?

A. You have often heard of men being murdered in the business.

Q. Do you believe that?

A. I do: it is common through the country; I have read the proclamations upon it, and you may have done so too.

Q. How soon, after you were sworn, did you see the magistrate?

A. I was sworn upon the 25th, and upon the 28th I was brought to Lord Portarlington; and in the interval of the two days, Hyland was with me and dined with me.

Q. Why did you not gc the next day?

A. Because I did not get clear of them, and they might murder me.

Q. Where did you sleep the first night after?

A. At my own place. I was very full—very drunk.

Q. Did either of them sleep there?

A. No.

Q. Where did you live?

A. In Keven street, among some friends good to the same cause.

Q. Where did you see Hyland the next day?

A. He came to me next morning before I was out of bed, and stayed all day, and dined: we drank full in the evening.

Q. What became of you the next day?

A. Hyland came early again, and stayed all day. I was after getting two guineas from my brother. I was determined to see it out—to know their conspiracies after I was sworn.

Q. Then, you meant to give evidence?

A. I never went to a meeting that I did not give an account of it.

* * * * * *

Q. Do you know Charles Clarke, of Blue Bell?

A. I have heard of such a man.

Q. You do not know him?

A. I do: I do not mean to tell a lie.

Q. You did not know him at first?

A. There are many men of the name of Clarke; I did not know but it might be some other. It did not immediately come into my memory.

Q. You thought it might be some other Clarke?

A. There is a Clarke came in to me yesterday.

Q. Did you ever get money from Clarke, of Blue Bell, as an excise officer?

A. I got 3*s.* 3*d.* from him not to tell Fitzpatrick: he did not know me, and I bought spirits there; and seeing me walk with an exciseman, he was afraid I would tell of him, and he gave me 3*s.* 3*d.*

Q. And you put it in your pocket?

A. To be sure.

*   *   *   *   *   *

Q. Did you pass yourself as a revenue officer upon him?

A. No.

Q. You swear that?

A. I do.

Q. You know a man of the name of Edward Purcell?

A. That is the man that led me into everything. He has figured among United Irishmen. He got about £40 of their money, and went off. He has been wrote to several times.

Q. How came you to know him?

A. Through the friendship of Fitzpatrick. He had Fitzpatrick's wife, as a body might say, having another man's wife.

Q. He made you acquainted?

A. I saw him there, and Fitzpatrick well contented.

Q. Did you ever give him a recipe?

A. I did.

Q. Was it for money?

A. No.

Q. What was it?

A. It was partly an order, where Hyland, he, and I, hoped to be together. It was a pass-word I gave him to go to Hyland to buy light gold that I knew was going to the country.

Q. Did you ever give him any other recipe?

A. I do not know but I might: we had many dealings.

Q. Had you many dealings in recipes?

A. In recipes?

Q. I mean recipes to do a thing; as, to make a pudding, &c. Did you give him recipes of that nature?

A. I do not know but I might give him recipes to do a great number of things.

Q. To do a great number of things? What are they?

A. Tell me the smallest hint, and I will tell the truth.

Q. Upon that engagement, I will tell you. Did you ever give him a recipe to turn silver into gold, or copper into silver?

A. Yes; for turning copper into silver.

Q. You have kept your word?

A. I said I would tell everything against myself.

Q. Do you consider that against yourself?

A. I tell you the truth: I gave him a recipe for making copper money like silver money.

Q. What did you give it him for? Did he make use of it? Was it to protect his copper from being changed that you did it?

A. He was very officious to make things in a light easy way, without much trouble, to make his bread light: but I did it more in fun than profit.

Q. You did not care how much coin he made by it?

A. I did not care how much coin he made by it: he might put it upon the market cross.

Q. Do you say you do not care how many copper shillings he made?

A. I did not care whether he made use of it or not.

Q. Upon your solemn oath, you say that you did not care how many base shillings he made in consequence of the recipe you gave him?

A. I did not care how many he told of it, or what he did with it.

Q. Had you never seen it tried?

A. No, I never saw the recipe I gave him tried; but I saw others tried.

Q. For making copper look like silver?

A. To be sure.

Q. Do you recollect whether you gave him half-a-crown, upon which that recipe was tried?

A. I never saw it tried; but I gave him a bad half-crown. I did not give it him in payment: I did it more to humbug him than anything else.

* * * * * *

Q. Do you know Mr. Roberts?

A. What Mr. Roberts?

Q. Mr. Arthur Roberts of Stradbally?

A. I do.

Q. Did you ever talk to any person about his giving a character of you?

A. He could not give a bad character of me.

Q. Did you ever tell any person about his giving you a character?

A. I say now, in the hearing of the court and jury, that I heard of his being summoned against me; and, unless he would forswear himself, he could not give me a bad character.

Q. Did you ever say you would do anything against him?

A. I said I would settle him; but do you know how? There was a matter about an auction that I would tell of him.

Q. Had you a weapon in your hand at the time?

A. I believe I had a sword.

Q. And a pistol?

A. Yes.

Q. And you had them in your hand at the time you made the declaration?

A. I knew he was a government man; and I would not do any thing to him in the way of assassination.

While Mr. Curran was cross-examining O'Brien upon the point of his assuming the character of a revenue officer, the prisoner's agent accidentally heard, from some of the by-standers, that there was a man residing at the distance of a few miles from Dublin, whose testimony would place beyond a doubt that O'Brien was perjuring himself in the answers that he returned. A chaise was immediately despatched, to bring up this person; and, in the interval, it was proposed by Mr. Curran, that he, who, as senior, was to have commenced the prisoner's defence, should reserve himself for the speech to evidence, and that his colleague should state the case, and *continue speaking as long as he could find a syllable to say*, so as to give time to the chaise to return before the trial should be over. The latter, in whose character there was as little of mental as of personal timidity, accepted the proposal without hesitation, and for once belying the maxim that "brevity is the soul of wit," produced an oration so skilfully voluminous, that, by the time it was concluded, which was not until his physical strength was utterly exhausted, the evening was so far advanced, that the Court readily consented to a temporary adjournment, for the purpose of refreshment; and before it resumed its sitting, the material witness for the prisoner had arrived.*

For this important service rendered to their cause, Mr. Curran, in his address to the jury, paid his colleague a tribute, to which, as a man and an advocate, he was so well entitled. When, in the commencement of his speech, he alluded to the statement of his friend, and expressed "his reluctance to repeat any part of it, for fear of weakening it," he turned round to him, threw his arm affectionately over his shoulder, and, with that pathetic fervour of accent so peculiarly his own, addressed him thus: "My old and excellent friend, I have long known and respected the honesty of your heart, but never, until this occasion, was I acquainted with the extent of your abilities. I am not in the habit of paying compliments where they are undeserved." Tears fell from Mr. Curran as he hung over his friend, and pronounced these few and simple words; and, however unimposing they may appear in the repetition, it certainly was not the part of his defence of Finnerty that touched the jury the least.

His speech in this case (particularly in the imperfect report of it that has appeared) does not contain many passages calculated to delight in the closet. It is chiefly occupied in developing the atrocities of the detestable O'Brien; and this object he accom-

* Thomas Davis, who edited the last collection of Curran's speeches, possessed Leonard McNally's own copy (a gift from Curran himself) and left a memorandum to the effect that he spoke for three hours and a half.—M.

plished with signal success. That wretch, who had, in the early part of the trial, comported himself with so much triumphant insolence, was for a moment appalled by Mr. Curran's description of his villanies, and by the indignant fury of his glances. He was observed palpably shrinking before the latter, and taking shelter in the crowd which thronged the Court. The advocate did not fail to take advantage of such a circumstance. "What was the evidence of the innocent, unlettered, poor farmer Cavanagh; pursuing the even tenor of his way in the paths of honest industry, he is in the act of fulfilling the decree of his Maker—he is earning his bread by the sweat of his brow, when this villain, less pure than the arch-fiend who brought this sentence of laborious action on mankind, enters the habitation of peace and honest industry; and, not content with dipping his tongue in perjury, robs the poor man of two guineas. Where is O'Brien now?—Do you wonder that he is afraid of my eye?—that he has buried himself in the crowd?—that he crept under the shade of the multitude when this witness would have disentangled his evidence? Do you not feel that he was appalled with horror, by that more piercing and penetrating eye that looks upon him, and upon me, and upon us all? At this moment even the bold and daring villany of O'Brien stood abashed; he saw the eye of Heaven in that of an innocent and injured man; perhaps the feeling was consummated by a glance from the dock—his heart bore testimony to his guilt, and he fled for the same. Do you know him, gentlemen of the jury?—Are you acquainted with James O'Brien? If you are, let him come forward from the crowd where he has hid himself, and claim you by a look."

The religious character of Mr. Curran's addresses to juries, during these convulsed times, has been already adverted to; of this the conclusion of his defence of Finney affords a striking example:—

"This is the great experiment of the informers of Ireland, to ascertain how far they can carry on a traffic in human blood.

This cannibal informer, this demon, O'Brien, greedy after human gore, has fifteen other victims in reserve, if from your verdict he receives the unhappy man at the bar—fifteen more of your fellow-citizens are now in gaol, depending on the fate of the unfortunate prisoner, and on the same blasted and perjured evidence of O'Brien. Be you then their saviours; let your verdict snatch them from his ravening maw, and interpose between yourselves and endless remorse. The character of the prisoner has been given. Am I not warranted in saying that I am now defending an innocent fellow-subject on the grounds of eternal justice and immutable law? and on that eternal law I do call upon you to acquit my client. I call upon you for your justice! Great is the reward and sweet the recollection in the hour of trial, and in the day of dissolution, when the casualties of life are pressing close upon the heart, or when in the agonies of death you look back to the justifiable and honourable transactions of your life. At the awful foot of eternal justice, I do therefore invite you to acquit my client; and may God of his infinite mercy grant you a more lasting reward than that perishable crown we read of, which the ancients placed on the brow of him who saved in battle the life of a fellow-citizen? In the name of public justice I do implore you to interpose between the perjurer and his intended victim; and if ever you are assailed by the hand of the informer, may you find an all-powerful refuge in the example which, as jurors, you shall set this day to those that might be called to pass upon your lives, that of repelling, at the human tribunal, the intended effects of hireling perjury and premeditated murder. And if it should be the fate of any of you to count the tedious moments of captivity, in sorrow and pain, pining in the damps and gloom of a dungeon, while the wicked one is going about at large, seeking whom he may devour, recollect that there is another more awful tribunal than any upon earth, which we must all approach, and before which the best of us will have occasion to look back to what little good we may have done on this side the grave. In that awful trial—oh! may your verdict this day assure your hopes, and give you strength and consolation, in the presence of an adjudging God. Earnestly do I pray that the author of eternal justice may record the innocent deed you shall have done, and give to you the full benefit of your claims to an eternal reward, a requital in mercy upon your souls."

The fate of O'Brien is almost a necessary sequel to the trial of Finney. Mr. Curran, whom long observation in the exercise of his profession had familiarized to every gradation of atrocity, declared at the time, that, much as he had seen of crime, he had never met with such intense, unmitigated villany, as the conduct and countenance of this ruffian manifested; and he did not hesitate to predict, that some act of guilt would shorten his career. Two years after, O'Brien was tried for murder,* and by a kind of retributive justice, the two counsel who had rescued Finney were appointed to conduct the prosecution.

Mr. Curran's speech in O'Brien's case is not distinguished by much eloquence; but it possesses one quality, infinitely more honourable to him than any display of talent could have been. It is full of moderation, resembling as much the charge of a judge as the statement of a prosecutor, and contains no vindictive allusion to the previous crimes of the prisoner. This the following extract will show:

"The present trial is considered abroad as of some expectation. I am very well aware that when a judicial inquiry becomes the topic of public and general conversation, every conversation is in itself a little trial of the fact. The voice of public fame, the falsest witness that ever was sworn or unsworn, is always ready to bear testimony to the prejudice of an individual. The mind becomes heated, and it can scarcely be expected, even in a jury-box,

* An assemblage of persons of the lower orders having taken place in the suburbs of Dublin, for the purpose of recreation, the officers of the police, accompanied by O'Brien, proceeded to disperse them. The multitude fled, and in the pursuit one of them (named Hoey) was murdered by O'Brien.—C.

to find it cool, and reflecting, and uninterested. There are two tribunals to which every man must be amenable; the one a municipal tribunal, the other the great, and general, and despotic tribunal of public reputation. If the jury have any reason to suppose that any man who comes before them has been already tried by public fame, and condemned, I beg to remind them of the solemn duty that justice imposes on them; to turn their eyes away from the recollection that any sentence of that sort of condemnation has been pronounced by the voice of public reputation; and if they think that his character has sunk under such a sentence, I remind the jury, that the infamy of such a condemnation is enough without their taking it into their consideration. It is the duty of the jury to leave the decrees of that court to be executed by its own authority, for they have no right to pass sentence of condemnation upon any man because that ill-judging court may have passed sentence on his character. They ought to recollect, that the evidence given before that court was unsworn, and therefore they are bound to consider the evidence before them naked and simple, as if they had never heard the name of the man they are to try, and the sentence of condemnation that public fame had pronounced upon his character. There is but one point of view in which public character ought to be taken; that is where there is doubt. In such a case general good character ought to have great weight, and go towards the acquittal of the accused; but should it so happen that general bad character should be thrown into the scale, it ought not to have one twentieth part the weight that good character should have.

"The jury, I am satisfied, will deliberately and cautiously weigh the evidence to be produced; they must be perfectly satisfied in their minds of the guilt of the prisoner. They must feel an irresistible and coercive force acting on them, from the weight of the evidence, before, by their verdict, they pronounce that melancholy sentence which would remove a murderer from the face of the earth."

O'Brien was convicted and executed. The populace of most countries are too disposed to regard the death of the greatest criminals with sympathy and regret; but so predominant were the feelings of terror and detestation which O'Brien's character had excited, that his execution was accompanied by shouts of the most unusual and horrid exultation.

Before dismissing the subject of this wretched man, one observation should be made, of which the omission might seem to imply a reproach upon the conduct of the prosecutors in Finney's case. It may occur, that the information of such a person should not have gained a moment's attention, still less have endangered the lives of so many subjects. It is, therefore, only just to add, that the real character of O'Brien was unknown to the officers of the Crown, until it became developed in the progress of the trial. The Attorney-General, who conducted that prosecution, was the late Lord Kilwarden, a man the most reverse of sanguinary, and who, in those violent times, was conspicuous for correcting the sternness of his official duties by the tenderness of his own amiable nature. His expiring sentiments had been the maxim of his life: "Let no man perish but by the just sentence of the law."

CHAPTER X.

Rebellion of 1798—Its causes—Unpopular system of Government—Influence of the French Revolution—Increased intelligence in Ireland—Reform Societies—United Irishmen—Their views and proceedings—Apply for aid to France—Anecdote of Theobald Wolfe Tone—Numbers of the United Irishmen—Condition of the peasantry and conduct of the aristocracy—Measures of the Government—Public alarm—General insurrection.

THE order of this work has now brought us to the year 1798—*the year* '98!—a sound that is still so full of terrible associations to every Irishman's imagination. During the agitated period which followed the transactions of 1782, Ireland had seen the newly-acquired spirit of her people, inflamed by disappointment, by suffering, and by ignorance, discharging itself in bursts of individual or local turbulence, which were not much felt beyond the particular persons, or the immediate spot. But the hour, of which these were the prophetic signs, and of which so many warning and unheeded voices foretold the approach, at length arrived, bringing with it scenes of civil strife that struck dismay into every fibre of the community, sending thousands to the grave, thousands into exile, and involving many a virtuous and respected family in calamity and shame.

In adverting to the events of this disastrous era, it would be an easy task to recapitulate its horrors, or, according to the once popular method, to rail at the memory of its victims; but it is time for invective and resentment to cease; or, if such a feeling will irresistibly intrude, it is time at least to control and suppress it. Fifty years have now passed over the heads or the graves of the parties to that melancholy conflict, and their children may now see prospects of prosperity opening upon their country, not perhaps of the kind, or to the extent to which in her more ambitious days she looked, but assuredly a more rational description than could have been attained by violence; and such as, when realized, as they promise soon to be, will compensate for past reverses, or at all events console. At such a moment, in approaching this fatal year, we may dismiss every sentiment of personal asperity, or posthumous reproach; without wishing to disturb the remorse of those upon either side who may be repenting, or to revive the anguish of the many that have suffered, we may now contemplate it as the period of an awful historical event; and allude to the mutual passions and mistakes of those who acted or perished in it, with the forbearance that should not be refused to the unfortunate and the dead.

It has been seen, in the preceding pages, that the system by which Ireland was governed had excited general dissatisfaction, and that, in the year 1789, several of the most able and distinguished persons in the Irish Parliament formed themselves into a body, for the avowed design of opposing the measures of the Administration, and of conferring upon their country, if their exertions could enable them, all the practical benefits of a free constitution. While they were scarcely yet engaged in this arduous struggle, the French Revolution burst upon the world—not, as it has since been witnessed, presenting images of blood and disorder, but coming as the messenger of harmony and freedom to the afflicted nations. This character of peace and innocence it did not long retain, or was not allowed to retain; but, in the progress of its resistless career, its crimes seemed for a while almost justified by the grandeur of their results, and by the imposing principles which they were committed to establish. It soon appeared how popular talent, combined with popular force, could level all the old decrepit opinions against which they had confederated, and Europe was fixed with mingled wonder and dismay upon the awful spectacle of a self-emancipated people seated upon the throne, from which they had hurled the descendant of their former idols as an hereditary usurper.

The effects of this great event, and of the doctrines by which it was defended, were immense. Every day some long-respected maxim was tried and condemned, and a treatise sent forth to justify the decision. The passions were excited by addressing the reason—by bold and naked appeals to the primitive and undeniable principles of human rights, without allowing for the number less accidents of human condition by which those rights must inevitably be modified and restrained. Philosophy no longer remained to meditate in the shade; she was now to be seen directing the movements of the camp, or marching at the head of triumphal processions, or presiding at civic feasts and regenerating clubs. In all this there was absurdity; but there was enthusiasm. The enthusiasm spread with contagious fury. Every nation of Europe, every petty state became animated by a new-born vigour and unaccustomed pretensions; and, as if awaking from a long slumber, imagined that they had discovered in the old social bonds the shackles that enslaved them. "The democratic principal in Europe was getting on and on like a mist at the heels of the countryman, small at first and lowly, but soon ascending to the hills, and overcasting the hemisphere."* This principle made its way to England, where the better genius of the constitution prevailed against its allurements: it passed on to Ireland, where it was welcomed with open arms by a people who had been long since ripe for every desperate experiment.

During the twenty years which preceded the French Revolution, the progress of intelligence in Ireland had been unprecedented; a

* Mr. Grattan's Letter to the Citizens of Dublin.

The readers of Milton will not fail to recognise this image, and to observe the use which men of genius can make of their predecessors.

All in bright array
The cherubim descended—on the ground
Gliding meteorous, as evening mist
Risen from a river o'er the marish glides,
And gathers ground fast at the laborer's heels
Homeward returning.

Paradise Lost, Book xii.

circumstance which is to be in part attributed to the general diffusion of knowledge at the same period throughout the European community, but still more to the extraordinary excitement which her own domestic struggle had given to the Irish mind. In Ireland almost the whole of this accession of intellect was expended upon political inquiries, the most natural subjects of investigation in a country whose actual condition was so far below her most obvious claims; and this peculiar attention to local politics seems to have been the reason that her contributions to general science and literature have not been commensurate with the genius and increased acquirements of her people. It has already been shown how much of this new energy was exerted upon the Parliament for the reformation of the old penal system, which it was evident the nation had determined no longer to endure; but the Parliament was inexorable; and, by thus unnaturally opposing, instead of conducting, and sometimes indulging, sometimes controlling the public sentiment, left it at the mercy of all whose resentment or ambition might induce them to take advantage of its exasperation.

Of such there were many in Ireland. There were several men of speculative and enterprising minds, who, looking upon the obstinate defence of abuses at home, and the facility with which they had been banished from a neighbouring country, became convinced that a Revolution would now be as attainable as a Reform, and that there was a fund of strength and indignation in the Irish people, which, if skilfully directed, would vanquish every obstacle. There is no intention here of passing any unthinking panegyric upon those who were thus meditating a conspiracy against the State—upon the merits of such fatal appeals to chance and violence, no friend to law and humanity can hesitate a moment —but it is due to historical truth to state, that, in the present instance, they were not a band of factious demagogues, of desperate minds and ruined fortunes, who were looking to a Revolution as a scene of confusion and depredation. In the formation of such a confederacy there could, indeed, have been no scrupulous selection of persons. Several, no doubt, entered into the association from private motives; some from ambition—some from vanity—some from revenge; but there were many whose mental attainments, and personal virtues, and enthusiastic fidelity to the cause they had espoused, extorted the admiration and sympathy of those who were the least disposed to justify their conduct, or deplore their fate.

As early as the year 1791 the future leaders of the projected designs were taking measures for organizing the public force, by producing a general union of sentiment among the various classes upon whose co-operation they were to depend. As yet neither their plans nor objects were distinct and defined; but without any formal avowal of those objects to each other, and perhaps without being fully apprized themselves of their own final determinations, they took as effectual advantage of every public accident as if the whole had been previously digested and resolved. About this period several of the friends to constitutional monarchy, among whom appeared some of the most respected and exalted characters in the country, united in forming political societies,* for the purpose of collecting together all the rational supporters of freedom, and, by affording a legal and public channel of expression to the popular sentiment, of preventing the adoption of secret and more formidable combinations. Many of the persons, who were afterwards the most active promoters of more violent proceedings, became members of these societies, of which the avowed object was a simple

* The principal of these was the Whig Club, which was formed under the auspices of the late Lord Charlemont. The example was soon followed by the establishment of societies of United Irishmen at Belfast and Dublin, and finally in every part of the kingdom. It would be inconsistent with the limits of this work to trace minutely the progress of these societies; but it should be observed, that several who were leading members of the United Irishmen, when their designs had become revolutionary, were unconnected with them at an earlier period. It is also necessary to remark, that, though many of those who took an active part in their proceedings at every period of their existence would originally have been satisfied with a reform, there were exceptions. See the following note.—C.

redress of grievances—and with this there are reasons to believe that the future leaders of the conspiracy would in the first instance have been satisfied; but soon perceiving the improbability of such an event, while they continued, as members of the original and legal associations, ostensibly to limit their views to a Constitutional Reform, they were industriously establishing subordinate clubs* throughout the country, to which, in order to allure adherents, and to evade suspicion, they assigned the same popular denominations, and the same tests; but, by impressing on the minds of all who were admitted (and all of every class were admitted) that no hope of constitutional redress remained, they speedily formed them into a widely extended confederacy, under the name of the Irish Union, for revolutionizing Ireland, and establishing a Republic.

This statement refers more immediately to the north of Ireland, were a large portion of the inhabitants were Protestants or Dissenters, who, having no religious disabilities to exasperate them, and being to a considerable degree possessed of affluence and education, must be supposed to have been determined to republican principles upon purely speculative grounds. It should, however, be observed, that simultaneously with their proceedings, and

* Entitled "Societies of United Irishmen." By the test of the more early of these societies, the members pledged themselves "to persevere in endeavouring to form a brotherhood of affection among Irishmen of every religious persuasion, and to obtain an equal, full, and adequate representation of all the people of Ireland *in the Commons House of Parliament.*" In the year 1795 the latter words were struck out, in order to accommodate the test to the revolutionary designs that began to be generally entertained. *Report of the Secret Committee*, 1798. It is a received opinion, that the celebrated Thobald Wolfe Tone was the author of the Constitution of the later United Irishmen; but the writer of this work is informed that he himself denied this to be the fact. "He assured me (adds my authority) that Captain Thomas Russell, to whom he was for many years so warmly attached, was the person who drew up that remarkable paper, and that he (Tone) was not a member of the *close* society of United Irishmen till the eve of his embarking at Belfast for America, in the summer of 1795." It is, however, certain that Mr. Tone, as far back as 1791, strongly recommended to the societies of United Irishmen, then in their infancy, to attempt a Revolution, as appears from his letter written in that year to the society at Belfast.—*Report of the Secret Committee.* —(Appendix.)—C.

without any connexion or communication with them, a most formidable league existed among the poorer Catholics of several districts. These latter, assuming the name of Defenders,* had originally associated to repel the local outrages of their Protestant neighbours. The frequency and the length of the conflicts in which they were involved, had forced them into a kind of barbarous discipline and coherence; and having now become confident from their numbers, and from their familiarity with success or with danger, they began to despise the laws, of which they had vainly invoked the protection, and to entertain a vague idea that their strength might be successfully employed for the improvement of their condition. While their minds were in this state of confused excitation, emissaries were despatched from the united societies to explain to them their wrongs, and to propose the remedy. The Defenders were easily persuaded by the eloquence of doctrines, which only more skilfully expressed their previous sentiments; and, laying aside their religious resentments and distinctive appellation, adopted the more general views and title of United Irishmen.

Before the year 1796, societies of United Irishmen prevailed in every quarter of the kingdom. The great majority consisted of the lowest classes, of whom all that had the inducements of degradation, or of personal animosities, readily enlisted under a standard that was to lead them to freedom and revenge. In order to secure an uniformity of action, and habits of subordination, a regular and connected system (comprising committees, baronial, county, and provincial; and, finally, an executive) was established, and periodical returns of members admitted, arms procured, money contributed, and of every other proceeding, were made with all the forms and order of civil state.

* The Defenders first appeared about the year 1785: they increased rapidly, and soon attained a considerable degree of organization. From their oath and rules, which are couched in the rudest language, it sufficiently appears that the Association must have been composed of the lowest order in the community.—C.

Their numbers had soon become so great, that nothing but discipline seemed wanting to the accomplishment of their objects; and when we consider the description of men of whom the mass was composed, we cannot contemplate without surprise the spirit of ardour and secrecy that they displayed, and the enthusiastic patience with which they submitted to the irksomeness of delay, and to the labours and dangers by which alone any degree of discipline could be acquired. In the neighbourhood of the capital and the principal towns, where large bodies could not have assembled without discovery, they separated into very small parties, each of which appointed the most skilful to direct its manœuvres. The most active search was made for persons who had ever been in the military profession, to whom every motive of reward, and rank, and expected glory, were held out, and generally with success, to allure them into the association. Under these they met, night after night, to be instructed in the use of arms; sometimes in obscure cellars, hired for the purpose; sometimes in houses, where every inhabitant was in the secret; it even sometimes happened that in the metropolis these nocturnal exercises took place in the habitations of the more opulent and ardent of the conspirators. In the interior their evolutions were performed upon a more extensive scale. There, every evening that the moon, the signal of rendezvous, was to be seen in the heavens, the peasant, without reposing from the toils of the day, stole forth with his rude implement of war, to pass the night upon the nearest unfrequented heath, with the thousands of their comrades, who were assembled at that place and hour, as for the celebration of some unrighteous mysteries. It was also a frequent custom at this time, among the lower orders, to collect in large bodies, under the pretext indulging in some of the national games of force; but for the secret purpose of inspiring mutual confidence, by the display of their numbers, and their athletic forms, and of exercising in those mimic contests the alertness and vigour which they were so soon to employ in the real conflict. The general enthusiasm was kept alive by the distribution of songs in praise of freedom, arranged to popular native airs. Green, the old distinguishing colour of the island, and in itself, from its connexion with the face and restorative energies of nature, an excitant to the imaginations of men, who conceived themselves engaged in a struggle for the recovery of their natural rights, was adopted as their emblem. Their passions for spirituous liquors, a propensity that seems in some degree peculiar to those with whom it is the only luxury, and to those who have exhausted every other, was restrained, by explaining to them the embarrassment in which the sudden non-consumption of such a source of revenue would involve the Government. And so intense was the ardour for the general cause, that this inveterate indulgence was sacrificed to such a motive, and the populace became for a while distinguished by habits of unaccustomed, and it might be said, impassioned sobriety.*

The leaders of the United Irishmen began now (1796) to look with confidence to the success of their designs; but foreseeing that notwithstanding their strength and enthusiasm, the contest with the regular forces of the Government might be sanguinary and protracted, they were anxious to call in the aid of a disciplined army, which, by directing the movements and restraining the excesses of the insurgents, might enable them to decide the struggle at a blow. For such a reinforcement they turned their eyes towards France. The documents produced upon Jackson's trial had lately given them public intimation, that that country was disposed to assist the Irish malcontents. The latter were aware that France could have no interest in promoting a constitutional reform in Ireland, of which the obvious effect would have been an accession of strength to the British empire: they therefore applied for a military aid to effect a separation from England.† This

* Of the preceding facts, some are taken from the report of the secret committee and others are given upon the authority of individual information.—C.

† The United Irishmen despatched an agent to France for this purpose, about the middle of 1796 Mr. Tone was then at Paris, and exerted all his influence to the same effect.

would evidently be an important object with the French Government; and it was the necessity of holding out such an inducement that in some degree determined the Irish directory to the final and extreme measure of a Revolution. *The French authorities accepted the proposal, and immediately prepared for the embarkation of an army, to co-operate with the Irish insurgents. But the main dependence of the leaders of the conspiracy was upon the Irish populace; an agricultural population, full of vigour, burning for the conflict, and long inured to habits of insurrection. Of these, 500,000 were in arms.

If it should here be asked by any of the many subjects of the same empire, who still continue strangers to the former condition of Ireland, how so long and formidable a system of secret organization could have been carried by her people for the violent design of revolutionizing her country? the answer is not difficult. It

In the first memorial which Mr. Tone presented to the French directory in order to induce them to send an expedition to Ireland, he stated that at that period more than two-thirds of the sailors in the British Navy were Irish; that he was present when the Catholic delegates urged this to Lord Melville as one reason for granting emancipation, and that his lordship had not denied the fact. This statement was understood to have had great weight with the directory, who immediately committed the whole of the subject to the consideration of Carnot (then one of the directory) and Generals Clark and Hoche. The gentleman who has communicated the preceding circumstances has added the following anecdote: Soon after an expedition to Ireland had been left to the decision of Carnot, Clark, and Hoche, they named an evening to meet Tone at the palace of Luxembourg. Tone arrived at the appointed hour, eight o'clock. He was ushered into a splendid apartment. Shortly after the director and the generals made their appearance: they bowed coldly, but civilly, to Tone, and almost immediately retired, without apology or explanation, through a door opposite to that by which they had entered. Tone was a good deal struck by so unexpected a reception; but his surprise increased, when ten o'clock arrived, without the appearance of, or message of any kind from those on whom all his hopes seemed to depend. The clock struck eleven, twelve, one—all was still in the palace; the steps of the sentinels, on their posts without, alone interrupted the dead silence that prevailed within. Tone paced the room in considerable anxiety; not even a servant had entered of whom to inquire his way out, or if the director and the generals had retired. About two o'clock the folding doors were suddenly thrown open; Carnot, Clarke, and Hoche entered; their countenances brightened, and the coldness and reserve so observable at eight o'clock, had vanished. Clarke advanced quickly to Tone, and taking him cordially by the hand, said, "*Citizen! I congratulate you: we go to Ireland.*"—The others did the same; and having fixed the time to meet again, the persons engaged in this remarkable transaction separated.—C.

sprang from their degradation, and from the ignorance and revenge that accompanied it. The Rebellion of 1798 was a servile war. In Ireland her millions of peasantry were a mere collection of physical beings, to whom nature had amply dispensed every human passion, but whom society had imparted no motives to restrain them. The informing mind of a free constitution had never reached them; they never felt the tranquillizing consciousness that they were objects of respect. In Ireland the State was not the "great central heart," that distributed life and health, and secured them in return. The old Irish government was a mechanical, not a moral system; it was, what it has been so often likened to, a citadel in an enemy's country; its first and its last expedient was force; it forgot that those whom no force can subdue, nor dangers terrify, will kneel before an act of conciliation. But it obstinately refused to conciliate, and the people at length, prepared by the sufferings and indignities of centuries, listened with sanguine or desperate credulity to the counsel which reminded them of their strength, and directed them to employ it in one furious effort, which, whether it failed or prospered, could not embitter their condition.

The spirit of the Government found a ready and fatal co-operation in the gentry of the land. Never was there a class of men less amenable to the lessons of experience; adversity, the great instructor of the wise, brought to them all its afflictions without their antidote. Every fierce, inveterate resentment of the race lineally descended, with the title-deeds, from the father to the child. Year after year the landlord's house was fired, his stock was plundered, his rent unpaid, his land a waste, and each succeeding year he was seen effecting his escape, through scences of turbulence and danger, from his estate to the capital, to make his periodical complaint of his sufferings, and to give the minister another vote for their continuance.

The Irish landlord of the last century was the great inciter to insurrection. With a nominal superiority of rank and education.

he was in every ferocious propensity upon a level with the degraded dependants, whom he affected to contemn, and whose passions he vainly laboured to control; because he had never set them the example by controlling his own. Finding his efforts abortive, he next vindictively debased them; and the consequence was, that in a little time he shared the same fate with his victims. The condition of Ireland during the eighteenth century affords a striking and melancholy example of the certain retribution with which a system of misrule will visit those who so mistake their own interests as to give it their support. An inconsiderable order, or a single sect, may (however unjustly) be degraded with impunity; but the degradation of the mass of a nation will inevitably recoil upon its oppressors. The consequences may not always be visible in formidable acts of force; but there is a silent and unerring retaliation in the effects upon morals and manners, by which the tyrant is made eventually to atone for his crimes. In every condition of society the predominating sentiments and manners will spread and assimilate. In highly polished states they may be observed descending from the higher to the inferior ranks. The courtesy and humanity of the old French peer were found to give a tinge to the conversation of the mechanic. In uncivilized countries the progress is the reverse; the rudeness of the boor will ascend and taint his master. The latter was the case in Ireland; the Irish peasant, in his intercourse with his superiors, saw nothing of which the imitation could soften and improve him. The gentry, although conscious that their religion, and the violent means by which so many of them had acquired their properties, excited the suspicion and aversion of those below them, resorted to every infallible method of confirming these hostile impressions. Instead of endeavouring to eradicate them by mildness and protection, they insulted and oppressed. The dependant, unrestrained by any motive of affection or respect, avenged himself by acts of petty outrage. The outrage was resented and punished as an original unprovoked aggression. Fresh revenge ensued, and hence every district presented scenes of turbulent contention, in which the haughty lord lost whatever dignity he had possessed, and finally became infected with the barbarous passions and manners of the vassals whom he had disdained to civilize, till he required as much to be civilized himself.

The attachment of the Irish peasant to the government was suspected; but nothing could have been more unskilful than the means adopted to secure his fidelity. The Irish aristocracy, who imagined that because they were loyal, they might proceed to every violent extreme, were a band of political fanatics, and would have made proselytes by the sword. They knew nothing of the real nature of the allegiance which they were so zealous to establish, and which was never yet established by the sword. They were not aware that the allegiance of a nation to the state is a feeling compounded of a thousand others, half interest, half sentiment, of gratitude, of hope, of recollections, of the numberless minute and "tender influences," that reconcile the subject to his condition; that it is seldom a direct and defined attachment to the sovereign, but a collection of many subordinate attachments, of which the sovereign has all the benefit; that it is but the youngest of the group of private virtues, and, like them, must be reared in the bosom of domestic comfort; that it is upon the moral allegiance of each rank to its immediate relations, of the servant to his master, of the artisan to his employer, of the tenant to his landlord, that must be founded the political allegiance of the whole to the State.

Those mistaken loyalists supposed that they were teaching allegiance by a haughty and vindictive enforcement of the laws against its violation. They did not see that they were exacting from the laws what no laws could perform; that their positive provisions must be always impotent, where their spirit is not previously infused into the subject by manners and institutions. In Ireland these two were at perpetual variance. The Irish lawgiver passed his statute, setting forth, ir pompous phraseology, its wisdom and necessity, and denouncing the gibbet against the offender, and then returned to his district, to defeat its efficacy, by giving a practical continuance to the misery, the passions, the galling epithets, and the long train of customary insults and local provocations that were for ever instigating to crime. He did what was stranger and more absurd than this—he had the folly to put the State in competition with a power above it. He trampled upon the religion of the people*—not reflecting that, though by the doctrines of Christianity all injuries are to be forgiven, it had been the universal practice of its various sects, for successive centuries, to except the offences committed against themselves. He pointed to the peasant's chapel, and gloried in the reflection, that the disloyal bell which had called their fathers to worship should never sound upon the ears of their children—as if to approach his Maker with a little show of decent pomp was not the harmless pride of every man of every faith upon the surface of the globe. He thought he could drive them along the path of allegiance, where he had placed their religion to stop the way; and was surprised that, when the alternative was to be made, they should turn upon their driver rather than advance in the face of what they dreaded more than death.

The mass of the Irish people were tillers of the soil, and were thus systematically debarred, by those who should have been their patrons and instructors, from every motive to be tranquil. The country gentleman, the great bulwark (if he performs his duties) against extended projects of revolution, hated them and feared them. He received them with sullen reserve when they brought him his rent, and trembled at the vigorous hands that paid it; but there was no moral intercourse between them, no interchange of

* The first attacks upon the Irish Catholics originated in the English parliament; but the Irish aristocracy gave the penal code their fullest support. Had the latter performed their duty, and undeceived England upon the supposed necessity of continuing it, the fate of Ireland would have been very different; but upon this subject England was abused. and is to this hour abused.- C.

sympathy and endearing offices. The landlords, in constant alarm for their property and safety, would not convert the depredator into a protector. They opposed the tenant's education, which would have taught him to employ his idle hours in acquiring a love of order, instead of passing them in plans to recover in plunder what he had paid in rent, and looked upon as tribute. Erecting the nselves into the little deities of their own district, they would not let the tenant touch of knowledge, lest he should "become as one of them." They drew between themselves and their natural allies a proud line of separation, which effectually cut off all communications of reciprocal affection, but proved a barrier of air against irruptions of hatred and of force. In Ireland there were none of those feudal privileges which bring the persons and feelings of the Scottish dependants into closer contact with those of their superiors. The Irish peasant was never seen in the hall of his lord. He was left in his hovel to brood over his degradation—to solace or inflame his fancy with legendary traditions of his country's ancient glory, and with rude predictions of her coming regeneration, and to hail, in every factious spirit, the Messiah that was to redeem her.

These were the real causes of the avidity with which the Irish populace entered into this formidable conspiracy. The government was early apprised of its existence though not of its extent, and took very vigorous but ineffectual means to suppress it. Session after session it resorted to measures of terror or precaution, by penal acts and prosecutions, to try their efficacy; but, of the persons thus proceeded against, the acquittal of many only served to bring discredit upon the Administration, while the executions of such as were convicted were regarded by their party as so many acts of hostile severity, that called, not for submission, but revenge. The Ministers of the Crown conducted themselves, at this trying crisis, with a zeal which could not be too much applauded, if it were not so often carried to excess, and with the most undoubted fide ty to the powers whom they served; but throughout they committed one fatal error, which must for ever detract from their characters as able statesmen. Because it was evident that a few educated men were at the head of the popular combinations, they adopted, and to the last persisted in the opinion, or at least in the assertion, that the whole was essentially a conspiracy of a few speculative adventurers, who had *seduced* the nation from its allegiance, and that all the power and wisdom of the State was to be confined to the counteraction of the malignant design; and to this notion, notwithstanding its daily refutation, they adhered, with the spirit rather of persons engaged in an acrimonious controversy, than of ministers whose duty it was to save the country from the horrors of a civil war.* It was to no purpose that the sophistry by which they defended it was exposed—it was in vain that they were told, by men who knew the state of Ireland and the general course of the human passions as well as they did, that their reasonings would never satisfy the disaffected—that the dissatisfaction was not temporary or accidental, but radical—and that it was only a waste of time and of life to resort to unpopular laws and frequent executions, while the parent mischief remained untouched upon the statute book. The Irish Ministry not only spurned those counsels, which the event proved to have been prophetic, but, superadding a farther error, they reviled the advisers with so little discretion, that they gave the real conspirators official authority for believing that the opposers of the Administration were secretly the advocates of rebellion, and thus afforded them an additional incitement to persevere in their designs.†

* Even after the suppression of the Rebellion, when the Government possessed the fullest information regarding its origin and progress, the Viceroy, in his speech to the Parliament, was made to say, " the foulest and darkest conspiracy was formed and long carried on by the implacable enemy of this realm, for the total extinction of the Constitution, etc."—*Lord Lieutenant's Speech, October* 6, 1798.

† A leading member of the minority in the Irish House of Commons was the late Mr. George Ponsonby, a gentleman, who, if the purest constitutional views and personal dignity of deportment could have saved from insults, would have escaped them; but at this period no dignity was a protection. He, among others, impressed upon the Ministry that Ireland could be preserved from the threatened crisis by no means but by a complete

This glaring departure from the most obvious prudence has been variously accounted for. By many it has been attributed to incapacity. A more general opinion was, that the Government was fomenting the conspiracy, in order that the excesses to which it would lead might reconcile the nation to a Legislative Union: and, however vulgar and improbable the latter supposition may appear, it is still perhaps the only one that can satisfactorily explain the apparent inconsistencies and infatuation of their councils.

The enemy of Great Britain had already made an abortive effort*

reform of the Parliament, by Catholic emancipation, and by an equalization of commerce between England and Ireland. The following was the answer of one of the servants of the Crown (the solicitor-general) to Mr. Ponsonby's opinions: "What was it come to, that in the Irish House of Commons they should listen to one of their own members degrading the character of an Irish gentleman by language which was fitted but for hallooing a mob? Had he heard a man uttering out of those doors such language as that by which the honourable gentleman had violated the decorum of Parliament, he would have seized the ruffian by the throat, and dragged him to the dust!! What were the house made of who could listen in patience to such abominable sentiments?—sentiments which, thank God, were acknowledged by no class of men in this country, except the execrable and infamous nest of traitors, who were known by the name of United Irishmen, who sat brooding in Belfast over their discontents and treasons, and from whose publications he could trace, word for word, every expression the honourable gentleman had used."—*Irish Parl. Deb. Feb.* 1797.

George Ponsonby, one of the "Old Whigs," was a man of mediocre capacity, owing his position mainly to the circumstance of his aristocratic connexions. His father had been Speaker of the Irish House of Commons. His cousin was Earl of Bessborough; his father-in-law was the Earl of Lansborough. Born in 1755, he was called to the bar in 1780, and speedily was made King's Counsel, and Counsel to the Revenue Commissioners. Quarrelling with "the Castle," he was turned out of office, and became patriotic:

> "Here and there some stern, high patriot stood,
> Who could not get the place for which he cried."

In the Irish Parliament he was one of the Opposition leaders, and was made Lord Chancellor of Ireland in 1806. On the break up of the Fox ministry he lost his office, but was solaced with a pension of £4000, which he duly drew, year after year, until his death in July 1817. For some years after leaving Ireland, he was a Parliamentary leader of the Opposition in England.—M.

* In December 1796 the French Fleet was dispersed by a storm. A part of it anchored in Bantry Bay, where it remained for some days; but the vessel, on board of which Gen. Hoche (the commander of the expedition) was, not arriving, the French admiral, without attempting a landing, returned to France. It is well known that grievous complaints were made in the English Parliament against the Ministry, for having left the coast of Ireland

to transport an armament to Ireland, the landing of which was to have been the signal for the intended rising; but the leaders of the Irish Union, still depending upon the promised renewal of the attempt, had been anxious to restrain the impatience of the people until the foreign succours should arrive. Disappointed, however, in their expectations from abroad, and apprehending from any further delay, either the uncontrollable impetuosity or the desertion of their followers, they resolved, in the early part of this year, against their better judgment, to bring the matter to a final issue. The 23d of May was fixed as the day for a general insurrection.

so unprotected on this occasion. In explanation of this apparent negligence, Theobold Wolf Tone, who had been confidentially employed in the preparations for the French expedition (he was himself on board one of the vessels that anchored in Bantry Bay) related the following circumstances, as having come within his personal knowledge. While this formidable armament, which had so long fixed the attention of Europe, was fitting out at Brest, various conjectures prevailed as to its probable destination. The general opinion was that the invasion of either Ireland or Portugal was intented.—There was at this time (according to Mr. Tone's account) a secret agent of the British ministry at Brest, who, having discovered that a particular printer of that town had General Hoche's proclamations in his press, privately offered him a large sum for a single copy. With this offer the printer made General Hoche acquainted, who immediately drew up a proclamation, as addressed to the Portuguese by the commander of the French invading army. A few copies of this were accordingly, by the General's desire, struck off, and handed by the printer to the agent. The latter forwarded them to Mr. Pitt, whom the receipt of such a document is said to have so completely deceived, that he directed the British squadrons to make Portugal the peculiar object of their vigilance, and, in the first instance, treated the report of an actual descent upon Ireland with derision. Although the appearance of the French Fleet in Bantry Bay produced no movements of disaffection in the vicinity, it was yet at this period, or very shortly after, that the organization of the United Irishmen was most complete, and their prospect of success most promising. In 1797 they felt assured, that, in the event of a general insurrection, the greater number of the Irish militia regiments would have revolted. It is confidently asserted, that an attack upon Dublin having been proposed in that year, every soldier who mounted guard in that city on the night of the intended attempt was in their interests. The following occurrence, however ludicrous, is a striking proof of the prevailing sentiment among the native forces. At this time persons of democratic principles, in imitation of the French revolutionists, wore their hair short behind; from which custom Croppies and Rebels became synonymous terms. A commander of yeomanry in Dublin, while reviewing his corps, observed a false tail lying upon the parade. He held it up, and asked who had dropped it. By an instantaneous movement, every man of the corps raised his hand to the back of his head. This corps is said to have been, in consequence, disbanded on the following day.—C.

Of this intention the government having received information in the course of the preceding March, arrested several of the principal leaders in the capital; and, announcing by proclamation the existence of the conspiracy, authorised the military powers to employ the most summary methods of suppressing it.

This formal declaration of the impending crisis was followed by the most extreme agitation of the public mind. Every ear was catching, every tongue was faltering some tremendous confirmation that the hour was at hand. As it approached, the fearful tokens became too manifest to be mistaken. In the interior, the peasantry were already in motion. Night after night large masses of them were known to be proceeding by unfrequented paths to some central points. Over whole tracts of country the cabins were deserted, or contained only women and children, from whom the inquirers could extort no tidings of the owners. In the towns, to which, in the intervals of labour, the lower classes delighted to flock, a frightful dimunition of numbers was observed; while the few that appeared there, betrayed, by the moody exultation of their looks, that they were not ignorant of the cause. Throughout the capital, against which the first fury of the insurgents was to be directed, and where, from its extent, there could never be a certainty that the attack had not already begun, the consternation was universal. The spectacle of awful preparation, that promised security, gave no tranquillity. In the panic of the moment the measures for security became so many images of danger. The military array and bustle in some streets—the silence and desertion of others—the names of the inhabitants registered on every door—the suspension of public amusements, and almost of private intercourse—the daily proclamations—prayers put up in the churches for the general safety—families flying to England—partings that might be eternal—every thing oppressed the imagination with the conviction, that a great public convulsion was at hand. The Parliament* and the courts of justice, with a laudable attach-

* On the 22d of May (the day before the insurrection) the House of Commons voted an

ment to the forms of the constitution, continued their sittings; but the strange aspect of senators and advocates transacting civil business in the garb of soldiers, reminded the spectator that the final dependance of the state was upon a power beyond the laws. In Dublin the domestics of the principal citizens had disappeared, and gone off to join the insurgents; while those, who could not be seduced to accompany them, became the more suspected, from this proof of their fidelity: they could have remained, it was apprehended, for the sole purpose of being spies upon their masters, and co-operators in their intended destruction; and thus, to the real dangers of a general design against the government, were added all the imaginary horrors of a project of individual vengeance. The vigorous precautions of the Administration, instead of inspiring confidence, kept alive the public terror and suspense. In every quarter of the kingdom the populace were sent in droves to the prisons, till the prisons could contain no more. The vessels in the several bays adjoining the scenes of disturbance were next converted into gaols. The law was put aside: a non-commissioned officer became the arbiter of life and death. The military were dispersed through every house: military visits were paid to every house in search of arms, or other evidence of treason. The dead were intercepted on their passage to the grave, and their coffins examined, lest they might contain rebellious weapons. Many of the conspirators were informally executed. Many persons who were innocent were arrested and abused. Many who might have been innocent, were suspected, and summarily put to death.

Upon the appointed day the explosion took place. The shock was dreadful. The imagination recoils from a detail of the scenes that followed. Every excess that could have been apprehended from a soldiery, whom General Abercrombie, in the language of

address to the Viceroy, expressing their fidelity and their reliance upon the vigilance and vigour of his government. In order to render the proceeding more imposing, all the members of that house, with the Speaker at their head, walked through the streets, two and two, and presented the address to his Excellency.—C.

manly reproof had declared to be in a state of licentiousness that rendered it formidable to all but the enemy; every act of furious retaliation to be expected from a peasantry inflamed by revenge and despair, and, in consequence of the loss of their leaders, surrendered to the auspices of their own impetuous passions, distinguished and disgraced this fatal conflict.* After a short and sanguinary struggle, the insurgents were crushed. The numbers of them who perished in the field, or on the scaffold, or were exiled, are said to have amounted to 50,000;—the losses upon the side of the crown have been computed at 20,000 lives;—a solemn and memorable fact:—70,000 subjects sacrificed in a single year, whose energies, had other maxims of government prevailed, might have been devoted to what it is equally the interest of subjects and governments to promote—the cause of rational freedom, the possession of which can alone inspire a manly and enlightened attachment to the laws and the state.

* The high state of passion and resentment which prevailed at this unfortunate period may be collected from the single fact that in the House of Commons a member suggested that military executions should have a retrospective operation, and that the state prisoners, who had been for several weeks in the hands of government, should be summarily disposed of; but the secretary, Lord Castlereagh) with becoming dignity and humanity, vehemently discountenanced so shocking a proposal.—C. [There is something ludicrous in any one's gravely speaking of the "humanity" of Castlereagh!—M.]

CHAPTER XI.

Trial of Henry and John Sheares.

As soon as the public safety was secured (it was long before tranquillity was restored) by the defeat of the insurgents, a general amnesty was granted to all, except the actual leaders of the conspiracy, who should surrender their arms, and take the oath of allegiance to the King. Several of the leaders were in the hands of the Government, and it was now decided that the most conspicuous of them should be brought to immediate trial, in order that their fates should give a final blow to any still remaining hopes of their adherents.

The first of the persons thus selected were two young gentlemen, brothers, and members of the Irish bar, Henry and John Sheares.* Their previous history contains nothing peculiar. They were both of respectable and amiable characters. The elder of them "had given many hostages to fortune;" but with the ardour incidental to their years, and to the times, they had been induced to look beyond those sources of private happiness which they appear to have abundantly enjoyed, and to engage in the political speculations that were now to be expiated with their lives. When the original members of the Irish executive were committed to prison, in the month of March, the Sheareses were among those who were chosen to supply their place, and they took a very active part in arranging the plan of the approaching insurrection.

* The Sheareses were arrested on the 21st of May, 1798, two days before the rising of the people. They were two Cork gentlemen, "barristers by profession," says Davis, "both men of liberal education, but of very unequal characters. Henry, the eldest, was mild, changeful, weak: John was fiery and firm, and of much greater abilities."—M.

Of all these proceedings the Government obtained accurate information through a Captain Armstrong, an officer of the Irish militia, who had succeeded in insinuating himself into their confidence, for the purpose of discovery.* They were accordingly arrested two days previous to the explosion, and were now summoned to abide their trial for high treason.

Mr. Curran's defence of these unfortunate brothers was suppressed at the period, and is generally supposed to have altogether perished. A report of the trial has, however, been preserved, from which an account of the share that he bore in it shall now be given.†

The prisoners were brought to the bar, and arraigned, on the 4th of July, 1798.‡ In this stage of the proceedings, a very interesting and important discussion took place. Their counsel having discovered that one of the grand jury, who had found the bill of indictment, was a naturalized Frenchman,§ pleaded that

* Of Captain Armstrong, Davis says, "This frightful wretch had sought the acquaintance of the Sheareses—made it—encouraged their prospects—assisted them with military hints—professed tender love for them—mixed with their family, and used to dandle Henry Sheares's children. * * * He shared their hospitality—urged on their schemes—came to condole with them in prison—and then assassinated them with his oath." John Warneford Armstrong was Captain in the King's County Militia. He made the acquaintance of the Sheareses to get them into his clutches, and dined with John the day before the arrest. He had actually known them only ten days before that. Barrington says that Henry Sheares "was a participator in the treason, and aided in procuring emissaries to seduce the troops at Loughlinston. There Captain Armstrong became acquainted with the two brothers—pledged to them his friendship—persuaded them he would seduce his regiment—gained their implicit confidence—faithfully fulfilled the counter-plot—devised several secret meetings—and worked up sufficient guilt to sacrifice the lives of both."—M.

† The father of the Sheareses, a banker in Cork, had been a member of the Irish Parliament, and in that capacity had succeeded in carrying an act (5th George III.) by which was conceded to prisoners the right to have counsel assigned them by the Court and to have a copy of the indictment. Under this statute, Mr. Curran and Mr. McNally were assigned as counsel to John Sheares, and Mr. Plunket for Henry Sheares.—M.

‡ The trial took place before Lord Carleton, Barons Smith and George, and Justice Daly.—M.

§ It was McNally who filed the plea that John Decluzeau, one of the jurors who found the bills, for High Treason, against the Sheareses and for others, was an alien, not naturalised. The Crown lawyers argued against this plea, and then, in reply, Curran spoke in its support.—M.

fact against its legality. The following are parts of Mr. Curran's argument upon the occasion: *

"My lords; the law of this country has declared, that in order to the conviction of any man, not only of any charge of the higher species of criminal offences, but of any criminal charge whatsoever, he must be convicted upon the finding of two juries; first, of the grand jury, who determine upon the guilt in one point of view; and, secondly, by the corroborative finding of the petty jury, who establish that guilt in a more direct manner; and it is the law of this country, that the jurors, who shall so find, whether upon the grand or upon the petty inquest, shall be *probi et legales homines omni exceptione majores.* They must be open to no legal objection of personal incompetence; they must be capable of having freehold property, and in order to have freehold property, they must not be open to the objection of being born under the jurisdiction of a foreign prince, or owing allegiance to any foreign power. Because the law of this country, and indeed the law of every country in Europe, has thought it an indispensable precaution, to trust no man with the weight or influence which territorial possession may give him contrary to that allegiance which ought to flow from such possession of property in the country. This observation is emphatically forcible in every branch of the criminal law; but in the law of treason, it has a degree of force and cogency that fails in every inferior class of offence; because the very point to be inquired into in treason is the nature of allegiance. The general nature of allegiance may be pretty clear to every man. Every man, however unlearned he may be, can easily acquire such a notion of allegiance, whether natural and born with him, or whether it be temporary and contracted by emigration into another country; he may acquire a vague, untechnical

* Different statutes of Charles II. Geo. I. and Geo. III. enact, that naturalized aliens, performing certain specified conditions, "shall be deemed liege, free, and natural subjects, to all intents and purposes;" with a proviso "that they shall not be enabled to serve in Parliament, nor to be of his majesty's privy council, nor to hold any office of trust, civil or military, in the kingdom.—C.

idea of allegiance, for his immediate personal conduct. But I am warranted in saying that the constitution does not suppose that any foreigner has any direct idea of allegiance but what he owes to his original prince. The constitution supposes, and takes for granted, that no foreigner has such an idea of our peculiar and precise allegiance, as qualifies him to act as a juror, where that is the question, to be inquired into; and I found myself upon this known principle, that though the benignity of the English law has, in many cases, where strangers are tried, given a jury, half composed of foreigners and half natives, that benefit is denied to any man accused of treason, for the reason I have stated; because, says Sir W. Blackstone, 'aliens are very improper judges of the breach of allegiance.'* A foreigner is a most improper judge of what the allegiance is which binds an English subject to his constitution. And, therefore, upon that idea of utter incompetency in a stranger, is every foreigner directly removed and repelled from exercising a function that he is supposed utterly unable to discharge. If one Frenchman shall be suffered to find a bill of indictment between our Lord the King and his subjects, by a parity of reasoning may twenty-three men of the same descent be put into the box, with authority to find a bill of indictment. By the same reason, that the court may communicate with one man whose language they do not know, may they communicate with twenty-three natives of twenty-three different countries and languages. How far do I mean to carry this? Thus far: that every statute, or means by which allegiance may be shaken off, and any kind of benefit or privilege conferred upon an emigrating foreigner, is for ever to be considered by a court of justice with relation to that natural incompetency to perform certain trusts, which is taken for granted and established by the law of England.

"Therefore, my lord, my clients have pleaded, that the bill of indictment to which they have been called upon to answer has

* 4 Bl. Com. 352.—C.

been found, among others, by a foreigner, born under a foreign allegiance and incapable of exercising the right of a juror, upon the grand or the petty inquest. The stat. of Charles II. recites that the kingdom was wasted by the unfortunate troubles of that time, and that trade had decreased for want of merchants. After thus stating generally the grievances which had afflicted the trade and population of the country, and the necessity of encouraging emigration from abroad, it goes on and says, that strangers may be induced to transport themselves and families to replenish the country, if they may be made partakers of the advantages and free exercise of their trades without interruption and disturbance. The grievance was the scarcity of men; the remedy was the encouragement of foreigners to transport themselves, and the encouragement given was such a degree of protection as was necessary to the full exercise of their trades in the dealing, buying and selling and enjoying the full extent of personal security. Therefore it enacts, that all foreigners of the protestant religion, and all merchants, &c. who shall, within the term of seven years, transport themselves to this country shall be deemed and reputed natural-born subjects, and 'may implead and be impleaded,' and 'prosecute and defend suits.' The intention was to give them protection for the purposes for which they were encouraged to come here; and therefore the statute, instead of saying, generally, 'they shall be subjects to all intents and purposes,' specifically enumerates the privileges they shall enjoy. If the legislature intended to make them 'subjects to all intents and purposes,' it had nothing more to do than say so.* But not having meant any such thing, the statute is confined to the enumeration of the mere hospitable rights and privileges to be granted to such foreigners as come here for special purposes. It states, 'he may implead, and he shall be answered unto;' that 'he may prosecute and defend suits.' Why go on and tell a man, who is to all intents and purposes a natural-

* The statute does say this generally, in the first instance; but the subsequent enumeration of particular privileges supports the view that Mr. Curran took of it.—C.

born subject, that he may implead and bring actions? I say, it is to all intents and purposes absurd and preposterous. If all privileges be granted in the first instance, why mention particular parts afterwards? A man would be esteemed absurd, who by his grant gave a thing under a general description, and afterwards granted the particular parts. What would be thought of a man, who gave another his horse, and then said to the grantee, 'I also give you liberty to ride him when and where you please?' What was the case here? The government of Ireland said, 'we want men of skill and industry; we invite you to come over; our intention is, that if you be protestants, you shall be protected; but you are not to be judges, or legislators, or kings; we make an act of parliament, giving you protection and encouragement to follow the trades, for your knowledge in which we invite you. You are to exercise your trade as a natural-born subject. How? 'With full power to make a bargain and enforce it. We invest you with the same power, and you shall have the same benefit, as if you were appealing to your own natural forum of public justice. You shall be here as a Frenchman in Paris, buying and selling the commodities appertaining to your trade.'

"Look at another clause in the act of Parliament, which is said to make a legislator of this man, or a juror, to pass upon the life or death of a fellow-subject—no, not a fellow-subject, but a stranger. It says, 'you may purchase an estate, and you may enjoy it, without being a trustee for the crown.' Why was that necessary, if he were a subject to all intents and purposes? But, my lords, a great question remains behind to be decided upon. I know of no case upon it. I do not pretend to say that the industry of other men may not have discovered a case. But I would not be surprised if no such case could be found—if, since the history of the administration of justice, in all its forms, in England, a stranger had not been found intruding himself into its concerns—if, through the entire history of our courts of justice, an instance was not to be found of the folly of a stranger interfering upon so awful a subject as the breach of allegiance between a subject and his king. My lords, I beg leave upon this part to say that it would be a most formidable thing, that a court of justice would pronounce a determination big with danger, if they should say that an alien may find a bill of indictment involving the doctrine of allegiance. It is permitting him to intermeddle in a business of which he cannot be supposed to have any knowledge. Shall a subject of the Irish Crown be charged with a breach of his allegiance upon the saying of a German, an Italian, a Frenchman, or a Spaniard? Can any man suppose any thing more monstrous or absurd, than that of a stranger being competent to form an opinion upon the subject? I would not form a supposition upon it. At a time when the generals, the admirals, and the captains of France, are endeavouring to pour their armies upon us, shall we permit their petty detachments to attack us in judicial hostility? Shall we sit inactive, and see their skirmishes take off our fellow-subjects by explosions in a jury-room?

"When did this man come into this country? Is the raft upon which he floated now in court? What has he said upon the back of the bill? What understanding had he of it? If he can write more than his own name, and had written 'ignoramus' upon the back of the indictment, he might have written truly; he might say he knew nothing of the matter. He says he is naturalized. 'I am glad of it; you are welcome to Ireland, sir; you shall have all the privileges of a stranger, independent of the invitation by which you came. If you sell, you shall recover the price of your wares; you shall enforce the contract. If you purchase an estate, you shall transmit it to your children, if you have any; if not, your devisee shall have it. But you must know, that in this constitution there are laws binding upon the court as strongly as upon you. The statute itself, which confers the privileges you enjoy, makes you incapable of discharging offices. Why? Because they go to the fundamentals of the constitution, and belong only to those men who have an interest in that constitution transmitted to them from their ancestors.' Therefore, my lords, the foreigner must be content; he shall be kept apart from the judicial functions;—in the extensive words of the act of parliament, he shall be kept from 'all places of trust whatsoever.' If the act had been silent in that part, the court would, notwithstanding, be bound to say that it did not confer the power of filling the high departments of the state. The alien would still be incapable of sitting in either house of parliament—he would be incapable of advising with the king, or holding any place of constitutional trust whatever. What? shall it be said there is no trust in the office of a grand juror? I do not speak or think lightly of the sacred office confided to your lordships, of administering justice between the crown and subject, or between subject and subject;—I do not compare the office of grand juror to that;—but, in the name of God, with regard to the issues of life and death—with regard to the consequences of imputed or established criminality—what difference is there in the constitutional importance between the juror who brings in a verdict, and the judge who pronounces upon that verdict the sentence of the law? Shall it be said that the former is no place of trust? What is the place of trust meant by the statute? It is not merely giving a thing to another, or depositing it for safe custody; it means *constitutional* trust, the trust of executing given departments, in which the highest confidence must be reposed in the man appointed to perform them. It means not the trust of keeping a paltry chattel—it means the awful trust of keeping the secrets of the state and of the king. Look at the weight of the obligation imposed upon the juror—look at the enormous extent of the danger, if he violate or disregard it. At a time like the present, a time of war—what, is the trust to be confided to the conscience of a Frenchman? But I am speaking for the lives of my clients; and I do not choose even here to state the terms of the trust, lest I might furnish as many hints of mischief as I am anxious to furnish arguments of defence. But shall a Frenchman at this moment be entrusted with those secrets upon which your sitting on the bench may eventually depend? What is the inquiry to be made? Having been a pedlar in the country, is he to have the selling of the country, if he be inclined to do so? Is he to have confided to him the secrets of the state? He *may* remember to have had a *first* allegiance, and that he was *sworn* to it. He might find civilians to aid his perfidious logic, and to tell him that a secret, communicated to him by the humanity of the country which received him, might be disclosed to the older and better natured allegiance sworn to a former power! He might give up the perfidious use of his conscience to the integrity of the older title. Shall the power of calling upon an *Irishman* to take his trial before an *Irish* judge, before the country, be left to the broken speech, the *lingua franca* of a stranger, coming among you, and saying, 'I was naturalized by act of parliament, and I cannot carry on my trade without dealing in the blood of your citizens?' He holds up your statute as his protection, and flings it against your liberty, claiming the right of exercising a judicial function, and feeling, at the same time, the honest love for an older title to allegiance. It is a love which every man ought to feel, and which every subject of this country would feel, if he left his country to-morrow, and were to spend his last hour among the Hottentots of Africa. I do trust in God there is not a man that hears me, who does not feel that he would carry with him, to the remotest part of the globe, the old ties which bound him to his original friends, his country, and his king. I do, as the advocate of my clients, of my country—as the advocate for you, my lords, whose elevation prevents you from the possibility of being advocates for yourselves—for your children I do stand up; and rely upon it, that this act of parliament has been confined to a limited operation; it was enacted for a limited purpose, and I will not allow this meddling stranger to pass upon the life, fame, or fortune of the gentlemen at the bar—of me, their advocate—of you, their judges—or of any man in the nation. It is an intrusion not to be borne."

Mr. Plunket followed Mr. Curran on the same side; but, after a long discussion, it was ruled by the court, that the office of grand juror was not one of the *offices of trust* alluded to by the legislature, and, consequently, that the person objected to was competent to fill it. The prisoners were, therefore, in the language of the law, "awarded to answer over." Their trial was, upon their own application, in consequence of the absence of witnesses, postponed till the 12th of July, when it came on for final decision before Lord Carleton, Mr. Justice Crookshank, and Mr. Baron Smith.*

Mr. Curran's speech upon this occasion,† which was considered as the most moving that he had ever pronounced, was rendered peculiarly affecting, by the circumstances that accompanied its delivery. Notwithstanding the length of many of the state trials of this period, the courts seldom adjourned till the proceedings were concluded, so that their sittings were not only protracted to a late hour of the night, but it was not unusual for the returning morning to find them still occupied with their melancholy labours.‡

* The Attorney-General of that day, who stated the case for the Crown, was John Toler,—afterwards known as Lord Norbury, "the hanging judge," who would jest with the culprit as he sentenced him to the Gallows.—Alderman Alexander proved that he had found in the open desk of Henry Sheares, in Baggot Street, a rough draft of a rebellious proclamation to the People of Ireland, in the handwriting of John Sheares. Armstrong was examined for the Crown by Saurin.—On the trial it was for Henry Sheares in particular, that Curran spoke. Mr. Davis, who had seen the brief of prisoners' Counsel, and knew that John Sheares had actually dictated the defence, states that they admitted his part in the proceedings against the Government, and, in fact, indicated to Counsel his desire to save his brother Henry even at the risk of his (John's) life.—M.

† This speech in its reported state, is by no means the most favourable specimen of Mr. Curran's eloquence. Several passages in it are broken and unconnected, which may be attributed either to the incorrectness of the reporter, or to the extreme exhaustion of the speaker. If the defect arose from the latter cause, the solemnity of his delivery atoned for it with his auditors; for nothing could exceed the effect which it produced upon them. The suppression of this defence has been so often the subject of public regret, that the whole of it, as it has been preserved, is given here.—C. [This is an error. In Davis's edition of Curran's speeches, a fuller report is given.] M.

‡ George Ponsonby opened for Henry and Plunket for John Sheares. M'Nally pressed some law points with little effect. Three witnesses were then examined to prove Captain Armstrong an Atheist: two that he was an avowed Republican and rebel. Several witnesses testified as to the character of the Sheareses. The trial had commenced at nine

It was midnight when Mr. Curran rose to address the jury; and the feelings with which he entered on the task cannot be perfectly conceived, without adverting to the persons who were grouped around him. At the bar stood his clients, connected with each other by blood, with their advocate, and many more of the surrounding audience, by profession, and with the presiding judge by the ties of hereditary friendship.* Upon the bench he saw in Lord Carleton one of his own oldest and most valued friends, with whom he was now to intercede, if intercession could avail, for those who had so many tender claims to his merciful consideration; while upon the jury appeared several whom Mr. Curran (and probably his clients) had long known as acquaintances and companions, and with more than one of whom he had lived, and was still living, upon terms of the most confidential intimacy. When to this collection of private relations, so unusual upon such an occasion, are added the other attending public circumstances, it is not surprising that the surviving spectators of this memorable scene should speak of it as marked by indescribable solemnity. The fate that impended over the unfortunate brothers—the perturbed state of Ireland—the religious influence of the hour—the throng of visages in the galleries, some of them disfigured by poverty, others betraying, by their impassioned expression, a consciousness of participation in the offence for which the accused

in the morning. At midnight, after fifteen hours' sitting, in a crowded court, in midsummer, Curran entreated the delay of a few hours "for repose, or rather for recollection." If necessary, said he, "I will go on, if I sink." Lord Carleton, instead of adjourning until the next morning, which he could have done, asked the Attorney-General's opinion. Toler declined assenting to any adjournment, and said if the Sheareses' counsel did not speak to the evidence, the Crown lawyer would waive their right to speak, and leave the matter at once to the Court. Then, after a sitting of 16 hours, with only twenty minutes' interval, Carleton decided on going on. And the trial actually proceeded eight hours longer—making *twenty-four* in all! It was under such circumstances that Curran made his speech for Henry Sheares, one of the greatest forensic efforts ever made in any Court of law.—M.

* Lord Carleton had been the intimate friend of the parents of the prisoners—(see the conclusion of the trial:)—a report even prevailed that he had been the guardian of the latter; but this, it is presumed, was incorrect.—C.

were about to suffer, and all of them rendered haggard and spectral by the dim lights that discovered them—the very presence of those midnight lights so associated in Irish minds with images of death—every thing combined to inspire the beholders, who were now enfeebled by exhaustion, with a superstitious awe, and to make the objects, amidst which the advocate rose to perform the last offices to his sinking clients,* appear not so much a reality as the picture of a strained and disturbed imagination.

Mr. Curran.†—"My lord, before I address you or the jury, I would wish to make one preliminary observation. It may be an

* Mr. Curran was nominally counsel for only one of the prisoners: he had originally been the assigned counsel for both; but before the trial commenced, at the request of John Sheares, Mr. Ponsonby was assigned one of his counsel in the room of Mr. Curran, in order to give the prisoners four counsel between them. The other two were Mr. Plunket and Mr. M'Nally. But as the charge and evidence against both the prisoners were the same, the counsel for one was virtually defending the other.—C.

† That the reader may more fully comprehend the topics of Mr Curran's speech for the prisoners, the following summary of the leading articles of the evidence is inserted. The principal witness for the crown, John Warnford Armstrong, of the King's County militia, proved the overt-acts of high treason laid in the indictment. He swore that he was introduced by Mr. Byrne, a bookseller of Dublin, to the prisoners, who, supposing him (Armstrong) to be an United Irishman, freely communicated to him their treasonable designs. He had subsequent interviews with them at their own homes, the subjects of which he regularly reported to Colonel L'Estrange and Captain Clibborn of his own regiment, to Mr. Cooke of the Castle, and to Lord Castlereagh. Doubts having been entertained of the witness' belief in the existence of a Deity, a future state of rewards and punishments, Mr. Curran, who cross-examined him, pressed him upon those points. Captain Armstrong swore that he had always professed that belief, and that he had never derided the obligation of an oath.

He also swore that he had never said, "that if no other person could be found to cut off the head of the King of England, that he (the witness) would do it;" and that he had never declared "that the works of Paine contained his creed."

To these latter articles of Armstrong's, evidence was opposed, that of T. Dought, Esq., who swore that Armstrong, with whom he was very intimate, had frequently uttered atheistical opinions; and, with his usual calmness of manner, had spoken of the future state of the soul of man as an "eternal sleep—annihilation—non-existence."

R. Bride, Esq., barrister at law, swore that he had heard Armstrong speak slightingly of the obligation of an oath.

C. R. Shervington, Esq., (Lieutenant, 41st regiment, and uncle to Armstrong) swore that Armstrong had said in his presence, that if there was not another executioner in the kingdom for George the Third, he would be one, and pique himself upon it; and that upon another occasion Armstrong handed him Paine's Rights of Man, saying, "Read this, it is my creed."

observation only—it may be a request. For myself I am indifferent; but I feel I am now unequal to the duty—I am sinking under the weight of it. We all know the character of the jury: the interval of their separation must be short, if it should be deemed necessary to separate them. I protest I have sunk under this trial. If I must go on, the Court must bear with me;—the jury may also bear with me:—I will go on until I sink;—but, after a sitting of sixteen hours with only twenty minutes' interval, in these times, I should hope it would not be thought an obtrusive request, to hope for a few hours' interval for repose, or rather for recollection."

Lord Carleton.—"What say you, Mr. Attorney-General?"

Mr. Attorney-General Toler.—"My lords, I feel such public inconvenience from adjourning cases of this kind, that I cannot consent. The counsel for the prisoners cannot be more exhausted than those for the prosecution. If they do not choose to speak to the evidence, we shall give up our right to speak, and leave the matter to the Court altogether. They have had two speeches already; and leaving them unreplied to is a great concession."

Lord Carleton.—"We would be glad to accommodate as much as possible. I am as much exhausted as any other person; but we think it better to go on."

Mr. Curran.—"Gentlemen of the jury: it seems that much has been conceded to us. God help us! I do not know what has been conceded to me—if so insignificant a person may have extorted the remark. Perhaps it is a concession that I am allowed to rise in such a state of mind and body, of collapse and deprivation, as to feel but a little spark of indignation raised by the remark, that much has been conceded to the counsel for the prisoners; much has been conceded to the prisoners! Almighty and merciful God, who lookest down upon us, what are the times to which we are reserved, when we are told that much has been conceded to prisoners who are put upon their trial at a moment like this—of more darkness and night of the human intellect than a darkness of the natural period of twenty-four hours; that public convenience can not spare a respite of a few hours to those who are acc sed for their lives; and that much has been conceded to the advocate, almost exhausted, in the poor remark which he has endeavoured to make upon it!

"My countrymen, I do pray you, by the awful duty which you owe your country—by that sacred duty which you owe your character (and I know how you feel it) I do obtest you, by the Almighty God, to have mercy upon my client—to save him, not from the consequences of his guilt, but from the baseness of his accusers, and the pressure of the treatment under which I am sinking. With what spirit did you leave your habitations this day? In what state of mind and heart did you come here from your family? With what sentiments did you leave your children, to do an act of great public importance; to pledge yourselves at the throne of Eternal Justice, by the awful and solemn obligation of an oath, to do perfect, cool, impartial, and steady justice, between the accuser and the accused? Have you come abroad under the idea that public fury is clamorous for blood; that you are put there under the mere formality or ceremonial of death, and ought to gratify that fury with the blood for which it seems to thirst? If you are, I have known some of you,* more than one, or two,

* One of the persons on the jury to whom the observation was particularly directed, was Sir John Ferns, with whom Mr. Curran had been long connected by habits of private friendship, and in whose society he had passed many of his happiest hours of convivial relaxation.

The following little impromptu shows, in a striking point of contrast, the different styles in which different occasions induced the writer to address the same individual:—

TO SIR JOHN FERNS.

WITH A BOTTLE OF CHAMPAIGNE.

This bottle I've raised from the dust,
Where for many a year it had lain,
In hope that one day with the just
It might rise and might sparkle again.

And now, my dear Sir John, I send
This type of good tidings to come,
That the grave-digger's empire must end,
And his prisoners get loose from the tomb.

J. P. C.

or three, in some of those situations, where the human heart speaks its honest sentiments. I think I ought to know you well; you ought to know me; and there are some of you who ought to listen to what so obscure an individual may say, not altogether without some degree of personal confidence and respect. I will not solicit your attention, by paying the greatest compliment which man can pay to man; but I hold you in regard as being worthy of it; I will speak such language as I would not stoop to hold if I did not think you worthy of it. Gentlemen, I will not be afraid of beginning with what some may think I should avoid, the disastrous picture which you must have met upon your way to this court. A more artful advocate might endeavour to play with you, in supposing you to possess a degree of pity and of feeling beyond that of any other human being. But I, gentlemen, am not afraid of beginning by warning you against those prejudices which all must possess; by speaking strongly against them; by striking upon the string, if not strong enough to snap it, I will wake it into vibration. Unless you make an exertion beyond the power almost of men to make, you are not fit to try this cause. You may preside at such an execution as the witness would extol himself for,* at the sentence flowing from a very short inquiry into reason. But you are not fit to discharge the awful trust of honest men coming into the box, indifferent as they stood unsworn, to pronounce a verdict of death and infamy, or of existence and of honour. You have only the interval between this

* Captain Armstrong, the witness in this case, having been questioned by Mr. Curran regarding the death of two countrymen, replied, "We were going up Blackmore Hill, under Sir James Duff; there was a party of rebels there. We met three men with green cockades: one we shot—another we hanged—and the third we flogged and made a guide of." Thomas Drought, Esq., (one of the witnesses for the prisoners) gave in evidence a conversation which he had held with Armstrong, respecting this transaction. "I asked him, (said Mr. Dought) how he could possibly reconcile it to himself to deprive those wretches of life, without even the form of a trial. He acknowledged that he did so. I asked him whether he expected any punishment for it; and though he did not expect it from Government, yet that there was an all-powerful Being who would punish him. He said, 'You knew my opinion long ago upon this subject.'" This was the execution to which Mr. Curran above alluded—C.

and pronouncing your verdict to reflect; and the other interval, when you are resigning up your last breath, between your verdict and your grave, when you lament that you did not as you ought.

"Do you think I want to flatter your passions? I would scorn myself for it. I want to address your reason; to call upon your conscience; to remind you of your oaths, and the consequence of that verdict, which upon the law and the fact, you must give between the accuser and the accused. Part of what I shall say must of necessity be addressed to the Court, for it is a matter of law. But upon this subject, every observation in point of law is so inseparably blended with the fact, that I cannot pretend to say that I can discharge your attention, gentlemen, even when I address the Court. On the contrary I shall the more desire your attention, not so much that you may understand what I shall say, as what the Court shall say.

"Gentlemen, this indictment is founded upon the statute 25 Ed. III. The statute itself begins with a melancholy observation upon the proneness to deterioration, which has been found in all countries, unfortunately, to take place in their criminal law, particularly in the law respecting High Treason. The statute begins with reciting, that, in the uncertainty of adjudications, it became difficult to know what was treason, and what was not: and, to remove further difficulty, it professes to declare all species of treason that should thereafter be so considered; and, by thus regulating the law, to secure the state and the constitution, and the persons of those interested in the executive departments of the government, from the common acts of violence that might be used to their destruction. The three first clauses of the statute seem to have gone a great way indeed upon the subject; because the object of the provisions was to protect the person; and I beg of you to understand what I mean by person—I mean the *natural person;* I mean no figure of speech—not the monarch in the abstract, but the natural man; the first clause was made without the smallest relation to the executive power, but solely to the natural body and person. The words are, 'When a man doth compass or imagine the death of the king, or of our lady his queen, or their eldest son and heir, and thereof be of sufficient proof attained of open deed by men of his condition, he shall be a traitor.' This, I say, relates only to the natural person of the king. The son and heir of the king is mentioned in the same manner; but he has no power, and therefore a compassing his death must mean the death of his natural person; and so must it be in the case of the king. To conceive the purpose of destroying a common subject was once a felony of death; and that was expressed in the same language, compassing and imagining the death of the subject. It was thought right to dismiss that severe rigour of the law in the case of the subject; but it was thought right to continue it in the case of the king, in contradistinction to all the subjects within the realm.

"The statute, after describing the persons, describes what shall be evidence of that high and abominable guilt; it must appear by open deed—the intention of the guilty heart must be proved by evidence of the open deed committed towards the accomplishment of the design. Perhaps in the hurry of speaking—perhaps from the mistakes of reporters; sometimes from one, and sometimes from the other, judges are too often made to say that such or such an overt act is, if proved to have been committed, ground upon which the jury must find the party guilty of the accusation. I must deny the position, not only in the reason of the thing, but I am fortified by the ablest writers upon the law of treason. In the reason of the thing; because the design entertained, and the act done, are matters for the jury. Whether a party compassed the king's death or not, is matter for the jury; and, therefore, if a certain fact be proved, it is nonsense to say that such a *conclusion* must follow; because a conclusion of law would then be pronounced by the jury, not by the court. I am warranted in this by the writers cited by Mr. Justice Foster; and therefore, gentlemen upon the first count in the indictment you are to decide a plain *matter of fact:* 1st, Whether the prisoner did compass and imagine the death of the king? or whether there be any act proved, or apparent means taken, which he resorted to for the perpetration of that crime? Upon this subject many observations have already been made before me. I will take the liberty of making one: I do not know whether it has been made before. Even in a case where the overt act stated has of its own nature gone to the person of the king, still it is left to the jury to decide whether it was done with the criminal purpose alleged or not? In Russel's case there was an overt act of the conspiracy to seize the guards; natural consequence threatened from an act of gross violence so immediately approaching the king's person, might fairly be said to affect his life; but still it was left to the jury to decide whether that was done for the purpose of compassing the king's death. I mention this, because I think it a strong answer to those kinds of expressions, which in bad times fall from the mouths of prosecutors, neither law nor poetry, but sometimes half metaphysical. Laws may be enacted in the spirit of sound policy, and supported by superior reason; but when only half considered, and their provisions half enumerated, they become the plague of government, and the grave of principle. It is that kind of refinement and cant which overwhelmed the law of treason, and brought it to a metaphysical death; the laws are made to pass through a contorted understanding, vibratory and confused; and therefore, after a small interval from the first enaction of any law in Great Britain, the dreams of fancy get around, and the law is lost in the mass of absurd comment. Hence it was, that the statute gave its awful declarations to those glossarists, so that if any case should arise, apparently within the statute, they were not to indulge themselves in conjecture, but refer to the standard, and abide by the law as marked out for them. Therefore, I say, that the issue for the jury here is to decide, in the words of the statute, whether the prisoners "did compass the death of the king," and whether they can say, upon their oaths, that there is any overt act proved in evidence, manifesting an intention of injury to the natural person of the king.

"I know that the semblance of authority may be used to contradict me. If any man can reconcile himself to the miserable toil of poring over the records of guilt, he will find them marked, not in black, but in red, the blood of some unfortunate men, leaving the marks of folly, barbarity, and tyranny. But I am glad that men, who in some situations, appear not to have had the pulse of honest compassion, have made sober reflections in the hour of political disgrace. Such has been the fate of Lord Coke; who, in the triumph and insolence of power, pursued a conduct, which, in the hour of calm retreat he regretted in the language of sorrow and disappointment. He then held a language which I willingly repeat, 'that a conspiracy to levy war was no act of compassing the murder of the king.' There he spoke the language of law and good sense; for a man shall not be charged with one crime, and convicted of another. It is a narrow and a cruel policy to make a conspiracy to levy war an act of compassing the king's death, because it is a separate and distinct offence; because it is calling upon the honest affections of the heart, and creating those pathetical effusions which confound all distinct principles of law, a grievance not to be borne in a state where the laws ought to be certain.

"This reasoning is founded upon the momentary supposition that the evidence is true, for you are to recollect the quarter from whence it comes: there has been an attempt, by precipitate confession, to transfer guilt to innocence, in order to escape the punishment of the law. Here, gentlemen, there is evidence of levying war, which act, it is said, tends to the death of the king. That is a constructive treason, calculated as a trap for the loyalty of a jury, therefore you should set bounds to proceedings of that kind; for it is an abuse of the law to make one class of offence, sufficiently punished already, evidence of another. Every court, and every jury, should set themselves against crimes, when they come to determine upon distinct and specified guilt; but they are not to encourage a confusion of crimes by disregarding the distinction of punishments, nor to show the effusion of their loyalty by an effusion of blood.

"I cannot but say, that when cases of this kind have been under judgment in Westminster Hall, there was some kind of natural reason to excuse this confusion in the reports—the propriety of making the person of the king secure: a war immediately adjoining the precincts of the palace—a riot in London—might endanger the life of the king. But can the same law prevail in every part of the British empire? It may be an overt act of compassing the king's death to levy war in Great Britain; but can it be so in Jamaica, in the Bahama Islands, or in Corsica, when it was annexed to the British empire? Suppose at that time a man had been indicted there for compassing the king's death, and the evidence was that he intended to transfer the dominion of the island to the Genoese or the French; what would you say, if you were told that was an act by which he intended to murder the king? By seizing Corsica he was to murder the king! How can there be any immediate attempt upon the king's life by such a proceeding? It is not possible, and therefore no such consequence can be probably inferred; and therefore I call upon you to listen to the court with respect; but I also call upon you to listen to common sense, and to consider whether the conspiring to raise war in this country be an overt act of compassing the king's death in this country.* I will go further. If the statute of Edward III. had been conceived to make a conspiracy to levy war an over act of compassing

* This point was strongly urged by Mr. Ponsonby, counsel for John Sheares, and by Mr. Curran's colleague, Mr. Plunket; but the Court decided that it was untenable. The Prime Serjeant observed upon it with more zeal than logical consistency:—"It was *for this day* reserved to broach the alarming and monstrous position. I trust in God that the authority of such opinions has not gone abroad; and that the rebellion, which has for some time ravaged the country, has not been matured by such a doctrine." Lord Carleton, instead of countenancing so absurd an insinuation against the counsel, answered their arguments in the language of compliment and respect.—C.

the king's death, it would be unnecessary to make it penal by any subsequent statute; and yet subsequent statutes were enacted for that purpose, which I consider an unanswerable argument, that it was not considered as coming within the purview of the clause against compassing the king's death. Now, gentlemen, you will be pleased to consider what was the evidence brought forward to support the indictment. I do not think it necessary to exhaust your attention by stating at large the evidence given by Captain Armstrong. He gave an account which we shall have occasion to examine with regard to its credibility. He stated his introduction, first, to Mr. Henry Sheares, afterwards to his brother; and he stated a conversation, which you do not forget, so strange has it been! But, in the whole course of his evidence, so far from making any observation, or saying a word of connexion with the power at war with the king, he expressly said, that the insurrection, by whomsoever prepared, or by what infatuation encouraged, was to be a *home* exertion, independent of any foreign interference, whatever. And, therefore, I am warranted in saying, that such an insurrection does not come within the first clause of the statute. It cannot come within the second, of adhering to the king's enemies, because that means his foreign enemies; and here, so far from any intercourse with them, they were totally disregarded.

" Adhering to the king's enemies means co-operating with them, sending them provisions, or intelligence, or supplying them with arms. But I venture to say, that there has not been any one case, deciding that any act can be an adherence to a foreign enemy, which was not calculated for the advantage of that enemy. In the case of Jackson, Hensey, and Lord Preston, the parties had gone as far as they could in giving assistance. So it was in Quigley's. But, in addition to this, I must repeat, that it is utterly unnecessary that the law should be otherwise, for levying war is of itself a crime; therefore it is unnecessary, by a strained construction, to say, that levying war, or conspiring to levy war, should come within any other clause equally penal, but not so descriptive.

"But, gentlemen, suppose I am mistaken in both points of my argument—suppose the prisoners (if the evidence were true) did compass the king's death, and adhere to the king's enemies: what are you to found your verdict upon? Upon your oaths: what are they to be founded upon? Upon the oath of the witness: and what is that founded upon?—upon this, and this only—that he does believe there is an eternal God, an intelligent supreme existence, capable of inflicting eternal punishment for offences, or conferring eternal compensation upon man after he has passed the boundary of the grave. But where the witness believes that he is possessed of a perishing soul, and that there is nothing upon which punishment or reward can be exerted, he proceeds, regardless of the number of his offences, and undisturbed by the terrors of exhausted fancy, which might save you from the fear that your verdict is founded upon perjury. Suppose he imagines that the body is actuated by some kind of animal machinery—I know not in what language to describe his notions—suppose his opinion of the beautiful system framed by the almighty hand to be, that it is all folly and blindness compared to the manner in which he considers himself to have been created—or his abominable heart conceives his ideas, or his tongue communicates his notions;—suppose him, I say, to think so—what is perjury to him? He needs no creed, if he thinks his miserable body can take eternal refuge in the grave, and the last puff of his nostrils can send his soul into annihilation! He laughs at the idea of eternal justice, and tells you, that the grave, into which he sinks as a log, forms an intrenchment against the throne of God and the vengeance of exasperated justice!

"Do you not feel, my fellow-countrymen, a sort of anticipated consolation in reflecting upon the religion which gave us comfort in our early days, enabled us to sustain the stroke of affliction, and endeared us to one another; and, when we see our friends sinking into the earth, fills us with the expectation that we rise again—that we but sleep for a while to wake for ever. But what kind of communion can you hold—what interchange expect—what confidence place in that abject slave—that condemned, despaired-of wretch, who acts under the idea that he is only the folly of a moment—that he cannot step beyond the threshold of the grave—that that, which is an object of terror to the best, and of hope to the confiding, is to him contempt or despair?

"Bear with me, my countrymen; I feel my heart running away with me—the worst men only can be cool. What is the law of this country? If the witness does not believe in God, or a future state, you cannot swear him. What swear him upon? Is it upon the book or the leaf? You might as well swear him by a bramble or a coin. The ceremony of kissing is only the external symbol by which man seals himself to the precept, and says, 'May God so help me, as I swear the truth.' He is then attached to the Divinity upon the condition of telling the truth; and he expects mercy from Heaven, as he performs his undertaking. But the infidel! By what can you catch his soul? or by what can you hold it? You repulse him from giving evidence; for he has no conscience—no hope to cheer him—no punishment to dread! What is the evidence touching that unfortunate young man? What said his own relation, Mr. Shervington? He had talked to him freely—had known him long. What kind of character did he give of him? Paine was his creed and his philosophy. He had drawn his maxims of politics from the vulgar and furious anarchy broached by Mr. Paine. His ideas of religion were adopted from the vulgar maxims of the same man—the scandal of inquiry—the blasphemer of his God as of his king. He bears testimony against himself, that he submitted to the undertaking of reading both his abominable tracts—that abominable abomination of all abominations, Paine's 'Age of Reason;' who professes to teach mankind, by acknowledging that he did not learn himself! Why not swear the witness upon the vulgar maxims of that base fellow, that wretched outlaw and fugitive from his country and his God? Is it not lamentable to see a man labouring under an incurable disease, and fond of his own blotches? 'Do you wish,' says he, 'to know my sentiments with regard to politics? I have learned them from Paine! I do not love a king; and, if no other executioner could be found, I would myself plunge a dagger into the heart of George III., because he is a king. And because he is my king, I swear, by the sacred missal of Paine, I would think it a meritorious thing to plunge a dagger into his heart, or whom I had devoted a soul which Mr. Paine says I have not to lend.' Is this the casual effusion of a giddy young man, not considering the meaning of what he said? If it were said among a parcel of boarding-school misses, where he might think he was giving a specimen of his courage, by nobly denying religion, there might be some excuse. There is a latitude assumed upon some such occasions. A little blasphemy and a little obscenity passes for wit in some companies. But recollect it was not to a little miss, whom he wished to astonish, that he mentioned these sentiments, but to a kinsman, a man of that boiling loyalty. I confess I did not approve of his conduct in the abstract, talking of running a man through the body;* but I admired the honest boldness of the soldier who expressed his indignation in such warm language. If Mr. Shervington swore truly, Captain Armstrong must be a forsworn witness—it comes to that simple point. You cannot put it upon other ground. I put it to your good sense—I am not playing with your understandings—I am putting foot to foot, and credit to credit. One or other of the two must be perjured: which of them is it? If you disbelieve Captain Armstrong, can you find a verdict of blood upon his evidence?

* This alludes to a part of Mr. Shervington's testimony. "I met Captain Clibborn, and told him I was sorry to find that John Armstrong was finding the secrets of men, in order to discover them. He told me it was a different thing—that the Sheareses wanted to seduce him from his allegiance. 'Damn him!' said I, 'he should have run them through the body.'"

"Gentlemen, I go further. I know your horror of crimes—your warmth of loyalty. They are among the reasons why I respect and regard you. I ask you, then, will you reject such a witness? or would you dismiss the friend you regarded, or the child you loved, upon the evidence of such a witness? Suppose him to tell his own story. 'I went to your friend or your child—I addressed myself in the garb of friendship, in the smile of confidence, in order to betray it. I traduced you—spoke all the evil I could against you, to inflame him. I told him your father does not love you.' If he went to you, and told you this—that he inflamed your child, and abused you to your friend, and said, 'I come now to increase it, by the horror of superadded cruelty,' would you dismiss from your love or affection the child or the friend you loved for years? You would not prejudge them. You would examine the consistency of the man's story; you would listen to it with doubt, and receive it with hesitation.

"Says Captain Armstrong, Byrne was my bookseller; from him I bought my little study of blasphemy and obscenity, with which I amused myself.—'Shall I introduce Mr. Sheares to you?'—not saying which. What was done then? He thought it was not right till he saw Captain Clibborn. Has he stated any reason why he supposed Mr. Sheares had any wish at all to be introduced to him? any reason for supposing that Byrne's principles were of that kind? or any reason why he imagined the intercourse was to lead to any thing improper? It is most material that he says he never spoke to Byrne upon political subjects: therefore he knew nothing of Byrne's principles, nor Byrne of his. But the proposal was made; and he was so alarmed, that he would not give an answer until he saw his captain. Is not this incredible? There is one circumstance which made an impression upon my mind, that he assumed the part of a public informer; and, in the first instance, came to the field with pledgets and bandages. He was scarcely off the table when a witness came to his credit. It is the first time that I saw a witness taking fright at his own credit, and sending up a person to justify his own character.

"Consider how he has fortified it. He told it all to Captain Clibborn! He saw him every evening, when he returned, like a bee, with his thighs loaded with evidence. What is the defence? that the witness is unworthy of belief. My clients say their lives are not to be touched by such a man: he is found to be an informer; he marks the victim. You know the world too well, not to know that every falsehood is reduced to a certain degree of malleability by an alloy of truth. Such stories as these are not pure and simple falsehoods. Look at your Oateses, your Bedloes, and Dugdales! I am disposed to believe, shocking as it is, that this witness had the heart, when he was surrounded by the little progeny of my client; when he was sitting in the mansion in which he was hospitably entertained; when he saw the old mother, supported by the piety of her son, and the children basking in the parental fondness of the father; that he saw the scene, and smiled at it; contemplated the havoc he was to make, consigning them to the storms of a miserable world, without having an anchorage in the kindness of a father!* Can such horror exist, and not waken the rooted vengeance of an eternal God? But it cannot reach this man beyond the grave; therefore I uphold him here. I can imagine it, gentlemen; because when the mind becomes destitute of the principles of morality and religion, all within the miserable being is left a black and desolated waste, never cheered by the rays of tenderness and humanity; when the belief of eternal justice is gone from the soul of man, horror and execution may set up their abode; I can believe that the witness (with what view I cannot say; with what hope I cannot conjecture; you may) did meditate the consigning of these two men to death, their children to beggary and reproach; abusing the hospitality with which he was received, that he might afterwards come here and crown his

* The writer of this is assured, by a gentleman now in Dublin, and who is free from any political zeal which could induce him to invent or distort a fact, that, upon his dining one day at the house of Henry Sheares, immediately before his arrest, he observed Armstrong, who was one of the guests, taking his entertainer's little children upon his knee, and, it was then thought, affectionately caressing them.—C. [Armstrong strongly denied this accusation.]—M.

work, having first obtained the little spark of truth, by which his mass of falsehood was to be put into animation.

"I have talked of the inconsistency of the story. Do you believe it, gentlemen? The case of my client is, that the witness is perjured; and you are appealed to, in the name of that ever living God whom you revere, but whom he despiseth, to consider that there is something to save him from the baseness of such an accuser.

"But I go back to the testimony. I may wander from it; but it is my duty to stay with it. Says he, 'Byrne makes an important application: I was not accustomed to it; I never spoke to him; and yet he, with whom I had no connexion, introduces me to Sheares. This is a true brother.' You see, gentlemen, I state this truly: he never talked to Byrne about politics; how could Byrne know his principles? by inspiration! He was to know the edition of the man as he knew the edition of books. 'You may repose all confidence.' I ask not is this true; but I say it can be nothing else than false. I do not ask you to say it is doubtful; it is a case of blood; of life or death. And you are to add to the terrors of a painful death the desolation of a family, overwhelming the aged with sorrow, and the young with infamy! Gentlemen, I should disdain to trifle with you; I am pinning your minds down to one point, to show you to demonstration that nothing can save your minds from the evidence of such perjury; not because you may think it false, but because it is impossible it can be true. I put into the scales of justice that execrable perjury; and I put into the other the life, the fame, the fortune, the children of my client. Let not the balance tremble as you hold it: and, as you hold it now, so may the balance of eternal justice be held for you.

"But is it upon his inconsistency only I call upon you to reject him? I call in aid the evidence of his own kinsman, Mr. Shervington, and Mr. Drought; the evidence of Mr. Bride, and Mr. Graydon. Before you can believe Armstrong, you must believe that all these are perjured. What are his temptations to perjury? the hope of bribery and reward:—and he did go up with his sheets of paper in his hand here is one: it speaks treason; here is another: the accused grows paler; here is a third: it opens another vein. Had Shervington any temptation of that kind? No: let not the honest and genuine soldier lose the credit of it. He has paid a great compliment to the proud integrity of the King his master, when he did venture, at a time like this, to give evidence, 'I would not have come for a hundred guineas!'* I could not refuse the effusion of my heart, and avoid exclaiming, 'May the blessings of God pour upon you; and may you never want a hundred guineas!'

"There is another circumstance. I think I saw it strike your attention, my lords. It was the horrid tale of the three peasants whom he met upon the road: they had no connexion with the rebels. If they had, they were open to a summary proceeding. He hangs up one, shoots a second, and administers torture to the body of the third in order to make him give evidence. Why, my lords, did you feel nothing stir within you? Our adjudications have condemned the application of torture for the extraction of evidence. When a wild and furious assassin had made a deadly attempt upon a life of much public consequence, it was proposed to put him to the torture in order to discover his accomplices. I scarcely know whether to admire most the awful and impressive lesson given by Felton, or the doctrine stated by the judges of the land. 'No,' said he, 'put me not to the torture; for, in the extravagance of my pain, I may be brought to accuse yourselves.' What say the judges?—'It is not allowable, by the law and constitution of England, to inflict torture upon any man, or to extract evidence under the coercion of personal sufferings.' Apply that to this case; if

* When Mr. Shervington was asked, upon his cross-examination by the counsel for the Crown, "if he had not kindly come forward, upon hearing that Captain Armstrong was to be a witness against the Sheareses," he answered, "No: I was summoned. I would not have appeared for a hundred guineas."—C.

the unfortunate man did himself dread the application of such an engine for the extraction of evidence, let it be an excuse for his degradation, that he sought to avoid the pain of body, by public infamy. But there is another observation more applicable: says Mr. Drought, 'Had you no feeling, or do you think you will escape future vengeance?' 'Oh! sir, I thought you knew my ideas too well to talk in that way. Merciful God! do you think it is upon the evidence of such a man that you ought to consign a fellow subject to death? He who would hang up a miserable peasant to gratify caprice, could laugh at remonstrance, and say, 'you know my ideas of futurity.' If he thought so little of murdering a fellow creature without trial, and without ceremony, what kind of compunction can he feel within himself when you are made the instruments of his savage barbarity? He kills a miserable wretch, looking perhaps for bread for his children, and who falls unaccused and uncondemned. What compunction can he feel at sacrificing other victims, when he considers death as eternal sleep, and the darkness of annihilation? These victims are at this moment led out to public execution; he has marked them for the grave; he will not bewail the object of his own work; they are passing through the vale of death, while he is dozing over the expectancy of mortal annihilation.

"Gentlemen, I am too weak to follow the line of observation I had made; but I trust I am warranted in saying, that if you weigh the evidence, the balance will be in favour of the prisoners.

"But there is another topic or two to which I must solicit your attention. If I had been stronger, in a common case I would not have said so much; weak as I am, here I must say more. It may be said that the parol evidence may be put out of the case; that, attribute the conduct of Armstrong to folly, or passion, or whatever else you please, you may safely repose upon the written evidence. This calls for an observation or two. As to Mr. Henry Sheares, that written evidence,* even if the hand-writing were fully proved,

* This written evidence was an address to the United Irishmen, in the hand-writing of John Sheares.—C.

does not apply to him: I do not say it was not admissible. The writings of Sidney, found in his closet, were read; justly according to some; but I do not wish to consider that now. But I say the evidence of Mr. Dwyer has not satisfactorily established the handwriting of John. I do not say it is not proved to a certain extent, but it is proved in the very slightest manner that you ever saw paper proved; it is barely evidence to go to you, and the witness might be mistaken. An unpublished writing cannot be an overt act of treason; so it is laid down expressly by Hale and Foster. A number of cases have occurred, and decisions have been pronounced, asserting that writings are not overt acts, for want of publication; but if they plainly relate to an overt act proved, they may be left to the jury for their consideration. But here it has no reference to the overt act laid; it could not have been intended for publication until after the unfortunate event of revolution had taken place, and therefore it could not be designed to create insurrection. Gentlemen, I am not counsel for Mr. John Sheares, but I would be guilty of cruelty if I did not make another observation. This might be an idle composition, or the translation of idle absurdity from the papers of another country; the manner in which it was found leads me to think *that* the more probable. A writing designed for such an event as charged would hardly be left in a writing-box, unlocked, in a room near the hall door. The manner of its finding also shows two things; that Henry Sheares knew nothing of it, for he had an opportunity of destroying it, as Alderman Alexander said he had; and further, that he could not have imagined his brother had such a design; and it is impossible, if the paper had been designed for such purposes, that it would not be communicated to him.

"There is a point to which I will beseech the attention of your Lordships. I know your humanity, and it will not be applied merely because I am exhausted or fatigued. You have only one witness to any overt act of treason. There is no decision upon the point in this country.* Jackson's case was the first: Lord Clon-

* This is not correct: it was the unanimous opinion of the three judges of the Court of

mel made an allusion to the point; but a jury ought not to find guilty upon the testimony of a single witness. It is the opinion of Foster, that by the common law, one witness, if believed, was sufficient. Lord Coke's opinion is that two were necessary. They are great names; no man looks upon the works of Foster with more veneration than myself, and I would not compare him with the depreciated credit of Coke; I would rather leave Lord Coke to the character which Foster gives him; that he was one of the ablest lawyers, independent of some particulars, that ever existed in England. In the wild extravagance, heat, and cruel reigns of the Tudors, such doctrines of treason had gone abroad as drenched the kingdom with blood. By the construction of crown lawyers and the shameful complaisance of juries, many sacrifices had been made, and therefore it was necessary to prune away these excesses by the stat. of Edward VI., and therefore there is every reason to imagine, from the history of the times, that Lord Coke was right in saying, that not by new statute, but by the common law, confirmed and redeemed by declaratory acts, the trials were regulated. A law of Philip and Mary was afterwards enacted; some think it was a repeal of the stat. of Edward VI., some think not. I mention this diversity of opinions with this view, that in this country, upon a new point of that kind, the weight of criminal prosecution will turn the scale in favour of the prisoner; and that the court will be of opinion that the stat. 7 William III. did not enact any new thing unknown to the common law, but redeemed it from abuse. What was the state of England? The king had been declared to have abdicated the throne: prosecutions, temporising juries, and the arbitrary construction of judges, condemned to the scaffold those who were to protect the Crown; men who knew, that, after the destruction of the cottage, the palace was endangered. It was not, then, the enaction of anything new; it was founded in the caution of the times, and derived from the maxims of the consti-

King's Bench, before whom Jackson was tried, that in Ireland two witnesses were not necessary in cases of High Treason.—See Jackson's Trial.—C. [It is altered now.—M.]

tution. I know the peevishness with which Burnet observed upon that statute. He is reprehended in a modest manner by Foster. But what says Blackstone, of great authority, of the clearest head and the profoundest reading? He differs from Montesquieu, the French philosopher.

"'In cases of treason there is the accused's oath of allegiance to counterpoise the information of a single witness; and that may, perhaps, be one reason why the law requires a double testimony to convict him: though the principal reason, undoubtedly, is to secure the subject from being sacrificed to fictitious conspiracies, which have been the engines of profligate and crafty politicians in all ages.'*

"Gentlemen, I do not pretend to say that you are bound by an English act of parliament. You may condemn upon the testimony of a single witness. You, to be sure, are too proud to listen to the wisdom of an English law. Illustrious independents! You may murder under the semblance of judicial forms, because you are proud of your blessed independence! You pronounce that to be legally done which would be murder in England, because you are proud! You may imbrue your hands in blood, because you are too proud to be bound by a foreign act of parliament: and when you are to look for what is to save you from the abuse of arbitrary power, you will not avail yourself of it, because it is a foreign act of parliament! Is that the independence of an Irish jury? Do I see the heart of any Englishman move when I say to him, 'Thou servile Briton, you cannot condemn upon the perjury of a single witness, because you are held in the tight waistcoat of the cogency of an act of parliament? If power seeks to make victims by judicial means, an act of parliament would save you from the perjury of abominable malice. Talk not of proud slavery to law, but lament that you are bound by the integrity and irresistible strength of right reason; and, at the next step, bewail that the all-

* 4 Blackstone's Commentaries, 358.

powerful Author of nature has bound himself in the illustrious servitude of his attributes, which prevent him thinking what is not true, or doing what is not just.' Go, then, and enjoy your independence. At the other side of the water your verdict, upon the testimony of a single witness, would be murder. But here you can murder without reproach, because there is no act of parliament to bind you to the ties of social life, and save the accused from the breath of a perjured informer. In England a jury could not pronounce a conviction upon the testimony of the purest man, if he stood alone; and yet what comparison can that case bear with a blighted and marred informer, where every word is proved to be perjury, and every word turns back upon his soul?

"I am reasoning for your country and your children, to the hour of your dissolution: let me not reason in vain. I am not playing the advocate: you know I am not. I put this case to the bench: the stat. 7 W. 3 does not bind this country by its legislative cogency; and will you declare positively, and without doubt, that it is common law, or enacting a new one? Will you say it has no weight to influence the conduct of a jury from the authority of a great and exalted nation? the only nation in Europe where Liberty has seated herself. Do not imagine that the man who praises Liberty is singing an idle song: for a moment it may be the song of a bird in his cage: I know it may. But you are now standing upon an awful isthmus, a little neck of land, where Liberty has found a seat. Look about you—look at the state of the country—the tribunals that dire necessity has introduced. Look at this dawn of law, admitting the functions of a jury. I feel a comfort. Methinks I see the venerable forms of Holt and Hale looking down upon us, attesting its countenance. Is it your opinion that bloody verdicts are necessary—that blood enough has not been shed—that the bonds of society are not to be drawn close again, nor the scattered fragments of our strength bound together to make them of force; but that they are to be left in that scattered state, in which every little child may break them to pieces? You will do more towards tranquillizing the country by a verdict of mercy. Guard yourselves against the sanguinary excesses of prejudice or revenge; and, though you think there is a great call for public justice, let no unmerited victim fall.

"Gentlemen, I have tired you. I durst not relax. The danger of my client is from the hectic of the moment, which you have fortitude, I trust, to withstand. In that belief, I leave him to you; and, as you deal justice and mercy, so may you find it. And I hope that the happy compensation of an honest discharge of your duty may not be deferred till a future existence—which this witness [Armstrong] does not expect—but that you may speedily enjoy the benefits you will have conferred upon your country."*

It was between seven and eight o'clock, on the morning of the 13th of July, when the jury retired to consider their verdict. After the deliberation of a few minutes, they returned it, finding both the prisoners guilty. As soon as the verdict was pronounced, the unfortunate brothers clasped each other in their arms. They were brought up for judgment at three o'clock on the same day upon which occasion, they both addressed the court.

Henry, who had a numerous family, was proceeding to request a short respite; but, when he came to mention his wife and children, he was so overwhelmed with tears, that he found it impossible to go on. His brother spoke with more firmness, and at more length. He began by strenuously disavowing the sanguinary intentions that had been imputed to him in consequence of the unpublished address to the insurgents which had been found in his handwriting, and produced in evidence against him. "The accusation," said he, "of which I speak, while I linger here yet a few minutes, is 'that of holding out to the people of Ireland a

* The Prime-Sergeant replied for the Crown. Henry Sheares, who was then allowed to say a few words, strongly denied all knowledge of the paper found in his desk, and asked was it likely that, having the dearest sources of happiness around him, he should sacrifice them and himself by leaving such a document in an open writing-box? Lord Carleton charged the jury, the two other judges concurring, and the verdict was returned after a deliberation of *seventeen* minutes.—M.

direction to give no quarter to the troops fighting for its defence.' I cannot only acquit my soul of such an intention, but I declare, in the presence of that God before whom I must shortly appear, that the favourite doctrine of my heart was—*that no human being should suffer death, but where absolute necessity required it.*"

After having spoken for a considerable time to the same effect, he proceeded. "Now, my lords, I have no favour to ask of the Court. My country has decided that I am guilty; and the law says that I shall suffer. It sees that I am ready to suffer. But, my lords, I have a favour to request of the Court that does not relate to myself. I have a brother, whom I have ever loved dearer than myself;—but it is not from any affection for him alone that I am induced to make the request; he is a man, and therefore, I hope prepared to die, if he stood as I do—though I do not stand unconnected; but he stands more dearly connected. In short, my lords, to spare your feelings and my own, I do not pray that I should not die; but that the husband, the father, the brother, and the son, all comprised in one person, holding these relations, dearer in life to him than any man I know; for such a man I do not pray a pardon, for that is not in the power of the Court, but I pray a respite for such a time as the Court, in its humanity and discretion, shall think proper. You have heard, my lords, that his private affairs require arrangement. I have a further room for asking it. If immediately both of us be taken off, an aged and reverend mother, a dear sister, and the most affectionate wife that ever lived, and six children will be left without protection or provision of any kind. When I address myself to your lordships, it is with the knowledge you will have of all the sons of our aged mother being gone: two perished in the service of the king, one very recently. I only request, that, disposing of me with what swiftness either the public mind or justice requires, a respite may be given to my brother, that the family may acquire strength to bear it all. That is all I wish. I shall remember it to my last breath; ana I will offer up my prayers for you to that Being who has endued us all with sensibility to feel. This is all I ask."

To this affecting appeal, Lord Carleton replied: "In the awful duty imposed on me, no man can be more sensibly affected than I am, because I knew the very valuable and respectable father and mother from whom you are both descended. I knew and revered their virtues. One of them, happily for himself, is now no more: the other, for whom I have the highest personal respect, probably, by the events of this day, may be hastened into futurity. It does not rest with us, after the conviction which has taken place, to hold out mercy—that is for another place; and I am afraid, in the present situation of public affairs, it will be difficult to grant even that indulgence which you, John Sheares, so pathetically request for your brother. With respect to the object of your soliciting time for your brother, unfortunately it could be of no use; because, by the attainder, he will forfeit all his property, real and personal: nothing to be settled will remain."

His lordship then, after some preliminary observations, pronounced sentence of death upon the prisoners; and, at the prayer of the attorney-general, directed that it should be executed on the succeeding day.*

* A few hours before his execution, Henry Sheares wrote a letter to Mr. (afterwards Sir Jonah) Barrington, a facsimile of which is to be found in the latter's "Historic Anecdotes of the Legislative Union between Great Britain and Ireland." Barrington says: "There never was a more affecting picture of a feeling, agonized mind, at the approach of a violent death, than is this facsimile. Had but three hours been granted for the unhappy culprit's preparation for his fate, he would have been respited. Lord Clare was disposed to act with great humanity towards this amiable, but misguided man, having discovered that he was utterly ignorant of the sanguinary proclamation, which was found in his secretaire—he had never seen it." In Henry Sheares' letter, he besought Barrington to fly to the Lord Chancellor—"Ah, save a man whose fate will kill his family!"—to tell the Chancellor that he would pray for him for ever, "and that *the Government shall ever find me what they wish*,"—that the papers found in his office he knew nothing of—that he had been duped, misled, deceived—that he never was for violence—that his whole happiness was centred in his family, "with them I will go to America, if the Government will allow me; or that I will stay here, *and be the most zealous friend they have*," and would be under *any* conditions the Government might choose to impose on him, if they would but restore him to his family. This letter is dated 8 o'clock, but did not reach Barrington

The following is a copy of Mr. John Sheares' farewell letter to his fan ily. It is addressed to his sister, to whom he had been most tenderly attached. It may not have much literary merit; "but nature is there, which is the greatest beauty."

"KILMAINHAM PRISON.—Wednesday night.

"The troublesome scene of life is nearly closed; and the hand that now traces these lines, in a short time will be no longer capable of communicating to a beloved family the sentiments of his heart.

"It is now eleven o'clock, and I have only time to address my beloved Julia in a short, eternal farewell. Thou sacred Power!—whatever be thy name and nature—who has created us the frail and imperfect creatures that we are, hear the ardent prayer of one now on the eve of a most awful change. If thy Divine Providence can be affected by mortal supplication, hear and grant, I most humbly beseech thee, the last wishes of a heart that has ever adored thy greatness and thy goodness. Let peace and happiness once more visit the bosom of my beloved family. Let a mild grief succeed the miseries they have endured; and, when an affectionate tear is generously shed over the dust of him who caused their misfortunes, let all their ensuing days glide on in union and domestic harmony. Enlighten my beloved brother: to him and his invaluable wife grant the undisturbed enjoyment of their mutual love; and, as they advance, let their attachment increase. Let my Julia, my feeling, my too feeling Julia, experience that

until 11 o'clock of the morning after the trial. He hastened to Lord Clare, and showed him the letter. It moved him; and he exclaimed, naturally enough, "What a coward he is!" He said it was impossible to save John Sheares, and the doubt was how the Viceroy could draw the distinction between them. At last, anticipating that Henry would make any disclosures to save his life, he desired Barrington to go to the prison, see Henry Sheares, and put the question to him. "I lost no time," says Barrington, "but I found, on my arrival, that orders had been given, that nobody should be admitted without a written permission. I returned to the Castle—they were all in council. Cooke [the Secretary] was not in his office—I was delayed. At length the Secretary returned—gave me the order. I hastened to Newgate, and arrived at the very moment the executioner was holding up the head of my friend, saying: '*Here is the head of a traitor!*'"—M.

consolation which she has so often imparted to others; let her soul repose at length in the consummation of all the wishes of her excellent heart; let her taste that happiness her virtues have so well merited. For my other sisters provide those comforts their situation requires. To my mother—O, Eternal Power! what gift shall I wish for this matchless parent? Restore her to that peace which I have unfortunately torn from her: let her forget me in the ceaseless affections of my sisters, and in their prosperity; let her taste that happiness which is best suited to her affectionate heart; and, when at length she is called home, let her find, in everlasting bliss, the due reward of a life of suffering virtue.

"Adieu, my dear Julia! My light is just out. The approach of darkness is like that of death, since both alike require me to say farewell! farewell, for ever! O, my dear family, farewell!—Farewell, for ever!

"J. S."

In the cemetery of the Church of St. Michan's, in Dublin, there are vaults for the reception of the dead, of which the atmosphere has the peculiar quality of protracting for many years the process of animal decay. It is not unusual to see there the coffins crumbling away from around what they were intended for ever to conceal, and thus giving up once more to human view their contents, still pertinaciously resisting the influence of time. In this place the unfortunate brothers were deposited;* and in this state of undesigned disinterment their remains may be seen to this day, the heads dissevered from the trunks, and "the hand that once traced those lines" not yet mouldered into dust.*

* They were hanged and beheaded in the front of Newgate. Davis says of John Sheares: "He died (as did Henry, too, when he really came to his doom), placidly and well." On the other hand, Barrington records that "They came hand in hand to the scaffold: Henry died without firmness—the brother met his death with sufficient fortitude."—M.

† This reproach is out of date in 1855. In consequence of what Mr. W. H. Curran stated on this subject, in these pages and elsewhere, the mortal remains of the Sheareses were put out of public view, into substantial oak coffins.—M.

CHAPTER XII.

Trials of M'Cann, Byrne, and Oliver Bond—Reynolds the informer—Lord Edward Fitzgerald—His attainder—Mr. Curran's conduct upon the State Trials—Lord Kilwarden's friendship—Lines addressed by Mr. Curran to Lady Charlotte Rawdon—Theobald Wolfe Tone—His trial and death.

The trial of the Sheareses was followed by that of John M'Cann of the 17th of July, 1798, of William Michael Byrne on the 20th, and Oliver Bond on the 23d of the same month. These were among the persons who had been at the head of the United Irishmen in the metropolis, and whom the Government, upon information communicated by one of their associates, had arrested in the preceding March. Mr. Curran acted as leading counsel for them all; but his speeches in the two former cases having been entirely suppressed,* the present account must be confined to his defence of Bond.

[Oliver Bond was an eminent woollen-draper, residing in Bridge Street, Dublin, and is described by Davis as "a shrewd, kind man." He was indicted for high treason,—that is for having administered unlawful oaths, on the 20th of May, 1798, to Thomas Reynolds and others, for conspiring to cause a rebellion to overthrow the King's government, for collecting money to furnish arms and ammunition for that purpose, for aiding and causing Reynolds to be a rebel Colonel in the county of Kildare, and for aiding and assisting the French to invade Ireland, &c.

The principal witness, Thomas Reynolds, of Kilkea Castle, "swore hard" but many persons testified that he was not to be believed upon his oath. In fact, he was steeped to the eyes in

* M'Cann and Byrne were convicted and executed.—C.

crime. He stole jewels, and silks from his mother,—swindled a servant out of a bond of £175,—and was accused, by his own brother-in-law, under circumstances of the strongest suspicion, of having poisoned his wife's mother, for the sake of robbing her of £300. His infamy, as will be seen by the extracts from his evidence, was proven, out of his own lips.*]

This was considered by the bar as the most powerful of his efforts upon the state trials of this year. Mr. Curran has been represented, by the detractors of his reputation, as surrounded, during those trials, by an admiring populace, whose passions, instead of endeavouring to control, he was rather anxious to exasperate, by presenting them with exaggerated pictures of the calamities of the times. It is not true that his audiences were of this description: one of the most honourable circumstances of his life is the fact that they were of a far different kind. He was encompassed, indeed, by men whose passions were sufficiently inflamed, but they were passions which it required no ordinary courage in the advocate to brave, and to despise. In his defence of Bond he was repeatedly interrupted, not by bursts of applause, but by violence and menace; with what effect will appear in the course of the following passages.

"Gentlemen, much pains has been taken to warm you, and then you are intreated to be cool; when the fire has been kindled, it has been spoken to, and prayed to be extinguished. What is that?"† [Here Mr. Curran was again interrupted by the tumult of the auditors; it was the third time that he had been obliged

* Reynolds's family did not like to rest under the imputation of his having been an informer and perjurer. His son, some years since, published an apology for his life. It failed to clear him. Reynolds was rewarded with two consular appointments, and, for some time was postmaster of Lisbon during the Peninsular war. In all he received £45,000 for swearing men's lives away, and one of his family still receives the pension settled on him, literally as the price of blood.—M.

† This question was occasioned by a clash of arms among the military that thronged the court; some of those who were nearest to the advocate appeared, from their looks and gestures, about to offer him personal violence, upon which, fixing his eye sternly on them, he exclaimed, "You may assassinate, but you shall not intimidate me."—C.

to sit down: on rising he continued,] "I have very little, scarcely any hope of being able to discharge my duty to my unfortunate client,—perhaps most unfortunate in having me for his advocate. I know not whether to impute these inhuman interruptions to mere accident; but I greatly fear they have been excited by prejudice."

[The Court said they would punish any person who dared to interrupt the counsel for the prisoner. "Pray, Mr. Curran, proceed on stating your case; we will take care, with the blessing of God, that you shall not be interrupted."]

"You have been cautioned, gentlemen, against prejudice. I also urge the caution, and not with less sincerity: but what is the prejudice against which I would have you armed? I will tell you: it is that pre-occupation of mind that tries the accused before he is judicially heard; that draws those conclusions from passion which should be founded on proof, and that suffers the temper of the mind to be dissolved and debased in the heat of the season. It is not against the senseless clamour of the crowd, feeling impatient that the idle discussion of facts delays the execution, that I warn you. No: you are too proud, too humane, to hasten the holiday of blood. It is not against any such disgraceful feelings that I warn you. I wish to recall your recollections to your own minds, to guard you against the prejudice of elevated and honest understanding, against the prejudice of your virtues.

"It has been insinuated, and with artful applications to your feelings of national independence, that I have advanced, on a former occasion, the doctrine that you should be bound in your decisions by an English act of parliament, the statute of William III. Reject the unfounded accusation; nor believe that I assail your independence, because I instruct your judgment and excite your justice. No: the statute of William III. does not bind you; but it instructs you upon a point which before was enveloped in doubt. The morality and wisdom of Confucius, of Plato, of Socrates, or of Tully does not bind you, but it may elevate and illuminate you; and in the same way have British acts of parliament reclaimed you from barbarism. By the statute of William III. two witnesses are necessary, in cases of high treason, to a just and equal trial between the Sovereign and the subject; and Sir William Blackstone, one of the wisest and best authorities on the laws of England, states two witnesses to be but a necessary defence of the subject against the profligacy of ministers. In this opinion he fortifies himself with that of Baron Montesquieu, who says, that, where one witness is sufficient to decide between the subject and the state, the consequences are fatal to liberty; and a people so circumstanced cannot long maintain their independence. The oath of allegiance, which every subject is supposed to have taken, stands upon the part of the accused against the oath of his accuser; and no principle can be more wise or just than that a third oath is necessary to turn the balance. Neither does this principle merely apply to the evidence of a common and impeached informer, such as you have heard this day, but to that of any one witness however high and respectable his character."

The informer in question was Thomas Reynolds,* a name that

* Reynolds was a silk-mercer of Dublin, who had taken a very active part in the conspiracy. He was, in 1797, a colonel of the United Irishmen, afterwards treasurer and representative of a county, and finally a delegate for the Province of Leinster. As the time of the general insurrection approached, either remorse, or the hope of reward induced him to apprise the Government of the danger. Having previously settled his terms (500 guineas in hand, and personal indemnity) through Mr. Cope, a Dublin Merchant, he gave information of an intended meeting of the Leinster delegates at Mr. Bond's house, upon which those persons, among whom were M'Cann and Byrne, were arrested in the month of March. The evidence of Reynolds, when connected with the papers that were seized, was so conclusive against the three who were tried, that no line of defence remained but to impeach his testimony. The following extracts from Mr. Curran's cross-examination of him will show the manner in which this was attempted.

THOMAS REYNOLDS CROSS-EXAMINED BY MR. CURRAN.

Q. You talked of yourself as a married man; who was your wife?

A. Her name was Witherington.

Q. Whose daughter?

A. The daughter of Catherine and William Witherington, of Grafton-street.

Q. She has brothers and sisters?

A. One sister and two brothers.

will be long remembered in Ireland, and of which the celebrity has been extended to England, by some late discussions of his character in the British Parliament. This man had been the principal

Q. How long are you married?
A. I was married upon the 25th of March, 1794.
Q. You were young when your father died?
A. I was about sixteen years of age.
Q. I think your mother carried on the business after his death?
A. She did.
Q. Do you recollect at that time whether, upon any occasion, you were charged, perhaps erroneously, with having taken any of her money?
A. No, sir, I do not recollect having heard any such charge.
Q. You have sisters?
A. I have, and had sisters.
Q. Some of them were living at the time of your father's death?
A. All that are now living were: there were more but they died.
Q. Do you recollect having had any charge made of stealing trinkets or any thing valuable belonging to those sisters?
A. Never. I never was charged with taking any thing valuable belonging to any of my sisters.
Q. Were you ever charged with having procured a skeleton key to open a lock belonging to your mother?
A. I was.
Q. I do not ask you whether the charge were true or not; but you say there was a charge of that kind?
A. I say I was told my mother said so.
Q. She did not believe it I suppose?
A. She did not say anything she did not believe.
Q. And she said it?
A. I heard so; and I have no reason to doubt it.
Q. It was to open a drawer?
A. No: it was to open an iron chest.
Q. Where there were knives and forks kept?
A. It is not usual to keep such things there. I believe papers were kept there. Mr. Warren was my mother's partner: he kept her in ignorance, and did not supply her with money.
Q. Do you not believe that your mother made this charge?
A. I believe she thought it at the time. She was a woman of truth: though, at times extremely passionate. I wish to say this:—You ask me whether I ever was accused of stealing money, or other valuables or trinkets, from my sisters: I was not; but I was accused of stealing my mother's trinkets. I was then about sixteen years of age.
Q. During the partnership between Mr. Warren and your mother, do you recollect any thing about a piece of lutstring?
A. I do perfectly well.
Q. Was any charge made of stealing that?

witness foı the Crown upon the trial of M'Cann and Byrne, and it is not improbable that a tenderness for his reputation had occasioned the suppression of Mr. Curran's defences in those cases.

A. The very same charge. I was charged with stealing the lutstring to give it to a girl, and that I also took my mother's jewels for the same purpose.

Q. Then the charge consisted of two parts—the taking, and the manner in which they were given away?

A. If you will have it so.

Q. I am not asking you whether you committed any facts of this kind or not, but whether the charges were made?

A. I tell you the charges were made; and I took the things.

Q. Then you committed the theft; and you were charged with the stealing?

A. Both of the facts were true.

Q. I did not ask you as to the skeleton key?

A. That charge was untrue.

Q. It did not fit the lock?

A. I had no such key: the charge was unfounded: the others were true.

Q. How long is Mrs. Witherington, your mother-in-law, dead?

A. Twelve months, last April.

Q. Where did she die?

A. In Ash-street: a part of the house was my office, and connected with the house.

Q. How long did she live there?

A. About ten months.

Q. Do you recollect what the good old lady died of?

A. I do not know; but heard it was a mortification in her bowels; she was complaining badly for some days.

Q. Had there been any medicine brought to her?

A. I recollect perfectly well, after she was ill, medicine was brought her.

Q. By whom?

A. By me.

Q. Are you a physician?

A. No: but I will tell you. A Mr. Fitzgerald, a relation of our family, who had been an apothecary, and quitted business, left me a box of medicines, containing castor oil, cream of tartar, rhubarb, tartar emetic, and such things. I had been subject to a pain in my stomach, for which he gave me a quantity of powders in small papers, which I kept for use, and found great relief from: they saved my life. I asked Mrs. Reynolds for one of these papers to give Mrs. Witherington, and it was given to her.

Q. It did not save her life?

A. No, sir; and I am sorry for it.

Q. You paid her a sum of money?

A. I did.

Q. How much?

A. £300.

Q. How long before her death?

A. About a fortnight or three weeks; I got her receipt, and made my clerk account for it in my books.

The following description of him by Mr. Curran, in Bond's case, has been omitted in the common report:

"I know that Reynolds has laboured to establish a connection between the prisoner and the meeting held at his house; but how does he manage? he brings forward asserted conversations with persons who cannot confront him—with M'Cann, whom he has sent to the grave, and with Lord Edward Fitzgerald, whose premature death leaves his guilt a matter upon which justice dares not to pronounce. He has never told you that he has spoken to any of these in the presence of the prisoner. Are you then prepared, in a case of life and death, of honor and of infamy, to credit a vile informer, the perjurer of an hundred oaths—a wretch whom pride, honour, or religion could not bind? The forsaken prostitute of every vice calls upon you, with one breath, to blast the memory of the dead, and to blight the character of the living. Do you think Reynolds to be a villain? It is true he dresses like a gentleman; and the confident expression of his countenance, and the tones of his voice, savour strong of growing authority. He measures his value by the coffins of his victims; and, in the field of evidence, appreciates his fame as the Indian warrior does in fight—by the number of scalps with which he can swell his triumphs. He calls upon you, by the solemn league of eternal justice, to accredit the purity of a conscience washed in his own

Q. Were you ever charged with stealing that money?

A. I never heard that such a charge was made: none of the family ever spoke of it to my face.

Q. Captain Witherington is the son of your mother-in-law?

A. He is.

Q. Did he make that charge?

A. Not to myself. I will mention a circumstance; she had a bond, and gave it to Mr. Jones to purchase a commission: he said the money could not be got; and the £300 was asked to purchase the commission; and I always thought that her son, Edward Witherington got that money. She died suddenly, and had not made a will.

Q. She died suddenly?

A. She died unexpectedly.

Q. She died in forty-eight hours after taking the powder, which you gave to cure her?

A. She took the paper n Friday evening, and died on Sunday morning.

atrocities. He has promised and betrayed—he has sworn and forsworn; and, whether his soul shall go to heaven or to hell, he seems altogether indifferent, for he tells you that he has established an interest in both. He has told you that he has pledged himself to treason and to allegiance, and that both oaths has he contemned and broken.* At this time, when reason is affrighted from her seat, and giddy prejudice takes the reins—when the wheels of society are set in conflagration by the rapidity of their own motion—at such a time does he call upon a jury to credit a testimony blasted by his own accusation. Vile, however, as this execrable informer must feel himself, history, alas! holds out too much encouragement to his hopes; for, however base, and however perjured, I recollect few instances, in cases between the subject and the crown, where informers have not cut keen and rode

* The following is the list of Reynolds' oaths:

Q. (By Mr. Curran). Can you just tott up the different oaths that you took upon either side?

A. I will give the particulars.

Q. No, you may mention the gross.

A. No; I will mention the particulars. I took an oath of secrecy in the county meeting—an oath to my captains, as colonel. After this I took an oath, it has been said—I do not deny it, nor do I say I took it, I was so alarmed; but I would have taken one if required—when the United Irishmen were designing to kill me, I took an oath before a county member, that I had not betrayed the meeting at Bond's.* After this I took an oath of allegiance.

Q. Had you ever taken an oath of allegiance before?

A. After this I took an oath before the privy council. I took two, at different times, upon giving information respecting these trials. I have taken three since, one upon each of the trials; and, before I took any of them, I had taken the oath of allegiance.

* Upon one occasion Reynolds saved himself from the vengeance of those whom he had betrayed, in a way that was more creditable to his presence of mind. Before he had yet publicly declared his infidelity to the cause of the United Irishmen, as one of their leaders, Samuel Neilson, was passing at the hour of midnight through the streets of Dublin, he suddenly encountered Reynolds, standing alone and unarmed. Neilson, who was an athletic man, and armed, rushed upon him, and commanded him, upon pain of instant death, to be silent and to accompany him. Reynolds obeyed, and suffered himself to be dragged along through several dark and narrow lanes, till they arrived at an obscure and retired passage in the liberties of Dublin. Here Neilson presented a pistol to his prisoner's breast—"What," said the indignant conspirator, "should I do to the villain who could insinuate himself into my confidence for the purpose of betraying me?" Reynolds, in a firm tone, replied, "You should shoot him through the heart." Neilson was so struck by this reply, that, though his suspicions were not removed, he changed his purpose, and putting up his pistol, allowed the other to retire. This fact is given as related by an eminent Irish barrister, to whom it was communicated by one of the parties.—C.

awhile triumphant on public prejudice. I know of few instances wherein the edge of his testimony has not been fatal, or only blunted by the extent of its execution, and retiring from the public view beneath an heap of its own carnage."

Mr. Curran's parting words to the jury in this case have been also omitted in the printed collection of his speeches.

"You have been emphatically called upon to secure the state by a condemnation of the prisoner. I am less interested in the condition and political happiness of this country than you are, for probably I shall be a shorter while in it. I have then the greater claim on your attention and confidence, when I caution you against the greatest and most fatal revolution—that of the sceptre, into the hands of the informer. These are probably the last words I shall ever speak to you; but these last are directed to your salvation, and that of your posterity, when they tell you that the reign of the informer is the suppression of the law. My old friends, I tell you, that, if you surrender yourselves to the mean and disgraceful instrumentality of your own condemnation, you will mark yourselves fit objects of martial law—you will give an attestation to the British minister that you are fit for, and have no expectation of any other, than martial law—and your liberties will be flown, never, never to return! Your country will be desolated, or only become the gaol of the living; until the informer, fatigued with slaughter, and gorged with blood, shall slumber over the sceptre of perjury. No pen shall be found to undertake the disgusting office of your historian; and some future age shall ask—what became of Ireland? Do you not see that the legal carnage which takes place day after day has already depraved the feelings of your wretched population, which seems impatient and clamorous for the amusement of an execution. It remains with you—in your determination it lies—whether that population shall be alone composed of four species of men—the informer to accuse, the jury to find guilty, the judge to condemn, and the prisoner to suffer. It regardeth not me what impressions your verdict shall make on the fate of this country; but you it much regardeth. The observations I have offered, the warning I have held forth, I bequeath you with all the solemnity of a dying bequest; and oh! may the acquittal of your accused fellow-citizen, who takes refuge in your verdict from the vampire who seeks to suck his blood, be a blessed and happy promise of speedy peace, confidence, and security, to this wretched, distracted, and self-devouring country!" *

The preceding trials were immediately followed by an act of attainder against three of the conspirators who had previously perished, and whose property and consideration pointed them out as objects of this measure of posthumous severity. One of these was Lord Edward Fitzgerald,† a young nobleman, whose high connections and personal qualities excited the most lively sympathy for his unfortunate end. He was one of the leaders against whom Reynolds had given information; and for some weeks had contrived, by disguising and secreting himself, to elude the pursuit of the officers of justice. At length he was traced to an obscure house in the metropolis, and apprehended. He made a desperate resistance, and shortly after died in prison, from the wounds which he had received in the struggle. His widow and infant children petitioned against the bill of attainder, upon which occasion Mr. Curran was heard as their counsel at the bar of the House of Commons.‡

[Lord Camden, the Viceroy, was vainly appealed to by Lord Edward's family, to take compassion on the widow and three babes, the eldest not four years old, and protect their estate for

* Mr. Bond was convicted, and sentenced to die: but, in consequence of a negociation entered into between the government and the state prisoners, of which one of the articles proposed by the latter was that his life should be spared, he was respited. He was shortly after carried off by an attack of apoplexy.—C. [Thomas Davis, giving credence to a charge made by Dr. Madden, in his "United Irishmen," says that there is much evidence to show that Bond was murdered. I confess that I do not see the motive of such a crime.—M.]

† The other two were Messrs. Cornelius Grogan, and Beauchamp Bagenal Harvey.—C

‡ August 20th, 1798.—C.

them from violence and plunder. The Viceroy would not, or could not, exercise humanity. On the 27th July, 1798, Toler (afterwards Lord Norbury) introduced a bill into the Irish House of Commons, to attaint Lord Edward, and Messrs. Grogan and Harvey. All efforts against this vicarious trial of dead and unconvicted men were fruitless. Arthur Moore (afterwards a judge), Jonah Barrington, and Plunket spoke, as members of Parliament, on the side of humanity. Reynolds, who had been implicitly trusted by Lord Edward, established the case against him. Still, it appeared (as it was) against law and justice to attaint an *untried* man—every accused person being presumed innocent until convicted, *on trial.* Mr. Curran's appeal, though powerful, was hopeless.]

His speech upon this question is imperfectly reported; but even had it been more correctly given, the leading topics would be found of too abstract a nature to attract the general reader. It still contains, like almost all his arguments upon the most technical subjects, passages of feeling and interest. At this period, he could never refrain, no matter what the occasion might be, from giving expression to the mingled sentiment of melancholy and indignation with which the scenes that were passing before him had filled his mind.

"Upon the previous and important question, namely, the guilt of Lord Edward (without the full proof of which, no punishment can be just), I have been asked by the committee if I have any defence to go into. I was confounded by the question, which I could not answer; but, upon a very little reflection, I see, in that very confusion, the most conclusive proof of the injustice of the bill; for, what can be more flagrantly unjust than to inquire into a fact, of the truth or falsehood of which no human being can have knowledge, save the informer who comes forward to assert it? Sir, I now answer the question: *I have no defensive evidence —it is impossible that I should. I have often of late gone to the dungeon of the captive, but never have I gone to the grave of the* *dead to receive instructions for his defence—nor, in truth, have I ever before been at the trial of a dead man:** I, therefore, offer no evidence upon this inquiry, against the perilous example of which I do protest, on behalf of the public, and against the cruelty and injustice of which I do protest in the name of the dead father, whose memory is sought to be dishonoured, and of his infant orphans, whose bread is sought to be taken away."

The allusion in the following passage to the amiable character of Lord Edward Fitzgerald, will lose much of its force to those who have heard nothing of that unfortunate nobleman, except his fate. His private excellencies were so conspicuous, that the officer of the Crown [Toler], who moved for leave to bring in the bill of attainder, could not refrain from bearing ample testimony to them: "his political offences he could not mention without grief; and, were it consistent with the principles of public justice, he would wish that the recording angel should let fall a tear, and wash them out for ever."

"One topic more," said Mr. Curran, "you will permit me to add.† Every act of this sort ought to have a practical morality

* Lord Brougham has more than once mentioned to me that, in the whole range of forensic eloquence with which he was acquainted, he remembered nothing more pathetic and touching than this passage which I have printed in Italics. The Bill of attainder passed despite of many strenuous efforts to interest George III. in favour of the widow and her orphans. Lord Edward's estate was then sold in Chancery, to satisfy a mortgage, and bought for £10,500 by Mr. W. Ogilvie, Lord Edward's stepfather, who cleared the property, and restored it to the widow. The poor woman (better known, perhaps, as Pamela, the reputed daughter of Madame de Genlis and Egalité), quitting Ireland, went to live at Hamburg, where she married within two years of Lord Edward's death. The union was disunion. She died, at Paris, poor and miserable, in 1831. The British Government promised to reverse the act of attainder, when the Irish "troubles" were over, but this merciful act of justice was not accomplished until 1819. The reader may recollect Byron's graceful sonnet of thanks to George IV. (then Prince Regent), for this act.—M.

† The gist and law of the case were thus put by Curran into a single sentence: "But if he died without attainder, a fair trial was impossible, because a fair defence was impossible; a direct punishment upon his person was impossible, because he could not feel it; and a confiscation of his estate was equally impossible, because it was then no longer his, but was vested in his heir, to whom it belonged by a title as good as that by which it had ever belonged to him in his lifetime, namely, the known law of the country."—M.

flowing from its principle. If loyalty and justice require that these infants should be deprived of bread, must it not be a violation of that principle to give them food or shelter? Must not every loyal and just man wish to see them (in the words of the famous Golden Bull) always poor and necessitous, and for ever accompanied by the infamy of their father; languishing in continued indigence, and finding their punishment in living and their relief in dying; and if the widowed mother should carry the orphan heir of her unfortunate husband to the gate of any man who might feel himself touched by the sad vicissitudes of human affairs—who might feel a compassionate reverence for the noble blood that flowed in his veins, nobler than the loyalty that first ennobled it; that, like a rich stream, rose till it ran and hid its fountain—if remembering the many noble qualities of his unfortunate father, his heart melted over the calamities of the child; if his bosom swelled, if his eyes overflowed, if his too precipitate hand was stretched out by his pity or his gratitude to the poor excommunicated sufferers, how could he justify the rebel tear, or the traitorous humanity?"

Mr. Curran's conduct upon these memorable causes exposed his character at the time to the foulest misrepresentation. The furious and the timid considered it an act of loyalty to brand as little better than a traitor the advocate who, in defending the accused, ventured to demand those legal privileges, and that fair, impartial hearing, to which, by the constitution of their country, they were entitled. He often received, as he entered the Court, anonymous letters threatening his life, if he should utter a syllable that might bring discredit upon the public measures of the day. Even in the House of Commons, he had, in the preceding year, to meet the charge of having forfeited the character of a "good subject" by his efforts for his clients. "I am heavily censured," said he, "for having acted for them in the late prosecutions. I feel no shame at such a charge, except that of its being made at such a time as this; that to defend the people should be held out as an imputation upon the King's counsel, when the people are prosecuted by the state. I think every counsel is the property of his fellow subjects. If, indeed, because I wore his Majesty's gown I had declined my duty, or had done it weakly or treacherously—if I had made that gown a mantle of hypocrisy, and had betrayed my client, or sacrificed him to any personal view—I might, perhaps, have been thought wiser by those who have blamed me, but I should have thought myself the basest villain upon earth." And, in a letter to Mr. Grattan, some years after, alluding to the same subject, he says: "But what were those attacks? Slanders provoked by a conduct of which my friends, as well as myself, had reason to be proud—slanders cast upon me by the very men whose want of wisdom or humanity threw upon me the necesssity of pursuing that conduct which provoked their vengeance and their misrepresentations. Thank God! I did adopt and pursue it, under the pressure of uninterrupted attacks upon my character and fortune, and frequently at the hazard of my life. I trust, that while I have memory, that conduct will remain indelibly engraven upon it, because it will be there a record of the most valuable of all claims—a claim upon the gratitude of my own conscience."

In resisting such attacks, or in braving any more aggravated measures of political hatred, Mr. Curran might have stood alone, and have looked with calmness to the result; but gratefully to his own feelings, and honourably for others, he was not thus abandoned to his own protection. It was now that he was enabled to appreciate the full value of some of the intimacies of his youth, by finding in his own case how tenderly the claims of the ancient friend and companion were respected in a season of general alarm, distrust, and unnatural separation. Had it not been for the interference of Lord Kilwarden, his character and repose would have been more frequently invaded; but that virtuous person, whose mind was too pure to be sullied by party rancour, discountenanced every proposal to prosecute his friend; and never failed to check, as far as his authority could do so, any acts of malignity which might have been adopted without his knowledge.*

It would be defrauding Lord Kilwarden of his greatest praise, to attribute this generous interposition to considerations of mere private friendship: it was only a part of that system of rare and manly toleration which adorned his whole public career. It is

* As an example of the spirit of petty persecution to which he was exposed from persons in subordinate authority, it may be mentioned, that in the year 1798, when the military were billeted throughout the country, a party of seventeen soldiers, accompanied by their wives, or their profligate companions, and by many children, and evidently selected for the purpose of annoyance, were, without any previous notice, quartered on Mr. Curran's house; but the moment that Lord Kilwarden heard of the circumstance, the nuisance was removed. There is another instance of similar interposition to which Mr. Curran alludes in his speech on behalf of Hevey, and of which the particulars are too honourable to Lord Kilwarden to be omitted. Mr. Curran, in that case, mentioned, that "a learned and respected brother barrister had a silver cup, and that Major Sandys (the keeper of the provost prison) having heard that it had for many years borne the inscription of 'Erin go brach,' or 'Ireland for ever,' considered this perseverance in guilt for such a length of years as a forfeiture of the delinquent vessel; and that his poor friend was accordingly robbed of his cup." The gentleman in question was Mr. M'Nally. The manner of the robbery is characteristic of the times; a serjeant waited upon him, and delivered a verbal command from Major Sandys to surrender the cup; Mr. M'Nally refused, and commissioned the messenger to carry back such an answer as so daring a requisition suggested. The serjeant, a decent, humane Englishman, and who felt an honest awkwardness at being employed on such a service, complied; but respectfully remonstrated upon the imprudence of provoking Major Sandys. The consequences soon appeared: the serjeant returned with a body of soldiers, who paraded before Mr. M'Nally's door, and were under orders to proceed to extremities if the cup was not delivered up. Upon Mr. M'Nally's acquainting Lord Kilwarden with the outrage, the latter burst into tears, and exclaiming, that "his own sideboard might be the next object of plunder, if such atrocious practices were not checked," lost not an instant in procuring a restitution of the property. The cup was accordingly sent back with the inscription erased. "And here," continued Mr. Curran, observing upon this transaction, "let me say, in my own defence, that this is the only occasion upon which I have ever mentioned it with the least appearance of lightness. I have often told the story in a way that it would not become me to tell it here: I have told it in the spirit of those feelings that were excited at seeing that one man could be sober and humane, at a moment when so many thousands were drunk and barbarous; and probably my statement was not stinted, by the recollection that I held that person in peculiar respect and regard. But little does it signify whether acts of moderation and humanity are blazoned by gratitude, by flattery, or by friendship: they are recorded in the heart from which they sprung: and, in the hour of adverse vicissitude, if it should ever come, sweet is the odour of their memory, and precious the balm of their consolation."—C.

often the face of the most splendid characters, who mingle in political contentions, to be misunderstood and traduced, until the turbulence of the scene is past, or until the appeasing influence of the grave extorts an admission of their virtues. With Lord Kilwarden it was otherwise, so conspicuous were (if not his talents) his integrity and humanity, more admirable than the most exalted talents, that Ireland, in her most passionate moments, thought and spoke of him while he lived as she now does of his memory. His conduct in the situation of Attorney-General would alone have entitled him to the lasting gratitude of his country. This trying and so frequently unpopular office he filled during the most agitated period of her history. From the year 1790 to 1798 it devolved upon him to conduct the state prosecutions, a task so difficult to perform without reproach; and, to his honour it is recorded, that he did not escape reproach—the reproach of an extreme respect for human life. He delighted in mercy; and though, "like the noble tree, that is wounded itself, while it yields the balm," the indulgence of his nature exposed him to censure, he was still inflexibly merciful, screening the deluded, mitigating, where it could be done, the punishment of the convicted, abstaining, in the most aggravated cases, from embittering the agonies of the criminal by official invective, or by more inhuman levity. Such were the arts by which this excellent man collected arround him the applause of the good, and earned for his memory that epitaph which is never separated from an allusion to his fate—" *the lamented* Lord Kilwarden."

As soon as the first interval of professional occupation permitted him, Mr. Curran seized the opportunity of passing over to England, and of seeking in a more tranquil scene, and in the consolations of private friendship, a temporary relief from the anguish with which he had witnessed the spectacle of turbulence and suffering at home. Upon the present occasion, his feelings of personal respect, and his certainty of finding a generous sympathy for the calamities of their common country, directed his steps to the residence of the Earl of Moira,* a nobleman for whose public and private virtues he had long entertained the most ardent veneration; and it would here be depriving Mr. Curran's memory of one of the titles of honour, upon which he always set the highest value, if it were not added, that, from his first acquaintance with his lordship, and with his accomplished mother, he continued ever after to enjoy their most perfect confidence and esteem. During this visit to them, he addressed to the latter the following little poem, in which the prevailing sentiment will be found to be the despondency that oppressed his own mind at the unfortunate period.

LINES ADDRESSED TO LADY CHARLOTTE RAWDON, AND WRITTEN ON A BLANK LEAF OF CAROLAN'S IRISH AIRS. DONNINGTON PARK, OCTOBER, 1798.

And she said unto her people, Lo! he is a wanderer and in sadness; go therefore, and give him food, that he be not hungry, and wine, that he be comforted. And they gave him food and wine, and his heart was glad: and, when he was departing, he said unto her, I will give thee a book—it containeth the songs of the bards of Erin, of the bards of the days that are gone! and these bards were prophets, and the griefs of the times to come were known unto them, and their hearts were sore troubled; and their songs, yea, even their songs of joy, were full of heaviness! This book will I give unto thee; and it shall be a memorial of the favour thou showedst unto me. And I will pray a prayer for thee, and it shall be heard—that thy days may be happy; and that, if sorrow should come unto thee, it may only be for a season, and that thou mayest find comfort even as I have done, so that thou mayest say, even as I have said, I did not take heed unto my words, when I said I was as one without hope. Surely I am not a wanderer, neither am I in the land of strangers!

* The Earl of Moira here named served, in this country, as Aide-de-camp to Sir Henry Clinton, and subsequently as Adjutant-General of the British forces. He was then Lord Rawdon, and, on his father's death, became Earl of Moira. He ruined his fortune by intimacy with George, Prince of Wales—was sent to India, as Governor-General to repair it—remained there nine years, and was made Marquis of Hastings in his absence. He returned to England in 1822, and was made Governor of Malta in 1824, and died in 1826. He was father of Lady Flora Hastings, so foully "done to death by lying-tongues," in Queen Victoria's Court, some years since.—M.

By the waters of Babylon we sat down and wept, when we remember thee, O Sion!

Carolan, thy happy love
No jealous doubt, no pang can prove.
Thy generous lord is kind as brave;
He loves the bard, and scorns the slave:
And Charlotte deigns to hear thy lays,
And pays thee not with thoughtless praise.
With flowery wreaths the cup is crown'd:
The frolic laugh, the dance goes round
"The hall of shells:" the merry throng
Demand thy mirth, demand thy song.
Here echoes wait to catch the strain,
And sweetly give it back again.
Then, happy bard! awake thy fire—
Awake the heart-string of thy lyre—
Invoke thy Muse. Thy Muse appears;
But robed in sorrow, bathed in tears.
No blithesome tale, alas! she tells—
No glories of the "hall of shells"—
No joy she whispers to thy lays—
No note of love, no note of praise;—
But to thy boding fancy shows
The forms of Erin's future woes,
The wayward fates, that crown the slave,
That mar the wise, that crush the brave,
The tyrant's frown, the patriot's doom,
The mother's tears, the warrior's tomb.
In vain would mirth inspire thy song:
Grief heaves thy breast, and claims thy tongue:
Thy strain from joy to sadness turns:
Thy bard would smile—the prophet mourns.*

Mr. Curran had scarcely returned to Ireland to resume his public duties, when it was his fate to be engaged, while performing them, in another scene, which bore a striking resemblance to the melan-

* These verses were written in answer to a question from Lady Rawdon, upon the cause of the mixture of liveliness and melancholy which distinguishes the compositions of Carolan.—C.

choly catastrophe in Jackson's case. The circumstances alluded to were those which followed the trial and conviction of Theobald Wolfe Tone.

Mr. Tone was one of the most active promoters of the designs of the United Irishmen; and, according to the concurring testimony of all his cotemporaries, was the ablest man who had given his support to that cause. He was originally a member of the Irish bar, where his talents could not have failed to have raised him to distinction; but the principles of the French Revolution, and the hope of successfully applying them to change the condition of his own country, soon diverted his ardent mind from legal pursuits, and involved him in that political career which subsequently occupied his life. In this new field he, at a very early period, became conspicuous for his zeal in supporting the claims of the Roman Catholics, who appointed him a secretary to their committee, and voted him a sum of money as the reward of his exertions. He was also one of the original projectors of the plan of combining the popular strength and sentiment, which was afterwards matured into the Irish Union. That association existed some years before its object was to effect a revolution; but it has already been shown, that, as early as 1791, Mr. Tone recommended precisely the same views which the future leaders vainly attempted to accomplish. In 1794, when Jackson arrived in Ireland upon his secret mission from the French Government, he soon discovered that Mr. Tone was one of the persons the most likely to approve and assist his designs. He accordingly communicated them to him, and was not disappointed in his expectation. Mr. Tone so cordially embraced the proposal of an invasion of Ireland by the French, that, had not the urgency of his private affairs prevented, he would have passed over to France, in order to confer in person with the French authorities upon the subject. Some of the discussions upon this topic took place in the prison of Newgate, in the presence of Cockayne and Mr. Hamilton Rowan, the latter of whom was at that time under sentence of confinement for the publication of a libel. Jackson being shortly after arrested upon the information of Cockayne, Mr. Rowan, who was aware that the evidence of that witness would equally involve himself, effected his escape, and fled to France. Mr. Tone remained. Whatever his more private communications might have been with Jackson, upon whose fidelity he relied, he conceived that the amount of Cockayne's testimony could convict him of no higher an offence than misprision of treason. Considerable exertions were also used by his private friends to dissuade the Government from a prosecution; and, in consequence, he was not arrested. The evidence upon Jackson's trial, however, having publicly shown that some degree of treasonable connexion had subsisted between him and Mr. Tone, the latter was advised, if he consulted his safety, to withdraw from Ireland. He accordingly, in the summer of 1795, transported himself and his family to America.* Here he did not remain many months. He tendered his services to the French Directory, and having met with all the encouragement he could desire, he procured a passage to France, where he arrived in the beginning of the year 1796. He was most favourably received, and appointed to a commission in the French army. His efforts to persuade the Directory to send an armament to Ireland have been previously mentioned. The first expedition having failed, a second attempt was made in the autumn of 1798. This was equally unsuccessful; and Mr. Tone, who was on board the *Hoche* French line-of-battle-ship, one of the vessels captured by Sir J. B. Warren's squadron off the Irish coast, fell into the hands of the English Government, and was brought to trial by court-martial in Dublin, on the 10th of November, 1798.†

* The vessel, in which he was a passenger, no sooner arrived in sight of an American port, than she was boarded by a boat from a British man of war. Mr. Tone was (among others) impressed to serve as a sailor in his majesty's navy; but, after considerable difficulties, his own remonstrances, and the solicitations of Mrs. Tone, obtained his release.—C.

† There is no report, in Thomas Davis's excellent edition of Curran's speeches, of his defence of Wolfe Tone.—M.

Mr. Tone appeared in court in the dress of a French officer. When called on for his defence, he admitted the facts of which he was accused;* but pleaded (of course ineffectually) his French commission. He then proceeded to read a paper which he had drawn up in justification of his conduct, from the conclusion of which it was evident that he had entertained no hope that any defence could avail him. "I have little more to say. Success is all in this life; and, unfavoured of her, virtue becomes vicious in the ephemeral estimation of those who attach every merit to prosperity. In the glorious race of patriotism, I have pursued the path chalked out by Washington in America, and Kosciusko in Poland. Like the latter, I have failed to emancipate my country; and, unlike them both, I have forfeited my life. I have done my duty, and I have no doubt the Court will do theirs. I have only to add, that a man who has thought and acted as I have done, should be armed against the fear of death. I conceive," continued he, "that I stand here in the same light with our *émigrés*; and, if the indulgence lay within the power of the court, I would only request what French magnanimity allowed to Charette and to the Count de Sombreuil—the death of a soldier, and to be shot by a file of grenadiers. This is the only favour I have to ask; and I trust that men, susceptible of the nice feelings of a soldier's honour, will not refuse the request. It is not from any personal feeling that I make this request, but from a respect to the uniform which I wear, and to the brave army in which I have fought."

This final request was not granted. It was directed by the Government that he should be executed in the ordinary form, and in the most public manner; but this the prisoner took the resolution of preventing, by an act, which, in his case, shows the uncertain security of any speculative determinations respecting suicide, against the pressure of the actual calamity, or of the many

* When asked what he would plead, he exclaimed, "Guilty; for I have never, during my life, stooped to a prevarication."—C.

other motives which impel a man to raise his hand against himself.

Upon the evening before the Hoche sailed from Brest, the subject of suicide was fully discussed among the Irish, who formed a part of the expedition. They felt confident of success, should the French troops debark in safety upon the coast of Ireland; but they were equally certain, that, if captured at sea, they would all be condemned, and executed. Upon this a question arose, whether in the latter event, they should suffer themselves to be put to death according to the sentence and forms of law. Mr. Tone maintained that they ought; and, with his usual eloquence and animation, delivered his decided opinion, that, in no point of view in which he had ever considered suicide, could he hold it to be justifiable. It is supposed, that, in his own particular instance, he did not at this time anticipate an ignominious mode of death; but that he expected, in case of capture and condemnation, to be allowed the military privilege which he afterwards so earnestly claimed.† Disappointed in this hope, he now committed the act which he had so lately reprobated. He was induced to do so either by a natural impulse of personal pride, of which he had not previously contemplated the powerful influence, or (as is conjectured by those who best knew him) out of consideration for the army of which he was a member, and for whose honour, in his estimation, no sacrifice could be too great.

Mr. Tone's execution was fixed for Monday, the 12th of Novem-

† The gentleman who has communicated the above circumstances was present at the conversation. Independent of the moral arguments adduced against suicide, it was suggested by one of the company, that from political considerations, it would be better not to relieve, by any act of self-murder, the Irish government from the discredit in which numerous executions would involve it—an idea which, he says, Mr. Tone warmly approved. He adds, that when it appeared that the Hoche was likely to be captured, a boat was despatched to her from the *Biche* (a small, fast sailing vessel, which afterwards escaped into Brest) in order to bring off all the Irish on board; but that Mr. Tone could not be persuaded to avail himself of the opportunity.—C. [Wolfe Tone's own Memoirs tell every thing about him.—M.]

ber. At an early hour upon that morning the sentinel who watched in his room having approached to awaken him, found him with his throat cut across, and apparently expiring. A surgeon was immediately called, who, on examining the wound, pronounced it not mortal, though extremely dangerous; to which Mr. Tone faintly answered, "I find, then, I am but a bad anatomist." The wound was dressed, with the design of prolonging life till the hour of one o'clock, the time appointed for his execution. In the interval a motion was made in the court of King's Bench by Mr. Curran, on an affidavit of Mr. Tone's father, stating that his son had been brought before a bench of officers, calling itself a court-martial, and by them sentenced to death. "I do not pretend to say," observed Mr. Curran, "that Mr. Tone is not guilty of the charges of which he was accused; I presume the officers were honourable men; but it is stated in the affidavit, as a solemn fact, that Mr. Tone had no commission under his majesty, and therefore no court-martial could have cognizance of any crime imputed to him, while the court of King's Bench sat in the capacity of the great criminal court of the land. In times when war was raging, when man was opposed to man in the field, courts martial might be endured; but every law authority is with me while I stand upon this sacred and immutable principle of the constitution—*that martial law and civil law are incompatible;* and that the former must cease with the existence of the latter. This is not the time for arguing this momentous question. My client must appear in this court. *He is cast for death this day.* He may be ordered for execution while I address you. I call on the court to support the law. I move for a habeas corpus to be directed to the provost-marshal of the barracks of Dublin, and Major Sands to bring up the body of Mr. Tone."

Chief Justice.*—"Have a writ instantly prepared."

* Lord Kilwarden.—C.

Mr. Curran.—"My client may die while this writ is preparing."

Chief Justice.—"Mr. Sheriff, proceed to the barracks, and acquaint the provost-marshal that a writ is preparing to suspend Mr. Tone's execution; and *see that he be not executed.*"

The Court awaited, in a state of the utmost agitation, the return of the Sheriff.

Mr. Sheriff.—"My lords, I have been at the barracks, in pursuance of your order. The provost-marshal says he must obey Major Sands. Major Sands says he must obey Lord Cornwallis."

Mr. Curran.—"Mr. Tone's father, my lords, returns, after serving the habeas corpus: he says General Craig will not obey it."

Chief Justice.—"Mr. Sheriff, take the body of Tone into your custody. Take the provost-marshal and Major Sands into custody: and show the order of this court to General Craig."

Mr. Sheriff, who was understood to have been refused admittance at the barracks, returns.—"I have been at the barracks. Mr. Tone, having cut his throat last night, is not in a condition to be removed. As to the second part of your order, I could not meet the parties."

A French emigrant surgeon, whom General Craig had sent along with the Sheriff, was sworn.

Surgeon.—"I was sent to attend Mr. Tone this morning at four o'clock. His windpipe was divided. I took instant measures to secure his life, by closing the wound. There is no knowing, for four days, whether it will be mortal. His head is now kept in one position. *A sentinel is over him, to prevent his speaking.* His removal would kill him."

Mr. Curran applied for further surgical aid, and for the admission of Mr. Tone's friends to him. Refused.

Chief Justice.—"Let a rule be made for suspending the execution of Theobald Wolfe Tone; and let it be served on the proper person."

The prisoner lingered until the 19th day of November, when he expired, after having endured the most excruciating pain;* and with his fate shall close the account of the part which Mr. Curran bore in the public transactions of this calamitous year.

* Mr. Tone had reached only his thirty-fourth year. His father was an eminent coachmaker in Dublin: he had sixteen children (thirteen sons and three daughters), of whom only five attained the age of maturity, and whose fates afford a singular instance of the wanderings and calamities of a single family. Theobald died as before related. Matthew was executed the same year, in Dublin barracks, for high treason: it is said that no more than five persons were present at the execution. William was killed in India, a major in Holkar's service. Arthur accompanied his brother Theobald to America; and was subsequently, at the early age of eighteen, appointed to the command of a frigate in the service of the Dutch republic: he is supposed to have perished at sea, as no account was ever after received of him. Mary was married to a foreign merchant, and died at St. Domingo. Their aged mother survives, and now [1819] resides in Dublin. After the death of Mr. Wolfe Tone, his widow and infant children were protected by the French republic; and, on the motion of Lucien Bonaparte, a pension granted for their support.—C.

CHAPTER XIII.

Effects of the Legislative Union upon Mr. Curran's mind—Speech in Tandy's case—Speech in behalf of Hevey—Allusion in the latter to Mr. Godwin—Mutual friendship of Mr. Curran and Mr. Godwin.

MR. CURRAN's history, during the eight remaining years of his forensic life, consists almost entirely of the causes of interest in which he was engaged. He was no longer in Parliament when the question of the Union was agitated and carried. This measure, which he had always deprecated as ruinous and disgraceful to his country, completed those feelings of political despondency to which the scenes of the rebellion, and the uniform failure of every struggle to avert them, had been habituating his mind.* With the Union, which he considered as "the extinction of the Irish name," all his long cherished hopes for Ireland vanished for ever. From this last shock to his affections and his pride he never recovered. It was ever after present to his imagination, casting a gloom over all his political speculations, and interfering with the repose of his private hours. This sensibility to what so many others bore with complacency as a mere national disaster, will, perhaps, be ridiculed as affected, or doubted as incredible; but those who best knew

* Years before, while in Parliament, he had thus predicted the results of an Union:—"It is very easy to conceive, that in case of such an event the inevitable consequence would be, *an union with Great Britain.* And if any one desires to know what that would be, I will tell him: *It would be the emigration of every man of consequence from Ireland; it would be the participation of British taxes without British trade; it would be the extinction of the Irish name as a people. We should become a wretched colony, perhaps leased out to a company of Jews, as was formerly in contemplation, and governed by a few tax-gatherers and excisemen, unless possibly you may add fifteen or twenty couple of Irish members, who might be found every session sleeping in their collars under the manger of the British Minister.*"—M.

him can attest the sincerity and extent of his affliction. It was so deep, that he began seriously to meditate a final departure from Ireland.* At one time he looked towards America, at another to the English bar; but the better influence of duties and old attachments prevailed over these suggestions of melancholy, and he remained to conclude his fortunes on the scene where they had commenced.

CASE OF JAMES NAPPER TANDY.

ONE of Mr. Curran's speeches, which has been omitted in all the editions of the published collection,† was that in behalf of Mr. James Napper Tandy. Mr. Tandy had been a conspicuous member of the early societies of United Irishmen. In 1795, he was indicted for High Treason, and fled to the Continent, where he became an officer in the French service. He was one of the persons excluded from the benefit of the bill of general amnesty, which was passed after the suppression of the rebellion of 1798. The other particulars of his case may be sufficiently collected from Mr. Curran's statement. The trial took place in the King's Bench, before Lord Kilwarden and the other judges of that Court, on the 19th of May, 1800.‡

Mr. Curran (for the prisoner).—"My lords, and you, gentlemen

* "That country (as he observes in one of his latest speeches at the bar) of which I have so often abandoned all hope, and which I have been so often determined to quit for ever—

Sæpe vale dicto, multa sum deinde locutus,
Et quasi discedens oscula summa dabam,
Indulgens animo, pes tardus erat."

Speech in Judge Johnson's Case.

† It is to be found in Davis's edition.—M.

‡ Napper Tandy had been a merchant in Dublin, of good family; and became an active member of the Corporation fully twenty-five years before 1798. In the struggle for Irish Independence, he commanded the Artillery of the Volunteers, and had his guns cast with "Free Trade or else——" upon them. He led the Radical party in the Corporation, in 1790, and was much mixed up with the United Irishmen from 1791. He fled to America, from prosecution, in 1794, left it in 1798, and headed the Irish Government's list of persons to be held as traitors, if they did not come in to be tried before December 1798. Eventually, he was seized at Hamburgh, (a neutral German city) deported to Ireland,

of the jury, I am in this case of counsel for Mr. Tandy, the prisoner at the bar. I could have wished it had been the pleasure of the gentlemen who conduct this business on the part of the Crown to have gone on first: the subject itself is of a very novel nature in this country; but certainly it is the right of the Crown, and which the gentlemen have thought proper to follow, to call on the counsel for the prisoner to begin; and, therefore, it is my duty, my lords, to submit to you, and to explain, under the direction of the Court, to you, gentlemen of the jury, what the nature of the question is that you are sworn to try.

"An act of parliament was passed in this country, which began to be a law on the 6th of October, 1798; on that day it received the royal assent. By that law it is stated, that the prisoner at the bar had been guilty of acts of treason of many different kinds: and it enacted, that he should stand attainted of high treason except he should, on or before the first day of December following, surrender himself to one of the Judges of this Court, or to one of his Majesty's justices of the peace, for the purpose of becoming amenable to that law, from which he was supposed to have fled, in order to abide his trial for any crime that might be alleged against him.

"It was a law not passed for the purpose of absolutely pronouncing any judgment whatsoever against him, but for the purpose of compelling him to come in and take his trial: and nothing can show more strongly that that act of Parliament has not established anything touching the fact of the prisoner's guilt; because it would be absurd, in one and the same breath, to pronounce that he was guilty of high treason, and then call upon him to come in and abide his trial: and the title of the act speaks that it is an act not pronouncing sentence against the prisoner, but that it is an act in order to compel him to come forward.

tried, defended by Curran, and acquitted. In April 1801, he was again tried for "invading" Ireland, convicted, sentenced to be hanged, and was finally exchanged against a general officer taken by the French, and died there, soon after.—M.

"This act creates a Parliamentary attainder, not founded on the establishment of the prisoner's guilt of treason, but on his contumacious avoidance of trial, by standing out against a trial by law. I make this observation to you, gentlemen of the jury, in order that you may, in the first instance, discharge from your minds any actual belief of any criminality in the prisoner at the bar, and that for two reasons—first, because a well-founded conviction of his guilt, on the authority of this statute, might have some impression on the minds of men sitting in judgment on the prisoner; but for a more material reason I wish to put it from your minds, because his guilt or innocence has nothing to do with the issue you are sworn to try.

"Gentlemen, the issue you are called to try is not the guilt or innocence of the prisoner; it is therefore necessary you should understand exactly what it is. The prisoner was called on to show cause why he should not suffer death, pursuant to the enacting clause of the statute; and he has put in a plea, in which he states, that before the time for surrender had expired, namely, on the 24th of November, 1798, seven days before the day that he had for surrendering had expired, he was, by the order of his Majesty, arrested, and made a prisoner in the town of Hamburgh; and that in consequence of such arrest, it became impossible for him to surrender himself and become amenable to justice within the time prescribed: and the counsel for the crown have rested the case on the denial, in point of fact, of this allegation; and, therefore, the question, that you are to try is simplified to this—'I was arrested,' says the prisoner, 'whereby it became impossible for me to surrender'—to which the counsel for the crown reply, 'You have not been arrested at the time alleged by you, whereby it became impossible for you to surrender.' This I conceive to be the issue, in point of fact, joined between the parties, and on which it is my duty to explain the evidence that will be offered.

"Mr. Tandy is a subject of this country, and had never been in it from the time this act of parliament passed, until he was brought into it after his arrest on the 24th of November, 179.. on that day he was in the town of Hamburgh. He had seven days, in which time it was practicable for him to arrive in this country, and surrender himself, according to the requisitions of the act of attainder. Every thing that could be of value to man was at stake, and called on him to make that surrender. If he did not surrender, his life was forfeited—if he did not surrender, his fortune was confiscated—if he did not surrender, the blood of his family was corrupted; and he could leave them no inheritance, but the disgrace of having suffered as a traitor.

"Your common sense, gentlemen, will show you, that where a man is to forfeit his life unless he complies with the conditions of an act of parliament—your common sense, your common humanity must show you, that a man ought to be suffered to perform the conditions on which his life depends. It can require no argument to impress upon your mind, that to call on a man to surrender himself on pain of death, and by force to prevent him from surrendering, goes to an atrocity of oppression that no human mind can contemplate without horror.

"But it seems that the prisoner at the bar was a man of too much consequence to the repose of all civilized nations; to the great moral system, I might almost say, to the great physical system of the universe, to be permitted to act in compliance with the statute that called upon him to surrender himself upon pain of death. The wisdom of the entire continent was called upon to exercise its mediation on this most momentous circumstance—the diplomatic wisdom of Germany was all put into action on the subject—the enlightened humanity of the north was called on to lend its aid. Gentlemen, you know as well as I the princely virtues, and the imperial qualifications, the consummate wisdom and sagacity of our stedfast friend and ally, the Emperor of all the Russias; you must feel the awe with which he ought to be mentioned: his sacred person has become embodied in the criminal law of England, and it has become almost a misprision to deem of him or speak of him but with reverence. I feel that reverence for him; and I deem of him and conceive him to be a constellation of all virtue—compared with whose radiance the Ursamajor twinkles only as the glow-worm. And, gentlemen, what was the result of the exercise of this combination of wisdom? That James Napper Tandy ought not to be got rid of in the ordinary way. They felt an honest and a proper indignation, that a little community like Hamburgh should embezzle that carcase which was the property of a mild and merciful Government: they felt a proper indignation that the senate of Hamburgh, under the present sublime system, should defraud the mercy of the Government of the blood of the prisoner, or cheat the gibbet of his bones, or deprive the good and loyal ravens of this country of his flesh—and accordingly by an order issued to these miserable inhabitants of the town of Hamburgh, who were made to feel that common honesty and common humanity can only be sustained by a strength not to be resisted; they were obliged to break the ties of justice and hospitality—to trample on the privileges that every stranger claims; they were obliged to suffer the prisoner to be trampled on, and meanly, and cruelly, and pitiably to give up this unfortunate man to the disposal of those who could demand him at such a price.

"If a surrender, in fact, had been necessary on the part of the prisoner, certainly a very material object was achieved by arresting him: because they thereby made it impossible for him to avail himself of the opportunity. They made it impossible for him to avail himself of the surrender, if the reflection of his mind led him to it. If a sense of the duty he owed his family led him to a wish, or to an intention, of availing himself of the remaining time he had to surrender, they were determined he should not take advantage of it. He had been guilty of what the law deems a crime, that is, of flying from justice, though it does not go to the extent of working a corruption of blood: but by this act of power—by this act of tyrannic force, he was prevented from doing that which every court of justice must intend he was willing to do: which the law intends he would have done—which the law gave him time to do—which the law supposes he might have done the last hour, as well as the first. He was on his passage to this country; that would not have taken up a third part of the time that had now elapsed—but by seizing on him in the manner he was arrested, it became impossible for him to surrender himself, or become amenable to justice.

But, gentlemen, the prisoner, when he was arrested, was treated in a manner that made it impossible for him to do any act that might have been considered as tantamount to a surrender. He was confined in a dungeon, little larger than a grave—he was loaded with irons—he was chained by an iron that communicated from his arm to his leg; and that so short, as to grind into his flesh. In such a state of restriction did he remain for fifteen days; in such a situation did he lie in a common vault; food was cut into shapeless lumps, and flung to him by his filthy attendants as he lay on the ground, as if he had been a beast; he had no bed to lie on; not even straw to coil himself up in, if he could have slept. In that situation he remained in a foreign country for fifteen days of his long imprisonment; and he is now called to show good cause why he should not suffer death, because he did not surrender himself and become amenable to the law. He was debarred all communication whatsoever; if he attempted to speak to the sentinels that guarded him, they could not understand him: he did make such kind of indications of his misery and his sufferings as could be conveyed by signs, but he made them in vain; and he is now called on to show good cause wherefore he did contumaciously and traitorously refuse to surrender himself, and become amenable to the law.

"Gentlemen of the jury, I am stating facts that happened in a foreign country; will you expect that I should produce witnesses to lay those abominable offences before you in evidence? It was not in the power of the prisoner at the bar to procure witnesses he was not of importance enough to call on the armed civilization of Europe, or on the armed barbarity of Europe, to compel the inhabitants of the town where he was imprisoned to attend at the bar of this court to give evidence for the preservation of his life; but though such interposal could not be obtained to preserve his life, it could be procured for the purposes of blood.

"And this is one reason why the rights of neutral states should be respected: because, if an individual, claiming those privileges, be torn from that sanctuary, he comes without the benefit of the testimony of those that could save his life. It is a maxim of law, that no man shall lose any thing, much less his life, by the non-performance of a condition, if that non-performance had arisen by the act of God, or of the party who is to avail himself of the condition; that the impossiblity so imposed shall be an excuse for the non-performance of the condition: that is the defence the prisoner relies upon here. 'Why did you not surrender, and become amenable to justice? Because I was in chains.'—'Why did you not come over to Ireland? Because I was a prisoner in a grave in the town of Hamburgh.' 'Why did you not do something tantamount to a surrender? Because I was unpractised in the language of the strangers, who could not be my protectors, because they were also my fellow-sufferers.'

"But he may push this reasoning much farther: the statute was made for the express purpose of making him amenable. When the crown seized him at Hamburgh, it thereby made him amenable, and so satisfied the law. It could not seize him for execution as an attainted person, for the time had not arrived at which the attainder could attach. The King, therefore, seized him as a man liable to be tried, and yet he calls upon him to suffer death, because he did not make himself amenable by voluntary surrender; that is, because he did not do that which the King was pleased to do for him, by a seizure which made it at once unnecessary and impossible for him to do by any voluntary act.

"Such is the barbarity and folly that must ever arise, when force and power assume the functions of reason and justice.

"As to his intention after the arrest, it is clearly out of the question. The idea of intention is not applicable to an impossible act. To give existence to intention, the act must be possible, and the agent must be free. Gentlemen, this, and this only, is the subject on which you are to give a verdict. I do think it is highly honourable to the gentleman who has come over to this country, to give the prisoner at the bar the benefit of his evidence; no process could have compelled him: the inhabitants of foreign countries are beyond the reach of process to bring witnesses to give evidence. But we have a witness, and that of the highest respectability, who was himself at Hamburgh at the time Mr. Tandy was arrested, in an official situation. We will call Sir James Crawford, who was then the King's representative in the town of Hamburgh. We will show you, by his evidence, the facts that I have stated; that before the time allowed to the prisoner to surrender had elapsed, Sir James Crawford did in his official situation, and by orders from his own Government, cause the person of Mr. Tandy to be arrested in Hamburgh. Far am I from suspecting, or insinuating against Sir James Crawford, that any of the cruelties that were practised on that abused and helpless community, or on my abused client, were committed at his instance or personal sanction; certain am I that no such fact could be possible.

"I told you before, gentlemen, that the principal question you had to try was, the fact on which the parties had joined issue: the force and arrest alleged by the prisoner; and the denial of that force by the counsel for the Crown. There is one consideration, that I think necessary to give some attention to. What you may think of the probable guilt or innocence of the prisoner, is not within the question that you are to decide; but if you should have any opinion of that sort, the verdict given in favour of the prisoner can be no preclusion to public justice, if after your verdict they still call for his life; the utmost that can follow from a verdict in his favour will be, that he will be considered as a person who has surrendered to justice, and must abide his trial for any crime that may be charged against him. There are various ways of getting rid of him, if it is necessary to the repose of the world that he should die.

"I have said, if he has committed any crime, he is amenable to justice, and in the hands of the law: he may be proceeded against before a jury, or he may be proceeded against in another and more summary manner; it may so happen that you may not be called upon to dispose finally of his life or of his character.

"Whatever verdict a jury can pronounce upon him can be of no final avail. There was, indeed, a time when a jury was the shield of liberty and life: there was a time, when I never rose to address it without a certain sentiment of confidence and pride; but that time is past. I have no heart now to make any appeal to your indignation, your justice, or your humanity. I sink under the consciousness that you are nothing. With us, the trial by jury has given place to shorter, and, no doubt, better modes of disposing of life. Even in the sister nation, a verdict can merely prevent the duty of the hangman; but it never can purge the stain which the first malignity of accusation, however falsified by proof, stamps indelibly on the character of an 'acquitted felon.' To speak proudly of it to you would be a cruel mockery of your condition; but let me be at least a supplicant with you for its memory. Do not, I beseech you, by a vile instrumentality, cast any disgrace upon its memory.

"I know you are called out to-day to fill up the ceremonial of a gaudy pageant, and that to-morrow you will be flung back again among the unused and useless lumber of the constitution: but, trust me, the good old trial by jury will come round again; trust me, gentlemen, in the revolution of the great wheel of human affairs, though it is now at the bottom, it will reascend to the station it has lost, and once more assume its former dignity and respect; trust me, that mankind will become tired of resisting the spirit of innovation, by subverting every ancient and established principle, and by trampling upon every right of individuals and of nations. Man, destined to the grave—nothing that appertains to him is exempt from the stroke of death—his life fleeth as a dream, his liberty passeth as a shadow. So, too, of his slavery—it is not immortal; the chain that grinds him is gnawed by rust, or it is rent by fury or by accident, and *the wretch is astonished at the intrusions of freedom, unannounced even by the harbinger of hope*.* Let me therefore conjure you, by the memory of the past, and the hope of the future, to respect the fallen condition of the good old trial by jury, and cast no infamy upon it. If it is necessary to the repose of the world that the prisoner should die, there are many ways of killing him—we know there are; it is not necessary that you should be stained with his blood. The strange and still more unheard of proceedings against the prisoner at the bar, have made the business of this day a subject of more attention to all Europe than is generally excited by the fate or the suffering of any individual. Let me, therefore, advise you seriously to reflect upon your situation, before you give a verdict of meanness and of

* There is a passage in Dante descriptive of the same state of amazement, produced by an unexpected escape from danger.

> E come quei che con lena affanata,
> Uscito del pelago alla riva,
> Si volge all' acqua perigliosa, e *guata*.
>
> (And, as a man with difficult short breath,
> Forespent with toiling, 'scaped from sea to shore,
> Turns to the perilous wide waste, and stands
> At gaze.)
>
> *Cary's Translation.*

A distinguished Italian writer, (Ugo Foscolo, in the *Quarterly Review*) now in England, commenting upon this passage in a late number of a periodical work, observes, nearly in the words of Mr. Curran, "The concluding verse places the man in that state of stupor which is felt upon passing at once to safety from despair, without the intervention of hope: he looks back upon perdition with a stare, unconscious how he had escaped it."—C.

blood that must stamp the character of folly and barbarity upon this already disgraced and degraded country."*

[A trial of great local interest, in which Mr. Curran was engaged, came off at the Spring Assizes of Cork, on April 13th, 1801, when Sir Henry Hayes was capitally indicted for the abduction of Miss Pike. The facts were these; Hayes was son of the Alderman of Cork, and had ran through a large property. He was fashionable and expensive in his habits. A widower, with several children, he determined to retrieve his fortune by marriage. Samuel Pike, a Quaker, was a banker in Cork, on whose death, Mary Pike, his daughter, became possessed of £20,000. She was 21 years of age, in weak health, and when the cause for action took place, was living with her relation, Mr. Cooper Penrose, at his beautiful seat called Wood Hill, on the Glanmire road, near Cork. On Sunday, July 2, 1797, Sir Henry Hayes, who was unacquainted with Mr. Penrose, rode over to Wood Hill, was shown round the demesne, and finally, in the full spirit of hospitality, was asked to remain and dine. At table, he first saw Miss Pike, but had no conversation with her as she sat at a side tablé, with Mr. Penrose's daughters.

Hayes returned to Cork, and having ascertained that Miss Pike's mother was a patient of Dr. Gibbings, wrote to him on some trifling pretence, obtained a reply, and then, closely imitating the handwriting, sent a note to Mr. Penrose, intimating that Mrs. Pike was taken suddenly ill and wished to see her daughter, and to command dispatch as she was not expected to live many hours. This missive reached Mr. Penrose after midnight, on July 22nd, 1797, and Miss Pike, accompanied by Miss Penrose and another relative, set off in Mr. Penrose's carriage. The night was tempestuous and dark. The carriage had not proceeded very far before it was stopped by a body of armed men. Miss Pike was identified by a muffled man, placed in another carriage with a lady, and driven off, sur-

* The jury found a verdict for the prisoner. He was afterwards permitted to retire to the continent, where he ended his days.—C.

rounded by an armed escort, to Mount Vernon, the seat of Sir Henry Hayes, in the suburbs. The muffled man was Hayes, the lady was his sister. The traces of Mr. Penrose's carriage were cut to prevent pursuit. The muffled man took Miss Pike in his arms, out of the carriage, into his house, and placed her for that night, under charge of two women. Next morning, at day-break, she was forced into an upper room by Sir Henry and Miss Hayes, and a man in priest's habits was introduced, who performed a sort of marriage ceremonial, in which Sir Henry attempted to force a ring upon her finger, which she threw away. She was then locked up in the room, which contained only a table and bed, and after tea had been given to her, Sir Henry, (to use her own words,) was "coming in and out, and behaving in the rudest manner," and saying she was his wife. However, he did not perpetrate the worst outrage. She insisted on writing to her friends, who liberated her the next day.

If Sir Henry Hayes was popular, Miss Pike's friends were wealthy, persevering, and determined. They appealed to the law, such abduction being then a capital felony under the statute. Hayes fled. A reward of £2000 was offered by the Government and Miss Pike's friends, but in vain. Hayes was outlawed, but actually returned to Cork, where he lived, unconcealed and unmolested. At last, Hayes wrote to Miss Pike, politely offering to stand his trial, which took place (the outlawry being reversed, by consent,) nearly four years after the commission of the offense. Mr. Justice Day was the presiding Judge. There was a great array of counsel on both sides. For the Crown, Mr. Curran and six others; for the prisoner, Mr. Quin and seven more. Hayes came into Court attended by "host of friends." Curran's speech was earnest, eloquent, grave, and at times pathetic. He dwelt on the anomaly of Miss Pike, the victim, being compelled to fly to England, for security, during two years that the ravisher was "basking in the favours of a numerous kindred and acquaintance, in a widely-extended city," where every man knew his person. Hayes called no witnesses, his counsel pressing for an acquittal in law, from the insufficiency of evidence under the statute of abduction. Curran replied. The jury returned a verdict of "Guilty," with a recommendation to mercy. The point of law raised by Sir Henry's counsel was referred to the twelve judges and decided against him. The capital punishment was not inflicted, being commuted to transportation for life. In a few years, a full pardon was granted. Hayes returned to Cork, and died over twenty years after the trial.*]

The next of Mr. Curran's professional efforts which shall be noticed was that in behalf of Mr. John Hevey, who brought an action for false imprisonment against Charles Henry Sirr, town-major of Dublin.† This, though a private case, was intimately connected with the public events in which the preceding state trials originated. It also resembles them in the examples of suffering and depravity which it exhibits. It presents a picture of a race of beings, the greatest scourge of an agitated country—political middle-men, who, conscious that the restoration of tranquillity must throw them out of employment and plunder, feel an interest in aggravating the public disorders by every art of violence and persecution, which, under the pretext of proving their zeal, can prolong the necessity of their office. Of this office and its detest-

* The popular voice was wholly in favor of Sir Henry Hayes. A ballad-singer made a good deal of money by selling a song, the refrain of which was

Sir Henry kissed—Sir Henry kissed
Sir Henry kissed the Quaker.
And what if he did? You ugly thing,
I'm sure he did not *ate* her!

On the morning of the trial, as Mr. Curran was going into the Court-House, some of the populace, who greatly admired him, called out "God bless you, Mr. Curran! I hope you'll win the day!" Curran, who was *against* their favorite, answered "If I do, you'll lose the *Knight!*" I recollect having seen Sir Henry Hayes, in the streets of Cork, in 1825. He was a low-statured, thick-set man, wearing a broad-brimmed hat. It was said that his constant companion was a man who used to walk with his head on one side, the effect, I have heard, of his having been hanged in the rebellion of 1798.—M.

† May 17th, 1802.—C. [The trial took place before Lord Kilwarden and a special jury.—M.]

able abuses, a tolerable idea may be formed from a sketch of Mr. Curran's statement.

"It was at that sad crisis (1798) that the defendant, from an obscure individual, started into notice and consequence. It is the hot-bed of public calamity that such inauspicious products are accelerated without being matured. From being a town major, a name scarcely legible in the list of public incumbrances, he became at once invested with all the real powers of the most absolute authority.

"With this gentleman's extraordinary elevation began the story of the sufferings and ruin of the plaintiff. A man was prosecuted by the state; Hevey, who was accidentally present at the trial, knowing the witness for the prosecution to be a person of infamous character, mentioned the circumstance in court. He was sworn, and on his evidence the prisoner was acquitted. In a day or two after, Major Sirr met the plaintiff in the street, asked how he dared to interfere in *his* business? and swore, by God, he would teach him how to meddle with 'his people.' On the following evening poor Hevey was dogged in the dark into some lonely alley—there he was seized, he knew not by whom, nor by what authority—his crime he soon learned, it was the treason he had committed against the majesty of Major Sirr. He was immediately conducted to a new place of imprisonment in the Castle-yard, called the provost. Of this mansion of misery Major Sandys was the keeper, a gentleman of whom I know how dangerous it is to speak, and of whom every prudent person will think and talk with all due reverence. Here Hevey lay about seven weeks; he was at last discovered among the sweepings of the prison. 'Hevey' (said the Major) 'I have seen you ride, I think, a smart sort of mare—you can't use her here—you had better give me an order for her.' Hevey, induced by hope and by fear, gave the order. The Major accepted the order, saying, 'Your courtesy will not cost you much—you are to be sent down to-morrow to Kilkenny, to be tried for your life—you will most certainly be hanged—and you can scarcely think that your journey to the other world will be performed on horseback.' Hevey was accordingly transmitted to Kilkenny, tried by a court-martial, and convicted upon the evidence of a person under sentence of death, who had been allured by a proclamation offering a reward to any man who would come forward and give any evidence against the traitor Hevey. Lord Cornwallis read the transmiss of Hevey's condemnation—his heart recoiled from the detail of stupidity and barbarity. He dashed his pen across the odious record, and ordered that Hevey should be forthwith liberated. On his return to Dublin the plaintiff met Major Sandys, and demanded his mare;—'Ungrateful villain,' (says the Major) 'is this the gratitude you show to his Majesty and to me, for our clemency to you—you shan't get possession of the beast.' Hevey brought an action for the mare; the Major, not choosing to come into court and suggest the probable success of a thousand actions, restored the property.

"Three years," continued Mr. Curran, "had elapsed since the deliverance of my client; the public atmosphere had cleared; the private destiny of Hevey seemed to have brightened, but the malice of his enemies had not been appeased. On the 8th of last September, Mr. Hevey was sitting in a public coffee-house; Major Sirr was there; Mr. Hevey was informed that Major Sirr had at that moment said, that he (Hevey) ought to have been hanged. The plaintiff was fired at the charge; he fixed his eyes on Sirr, and asked if he had dared to say so? Sirr declared that he had, and had said truly. Hevey answered, that he was a slanderous scoundrel. At that instant Sirr rushed upon him, and, assisted by three or four of his satellites, who attended him in disguise, secured him and sent him to the Castle guard, desiring that a receipt might be given for the villain. He was sent thither. The officer of the guard chanced to be an Englishman, but lately arrived in Ireland—he said to the bailiffs, 'If this was in England, I should think this gentleman entitled to bail, but I don't know the laws of this country; however I think you had better loosen those irons on his wrists, or they may kill him.'

"Major Sirr, the defendant, soon arrived, went into his office, and returned with an order which he had written, and by virtue of which Mr. Hevey was conveyed to the custody of his old friend and gaoler, Major Sandys. Here he was flung into a room of about thirteen feet by twelve; it was called the hospital of the provost; it was occupied by six beds, in which were to lie fourteen or fifteen miserable wretches, some of them sinking under contagious disorders. Here he passed the first night without bed or food. The next morning his humane keeper, the Major, appeared. The plaintiff demanded why he was so imprisoned, complained of hunger, and asked for the gaol allowance? Major Sandys replied with a torrent of abuse, which he concluded by saying, 'your crime is your insolence to Major Sirr; however, he disdains to trample on you; you may appease him by proper and contrite submission; but unless you do so you shall rot where you are. I tell you this, that if Government will not protect us, by God, we will not protect them. You will probably (for I know your insolent and ungrateful hardiness) attempt to get out by an habeas corpus, but in that you will find yourself mistaken, as such a rascal deserves.' Hevey was insolent enough to issue a habeas corpus, and a return was made on it, 'that Hevey was in custody under a warrant from General Craig, on a charge of treason.' That this return was a gross falsehood, fabricated by Sirr, I am instructed to assert. The judge, before whom this return was brought, felt that he had no authority to liberate the unhappy prisoner; and thus, by a most inhuman and malicious lie, my client was again remanded to the horrid mansion of pestilence and famine. Upon this Mr. Hevey, finding that nothing else remained, signed a submission dictated by Sandys, was enlarged from confinement, and brought the present action."

The foregoing is a very curtailed sketch of the particulars of this case; those who partake of the prevailing taste for strong emotions are referred to the entire report, where they will find in every line abundant sources of additional excitement.

Of the style in which the advocate commented upon these

extraordinary facts, the following is among the most striking examples:

Adverting to the ignorance in which England was kept regarding the sufferings of Ireland, and to the benefit to be derived from sending her one authenticated example, Mr. Curran goes on—" I cannot also but observe to you, that the real state of one country is more forcibly impressed on the attention of another by a verdict on such a subject as this, than it could be by any general description. When you endeavour to convey an idea of a great number of barbarians practising a great variety of cruelties upon an incalculable number of sufferers, nothing defined or specific finds its way to the heart; nor is any sentiment excited, save that of a general, erratic, unappropiated commiseration. If, for instance, you wished to convey to the mind of an English matron the horrors of that direful period, when, in defiance of the remonstrance of the ever to be lamented Abercromby,* our poor people were surrendered to the licentious brutality of the soldiery, by the authority of the State—you would vainly endeavour to give her a general picture of lust, and rapine, and murder, and conflagration. By endeavouring to comprehend every thing, you would convey nothing. When the father of poetry wishes to pourtray the movements of contending armies and an embattled field, he exemplifies only, he does not describe—he does not venture to describe the perplexed and promiscuous conflicts of adverse hosts, but by the acts and fates of a few individuals he conveys a notion of the vicissitudes of the fight and the fortunes of the day. So should your story to her keep clear of generalities; instead of exhibiting the picture of an entire province, select a single object, and even in that single object do not release the imagination of your hearer from its task, by giving more than an outline. Take a cottage—place the affrighted mother of her orphan daughters at the door, the paleness of death in her face, and more than its agonies in her heart—

* Sir Ralph Abercromby (born in 1738, died in 1801) commanded the troops in Ireland during the early part of the Rebellion of 1798; but his disgust at the system of cruelty and tyranny sanctioned there by the Government, caused him to make indignant remonstrances, which were answered by his recall.—M.

her aching heart, her anxious ear struggling through the mist of closing day to catch the approaches of desolation and dishonour. The ruffian gang arrives—the feast of plunder begins—the cup of madness kindles in its circulation—the wandering glances of the ravisher become concentrated upon the shrinking and devoted victim: you need not dilate—you need not expatiate—the unpolluted mother, to whom you tell the story of horror, beseeches you not to proceed; she presses her child to her heart—she drowns it in her tears—her fancy catches more than an angel's tongue could describe; at a single view she takes in the whole miserable succession of force, of profanation, of despair, of death. So it is in the question before us. If any man shall hear of this day's transaction, he cannot be so foolish as to suppose that we have been confined to a single character like those now brought before you. No, gentlemen, far from it—he will have too much common sense not to know, that outrages like these are never solitary; that where the public calamity generates imps like these, their number is as the sands of the sea, and their fury as insatiable as its waves."

The jury awarded Mr. Hevey £150 damages:* out of Ireland this verdict excited some surprise and indignation, feelings which sufficiently corroborate Mr. Curran's assertion, that the internal condition of his country was but little known in the sister kingdom. A story of such complicated sufferings and indignities would have found a far different reception from an English jury—but the plaintiff in this action was a person to whom, in Ireland, it would have been deemed disloyal to have granted a just remuneration. Hevey was suspected of disaffection in 1798, and the men who were thus regardless of his appeal to their sympathy, were avenging the popular excesses of that year.

In the course of Mr. Curran's observations upon the persecution of his client in this case, he took an occasion of introducing a happy

* Plunket was counsel for Major Sirr. Despite the favourable verdict, Hevey was ruined. The long imprisonment made him bankrupt. Poverty and sorrow broke his mind (said Davis), and he died a pauper lunatic shortly after.—M.

and well-merited compliment to a friend and a man of genius. "No country" (said he) "governed by any settled laws, or treated with common humanity, could furnish any occurrences of such unparalleled atrocity; and if the author of Caleb Williams, or of the Simple Story,* were to read the tale of this man's sufferings, it might, I think, humble the vanity of their talents (if they are not too proud to be vain) when they saw how much more fruitful a source of incident could be found in the infernal workings of the heart of a malignant slave, than in the richest copiousness of the most fertile and creative imagination."

Among his English friends, the author of Caleb Williams was the one to whom Mr. Curran, during the last twenty years of his life, was the most attached, and in whose society he most delighted. However he may have dissented from some of Mr. Godwin's speculative opinions, he always considered him as a man of the most decidedly original genius of his time, and uniformly discountenanced the vulgar clamour with which it was the fashion to assail him. There are many who well remember his fervour and eloquence upon this topic, the tears which he so frequently excited by his glowing descriptions of the private excellencies of his friend, and of the manly, philosophic equanimity by which he triumphed over every accident of fortune. Mr. Curran's affection and respect were not unreturned—Mr. Godwin attended him in his last illness, watched over him till he expired, accompanied him to his grave, and has since his death omitted no occasion, in public or private, of honouring his memory.†

* Mrs. Inchbald.—M.

† His work, Mandeville, is dedicated to the memory of Mr. Curran, "the sincerest friend he ever had," a tribute of generous and disinterested regard, of which the motives are above all suspicion.—C. [Godwin, who was six years younger than Curran, survived him, not departing this life until 1836. At the time when Curran complimented Godwin, in his speech for Hevey, the novelist, who was on a visit at the Priory, was in Court. On returning, Curran, who expected at least a word or two of acknowledgment, and received none, asked Godwin what he thought of the trial? "Oh," said Godwin, "I had forgotten. I am glad that I heard you, as I have now *some idea of your manner*." The very last note written by Curran was an invitation to Charles Phillips to meet Godwin at dinner."—M.]

CHAPTER XIV.

Mr. Curran visits Paris—Letter to his son—Insurrection of 1803—Defence of Kirwan—Death of Lord Kilwarden—Intimacy of Mr. Robert Emmett in Mr. Curran's family, and its consequences—Letter from Mr. Emmett to Mr. Curran—Letter from the same to Mr. Richard Curran.

THIS year (1802) Mr. Curran, taking advantage of the short peace, revisited France. His journey thither now was undertaken with views and anticipations very different from those which had formerly attracted his steps towards that country. He had this time little hope of any gratification; he went from an impulse of melancholy curiosity, to witness the extent of his own disappointments, and to ascertain in person whether anything worth saving, in morals and institutions, had escaped the general wreck; for he was among those whose general attachment to freedom had induced them to hail with joy the first prospects which the revolution seemed to open upon France. His own early admiration of the literary and social genius of her people had made him watch, with the liveliest interest, the progress of their struggles, until they assumed a character which no honourable mind could contemplate without anguish and horror.

To Mr. Curran, too, every painful reflection upon the destiny of France was embittered from its connexion with a subject so much nearer to his heart, the fate of Ireland: for to whatever cause the late rebellion might be attributed, whether to an untimely and intemperate spirit of innovation in the people, or to an equally violent spirit of coercion in the state, it was in the influence of the French revolution that the origin of both might be found.

It will be seen, from some passages in the following letter to one of his sons, that he found little in France under its consular government to diminish his regrets or justify a return to hope.

"PARIS, *October* 5, 1802.

"DEAR RICHARD,

"Here I am, after having lingered six or seven days very unnecessarily in London. I don't know that even the few days tnat I can spend here will not be enough; sickness long and gloomy; convalescence disturbed by various paroxysms; relapse confirmed; the last a spectacle soon seen and painfully dwelt upon. I shall stay here yet a few days. There are some to whom I have introductions that I have not seen. I don't suppose I shall get myself presented to the consul. Not having been privately baptized at St. James's would be a difficulty; to get over it a favour; and then the trouble of getting one's self costumed for the show; and then the small value of being driven, like the beasts of the field before Adam when he named them; I think I sha'n't mind it. The character of this place is wonderfully different from that of London. I think I can say without affectation, that I miss the frivolous elegance of the old times before the Revolution, and that in the place of it I see a squalid, beard-grown, vulgar vivacity; but still it is vivacity, infinitely preferable to the frozen and awkward sulk that I have left. Here they certainly wish to be happy, and think that by being merry they are so. I dined yesterday with Mr. Fox, and went in the evening to Tivoli, a great planted, illuminated garden, where all the *bourgeoisie* of Paris, and some of better description, went to see a balloon go up. The aeronaut was to have ascended with a smart girl, his *bonne amie*; for some reason that I know not, some one else went up in her place; she was extremely mortified; the balloon rose, diminished, vanished into night; no one could guess what might be its fate, and the poor dear one danced the whole evening to shake off her melancholy.

"I am glad I have come here I entertained many ideas of it,

which I have entirely given up, or very much indeed altered. Never was there a scene that could furnish more to the weeping or the grinning philosopher; they well might agree that human affairs were *a sad joke**. I see it every where, and in every thing. The wheel has run a complete round; only changed some spokes and a few 'fellows,' very little for the better, but the axle certainly has not rusted; nor do I see any likelihood of its rusting. At present all is quiet except the tongue, thanks to those invaluable protectors of peace, the army!! At Tivoli last night we had at least an hundred soldiers, with fixed bayonets. The consul now *lives* at St. Cloud in a magnificence, solitary, but still fitting his marvellous fortune. He is very rarely seen—he travels by night—is indefatigable—has no favourite, &c.

"As to the little affairs at the Priory,† I can scarcely condescend, after a walk in the Louvre, amid the spirit of those arts which were inspired by freedom, and have been transmitted to power, to think of so poor a subject. I hope to get a letter from you in London, at Osborne's, Adelphi. Many of the Irish are here—not of consequence, to be in danger: I have merely heard of them. Yesterday I met Arthur O'Connor in the street, with Lord and Lady Oxford. Her ladyship very kindly pressed me to dine: but I was engaged. I had bargained for a cabriolet, to go

* This idea occurs again in a speech, delivered by Mr. Curran two years subsequent to the date of the above letter. "I find, my lords, I have undesignedly raised a laugh. Never did I less feel merriment—let me not be condemned—let not the laugh be mistaken. Never was Mr. Hume more just than when he says, 'that in many things the extremes are nearer to one another than the means.' Few are those events, that are produced by vice and folly, which fire the heart with indignation, that do not also shake the sides with laughter. So when the two famous moralists of old beheld the sad spectacle of life, the one burst into laughter, and the other melted into tears; they were each of them right and equally right.

Si credas utrique
Res sunt humanæ flebile ludibrium.

But these are the bitter ireful laughs of honest indignation, or they are the laughs of hectic melancholy and despair."—*Speech in behalf of Mr. Justice Johnson.*

† Mr. Curran's country seat in the vicinity of Dublin.—C.

and see my poor gossip. Set out at two: at the end of five miles found I was totally misdirected—returned to St. Denys—got a miserable dinner, and was fleeced as usual. I had some vengeance of the rascal, however, by deploring the misery of a country where a stranger had nothing for his dinner but a bill. You feel a mistake in chronology in the two "yesterdays;" but, in fact, part of this was written yesterday, and the latter part now. I need not desire you to bid any one remember me; but tell them I remember them. Say how Eliza does. Tell Amelia and Sarah I do not forget them. God bless you all.

"J. P. C."

A more detailed and elaborate exposition of Mr. Curran's opinions upon the condition of France at this period, and upon the merits of its ruler's system, is contained in a speech which he made the following year in defence of Owen Kirwan,* one of the persons engaged in the insurrection of the 23d of July, 1803. He undertook the office of counsel for some of these deluded insurgents, not in the expectation that any aid of his could save them, but because it afforded him an opportunity of warning his countrymen against a recurrence to such fatal enterprises, by publicly protesting against their folly and criminality, and by exposing the fatuity of those who imagined that a revolution, achieved by the assistance of France, could have any other effect than that of subjecting Ireland to the merciless control of that power. His

* The trial of Owen Kirwan arose out of Robert Emmett's unsuccessful attempt at a general insurrection, in 1803. The revolt was over almost before it commenced. Government made numerous arrests. A special commission was issued for the trial of the prisoners, and the judges were Lord Norbury, Mr. Justice Finucane, and Barons George and Daly. Nineteen persons were tried; one was acquitted, one was respited, and Robert Emmett, with sixteen more, were convicted and executed. Several of the prisoners were defended by Curran, Ponsonby, and McNally; but Curran's only speech was for Owen Kirwan, who was convicted. No other verdict could have been given on the evidence, proof being given of the outbreak, and of Kirwan (a tailor in Plunket street, Dublin) having turned out from his shop with a pike on his shoulder, at the head of several men. It was attempted to be shown, but without success, that Kirwan had slept at home on the night in question. He was executed on September 3, 1803.—M.

opinions and advice upon this subject he gave at considerable length in the speech alluded to, which, independent of any other claims to praise, remains an honourable testimony of his promptness in opposing the passions of the people, where he did not conceive that they were the necessary result of more reprehensible passions in a higher quarter. He has hitherto been seen almost uniformly exclaiming against the latter as the principal causes of his country's disasters; it is therefore due to him, and to the Government of 1803, to give an example of the different language that he used where he considered it deserved.

"I cannot but confess that I feel no small consolation when I compare my present with my former situation upon similar occasions. In those sad times to which I allude, it was frequently my fate to come forward to the spot where I now stand, with a body sinking under infirmity and disease, and a mind broken with the consciousness of public calamity, created and exasperated by public folly. It has pleased heaven that I should live to survive both these afflictions, and I am grateful for its mercy. I now come here through a composed and quiet city—I read no expression in any face, save such as marks the ordinary feelings of social life, or the various characters of civil occupation—I see no frightful spectacle of infuriated power or suffering humanity—I see no tortures—I hear no shrieks—I no longer see the human heart charred in the flame of its own vile and paltry passions, black and bloodless, capable only of catching and communicating that destructive fire by which it devours, and is itself devoured—I no longer behold the ravages of that odious bigotry by which we were deformed, and degraded, and disgraced; a bigotry against which no honest man should ever miss an opportunity of putting his countrymen, of all sects, and of all descriptions, upon their guard.

"Even in this melancholy place I feel myself restored and re-created by breathing the mild atmosphere of justice, mercy, and humanity—feel I am addressing the parental authority of the law. I feel I am addressing a jury of my countrymen, of my fellow-subjects, and my fellow-Christians, against whom my heart is waging no concealed hostility, from whom my face is disguising no latent sentiment of repugnance or disgust. I have not now to touch the high-raised strings of an angry passion in those that hear me; nor have I the terror of thinking, that, if those strings cannot be snapped by the stroke, they will be only provoked into a more instigated vibration.

"I have heard much of the dreadful extent of the conspiracy against this country, of the narrow escape of the Government: you now see the fact as it is. By the judicious adoption of a mild and conciliatory system of conduct, what was six years ago a formidable rebellion has now dwindled down to a drunken, riotous insurrection—disgraced, certainly, by some odious atrocities: its objects, whatever they were, no doubt highly criminal; but, as an attack upon the state, of the most contemptible insignificance.

"I have no pretension to be the vindicator of the Lord Lieutenant of Ireland, whose person I do not know that I have ever seen; at the same time, when I am so necessarily forced upon the subject, I feel no disposition to conceal the respect and satisfaction with which I saw the King's representative comport himself as he did, at a crisis of no little anxiety, though of no considerable danger. I think it was a proof of his excellency's firmness and good sense, not to discredit his own opinion of his confidence in the public safety, by an ostentatious display of unnecessary open preparation;* and I think he did himself equal honour, by preserving his usual temper, and not suffering himself to be exasperated by the event, when it did happen, into the adoption of any violent or precipitate measures. Perhaps I may even be excused, if I confess that I was not wholly free from some professional vanity when I saw that the descendant of a great lawyer†

* Preparation was *not* made. Had Emmett's followers congregated in a compact force and assailed the Castle, it must have been taken; for, so unprepared was the Government, that, whether from carelessness or design there was not a single ball in the arsenal which would fit the artillery!—M.

† Lord Hardwicke.—M.

was capable of remembering what, without the memory of such an example, he perhaps might not have done, that, even in the moment of peril, the law is the best safeguard of the constitution. At all events, I feel that a man, who, at all times, has so freely censured the extravagancies of power and force as I have done, is justified, if not bound, by the consistency of character, to give the fair attestation of his opinion to the exercise of wisdom and humanity wherever he finds them, whether in a friend or in a stranger."

Upon the subject of the mere political folly, setting even apart all moral tie of duty or allegiance, or the difficulty or the danger" of Ireland's desiring to separate from England, and fraternize with France, Mr. Curran observes, "Force only can hold the acquisitions of the French Consul. What community of interest can he have with the different nations that he has subdued and plundered? clearly none. Can he venture to establish any regular and protected system of religion among them? Wherever he erected an altar, he would set up a monument of condemnation and reproach upon those wild and fantastic speculations which he is pleased to dignify with the name of philosophy, but which other men, perhaps because they are endowed with a less aspiring intellect, conceive to be a desperate, anarchical atheism, giving to every man a dispensing power for the gratification of his passion, teaching him that he may be a rebel to his conscience with advantage, and to his God with impunity. Just as soon would the government of Britain venture to display the crescent in their churches, as an honorary member of all faiths to show any reverence to the cross in his dominions. Apply the same reasoning to liberty. Can he venture to give any reasonable portion of it to his subjects at home, or his vassals abroad? The answer is obvious: sustained merely by military force, his unavoidable policy is to make *the army every thing* and *the people nothing.* If he ventured to elevate his soldiers into citizens and his wretched subjects into freemen, he would form a confederacy of mutual interest between both, against which he could not exist a moment.

"I may be asked are these merely my own speculations, or have others in Ireland adopted them. I answer freely, *non meus hic sermo est.* It is to my own knowledge, the result of serious reflection in numbers of our countrymen. In the storm of arbitrary sway, in the distraction of torture and suffering, the human mind had lost its poise and tone, and was incapable of sober reflection; but, by removing those terrors from it, by holding an even hand between all parties, by disdaining the patronage of any sect or faction, the people of Ireland were left at liberty to consider her real situation and interest; and happily for herself, I trust in God, she has availed herself of the opportunity. With respect to the higher orders, even of those who thought they had some cause to complain, I know this to be the fact—they are not so blind as not to see the difference between being proud, and jealous, and punctilious, in any claim of privilege or right between themselves and their fellow subjects, and the mad and desperate depravity of seeking the redress of any dissatisfaction that they might feel, by an appeal to force, or the dreadful recourse to treason and to blood. As to the humbler order of our people, for whom, I confess, I feel the greatest sympathy, because there are more of them to be undone—I have not the same opportunity of knowing their actual opinions; but if their opinions be other than I think they ought to be, would to God they were present in this place, or that I had the opportunity of going into their cottages—and they well know I should not disdain to visit them, and to speak to them the language of affection and candour on the subject—I should have little difficulty in showing to their quick and apprehensive minds how easy it is, when the heart is incensed, to confound the evils which are inseparable from the destiny of imperfect man, with those which arise from the faults or errors of his political situation. I would put a few questions to their candid, unadulterated sense: Do

15*

you think you have made no advance to civil prosperity within the last twenty years? Are your opinions of modern and subjugated France the same that you entertained of popular and revolutionary France fourteen years ago? Have you any hope, that, if the first Consul got possession of your island, he would treat you half so well as he does those countries at his door, whom he must respect more than he can respect or regard you? Can you suppose that the perfidy and treason of surrendering your country to an invader would, to your new master, be any pledge of your allegiance? Can you suppose that, while a single French soldier was willing to accept an acre of Irish ground, he would leave that acre in the possession of a man who had shown himself so stupidly dead to the suggestions of the most obvious interest, and to the ties of the most imperious moral obligations? Do you think he would feel any kind-hearted sympathy for you? Answer yourselves by asking, what sympathy does he feel for Frenchmen, whom he is ready by thousands to bury in the ocean, in the barbarous gambling of his wild ambition? What sympathy, then, could bind him to you? He is not your countryman: the scene of your birth and your childhood is not endeared to his heart by the reflection that it was also the scene of his. He is not your fellow-Christian: he is not, therefore, bound to you by any similarity of duty in this world, or by any union of hope beyond the grave; what, then, could you suppose the object of his visit, or the consequence of his success? Can you be so foolish as not to see that he would use you as slaves while he held you; and that when he grew weary, which he would soon become, of such a worthless and precarious possession, he would carry you to market in some treaty of peace, barter you for some more valuable concession and surrender you to expiate by your punishment and degradation, the advantage you had given him by your follies and your crimes."

The particulars of the scene on the night of the 23d of July are not inserted here.* It resembled a riot rather than insurrection, and was alarming only because it was unexpected; for, notwithstanding the momentary panic which it excited, in a few hours the public tranquillity was restored; yet however innocuous to the state, it was to Ireland a great calamity. It revived and confirmed many sentiments of internal animosity and distrust, by fatally proving that the elements of disorder were not extinct; it violently tore from the services of his country the respected Lord Kilwarden, one of the most upright of her magistrates; the wisest, because the gentlest, in her councils; the man who of all others least required such a martyrdom to consecrate his name. It is scarcely necessary to add, that to Mr. Curran the fate of a person whom he had so long loved and honoured, and who in the season of trial had proved so tender a friend to him, and to their common country, was a source of profound and lasting affliction.†

* The account of the plan of insurrection, drawn up by Mr. Robert Emmett during his imprisonment, has been published.—C.

† It is universally agreed that the murder of this excellent man was the unpremeditated act of a ferocious rabble; but there are various accounts of their probable motives in wantonly sacrificing so upright and humane a judge to their fury. A popular explanation of this is, that that the perpetrators mistook him for another person. There is also an account which admits the mistake in the first instance, but subjoins other particulars which appear sufficiently probable; and as some of the facts, of which there are no doubt, reflect the highest honour upon Lord Kilwarden's memory, the whole shall be given here. In the year 1795, when he was Attorney-General, a number of young men (all of whom were between the age of fifteen and twenty) were indicted for high treason. Upon the day appointed for their trial they appeared in the dock, wearing shirts with tuckers and open collars, in the manner usual with boys. When the Chief Justice of the King's Bench, before whom they were to to be tried, came into court and observed them, he called out, "Well, Mr. Attorney, I suppose you're ready to go on with the trial of these tuckered traitors?" The Attorney-General was ready, and had attended for the purpose; but indignant and disgusted at hearing such language from the judgment seat, he rose, and replied, "No, my lord, I am not ready; and, (added he, in a low tone to one of the prisoners' counsel who was near him) if I have any power to save the lives of these boys, whose extreme youth I did not before observe, that man shall never have the gratification of passing sentence of death upon a single one of these tuckered traitors." He performed his promise, and soon after procured pardons for them all, upon the condition of their expatriating themselves for ever; but one of them obstinately refusing to accept the pardon upon that condition, he was tried, convicted and executed. Thus far the facts rest upon credible authorities; what follows is given as an unauthenticated report. After

But it was not solely in this point of view that the late events affected Mr. Curran: there were some accompanying circumstances which more intimately related to himself; and however painful their introduction may be, it yet becomes every one who has a sense of the fidelity which is due to the public whom he addresses, not to screen himself behind his personal feelings, where a paramount duty demands their sacrifice; still less would he, upon whom that duty at present devolves, be justified under such a pretext, in leaving the possibility of any misconception or reproach regarding one whose memory the combined sentiments of nature, of country, and of individual respect, impel him to cherish and revere. In the following facts, as far as they are generally connected with Mr. Curran, there is indeed no new disclosure. It is a matter of notoriety, that at this period his house was searched—that he appeared himself before the members of the Privy Council; that a rumour prevailed, to which his political enemies gave a ready credit, and as far as they could, a confirmation, that he was personally implicated in the recent conspiracy. To be silent, therefore, upon a subject so well known, would be a fruitless effort to suppress it; to allude to it remotely and timidly would be to imply that the whole could not bear to be told: it only remains then to give an explicit statement of the particulars, and to subjoin one or two original documents, which will be found to corroborate it in every essential point.

The projector of the late insurrection, Mr. Robert Emmett, who was a young gentleman of a highly respectable family, of very striking talents and interesting manners, was in the habit of visit-

the death of this young man, his relatives (it is said) readily listening to every misrepresentation which flattered their resentment, became persuaded that the Attorney-General had selected him alone to suffer the utmost severity of the law. One of these (a person named Shannon) was an insurgent on the 23d of July, and when Lord Kilwarden, hearing the popular cry for vengeance, exclaimed from his carriage, "It is I, Kilwarden, Chief Justice of the King's Bench!" "Then," cried out Shannon. "you're the man that I want!" and plunged a pike into his lordship's body. This story was current among the lower orders in Dublin, who were most likely to know the fact.—C.

ing at Mr. Curran's house: here he soon formed an attachment for [Sarah] Mr. Curran's youngest daughter. Of the progress of that attachment, and of the period and occasion of his divulging it to her, Mr. Emmett's letters, inserted hereafter, contain all that is to be told. It is necessary, however, to add, as indeed will appear from those letters, that her father remained in total ignorance of the motive of Mr. Emmett's visits, untill subsequent events mad it known to all. To a man of his celebrity and attractive conversa tion, there seemed nothing singular in finding his society cultivated by any young person to whom he afforded (as he so generally did to all) the opportunities of enjoying it. As the period, however, of the intended insurrection approached, Mr. Curran began to suspect, from minute indications, which would probably have escaped a less skilful observer, that his young visiter was actuated by some strong passions, which it cost him a perpetual effort to conceal; and in consequence, without assigning to those appearances any precise motive, or giving the subject much attention, he, in general terms, recommended to his family not to allow what was at present only a casual acquaintance to ripen into a greater degree of intimacy.

Upon the failure of the insurrection, its leader escaped, and succeeded for some weeks in secreting himself. There is reason to believe, that had he attended solely to his safety, he could have easily effected his departure from the kingdom; but in the same spirit of romantic enthusiasm which distinguished his short career, he could not submit to leave a country to which he could never more return, without making an effort to have one final interview with the object of his unfortunate attachment, in order to receive her personal forgiveness for what he now considered as the deepest injury. It was apparently with a view to obtaining this last gratification that he selected the place of concealment in which he was discovered: he was arrested in a house situated midway between Dublin and Mr. Curran's country seat. Upon his person were found some papers, which showed that subsequent to the insurrection he had corresponded with one of that gentleman's family: a warrant accordingly followed as a matter of course, to examine Mr. Curran's house, where some of Mr. Emmett's letters were found, which, together with the documents taken upon his person, placed beyond a doubt his connection with the late conspiracy, and were afterwards used as evidence upon his trial.

It was from this legal proceeding that Mr. Curran received the first intimation of the melancholy attachment in which one of his children had been involved. This is not the place to dwell upon the agony which such a discovery occasioned to the private feelings of the father. It was not the private calamity alone which he had to deplore; it came embittered by other circumstances, which, for the moment, gave his sensibility an intenser shock. He was a prominent public character, and from the intrepid resistance which he had uniformly made in the senate and at the bar to the unconstitutional measures of the state, was inevitably exposed to the political hatred of many, who would have gloried in the ruin of his reputation as in a decisive triumph over those principles which he had all his life supported. He had seen and experienced too much of party calumny not to apprehend that it would show little respect for a misfortune which could afford a pretext for accusation; and however secure he might feel as to the final results of the most merciless investigation, he still could not contemplate without anguish the possibility of having to suffer the "humiliation of an acquittal." But his mind was soon relieved from all such distressing anticipations. He waited upon the Attorney-General,* and tendered his person and papers to abide any inquiry which the government might deem it expedient to direct. That officer entered into his situation with the most prompt and manly sympathy, and instead of assuming the character of an accuser of

* The right honourable Standish O'Grady, the present Chief Baron of the Exchequer in Ireland.—C. [Standish O'Grady, was created Baron O'Grady of Rockbarton, and Viscount Guillamore, of Caher Guillamore, in the County of Limerick, in 1831, when he quitted the Bench. He died in April, 1840, aged 74 years.—M.]

the father, more generously displayed his zeal in interceding for the child. At his instance Mr. Curran accompanied him to the Privy Council. Upon his first entrance there was some indication of the hostile spirit which he had originally apprehended. A noble lord, who at that time held the highest judicial situation in Ireland,* undertook to examine him upon the transaction which had occasioned his attendance. To do this was undoubtedly his duty; but overstepping his duty, or at least his prudence, he thought proper to preface his intended questions by an austere authoritative air, of which the palpable meaning was, that he considered intimidation as the most effectual mode of extracting the truth. He fixed his eye upon Mr. Curran, and was proceeding to cross-examine his countenance, when (as is well remembered by the spectators of the scene) the swell of indignation, and the glance of stern dignity and contempt which he encountered there, gave his own nerves the shock which he had meditated for another's, and compelled him to shrink back into his chair, silent and disconcerted at the failure of his rash experiment. With this single exception, Mr. Curran was treated with the utmost delicacy; for this he was principally indebted to the friendship of the Attorney-General, who finding that every inquiry and document upon the subject explained all the circumstances beyond the possibility of an unfavourable conjecture, humanely and (where it was necessary) firmly interposed his authority, to save the feelings of the parent from any additional affliction.

The following are the letters which it seems requisite to introduce. There was a time when the publication of them would have excited pain, but that time is past. The only persons to whom such a proceeding could have given a pang, the father and the child, are now beyond its reach; and their survivor, who from a sense of duty permits them to see the light, does so under a full persuasion, that all those who from personal knowledge, or

* The Earl of Clare, his old antagonist.—M.

from report, may sometimes recall their memories with sentiments of tenderness or esteem, will find nothing in the contents of those documents which can provoke the intrusion of a harsher feeling.

FROM MR. ROBERT EMMETT TO JOHN PHILPOT CURRAN, ESQ.

"I did not expect you to be my counsel.* I nominated you, because not to have done so might have appeared remarkable. Had Mr. —— been in town, I did not even wish to have seen you; but as he was not, I wrote to you to come to me once. I know that I have done you very severe injury, much greater than I can atone for with my life: that atonement I did offer to make before the Privy Council, by pleading guilty, if those documents were suppressed.† I offered more—I offered, if I was permitted to consult some persons, and if they would consent to an accommodation for saving the lives of others, that I would only require for my part of it the suppression of those documents, and that I would abide the event of my own trial. This also was rejected; and nothing but individual information (with the exception of names) would be taken. My intention was, not to leave the sup-

* Curran had originally been named as one of Emmett's counsel, but the delicacy of his situation forbade his acting. He had the highest opinion of him, and subsequently said: "I would have believed the word of Emmett as soon as the oath of any man I ever knew."—M.

† His letters to Sarah Curran.—In fact, the letters were not brought before the Court, on the trial, and, in fulfilment of the compact, Emmett made no legal defence. His celebrated speech was *after* conviction, when he was called up to offer any cause why sentence should not be passed. The reader of Washington Irving (the whole world), will recollect that the unhappy loves of Emmett and Sarah Curran, supplied a subject for one of the most touching and pathetic papers in "The Sketch Book." After Emmett's execution, home became changed to Sarah Curran, and she went to live in the house of Mr. Penrose near Cork. There, Captain Sturgeon prevailed upon her to marry him, which she did, telling him that her affections were in the grave. He took her to Sicily, where, in a few months, she died of a broken heart. Captain Sturgeon, who survived her several years, was killed in battle, during the Peninsular War,—Emmett wore a tress of her hair next his heart, when he was executed; and, only an hour before his death, he bade her farewell in this brief note, "My love, Sarah! it was not thus that I thought to have requited your affection, I did hope to be a prop around which your affections might have clung and which never have been shaken; but a rude blast has snapped it, and they have fallen over a grave!"—He died, as he had lived, fearlessly.—M.

pression of those documents to possibility, but to render it unnecessary for any one to plead for me, by pleading guilty to the charge myself.

"The circumstances that I am now going to mention, I do not state in my own justification. When I first addressed your daughter, I expected that in another week my own fate would be decided. I knew that in case of success, many others might look on me differently from what they did at that moment; but I speak with sincerity, when I say that I never was anxious for situation or distinction myself, and I did not wish to be united to one who was. I spoke to your daughter, neither expecting, nor, in fact, under those circumstances wishing that there should be a return of attachment; but wishing to judge of her dispositions, to know how far they might be not unfavourable or disengaged, and to know what foundation I might afterwards have to count on. I received no encouragement whatever. She told me that she had no attachment for any person, nor did she seem likely to have any that could make her wish to quit you. I staid away till the time had elapsed when I found that the event to which I allude was to be postponed indefinitely. I returned by a kind of infatuation, thinking that to myself only was I giving pleasure or pain. I perceived no progress of attachment on her part, nor anything in her conduct to distinguish me from a common acquaintance. Afterwards I had reason to suppose that discoveries were made, and I should be obliged to quit the kingdom immediately; and I came to make a renunciation of any approach to friendship that might have been formed. On that very day she herself spoke to me to discontinue my visits; I told her that it was my intention, and I mentioned the reason. I then, for the first time, found, when I was unfortunate, by the manner in which she was affected, that there was a return of affection, and that it was too late to retreat. My own apprehensions, also, I afterwards found, were without cause, and I remained. There has been much culpability on my part in all this, but there has also been a great deal of that misfortune which seems uniformly to have accompanied me. That I have written to your daughter since an unfortunate event has taken place, was an additional breach of propriety, for which I have suffered well; but I will candidly confess, that I not only do not feel it to have been of the same extent, but that I consider it to have been unavoidable after what had passed; for though I will not attempt to justify in the smallest degree my former conduct, yet when an attachment was once formed between us—and a sincerer one never did exist—I feel that, peculiarly circumstanced as I then was, to have left her uncertain of my situation would neither have weaned her affections, nor lessened her anxiety; and looking upon her as one, whom, if I had lived, I hoped to have had my partner for life, I did hold the removing her anxiety above every other consideration. I would rather have had the affections of your daughter in the back settlements of America, than the first situation this country could afford without them. I know not whether this will be any extenuation of my offence—I know not whether it will be any extenuation of it to know, that if I had that situation in my power at this moment, I would relinquish it to devote my life to her happiness—I know not whether success would have blotted out the recollection of what I have done—but I know that a man, with the coldness of death on him, need not be made to feel any other coldness, and that he may be spared any addition to the misery he feels not for himself, but for those to whom he has left nothing but sorrow."*

FROM THE SAME TO RICHARD CURRAN, ESQ.

"MY DEAREST RICHARD,

"I find I have but a few hours to live, but if it was the last moment, and that the power of utterance was leaving me, I would

* The original, from which the above has been copied, is not signed or dated. It was written in the interval between Mr. Emmett's conviction and execution.—C.

thank you from the bottom of my heart for your generous expressions of affection and forgiveness to me. If there was any one in the world in whose breast my death might be supposed not to stifle every spark of resentment, it might be you; I have deeply injured you; I have injured the happiness of a sister that you love, and who was formed to give happiness to every one about her, instead of having her own mind a pray to affliction. Oh! Richard, I have no excuse to offer, but that I meant the reverse; I intended as much happiness for Sarah as the most ardent love could have given her. I never did tell you how much I idolised her: it was not with a wild or unfounded passion, but it was an attachment increasing every hour, from an admiration of the purity of her mind, and respect for her talents. I did dwell in secret upon the prospect of our union. I did hope that success, while it afforded the opportunity of our union, might be the means of confirming an attachment which misfortune had called forth. I did not look to honours for myself—praise I would have asked from the lips of no man; but I would have wished to read in the glow of Sarah's countenance that her husband was respected. My love, Sarah! it was not thus that I thought to have requited your affection. I did hope to be a prop round which your affections might have clung, and which would never have been shaken; but a rude blast has snapped it, and they have fallen over a grave.*

"This is no time for affliction. I have had public motives to sustain my mind, and I have not suffered it to sink, but there have been moments in my imprisonment when my mind was so sunk by grief on her account, that death would have been a refuge.

"God bless you, my dearest Richard. I am obliged to leave off immediately.

"ROBERT EMMETT."

* In 1847 a London journal mentioning the death of Miss Curran, at Rome, declared that the lady was "the betrothed of Robert Emmett," and the heroine of Moore's song and Irving's touching story. This was an error. It was Amelia, Curran's eldest daughter, who thus died at Rome. His youngest daughter, Sarah, had passed away some thirty years before.—M.

This letter was written at twelve o'clock on the day of Mr. Emmett's execution,* and the firmness and regularity of the original hand-writting contain a striking and affecting proof of the little influence which the approaching event had over his frame. The same enthusiasm which allured him to his destiny, enabled him to support its utmost rigour. He met his fate with unostentatious fortitude; and although few could ever think of justifying his projects or regreting their failure, yet his youth, his talents, the great respectability of his connexions, and the evident delusion of which he was the victim, have excited more general sympathy for his unfortunate end, and more forbearance toward his memory, than is usually extended to the errors or sufferings of political offenders.†

* The best account of Emmett's trial is given by Dr. Madden. He pleaded "Not guilty," but made no defence. Nor, in his speech after conviction, did he allude to Plunket. O'Grady was Attorney-General, James McClelland was Solicitor General, and it was his duty to speak to evidence. But Plunket performed that task—and is accused of having *volunteered* to do it. Neither of the two law officials had thought it necessary to speak —so clear was the case against Emmett, but Plunket (as one of his own biographers admits) "assailed the sad enthusiast, in that form of his deepest suffering, in a theme of invective which might well have been spared." It would seem as if Plunket wished to show how his own strong liberality had declined down to the Government gauge. In two months from that date, Plunket was in office as Solicitor-General.—M.

† In Ireland, the Emmett family have invariably spelled their name with a double *t*. In this country, they have economized, and write *Emmet*.—M.

CHAPTER XVI.

Mr. Curran's domestic affairs—Forensic efforts—Appointed Master of the Rolls in Ireland—His literary projects—Letter to Mr. M'Nally—Account of a visit to Scotland in a letter to Miss Philpot—Letter to Mr. Leslie—Letters to Mr. Hetherington.

[This seems to be the proper place to introduce a notice of Mr. Curran's domestic relations, which it was very pardonable in his son, to have avoided any mention of. His two other biographers, Phillips and O'Regan, were not in a situation to be affected by such delicacy, and have spoken what they knew. Phillips says:—

"There is no doubt there were times when he was subject to the most extreme despondency; but the origin of this was visible enough, without having recourse to any mysterious inquiries. It was the case with him as it is with every person whose spirits are apt to be occasionally excited—the depression is at intervals in exact proportion. Like a bow overstrained, the mind relaxes in consequence of the exertion. He was naturally extremely sensitive—domestic misfortunes rendered his home unhappy—he flew for a kind of refuge into public life; and the political ruin of his country, leaving him without an object of private enjoyment or of patriotic hope, flung him upon his own heart-devouring reflections. He was at those times a striking instance of his own remark upon the disadvantages attendant upon too refined a sensibility. 'Depend upon it, my dear friend,' said he, 'it is a serious misfortune in life to have a mind more sensitive or more cultivated than common; it naturally elevates its possessor into a region which he must be doomed to find *nearly uninhabited!*' It was a deplorable thing to see him, in the decline of life, when visited by this constitutional melancholy. I have not unfrequently accompanied him in his walks upon such occasions, almost at the hour of midnight. He had gardens attached to the Priory, of which he was particularly fond; and into these gardens, when so affected, no matter at what hour, he used to ramble. It was then almost impossible to divert his mind from themes of sadness. The gloom of his own thoughts discolored everything, and from calamity to calamity he would wander on, seeing in the future nothing for hope, and in the past nothing but disappointment. You could not recognize in nim the same creature who, but an hour preceding, had 'set the table in a roar'—his gibes, his merriment, his flashes of wit, were all extinguished. He had a favorite little daughter, who was a sort of musical prodigy. She had died at the age of twelve, and he had her buried in the midst of a small grove just adjoining this garden. A little rustic memorial was raised over her, and often and often have I seen him, the tears 'chasing each other' down his cheeks, point to his daughter's monument, and 'wish to be with her, and at rest.' Such, at times, was the man before whose very look not merely gravity, but sadness has often vanished—who has given birth to more enjoyment, and uttered more wit, than perhaps any of his contemporaries in any country—who had in him materials for social happiness such as we can not hope again to see combined in any one; and whose death has cast, I fear, a permanent eclipse upon the festivities of his circle. Yet even these melancholy hours were not without their moral. They proved the nothingness of this world's gifts—the worse than inutility of this world's attainments; they forced the mind into involuntary reflection; they showed a fellow-creature enriched with the finest natural endowments, having acquired the most extensive reputation, without a pecuniary want or a professional rival, yet weighed down with a constitutional depression that left the poorest wealthy and the humblest happy in the comparison. Nor were they without a kind of mournful interest: he spoke as under such circumstances no human being but himself could have spoken—his mind was so very strangely constituted; such an odd medley of the romantic and the humorous; now soaring into regions of light and sublimity for illustrations, and now burrowing under ground for such ludicrous and whimsical examples; drawing the most strange inferences from causes so remote, and accompanied at times with gestures so comic, that the smile and the tear often irresistibly met during the recital. Perhaps, after one of those scenes of misery, when he had walked himself tired and wept himself tearless, he would again return into the house, where the picture of some friend, or the contingency of some accident, recalling an early or festive association would hurry him into the very extreme of cheerfulness! His spirits rose—his wit returned—the jest, and the tale, and the anecdote pushed each other aside in an almost endless variety, and day dawned upon him, the happiest, the pleasantest, and the most fascinating of companions. The friends whom he admitted to intimacy may perhaps recognize him, even in this hurried sketch, as he has often appeared to them in the hospitalities of the Priory; but, alas! the look all eloquent—the eye of fire—the tongue of harmony, the exquisite address that gave a charm to everything, and spell-bound those who heard him, are gone for ever!"

The domestic misfortunes which rendered his home unhappy, are thus mentioned by O'Regan;—

"Mr. Curran had been married very early to a Miss Creagh, of the county of Cork, with whom for many years he lived very happily. She was of an ancient and highly esteemed family, in the neighbourhood of Newmarket. His union with this lady was founded on affection; her fortune, though small, yet enabled him to pursue his career of study and ambition, and took off many difficulties to which his youth might otherwise have been exposed. He built on a glen in his native country a tasty and rather an handsome cottage, which he called the *Priory*. This became the residence of his family, and the occasional resort of many of the first men of his time and of his country, while his yet limited fortune did not permit a suitable residence in the capital. From this connection commenced under the happiest auspices of mutual affection, afterwards sprang the sorest tortures of his life: it was here began the tempest to his soul. He had many children by this marriage; and so unhappy became his mind by the dishonour which afterwards ensued, that it rent asunder the finest charities of the heart; and for ever afterwards were broken up those great ties and ligaments, by which nature binds the savage and the sage in delicious bondage to the sovereignty of this protecting contrivance. Yet, by permitting his mind to dwell too ardently on this domestic and deplorable calamity, he appears to have suffered under its influence, and to have permitted his own peace to be poisoned. These matters had a powerful re-action on his own happiness; and, thus swung from his moorings, he seemed never after to have had any safe anchorage to ride upon. It is true his vivacity, though impaired, was not extinguished; it burst forth like gleams of light, and vanished; its fiery track left a burning ember after it. The moral aliment by which he was accustomed to be nourished was gone, or, if it remained, it did so remain, but to sour upon his stomach; and to the morbid state of the affections of the heart, succeeded a distracting and a malady of soul, for which society gave but the peace of its presence. Such was the distress, so deep and so afflicting, that with all the elasticity of his temperament, it took him years to consent to be concerned in actions of that nature which unbound his own wounds; and, in his own words, 'let in the brine of the salt sea through the chinks of a vessel, not yet sufficiently staunched or seasoned to keep it out.' At length, however, he conquered those sensations; and we find him the advocate in the famous case of the Rev. Charles Massy, against the Marquis of Headford, tried at Ennis, in the county of Clare, in July 1804, where damages were laid at £40,000 and £10,000 were recovered,—a tribute to eloquence; but how can money heal a wounded spirit? This he spoke of as a gigantic victory over his own feelings; and, in this trial, the philosopher might have traced the history of human suffering amidst the most glowing eloquence; he could have deduced what might have supplied the moral chair with maxims and illustrations, fresh from the mint of nature, by perceiving the agonies of two sufferers identified in the client and in the advocate. Here he had nothing to dramatize, nothing unreal. He had but to spread upon the canvas the picture of woe familiar to his own sufferings: he did so; and if the reporter (the editor of this collection) were faithful, or fortunate to preserve the genuine features of the figure, such might have been placed among the works of the first masters: but to those who heard him, and felt the effect of his overwhelming eloquence, to such it was as electric, and as affecting a piece of pathos, as ever yet was addressed to human feelings: it bore down every thing before it; and he who wrote was often suspended in his labours; and those who heard it were entranced and amazed. Mr. Curran was much flattered on hearing that it drew tears from the eyes of our gracious Queen* on the reading of it.† But, had

* Charlotte; wife of George III.—M.

† Mr. Phillips states that a few years after this speech had been delivered, Mr. Curran was introduced, through the jocularity of a common friend, to the noble defendant, in St. James's Street. It is a mistake to suppose, as has been asserted, that he declined all advocacy in actions of criminal conversation from the period of his own domestic calamity down to that of the trial for Lord Headford. The fact is, in the very year preceding, he obtained one thousand pounds damages in the case of Pentland against Clarke. This case is not reported in the printed volume, but it was tried before Lord Avonmore, the very same judge who presided on the trial of Mr. Curran's own action. The chief argument against him on that lamentable occasion was his alleged inconstancy; and there is a most curious passage in the speech before me, in which he takes occasion to anticipate that ground of defense, and leaves his own opinions on a subject on which, whether justly or unjustly, he was supposed to be so much interested. This speech is very little known.—"There is a species of defense, which perhaps the gentlemen on the other side may attempt to set up—I mean that of recrimination; and I have been led to think that acts of this kind proved against the husband ought not to prevent him from recovering damages for the seduction of his wife; for the consequence arising from illicit connections is widely different with respect to the husband and the wife: casual revelry and immorality in the husband is not supposed to cast an indelible disgrace upon the wife, and can not defraud the children of their property, by introducing a spurious offspring

she heard it delivered, the native notes of Kotzebue would have been, in comparison, but mock heroic. Not quite apprised how Queens feel upon these occasions, certain it is, that her humble subjects, the Ennis ladies, enjoyed it in transports, and his name resounded through the rocks and groves of Edenvale.

"In the action for criminal conversation, brought by Mr. Curran against the Rev. Mr. Sandys, (not Sandes), Lord Clare was supposed not to be an indifferent spectator. It was on this occasion Mr. Saurin's talents were first drawn forth in a statement for defendant, at once solid, luminous, and vehement. Lord Avonmore, the early patron and friend of Mr. Curran, tried the case; and, in its progress, many interesting and affecting scenes took place; the private feelings of the man, his known partiality for the plaintiff, though occasionally interrupted by some small jealousies, the pity for his sufferings, frequently burst forth in some of the finest touches ever witnessed; but the sense of justice, the pride and purity of his mighty mind, quickly deposed the brief authority of the most generous feelings; and the judge, resuming his great functions, shook off the dew-drops from the lion's mane. By the sovereignty of that character it was, that the judge alone presided. On his trial, as well of men as of the case, Mr. Plunket, (to whom Lord Avonmore had been a friend, and whose infancy had been protected since the loss of his father by that excellent nobleman, was employed on the part of Mr. Sandys. Amidst the clashing of opposite arguments, and many animated contentions with Lord Avonmore sustained for a long time in undecided conflicts, Mr. Plunket rallied with fresh forces,

to which the infidelity of the wife may lead. Errors of this kind in the husband may not arise from an actual turpitude of heart; he may have committed errors of this kind, and yet be a good father; he may be a good citizen, he may be a good husband, notwithstanding he may not be entirely without blemish. I am not speaking of a constant scene of riot and excessive debauchery, but of acts which, though they are to be condemned, it is possible to atone for by subsequent good conduct. Could the ill conduct of the husband entail upon the wife the character of a prostitute? No. But the consequences resulting from the conduct of the wife are of a very different nature indeed."—M

and drew upon those great stores, with which nature has so abundantly supplied him: sometimes playing off the light artillery of that wit, which his pride so chastens, that it lies back like that recondite matter in animal nature which is produced for sustenance, but upon great and important occasions; sometimes riding on the wiry edge of irony, his own appropriate figure; and which nor Swift nor Lucian ever possessed in a richer vein. In the indulgence of some of those sallies thrown off in the impetuosity of feeling, the ardent sensibility of the patron, the friend and the judge, kindled, and rapidly rising into one of those impassioned blazes, to which his great nature was subject, he burst forth into this short exclamation, *et tu fili—and thou also, my son.* The effect was overpowering on Mr. Plunket; the sense of gratitude, the reverence for the venerable judge; the obligations imposed on him by the duty he owed his client, and other emotions of a nobler kind, became, by their varied combinations, irresistible; while he, overwhelmed by the impetuosity of mingled, yet contradictory forces, muffling his face in his mantle, sunk down, and was dissolved in tears—tears more creditable to him, than all that eloquence, less popular than argumentative, of which he of most men, may be truly said to be one of the greatest masters.

"Mr. Curran obtained a verdict, and damages, which the defendant was never afterwards called upon to pay; he was scarcely ever heard of after; whilst the unhappy woman, sustained by the bounty of the afflicted husband, made the best atonement by a conduct ever after without reproach or censure. This event discoloured the stream of his future life; and, from the change in his domestic habits, furnished many topics for unkind observation. It is certain he did not refuse to her the consolation of a requested interview, when she lay on the bed of sickness, and, as she thought, of death. If he did not totally forget the injuries he had suffered, he generously consented to see her, which she sought as a consolation, and which to him was the severest trial. This occurred in London some years after the action: but a message, announcing the certainty of her recovery, made this melancholy visit unnecessary."]

Upon the death of Mr. Pitt, * [1806] the political party with whom Mr. Curran had so long been acting having come into office, he was appointed Master of the Rolls in Ireland, and a member of the Privy Council. † With this appointment he was dissatisfied

* In the interval between 1803 and the period of his elevation to the bench (1806) Mr. Curran farther distinguished himself at the bar in the prosecution of Ensign John Castley, for conspiracy to murder the Rev. W. Ledwich, a Roman Catholic Clergyman, (Feb. 1804,) and obtained a conviction for assault; in the case of Massey against the Marquis of Headfort (July 1804) and in the case of Mr. Justice Johnson (February, 1805.) His speeches upon those occasions are among his most vigorous efforts; but ample specimens of his forensic eloquence having been already introduced, the reader is referred to the published collection.—C. [It was in his speech, made on Feb. 4, 1805, for Judge Johnson, that Curran introduced the well-known, and already-quoted, eulogium on Lord Avonmore, with a touching allusion to their former friendship.]

† Upon this occasion the Irish bar convened a meeting, and voted the following address to Mr. Curran:—

"SIR—In your recent appointment to a high and dignified situation, the first pride of the Irish bar feels itself gratified, that independent spirit, preëminent talents, and inflexible integrity have recommended their possessor to the royal favour, and procured his advancement to the bench of justice.

"Yes, Sir, we trust that the lustre which shone upon your distinguished progress as an advocate will beam with a milder but more useful influence from the bench; and the unbiased, impartial, and upright judge will be found in the person who exalted the character of the Irish bar, by his eloquence, and uniformly supported the rights and privileges of an honourable profession."

MR. CURRAN'S ANSWER.

"GENTLEMEN—I thank you from my heart for this proof of your confidence and affection. The approving opinion of so enlightened and independent a body as the Irish bar would be a most valuable reward of merit much superior to mine, which I am conscious has gone little beyond a disposition, but I trust an honest and ardent disposition, so to act in my public and professional characters, as not to be altogether unworthy of the name of an Irishman of that disposition. I receive your kind commendation with pride. I feel that probity of intention is all that we can be responsible for.

"I am peculiarly gratified by the flattering attestation you are pleased to bestow on my endeavours to support the privileges of our profession. They are vitally and inseparably connected with the enjoyment of constitutional liberty and the effectual administration of justice. The more active part which I may have taken in the defence of these privileges I bequeath to you; but be assured that I bring with me the most perfect conviction, that in continuing to maintain them, I shall co-operate with you in the discharge of one of the most important duties that can bind us to our country."

at the time, and he never became entirely reconciled to it. It imposed upon his mind a necessity of unaccustomed labour and unaccustomed restraint, to which opposite habits of so many years did not allow him easily to submit.

[O'Reagan says: "The truth is well known, that Mr. Curran's practice was not so much in the courts of equity. This has been partly accounted for already; the minuter details of practice he was not well acquainted with, and at the time of life when he wa appointed to that office, the character of the mind had acquired a stiff and unbending rigour unfit for pursuits which to him were ever uncongenial. Forms were not habitual to his taste, or to the elevation of his mind; its aspirations were loftier. Of forms he once observed that they were bullet moulds: if once, said he, you have them, you may cast on *ad infinitum*. He should have condescended to them, however, and because he did not do so, and because his mind was accustomed to the common, criminal, and constitutional codes, he was not in his proper element in the Rolls. He unwillingly yielded to be placed there.]

Whatever might be its dignity or emolument, it had no political consequence; and therefore, to him, who had acted such a part in the history of his country, it seemed rather like a compensation for former services, than as a means of taking that honourable share to which he felt himself entitled, in an administration that promised such benefits to Ireland. These sentiments of disgust, in which he perhaps indulged to an unreasonable excess, disturbed the friendship which had so long subsided between him and the late Mr. George Ponsonby, whom Mr. Curran considered as having, by his acquiescence in his appointment to the Rolls, attended to his nominal interests at the expense of his feelings and his reputation. In this opinion, however encouraged by some subsequent circumstances, it is due to the memory of Mr. Ponsonby to state, that Mr. Curran was mistaken. Mr. Ponsonby made no such intentional sacrifice of his friend. He imagined that he was observing, with the strictest honour, the spirit of every former engagement, although it cannot be too much lamented that he should have withheld all explanation on the subject, until a mutual alienation had taken place, which no explanation could recall. The impression was never removed from Mr. Curran's mind, that he had, upon this occasion, been unkindly treated; but it is pleasing to observe, that his resentment was softened and finally subdued by the recollection of his former regard and respect. He visited Mr. Ponsonby in his last illness, and after his lamented death took every opportunity of dwelling upon his virtues, and attesting the claims, which the long and disinterested services of himself and his family had given their name to the gratitude of their country.

[Mr. Curran felt himself driven into the publication of a letter to Mr. Grattan, in which he shewed that he had full grounds for being dissatisfied with the manner in which his party, and particularly Mr. George Ponsonby, had treated him. Passages of this letter, explaining his position, can scarcely be out of place here—particularly as the document itself had a limited circulation at first, and has long been out of print. Mr. Curran says:

"You will remember the state of Ireland in 1779; and the necessity under which we found ourselves, forming some bond of honourable connexion, by which the co-operation of even a small number might be secured, in making some effort to stem that torrent, which was carrying every thing before it. For that purpose our little party was formed;—it consisted of yourself the Duke of Leinster, (that excellent Irishman) the late Lord Ponsonby, Mr. B. Daly, Mr. G. Ponsonby, Mr. Forbes, myself, and some very few others. It may not be for us to pronounce encomiums upon it, but we are entitled to say, that had it been as successful as it was honest, we might now look back to it with some degree of satisfaction. The reason of my adverting to it is, that, under the sanction of that party, and in its presence, it was agreed between Mr. G. Ponsonby and me, that if any circumstances should arise under which it might be honourably open to us to accept office, it should be on the terms of his taking the first, and my taking the second place in the course of professional advancement. Upon the basis of this compact, which was always publicly known, and adopted by Lord Fitzwilliam, in 1795, Mr. G. Ponsonby was then nominated to the office of Solicitor General. The completion of that arrangement was prevented by the change of the Irish Administration; the compact itself continued with increased force, (if by the continued fidelity of observance, compact can be susceptible of accessional obligation) till the late change in 1806; it was again acted upon by the parties to it. On that occasion I was the only interested member of that party that remained in Ireland. I did not write to any of my friends then in London; not to Lord Ponsonby; not even to you. I knew your zeal for my interest; I knew the friendship and purity of Lord Ponsonby—I was sensible of the warm protection of Mr. Fox, to which I had no claim, save what might be suggested to a noble and generous spirit, like his, by my conduct as a public man; I knew also, the protection my interests would have found in Lord Moira, Lord Erskine, or Lord Howick, had such protection been necessary. I felt no solicitude for myself; I remained at home; the event justified my confidence; Mr. G. Ponsonby accepted the Seals; a proof, of itself, that I must have been appointed to the next attainable situation. The next situation could be no other than the office of Attorney-General; it was the only place in the power of the new Administration to vacate; from its official rank in the Government it was the natural passage to that place on the King's Bench, to which, as next in professional advancement, I had a right to succeed. But on this fact I was not left to conjecture. I was apprised by letter from you, and also Mr. G. Ponsonby, that my interests had been taken care of; Mr. G. Ponsonby communicated the same to a relation of mine, then in London; directing him to inform me that my place as Attorney-General was fixed, and that my coming over would be but unnecessary trouble."

The Duke of Bedford, was sent over as Viceroy to Ireland, and on Mr. Ponsonby's appointment as Chancellor, he assured Mr. Curran that every thing would be done for him to his satisfaction. But instead of getting the appointment of Irish Attorney-General, (the stepping stone to the Chief Justiceship, for which, as a common lawyer, he was well qualified, Mr. Curran found that Mr. Plunket was to be continued in that office. After some delay, he saw the Viceroy, who told him that the Mastership of the Rolls was reserved for him. What follows can best be related in Mr. Curran's own words:

"You may easily judge of my feelings on this communication; but it was the first time I had ever seen the Duke of Bedford; I had no shadow of claim upon his Grace; he was not the person to whom I could complain, that I was humbled or ill-treated; I barely said that "that I was grateful to his Grace for the courtesy of the communication;" and retired with an almost decided purpose to decline the appointment. This substitution I considered a direct departure from the compact with Mr. G. Ponsonby, and accompanied by the aggravation of withholding that consultation and explanation, without which, and without my own express consent, I ought not to have been so disposed of. As to the place itself, it was the last I should have chosen; it imposed upon me a change of all my habits of life; it forced my mind to a new course of thinking, and into new modes of labour, and that, increased labour; it removed me from that intellectual exercise which custom and temper had rendered easy and pleasant; it excluded me from the enjoyment of the honest gratification of an official share in an administration which I then thought would have consisted principally, if not altogether, of the tried friends of Ireland. When the party with which I had acted so fairly, had, after so long a proscription, come at last to their natural place, *I did not expect to have been stuck into a window, a spectator of the procession.* From the station, which I then held at the Bar, to accept the neutralized situation of the Rolls, appeared to me a descent, and not an elevation:—It had no allurement of wealth, for diminished as my income had been by the most remorseless persecution for years, by which I was made to expiate the crime of not being an alien to my country, by treachery, or by birth, it was still abundant when compared with my occasions, and was likely to continue so, long as the occasions should last.

"To this intended refusal, however, my friends in Ireland thought there were strong objections; they thought it would look like an accusation of the party at large, to the great majority of whom I had reason to be more attached than ever—they urged other inducements unnecessary to detail—and which I thought worthy my attention. There remained a still superior motive to decide me: to have yielded to resentment, or disgust, and refused the offered situation, might be to carry disturbance and irritation to the bed of a dying friend; I knew the untemporising nature of Lord Ponsonby, where he thought his honour concerned, and I saw that the whole arrangement of the administration for Ireland, as far as it depended upon him, might be dissolved, if he thought me ill-treated; I had a similar apprehension from the part you yourself would pursue upon such an occasion; and I could not but see, that if you and Lord Ponsonby were to withdraw your support from the Irish Administration, that unhappy country could have little to hope from any new order of things. I resolved therefore to submit, and to do so with an appearance of as much good humour as I could affect."

He submitted, therefore, rather than break up his "party." He saw Mr. Ponsonby, who informed him that Sir Michael Smith, (then Master of the Rolls) should be "treated with on the subject of his resignation," and Mr. Curran had the mortification of seeing that instead of coming into the stipulated situation "by an undisputed claim of *right* (?) and without the burthen of one shilling expense to the country," he was flung upon the precarious chance of a place, which if achieved at all could be obtained only by a charge on the public, and rendered additionally disgusting to himself by the appearance of a job. He says:

"At last, after delays perhaps not easy to be avoided, but certainly affording ample time for the triumph of my enemies, and the vexation of my friends, both of whom looked upon me as insulted and abandoned, that treaty took place, without any participation of mine, and without the remotest hint that it could involve any stipulation and guarantee on my part. I was informed by Mr. G. Ponsonby that the arrangement was completed: That Sir Michael was to resign on the terms of receiving the retiring salary; and also, upon the promise by the government, that his deputy Mr Ridgeway, should get a place of 600*l.* per annum, if such place should become vacant before the 25th of March ensuing, until which time no addition could be made to the pension list; and if no such vacancy should occur before that day, he should then be placed on the pension establishment for 500*l.* a year, for his life, and that a provision by pension, to the amount altogether of 300*l.* a year, was also to be made for three inferior officers of Sir Michael's Court.

"Had any idea of any stipulation whatever on my part been suggested, feeling as I did, I could not have borne it—for, see how it would have stood: on my part, it would have been a direct purchase of a judical office. The purchase could not be made good out of its own income, which could last only to my death or resignation: for these annuities were for the lives of four other persons, and worth at least 8000*l.*; with these 8000*l.* therefore, I was eventually to charge my private fortune; for this sum I was to buy the disappointment of an expectation, which I thought certain, and to commit a breach of the law and the constitution.

"But if I could have dispensed with the matter of purity, another question remained: Was this change between my professional and judicial situation so to be obtained, worth the sum of

8000*l.*? There would have been, therefore, two previous questions to decide, a question of crime, and a question of prudence: if I had consulted a moralist upon the one and a Jew upon the other, what would have been the answer? I would not therefore have submitted for a moment, I would have snapped the thread in such a manner as would have made it impossible to splice it, and have felt pleasure in being restored to my liberty."

Five months elapsed before Sir Michael Smith resigned the Rolls. Mr. Curran was then appointed. Time passed on. No place was given, as promised, to Mr. Ridgeway. The Ministry fell to pieces, by the death of Mr. Fox, and finally broke up in April 1807. No pensions had been granted to Mr. Ridgeway and the three other officers of Sir Michael Smith's court, and it was then endeavored to throw upon Mr. Curran the liabilities of the non-performance of a promise to Sir Michael Smith actually made without his consent, or even knowledge. He refused to allow his salary as judge to be burthened with the payment of 800*l.* a year for life to the deputy, trainbearer, tipstaff, and crier of his predecessor. He adds:

"I some time after, heard that Mr. G. Ponsonby had made a grant of 800*l.* per annum to Mr. Ridgeway, and those three inferior officers, and this act has been represented to the public as occasioned by want of gratitude to Mr. G. Ponsonby, my benefactor, and of personal honor as a member of the party; as to the first part of the charge, you well know how unfounded it is; thank God, I have had many friends; I am now addressing the most valued of them; but, in the sense intended, I never had a benefactor: If I had entertained any views of ambition, I could have been lifted only by a stronger wing than my own; but my journey has been on the ground, and performed on foot, and I was able to walk without the crutches of patronage. As to the allegation of my breach of just or honorable engagement, the fact of such engagement must have been with the knowledge of the Duke of Bedford, of Mr. G. Ponsonby, and of Sir Michael Smith; and I aver that I never was required to take any part in guaranteeing to Sir Michael Smith that agreement of government, or of being liable to him in any event for the performance; and that I never did, directly or indirectly, make any promise on the subject; and that I know not of any act whatsoever, which, to the best of my judgment, after the maturest consideration, can warrant the allegations that have been made against me. Of these allegations, I now feel it necessary to take some farther notice: I well knew how incapable Mr. G. Ponsonby must be of making them; if he had heard them, he had too much honour to repel them with indignation; it is therefore the more necessary for me to advert to them. It is said, the substitution, of which I complained, was for my benefit: I answer, first, that it was a question upon which I alone was competent to decide; a question for the feelings of a gentleman; not the calculation of a notary public. Had it been referred to me, as I think it ought, I should have seen, as the public did see, and did say, that it went to sink me, by excluding me from all political confidence. Between such discredit and pecuniary compensation, no honorable mind could balance. But the assertion itself is untrue in fact. The place which I hold was as inferior to that of Attorney-General, in point of pecuniary emolument, as of political consequence. The professional and official income I should have derived from the latter, could not have been less than double the amount of what I now enjoy. I should have made no deduction for any precariousness of tenure, for never was there an administration less likely to be changed. That income, therefore, I should have counted upon as certain, till I passed to the chief seat on the King's Bench; a situation of equal certainty with that of the Rolls; of far more dignity; of, I believe twice the annual value; far more congenial with my habits and temper; which I should have filled with, perhaps, more advantage to the public; certainly, with much greater to myself

And to that place, the office of Attorney-General would have led by the course of ordinary usage. And to that place it must have led me, because in no other way could the compact have been finally fulfilled. I say, then, it was not for my benefit; and I say further, it was for the benefit of Mr. G. Ponsonby himself; as, without some arrangement in which I should acquiesce, his own compact must have been an insurmountable bar to his acceptance of office. I say, also, that if the compact with me had been observed, the arrangement with Sir Michael Smith could never have existed; nor of course any person be called upon to compensate for its non-performance. And yet the charge against me is, that having received a part payment of a debt, I was bound in honour, out of that payment, to defray the expense of the disappointment which prevented my receiving the whole."

Further on, he thus records his claim for consideration from his "party."

"I came into Parliament at a very early period; having no hereditary fortune, I could have little property. During the whole time of my sitting there, I never deviated from those principles which have bound us together; I continued, from Parliament to Parliament, to come in at my own expense. It is apparent how heavy such a burthen must have been. I was not like other men, who came into Parliament without any expense; who had great family interest to support them; I had not the same means nor the same inducements. To this, perhaps, it might be objected, that at my first coming into the House of Commons I did accept a seat from a particular friend; and the fact is so: but it is also true, that having soon differed on political subjects with that gentleman, I purchased a seat for a friend of his, there being then no way of vacating; though, to do him justice, he endeavoured to dissuade me from it; having given me the seat on the express condition of perfect freedom on my part. From the first, I adopted your principles, and on those we acted until the forming of our party, 1789. In the mere personal compact between Mr. G. Ponsonby and me, you (Mr. Grattan) could have no interest; for it was known that you would not accept any emolument of office. The compact itself was not a stipulation for gain, but simply a bond of cohesion in the faithful discharge of that agreement. I made no compromise with power; I had the merit of provoking and despising the personal malice of every man in Ireland who was the known enemy of the country. Without the walls of the courts of justice, my character was pursued by the most persevering slander; and within those walls, though I was too strong to be beaten down by any judicial malignity—it was not so with my clients; and my consequent losses in mere professional income, have never been estimated at less, as you must have often heard, than 50,000*l.*; and yet for these losses, it seems I am to be considered as compensated. It is with no little pain that I descend to such paltry topics, but when accusation is vile and grovelling, what dignity can be expected in defence? It seems the privilege of vulgar calumny, that the victim must be humbled by the one, if he be not disgraced by the other."

Mr. Curran concluded his letter to Mr. Grattan by requesting him to communicate with Mr. Ponsonby (then receiving 4000*l.* a year, as pension for having been Chancellor for less than a twelvemonth), and ascertain whether he had any claims on Mr. Curran, as regards the pensions to Sir M. Smith's ex-officers. If he had, Mr. Curran offered to refer it to Mr. Grattan, Lord Moira, Lord Grey, Lord Erskine, Lord Holland, or Lord Ponsonby, or any other friend or friends that might be appointed. Lords Moira, Grey, and Holland were accordingly named as arbitrators. The matter remained in dispute until May 1810, when it dropped, on Mr. Ponsonby's declaring that *he* had nothing to be referred; and that, therefore, it was for Mr. Curran to open the case, which Mr. Curran, in the absence of his friends, declined doing. Very properly Mr. Ponsonby, not Mr. Curran, was saddled with the payment of Sir M. Smith's ex-officers; while in power, he might have obtained employment or provision for them, and, not having done so, suffered for his default or neglect.

The fact is, Mr. Ponsonby, who had aristocratic connexions (his brother and cousin were Peers), was made Chancellor by the English party, who disliked Curran, the maker of his own fame and fortune, as being "too Irish." Mr. Ponsonby would have cast aside Mr. Curran if he dared, and alleged that his private character would not justify his being made Attorney-General. That this assertion was untrue, may be judged from the fact, that he was made Master of the Rolls—the second equity judge in Ireland. Mr. Grattan is said, when the "party" were puzzled what to do with Mr. Curran, to have suggested, with most unbecoming levity, that he should be made an Irish bishop. This is recorded by Mr. Phillips.

Mr. Davis states the professional opinion of the time, when he declares that "Curran was unsuited to the technicalities and minute business of the Rolls. He had neither knowledge nor taste for it. He felt this, and the moment he could rise was one he anxiously looked to. It may be guessed that his orders or details were not very sound nor convenient. The only memorable decision he made was that in Merry *v.* Power."

The facts of this case may be stated thus. In 1804, Mary Power made her will, bequeathing a considerable portion of her property to the Rev. Dr. John Power (Roman Catholic bishop of Waterford) and others, in trust for charitable purposes. Mr. Merry, her brother, a merchant in Spain, was her next of kin, and died intestate. Her son administered, and brought a suit in the Spiritual Court to set aside the will as unduly obtained and as disposing a large property to "Papists," and for superstitious purposes. His application as an administrator, *pendente lite*, was refused. He then filed a bill praying that the effects be brought into Court by Dr. Power, the acting executor of Mary Power, and her counsel, contending that the will was caused by fraud, by Dr. Power, whom he contumeliously described as "one John Power, a Popish priest." On the other hand, it was argued that there was no color for impeaching the transaction; that the bequests had been most praiseworthy—that the Court had already affirmed the legality of the trusts,—and that it would be unprecedented for a Court to interfere, as was prayed, before the defendant had answered, or had even time to put in an answer.

In giving judgment, the Master of the Rolls (Mr. Curran), said, on the allegation that the will was obtained by fraud practised by "one John Power:"

"I see no semblance of fact to sustain such a charge. Who does this '*one John Power, a Popish priest,*' turn out to be? I find he is a Catholic clergyman—a doctor in divinity, a titular bishop in the diocese of Waterford. And yet I am now pressed to believe this gentleman has obtained this will by fraud. Every fact now appearing repels this charge; I cannot but say that the personal character of the person accused, repels it still more strongly. Can I be brought, on grounds like those now before me, to believe, that a man, having the education of a scholar, the habits of a religious life, and vested with so high a character in the Ministry of the Gospel, could be capable of so detestable a profanation as is flung upon him? Can I forget that he is a Christian bishop, clothed not in the mere authority of a sect, but clothed in the indelible character of the Episcopal order; suffering no diminution from his supposed heterodoxy, nor drawing any increase or confirmation from the merits of his conformity, should he think proper to renounce what we call the errors of faith? Can I bring my mind on so slight, or rather no grounds, to believe, that he could so trample under his feet all the impressions of that education, of those habits, and of that high rank in the sacred ministry of the Gospel, which he holds, as to sink to the odious impiety imputed to him? Can I bring myself to believe such a man, at the dying bed of his fellow-creature, would be capable with one hand of presenting the cross before her uplifted eye, and with the other, of basely thieving from her those miserable dregs of this world, of which his perfidious tongue was employed in teaching her a Christian's estimate? I do not believe it; on the contrary, I am (as far as it belongs to me in this interlocutory way, to judge of the fact) as perfectly convinced that the conduct of Doctor Power was what it ought to be, as I am that the testatrix is dead."

On the allegation that it was a foolish bequest to superstition and Popish uses, he said that, on examination, he had found the object of these bequests to be to provide shelter and comfortable support for poor helpless females; and clothes, and food, and instruction, for poor orphan children.

"How can we behold such acts, without regarding them as forming a claim to, as springing from a consciousness of immortality? In all ages the hour of death has been considered as an interval of more than ordinary illumination: as if some rays from the light of the approaching world had found their way to the darkness of the parting spirit, and revealed to it an existence that could not terminate in the grave, but was to commence in death.

"But these uses are condemned, as being not only superstitious but Popish uses. As to that, I must say that I feel no disposition to give any assistance even to the orthodox rapine of the living, in defeating even the heterodox charity of the dead. I am aware that this objection means somewhat more than directly meets the ear, if it means anything. The objects of these bequests, it seems, are Catholics, or, as they have been called, *Papists;* and the insinuation clearly is, that the religion of the objects of this woman's bounty, calls upon me to exercise some peculiar rigour of interference to abridge or defeat her intentions. Upon this point I wish to be distinctly understood; I do not conceive this to be the spirit of our existing law; nor, of course, the duty of this court to act upon that principle in the way contended for. In times, thank

God, now past, the laws would have warranted such doctrines. *Those laws owed their existence to unfortunate combinations of circumstances that were thought to render them necessary. But if we look back with sorrow to their enactment, let us look forward with kindness and gratitude to their repeal. Produced by national calamity, they were brought by national benevolence, as well as by national contrition, to the altar of public justice and concord, and there offered as a sacrifice to atone, to heal, to conciliate, to restore social confidence, and give us the hope of prosperity and safety, which no people ever had, or deserved, or dared to have,* except where it is founded on the community of interests, a perfectly even and equal participation of just rights, and a consequent contribution of all the strength—of all the parts so equally interested in the defence of the whole.

"I know they have been supposed to originate in religious bigotry—that is, religious zeal carried to excess—I never thought so. The real spirit of our holy religion is too incorruptibly pure and beneficent to be depraved into any such excess. Analyse the bigot's object, and we see he takes nothing from religion but a flimsy pretext in the profanation of its name; he professes the correction of error and the propagation of truth. But when he has gained the victory, what are the terms he makes for himself? Power and profit. What terms does he make for religion? Profession and conformity. What is that profession? The mere utterance of the lips; the utterance of sounds, that after a pulsation or two upon the air, are just as visible and lasting as they are audible. What is the conformity? Is it the practice of any social virtue or Christian duty? Is it the forgiveness of injuries, or the payment of debts, or the practice of charity? No such things. It is the performance of some bodily gesture or attitude. It is going to some place of worship. It is to stand or to kneel, or to bow to the poor-box, but it is not a conformity that has anything to do with the judgment, or the heart, or the conduct. All these things bigotry meddles not with, but leaves them to religion herself to perform. Bigotry only adds one more, and that a very odious one, to the number of those human stains which it is the business of true religion not to burn out with the bigot's fire, but to expunge and wash away by the Christian's tears: such, invariably, in all the countries and ages, have been the motives to the bigot's conflicts, and such the use of his victories: not the propagation of any opinion, but the engrossment of power and plunder, of homage and tribute. Such, I much fear, was the real origin of the Popèry laws. But power and privilege must necessarily be confined to very few. In hostile armies you find them pretty equal, the victors and the vanquished, in the numbers of their hospitals and in the numbers of their dead; so it is with nations, the great mass is despoiled and degraded, but the spoil itself is confined to few indeed. The result finally can be nothing but the disease of dropsy and decrepitude. In Ireland this was peculiarly the case. Religion was dishonoured, man was degraded, and social affection was almost extinguished. A *few, a very few* still profited by this abasement of humanity. But let it be remembered, with a just feeling of grateful respect to their patriotic and disinterested virtue, and it is for this purpose that I have alluded as I have done, that *that few* composed the whole power of the legislature which concurred in the repeal of that system, and left remaining of it, not an edifice to be demolished, but a mere heap of rubbish, unsightly, perhaps pernicious, to be carted away.

"If the repeal of those laws had been a mere abjuration of intolerance, I should have given it little credit. The growing knowledge of the world, particularly of the sister nation, had disclosed and unmasked intolerance, had put it to shame, and consequently to flight! *But though public opinion may proscribe intolerance, it cannot take away powers or privileges established by law.* Those powers of exclusion and monopoly could be given up only by tne generous relinquishment of those who possessed them. And nobly were they so relinquished by those repealing statutes. Those lovers of their country saw the public necessity of the sacrifice, and most disinterestedly did they make it. If too, they have been singular in this virtue, they have been as singularly fortunate in their reward. In general, the legislator, though he sows the seed of public good, is himself numbered with the dead before the harvest can be gathered. With us it has not been so—with us the public benefactors, many of them at least, have lived to see the blessing of Heaven upon their virtue, in an uniformly accelerating progress of industry and comfort, and liberality, and social affection, and common interest, such as I do not believe that any age or nation has ever witnessed.

"Such I do know was the view, and such the hope, with which that legislature, *now no more!* proceeded so far as they went, in the repeal of those laws so repealed. And well do I know how warmly it is now remembered by every thinking Catholic, that not a single voice for those repeals was or could be given, except by a Protestant legislator. *With infinite pleasure do I also know and feel, that the same sense of justice and good will which then produced the repeal of those laws, is continuing to act, and with increasing energy, upon those persons in both countries, whose worth and whose wisdom are likely to explode whatever principle is dictated by bigotry and folly, and to give currency and action to whatever principle is wise and salutary. Such, also, I know to be the feelings of every court in this hall. It is from this enlarged and humanized spirit of legislation that courts of justice ought to take their principles of expounding the law.*

"At another time I should probably have deemed it right to preserve a more respectful distance from some subjects which I have presumed (but certainly with the best intentions, and I hope, no unbecoming freedom), to approach. But I see the interest the question has excited, and I think it right to let no person carry away with him any mistake, as to the grounds of my decision, *or suppose that it is either the duty or the disposition of our courts to make any harsh or jealous distinctions in their judgment founded on any differences of religious sects or tenets.* I think therefore, the motion ought to be refused; and I think myself bound to mark still more strongly my sense of its impropriety, by refusing it with full costs."]

The remaining years of Mr. Curran's life contain little of incident. His time was passed without much variety between the duties of his judicial situation, and the enjoyment of that social intercourse for which his taste continued undiminished to the last It was observed by his friends, to whom he was an object of so much interest that the slightest circumstance connected with him attracted their attention, that his spirits began to decline from the moment of his elevation to the bench. He felt sensible himself that the sudden discontinuance of those modes of intellectual exercise, which an uninterrupted habit of so many years had rendered almost a necessary of life, was impairing the health of his mind.* All his powers were still in the fullest vigor, and he

* It was at this time that Charles Phillips made the acquaintance of Mr. Curran. He thus describes its commencement;

"When I was called to the bar he was on the bench; and, not only bagless, but briefless, I was one day, with many an associate, taking the idle round of the hall of the Four Courts, when a common friend told me he was commissioned by the Master of the Rolls to invite me to dinner that day at the Priory, a little country villa about four miles from Dublin. Those who recollect their first introduction to a really great man, may easily comprehend my delight and my consternation. Hour after hour was counted as it passed, and, like a timid bride, I feared the one which was to make me happy. It came at last, the important *five o'clock*, the *ne plus ultra* of the guest who would not go dinnerless at Curran's. Never shall I forget my sensations when I caught the first glimpse of the little man through the vista of his avenue. There he was, as a thousand times afterward I saw him, in a dress which you would imagine he had borrowed from his tip-staff—his hands on his sides—his face almost parallel with the horizon—his under lip protruded, and the impatient step and the eternal attitude only varied by the pause during which his eye glanced from his guest to his watch, and from his watch reproachfully to his dining-room. It was an invincible peculiarity; one second after five o'clock, and he would not wait for the viceroy. The moment he perceived me, he took me by the hand, said he would not have any one introduce me, and with a manner which I often thought was *charmed*, at once banished every apprehension, and completely familiarized me at the Priory. I had often seen Curran—often heard of him—often read him, but no man ever knew any thing about him who did not see him at his own table with the few whom he selected. He was a little convivial deity! He soared in every region, and was at home in all; he touch-

could not but feel discontented and mortified at finding them (not so much released from toil as) condemned to repose. In the hope of removing this inquietude by indulging his faculties in their accustomed tastes, he began to project one or two literary works.* One of them, and which it is much to be regretted that he had not the firmness to execute, was memoirs of his own time; but all the entreaties of his friends, and all his own resolutions, gave way before his unconquerable aversion to written compositions. The only notice of this intended work found among his papers, was the following motto and preface:

ed every thing, and seemed as if he had created it; he mastered the human heart with the same ease that he did his violin. You wept, and you laughed, and you wondered: and the wonderful creature who made you do all at will never let it appear that he was more than your equal, and was quite willing, if you chose, to become your auditor. It is said of Swift that his rule was to allow a minute's pause after he had concluded, and then, if no person took up the conversation, he recommenced. Curran had no conversational rule whatever; he spoke from impulse; and he had the art so to draw you into a participation, that, though you felt an inferiority, it was quite a contented one. Indeed, nothing could exceed the urbanity of his demeanour. At the time I speak of he was turned of sixty, yet he was as playful as a child. The extremes of youth and age were met in him; he had the experience of the one and the simplicity of the other. At five o'clock we sat down to dinner, during which the host gave ample indications that it was one of his happy days. He had his moody ones: there was no one more uncertain. Joyous was my anticipation of a delightful evening. But, alas! what are the hopes of man? When the last dish had departed, Curran totally confounded me with a proposal, for which I was anything but prepared—'Mr. Phillips, as this is the first of, I hope, your very many visits to the Priory, I may as well at once initiate you into the peculiarities of the place. You may observe, though the board is cleared, there are no preparations for a *symposium:* it all depends upon you. My friends here generally prefer *a walk* after dinner. It is a sweet evening; but if you wish for wine, say so without ceremony.' Even now I can see Curran's star-like eyes twinkling at the disappointment no doubt visible in mine. I had heard, and truly, that he was never more delightful than with half a dozen friends, after dinner, over his bottle. The hope in which I had so long revelled was realized at last—and here came this infernal walk and the 'sweet evening!' Oh, how I would have hailed a thunder-storm! But, to say the truth, the sun was shining, and the birds were singing, and the flowers were blooming and breathing so sweetly on that autumn eve, that, wondering not at the wish of my companions, I also voted for the 'walk.' Never was man so mystified. We took the walk, no doubt, but it was only to the drawing-room, where, over a dessert freshly culled from his gardens, and over wines for which his board was celebrated, we passed those hours which formed an era in my life. It was the commencement of that happy intercourse which gave this world a charm it ought, perhaps, never to possess."

* He left a novel more than half finished, and a long criticism on Milton.—M.

"You that propose to be the historian of yourself, go first and trace out the boundary of your grave—stretch forth your hand and touch the stone that is to mark your head, and swear by the Majesty of Death, that your testimony shall be true, unwarped by prejudice, unbiassed by favour, and unstained by malice; so mayest thou be a witness not unworthy to be examined before the awful tribunal of that after time, which cannot begin, until you shall have been numbered with the dead.

"I have frequently conceived the design of writing some memoirs of myself, and of the times in which I have lived, but I have been prevented by other avocations, not very compatible with such a purpose. I was also deterred by the great hazard to which every man is exposed who ventures to take himself for a subject. What security can he offer to himself or to his reader against the glosses and perversions of false modesty and vain glory? How can he satisfy either that he is not an advocate, when he should be only a reporter? As to the strange and wayward destinies that have agitated this unhappy country during the interval I speak of—when I recollect the strong incitement that I felt as an observer or an actor, can I hope to subside into that unfevered moderation, without which I can scarcely be competent to the task of reviewing or recording them? And yet, perhaps, in my strong feeling of the difficulty and the danger, there may be some hope of escape. The consciousness may be some safeguard against myself, and the fairness of the avowal will naturally prevent the reader from following me when I am led astray. I have therefore resolved to make some attempts upon the subject, in such intervals of health or of leisure as I may be able to command; pursuing it in that way, I cannot hope for much minuteness of detail, or much exactness of connexion. But, however imperfect the performance may be, and indeed must be under such circumstances, yet if it shall contribute to preserve the memory of some acts, and of some actors, that ought not to perish, but should be preserved for the purpose of praise, or punishment, or example, my labour, however humble, will not be without its use."

He thus alludes to the same subject in one of his private letters: "I have long thought of doing something on the time in which I have myself lived, and acted, and suffered; from the bringing Ireland, in 1782, from the grave in which she had slept for so many centuries, to her reinterment in 1800; after so short an interval of hectical convalescence, and of hope so cruelly and effectually assailed and extinguished, probably for ever! This must, of necessity, draw me to collateral notice of myself in some small and very subordinate degree—the few events that befel myself—and the sentiments and opinions that I entertained upon public affairs, together with the notions that I formed as a public and professional man. Perhaps the strong terror which I anticipate at the possible seductions of silly vanity and egotism may be some antidote against their poison. And yet, perhaps, on this very point, my present feelings should convince me how little I have to hope from my own caution or discretion. I am conscious that I feel uneasy at thinking that the fooleries and falsehoods that have been published as memoirs of me during my life, will be more wantonly repeated when I am gone, which must be soon. And though I now think my only idea is to leave behind me some little postscript, merely to prevent misrepresentation, and modestly confining itself within the extreme insignificance of the subject, who, my dear Dick, will go bail for the quill that is born of a goose?"

Another and a more favourite design, which the same distaste to writing involved in a similar fate, was the composition of a novel, of which the scenes and characters were to be connected with the modern history of Ireland. Of this work, which since the period of the Union he had been meditating, his mind had completed the whole plan: he often repeated long passages, descriptive of the most interesting situations, and marked by a style of affecting eloquence, which would have rendered the work, had he submitted to the task of committing it to paper, a valuable and very original accession to that department of English literature.

However, although subsequent to Mr. Curran's leaving the bar, his mind produced little that could add to his previous reputation, there still remain many farther examples of his style and opinions, preserved in his letters on private and public subjects, and in occasional speeches, from which a selection shall be introduced in the remaining portion of his history. The greater number of the private letters are written from England, which, notwithstanding his constant complaints against what he considered the cold unsocial manners of its people, he seized every opportunity of visiting, and seldom quitted without reluctance and despondency. This was particularly the case since the Union, of which the effects had been so fatal to the society of the Irish capital.

TO LEONARD M'NALLY ESQ., DUBLIN.

"GODWIN'S, 41 SKINNER STREET, LONDON.*

"DEAR MAC,

"I got the cover yesterday, thinking to write a very long wise letter to you; now I have only the few moments that G.'s griskin takes to be burnt. Poor Tooke is, I fear, at his last. A singular man! One glory he has eminently—he has been highly valued by many good men of his day, and persecuted by almost every scoundrel that united the power with the will to do so. His talents were of the first stamp, his intellect most clear, his attachment to England, I think, inflexible, his integrity not to be seduced, and his personal courage not to be shaken. If this shall be admitted, he has lived long enough; and if it is not, he has lived too long.

"My health is much better; my breast quite free, the pain gone, my appetite rather better, sleep not so profound, spirits flatter, temper more even, altogether some gainer by the reduction of wine. At your side, I understand, my good friends have Sangradoed me, but I have taken only the water; no bleeding for me. I have written to Amelia; that may save you some three pages, which

* Godwin, the novelist, kept a book-shop in Skinner street, at this time.—M.

might be blank and written at the same time. I would beg a line, but I shall have set out too soon to get it. No news here, but what the papers give you; they are all mad about the convention; I differ from them totally, as I feel a disposition to do on every subject.

"I am glad to hear you are letting yourself out at Old Orchard; you are certainly unwise in giving up such an inducement to exercise, and the absolute good of being so often in good air. I have been talking about your habit without naming yourself, I am more persuaded that you and Egan are not sufficiently afraid of weak liquors. I can say, from trial, how little pain it costs to correct a bad habit. On the contrary, poor nature, like an ill-used mistress, is delighted with the return of our kindness, and is anxious to show her gratitude for that return, by letting us see how well she becomes it.

"I am the more solicitous upon this point from having made this change, which I see will make me waited for in heaven longer than perhaps they looked for. If you do not make some pretence for lingering, you can have no chance of conveying me to the wherry; and the truth is, I do not like surviving old friends. I am somewhat inclined to wish for posthumous reputation; and if you go before me, I shall lose one of the most irreconcilable of my trumpeters; therefore, dear Mac, no more water, and keep the other element, your wind, for the benefit of your friends. I will show my gratitude as well as I can, by saying handsome things of you to the saints and angels before you come. Best regards to all with you.

"Yours, &c.

"J. P. C."

TO MISS PHILPOT, DUBLIN.

LOUDON CASTLE (*Scotland*), *Sept.* 12, 1810.

"The day is too bad for shooting, so I write. We arrived in miserable weather at Donaghadee; thence we set sail for the

Port, where, after a prosperous voyage of ten hours, we arrived. Two English gentlemen had got before us to the inn, and engaged four horses, all there were; two might have drawn them one very short stage, and they saw us prepare to set out with a cart, which we did, and I trust with a cargo of more good manners and good humour aboard us than the two churls could boast in their chaise and four.

"I was greatly delighted with this country; you see no trace here of the Devil working against the wisdom and beneficence of God, and torturing and degrading his creatures. It seems the romancing of travelling; but I am satisfied of the fact, that the poorest man here has his children taught to read and write, and that in every house is found a Bible, and in almost every house a clock; and the fruits of this are manifest in the intelligence and manners of all ranks. The natural effect of literary information, in all its stages, is to give benevolence and modesty. Let the intellectual taper burn ever so brightly, the horizon which it lights is sure but scanty; and if it soothes our vanity a little, as being the circle of our light, it must check it also, as being the boundary of the interminable region of darkness that lies beyond it. I never knew any person of any real taste and feeling, in whom knowledge and humility were not in exact proportion. In Scotland what a work have the four and twenty letters to show for themselves!—the natural enemies of vice, and folly, and slavery; the great sowers, but still greater weeders, of the human soil. No where can you see the cringing hypocrisy of dissembled detestation, so inseparable from oppression, and as little do you meet the hard, and dull, and right lined angles of the southern visage; you find the notion exact and the phrase direct, with the natural tone of the Scottish muse.

"The first night, at Ballintray, the landlord attended us at supper; he would do so, though we begged him not. We talked to him of the cultivation of potatoes. I said I wondered at his taking them in place of his native food, oatmeal, so much more substantial.

His answer struck me as very characteristic of the genius of Scotland—frugal, tender and picturesque. 'Sir,' said he, 'we are not so much i' the wrong as you think; the tilth is easy, they are swift i' the cooking, they take little fuel; and then it is pleasant to see the gude wife wi' a' her bairns aboot the pot, and each wi' a potato in its hand.'

"We got on to Ayr. It was fortunate; it was the last day of the rain and the first of the races; the town was unusually full, and we stood at the inn door—no room for us. 'My dear Captain,'* said I, 'I suppose we must lie in the streets.' 'No, that you shall not,' says a good-looking man—it was Campbell of Fairfield—'my wife and I knew you were coming, and we have a warm bed ready for you; she is your countrywoman, and I am no stranger to you; I had a trial in Dublin eight years ago, and you were in the cause.' 'Oh! yes, sir, I remember; we beat the enemy.' 'Oh! yes, sir,' says Campbell of Fairfield, '*I* beat the enemy, though you were at his head.' I felt my appetite keen. I was charmed with the comical forgiveness of his hospitality. I assured him I heartily forgave him for thrashing my rascal client; and a few moments brought me to the kind greeting of my very worthy countrywoman. They went a little aside, and I overheard their whispers about dinner. Trouble, you may suppose, I did not wish to give; but the feeling of the possible delay by an additional dish, was my panic. 'My dear Madam, I hope you won't make me feel that I am not one of your family by adding any thing.' 'No, that I won't,' says she; 'and if you doubt my word, I'll give you the security of seven gentlemen against any extravagance.' So saying, she pointed to a group of seven miniatures of young men,

* The late Joseph Atkinson, Esq., of Dublin.—C. [He was one of Moore's earliest and best friends, and ample justice was done to his merits and his memory, by "the poets of all circles," in some beautiful stanzas on his death. It may be remembered that one of Moore's Juvenile Poems was a "Familiar Epistle," addressed to Mr. Atkinson, to whom, also, was written a missive from Bermuda, in Moore's Odes and Epistles from America.—M.]

that hung over the fire-place. 'Six of those poor fellows are all over the earth; the seventh, and these two little girls, are with us; you will think that good bail against the wickedness of extravagance. Poor fellows!' she repeated. 'Nay, madam, don't say "poor fellows," at the moment when you feel that hospitality prevents the stranger from being a poor fellow. You don't think this the only house in the world where the wanderer gets a dinner, and a bed; who knows, my dear countrywoman, but Providence is at this moment paying to some of your poor fellows far away from you, for what your kind heart thinks it is giving for nothing.' 'Oh, yes,' cried she; 'God bless you for the thought.' 'Amen, my dear madam,' answered I; 'and I feel that he has done it.'

"We were much pleased with the races; not, you may suppose, at a few foolish horses forced to run after each other, but to see so much order and cheerfulness; not a single dirty person nor a ragged coat. I was introduced to many of their gentry, Lord Eglington, Lord Casselis, Lord Archibald Hamilton, &c., and pressed very kindly to spend some time with them.

"Poor Burns!—his cabin could not be passed unvisited or unwept; to its two little thatched rooms—kitchen and sleeping-place—a slated sort of parlor is added, and 'tis now an alehouse. We found the keeper of it tipsy; he pointed to the corner on one side of the fire, and with a most *mal-à-propos* laugh, observed, 'there is the very spot where Robert Burns was born. The genius and the fate of the man were already heavy on my heart; but the drunken laugh of the landlord gave me such a view of the rock on which he foundered, I could not stand it, but burst into tears.

"On Thursday we dine with Lord Eglington, and thence I hope to pursue our little tour to Lochlomond, Glasgow, Edinburgh, &c. These places are, at this time of the year, much deserted: however, we shan't feel it quite a solitude; and, at all events, public buildings, &c., do not go to watering-places, so that still something will be visible. In this region the winter is always mild, but the rain is almost perpetual, and still worse as you advance to the north. An Englishman said to an Highlander, 'Bless me, Sir, does it rain for ever?' The other answered—'Oh! nay, Sir, it snaws whiles.'

"See what a chronicle I have written, &c., &c.

"J. P. C."

The preceding is not the only record that Mr. Curran has left of his admiration of Scotland. His defence of Mr. Hamilton Rowan contains a short but glowing eulogium upon the genius of that country, for whose splendid services in the cause of the human mind no praise can be too great. After speaking or the excessive terror of French principles, by which juries were governed in their verdicts, he proceeded:—"There is a sort of aspiring and adventurous credulity, which disdains assenting to obvious truths, and delights in catching at the improbability of circumstances, as its best ground of faith. To what other cause can you ascribe that in the wise, the reflecting, and the philosophic nation of Great Britain, a printer has been found gravely guilty of a libel, for publishing those resolutions to which the prime minister of that kingdom had actually subscribed his name? To what other cause can you ascribe what, in my mind, is still more astonishing;—in such a country as Scotland—a nation cast in the happy medium between the spiritless acquiescence of submissive poverty and the sturdy credulity of pampered wealth—cool and ardent—adventurous and persevering—winging her eagle flight against the blaze of every science, with an eye that never winks and a wing that never tires—crowned as she is with the spoils of every art, and decked with the wreath of every muse, from the deep and scrutinizing researches of her Hume to the sweet and simple, but not less sublime and pathetic, morality of her Burns—how from the bosom of a country like that, genius, and character, and talents, should be banished to a distant barbarous soil, condemned to pine under the horrid communion of vulgar vice and base-born profligacy, for twice the period that ordinary calculation gives to the continuance of human life?" *

TO PETER LESLIE, ESQ., DUBLIN.

"CHELTENHAM, Sept. 11, 1811.

"DEAR PETER,

"Don't open this till the little circle of our Hirish friends are together. You will be all glad to hear that an old friend is yet in the harbour of this stormy world, and has not forgotten you: in truth, it is only that sentiment that troubles you with this worthless despatch; but small as its value may be, it is worth at least what it costs you. I don't think these waters are doing me any good—I think they never did; they bury my poor spirits in the earth. I consulted yesterday evening (indeed chiefly to put so many moments to a technical death) our countryman B., a very obstinate fellow: though I paid him for his affability, and his 'indeed, I think so too, Mr. Shandy,' I could not work him into an admission that I had any malady whatsoever, nor even any to hope for by continuing the intrigue with Mrs. Forty:† so I have a notion of striking my tent, and taking a position behind the Trent, at Donington.‡ During my stay here I have fallen into some pleasant female society; but such society can be enjoyed only by those who are something at a tea-table or a ball. Tea always makes me sleepless; and as to dancing, I tried three or four steps that were quite the cream of the thing in France at one time, and which cost me something. I though it might be the gaiters that gave them a piperly air; but even after putting on my black silk stockings, and perusing them again before the glass, which I put on the ground for the purpose of an exact review, I found the the edition was too stale for republication.

"The cover of this contains a list of all the politicians now in

* Mr. Curran alludes to the sentence of Mr. Muir, Palmer, &c., who had been transported for sedition.—C.

† The person who dispensed the waters at Cheltenham.—C.

‡ The seat of Lord Moira.—C.

Cheltenham, and therefore you must see that I am out of work as well for my head as my heels. Even the newspapers seem so parched by the heat of the season, which is extreme, as to have lost all vegetation. In short, I have made no progress in anything except in marketing, and I fancy I can cast a glance upon a shoulder of Welsh mutton with all the careless indecision of an unresolved purchaser, and yet with the eye of a master; so I have contrived to have two or three at five o'clock, except when I dine abroad, which I don't much like to do.

"If you remember our last political speculations, you know all that is to be known; and that all being just nothing, you cannot well forget it. The smoke is thickest at the corners farthest from the chimney, and therefore near the fire we see a little more distinctly;* but as things appear to me, I see not a single ticket in the wheel that may not be drawn a blank, poor Paddy's not excepted. To go back to the fire—each party has the bellows hard at work, but I strongly suspect that each of them does more to blind their rivals, and themselves, too, by blowing the ashes about, than they do in coaxing or cherishing the blaze for the comfort or benefit of their own shins. Therefore, my dear Peter, though we have not the gift of prophecy, we have at least the privilege of praying. There is no act of parliament that takes away the right of preferring a petition to heaven; and therefore, while it yet is lawful, I pray that all may end well, and that we may have an happy escape from knaves and fools. In that hope there is nothing either popish or seditious. To-morrow I go to Gloucester, to the music-meeting, and then I think Mrs. Forty and I shall take the embrace of an eternal adieu. Do not forget me to all our dear friends about you, and assure them that, however kindly they may remember me, I am not, as far as grateful recollection

* This familiar image, almost similarly applied, was the subject of some perplexity to Dr. Johnson.—"Roscommon, foreseeing that some violent concussion of the State was at hand, proposed to retire to Rome, alleging, *that it was best to sit near the chimney when the chamber smoked*, a sentence of which the application seems not very clear."—*Life of Roscommon*.—C.

can go, in their debt. God grant we may all meet again in comfort here, or in glory somewhere else.

"Yours, dear Peter, very truly yours,

"John P. Curran."

TO RICHARD HETHERINGTON, ESQ.,* DUBLIN.

"London, 1811.

"Dear Dick,

"I merely write to say that I am alive. Never any thing so dull as this place; I shall soon steer towards you. You must know I have been requested by a great sculptor to sit for him, and we are now employed in making a most beautiful head in mud, which is to be the model for a piece of immortal Parian marble. Is that a small style of going, Dick? Having now disposed of what was most important, we come to smaller matters—politics and war. Wellington has been obliged to give up Rodrigo, and retire westward; I suppose to eat his Christmas pies at his old quarters in Torres Vedras, to which every hundred pound that is sent to him costs only one hundred and forty pounds here. As to politics, they seem quite relinquished by every one: nobody expects any material change of men or measures; nor, in truth, do I see any thing in the present state of things that can't be done as well by one set as another. I have little doubt that Perceval is as warlike a hero as Grenville, and just as capable of simplifying our government to the hangman and the taxgatherer. I am just interrupted; so, God bless you.

"J. P. Curran."

TO THE SAME.

"Holland House, 1811.

"Dear Dick,

"The allurement of a frank gives you this. Here I am, much better I think—all lonely. Burton here for a week—al-

* This gentleman held the situation of deputy keeper of the Rolls under Mr. Curran; all of whose letters in his possession he kindly communicated for insertion in this work.—C.

most every body else away. I am scarcely sorry for having come, one gets out of print; however, I have scarcely to complain, I find myself quite a proof copy. Dear Dick, a man loves to be cockered a little; and certainly I am not stinted here. I suspect it is all affectation when I talk cheaply of the great and the grand; for instance, I went to pay my devoirs to Lady D——, who was very kind; also to Lady A——, who was vastly gracious; also Godwin, as also Lord Holland. To-morrow I shall think of Denis O'Bryen and the Duke of Sussex; 'twill be well if I don't forget you and the hill, while I remember

"J. P. C."

"Some more lies from the continent:—another victory—three legs of Bonaparte shot away, the fourth foot very precarious. I really suspect that you have been here *incog.*, and bit every body; for they will believe nothing, even though authenticated by the most respectable letters from Gottingen. Farewell.

"J. P. CURRAN."

TO THE SAME.

"LONDON, *October* 12, 1811.

"DEAR DICK,

"I look forward to being very domestic for the winter. I feel my habits and feelings much upon the change: it puts me in mind of a couple of bad verses of my own growth,

And the long train of joys that charm'd before,
Stripped of their borrow'd plumage, charm no more.

I am weak enough to indulge in a conceited contrition for having done nothing, and the penitential purpose of doing something before I die. God help us! how poor the vanity that self accuses us of wasting funds that never existed, and draws for compensation upon the time that we are not destined to see! or upon efforts that we have not strength to make! You will think it odd that here in London I should be very studious; but so it has been. I have been always prone to metaphysical and theological subjects, though I well know the uncertainty and fruitlessness of such researches; however, I think to call another cause, and adjourn that, till I go thither where all must be plain and clear—where the evidence must be solid, and the judgment infallible.

"I have been only at one play, and that in company with the author, Moore.* I sleep three or four nights in the week in the country; so that in Ireland I look to be very good—like an old bachelor who proposes to marry, and take the benefit of an insolvent act.

"There is still no news here—people seem almost sick of conjecturing. As to my part, if I have any opinion, it is that a change would be only partial. The public undoubtedly have no enthusiasm for the outs, and Perceval unquestionably has risen much. In the City they think him a man of probity and of business, which they think much better than high and lofty tumbling. As to our miserable questions, they are not half so interesting as the broils in the Caraccas. What a test of the Union! And what a proof of the apathy of this blind and insolent country! They affect to think it glorious to struggle to the last shilling of their money, and the last drop of our blood, rather than submit their property and persons to the capricious will of France; and yet that is precisely the power they are exercising over us—the modest authority of sending over to us laws, like boots and shoes ready made for exportation, without once condescending to take our measure, or ask whether or where they pinch us.

"But enough, I think, of religion and politics.

"J. P. C."

* Thomas Moore. The play was operatic, and was damned. Its name was "M. P. or the Blue Stockings."—M.

CHAPTER XVI.

Mr. Curran is invited to stand for the borough of Newry—Speech to the electors—Letter to Sir J. Swinburne—Letter on Irish affairs to H. R. H. the Duke of Sussex.

From the period of Mr. Curran's elevation to the bench, his friends had been very desirous to see him a member of the British parliament. Independent of the service which they expected that his zeal and talents might render to Ireland, there mingled with their feelings on this subject a sentiment of national pride. His parliamentary abilities they considered as having been greatly underrated; notwithstanding the extensive circulation of his reported speeches, the admiration they had met in England was cold in comparison to the enthusiastic applause which their delivery had excited at home. They were therefore anxious that he should have an opportunity, before age or death should render it impossible, of justifying their preference, and confirming his own reputation by even a single display, before such an audience as the British senate, of those powers which his countrymen had so long been extolling as unrivalled.

These reasons—particularly the sense of duty, were frequently urged upon him, but with little effect. The only question, upon which it seemed to him that he could be useful, was that of Catholic Emancipation; and even here he could not venture to be sanguine. When he recollected that his illustrious friend, Mr. Grattan, who had made that question almost the business of a long life, was still (though supported by so much of the most exalted rank and talent in the British empire) vainly exerting his splendid abilities to drive or shame the bigot from his post, Mr. Curran feared that the accession of any strength that he possessed would prove of little value to the cause. The motives of personal vanity or ambition had still less influence. It is not surprising that he, who in the season of ardour and hope had been so negligent of fame, should continue equally indifferent, now that these incentives to action were passing or had passed away.

Such were his feelings (too full perhaps of despondency and indolence) when, upon the general election in 1812, the independent interest of the town of Newry proposed to elect him their member. A deputation from that borough having waited upon him for the purpose, he accepted the invitation,* and repaired to Newry;† but after a contest of six days, perceiving that the

* The feelings with which Mr. Curran accepted the invitation appear in his answer.

"TO THE WORTHY AND INDEPENDENT ELECTORS OF THE BOROUGH OF NEWRY.

"GENTLEMEN—I have just received an address, signed by a number of highly respectable members of your ancient borough, inviting me to offer myself a candidate to represent your town in parliament. To be thought worthy of such a trust, at so awful a crisis as the present, and to receive such an invitation, unsolicited and unexpected, is an honour that I feel deeply and gratefully.

"Gentlemen, I need not trouble you with many words. You know my principles, you know my conduct heretofore—I am not a stranger coming forward to menace, or to buy you, in order that I may sell you; nor do I rest my pretension on any contrition for the past, nor any premediated promise that I will at some future period begin to act honestly by you. From the earliest period of my life to see this ill-fated country retrieved from her sad condition of suffering and of shame has been the first and warmest wish of my heart, and warm it shall continue, till I myself am cold for ever.

"I know you will not impute it to a want of the most profound respect for you, when I say that I will not personally solicit the vote of any individual. I cannot run the risk of soliciting a suitor in the character of an elector—it would not benefit my judicial situation, and I think it would diminish that credit, which suffrage above all suspicion of bias, ought to give to your representative. It will therefore be sufficient that I attend you in such time before the election as will enable me to know your farther pleasure.

"I have the honour to be, Gentlemen, with a full sense of your confidence and favour,

"Your obedient servant,

"JOHN PHILPOT CURRAN.

"*Stephen's Green, October* 8, 1812."

† Mr. Curran's reception was most enthusiastic. He was met two miles outside Newry, and about 3000 persons joined in drawing him into the borough in his carriage, from which the horses had been taken. He made a brilliant speech (of which no report has been preserved), which occupied eighty minutes in the delivery, and was greatly applauded. His rival, who avowed Anti-Catholic opinions, was groaned. But some of the Catholic

strength of the other candidate (General Needham) left him no prospect of success, he declined any farther struggle. Upon this occasion, Mr. Curran delivered a speech of considerable length. It was his last great public effort, and was characterized by the same energy and fancy, and the same spirit of patriotic enthusiasm, which reign in all his former productions. After stating to the electors of Newry the circumstances under which he had been induced to appear among them, and the condition of the borough, which had baffled the exertions of his friends, Mr. Curran proceeded to impress upon his hearers that the long train of sufferings which Ireland had endured for centuries had originated in the dissension of her people, and that whatever of them remained could only be removed by mutual toleration. "Under this sad coalition of confederating dissensions, nursed and fomented by the policy of England, this devoted country has continued to languish with small fluctuations of national destiny, from the invasion of the second Henry to the present time. And here let me be just while I am indignant; let me candidly own that to the noble examples of British virtue, to the splendid exertions of British courage, to their splendid sacrifices, am I probably indebted for my feelings as an Irishmen and my devotion to my country. They thought it madness to trust themselves to the influence of any foreign country; they thought the circulation of the political blood could be carried on only by the action of the heart within the body, and could not be injected from without. Events have shown you that what they thought, was just; and that what they did, was indispensable: they thought they ought to govern themselves—they thought that at every hazard they ought to make the effort—they thought it more eligible to perish than to fail; and to the God of Heaven I pray that the authority of so splendid an example may not be lost upon Ireland."

After describing the condition of Ireland subsequent to the

voters were not true to their own cause, and this, backed by government influence, defeated Curran.—M.

revolution, Mr. Curran continued;—"At length, in 1782, a noble effort was made, and deathless ought to be the name of *him** that made it, and deathless ought to be the gratitude of the country for which it was made—the independence of Ireland was acknowledged. Under this system of asserted independence, our progress in prosperity was much more rapid than could have been expected, when we remember the conduct of a very leading noble person upon that occasion—never was a more generous mind or a purer heart—but his mind had more purity than strength. He had all that belonged to taste, and courtesy, and refinement; but the grand and the sublime of national reform were composed of colours too strong for his eye, and comprised an horizon too outstretched for his vision.† The Catholics of Ireland were in fact excluded from the asserted independence of their country. Thus far the result comes to this, that wherever perfect union is not found, complete redress must be sought in vain."

Passing on to the Union, Mr. Curran proceeded—"The whole history of mankind records no instance of any hostile Cabinet, perhaps even of any internal cabinet, actuated by the principles of honour or of shame. The Irish Catholic was therefore taught to believe, that if he surrendered his country he would cease to be a slave. The Irish Protestant was cajoled into the belief, that if he concurred in the surrender, he would be placed upon the neck of an hostile faction. Wretched dupe!—*You might as well persuade the gaoler that he is less a prisoner than the captives he locks up, merely because he carries the key in his pocket.*‡ By that

* Mr. Grattan.

† The person here alluded to was obviously the late Earl of Charlemont; but though that nobleman originally opposed the claims of the Roman Catholics, he had the honour in his latter years of rising above his early prejudides; he has also made Ireland amends for the delay, in having left a representative of his house, and of his more matured opinions, from whom all that his country can demand is that *he* may never change his present principles and conduct.—C.

‡ We loubt not that this is the origin of Byron's well known lines in *Don Juan:*

"The nations are
In prison—but the gaoler, what is he?

reciprocal animosity, however, Ireland was surrendered; the guilt of the surrender was most atrocious—the consequences of the crime most tremendous and exemplary. We put ourselves into a condition of the most unqualified servitude—we sold our country, and we levied upon ourselves the price of the purchase—we gave up the right of disposing of our properties—we yielded to a foreign legislature to decide whether the funds necessary to their projects or their profligacy should be extracted from us, or be furnished by themselves; the consequence has been, that our scanty means have been squandered in her internal corruption as profusely as our best blood has been wasted in the madness of her aggressions, or the feeble folly of her resistance. Our debt has accordingly been increased more than tenfold—the common comforts of life have been vanishing—we are sinking into beggary—our poor people have been worried by cruel and unprincipled prosecutions, and the instruments of our government have been almost simplified into the tax-gatherer and the hangman. At length, after this long night of suffering, the morning star of our redemption cast its light upon us, the mist was dissolved and all men perceived that those whom they had been blindly attacking in the dark were in reality their fellow sufferers and their friends. We have made a discovery of the grand principle in politics, that the tyrant is in every instance the creature of the slave—that he is a cowardly and a computing animal—and that in every instance he calculates between the expenditure to be made and the advantage to be acquired. And I therefore do not hesitate to say that if the wretched Island of Man, that *refugium peccatorum*, had sense and spirit to see the force of this truth, she could not be

No lesser victim to the bolt and bar.
Is the poor privilege to turn the key
Upon the captive, freedom? He's as far
From the enjoyment of the earth and air,
Who watches o'er the chain, as they who wear."

But Byron avowed that a poet had a right, whenever he found a good idea, to seize and use it.—M.

enslaved by the whole power of England. The oppressor would see that the necessary expenditure in whips, and chains, and gibbets, would infinitely countervail the ultimate value of the acquisition; and it is owing to the ignorance of this unquestionable truth, that so much of this agitated globe has, in all ages, been crawled over by a Manx population. This discovery Ireland at last has made. The Catholic claimed his rights—the Protestant generously and nobly felt as he ought, and seconded the claim; a silly government was driven to the despicable courage of cowardice, and resorted to the odious artillery of prosecutions—the expedient failed: the question made its way to the discussion of the senate—I will not tire you with the detail. A House of Commons who, at least, represented themselves, perhaps afraid, perhaps ashamed of their employers, became unmanageable tools in the hands of such awkward artists, and were dissolved; just as a beaten gamester throws the cards into the fire in hopes in a new pack to find a better fortune."

A little farther on, Mr. Curran, again adverting to the circumstances of the election, was interrupted by the other candidate's agent: when that person was made to sit down, Mr. Curran resumed. "I do not wonder at having provoked interruption when I spoke of your borough. I told you that from this moment it is free. Never in my life have I so felt the spirit of the people as among you; never have I so felt the throbs of returning life. I almost forgot my own habitual estimate of my own small importance; I almost thought it was owing to some energy within myself, when I was lifted and borne on the buoyant surge of popular sympathy and enthusiasm. I therefore again repeat it, it is the moment of your new birth unto righteousness. Your proved friends are high among you—your developed enemies are expunged for ever—your liberty has been taken from the grave, and if she is put back into the tomb, it can be only by your own parricide, and she must be buried alive."

"Ireland (said he, towards the conclusion of his address) can do more for herself now than she has done for centuries heretofore. She lay a helpless hulk upon the water; but now, for the first time, we are indebted to the Protestant spirit for the delicious spectacle of seeing her equipped with masts, and sails, and compass, and helm; at length she is sea-worthy. Whether she is to escape the tempest and gain the port is an event to be disposed of by the great Ruler of the waters and the winds. If our voyage be prosperous, our success will be doubled by our unanimity; but even if we are doomed to sink, we shall sink with honour. But am I over-sanguine in counting our Protestant allies? Your own county gives you a cheering instance in a noble Marquis,* retiring from the dissipation of an English court, making his country his residence, and giving his first entrance into manhood to the cause of Ireland. It is not from any association of place that my mind is turned to the name of Moira—to name him is to recognize what your idolatry has given to him for so many years; but a late transaction calls for a word or two. I thought anxiously upon it at the time, and from that time to this, if he required to be raised, he must have been raised in public opinion by the event of that negociation.† He saw that the public in either

* The Marquis of Downshire.—C.

† Mr. Curran had, a few weeks before, in an equally public manner, discountenanced the angry feelings with which he found some of his countrymen had regarded the conduct of his noble friend in the recent negotiations for a new administration. At a public dinner, given in Dublin to the Bishop of Norwich by the friends of religious freedom, and attended by many, the most distinguished for rank and talent in Ireland, Mr. Curran, in addressing the meeting, enumerated the several illustrious persons in the empire who supported the cause which they were that day celebrating: "But," said he, "I have not yet mentioned the name, which I was delighted to see you were on the tiptoe of expecting, and which, in whatever order it might be mentioned, you had in your own minds placed in its natural station, at the head of the list—the beloved child of Ireland, the ornament, and consoler, and intrepid defender of his country—the scholar of the camp—the philosopher of the senate—the exalted devotee of that high and unparlying honour, that will bend to no consideration of life, or death, or country, or even of fame: that man who, of all others, most distinctly sees into your character—your ardent, generous (do not be angry with me), your tender and excitable sensibility—your feather-springed disposability to affectionate and momentary jealousy, which evaporates in the breath that expresses it. He knows it well—he loves you for it—he knows the rapid condition of its

country could not have any hope from an arrangement, in which the first preliminary was a selfish scramble for patronage, that must have ended in a scramble for power; in which the first efforts of patriotism were for the surrender of mopsticks in the palace; to sink the head, and to irritate the man who wore the Crown, instead of making their first measure a restitution of representation to the people, who, if they were as strong as they ought to be, could have nothing to apprehend from the tinsel of a robe or the gilding of a sceptre.

"Little remains for me to add to what I have already said. I said you should consider how you ought to act—I will give you my humble idea upon that point. Do not exhaust the resources of your spirit by idle anger or idle disgust—forgive those who have voted against you here—they will not forgive themselves. I understand they are to be packed up in tumbrils with layers of salt between them, and carted to the election for the country, to appear again in patriotic support of the noble projector of the glories of Walcheren. Do not envy him the precious cargo of the raw materials of virtuous legislation—be assured all this is of use.

"Let me remind you before I go of that precept, equally profound and beneficent, which the meek and modest author of our blessed religion left to the world: 'and one command I give you, that you love one another.' Be assured that of this love the true spirit can be no other than probity and honour. The great analogies of the moral and the physical world are surprisingly coincident; you cannot glue two pieces of board together unless the joint be clean; you cannot unite two men together, unless the

recoil; but he ought not to be wounded, nor you humiliated by any formal ceremonial of that contrition. [*Loud applause.*] But I find I am not so bad a painter as I thought; you have made it unnecessary for me to put the name over the picture. May I be permitted to add, that although I have not been altogether unhonoured by some condescending notice from that illustrious and noble person, yet I am too proud to be swayed by any feeling which, if merely personal, must be despicable, and that it could not add a single pulsation to that energy of affection and respect with which my heart clings to him as an Irishman."—O. [The Earl Moira afterwards was created Marquis of Hastings.—M.]

cement be virtue: for vice can give no sanction to compact, she can form no bond of affection.

"And now, my friends, I bid you adieu, with a feeling at my heart that can never leave it, and which my tongue cannot attempt the abortive effort of expressing. If my death do not prevent it, we shall meet again in this place. If you feel as kindly to me as I do to you, relinquish the attestation which I know you had reserved for my departure. Our enemy has, I think, received the mortal blow; but though he reels, he has not fallen; and we have seen too much upon a greater scale of wretchedness of anticipated triumph. Let me therefore retire from among you in a way that becomes me and becomes you, uncheered by a single voice, and unaccompanied by a single man. May the blessing of God preserve you in the affection of one another."*

The following letters contain Mr. Curran's farther views upon the state of public affairs in Ireland at this period:

TO SIR J. SWINBURNE.

"Sir,

"I have just received the honour of your letter. I am very deeply, indeed, impressed by the honour of being thought by the committee not unworthy of the office of steward, at the meeting of the friends of religious freedom.

"If there were no obstacl in my way, but what was within my own control, most promptly, and with pride and gratitude, would I obey so flattering a summons; but the difficulty is what it does not belong to me to dispense with. The Court of Chancery will be sitting on the day of your meeting, and I could not be warranted in leaving my duty here, from any impulse, however strong, of

* In the middle of his speech Mr. Bell (a regularly ill-favoured gentleman), who was agent for the rival candidate, stood up, and fixed his eyes upon Mr. Curran, "with a very peculiar expression of countenance." On this Mr. Curran exclaimed, "Mr. Seneschal, I demand of you as returning officer, that I, a candidate, shall be protected, as you are in duty bound to do, from being disturbed by the obscene and unnatural grimaces of a baboon." Whereupon Mr. Bell sank into his seat—used up!—M.

personal gratitude or respect. I cannot look forward to any probable state of the court, that can leave me to my own disposal; but if such should occur, I shall certainly wait upon you. I am, however, not a little consoled in the reflection, that my absence from such a scene can be regretted only by myself, and that my presence could contribute little, or rather nothing, to the intended result. The sanction of illustrious personages,* who vouchsafe to patronise the meeting, must do much towards its object; and much also must be effected by the high rank and character of others, who I make no doubt will be zealous in following such an example, when the projects of intolerance are disclaimed by the authority of the enlightened and exalted; and when the great mass of the people are permitted to see what cannot be difficult in so reflecting a nation as England, that the cause of tolerance is really that of justice, and prudence, and true Christianity, in which they themselves are as deeply interested as their fellow-subjects can be. It is not, I trust, too sanguine to hope that practical bigotry must be driven to take refuge in flight; and that the empire may look forward to the adoption of such just and beneficent counsels as must ever compose the only certain basis of internal tranquillity, and of external safety. I know, sir, you will perceive that I allude principally to this part of the empire. I have passed not a short life in it; my notions respecting it are the fruit of long observation of it both in and out of parliament; and so deeply are these ideas graven upon my judgment, that upon a late occasion I was willing to forego every consideration of much labor passed, of advancing years, and declining health, and to undertake the duty of once more sitting in parliament. I could have no motive of ambition, or of party, or view to reputation; I looked not to be an advocate for my country, but I did venture to hope that a man so perfectly removed from all temptation to partiality, and with so much opportunity of knowledge, might be received as not an incredible witness, in point of fact, for this afflicted island. And from the discharge of so

* Dukes of Kent and Sussex, sons of George III.—M.

sacred a duty, I thought it would have been most unworthy to affect to excuse myself upon any etiquette of office, when the law had declared no incompatibility between official and public duty. I did think, and I yet think, that if the real state of this country be fairly and fully impressed upon the parliament and the public, it must appear to demonstration, that the hopes and the fears of the two parts of the empire are one and the same; that it is the critical moment in which every thing ought to be done to oppose the embankment of a consolidated nation to the hostile torrent, instead of leaving it even a chance of admission through the interstices of an incohering and porous population; and that those high persons, who saw things a year ago in this point of view, and were then willing to devote themselves to the public service, may, upon further consideration, think that the obstacles which then prevented their intention ought not for ever to deprive their country of the benefits of their virtue or capacity to serve it. Such an event as I allude to, they may be assured, would have a most consoling and cheering effect upon Ireland, because we should look with confidence to their acting upon that noble and conciliating principle of religious freedom, which has raised your illustrious patron, and those who think as he does, so high in the reverence of all men; they would be sure of retrieving Ireland from a state of suffering and peril; they would be sure of finding a co-operation in every honest Irishman infinitely superior to the zeal of party, or of sect, and founded on the pure devotion of public duty and public spirit. And it would convey to the heart of a loyal and ardent people a conviction that they were yet of a value in a quarter where their fondest hopes and affections had been fixed for years. But I fear my solicitude on this subject has led me to intrude farther than I had intended upon your attention. Permit me, therefore, only to request that you will be pleased to accept my cordial thanks for the courtesy of your communication, and to present my humble respects to the committee.

"I have the honour to be, sir, &c.,

"J. P. Curran."

TO HIS ROYAL HIGHNESS THE DUKE OF SUSSEX.

"I cannot, sir, express the pleasure with which I learn that the sanction of your illustrious rank and your great name are given to that noble principle of religious freedom, and that upon a ground perfectly distinct from all view whatsoever of political party. The relation in which you stand with respect to your country, and your august house, must remove all pretext for soiling our pure and modest religion, by blending it with the sordid spirit of party; or of advancing the projects of the latter, by an affected association with the former, in which heaven cannot be either interested or honoured, and in which the true principle of political wisdom and social virtue cannot fail to be degraded and depraved. Never, perhaps, have the fatal consequences of this monstrous union been more sadly proved and developed than in the late few years that we have passed; and more especially in this ill-fated country. In England your dissenters were pressed sorely enough by disabling and excluding statutes; but still the sharpness of those legal monopolies went rather against their interest than their honour. Still they were equal as Englishmen; and though shut out, perhaps very unwisely and very unjustly, from a part, and certainly no inconsiderable part, of the constitutional precincts of their country, they still had the uncontrollable range of the residue as freely and proudly as any other portion of the land; they had to complain of suffering rather than stigma or shame. With respect to other religious descriptions of sects, very unworthy indeed to be classed with dissenters—the strange combinations of persons connected together by the fantastical adoption of wild and extravagant opinions, much easier to be named than to be understood, England seems to have acted with the policy that might be expected from a discreet and thinking nation. You have most judiciously cut off the supplies, that martyrdom would have given them in their meek and ardent campaign against the sobriety and decorum of true religion. Your established clergy have stinted them in that food which refutation gives to folly. They have had too much good sense, and too much sound consideration for their sacred functions, to enter the lists of argument with these learned cobblers, and right reverend blacksmiths. However they may have been mortified by the scandal of their orgies, they have had forbearance enough to leave their diseases to cure themselves, and to consign them to the wholesome and cooling regime of silent commiseration and inflexible neglect. The Law has followed the example of the Church, and refused the honours of the pillory or the stake to the adventurous aspirants; and to this concurrence in good temper and good sense may it be attributed, in a great degree at least, that these contraband dealers and inventors of unheard-of forms of doctrine, and patterns of tenets, have not been still more successful in superseding the good order and sobriety of the national faith and practice. I should have hoped that this concurrence was founded on the adoption of a maxim, that forms the basis of that principle so fortunately adopted by your Royal Highness, the inviolability of religious freedom. But deeply concerned am I to see, that however acted upon in England, it has not been pursued in Ireland with the same dignity and temper. In saying this I do not mean to impute absolutely bad intentions to any party, or to say that neither has been betrayed into any step that may call for censure or regret; but I do think that in our late, or rather our present, unhappy conflicts here, a manifest distinction might be made. The Catholic was petitioning for a repeal of certainly very afflicting grievances, and it would be only fair to make some allowance for the tone and phrase in which he might utter what came simply to this:—'I am in bondage without having committed any crime. My degradation and suffering are justified by the most cruel imputation on my character and honour, and I humbly pray to be set at liberty.' If a man were to utter such an appeal with insolence or outrage, I do not say he ought to be kindly heard; but if he felt the right to freedom so coldly as to prefer his claim with an apathy that must freeze it, I should not hesitate to say, he ought not to be relieved; he has not yet arrived at that impatience of slavery, without which he cannot be yet ripe for freedom. I cannot, therefore, avoid saying that the mere ardour of the Catholics, in the pursuit of an object far more valuable than life, without which life could be of no value, was not a just ground for suspecting that their meeting to petition was a mere pretext to cover any other or any criminal design. The rank and property of the persons, which made them so firmly responsible to the State, should, I think, have repelled such a suspicion, and particularly when sanctioned by so numerous a co-operation of their Protestant fellow-subjects. I do not say that the government might not have intended well, or that a most unhappy mistake was any other than an error of judgment; but I do think that when the subsequent conduct of the people had proved their innocence beyond all doubt, a milder and more conciliating conduct might have been adopted with equal dignity and wisdom. But I fear a province is a bad school for a statesman to learn that the essence of dignity consists much more in rest than in action. It has not been so, and the consequence has been a state of trouble and fermentation, such as I never before witnessed in Ireland. Crimination and recrimination have gone on to an extent on all sides, most deeply to be deplored by every man who wishes well to Ireland or the empire. The discussions of those unhappy questions have been carried on in the shape of criminal prosecutions; of proceedings that never should be resorted to, except in cases of real guilt, and never as political measures of aspersion or counteraction. The result has been—No culpable intention whatsoever has been proved; no project has been defeated; the purity of the administration of justice itself has been exposed by the unhappy indiscretion of giving ground for actions, and the readiness of bringing forward prosecutions, in which every judgment and verdict for them has been a public calamity, by sinking them in the public opinion, and leading the people to entertain an idea, which I trust can never be true, that even the judicial authority may be degraded to an instrumentality to the State. A man of any party but that of public tranquillity and safety would probably speak a language very different from what I am holding to your Royal Highness. But my mind is profoundly impressed with the actual suffering and awful possible danger of such a state of things, which is not at all diminished by the real innocence of intention, which I am ready to concede to all parties. It is not the guilt of the parties, it is the fact of the conflict in which the peril consists. It was from this view of things, though not then so sadly matured as they are at present, that I was most anxious, a year ago, that the arrangement then proposed might take effect: every aspect of things seemed to indicate such an event as most practicable, and most salutary. The resolution of the House of Commons seemed to point it out as a measure of inevitable necessity: the exalted magnanimity of an illustrious personage, relinquishing every personal consideration, gave it complete facility, and that in a way the most endearing to the Irish people, by showing that his mind was perfectly untainted by bigotry.* Strange indeed would it be, if an individual of the first taste in England could be so tainted; for what is taste but the moral instinct of a highly cultivated understanding? The great talents and character of the noble persons concerned was a pledge to the empire of what might be expected from the measure. It held out a hope of friendly adjustment with America, instead of forcing her unnaturally into the ranks of our enemies, and driving her to waste her young blood in battle, instead of preserving it for growth; instead of recollecting that she might be destined to be the cradle of a Hercules, who, even in his infancy, was doomed to crush the snakes of despotism, and whose full-grown labours might be reserved, by the extirpation of monsters, to form a new system for freedom in the west, even after it had been banished, like the Americans themselves, from the east. It gave us at least an additional hope of an interval to breathe, by a peace with France; an event made probable by the known opinions of those noble persons upon the subject; and made

* The Prince Regent, afterwards George IV.—M.

still more probable by the incalculable addition to the actual force of the empire, in the perfect conciliation of Ireland, which they, and, I much fear, they alone, could be likely to effect; but in these prospects we were destined to be disappointed. Upon the cause of this failure there was a variety of opinions, but there was a perfect concurrence in the feeling, that it was a great misfortune to this nation: it doomed us to a continuance of disquiet, and an increase of burdens and of dangers; yet we did not hastily give up the hope that the difficulties might be yet got over. Nor can I now conceive how it is possible for those noble persons to allow the weight of a feather to those difficulties, when they see that every event that has happened from that hour to this is flung into the opposite scale, and is a call upon them to come forward and do their duty to their country.

"As an Irishman I own my heart sunk when all hope was at an end of seeing our favourite countryman * return to his native land bearing the olive branch; the only man who seemed peculiarly designated for the great work of conciliation; but even from the lip the cup has been dashed—the grating upon the mountain of Ararat was a delusive omen of the subsiding of the waters; and our miserable ark is still tossed, not upon a sinking but a rising and more angry flood. My own concern, at that time, did not spring from any personal bad opinion of the ministers; I gave them then and I give them now, full credit for perfect good intention. Indeed, I can scarcely conceive the possibility of a public man's having the heart not to intend most conscientiously for the best; but I could not avoid seeing that the vote of the house was a sort of presentment against them by the grand inquest of the nation; and that the readiness of their master to dismiss them was a full confirmation of the public opinion, that it was a blight under which, if they did not die, they must dwindle; and that their acts and their language could not but correspond with a dimi-

* The Earl of Moira.—M.

nished stature. They have verified their sad foreboding, peculiarly with respect to America and to Ireland; their tone and style has been undignified, peevish, and exasperating, sophisticated and insulting. What else have been their Orders in Council? 'The French are abusing your rights on the sea, we will retaliate by abusing them also:—the highwaymen rob you of half your property, we will retaliate upon the highwaymen by robbing you of the other half.' But this is a subject perhaps beyond my depth, and upon which my reasonings may be partial. There are many sad analogies that give us a deep and tender interest in the fate of that country. We cannot forget the fresh and daily increasing ties that bind us to them as brothers, or children, or kindred. An American war can never be popular in Ireland; and the same causes that make it impossible for us to be their enemies, make it improper to be their judges. My mind, therefore, returns to home the natural scene of every man's immediate solicitude. Upon this subject, to almost any other person than your Royal Highness, I should have much to say. To you, sir, I know how absurd it would be to affect to give information. The feeling and the splendid part which you have been pleased to take in our interests and our sufferings prove to us, not only how perfect a knowledge of them you possess, but also how much a patient and impartial judgment can contract questions which blindness and passion had dilated and perplexed, and to what a salutary degree you have been successful in simplifying the real objects to which the attention of the two countries ought to be confined. Any longer trespass upon your Royal Highness' patience can go no further, therefore, than very passingly to advert to the progress which I hope has been made in the happy work of conciliation.

"I think the good sense of England must now see, that the habits of reasoning and acting in Ireland are not to be judged by the interested and distorted misrepresentations that have been made of this country during centuries past. I understand with pleasure that those historical topics of abuse, which caught the public attention for some time, are now spurned or laughed at, as the venomous and silly effusions of reading without learning, or learning without knowledge; the real heads of inquiry are now plain. I know some weight was once given to the distinction, that mere exclusion was not privation. I believe there is now no rational man who does not see, that when it is justified upon the most degrading imputations, it is the bitterest of all privations, because in the same moment it takes away the privilege of the subject and the character of the man.

"It has been said, 'It is dangerous to give power to the Catholics as long as this objection was undefined.' This acted upon the nerves of, I am sure, many good men; but it could not but cease to do so, when they reflected that nothing like power was sought or intended to be given. Mere admissibility is nothing like power; mere admissibility can no more make a Catholic a gauger than it can make him a king. I am admissible to be Lord Chancellor of England; but would not any man in his senses imagine I had escaped from Bedlam if I called such admissibility by the name of power? It was said, that Emancipation would lead to attempts upon our establishments. It is not surely difficult to see that establishments can be altered or destroyed only by law or by force.

"As to law, the danger comes exactly to this; whether a few Catholic members could succeed in making proselytes of King, Lords and Commons, so as to subvert the Protestant Church? I confess, sir, that it is not my opinion of our Catholic gentry; if they became senators I suspect their ambition would have very little to do with religion, and that they would be seen going forth with the ministers of the day, as well as their Protestant brethren, in the mildest spirit of patriotic toleration.

"As to brutal force, I can't see that admissibility to sit in the House of Commons could be an inducement with any man to burn it. I cannot comprehend how giving men those interests in the state, without which no state can have any real value in their eyes, can increase their wish any more than their power to destroy it. I have heard of common sailors making off with a ship and cargo, but never of the proprietor joining in such an act. I never heard even of an Irish gentleman robbing himself and running away. If they are then asked—what do we solicit, and what can they give us? I cannot doubt that a generous nation will feel no little pain in being obliged to answer—'We cannot give you power, nor place, nor wealth; we cannot undo the sad consequences of continued oppression; we cannot restore you in a moment to national health; the most we can do is to remove the actual malady in which you have been so long consumed; and to put you into a state of possible convalescence, in which the progress, at the best, must be hectical and tardy.'

"I know the hopes of some men are damped by the petitions against us. My hope is, that they are favourable to us; when the motives and the means of procuring them are considered (and they cannot be unknown) they cannot fail of kindling a condign detestation of those who can resort, for any human object, to such obdurate and remorseless guilt, as that of exciting man against man; of loosening those bonds that should bind the subject to the state, and poisoning the sources of that Christian benevolence that ought to be the consolation of nations under those sufferings with which it has pleased Providence to permit almost the whole civilized world to be afflicted; nor can I deem it possible that so just a detestation of the oppression should not lead to a proportional sympathy for the sufferers. As to the petitions from ourselves, we know they are the natural consequences of our condition; they are much stronger proofs of deplorable prostration than of real malice; and happy is it for the quiet of Ireland, that they are so considered. When Verres was accused for his frightful maladministration in Sicily, a counter-petition was obtained; and if I forget not, at the head of the deputation who came to implore that no mercy should be extended to him, was advancing to the senate, an illustrious Sicilian, who had himself been the most distinguished victim of what authority may perpetrate in a province. I cannot imagine that the display of such a spectacle could do injury to the cause of the unfortunate supplicants; nor can I think, that if the Irish Catholic were now put upon his trial before an impartial tribunal of the English nation, his accusation weighed against his defence, his friends against his enemies, his conduct against his treatment; I cannot doubt that in such a situation, his character and claims would be so felt, that he might boldly say, 'I would to God that not only you, but all those who hear me this day, were both, almost and altogether such as I am, except these bonds.' I cannot, sir, in regard to the duty of perfect candor which I owe to your Royal Highness, avoid saying that the wild spirit of aggression which of late time has raved among us, has miserably reduced the respect in which every good government cannot fail to be held. These contests for dignity, without doubt, have been most disastrous. Alas, Sir, I much fear that dignity is a robe which he, that will box for it, must lay aside during the conflict, and there is great risk that when he has been soundly threshed, he may find, like Strap, that it has been taken away during the battle by the honest gentleman who undertook to keep it.

"But, sir, the baleful effects of this violence cannot stop here. It is too visible that manners, and morals too, must become ferociated; so that there can be no doubt, that if good sense and feeling shall not make the edge of authority more blunt, necessity must soon make it sharper even than it is. If the rider will not sit quietly on his saddle, but will hold his seat by grappling the sides of the animal with his spurs, he cannot avoid changing to a bridle of no ordinary force. No other way can remain for restraining the madness he provokes. This, sir, in my conscience I am convinced is the state of this country: things cannot stay as they are; temporizing palliatives will not avail; it will answer no end to draw upon our great grandsons in favour of the great grandsons of the Catholics, for liberty to be granted in the course of the next century.

"Mean time, for I more than feel how much I have passed the limits, I cannot but hope the best effects from the principle of religious freedom, which you are pleased to protect, and of which you will be so powerful a patron, and so bright an example.

"Be pleased, sir, to accept my humble thanks for your condescending wish, that I should have the honour of being present at the meeting of the friends of such a principle; as I find it is not to be immediate, I do not altogether give up the hope of being present, but, present or absent, it will have my most devout prayers for its success. I have the honour, sir, to be, with the most profound sense of attachment and respect,

"Your Royal Highness' dutiful servant,

"J. P. C."

CHAPTER XVII.

Mr. Curran's health declines—Letters to Mr. Hetherington—resignation of his judicial office—Letters from London to Mr. Lube—Letters from Paris to the same—His last illness and death.

In the beginning of 1813, the declining condition of Mr. Curran's health obliged him to meditate the resignation of his judicial office. While he was in London in the month of April of that year, he suffered a severe attack of inflammation in his chest. His illness, though by no means dangerous, was a subject of considerable alarm to his mind, in consequence of an old but unfounded opinion that his lungs were naturally weak; a mistake into which he had been led from confounding the temporary hoarseness and exhaustion which usually followed every great exertion in public speaking with a constitutional debility of that organ. There is something characteristic in his manner of announcing his illness upon this occasion to his friend in Dublin.

TO R. HETHERINGTON, ESQ.

"Dear Dick,

"Really I think rather an escape—I have been confined to to my bed these ten days; a violent attack on my breast—lungs not touched—better now, but very low and weak. I can't say with certainty when I can set out. Will you let Mr. Lockwood (or if he is not there the Chancellor) know my situation; a wanten premature effort might kill me.

"J. P. C."

TO THE SAME.

"DEAR DICK,

"I had hoped a quicker recovery, but the fit was most severe. I thought to have put myself into a chaise to-morrow, but the physician says it might be death, unless deferred some days longer. The malady was upon the breast; I think I caught it by walking from Kensington—the morning was snowy and the wind east. I had not even gone to a play but once—I am most uneasy at this absence from court, however involuntary. I have written to Lord Manners. I have no news; nothing could be kinder, or more general than the flattering reception I have met. Still I am not acting like a dying man. Surely I could not prepare to dance out of the world to a grand forte-piano; yet they talk of such a thing. The town is also full of rumours of a silver tea-pot, &c. &c.* What can all this mean? Doesn't it show a regard for our executors? My best regards to all about you, and with you.

"J. P. C."

Mr. Curran was in a little time so far recovered as to be able to resume his judicial functions. In the long vacation he returned as usual to England, from which he writes as follows.

TO RICHARD HETHERINGTON, ESQ. DUBLIN.

"CHELTENHAM, *September* 3, 1813.

"DEAR DICK,

"You ought to have heard from me before; I have been a truant; however, in fact I had little to say: I am here now ten days. I took the waters; as usual, they bore down whatever spirits I had to lose. Yesterday I went to the doctor; he told me

* When Mr. Curran was confined to his bed and suffering considerable pain, he could not abstain from the same playfulness. His medical attendant having observed one morning, that he found he coughed with more difficulty than on the preceding evening—"That's very surprising," replied the patient, "for I have been practising all night."—C.

I had taken them wrong and was wrong in taking them; that I had no symptom of any disease whatever; he mentioned also, in confidence, that notice had been taken of my intimacy with Mrs. Forty; that there were some ladies not far from the well, strangers altogether to my poor dear, in whom religion had turned from milk, and soured into vinegar; who had little hope of being talked ill of themselves, and who made it a moral duty to slide themselves in upon the market jury of every character, and give a verdict against them upon their own knowledge; particularly if there were any circumstance that made it an act of common mercy, in those canters of slanderous litanies, to be silent or merciful. 'My dear sir,' said he, 'let not women complain of their injuries from men, when they are such odious beasts in devouring one another.' In truth, my dear Dick, it is frightful to see how little they can spare their friends, when they can make them the pretexts for venting their infernal malice. I confess it has added to my sickness of heart against that country,* of which I have really deserved so much.

"You can scarcely believe what a difference I find here—courted and cherished by strangers; I assure you the question of celebrity between the royal tiger and me is not quite decided. The change of scene is amusing, so is the diversity of characters; there is a moral benefit in the change of scene; you look back to the niche you filled and you see it not: how minute then must be the little thing that filled it? Here too every body is as intimate with me as I permit. I really begin to think that the best tenure of earthly attachment is tenancy at will. You have the use of the soil, and the way-going crop; then nothing you plant shoots so deeply but you may remove it without injury to the soil or to itself. If affections strike their roots far into the heart, they cannot be pulled up without laceration and blood. I am not without an idea of cutting you altogether: I could easily get into Parlia-

* Ireland. The censorious ladies in question were his countrywomen.—C.

ment and on my own terms, but the object would not justify a purchase; and I need not tell you, I would not submit to restrictions.

"You will be surprised when I tell you that I have the highest authority for knowing that the silly malice of the Castle has not had the smallest impression on a certain high quarter. As I have jilted Mrs. Forty, my head is getting better, and I shall try and write. I may as well stay here sometime as any where else: I am afraid of London; however, I can't but pay a visit to the Duke of Sussex. Will you enclose "Wagram" to Mr. Reeves, and add my respects, and request that he will have the goodness to forward it to me to Cheltenham. The post is just going out—write to me by return; best regards to the hill. I begin to think that 'compliments to all *inquiring friends*' generally dwindles into a sinecure. What of the poor Priory? we have passed some happy and innocent days there. God bless you, dear Dick, prays very sincerely yours

"J. P. C.

"P. S. These senators are in bed, or this should pass more free than I have ever been able to do."

TO THE SAME.

"Dear Dick,

"My last was in spleen and haste; this is a postscript. I can scarcely add what I should have said, because I forget what I did say; no doubt I was too vain not to brag of the civility I have met, and consequently of the good taste of every body. Did I say any thing of the Italian countess, or the French count her uncle, whose legs and thighs are turned into grasshopper springs by a canister-shot at the battle of Novi? She talks of going westward; as Irish scandal does not talk Italian, and as she can't speak English, she may be safe enough, particularly with the assistance of a Venetian blind! Dear Dick, God help us! I find I am fast recovering from the waters; I think I'll drink no more of them; my nerves are much more composed, and my spirits, though far from good, are more quiet. Why may not the wretch of to-morrow be happy to-day? I am not much inclined to abstract optimism, but I often think Pope was right when he said that 'whatever is, is right,' though he was perhaps too shallow a moralist to know, not why he thought so, but why he said so probably 'twas like your own poetry, he made the ends of the lines jingle for the sake of the rhyme.

"Apropos of jingle. I forgot, I believe, to beg of you to send me two copies of 'O Sleep!' I wrote it for Braham. I suppose the air not correctly. *

"Did I beg of you to see and to direct James as to the erections at the barn? don't forget it; because, perhaps, I may see the Priory once again. I dreamt last night of your four-horse stable, and I was glad to find all well.

"You can scarcely believe what a good humoured compromise I am coming into with human malice, and folly, and unfixedness. By reducing my estimate of myself, every collateral circumstance sets out modestly on the journey of humility and good sense,

* TO SLEEP.

O Sleep, awhile thy power suspending,
  Weigh not yet my eye-lid down,
For Mem'ry, see! with Eve attending,
  Claims a moment for her own.
I know her by her robe of mourning,
  I know her by her faded light,
When faithful with the gloom returning,
  She comes to bid a sad good-night.

Oh! let me here, with bosom swelling,
  While she sighs o'er time that's past
Oh! let me weep, while she is telling
  Of joys that pine and pangs that last.
A' d now, O sleep, while grief is streaming,
  Let thy balm sweet peace restore,
While fearful hope through tears is beaming,
  Soothe to rest that wakes no more.

from the sign of the Colossus to that of the Pigmy, where the apartments are large and ample for the lodger and his train.

"Just as before, the post is on my heels; Richard has only time to put this in the office. I shall probably soon write more at my leisure. Compliments at the hill: ditto repeated *shaking the bottle.*

"J. P. C."

"The Scotch indorser of this gave me my dinner yesterday . champagne and soda. He votes with the Ministers. I gave a lecture, and got glory for rebuking a silly fellow that tried to sing an improper song in the presence of his son. 'Thunders of applause.'"

TO THE SAME.

"CHELTENHAM.

"DEAR DICK,

"I have not been well here—these old blue devils, I fear, have got a lease of me. I wonder the more at it, because I have been in a constant round of very kind and pleasant society. To-morrow Sir Frederick Faulkner and I set out for London. I don't turn my face to the metroplis *con amore*, but the Duke of Sussex might not take it well if I did not call upon him—so I go, being at once an humble friend and a patriot. Low as I have been myself in spirits, I could not but be attracted with the style of society and conversation here, particularly the talents and acquirements of females—I am sorry to say, few of them our countrywomen. The vulgarity too and forwardness of some of our heroes quite terrible. On the whole, however, perhaps, I'm the better for the jaunt."

Early in the following year, in consequence of the still declining condition of his health and spirits, Mr. Curran resigned his judicial situation. Upon which the following address was presented to him by the Catholic Board :—

"TO THE RIGHT HONOURABLE JOHN PHILPOT CURRAN,

"SIR,

"The general board of the Catholics of Ireland feel it their duty to address you on your resignation of the high office to which your talents were called, and the duties of which you have dis-discharged with the courtesy of a gentleman; the abilities of a lawyer; the dignity of a judge; and the characteristic integrity which has ever distinguished you. Taking a review of a life devoted to the service of your country, and the cause and the interest of public and private liberty, we shall ever hold in proud and grateful remembrance the energy which you displayed in resisting oppression, and defending the rights of the subject and the constitution; the independent spirit with which you met the frowns and seductions of power; the intrepidity with which you vindicated your insulted and maligned country, and the sacrifices which you made at the shrine of public virtue. The freedom and the privileges of your profession, so closely connected with those of the public, you upheld both at the bar and on the bench. The first flight of your juvenile genius was a noble and generous defence of an obscure but respectable individual against a lawless assault of tyrannical power. You have uniformly opposed that bigoted, that baneful policy, which impiously tries the principles of man by his religious creed. You have maintained the great and sound principle of religious liberty. A just, a liberal, and an enlightened mind abhors the pernicious system of excluding from equal rights those who contribute equally to the support of the state with their property and their lives; a system which sacrifies the liberty of the country to protect the monopoly of a party, and which, by perpetuating division and discord, saps the foundation of all social intercourse. You, Sir, and the other illustrious advocates of Irish prosperity, are well aware that the total extinction of such a system is absolutely essential to the consolidation and permanence of the general strength of the empire. Permit us, therefore, sir, to indulge our earnest hope, that your splendid talents, emerging from the eclipse of judicial station, and reviving under that name which has attached the hearts of your countrymen, will again be exerted in the service of Ireland."

MR. CURRAN'S ANSWER.

"GENTLEMEN,

"Be pleased to accept my warmest acknowledgment for this flattering mark of your approbation and regard. So far as honesty of intention can hold the place of desert, I can indulge even a proud feeling at this proof of your good opinion, because I have no secret consciousness that can blush while I receive it. I have early thought that the mere fact of birth imposes, by the authority of God, a loyalty to country, binding the conscience of man beyond the force of any technical allegiance, and still more devoted and excusable. To our unhappy country I know that this sentiment was little better than barren; however, what I had I gave. I might have often sold her—I could not redeem her. I gave her the best sympathies of my heart, sometimes in tears, sometimes in indignation, sometimes in hope, but oftener in despondence. I am repaid far beyond my claim; for what reward can be more precious than the confidence and affection of those for whom we could not think any sacrifice too great? I am still farther repaid by seeing that we have arrived at a season that gives us so fair a prospect of better days than we have passed. When I view these awful scenes that are daily marking the interposition of Providence in punishment or retribution, that teach rulers to reflect, and nations to hope, I cannot yield to the infidelity of despair, nor bring myself to suppose that we are destined to be an exception to the uniformity of divine justice, and that in Ireland alone the ways of God shall not, in his good time, be vindicated to man, but that we are to spend our valour and our blood in assisting to break the chains of every other nation, and in riveting our own; and that when the most gallant of our countrymen return to us, laden with glory and with shame, we are to behold them dragging about an odious fetter, with the cypress and the laurel intertwined. On the contrary, I feel myself cheered and consoled by those indications, which inspire the strong hope that the end of our affliction is rapidly advancing, and that we shall soon be placed in a condition where we shall cease to be a reproach to the justice and wisdom of Great Britan. The calumnies of our enemies have been refuted, and have left no impression behind them, save a generous regret that they could ever have been believed. It is with no ordinary feeling of condonation and respect that we should hail the awaking of a nation, formed to be illustrious, from the trance of a bigotry that cannot be refuted, because it does not reason; that, like every other intoxication, stupefies while it inflames, and evaporates only by sleep. It becomes us to congratulate on the recovery without retrospect to the time it may have cost. Within the short limits even of a year, the spirit of a just and liberal policy has assumed a station that scarcely could be hoped from the growth of centuries. That wise country has learned to see us as we are; to compare our sufferings with our merits and our claims; and to feel that every kind and tender sympathy that speaks to the heart or head of a man in favour of his fellow-subjects is calling upon her to put an end to the paroxysms of that gaol fever which must for ever ferment and fester in the imprisonment of a nation, and to do it in a way that shall attach while it redresses, and bind a blended empire in the bond of equal interest and reciprocal affection. We are asking for no restorative; the legislature has none to give; we ask only for what is perfectly in its power to bestow; that deobstruent which may enable the human creature, even by a slow convalescence, to exert the powers of his nature, and give effect, by the progress of his happiness and virtue, to the beneficence of that Being which could not have permanently designed him for the sufferings or the vices of a slave. In your anxiety for the honour of the bar, I cannot but see an auspicious omen of your near approach to the possession of such a treasure that deserves so high a protection. Short is the time that has passed since you could not have adverted to that subject without a mixture of shame and anguish; but you can now resort to persons of your own religious persuasions for those great talents for whose purity you are so justly anxious. You are certainly right in thinking the independence of the bar the only unfailing safeguard of justice, and of that liberty without which justice is but a name. It is the equal protection of the people against the state, and of the state against the people. If Erskine had lived in the dark times of the second James, it might have saved his country from the pain of reading the events of those days, when the Court could procure a bench, but the subject could not find a bar. It is with an emotion difficult to describe that I see how easily our hearts are betrayed into an exaggerated estimation of those we are supposed to love. You are pleased to bespeak the continuance of my poor efforts in the cause of Ireland. I cannot without regret reflect how feeble they would be; but I am fully consoled in the idea, that they would be as unnecessary as inefficient. It is still no more than justice to myself to say, that if an opportunity should occur, and God be pleased to let it be accompanied by health, my most ardent affections would soon find the channel in which they had flowed so long. A devoted attachment to our country can never expire but with my last breath. It is a sentiment that has been the companion of my life: and though it may have sometimes led to what you kindly call sacrifices, it has also given me the most invaluable consolation. And even when the scene shall come to a close, I trust that sentiment shall be the last to leave me, and that I shall derive some consolation in the reflection, that I have been a zealous, though an unprofitable, servant.

[This appears the proper place to introduce some of Charles Phillips' reminiscences of Mr. Curran. He says:

"It was during Mr. Curran's occupancy of the Rolls bench that I had the happiness of making his acquaintance. It soon became intimacy, and so continued to his death. A higher privilege could scarcely be enjoyed than his society conferred. Its simplicity was its greatest charm. He could afford to discard his greatness, and he did so. There was nothing of the senator, or the orator, or the judicial dignitary, or the superior in any way about him; but he was Curran, better and greater than all of them combined. Ostentation was a stranger to his home; so was formality of any kind. His table was simple, his wines choice, his welcome warm, and his conversation a luxury indeed. His habits were peculiar—some of them perhaps eccentric. For instance, an old person was scarcely ever seen within his dwelling. I can remember but three, and they were professionally connected with himself or his court. Although, as has been seen, risking his life recklessly enough, he had an aversion to anything that was associated with death. Hence the aspect of old age depressed him, while youth's joyousness semed to revive his own. Of his early bar associates, whose countenances indicated the ravages of time, I never remember one as a guest at the Priory. But it was a daily custom, when his court had risen, to stroll through the hall, recruiting his dinner company from the juniors. There were seldom more than half a dozen, and it was on such occasions he shone to most advantage. No one who did not see him when he was at his best can have any idea of his exquisite companionship. There was undoubtedly a reverse to the medal. He was occasionally the dullest of the dull, weighed down to the earth by some constitutional dejection. He was very far from being a happy man. Social misfortune aggravated a melancholy which was inherent in his nature. When irritated or discomposed, he could render himself, as I have heard, though I had no experience of it, inconceivably disagreeable. This, however, was rare, and, when he was in one of his happy veins, no one ever equalled him. Lord Byron wrote of him that he had fifty faces: he might have added fifty voices and fifty natures, in the assumption of which he, for the moment, merged his own identity. His powers of imitation were marvellous and irresistible. He was the parish. priest, the Munster peasant, the coal-quay fish-woman, the joval squireen, and the illiterate squire, each in their turn, and each a facsimile. He not merely aped the manner, but he either displayed the mind of the individual, or ascribed to him some drollery which much enhanced the humor of the assumption. Thus, when asked by Lord Byron to give him some idea of Mr. Grattan, bowing lowly to the ground, he expressed his gratitude that neither in person nor gesture was he obnoxious to imitation. That great man was composed of peculiarities. In stock stories his treasury was rich, and the perilous attempt to draw on it was generally assigned to me. However, failure was rare. He was too simple to suspect, and too facile to refuse. For instance, when the *vulgar pomposity* of the Mayor of Cork was to be elicited, the wine was tasted, the lips were smacked, and the glass held up scientifically to the candle. Mr. Curran, this strikes me as very fine claret. O dear! you are very good to say so; it's the red wax, the best I have. I can't compliment you as my cousin the Mayor of Cork did the Lord Lieutenant when he was entertaining him: 'Mr. Mayor this is very choice wine.' 'Does your Excellency think so? Why it is good wine, your Excellency, but *it's nothing at all to some I've got in my cellar.*' And then he followed up his own jest with the short, sharp, dry, familiar laugh, which he never refused to that of another. When Curran really enjoyed his evening, and the bottle had circulated sufficiently, it was sometimes his custom, when the weather permitted, to adjourn to the gardens. The walk was refreshing, and always preluded grilled bones, and plenty of what in Ireland was then called 'THE MATERIALS'—namely, scalding water, lemon, sugar, and the pottheen—for a definition of which, see Miss Edgeworth. There were always beds for the guests at the Priory—a precaution by no means inconsiderate. When breakfast came, it was somewhat problematical how the party were to return. If all was propitious, the carriage was in waiting; if a cloud was seen, however, the question came, 'Gentlemen, how do you propose getting to court?" Ominous was the silence which ushered in the summons

'Richard, harness the *mule* to the jaunting car, and take the gentlemen to town!' One of this worthy animal's most favorite pastimes was to carry the company into a pool of water which lay by the road side! Of course the host knew nothing of the mule's jocularity, and most certainly it never was suggested to him by any refusal of an invitation to the Priory.

"Although himself so admirable a mimic, he by no means relished being made a subject. One day being apprised that a gentleman then present personated him to the life, Curran affected to request a performance; entreaty and evasion were more than once repeated, when he terminated the scene: Well, indeed, my dear W., I'm sadly disappointed. It must be an amusing thing to see a cat running across a piano, and *calling it music.*

"Mr. Curran sprang from the people,* and he not only never forgot it, but was proud of it. His associates were not of the aristocracy, if, indeed, such a term was applicable to the very

* Mr. Curran was particularly sensitive to any mark of respect or confidence on the part of the lower orders. In one of his little poems he commemorates with much satisfaction.

"A croppy heifer sparèd by Holt."

This Holt was an extraordinary man. He was a farmer and dealer in wool, originally keeping aloof from politics. Of a liberal cast of mind, however, he refused to take any part against his Roman Catholic countrymen. This, in such times, was quite sufficient to render him a marked man, and being so, a domiciliary visit was paid to his house on the breaking out of the rebellion of 1798. He was not at home, and the visitors burned the house and property to ashes! Rendered desperate by this, he repaired to a cave in the Devil's Glen, in the county of Wicklow. Here he found some United Irishmen, refugees like himself, and, in the frame of mind in which he was, was easily persuaded to take the oath and become their general. In a week he was at the head of one hundred and sixteen men, and many hundreds afterward joined him. He became an admirable guerilla chief, and, during six months, kept the whole power of the government at bay. Well acquainted with the Wicklow mountains, and possessing both skill and intrepidity, Holt proved himself more than a match for the king's officers. At length some noble traits of character which he exhibited induced Lord Powerscourt to open a negotiation with him. Holt consented to expatriate himself to New South Wales, which he did; but soon receiving a free pardon, he returned to Ireland, where he died in 1826. Holt was a very superior man of his class, and proved himself a formidable antagonist. He wrote and published his life. His men, in one of their forays carried off, with other cattle, a cow of Curran's, whose house was near the mountains. However, when Holt saw the initials "J. P. C." branded on one of the horns, he guessed to whom the animal belonged and sent it home with a complimentary apology.

arrogant and very ignorant persons who at that time usurped it in Ireland. He heartily despised them. He never was of the Castle or *their set*. Before the Union he was generally in opposition, and after that the Viceroy appeared to him only as a titled memorial of the country's degradation. He used to talk, indeed, of his poor cottage, as he called it, having been graced by the choicest spirits of the land—not culled for their birth from a dull peerage, nor for their possessions from an ignorant proprietary, but from men risen from *the ranks*—from the Duquerys, Yelvertons, and Grattans, whose personal merits flung pedigree into the shade. There was in his own manner that easy and urbane courteousness which if not derived from nature, is very difficult of acquisition."]

Shortly after his resignation he passed over to London, in order to proceed to, and take a last look at, France, now once more accessible from the fall of Napoleon. He addressed several letters from London and Paris to one of his intimate friends in Ireland.* Of these the following selection will be found to contain his opinions at large upon the interesting events that had lately passed, and upon the state of society in those rival capitals:

TO DENIS LUBE, ESQ., DUBLIN.

"LONDON, *June*, 1814.

"MY DEAR LUBE,

"I AM not many days in London; yet am I as sick of it, as ever I was of myself. No doubt it is not a favourable moment for society; politics spoil every thing; it is a perpetual tissue of plots, cabals, low anxiety, and disappointment. Every thing I see disgusts and depresses me; I look back at the streaming of blood for so many years; and every thing everywhere relapsed into its former degradation. France rechained—Spain again sad-

* Mr. D. Lube, of the Irish bar; a gentleman of peculiarly estimable character, in whom Mr. Curran reposed the most unbounded confidence.—C.

dled for the priests—and Ireland, like a bastinadoed elephant, kneeling to receive the paltry rider: and what makes the idea the more cutting, her fate the work of her own ignorance and fury. She has completely lost all sympathy here, and I see no prospect for her, except a vindictive oppression and and an endlessly increasing taxation. God give us not happiness, but patience!

"I have fixed to set out for Paris on Tuesday with Mr. W. He is a clever man, pleasant, informed, up to every thing, can discount the bad spirits of a friend, and has undertaken all trouble. I don't go for society, it is a mere name; but the thing is to be found no where, even in this chilly region. I question if it is much better in Paris. Here the parade is gross, and cold, and vulgar; there it is, no doubt, more flippant, and the attitude more graceful; but in either place is not society equally a tyrant and a slave? The judgment despises it, and the heart renounces it. We seek it because we are idle, we are idle because we are silly; the natural remedy is some social intercourse, of which a few drops would restore; but we swallow the whole phial, and are sicker of the remedy than we were of the disease. We do not reflect that the variety of converse is found only with a very few, selected by our regard, and is ever lost in a promiscuous rabble, in whom we cannot have any real interest, and where all is monotony. We have had it some times at the Priory, notwithstanding the bias of the ball that still made it roll to a particular side. I have enjoyed it, not long since, for a few hours in a week with as small a number, where too there was no smartness, no wit, no petty affectation, no repartee; but where the heart will talk, the tongue may be silent—a look will be a sentence, and the shortest phrase a volume. No; be assured if the fancy is not led astray, it is only in the *coterie* that the thirst of the animal being can be slaked, or the pure luxury and anodyne of his life be found. He is endeared and exalted by being surpassed; he cannot be jealous of the wealth, however greater than his, which is expended for his pleasure, and which in fact, he feels to be his own. As well might an alderman become envious of the calabash in which his soul delights before the Lord. But we are for ever mistaking the plumage for the bird: perhaps we are justly punished by seeking happiness where it is not given by nature to find it. Eight or ten lines back I looked at my watch; I saw 'twas half-past six, the hour at which dinner, with *a friend or two*, was to be precisely on the table. I went—was presented to half a dozen dial plates that I never saw before, and that looked as if they had never told the hour of the day. I sat gagged—stayed twenty minutes—came back to write, leaving Richard to bring me word if, between this and to-morrow, the miserable mess shall be flung into the trough. How complete a picture this of glare without worth, and attitude without action. 'My temper,' to quote myself, 'and my dinner lost.' Can it have been the serious intention of Providence that affectation should obtain these triumphs over sense and comfort? and yet, really my host is a very good fellow in the main.

"'Tis now half-past seven—no Richard. I had just put on my hat to go to the next coffee-house, but I resolved to punish myself for the petty peevishness of being angry, because every one has not as much good sense as I think I have myself. I am now wishing there may be no dinner till ten, that I may have the glory of self-punishment—

'Judico me cremari,

in continuation—

'Et combustus fui.' *

"We sat down at eight, sixteen strong, but it had nothing of a

* Mr. Curran alludes to an anecdote related by Sir William Blackstone, in one of the notes to his Commentaries. In the reign of Henry the Sixth, the Chancellor of Oxford claimed the right of trying an action brought against himself; upon which occasion his counsel, Sergeant Rolfe, introduced the following curious argument in support of the claim:—*Jeo vous dirai un fable. En ascun temps fuit un pape et avoit fait un grand offence, et le cardinals vindrent a luy et disoyent a luy "peccasti:" et il dit, "judica me;" et ils disoyent, "non possumus, quia caput et ecclesiæ; judica teipsum:" et l'apostol dit, "judico me cremari," et fuit combustus; et apres fuit un sainct. Et in ceo cas il fuit son juge demene, et issint n'est pas inconvenient que un home soit juge demene.*—Bla. Com. Book 3, p. 299, *note.*

coterie. I sat next to a pleasantish sort of a lady; but alas! a look of attention is not a look of affiance: there are graciousnesses that neither identify nor attract; and as to the atmosphere that sported on her dimples, I would just as soon have had a thimbleful of common air. After all, how rare the coincidences that conciliate affection and exclusive confidence! how precarious!

> 'For either
> He never shall find out fit mate, but such
> As some misfortune bring him, or mistake;
> Or whom he wishes most shall seldom gain.
> Or if she love, withheld
> By parents, or his happiest choice too late
> Shall meet already linked and wedlock-bound
> To a fell adversary, his hate or shame.'

"Milton, you see, with all his rigour, was not insensible of these *lachrymæ rerum.* There is one thing that ought to make us humble and patient. When we are close enough for the inspection of others, we soon find that 'life is eternal war with woe.' Many, too, are doomed to 'suffer alone;' and, after all, would not a truly generous nature prefer the monopoly of its own ills rather than fling any part of them upon a kindred bosom?

"You ask me about politics. Regarding myself, my answer is—I had no object in parliament except the Catholic question, and that I fear is gone. Westminster will probably be a race of bribery, equally dangerous and precarious.* Burdett's conduct has been quite that of a friend and a man: he would have been most ardent, and what was to me most grateful, on a public ground. I dined with him yesterday; at first the party was numerous—the masquerade, about ten, drained them down to three, my *compagnon de voyage* and myself; till one it was quite

* It was expected at this time that there would shortly be a vacancy in the representation for Westminster, in which event Mr. Curran had been encouraged to offer himself as a candidate, but he never entered warmly into the scheme. This is the political project to which he adverts more than once in his subsequent letters.—C.

a *coterie;* with no wine, there's no playing on an instrument with many strings; half of them form only base accompaniments.

"I thought to have gone *incog.* to Paris, but my excellent friend, the Duke of Sussex, insisted on my taking a letter to Monsieur. [After Charles X.]

'So now cocked hats, and swords, and laces,
And servile bows and low grimaces:
For what at court the lore of Pascal
Weighed 'gainst the crouchings of a rascal?'

"As to my stay there, everywhere is to me nowhere; there fore, if it depends on me, I shall drop off when I'm full, or Mr. W will haul me along. If our friends have any wish, it ought to decide, and shall do so. I cannot endure to be conscious of any retaliating sulk in myself; and I know that heaven loveth the cheerful giver.

"Yours, &c.,
"J. P. C."

TO THE SAME.

"LONDON, *June*, 1814.

"DEAR LUBE,

"Just received your kind fragment. I cannot say I read it without some pain. When fortune deigns to favour, particularly if there is any port and dignity in her condescension, we are apt to feel any declination from the consistency of her kindness. If she has justly entitled herself to stand upon a high pedestal, she cannot sink into any pettishness without affliction to the votary, who may be too apt to fear that there may have been blindness in what she withholds.

Anne Howe* is an injudicious example of a woman of talents, favouring without much claim, inflicting without much cause, and diminishing the value of what she gives, and what would other-

* This is a fictitious name. The subject of this part of the above letter was entirely of a private nature, and is alluded to with a studied obscurity.—C.

wise rise above all price, by the levity of an unequal tenor that takes away from her the splendid of her own uniform judgment in her own justification; it lets down the giver, and abashes the taker. Our friends should not have made a point so much beneath their region; let them, therefore, review and correct. However, it should be ever the duty of gratitude, not to let even the breaking of a single string take away the merit of the residue of the octave, if that had given out all the luxury of harmony and feeling before that single key had lost its voice—but, perhaps too much of this.

"Since my arrival here my spirits have been wretchedly low: though treated with great kindness, I find nothing to my mind. I find heads without thinking, and hearts without strings, and a phraseology sailing in ballast—every one piping, but few dancing. England is not a place for society; it is too cold, too vain, without pride enough to be humble, drowned in dull fantastical formality, vulgarized by rank without talent, and talent foolishly recommending itself by weight rather than by fashion—a perpetual war between the disappointed pretension of talent and the stupid over-weening of affected patronage; means without enjoyment, pursuits without an object, and society without conversation or intercourse: perhaps they manage this better in France—a few days, I think, will enable me to decide. In that object I probably would have succeeded; I should have been strongly supported, but a conflict of corruption! surely not to be thought of. How would it mortify the discerning pride of our friends to see us decked and degraded in a mantle!

"So vilely purchased and so vilely wrought!"

and to find themselves disguising the pangs of wounded sympathy in the force semblance of gratulation. The advice of Longinus, 'consider how Homer would have expressed this idea,' applies equally to everything. How would the adviser have advised?—how feel? Will the 'promise so true,' 'for ever to partake the joy and the wo,' be performed in sharing the joy of what is right, or in the sad condolence at what is weak or wrong? If the latter, what would it be but the rising of the whirlwind, and drifting a mountain of sand upon the green spot that could never again appear? While fate permits that spot to bloom, sacred should it be kept, at least from voluntary weeds.

"One of our friends asked me how soon I meant to return. Instead of answering directly, I observed that the question implied no particular wish, or, if any, rather for a retarded than a precipitated return. If any wish had been intimated, it would have decided me. I did not impute the indecision to any want of interest, but I intended to have discussed it at large the day after my departure. What is the wish? Perhaps, on such a subject, the wisher might condescend to be also the amanuensis. I shall remain here, I think, just long enough to get a line—enclosed to J. Spencer, Esq. 28 Bury Street. If I am left to my own conjectures, my stay in France might be for the winter; it might lead to an excursion to Italy, in vainly pursuing 'phantoms that promise and afterwards disown.' A proposal towards such a plan has been mentioned to me, and by a pleasant man, who has been there already.

"Don't mistake me, in supposing that I meant anything peevish in the indecision of wish by our friends; quite the contrary. I really think it very difficult to know what wish to form, while all things are in such a state of vacillation. The post is just ringing. Farewell!

J. P C."

"PARIS, August, 3, 1814.

"DEAR L.

"I received your kind letter, and thank you for it; '*levius fit*,' &c. When I came here, I intended to have scribbled some little journal of what I met. I am now sorry I did not. Things so soon become familiar, and appear not worth notice: besides, I have not been well since I came here. If I had written, and sent it to you, it would have been a tissue of astonishment, or affliction, or disgust. I see clearly I am likely to be drummed out of this sad world. I fear war will soon unfold her tattered banners on the continent. This poor country is in a deplorable state—a ruined noblesse, a famished clergy, a depopulated nation, a state of smothered war between the upstarts and the restored; their finances most distressed; the military spirits divided; the most opposite opinions as to the lasting of the present form of things—every thing unhinged: yet I really sympathised with this worried, amiable, and perhaps contemptible people; so full of talent and of vice, so frivolous, so inconstant and prone to change, so ferocious too in their fickleness; about six revolutions within twenty years, and as fresh as ever for a new dance. These strange vicissitudes of man draw tears, but they also teach wisdom. These awful reverses make one ashamed of being engrossed by mere self, and examining a louse through a miscroscope, 'complain of grief, complain thou art a man.'

"I never so completely found my mind a magic-lantern; such a rapid succession of disjointed images! the past, the present, the future possible. One ought not to be hasty in taking of bad impressions, and I need not say that three weeks can give but little room for exact observation; but from what I do see, and learn from others who have seen long and deeply, I have conceived the worst of social Paris. Every thing on the surface is abominable; beastlinesses that even with us do not exist; they actually seem in talk and in practice to cultivate a familiarity with nastiness. In every public place, they are spitting on your shoes, in your plate, almost in your mouth. Such community of secretions, with, I think, scarcely any exception, is not to be borne. Then the contrast makes it worse—gaudiness more striking by filth: the splendid palace for the ruler, the hovels and the sink for the ruled; the fine box for the despot, the pigeon-holes for the people; and it strikes me with sadness, that the women can be little more than the figurantes, much more the property, and that a very abused property, than the proprietors; receiving a mock reverence, merely to carry on the drama, but neither cherished nor respected. What a reflection, if, as I fear, it is true that the better half of the species, (for such I really think them, when fitly placed) should be so sacrificed! How vile the feeling and the taste, that can degrade them from being the real directors and mistresses of man, to be the mere soubrettes of society, gilded and smart, and dextrous and vicious, giving up all that exalts and endears them in their proper characters of wives and friends, and partners in good, and consolers in adverse fortunes! Even before the revolution, manners were bad enough, but many causes since have rubbed off the gilding; the banishment of the nobles, the succession of low men to power, and more than all the elevation of plebeian soldiers to high rank, promoting of course their trulls to a station where manners and morals were under their influence; and this added to the horrible example set by Bonaparte himself in his own interior, putting every thing honest or sacred out of countenance and out of fashion. Add to this, what must have sent down the contagion to the lower orders—the conscription: the wretched men marrying without preference merely to avoid the army, and then running into that army to escape from their ill-chosen partners; all these causes must have conspired to make a frightful carnage in manners and morals too. In short, I am persuaded that a single monster has done more to demoralize and uncivilize this country than a century can repair. I am disposed to attribute to the same causes the growing fanaticism of England. In Ireland we had little to lose in civilization; but look at our late extravagances, and see at least how much we have lost in our own and in the opinion of others. For years to come, I see no hope; we have the anguish of being ourselves the cause of not going forward a little in the march of the world, but of still remaining a by-word among nations. Patriotic affectation is almost as bad as personal, but I declare I think these things do a good deal in sinking my health, which is far from good; my spirits quite on the ground; and yet as to Ireland, I never saw but one alternative—a bridewell or a guard-house; with England the first, with France the other. We might have had a mollification, and the bolts lightened, and a chance of progression; but that I now give up.

"I really wish the thing with myself over; and trust me that wish is not irreligious or peevish, but rather a good humoured feeling, that, not wishing to eat more, I may be better by rising from table; 'enough is as good as a feast.'

"I am every hour more and more confirmed as to my ideas of society; it is not for those that think or feel; it is not one fool getting on the back of many, to fly from himself. In France you can scarcely make even that experiment, for all here agree that at *the present moment* all society is dead. Nor is it wonderful, that, when all the actors on the great scene are changed, the parts should be badly performed; but still I have found society, as it is called, and met a great deal of kindness, and some persons of talent; but even there I found society an orchestra, where the fiddlers were putting one another out, or rather where one played a solo, and every other bow was soaped.

"At this moment my friend enters; he differs totally from my opinion, saying, 'I have lived single in a great city; few friends, many acquaintances; I think I have done right and shall continue. Sameness would cloy. How many happy matches have you seen? How many faithful friendships? Too much intimacy lays you bare; your little infirmities diminish respect, perhaps excite disgust, perhaps end in hatred. With the same persons and those few, what chance of having yourself, or finding in them, the attachment, the good temper, and good sense necessary for bearing and forbearing? You have complained of being spit upon—but you can easily curse them, make a polite bow, and go away; but that would be no cause for breaking a closer attachment. Are you not conscious, that you have observed, since we have been so much together some faults in me not observed before? Have you no suspicion of reprisal?' All this I treated as misanthropic cant—he retorted on me, 'What is your select attachment but general intolerance? What is the syrup of concentrated affection but extract from the wormwood of embittered irritability? When has any man ever found the male or the female inmate always equal, patient, and amiable? or even suppose it, will not sickness or death rend the bond, and leave you or them in a desert? As to me, I can bear almost every body; the grave-digger, I laugh at. I cannot weep over myself when I'm gone, and I will not over any body else.' He pressed me to say if I seriously thought there was nothing in these topics. I told him I had frequently been presented with them before, but was not exactly in a frame for an *ulterius concilium.* In truth, it was rather memory awakened, than opinion shaken, that made me disposed to silence; but of this enough for the present.

"I found myself all abaft. We agreed to go to *la chambre des Députés.* One of the members chanced to have heard of my name, was extremely courteous, lamented that I should be a mere auditor, but he would take care that I should be placed according to my high worthiness. We were accordingly placed *aux premières tribunes:* the question was to be of the liberty of the press, and of a previous censorship. The Baron had some difficulty in working us forward, and said how happy he was in succeeding. I assured him I was greatly delighted by the difficulty, as it marked the just point of solicitude of the public. The chamber is very handsome; the president faces the assembly; before him is a tribune, which the orator ascends, and reads his speech with his back to the president—we waited anxiously. I thought I shared in the throb of a public heart. We observed some bustle; the seats of the interior, reserved for the members, became crowded to excess by ladies admitted I know not how. The order for strangers to retire was read; the ladies would not stir. The president could find no remedy, and adjourned the house to next day. I was rather disgusted: the Baron asked me what we would have done in England? I said we had too much respect for our ladies to permit them to remain; he shook his head: I did not understand what he meant. But does not this prove, what I said a day or two ago (for this is written by starts) to be true, 'that women here have only a mock respect?' if real, would they have dreamed of such a silly termagancy? Does it not mark their unfeeling coxcombry and apathy in the public interest, and how fit they are to be the mothers of the Gracchi? And yet women here are vain of their sway. I can imagine nothing more humiliating than such Saturnalian licentiousness.

"However, I went next day. There was a previous list of the orators, pro and con: they mounted alternately, and read written speeches. The echo was strong; I lost much. But how can any man read his own speech? He may the speech of the dead or the absent; it is any thing but discussion. The orator swabs his face, notwithstanding the sedateness of the exertion; and when he stops to drink, which is a part of the performance, the whole assembly handle their 'kerchiefs, and trumpet in the most perfect time and unison, to the great animation and interest of the speech, and no doubt to the great comfort of the auditors, who must have had their secretions brimful during their attention. The question will not be decided probably in many days. The press is surely the great sentinel—it gives the light to see and the tongue to speak. They say the Russians always eat the candles before they swallow the people. I can't tell you how interested I am; I begin to doubt if man ought to be monopolized or his taper, however dim it may be, put under the bushel of mere private confined affection. Some, it seems, are afraid of the sudden mischiefs that might arise among a volatile people, if restraint were removed too soon; I own it never was my notion. But I know not how far these fears may be real or feigned. Such is the fate of revolutions—nothing certain but blood. The march of the captives begins through a Red Sea; and, after forty years in seeking new abodes and strange gods, the leader seldom sees the promised land, or, at least, dies before his foot has touched it. What is it, here at least, but the succession of wretches doing the duty of the hangman, till it is the turn of each to be the victim? These thoughts often console me. My dear friend, we must stay as we are; but let us look at the history of past and the acts of present men, and learn to be patient and modest.

"You can't forget my hatred of Bonaparte; everything I hear confirms it. When I went up to see his famous column at Boulogne, the poor muse, I thought was left behind, whispered at the moment,

'When ambition achieves her desire,
How fortune must laugh at the joke!
You mounted a pillar of fire,
You sink in a pillar of smoke.'

"I am greatly pleased to have this man's extinction marked by so much abject degradation. These butchers and robbers, called conquerers, have kept their vices up by the splendour of their rise or fall; but what a fall has this man had! He retires instead of falling like a brave highwayman, or as a Cataline did: he dwindles into an isl-icle, and plays the pitiful tricks of power among fishermen and washerwomen. After losing the game of the world, he sits down, like a child, to make castles with cards. Even his military talents are questioned. They say, that having no respect for property or person, he extorted such sums of money, and thousands of men, as made resistance physically impossible, even notwithstanding an infinite number of mistakes of head and violence of temper—but here you know I am speaking without book. Still he had laid hold of the gaudiness of many, and is talked of with regret; but his rising again is, I trust in God, impossible. I do believe the present rulers mean very well, though the King has none of the vices that might recommend him here. I believe he is well taught in the school of adversity, and has a respect for whatever is good and honest. Whatever he be bigoted, I don't know.

An attempt was made to shut the shops on Sunday, and to carry the host in procession, but both failed; they were, however, desisted from with great temper.

"I now regret that I did not throw upon paper the things that occurred every day; I have often regretted the omission. I would advise you to keep a journal of that kind; it will cost very little trouble, and will have the freshness of being ready gathered, not faded by forgetfulness and cold and laboured recollection. Even while I have been scribbling this, many incidents that glowed with life at the moment, have so lost their life, that though I rolled them they threw up nothing but water, and would be rotten before they could reach you, so I ceased all attempts to revive them. I had twenty things, the first few days to say of my host, and his wife, and his daughter. It seems they fled to Lubec at the first horrors of the revolution, and the children were born there; the girl, I thought, seemed to have a good opinion of me, and I thought her good taste ought to make amends for her want of beauty; and certainly she had brought a very scanty viaticum of charms from the north. About the end of the first week, meaning to be very sweet, she assured me I had the best English accent she ever heard, and that it was exactly the same as that of her English master. During this chat, in marches the teacher. The scoundrel is a German, who went to London at five and twenty, and returned, after four years, to teach the purity of their language in Paris. Poor girl! I turned her regimentals at the moment, and remanded her to her ugliness. However, all is well, for she knows nothing of the crime, or the sentence, or the pardon. The father and mother are very good sort of people, and have saved me from some small impositions; for really nothing can be so shameless and abject as the frauds upon strangers. Even at the coffee-house where I breakfast, the keeper of it, a very genteel woman, makes me almost every day pay a different price for the same thing. It is still only fair to say, the French are the civilest people upon earth, and I really believe sincerely good natured to strangers. Two nights ago I was overtaken by the national guard: I asked the officer my way; he answered so courteously, that I ventured a question or two more; he continued the same good nature, and the private next behind him assisted in doing the duties of hospitality. I said I was afraid he had led me to pass the line of respect to him, but his answer was, and in the kindest tone, 'Sir, a stranger *comme il faut* can never pass it in France.' I doubt if I should have found it so in England. Apropos! I am quite sure the two nations hate each other as devoutly as ever; and I think their respective imperfections of character will be kept alive by the mutual spirit of contempt. Paris will think it graceful to be volatile, as long as London thinks it dignified to be dull."

TO THE SAME.

"PARIS.

"MY DEAR LUBE.

"I write again, because I judge from myself, and how kindly I felt your last, that you would like to hear from me; perhaps the not being able to abstain from writing to the absent is the only certain proof that distance and memory are compatible: however, the compliment is not great, when you know that I have flung myself upon you as a correspondent only at those intervals when I could not bear my own company. The thermometer has been higher here lately than at any former time. Close, dirty streets, stewing play-houses, and a burning sun, have, perhaps naturally enough, completed the extreme depression of my spirits, and made me fit for nothing. I endeavour to dissipate, by wasting myself upon spectacle—but it wo 'nt do; this day I thought to look for something gay in the catacombs. It seems all Paris stands upon a vaulted quarry, out of which the stone to build it has been taken, and it is not very rare to see an entire house sink down to its original home, and disappear. Part of the excavation has been fitted up as a residence in remainder for a grave. We went down,

I think, seventy steps, and traversed more than half a mile by torch, or rather taper light, and we beheld more than 2,300,000 fragments of what once was life. They amount to four times the present population of Paris. The bones were very carefully built up, and at intervals were studded with projecting rows of skulls, with mottos occasionally written up in Latin or French. It was a sort of caravan, mostly women: one of them asked me to translate one of those; it was, I think, 'in nihilum revertitur quod ex nihilo fuit.' I asked whether it gave her a sentiment of grief, or fear, or hope? She asked me what room I could see for hope in a parcel of empty skulls? 'For that reason, madam, and because you know they cannot be filled with grief or fear, for all subjects of either is past.' She replied, 'oui, et cependant c'est jolie.' I could not guess to what she applied the epithet, so I raised the taper to her face, which I had not looked at before, and had it been any thing but the mirror of death, I should have thought she had looked into it, and applied the one reflection to the other, so perfectly unimpressed was her countenance. It did not raise her in my mind, though she was not ill-looking; and when I met her above ground, after our resurrection, she appeared fit enough for the drawing-rooms of the world, though not for the under-cellar. I do not remember ever to have had my mind compressed into so narrow a space: so many human beings, so many actors, so many sufferers, so various in human rank, so equalized in the grave! When I stared at the congregation, I could not distinguish what head had raved, or reasoned, or hoped, or burned. I looked for thought, I looked for dimples; I asked, whither is all gone—did wisdom never flow from your lips, nor affection hang upon them—and if both or either, which was the most exalting—which the most fascinating? All silent. They left me to answer for them, 'So shall the fairest face appear.'

"I was full of the subject. In the evening I went to distract at the comedy of le Misanthrope, the best of Moliere. The severe affection of Alceste, and the heartless coquetry of Celimene, were excellently done. It is not only tragedy that weeps—Golgotha was still an incubus upon me. I saw the moral of the piece went far beyond the stage—it only began there. Every good play ought to be just in the particular fable. It ought also (to be useful) to have a general analogy far more extensive and equally exact. Alceste is a man in the abstract—Celimene is the object of his wish, whatever that may be; she smiles, and caresses, and promises. He thinks he feels the blood in her heart, for he mistakes the pulse of his own for that of hers; he embraces the phantom, or thinks he does so, but is betrayed, and opens his eyes upon the desert: at the moment he does not recollect that the loss to him is little; 'tis only the loss of himself—to her it is nothing, for it is made up in the next conscription; and, at all events, whether sick or wounded, the march of man's warfare is never suspended; the moving infirmary never halts, and every day brings him a stage nearer *à la barrière d'enfer*, the entrance of the catacombs.

"This sad subject naturally turns me to another, that makes me suspect that my contempt of this world is not quite sincere. I mean the poor extravasated Irish that I meet here; I meet their ghosts as I pass, and view them as Eneas did,

> 'Quos abstulit atra dies et funere miscet acerbo.'

How can I affect to despise a scene where my heart bleeds for every sufferer? I wish to disperse my feelings as a citizen of the world, and break my own monopoly of them, but they all come back to our unhappy country. One of the most beautiful touches of the prince of sensitive poets is where he tinges the wanderings of Dido with patriotism,

> ———'Sæpe longum incomitata videtur
> Ire viam et Tyrios deserta quærere terra.'

By the by, it does some credit to the character of humanity that we sometimes exchange the suffering of egotism for a nobler sympathy, and lament over others instead of keeping all our tears for ourselves. What exquisite nectar must they be to those over whom they are shed! Nor perhaps should the assurance that they do n't suffer alone be always witheld, because it may not be always true; because for the purpose of consolation, it is enough if it be believed, whether true or not: if the payment is complete, is it worth while to inquire whether the coin be counterfeit or not? But with respect to our poor exiles the sympathy is most sincere as well as ardent: I had hopes that England might let them back. The season and the power of mischief is long past; the number is almost too small to do credit to the mercy that casts a look upon them. But they are destined to give their last recollection of the green fields they are never to behold, on a foreign death-bed, and to lose the sad delight of fancied visits to them in a distant grave.

"I continue to feel an increasing dislike of every thing here; I probably sha' n't remain long. I have left some things in Ireland unsettled that I must arrange, however I may dispose of myself hereafter. England can 't arrest me long; I have never found any good in watering-places. My malady, a constitutional dejection, can hope for no remedy in water or in wine. In general, the benefit of those places is attributed to the attendant temperance, but a person little given to excess any where has not much to add in that way; and as to evening parties, in a crowd of strangers, I never liked them, nor was fit for them: I have therefore given my evenings to the theatres—I prefer them to English, notwithstanding the difficulty of a foreign language. I prefer the style of their stage to ours: ours always appeared to me flat and dull, with never more than one or two of tolerable merit; on the contrary, here you never find any very bad. A comic nation is perpetually sending young aspirants to Paris, where of course there can be no dearth. In England you must put up with what you can get. No doubt, it is hard to find any exact principles of acting; 't is in a great degree arbitrary and accidental—still nature will assert certain boundaries. In France there may be bombast, and tinsel, and the eternal monotony of amour in their plays is liable to objections, lying much deeper than the mere criticism of the stage; it goes vitally to the morals and manners of the people—it goes to make the woman a bad sort of man, and the man a bad sort of woman; it goes to take away the solid basis of every virtue of either sex: it leaves the man little to wish, to the woman little to bestow; it annihilates the fine spirit of attachment. What can he feel for confidence given on a principle of good breeding? To fascinate, there must be no doubt of its being exclusive. When I am writing my bad verses, I would spurn the muse, if I suspected her of whispering the same idea to twenty other poetasters. On the same principle, if you have only the sixty-fourth part of a ticket in the lottery of regard, the prize is in fact a blank. How can you join in triumph with sixty-three other fortunate adventurers? Still these exhibitions amuse; the acting is flippant and graceful, and the music sometimes excellent. The English, who have no national music, affect to despise French. It is sometimes, perhaps, tinselish; but I own it frequently catches my fancy, and even my heart.

* * * * * * *

"I am not sorry for having come hither when I did—perhaps you see society better when cut into piece-meal, as in anatomy every thing is laid bare to the student—perhaps it is seen to great disadvantage. The best lesson that man can learn is toleration, and travelling ought to be the best school. There are many points in which this people must be allowed praise—lively, cheerful—a constitutional philosophy, disposing them to be always satisfied. I wish, as to government, they could be brought to an anchor; whether that is to happen, who can tell? Nothing can be more divided than the general sentiment: the higher military men have got safe into harbour, and wish perhaps for quiet; all under them most discontented; long arrears due. They can't employ them abroad, for want of money; and when the devil is raised, and can't be kept in work—we know the story. The favour to Bonaparte is the more singular, because, allowing for his extraordinary energy, I doubt if he had a single great quality. It is clear he was no statesman; force alone was sufficient for all he did. Men here of the best authority pronounce him a man of uncommon energy in action, but of no talent for retreat. The question is of more curiosity than moment. If otherwise, it might not be easy to ki ow what credit to give to these criticisms.

"22d. At last we have got our passports, and ordered a carriage for to-morrow. We shall go by Dieppe. Neither my fellow-traveller nor myself in the best health or spirits: I have a great kindness for him, though no human beings can be more different. I do n't think diversity is incompatible with friendship or affection; but strong contrariety, I fear, is. How different are they from the volatility of France, as well as from the loud, ardent, indiscreet vehemence of our poor people. Certainly it is not mere interest that forms the weight to the clock, through the utter want of any regulating power makes it a sad time-piece. But I consider it now as nearly a '*conclamatum est*,' and the insurrection act little other than a monumental inscription.

"London. Tuesday. (A new venue.) After a day spent at Dieppe, we sailed: and, after forty hours, landed at Brighton. I don't like the state of my health; if it was merely *maladie* under sailing orders for the undiscovered country, I should not quarrel with the passport. There is nothing gloomy in my religious impressions, though I trust they are not shallow: I ought to have been better—I know also that others have been as blameable; and have rather a cheerful reliance upon mercy than an abject fear of justice. Or were it otherwise, I have a much greater fear of suffering than of death.

"I had almost made up my mind to bestow a citizen to France, and I am mortified at finding any drag upon the intention—yet a drag there is. I have no doubt that the revolution has thrown that country a century back, yet she has qualities that might have hoped a better destiny. It has been suggested to me that a winter in Pa is might answer better.

"I just now return from a long conversation with the truly royal personage,* who saves you from the postage of this. A few days must, I now think, take me across. I think of meeting some persons at Cheltenham. As to waters, I suspect they are seldom o. use. I am quite decided against them, till Charon pledges me on the Styx.

"Yours, very truly,

"J. P. CURRAN."

The following letter, written in 1815, concludes the series of his private correspondence:

"LONDON.

"DEAR LUBE,

"As I sit down to write, I am broken in upon. In sooth I had little to say—the mere sending this is full proof that I have escaped being supped upon by Jonas's landlord, or any of his subjects. I sailed Wednesday night, and arrived here at half-past six this morning sound and sad. Kings and generals as cheap as dirt, and yet so much more valuable a thing as a lodging as dear as two eggs a penny. Saturday not being a day of business in the House, I met nobody; though I did not go to bed on my arrival: the little I have heard confirms the idea you know I entertained of a flatness of a certain political project; it could not pass unopposed, and in such a conflict, the expenditure of money to make a voter a knave, that you might be an honest senator, would, in such a swarm of locusts, surpass all calculation. However, I know nothing distinctly as yet, therefore I merely persevere in the notion I stated to you.

"I have just seen the immortal Blucher. The gentlemen and ladies of the mob huzza him out of his den, like a wild beast to his offal; and this is repeated every quarter of an hour, to their great delight, and for aught appears, not at all to his dissatisfaction. I am now going to dine with a friend, before whose house the illus-

* H. R. H. the Duke of Sussex.—C.

trious monarchs proceed to their surfeit at Guildhall. No doubt we shall have the newspapers in a state of eructation for at least a week. But I must close.

"J. P. C."

The short remainder of Mr. Curran's life was passed principally between Dublin and London.* Notwithstanding the decline of his health and spirits, the vigour of his mind continued unimpared, and probably added to his indisposition, by the constant impatience of inactivity in which it kept him. He occasionally returned to the literary projects already mentioned; but to speak had been the business of his life, and his mind could not now submit itself to the solitary labours of the closet. He still continued to look towards parliament, rather, perhaps, to give himself some nominal object, than from any hope or desire to be there. While in London he sometimes attended and spoke at public dinners. Both there and in Ireland his time was usually spent in the society of his intimate friends, whom his powers, as a companion, delighted to the last.

[Mr. Phillips may again be drawn upon here. He says:

"He also frequently visited both London and Cheltenham, and it was my good fortune generally to accompany him. On one occasion, however, having preceded him to town, he very kindly

* Mr. Curran, some short time before his death, had occasion to consult a physician in London on the general state of his health. He accordingly waited on a gentleman very eminent in that profession; he had no introduction to him, and was perfectly a stranger, The doctor made many enquiries as to the nature of his complaint, and of his constitution, and among other things asked him, had his father ever been afflicted by gout. Even then, the humor of Mr. Curran did not desert him: he perceived that the doctor did not see into the nature of his case, and, hoping little from him, he answered by assuring him, "that his father had left him neither *money* nor *malady*; that the only inheritance he ever got from him was a large stock of excellent advice; and that so careful was he of it, that he never broke bulk, never used any part of it, and that it was very likely to descend to posterity in the very same condition in which it had been left:"—wished the doctor a good morning, and left him *more puzzled about the man than the malady*.—O'REGAN.

offered me the following letter of introduction. I insert it, not merely as my credential to the reader, but because I cherish it as a precious and flattering relic of a friendship which was the honor and happiness of my youth.

"'*11th October*, 1816.

"'My Dear Friend—You know how squeamish I am of introducing. I do not make any attempt of that kind, for the bearer is Charles Phillips, whom you well know already, and I am paying a compliment to my own vanity by giving him this, as it tells two things I am proud of: one, that I know him; the second, that you are so good as to know

"'JOHN P. CURRAN.'"

"This at once gave me a passport to the splendid hospitality of Mr. Perry, the able proprietor of the *Morning Chronicle*, whose sumptuous board made me recollect the saying of Mr. Tierney when seated at it: 'I see now, Perry, how much better it is to publish speeches than to *make them*'.

"During Mr. Curran's visits to London, he occasionally, but not habitually, mingled in the political and literary society of the day. He was not fond of crowded rooms; his taste was rather a select circle of perhaps half a dozen, and those, if possible, intimates. Among the most remarkable whom he encountered—there is no other word for it—was Madame de Staël. Of this celebrated lady he gave me rather an extraordinary idea. After he had once or twice met her in society, she requested an interview with him at her residence on a particular day. 'I waited on her,' said he, 'as bound in gallantry so to do; and on being shown into her drawing-room, she desired that no one else should be admitted.

"'And now, Mr. Curran,' said she, 'on the reply you make to me, I apprise you our future intercourse must depend.' This was rather startling, but you may imagine my amazement when she commenced reciting a kind of indictment against my character! Ay, with due emphasis and little reservation, believe me. There was not a single item in the scandalous account which calumny had fabricated against me with which she was not perfectly familiar. Every misfortune of my private life, and every aspersion on my public conduct, she poured forth with a most marvellous volubility. The audacity of the whole procedure almost stunned me. I was at first inclined to plead to the jurisdiction and make my bow, but then I remembered she had a tongue, and I saw how she could use it, so I entered on the defence.' He then recapitulated, *seriatim*, the charges she had made and the exculpations he had essayed. How any person, and especially a female, could have originated such a discussion, seems inexplicable. Her oration, as he gave it, and his reply, occupied fully half an hour. The allegations on which she entered were coarse and cruel in the extreme—the sweepings of the Dublin streets for thirty years preceding, furnished, no doubt, by some of the party scavengers who sedulously collected them. However, in this instance it was labor lost, as the lady pronounced a verdict of acquittal.

"I had once myself an opportunity of seeing him suddenly put on his defence, and by one of the fair sex also. We were walking together in a public thoroughfare, when a lady, confronting and impeding us, thus commenced: 'Mr. Curran, I really am of opinion that you might be better employed than in vilifying me and my boarding-house.' 'Madam,' said Curran, 'I know well that I have many sins to answer for, but, before Heaven, I protest, the having wasted a word upon yourself, or a thought upon your boarding-house, will not be found in the catalogue,' and he bowed himself away.

"With Lord Erskine, his celebrated rival at the English bar, he was in habits of intimacy. He had a very high respect for his powers, but, aware of the comparison which the world naturally instituted between them, he rather avoided the topic. His lordship, it is said, once provoked a sarcasm from Curran: very unusual indeed, for his wit was not ill-natured. It was a few years after the Irish Union, and immediately after Mr. Grattan's *début* in the Imperial Parliament. The conversation after dinner naturally turned on the very splendid display of the Irish orator. Lord Erskine, as Curran imagined, exhibited rather an uncalled-for fastidiousness, and of Mr. Grattan's fame he was almost as jealous as of his own. The conversation proceeded. 'Come, come,' said his lordship, 'confess at once, Curran, was not Grattan a little intimidated at the idea of a first appearance before the British Parliament?' The comparison galled Curran to the quick. 'Indeed, my lord, I do not think he was, nor do I think he had any reason. When he succeeded so splendidly with so eloquent and so discriminating a body as the Irish House of Commons, he need not have apprehended much from any foreign criticism.' 'Well, but, Curran, did he not confess he was afraid, no matter what might be the groundlessness of his apprehensions —did you not *hear him* say so? Come, come,' continued his lordship, a little pertinaciously. 'Indeed, my good lord, I never did. Mr. Grattan is a very modest man—*he never speaks for himself*,' was the sarcastic and silencing rejoinder. It is well known that Cicero, and not Grattan, was Lord Erskine's model in this particular.

"Some time afterwards they met at the table of an illustrious personage.* The royal host, with much complimentary delicacy, directed the conversation to the profession of his celebrated visitors. Lord Erskine very eloquently took the lead. He descanted in terms which few other men could command on the interesting duties of the bar, and the high honors to which its success conducted. 'No man in the land,' said he, 'need be ashamed to belong to such a profession. For my part, of a noble family myself, I felt no degradation in practicing it: it has added not only to my wealth, but to my dignity.' Curran was silent, which the host observing, called for his opinion. 'Lord Erskine,' said he, 'has so eloquently described all the advantages to be derived from the profession, that I hardly thought my poor opinion was

* The Prince Regent—afterwards George IV.—M.

worth adding. But perhaps it was—pernaps I am a better practical instance of its advantages even than his lordship—he was ennobled by birth before he came to it, but it has,' said he, making an obeisance to his host, 'it has, in my person, raised the *son of a peasant to the table of his prince.*' Nothing, perhaps, could be more dignified than the humility of the allusion. But Mr. Curran had too great a mind not to feel that in fact he was ennobled by the obscurity of his origin. The accident of birth is surely no personal merit of its possessor; and too true it is that the pure fountain of hereditary honor too often flows through a polluted channel. Between these two great contemporary rivals a comparison has been often instituted. It is, perhaps, scarcely admissible. There was very little in common between them: they were rather to be contrasted than compared. Each had his own peculiar merits, and each did honor to his profession and his country. The following playful description, by Byron, is amusing and truthful, though, as the reader has already seen, he altered his opinion much in Mr. Curran's favor. The noble poet is enumerating the guests at a dinner party:

"There also were two wits by acclamation,
Longbow from Ireland, Strongbow from the Tweed,
Both lawyers, and both men of education;
But Strongbow's wit was of more polished breed:
Longbow was rich in an imagination,
As beautiful and bounding as a steed,
But sometimes stumbling over a potatoe,
While Strongbow's best things might have come from Cato.

Strongbow was like a new-tuned harpsichord;
But Longbow, wild as an Æolian harp,
With which the winds of Heaven can claim accord,
And make a music either flat or sharp.
Of Strongbow's talk you would not change a word;
At Longbow's phrases you might sometimes carp:
Both wits—one born so and the other bred—
This by the heart—his rival by the head."

"In the Autumn of 1816 I accompanied him to Cheltenham for the purpose of consulting Sir Arthur Brooke Faulkener (a friend and physician whom he much valued) on the state of his health. During his visit, though at times depressed, he occasionally rallied and even went a little into society.

"I had introduced him to two very lovely and accomplished sisters, who have since gone to increase the treasures of the East. After passing an evening in the enjoyment of conversation rarely to be met with, he said to me, 'I never saw such creatures: even to my old eyes it is quite refreshing to see *the sunshine of genius flying over their beautiful countenances.*'

"On the walk, one morning, we met an Irish gentleman who certainly most patriotically preserved his native pronunciation. He had acquired a singular habit of lolling out his tongue. 'What can he possibly mean by it?' said I to Curran. 'I think it's clear enough,' said he, '*the man's trying to catch the English accent.*'

"On another occasion, passing a person whom he much disliked, he said, 'Observe that solemn blockhead—that pompous lump of dulness. Now, if you breakfasted and dined with that fellow for a hundred years, you could not be intimate with him—he would not even be seen to smile, lest any body might suppose he was *too familiar with himself!*'

"Curran used to relate a ludicrous encounter between himself and a fish-woman on the quay at Cork. This lady, whose tongue would have put Billingsgate to the blush, was incited one day to assail him, which she did with very little reluctance. 'I thought myself a match for her,' said he, 'and valorously took up the gauntlet. But such a virago never skinned an eel. On the contrary, she was manifestly becoming more vigorous every moment, and I had nothing for it but to beat a retreat. This, however, was to be done with dignity; so, drawing myself up disdainfully, I said, 'Madam, I scorn all farther discourse with such an *individual.*' She did not understand the word, and thought it, no doubt, the very hyperbole of opprobrium. 'Individual, you wagabone!' she screamed; 'what do you mean by that? I'm no more an individual than your mother was!' Never was victory more complete. The whole sisterhood did homage to me, and I left the quay of Cork covered with glory."]

In the spring of 1817, he began to sink rapidly. While dining with his friend, Mr. Thomas Moore, he suffered a slight paralytic attack in one of his hands. He was also incommoded by frequent oppression in his chest, for which, as well as for his general health. his medical advisers recommended him to visit the milder climate of the south of Europe. Preparatory to following that advice, he passed over to Dublin, in July, to arrange his private affairs. But his friends could perceive, by his altered looks, that the hour of final separation was fast approaching. Of this he was not insensible himself. As he walked through the grounds of his country seat, with Mr. M'Nally, he spoke of the impending event with tranquillity and resignation.

"I melt (said he) and am not
Of stronger earth than others.

I wish it was all over."

On the day of his departure for England, after having parted in the ordinary way from another of his friends, he returned suddenly and grasped his hand, saying, in a affectionate, but firm tone, "You will never behold me more." He had a short time before, when leaving Cheltenham, handed the following little impromptu, as a final adieu to a family there (Sir Arthur Brooke Faulkener's), from whom he had received peculiar marks of hospitality and kindness:

"For welcome warm, for greeting kind
The present thanks the tongue can tell;
But soon the heart no tongue may find,
Then thank thee with a sad farewell!"

As Mr. Curran travelled between Holyhead and Cheltenham he was re-visited by paralytic symptoms. Upon his arrival at the latter place, doubtful of the nature of the recent attack, he requested of a medical friend to examine his pulse, and to declare explicitly whether it indicated any disposition to palsy. The physician assured him, that there was no indication of the kind. "Then," said Mr. Curran, "I suppose I am to consider what has lately happened as a runaway knock, and not a notice to quit."

"In the summer of 1817 he returned to Ireland for the last time, and in the September of that year again joined me at Cheltenham, under what mental disquietude the following letter, written a few days before to a friend there, will evince much better than any words of mine:

"'My Dear Friend—You'll think me a sad fellow—so I think too. However, you are too clear-sighted in diagnostics not to see the causes of my being so low-pulsed a correspondent. The truth is, I was every day on the point of leaving a country *where folly and suffering were lying like lead upon my heart;* and, in the mean time, I could only make one communication, the most unnecessary in the world, namely, that I never suspend the respect and solicitude which I always feel for you, and to which you are so well entitled.

"'Now I think you may look to a call at least. I may not be able, perhaps, to linger long, but I could not find myself within shot of you without coming mechanically to a *present* and a *snap*, even though it should be no more than a *flash in the pan.* I had hopes of seeing your brother, but he has deceived my hope. As to *Hope* herself, I have closed my accounts altogether with her. Drawing perpetually upon my credulity, I now find her, too late, an insolvent swindler. Meantime my entire life passed in a wretched futurity—breathing, I may say, in the *paulo post futurum:* I have happily, however, found out the only remedy, and that is, *to give over the folly of breathing at all.* I had some hope for this persecuted country, but that, I fear, is over. If our heads were curled like the Africans, I suppose we should go snacks with them in the justice and sympathy of that humane and philanthropic nation of yours; but if her tears of commiseration should make the hair of the Africans lank like ours, I make no doubt but you would send a coxcomb or two politically and madly like ——— and ———* to Ireland.

"'Ever yours, J. P. CURRAN.'

"His short stay at Cheltenham could scarcely be called existence. During that time he was with difficulty induced to pass the week of the Gloucester musical festival at Hynham Court, near that city. Here he became restless and unmanageable. Music, of which he had been so passionately fond, only irritated and incensed him. All of a sudden, at one of the morning performances at the Cathedral, he took it into his head that the whole proceeding was a blasphemy, and insisted on elbowing himself out through the aisle! Remonstrance was in vain. 'I'll stand it no longer!' he exclaimed, while all eyes were turned towards him; 'it's shameful—it's sinful—just hear him—the black, odious——baboon, yelling out that "the Lord is a man of war." I'll not countenance it'—and away he went! Nothing whatever could induce him again to enter the Cathedral, and he abruptly returned to Cheltenham on the next day, whither, under the circumstances, I felt it a duty to follow him. He had had, it seems, some premonitory symptoms in the spring of the year, at which his physicians felt no alarm, but which greatly added to his own depression. It was but too clear, however, that nature was almost exhausted. He fell asleep in the daytime, and even after dinner, and when he awoke it was to thoughts of sadness. It was in this frame of mind

* I have left an hiatus here, out of my high respect for the Attorney-General.—C. PHILLIPS.

that he once said to Mr. Grattan, 'I begin to tremble for Ireland. I almost wish to go to Spain, and borrow a beard, and turn monk. I am weaning off my early affections, and almost wish the grave-digger would overtake me in another country.' He was perpetually fancying things which never had existence, and misinterpreting those which had. He told me he was dying.

"Poor fellow! little did I then think that, in a very few days, I was to see the verification of his forebodings! The heart, indeed, was still beating, but the tongue—that tongue so eloquent—was mute forever. On Wednesday, the 8th of October, I called on him at his lodgings in Brompton. One of his eyes was swollen, and partly closed; but so little was it heeded, that he asked me to dine with him on the day following, to meet Mr. Godwin. It was, however, alas! a fatal premonitory symptom. At eleven o'clock at night he wrote the following note to me—*the last he was to write!* It is remarkable that there is not a superfluous word in it. In fact, he was struck with apoplexy in two hours after.

"'Dear Phillips—Just got a note: Mrs. Godwin is sick; he'll dine here Sunday. If you prefer an invalid, come to-morrow—You'd be more gratified on Sunday. *Utrum horum?* Yours,

'J. P. CURRAN.

"'*Wednesday.*'

"This note I received at my hotel at seven o'clock on Thursday morning, and with it the mournful intelligence of what had occurred. I hastened at once to Brompton, and, alas! what a spectacle awaited me! There he lay upon the bed of death—scarcely breathing—one eye closed, and one side quite inanimate.

"And this was all that now remained of CURRAN—the light of society—the glory of the forum—the Fabricius of the senate—the idol of his country. The only symptom of intelligence he gave was his squeezing my hand when I asked if he recognised me. A few days afterward he seemed conscious of the presence of one of his oldest and most valued friends, the late Judge Burton. All that filial piety could do, aided by the most eminent of the faculty, to alleviate his sufferings, was done. At seven o'clock on the evening of the fourteenth of October, I saw him for the last time: at nine we lost him. He expired at 7 Amelia Place Brompton, in the sixty-eighth year of his age."*]

He had arrived in London in September, where he proposed to pass the winter, still intending to proceed to the south of France, or Italy, in the commencement of the ensuing spring. His spirits were now in a state of the most distressing depression. He complained of having "a mountain of lead upon his heart." This despondency he increased by dwelling perpetually upon the condition of Ireland, which his imagination was for ever representing to him as doomed to endless divisions and degradation. A few days before his last illness he dined with his friend, the late Mr. Thomas Thompson. After dinner he was for a while cheerful and animated, but some allusion having been made to Irish politics, he instantly hung down his head, and burst into tears. On the 7th of October, a swelling appeared over one of his eyes, to which, attributing it to cold, he gave little attention. On the night of the 8th, he was attacked by apoplexy. He was attended by two eminent physicians, Doctors Badham and Ainslie, and by Mr. Tegart, of Pall Mall, all of whom pronounced his recovery to be impossible. The utmost efforts of their skill could not protract his existence many days.† Mr. Curran expired at nine o'clock at night, on the 14th of October, 1817, in the 68th year of his age. During his short illness, he appeared entirely free from pain; he was speechless from the commencement of the attack, and with the excep-

* From Phillip's Recollections.—M.

†His last moments were so tranquil that those around him could scarcely mark the moment of expiration. Though surprised by sickness at a distance from his home, he was not condemned to receive the last offices from the hands of strangers: three of his children, Captain Curran of the Navy, his son at the Irish Bar, and his daughter, Mrs. Taylor, were fortunately in London, and had the mournful gratification of paying the last duties to their illustrious father.—O'REGAN.

tion of a few intervals, quite insensible. His last minutes were so placid, that those who watched over him could not mark the exact moment of expiration. Three of his children, his son-in-law, and daughter-in-law, and his old and attached friend, Mr Godwin, surrounded his death-bed, and performed the last offices of piety and respect.

Mr. Curran's funeral did not take place till the 4th of November. His will, which it was supposed would have contained his own instructions upon the subject, having been left in Ireland, it was found necessary to await the examination of that document, and the directions of the executors.* In the interval, Mr. Daniel O'Connell, who was at Bath, and on the point of setting out with his family for Dublin, having received information of Mr. Curran's death, very generously sacrificed every consideration of private convenience, and hastened up to London, to attend his deceased

* O'Regan (who wrote in 1817) says: "The children of Mr. Curran who now survive him are Richard, who was called to the Irish bar, and for some years has retired from it, under the visitation of a settled melancholy; John, a captain in the Navy; William, now an Irish barrister, and a gentleman of considerable promise. Mrs. Taylor, the wife of an English clergyman; Amelia, unmarried. He had another son, James, who died in the East Indies; and a daughter, who is also dead. Of his brothers I knew two: one who is seneschal of Newmarket; the other was bred an attorney, and was considered a young man of as much natural genius as Mr. Curran himself.

"The date of the will is the 19th of September, 1816, and was opened in presence of Mr. Burton, Mr. Richards, Mr. M'Nally, Mr. John Franks, barristers, and Mr. Ponsonby Shaw. It was deposited at Mr. Shaw's bank; and the abstract, which I know to be authentic, is as follows: 'His real and personal property is left in trust to Philpot Fitzgerald for his life-use, with remainder to Mr. Curran's collateral relations; subject to a charge of £5000 for Henry Fitzgerald, brother to Philpot Fitzgerald, called his nephews; a provision on the estate of £80 a year for Mrs. Curran for her life; an annuity of £50 a-year to his daughter Amelia Curran, in addition to such provision as he before had made for her; a sum of £300 was bequeathed to Mrs. Dickson, of Brompton: some small legacies; but neither of his sons Richard, John, or William, were mentioned in the will or codicil; nor his daughter Mrs. Taylor. Thomas Quin, John Franks, John Glover, and Charles Burton, Esquires, were named trustees and executors.—He had in the Irish funds from ten to twelve thousand pounds in the 3½ per cents, stock in his own name. The Priory was the whole of his freehold estate. The interest he had in a lease of his former residence in the county of Cork had expired. He also had some property in the American funds, but I cannot at present ascertain its amount: it is supposed not to have been considerable."—M.

countryman to the grave: an act of affectionate respect which was peculiarly honourable to that gentleman, between whom and Mr. Curran a considerable misunderstanding had latterly existed upon the subject of Catholic politics. It was the anxious desire of Mr. O'Connell, and of several other friends of Mr. Curran, who were upon the spot, that his remains should be transported to his own country, in order to give a people, with whose interests and destiny the departed advocate had so entirely identified his own, a final opportunity of publicly testifying their admiration and regrets. Those who advised this measure were aware that he had himself (when he felt his end approaching) found a source of affecting consolation in the hope that, wherever it should be his fate to expire, Ireland would claim him. "The last duties (he pathetically observed in one of his latest letters) will be paid by that country on which they are devolved; nor will it be for charity that a little earth shall be given to my bones. Tenderly will those duties be paid, as the debt of well-earned affection, and of gratitude not ashamed of her tears." But with this last wish it was now found impossible to comply. His will was altogether silent regarding his interment; and of the four executors whom he had appointed only one was present in Dublin. That excellent person (Mr. John Franks of the Irish bar), had he been left to the exercise of his sole discretion, would have yielded to none in performing any act of honour or affection to the memory of his friend; but in consequence of the absence of the other executors, and from several legal considerations, he could not feel himself justified in authorising any departure from the ordinary course. Mr. Curran's remains were, therefore, privately interred in London, in one of the vaults of the Paddington church.*

* The persons who attended his funeral were (besides the members of his own family) Mr. Tegart, Messrs. Lyne and P. Phillips, of the Irish bar, Mr. P. Finnerty, the late Mr. Thomas Thompson, the Rev. George Croly, Mr. Thomas Moore, and Mr. Godwin. Mr. O'Connell's professional engagements had obliged him reluctantly to depart for Ireland before the day of Mr. Curran's interment.—C. [Mr. O'Connell was at Bath when Curran died. He immediately wrote to Mr. Phillips, at London, strongly recommending a public

[In 1834, seventeen years after the death of Mr. Curran, a committee of gentlemen was formed in Dublin, to provide for the removal of his mortal remains to Ireland. Prospect Cemetery, Glasnevin, Dublin, was the locality selected for his last earthly resting-place. The consent of his son (and biographer) was obtained,—a faculty permitting the removal of the body from Paddington Church was procured,—the exhumed body was removed to the house of Alderman Sir Matthew Wood, in George Street,—it was thence taken to Dublin, where it was received by Mr. W. H. Curran and one of the Committee,—was temporarily deposited in the private Mausoleum at Lyons, the residence of Lord Cloncurry, the friend of Curran,—and was finally removed to a grave at Glasnevin. The attendants were Messrs. W. H. Curran, John Finlay, Con. Lyne, and Andrew Carew O'Dwyer—the last-named being the person with whom originated the proposition for restoring the remains to their native soil. This re-interment was private. The pageantry of a national procession which was suggested, was respectfully and judiciously declined by Mr. W. H. Curran. A massive sarcophagus in Glasnevin contains the remains of Ireland's great orator and patriot, and the inscription, far more expressive than a laboured epitaph, is simply the one word

CURRAN.

There is a monument to Curran in St. Patrick's Cathedral, Dublin—a bust by Moore, on a sarcophagus. It is copied from Lawrence's portrait, and, Mr. Davis says, "is the finest monument, so simply made, I ever saw. It is most like him in his glorified

funeral, declaring that of *all*, he was "the only incorrupted and faithful," adding, "There is a loveliness and a heartiness over me when I think of this great man whom we have lost. Charles, there never was *so* honest an Irishman. His very soul was republican Irish. Look to his history in 1778, in '82, in 1790—at the Union—at all times—in all places." He suggested that the Irish of all classes in London should be invited to attend the funeral, each wearing a shamrock, and that "on *his* coffin should be laid a broken harp and a wreath of shamrock."—The funeral was private.—M.]

mood, full of thought and action. In an Irish Pantheon, our greatest orator should be represented at full length, and the bas-reliefs of his sarcophagus should be his receiving Father Neale's blessing, his rising to defend the Sheareses, his delivery of the judgment on Merry and Power, and his weeping for Ireland near his child's grave at the Priory."]

CHAPTER XVIII.

Observations on Mr. Curran's Eloquence—Objections to his Style considered—His habits of preparation for Public Speaking—His Ideas of Popular Eloquence—His Pathos—Variety of his powers—His Imagination—Peculiarity of his Images—His use of Ridicule—Propensity to Metaphor—Irish eloquence—Its origin—Mr. Curran's and Burke's eloquence compared.

For the last twenty years of his life, Mr. Curran enjoyed the reputation of being the most eloquent advocate that had ever appeared at the Irish bar; and if future times shall hold his genius in estimation, it is eloquence which must entitle him to that distinction.* His name may, indeed, derive a still more splendid

* O'Regan says: "Whatever criticism may have torn from him,—however mutilated he may have been by the shallowness or inaccuracy of his reporters, his effect has been as described; in one comparatively subordinate power of mind, so frequently mistaken for genius or high understanding, he manifested taste in almost every subject connected with literature. His skill in music made him attentive to the structure and harmony of his periods. He well knew that eloquence charmed the ear, and opened the widest entrance to the heart; and he studied with great earnestness the principles of this art. So fastidious was he of pedantry, that, amidst his profuse quotations from the ancient classics, he studiously avoided this error: when he used them, they were employed as powerful illustrations, or beautiful ornaments. He was one of those few scholars who stripped literature of that affectation which encumbers it; he broke and flung away the husk and shell by which it is too frequently surrounded; and his delicacy fused the original sentiments into his native language, enriching both by the medium through which both were delivered. You drank the Falernian in all its richness and raciness. You looked not to the musty casks of antiquity for the mark of the consulate, in which it had been stored; but you got it defœcated and poured forth in profusion into the clear modern glass, sparkling and mantling in all the purple colours, and in all the odour and flavour of its best vintage. To this exquisite delicacy of taste Mr. Curran had not an exclusive title; in the fine and cultivated mind of Mr. Bushe, redolent with classics, he may have found a rival." He adds—"Such was the effect produced, that in taking the note of his speech in the case of Massy and Headfort, in which I was of counsel with him, I became suspended; the hand forgot its office, and, till roused from the delicious transport by some friend near me, I was not conscious that I left the paper unstained by any one note. On observing this circumstance to Mr. Curran in a few days after, he said, 'Possibly at that very moment you were taking the best impression, perhaps then drinking deeply. It is probable it was then you were doing me and yourself the greatest justice.'"—M.

claim to posthumous respect, for the purity and manliness of his public conduct, during times when the hearts and nerves of so many others were tried, and sunk beneath the proof. Divested of this, his eloquence would have been comparatively worthless. Orators are common characters; but it is not so common to find a man, upon every occasion of his life preferring his public duty to his personal advancement—conducting himself, amidst the shock of civil contentions, with danger and allurements on every side, so as to command the entire approbation of his own conscience and the more impartial, though not more valuable, applause of that succeeding time which is a stranger to the particular interests and passions that might bias its decisions. This period has not yet come; but it may be asserted that it is approaching, and that when it shall actually arrive, Mr. Curran's memory has nothing to fear from its judgment. Before this tribunal it will be admitted that he, and the few who joined him, in making (in defiance of much momentary opprobrium) an undaunted stand against those sinister measures upon which the framers have subsequently reflected with shame, were but exercising the right of superior minds, whose privilege it is to discern, amidst all the tumult of conflicting opinions, and the hasty expedients of ephemeral sagacity, what alone is permanently wise and good—to judge the men and acts of their own day, with the same unbetraying firmness with which they judge the times that have passed, and with which posterity will judge themselves. It will not be overlooked, that it is the ordinary fate of such persons to be misconceived and reviled; that in the hour of general intoxication, the most grievous of offenders is he who passes the cup, and will not be degraded, rebuking, by his importunate sobriety, the indecent revelry that surrounds him. To have done this will be considered more rare and honourable in Mr. Curran's history, than to have been distinguished by the most commanding abilities; but in his case it is needless to dwell upon his conduct as separated from his oratory. " Words," said Mirabeau, " are things." In Mr. Curran's public life, his speeches were his acts; and all that the reader of them requires to know is, that his practice never discredited his professions. If what he said was honest, what he did was not less so. His language and his actions had a common origin and object, and cannot now be dissociated for the purpose of separate encomium or condemnation; it is out of his own mouth that he must now be judged.

His eloquence was original, not formed by the imitation of any preceding model, so much as resulting from his individual constitution of mind and temperament, and from the particular nature of the society and the scenes upon which he was thrown. With the same advantages of education elsewhere, he would undoubtedly have risen above the ordinary level—he possessed powers too uncommon to keep him long in obscurity; but it required the theatre upon which his life was passed, to give them that exact direction to which his oratory is indebted for its peculiar character.* The history of his mind is, in this respect, intimately connected with that of his country.

By nature ardent, of the most acute sensibility, instinctively alive to every social gratification, he passed his infancy and youth among those ranks where such qualities are the peculiar objects of applause. The heart naturally cherishes the scenes and authors of its first indulgences; and Mr. Curran entered upon his career of public

* Mr. O'Regan says: "He found within himself the happy power of giving shapes and exquisite forms to the beings of his own creation. Whether passing from images of terror to the soft and tender touches of pathos; whether he sported in the laugh of comedy, or in the broad grin of farce, he was equally successful in all. If he would hurl the bolt of a Jupiter, shake thrones, and appal tyrants, you might conceive it was the work of Homer! Would he move to pity, you had all the effect of Virgil; and would he excite to mirth or laughter, you might have fancied yourself conversing with a Congreve. Such was his excellence in each of these departments, that he may have placed himself nearly at the head of each; yet, though he rejected with fastidiousness to form himself either on the plans of the sophists, or of those societies which prefer words to ideas, talking to thinking, he furnished his mind from the great stores of antiquity, and enriched it with much of the best and purest modern literature. By both he chastened the wanderings of his own luxuriant imagination, and regulated the branches without injuring the tree; the sap was directed to feed the trunk, not to waste its aliment in idle foliage, or in gaudy flowers."—M.

life strongly attached to that order of the community which he had first known and of which, notwithstanding his accidental elevation, he considered himself as a part, and as bound to their interests by every motive of sympathy and duty. This early inclination to the popular cause could not fail to be encouraged by the condition of the times—by the successful efforts of America, which excited so much imitative enthusiasm in Ireland—and by those consequent movements of patriotic spirit which preceded the revolution of 1782. But, above all, there was in his daily view the degraded condition of his fellow-subjects; a spectacle which, without any farther incentive, might readily awaken, in a feeling breast, much suspicion of the wisdom and humanity of the government that could countenance such a system. Nor did his mind, when it ascended from his own personal impulses to the less questionable conclusions of England's great legal and constitutional authorities, discover anything that should make him pause in his estimate of the importance of the people's privileges. In contemplating the British constitution, to the fullest benefits of which he never ceased to vindicate his country's most undoubted claim, his first and his last conviction was, that no matter by what terms it might be described, it was essentially popular; that the original elemental principle which gave it life and vigour, and which alone could give it permanency, was the subject's freedom; that this, the most vital part, experience had shown to be most exposed to unconstitutional invasion; and that, as long as this practical tendency subsisted, it behoved every friend to the throne and the laws to demonstrate his attachment, not by a parade of simulated or fanatic loyalty, but by upholding, on every occasion, the dignity and the spirit of the subject. But, whatever was the cause, whether the original character of his mind, or the influence of early associations, or his education, or the passing scene, or, as seems most probable, all of them combined, he no sooner appeared than he declared himself the advocate of the people's rights, a title which he ever after supported with an ardour and constancy that leave no doubt of his sincerity.

It was the intensity of his feeling, which obstacles soon matured into a passion, that gave such an uncommon interest to his oratory. Whatever may be the opinion of the expediency of such popular tenets, there is a natural magnificence about them, when presented through the medium of a fervid imagination, to which the most unsympathising are compelled to pay a momentary homage—to those who are persuaded of their truth, and who feel that they have been defrauded of their benefits, they come as oracles fraught with rapture and consolation.

In all Mr. Curran's political speeches this sentiment of devoted attachment to liberty and to the country is conspicuous, animating and dignifying every topic that he advances. It cannot be too frequently repeated (and to attest it is a debt that Ireland owes his memory) that in his most vehement assertion of her rights, he was most conscientiously sincere. His love of Ireland was of no vulgar and fickle kind, originating in interest, vanity or ambition. Ireland was the choice of his youth, and was from first to last regarded by him, not so much with the feelings of a patriot as with the romantic idolatry of a lover. To her his heart was contracted for better and for worse; to her "what he had to give he gave," confederating all his most cherished projects with her wayward fortunes, and surrendering to her service all the resources of his genius, in the successive stages of her pride, her hopes, her struggles, and her despair. In him every man who knew him knew that these were not common-place pretences, which he put forth as mere instruments of rhetoric: the most sensitive of his audience were never under more subjection to his enthusiasm than he was himself; and it was in the evidence of this fact, more than in any art, that lay the extraordinary fascination of his manner. There was no elaborate ardour, no technical impetuosity; nothing to imply that while his lips were on fire his heart might be cold; but every look, tone, and gesture, carried with them the conviction, that if he were deluding them he was deluding himself.

Much of this fervour may be collected from his printed speeches, but let the reader of them, in justice to their author, recollect that he is a reader, not an auditor; that though he may find the words, and even these imperfectly recorded, he finds not all those accompaniments, without which the language is but a cold monumental image of the thoughts that once glowed with living energy. The words remain, but the eye before which judges and juries have so often shrunk—the unaffected and finely varying tones of indignant remonstrance, or of tender expostulation—the solemn and pathetic pause that embodied in a moment's silence more passion and persuasion than any spoken eloquence could convey—for these, and for much more than these, the reader must necessarily look in vain; and without them his estimate of the orator's entire powers must be as conjectural, as if he should undertake to appreciate the merits of some departed ornament of the stage from a tame perusal of the scenes to which he alone had imparted all the warmth and dignity of life.

Mr. Curran's speeches have met with some unfavourable criticism out of Ireland; and, though many of the objections may be founded, many have also been made without a sufficient advertence to the scenes which accompanied their delivery. It is found that there are passages and descriptions too strong, and even shocking for the closet. One of their principal merits was, that they were never intended for the closet: they were intended for occasions of emergency and despair; to excite passions of such force as to counteract the violence of those that already raged; to rescue the accused, and not to propitiate the critic. Yet even the critic, who condemns the taste that could paint the perjured informer, and other public delinquents, in such loathsome colours as the Irish advocate employed, should remember, that upon this subject his own rules will justify an important distinction. A writer who, in works of mere invention where he has the selection of his topics, takes a delight in dwelling upon revolting ideas, may be justly accused of being unhappy and perverted in his taste; but this is only where the introduction of such images is gratuitous, and not naturally arising from the horror of the situation. We should proscribe such situations altogether, were we fastidiously to reject the only colors in which they could be painted. We do not complain of Burns for the "father's grey hairs sticking to the heft,"* nor of Campbell for the "life-blood oozing through the sod."† Juliet is not hissed off the stage for her anticipated loathings in the tomb of the Capulets: so also it is but fair to judge of similar passages of Mr. Curran's oratory, and with this additional consideration, that instead of inventing, he was but describing existing facts and characters, in portraying which no language or illustration could surpass the nauseous. Before he had described the perjured witness as emerging from "those catacombs of living death, where the wretch that is buried a *man* lies till his heart has time to fester and dissolve, and is then dug up an *informer*," he had day after day seen those horrid apparitions stalk upon the public table, and he had himself been almost scared from his duty by the frightful glarings with which they would have converted the general execration into general dread, into the undissembled homage of deferential horror.‡

A more sustainable objection to his style is the exuberance and occasional extravagance of his imagery. It would be no defence of him to say that he could not avoid it; that in the ardour of extemporaneous creation, his mind frequently lost all authority over its associations. It was, indeed, the fact, that his imagination did often tyrannize over his other faculties, and that many wayward ideas were precipitated into existence by the still pressing throng that

* Tam O'Shanter. † O'Connor's child.

‡ "I have been eighteen years at this bar, and never until this year (1794) have I seen such witnesses supporting charges of this kind with such abandoned profligacy. In one case where men were on their trial for their lives, I felt myself involuntarily shrinking under your lordship's protection from the miscreant who leaped upon the table and announced himself a witness. I was trusting in God, that these strange exhibitions would be confined to the remote parts of the country. I was astonished to see them parading through the capital; but I feel that the night of unenlightened wretchedness is fast approaching, when a man shall be judged before he is tried—when the advocate shall be libelled for performing his duty to his client, that right of human nature—when the victim shall be hunted down, not because he is criminal, but because he is obnoxious."—*Mr. Curran's Defence of Dr. Drennan*, 1794.

followed before his taste had time to suppress or adorn them. This defect was perhaps in some degree organic; perhaps discipline and caution might have corrected it; but unless he had altogether changed his modes of intellectual exercise, it could scarcely be expected that any care could have entirely removed it.

The dangers of offending against good taste depend in a great measure upon the class of the mental powers that are employed. They who confine themselves to the exercise of those of reasoning, may continue from day to day to give extemporaneous utterance to every idea; and though they fail in their logic with every breath, may still avoid the smallest violation of good taste. But when the mind ascends to subjects of invention and imagination, there is no longer this security. Where is the poet, the most intuitively correct, who does not reject much which at first had pleased; whose mind has not been even incommoded by the intrusion of many fantastic combinations, which instead of venturing to express in language, he crushes at the moment of their birth? And it is only by exercising this right over the children of its fancy, by condemning the deformed to an early death, that of those who are permitted to survive, none are without beauty and proportion. The orator who in the same way aspires to create, and who, like Mr. Curran, defers the work till he is excited by the presence of a public audience, has to encounter all the dangers of the poet, without enjoying his privileges. The same fervour and impetuosity that lead to felicity, will often hurry him into extravagance: the latter, once produced, cannot be recalled—he has no leisure to soften, and mould, and reconcile; and hence conceptions, which in his cooler moments he would have suppressed, or have rendered worthy of himself, remain irrevocably accusers of his taste.

But perhaps this subject will be most readily explained, by adverting to Mr. Curran's habits of preparation for public speaking. From the first experiment of his talents, in London, till he had attained some eminence at the bar, he never composed his speeches for the purpose of delivering them from memory; but both at the debating societies, and during his early years at the bar, he used to assist his mind by ample notes upon the questions to which he had to speak. When his reputation rose, he for a while adopted the former method; but such written attempts having proved comparatively stiff and cold, and in every way greatly inferior to his more extemporaneous effusions, his own judgment, and the advice of his friends, induced him for ever to abandon that plan, and adhere to the one more suited to the habits and character of his mind.

There was something peculiar and desultory in his manner of considering the important questions that he had to meet. He very rarely retired formally to his closet: it was as he walked in the hall of the courts, or as he rode between Dublin and his country seat, or during his evening strolls through his own grounds,* that

* On letting his beautiful and tasty residence in the county of Cork, which was distant from the lakes of Killarney but one short day's journey, he became the purchaser of a country-seat near Rathfarnham, on the slope of those delightful hills hanging over the Marquis of Ely's demesne. The scenery before the windows is of interminable expanse, and commanding one of the richest and best dressed landscapes in Ireland, including the Bay of Dublin, the ships, the opposite hill of Howth, the pier, the light-house, and a long stretch of the county of Dublin; on the eastern side May-puss Craggs and obelisks, and a long range of hills. The house is plain, but substantial, and the grounds peculiarly well laid out, and neatly kept; sheltered to the south by a bridge of mountains; and though its elevation is considerable and commanding, it is relatively a plain or flattening on the mountain's side; its prospects are delightful. It was, as he said, a *toilette*, at which one might dress and shave for eternity. Situated about four miles from Dublin, and a sort of centre between the seats of his friend Mr. G ttan in the county of Wicklow, and the late Mr. George Ponsonby in the county of Kildare, and about eight miles from each. The country surrounding it is enchanting, and the neighbourhood populous and good. Within the short distance of two miles on the city side, was Lord Avonmore's seat of Fortfield, the residence of the present Master of the Rolls, Sir William M'Mahon. The houses of many other gentlemen of his friendship and of his profession were thickly crowded round him. Here it was he chose to pass in study, or in society, those hours which were not devoted to business; and here he generally entertained his friends. He brought nothing from his former country residence but its name (the Priory). His table was frugal; plain, yet comfortable; but his wines were the best and choicest, in which he did not generally more indulge, than in the ordinary manner of a gentleman. His deviations from sobriety were not frequent, and made but exceptions to his usual habits of temperance. Here it was, like Achilles in his tent, he delighted his heart with his harp; the violoncello was his instrument, and from this he did not desire reputation for skill in that de-

he meditated his subjects. Sometimes as he lay in bed, he had (like Rousseau,† and with a more fortunate memory) creative visitations, which he often declared were to him more delightful than repose. One of his most usual and favourite times of meditation, was when he had his violin or violoncello in his hand: he would thus forget himself for hours, running voluntaries over the strings, or executing some trivial air, while his imagination was far away, collecting its forces for the coming emergency.

Many of his finest passages were extemporaneous bursts, but many were thus prepared. It is, however, worth observing, that he seldom committed them *verbally* to memory. He contemplated the

lightful art. He sought no more than to feel the pleasure it imparted; nor am I apprised that he ever aspired to the glory of exhibiting even at a concert. An Irish giant used to come from the mountains to play upon it, and said it was the biggest fiddle he ever met; but that it was very awkward with but three strings, for so he sometimes found it. Here also it was that he composed much more than as yet has met the eye. Still it may be hoped, that a criticism of Milton's Paradise Lost may survive the wreck of works which a fastidious and refined taste may have too rapidly condemned. Leisure and revision may give a finish which may not satisfy himself, yet the efforts of such a mind, however carelessly flung off, must always be gratifying to curiosity. At his dinners two peculiarities appeared: one constantly, that of having dinner served to the minute of five o'clock. This was frequently inconvenient to others, but as he defined a good dinner to be two dishes and five o'clock, it sometimes occurred, that there were no other terms to be included in this definition. He drank a few glasses of port at dinner, "to keep," as he said, "the wet of the claret out of his stomach." The second peculiarity was, that you frequently met at his table persons seldom undistinguished, though often unknown to each other. And in this he often resembled his friend John Horne Tooke, who at his feasts at Wimbledon had persons of all tongues, nations, characters, and qualities. His own habits were plain and frugal, though the pomp and parade of good living did not appal him. He sustained through life a preference of the comforts to the luxuries of the table. *Liqueurs* being served after dinner, noyeau, persico, and everything *recherché*; malmsey, Madeira, hock, &c., Mr. Curran being asked which he would prefer, seized a bottle of the latter, and said, "*Hoc erat in votis*. A young gentleman who sat near him observed that the *liqueurs* were much better, and importunately recommended persico, adding that he who was fond of the *Medes*, should love the Persians also: to which Mr. Curran instantly replied, *Persicos odi puer*.—O'REGAN.

* "Je meditois dans mon lit a yeux fermes, et je tournois et retournois dans ma tete mes periodes avec des peines incroyables; puis quand j'etois parvenu a en etre content, je les deposois dans ma memoire, jusqu'a ce que je pusse les mettre sur le papier; mais le temps de me lever et de m'habiller me faisoit tout perdre, et quand je m'etois mis a mon papier, il ne me venoit presque plus rien de ce que j'avois compose."—*Confessions de Rousseau.*

topics and images until he had secured them beyond the danger of escape, and when the occasion came, and the same train of associations was revived, his mind not so much recollected, as repeated anew the operations by which it had originally created. He had not the words of a single sentence by heart; he had the leading ideas, and trusted to their reappearance to recall the same diction and imagery which had been suggested at the first interview. But it almost invariably happened that his own expectations were far exceeded, and that when his mind came to be more intensely heated by his subject, and by that inspiring confidence which a public audience seldom fails to infuse into all who are sufficiently gifted to receive it, a multitude of new ideas, adding vigour or ornament, were given off; and it also happened, that in the same prolific moments, and as almost their inevitable consequence, some crude and fantastic notions escaped; which, if they impeached their author's taste, at least leave him the merit of a splendid fault which none but men of genius can commit.

This was the account that he gave of his own intellectual habits, which he recommended to the imitation of all who aspired to excel in oratory; for according to his idea of popular eloquence, a facility of extemporaneous creation and arrangement, and of adapting and modifying according to the occasion, the produce of previous meditation, was indispensable: without it a person might be an elegant composer, and a skilful reciter and actor, but being necessarily at the mercy of every unforeseen contingency, could never be an orator. The practice of writing speeches and delivering them from memory, he strongly reprobated; he considered that it not only cut off the speaker from the benefit of those accidental bursts which so often turn the fortune of the day, and for which no anticipating sagacity can provide; but that when exclusively persevered in for any time, it directly tended to debilitate his mind; that instead of habituating him to a manly confidence in his own resources, and to that generous surrender of himself to the enthusiasm of the moment, which can almost impart the gift of miracles to those who put their faith in it, and which, even where it leads astray, will carry away the audience in its train, it generated a noxious taste for verbal finery —for epigram, antithesis, and inanimate declamation; and along with this, a pusillanimous and irrecoverable apprehension of failing to be correct, so destructive of that spirit of adventure, and occasionally heedless intrepidity, without which there is no plunging into the deeper recesses of human passions. So strongly was he impressed with the opinion that real eloquence demanded the fullest measure of extemporaneous ardour and ability, that when, about a year before his death, he was urgently solicited to address a jury in defence of a friend against whom an action for a libel was depending, he could not bring himself to comply with the request, however honourable and complimentary;* assigning as one of his reasons, his suspicion that after a *desuetude* of ten years, added to the more temperate and hesitating views which his judicial functions during that period had imposed, his mind might have become too rigid to yield to all the impulses of popular emotion with the same prompt and fortunate reliance which had secured the triumphs of his younger days.†

He was unaffectedly communicative to his young friends of the bar who consulted him on these subjects.‡ Amongst other

* To have done so would have been a violation of all professional precedent. In Great Britain and Ireland, a man who has once occupied the Bench *never* returns to the Bar.—M.

† One of Mr. Curran's greatest and longest efforts was his defence of Mr. Hamilton Rowan. The following is a copy of the notes from which he spoke upon that occasion, and their small number will show his dependence upon his own mind, without much mechanical aid.

"To *arms*.—2°. Reform—3°. Catholic emancip.—4°. Convention—now unlawful—Consequence of conviction—Trials before revolution—Drowned—Lambert—Muir—Character of R.—furnace, &c.—Rebellion smothered stalks—Redeeming spirit."—C.

‡ O'Regan says, "For the many years of his practice in the hall, his wit made an æra; there went by no day that did not furnish something new from him. The young and old of the bar were so fascinated with his effusions, that they got rapid circulation; they were echoed through the courts, and did, like sound, propagate themselves in every direction. You had them in the streets, and at the table; they were as certainly supplied, and made as necessary a part of the entertainment, as the wine: they travelled

particulars, he used to tell them, that the peculiarities of his own person had had an influence in forming his style of public speaking. He was conscious that it wanted dignity and grace, and in the apprehension that vehemence might expose him to ridicule, he originally proposed to himself to become persuasive by a mild, expostulatory manner; but when he formed this resolution he was unaware of his own resources; his genius, as soon as exasperated into an exertion of its force, prevailed over all the suggestions of modest precaution. Still it may be observed in almost all his speeches, that the first propensity is perpetually declaring itself; that in the midst of all his arguments, and impetuosity, and invective, he never forgets to implore.

But independent of any study and design upon his part, it was here that he was by nature pre-eminently qualified to succeed. His speeches upon political subjects contain many affecting specimens of his pathetic powers; but it was in questions confined to individual interests, where the domestic or social relations had been abused, that he exhibited the entire extent of his command over all the softer emotions of the human breast. For the secret of this power he was little indebted to books, or to the artifices of rhetoric. Its source was in his habitually intense sensibility to the affecting scenes of real life, more peculiarly to those of domestic happiness or affection, as he witnessed them in their most natural and tender forms, among those humble classes with which his original condition had first familiarised him. While yet a boy he caught an inspiration of the plaintive genius of his country, where, after all, the national genius prefers to dwell—beneath the peasant's roof. According to his own account, it was in the Irish cabin that he first learned to weep for others. He found there, what all who stoop to enter may find, the rude elements of the

with you into the country; they were domesticated everywhere; they pleased youth and delighted old age. When he left the practice of his profession, he did not leave the hall. He frequently descended from the bench, and distracted in groups of admirers his over active and over ardent mind."—M.

finest and softest affections. It was there that his young fancy, powerfully impressed with the living spectacle of all those homely but vigorous movements of undisguised nature which touch the heart the most, unconsciously prepared itself for those pathetic descriptions at which future assemblies were to melt: and when the occasion came of calling upon his hearers for their sympathy, he had only to present to their imagination some of those pictures of tenderness or distress over which he had so often wept himself.

His pathos, however, was not confined to such delineations; much of its influence depends upon the solemn associations which it raises, upon its alliance with emotions of a higher order than individual suffering can produce. The pangs of a single victim may appeal most forcibly to our pity, but the more intense the feeling, the more it is in danger of failing in dignity. One of the charms of Mr. Curran's pathos is, that it is so often connected with patriotic sorrow, or with more extensive and enlightened regrets for the general fate of nations. He represents the great principles of freedom as outraged and depressed, and deplores their fall; but we are perpetually reminded that they deserved a nobler destiny, and are made to feel the same sentiment of exalted melancholy, with which we would bend over the grave of one of the illustrious dead. We may lament the loss as irretrievable, but in the utmost extremity of our grief, we are elevated by the consciousness that we bear an honourable testimony to our own sensibility to departed worth.

But it was not only by successful appeals to any single passion that he surpassed every forensic speaker of his country; the wonder that he excited was owing to the rapidity of his transitions from passion to passion, from the deepest emotions that agitate the soul up to the liveliest combinations of a playful imagination. And yet this, the most extraordinary and distinguishing of his powers, can never be fully comprehended by those who know him only through his graver and recorded efforts. It is upon the latter that his general and lasting fame nust now depend; but in

Ireland, while any of his cotemporaries who heard him survive, and perhaps long after they all shall have followed him to the grave, his name will enjoy a peculiar and scarcely less brilliant reputation in the traditional accounts of the numberless unpremeditated and magical effusions that have been no otherwise preserved; and which in the estimation of his admiring hearers would alone have rendered him the ornament and boast of the Irish bar. For more than twenty years those astonishingly varied talents, upon which the critic may now fear to pass too unqualified an encomium, converted the Irish courts of justice into a theatre of popular recreation, whither day after day the multitude delighted to flock to behold the orator in whom they gloried, going, in the space of a few moments, his rounds of the human passions, and the human faculties; alternately sublime, indignant, sarcastic, subtle, playful, pathetic.

This extreme versatility, if Mr. Curran be contemplated as a model, may be deemed a defect, but for every practical purpose its success was so decided as to justify his adopting it. Had his eloquence been more scholastic, had every topic of persuasion been selected with an eye to rhetorical observances, he would have escaped some literary reproaches, but he would have gained fewer triumphs. The juries among whom he was thrown, and for whom he originally formed his style, were not fastidious critics; they were more usually men abounding in rude unpolished sympathies, and who were ready to surrender the treasure, of which they scarcely knew the value, to him that offered them the most alluring toys. Whatever might have been his own better taste, as an advocate he soon discovered, that the surest way to persuade was to conciliate by amusing them. With them he found that his imagination might revel unrestrained; that, when once the work of intoxication was begun, every wayward fancy and wild expression was as acceptable and effectual as the most refined wit; and that the favour which they would have refused to the unattractive reasoner or to the too distant and formal orator, they had not the firmness to withhold, when solicited with the gay persuasive familiarity of a companion. These careless or licentious habits, encouraged by early applause and victory, were never thrown aside, and we can observe in almost all his productions, no matter how august the audience, or how solemn the occasion, that his mind is perpetually relapsing into its primitive indulgences.

But whatever judgment may now be passed upon those wanderings of fancy by which those who were actually allured away were too charmed to utter a reproach, it is impossible to withhold our admiration of those mental qualities in which the beauties and imperfections of Mr. Curran's eloquence had equally their origin. They both originated in that intense activity of the imaginative faculty which was the predominant characteristic of his mind. It was in the exceeding richness of this, that consisted the essential distinctive originality of his style. It was not that his reasonings were subtle, his topics imposing, or his periods flowing; all of these may be found in others; but that what he passionately conceived, he could convey in passion's proper idiom; that his mird had familiar access to a world of splendid and vigorous illustration, whence it could select at pleasure the clothing that might best adorn, or ennoble every favourite idea; it was that nature, in the profuseness of her bounty, "filling even to overflowing," had "o'er informed" him with that supplemental poetic sense, which, disdaining to recognise in objects their homely realities, is for ever delighting to invest them with attributes not their own, raising what is low, animating what is cold, veiling what is deformed, or again fearlessly tearing away the veil where some high moral purpose demands that the deformity beneath should be exposed and exaggerated, and thus by the agency of its own creations, imparting to what the vulgar eye might view with most indifference, imagined charms or visionary horror.

The images in which Mr. Curran excelled were not of that order which it requires, but a simple process of intellect, unconnected with much mental or physical emotion to produce. There are some cultivated minds, to which so much varied knowledge is at all times present, that whatever be the subject of their thoughts, innumerable resemblances force themselves upon them, rendering them profusely figurative, but evidently without for a moment disturbing their tranquillity. But the Irish advocate's finest conceptions were the growth of the deepest sensibility. In his pathetic and descriptive bursts, so impressively did his language communicate to others the full extent of his emotions, that it might be said of him that at such moments he "felt aloud;" that his words were but the audible throbbings of his bosom labouring to vent itself in rapid, irregular, and abrupt gushes from the excess of feeling that oppressed it.

In producing this electric sympathy between the orator and his audience, there was something more than art can teach or than nature gives to many. Its original source was in his heart and spirit as much as in his talents; in his uncompromising and impassioned identification of himself with his subjects; in that chivalrous devotion to whatever principle he espoused, which impelled him boldly to defy and silence its adversaries, by the proud tender of his own individual responsibility for its truth and honour. In this, there was much that belonged to the man, no less than to the advocate—much of previous character—of personal and mental intrepidity—of profound moral sensibility, and its companion, moral pride, upon all the great questions of human rights and obligations. It was this extreme sensibility, combined (if not itself occasioned by) a superior intellect, that filled Mr. Curran's style with so much bold and vivid imagery. For it would be most unjust to attribute to him any deficiency of logical powers, because he so frequently supported the cause of freedom and morals, by sentiment and imagination. The very reverse was the fact. Of the dignity and importance of that cause, every sound understanding which reflects upon it is convinced; but there is a degree of intense conviction, known only to a few privileged minds, whose conclusions, instead of being the result of cold and wary deduction, flash upon them at once with all the light and warmth of instincts; and the consequence of this rapid perception is, that they either neglect or will not submit to a formal demonstration of what they have themselves thus intuitively acquired, or that assuming the truth to be equally evident to all, they think not so much of proving as of enforcing it by imposing illustration, and by addressing their hearers' imagination and passions, in order to kindle in them the courage or the shame, without which, in defiance of their conviction, the truth may be sacrificed to their fears or interests. This was constantly Mr. Curran's great object, and it was in effecting it that so much of his extraordinary power lay. Few speakers ever possessed such despotic controul over the honest passions of their audience, for few ever so unhesitatingly surrendered themselves to the inspiration of their own. He had the true popular temperament; there was no cold philosophic tranquillity about him, but all was life and action. His thoughts, style, and manner, "had certain vital signs." He was all his life contending for a cause, and he did it with no "half-faced fellowship;" he loved it "not wisely but too well," and not the less because it wanted friends. His cause was his religion, to which he adhered, under what he considered its persecution, with all the confiding, "desperate fidelity" of a martyr; and though his zeal might to many appear mistaken, still it was zeal, real, disinterested and fervent, affecting from its sincerity even where its tendency was least approved, and not unfrequently communicating its flame by surprise to those who were most active in extinguishing it. At the period of those displays to which these observations more particularly refer, the times were "too deeply commoved" for affectation; his audiences saw and knew that he had none; his very irregularities proved it. He was not for ever reminding them that he was an orator; he had, not the art, but what was above art, the feeling and manliness to forget it himself. He did not consider that he was only acting a part of which the world might hereafter say, that it was well or ill supported; but that a great constitutional trust had devolved upon him, of which, heedless of the world's sentence upon his skill or conduct, he would rigidly perform all the solemn obligations. When midnight after midnight* he rose, "with darkness and with dangers compassed round," not so much with the expectation of averting his clients' doom, as to show that all the decent rites of defence should be observed, or to give utterance to his own anguish at his country's fate, he took little thought of the future critic's comments. When "his soul was sick even unto fainting," he was not studying how "the stream of agony might flow decorously down his brow; how he should writhe with grace and groan in melody." Upon all those terrible occasions, he felt himself to be much more than the advocate of the mere individuals under trial; he had much to say that was not contained in his instructions. However, as a subject and a man, he might have condemned their projects or have bewailed their delusion, he still considered it his paramount duty, as the advocate of the thousands who were yet hesitating ere they plunged, and whom a gleam of mercy might recall and save—as the advocate of himself, of society, and of the last remnant of the constitution, the privilege of complaint—to discountenance the rage of public accusation, and to protest in his own person against the continuance of those fatal counsels, to which he referred so much of the disasters that he witnessed and predicted.

It is impossible to read a page of his speeches without observing how much the power depends upon this impassioned feeling; and how strikingly expressive of such a high temperature are the images that he employed. Numberless examples might be given, as the descriptions of the trial and execution of Orr—of the horrors of those distracted times—of the Irish informer—of "the perjured O'Brien,† a wretch who would dip the evangelists in blood"—of Reynolds, "who measured his importance by the coffins of his vic-

* Several of his speeches on the state trials were delivered at that hour.—C.

† "I have heard of assassination by sword, by pistol, and by dagger; but here is a wretch who would dip the evangelists in blood."—C.

tims, and appreciated his fame in the field of evidence, as the Indian warrior did in fight, by the number of scalps with which he could swell his triumphs." Many of his images, when stript of the imposing phraseology, are remarkable for their simplicity and familiarity, and for that reason came more home to the bosoms of their hearers, as where he exclaims—"Is it possible you can bring yourselves to say to your country, when the measures of government are pregnant with danger, that at such a season the press ought to slumber upon its post, or sound nothing but adulation and praise, acting like the perfidious watchman on his round, who sees the robber wrenching the bolts, or the flames bursting from the windows, while the inhabitant is wrapt in sleep, and cries out that 'the morning is fair and all is well?'" Or where, describing the extinction of the press, he thus concludes—"It is then that freedom is at its last grasp—it is then the honest man dares not speak, because truth is too dreadful to be told—it is then the proud man scorns to speak, but, like a sturdy physician, baffled by the wayward excesses of a dying patient, retires indignantly from the bed of an unhappy wretch, whose ear is too fastidious to bear the sound of wholesome advice—whose palate is too debauched to bear the salutary bitter that might redeem him, and therefore leaves him to the felonious piety of the slaves that talked to him of life, and strip him before he's cold."

To this extreme sensibility Mr. Curran could, for the most part, give expression in grave, energetic, and elevated language. Where the subjects before his mind were those of pity or eulogium, or of general description, passages without number may be cited, in which the most fastidious cannot complain that the dignity is unsustained. But when he was called upon, as he so often found himself, to speak in terms of reprobation; when some great public wrongs, of which he had as quick a sense as of a personal outrage, awakened his indignation, in the midst of more regular declamation, there were frequent intrusions of ludicrous association, which, at first view, may seem to form an unappropriate contrast with the prevailing solemnity of the occasion. In the generality of such instances, however, it will appear, upon a little consideration, that the levity is in the language and not in the ruling sentiment. Ordinary disapprobation may be conveyed in terms of ordinary and serious reproach; but in ardent natures, whose habit it is to *over-feel* upon every subject, whether of praise or censure, the sense of wrong, that in a common mind would stop at comparatively moderate indignation, becomes inflamed by their fancy into feelings of intense execration quite beyond the reach of formal invective to express. Such persons are seldom satisfied with gravely reproving what they condemn; it is not enough "to tell it how they hate it;" they know that the expression of their hatred alone will not detract from the dignity of its object; that it is often but the impotent railing of an inferior. Whether it be a public or a private delinquent that they denounce, they feel that they would be allowing him to escape almost with impunity, if they did not degrade him from his social or personal rank down to the level of his offence. To hatred they therefore add bitter ridicule; for ridicule, though not the test of truth, is the test of scorn and contempt. Humour for such a purpose (and it was for this that Mr. Curran most frequently employed it) is not levity; it has nothing of the sportings of a heart at ease, but its source is in the profoundest passion, and in that indignant haughtiness peculiar to the extreme of passion, which in its most violent paroxysm will assume a proud vindictive playfulness of exterior, lest the detested object should glory in the discovery of all the agitation that he excites, or lest it might be taken as a tribute to his importance to deem him worthy of a frown. It was in this impassioned, exaggerating spirit, upon which the particular talent of an advocate so much depends, that Mr. Curran approached every person or measure that he had occasion to arraign; whether the subject of his sarcasm happened to be a rival candidate, "whose voters might be seen coming in like the beasts of the field, in droves, from their pastures, presenting a picture of human nature in a state of degradation such as never had been witnessed since Nebuchadnezzar was at grass;" or an Irish secretary, "regarding whom he would not imitate the ancient tyrant's practice of *torturing insects*;" or an English ministry, "a motley group, without virtue, or character, or talents—the sort of cabinet that we have laughed at on the stage, where 'the potent, grave, and reverend seniors' were composed of scene-shifters and candle-snuffers, robed in old curtains and wigged from the stores of the theatre;" or even though he should have to call the public attention to "the princely virtues and the imperial qualifications, the consummate wisdom and sagacity of our steadfast friend and ally, the Emperor of all the Russias—a constellation of all virtue, compared with whose radiance the Ursa Major but twinkles as the glow-worm."

Over this, the most popular, and when skilfully managed, one of the most effective modes of attack, Mr. Curran's fancy gave him the entire command; and if he ever employed it to excess, or out of place, he but shared in the common failing of indolence and facility, that of preferring as best what is found the most easy and most successful. And here, in speaking of his facility in creating resemblances, whether of a humorous or a more elevated order, it is worthy of remark, that the history of his mind, in this respect, strongly favours the opinion that the powers of the imagination are as capable of improvement from cultivation as any other of the mental faculties. In Mr. Curran these powers were strikingly progressive; in his earlier attempts there is little of the usual exuberance of a juvenile imagination; they are, on the contrary, compared with his subsequent compositions, cold and prosaic, and, when considered as specimens of fancy, unworthy of the mind that produced them. The same remark applies to his conversation. It was by his conversation that he first attracted notice; but, however delightful in other respects, it was for a long time unilluminated by those gleams of poetic conception, which in his maturer years were incessantly bursting forth. The fact was (and in this his mind was peculiar) that his imagination developed itself with such extreme slowness, that it was not till he had been for some years a candidate for public distinction that he became aware of the particular powers that were to secure his success. The consciousness of them came gradually, and was, as it were, forced upon him by the unlooked for effect of accidental and unpremeditated efforts: but becoming at length assured of the secret of his strength, his confidence, ambition, and industry were excited, and he then, almost for the first time, began formally and assiduously to encourage, both in public and private, those habits of imaginative creation, which were subsequently to form the prominent character of his mind. The consequence of thus keeping his imagination in perpetual exercise was most conspicuous, and as a mere metaphysical fact is not incurious or unimportant. So great was the facility and the fertility which it produced, that, in his later years, scarcely an idea presented itself which did not come accompanied by some illustrative image. It was by the image that he generally preferred to express the idea, and accordingly his ordinary conversation, where he indulged in this propensity with the least reserve, presented such a series of original and apparently unlaboured illustrations, that he might almost be said to have habitually thought in metaphors.

Mr. Curran's speeches are generally referred to as instances of what is now denominated the Irish school of eloquence, the distinguishing quality of which is said to be the predominance of passion and imagination over solid argument. The correctness of this definition is questionable. It is true that the eminent persons who have employed this style perpetually express their thoughts in impassioned and figurative language, but there is no incompatibility between such a mode of expression and the profoundest reasoning. When a person addresses a public body, he does not proceed, like a mathematician, rigidly to demonstrate through each link of the chain the validity of every conclusion. A speaker who should attempt to make such a parade of logical exactness would soon discover that his audience would never submit to so harassing a tax upon their attention. The popular orator is necessarily obliged to throw out his conclusions, in separate unconnected masses. To try their value, we are not to ask if they are deducible from what has immediately preceded. They often are not so: they are often the results of previous meditation which he has stored in his memory, and takes occasion to advance as they happen to be *suggested* by the topics under discussion; although, strictly speaking, there may be no logical connexion between them. Their value is, therefore, to be ascertained, not by examining them as deductions from his previous matter, but by inquiring into the correctness of that original process of reasoning by which alone his mind could have acquired them; and if what the orator puts forward in the form of assertions appear, upon investigation, to be capable of demonstration, it is manifest that his matter is not less argumentative because he conveys it in a figurative diction. The profoundest moral and political truths may be conveyed as well in figurative as in literal language. The strength of a thought depends as little as that of a man upon dress. We may disapprove of the taste which needlessly decks it out in gaudy attire; but we are not, for that reason, to question its native force, and still less when it comes appropriately adorned with the richest clothing of a poetic imagination.

But whatever may be the merits of this style, it does not appear to have been for any length of time peculiar to the Irish people.* It was unknown in Ireland before the present reign. We do not find it to any extent in the productions of Swift, Goldsmith, or Sterne, the three most popular writers of that country. There is infinitely more of passion, and of the higher order of fancy, which is termed imagination, in the prose works of some

* This observation is to be understood to apply to the literary productions of the educated classes. The idiom of the native Irish language is highly figurative, and has a sensible influence upon the minds of the lower orders; but it would be difficult to show that this influence has ever extended much beyond them.—C.

of the eminent English writers of the seventeenth century.* This figurative style was introduced into the Irish House of Commons about the period of Ireland's great struggle for her independence. An opinion prevails that Burke was its original founder; but though Burke might have employed it in the British senate a few years before that period, it is a violent assumption to suppose that the eminent leaders in the Irish Parliament should have unanimously dismissed their previous ideas of oratorical composition, in order to become his imitators. There is also the strongest internal evidence against the supposition. An imitator does not copy merely the leading qualities of his model; he unconsciously conforms to it in every particular—in the structure of his periods, favourite forms of expressions, and other minute observances, which perpetually betray his secret. Let the speeches of Burke be compared with those of Mr. Grattan, the most eloquent of the Irish senators, and not a trace of such imitation can be detected: no two styles (as far as regards the diction and verbal construction) can be more different. Burke's language is rhetorical and copious, even to profuseness. He leaves nothing to be supplied by his hearers. He addresses them as persons previously unacquainted with the subject, and becomes so explanatory, that he seems determined not to leave off till he forces them to understand it. Mr. Grattan is the reverse—abrupt, condensed, and epigrammatic, rejecting the connecting particles of speech, and often the connecting ideas, as expletives and incumbrances. He throws off his matter in the form of a table of the contents of his mind.

If any single individual could be said to have laid the foundation of this style, it might equally be traced to the great Lord Chatham, many of whose impassioned bursts belong to that order of eloquence which was so general in the Irish House of Commons: but its prevalence in that assembly can be more naturally and satisfactorily

* Of this, numerous examples might be produced from the prose works of Milton, the writings of Jeremy Taylor, Lord Bacon, &c.—C.

explained by the condition of the times, and the nature of the subjects which agitated the nation. In the various stages of political society, there is none so favourable to popular eloquence as that in which the advantages of freedom are fully appreciated by the intellectual classes, but are in danger of being lost, or are unjustly withheld. This may be either at that period of national decline, when, from the corruption of morals, and its unerring signs, the venality of every rank, and a general contempt for established institutions, liberty is imperfectly secured against foreign invasion, or the licentious ambition of powerful subjects. Such was the case when eloquence most flourished in Greece and Rome. Or it may be when a people is just emerging from bondage—in that anxious interval between the first signs of returning life in the national body and its perfect reanimation, when violent and repeated shocks are necessary to rekindle its spirit, and preserve it from relapsing into torpor. This was the condition of Ireland. At such a period the advocates of popular rights could not confine themselves within the limits of temperate discussion. The flagrant abuses—the shameless stand made against their reformation—the notorious venality and worthlessness of those who made it—the natural pride and generous impatience of men, who found their honest efforts counteracted by a race of beings whom they despised, necessarily impelled them to give utterance to their indignation in all the vehemence of the most passionate remonstrance. These circumstances of themselves—the deep sense of their country's wrongs, and of the necessity of animating it, and exposing its oppressors—will sufficiently explain the peculiarities of their oratory. Figurative language is the natural idiomatic style of invective and complaint; the sufferer (or the advocate who represents him) finds a melancholy consolation in painting his misery in the most vivid colours that an exasperated imagination can supply. There is a feeling of high-minded self-love in the victim, whose spirit is not utterly enslaved, which leads him to exaggerate, if possible, the injustice under which he groans, and proudly to justify himself against his destiny.

The English House of Commons affords a corroboration of these remarks. Whenever the same impassioned style of eloquence has been heard there, it has almost invariably proceeded, not from the ministerial members defending the wisdom and expediency of their acts, but from the leaders of the Opposition inveighing against measures which they held to be dishonourable or oppressive.

In addition to the general influence which Burke is supposed to have had upon the oratory of his countrymen, it has been often observed, that a strong individual resemblance may be discovered between him and Mr. Curran. It is very doubtful praise to say of any one that he differed from Burke: still, if the two men be attentively compared, it must be admitted, that in many leading points, they were strikingly dissimilar. Thus (without attempting an elaborate analysis of their respective qualities), to advert to the most obvious differences. Both possessed the faculties of reason and imagination in a high degree; but the general maxims to which those powers conducted them were strongly contrasted. In all his general views of society, Burke's mind discovers a deep respect for power, for "rank, and office, and title, and all the solemn plausibilities of the world." He reviewed the history of the world, and, pausing over the institutions which had affected its destiny, reverenced them for the greatness of their effects. Mr. Curran looked at institutions as connected with freedom; and, where he found a tendency in them to enslave the human mind, forgot all their imposing grandeur in that single evil. Thus Burke's imagination contemplated, "with an awful gravity," the age of chivalry (the time of our "canonized forefathers," as a splendid array of pageantry, gallantry, and deeds of arms, with its proud "bearings and ensigns armorial," and all those images of power which "carry an imposing and majestic aspect." The other remembered its oppressions, and was never heard to lament that "the age of chivalry was gone. The same leaning to power may be observed in Burke's pathetical effusions. His most affecting lamentations are over fallen greatness. Mr. Curran's pathos was less ambitious, but more social and extensive, embracing the sufferings of every rank. The pathos of the one was more that of the schools: the sublime epic pathos of antiquity. He was most touched by historical viscissitudes. He hung over the royal corse and wept from the recollection that the head, now prostrate in the dust, had lately worn a crown. The other's tears were not reserved for the misfortunes of the great—he did not disdain to shift the scene of distress from the palace to the cottage or the dungeon, and to sympathise with those obscure afflictions which history does not condescend to record, but which man is destined hourly to endure.

Burke's acquired knowledge was more extensive, and his mind more scientific and discursive. He looked upon the great scene of human affairs as a problem for a philosopher to resolve, and delighted in those wide comprehensive views where much intermediate balancing and combination must precede the final result. No one could better describe the spirit of a particular age, or the condition and resources of a powerful empire. Mr. Curran's genius was less philosophic, but more popular. He had more confined his studies to the human passions and feelings as he observed them in active operation before him. His general views were derived from his own experience rather than from historical instruction. He had witnessed so much of the abuses of power, that he acquired a hatred of and contempt for it; and his chief skill lay in exposing those abuses. He could best describe a scene of local or individual oppression, and lay bare, for public execration, "the infernal workings of the hearts of the malignant slaves" who were its instruments.

Many particulars in which they differed may be attributed to their respective situations. They were cotemporaries; but they lived in such different countries, that they might be said to have lived in a different age. Burke's life was passed under a political system, which (whatever might be its theoretic imperfections) was diffusing real blessings all around; and to leave it as he found it was the wise end of all his efforts. The other lived under a system, which, with "many shows of seeming pure," was an actual curse; and his life was a long struggle to inspire his country with the spirit to reform it. These different objects of each—of the one to preserve freedom, of the other to obtain it—gave a different character to their oratory. Burke's wisdom had taught him the dangers of popular innovation; and he would have protected, even under the shield of superstition, the institutions over which he watched. There is a certain oracular pride and pomp in his manner of announcing important political truths, as if they were awful mysteries which the uninitiated crowd were to reverence from afar. Like the high priests of old, he would have inspired a sacred dread of approaching the inmost temple, lest some profane intruder should discover and proclaim that the god was not there. The spectacle of misrule in Ireland had, on the contrary, impressed upon Mr. Curran's mind the necessity of animating the people with a spirit of fearless inquiry. To do this he had to awaken them to a sense of their importance and their claims, by gratifying their self-love, and filling them with the persuasion, that there was no truth which they were not fitted to examine and comprehend.

Burke is more instructive and commanding than persuasive. He looked upon the people from an eminence, from which he saw them under their diminished forms, and betrayed a consciousness that he was above them. The other remained below—threw himself among them—and, persuading them that they were his equals, by that means became the master of their movements.

This is the most striking distinction in the impressions which they make upon us—that we feel the one to be our superior, and imagine the other to be only a companion. In Burke's most exalting conceptions there is a gorgeous display of knowledge and intellect, which reminds us of our inferiority and our incapacity to ascend without his aid. The popular charm of the other's eloquence is, that it makes us only feel more intensely what we have felt before. In his loftiest flights, we are conscious of being elevated with him, and for the moment forget that we soar upon another's wing; for the elements of his sublimity are the passions in which we all partake; and, when he wakes the living chords to their highest ecstasy, it is not that he strikes one which was never touched before, but that he gives a longer and louder vibration to the chords which are never still.

The history of each exemplifies their characters. Burke was a philosopher, and could transplant his sympathies. He went abroad, and passed his life admiring and enjoying the benefits of "his adopted, and dearer, and more comprehensive country." Mr. Curran was a patriot, whose affections, could he have torn them from their native bed, would have drooped in another soil. He stayed at home, and closed his days in deploring the calamities which he had vainly labored to avert.

CHAPTER XIX.

Mr. Curran's skill in cross-examination—His general reading—His conversation—His wit—Manuscript thoughts on various subjects—His manners, person—Personal peculiarities—Conclusion.

Next to the force of Mr. Curran's eloquence was the skill of his cross-examinations, a department of his profession in which he was, perhaps, still more unrivalled than as a speaker. Of the extent of this talent it is impossible that any description or examples can convey an adequate idea to those who have never witnessed the living scene; but the bar, who alone could fully appreciate his resources, for they alone were fully sensible of the difficulties in each case against which he had to contend, have unanimously allowed that his address and sagacity as a cross-examiner were altogether matchless. It was, perhaps, here that as an advocate he was most feared and most resistless.* In cases where there

* In the cross-examination of witnesses, Mr. Curran's scrutiny was tremendous. Instinctive and intuitive as Shakespeare, he knew all the fastnesses, passes and windings of the human heart, into which truth seeks to retire and to conceal itself. He knew all the weaknesses, the passions of hope and of fear, of interest and of resentment; and such was his knowledge of human nature, and so much was he in her confidence, that he silently inhaled all the operations of the villain he would expose; dragged Cacus from his cave, penetrated into the mysteries of hell, and threw open to the common observer the secrets of those dark regions. Keen and ardent in the pursuit, he was always sure of his game; eager and intrepid in the chase, he was ever in at the death; whether playful or severe, he never relaxed; whether his weapon was ridicule, or open and direct attack; whether it was the power of reason cutting through a weak and fluttering conscience, his edge was unerring: the mole which hid its head in the earth, he perceived by the kicking of its feet; when it could see nothing, it thought itself secure and unseen. If truth lay at the bottom of her well, he plunged in, and plucked up drowned honour by the locks; or did she escape to the mountain top, he would round its slopes and gain its heights with the activity of an Arab warrior. He had the power to elicit it from the flint; and by his touch, as if with a wand, he caused it to gush forth from the hardest rock. It may justly be said of him, that "The Gordian knot of it he could untie familiar

was some latent fraud or perjury, in exposing which his whole strength was always most conspicuously developed, he uniformly surprised his own profession no less than the general spectator, by the singular versatility of his powers, and by his familiarity with every variety of human character, at once so extensive and so minute, that he could discover at a glance the exact tone and manner best calculated to persuade, terrify or entrap into a confession of the truth, the particular description of person upon whom he had to work. In managing a sullen or dishonest witness there was nothing that he left untried; solemnity, menace, ridicule, pathos, flattery, and even for the moment respectful submission. In contests of this kind he had, in an eminent degree, the art of "stooping to conquer." If a few insidious compliments to the witness's understanding, and an apparently cordial assent to all his assertions and opinions, or a long series of jests, no matter whether good or bad, seemed likely to throw him off his guard, he never hesitated;* his favourite method was by some such artifice to divert his attention, or to press him with pretended earnestness upon some trivial irrelevant point until he found the witness elated with his fancied security, and then to drop, as it were incidentally,

as his garter." Jurors latterly began to doubt themselves, and to be frighted at the magic of his address; while he who bore false witness against his neighbours was often seen, like Festus, to have trembled. In variety and effect in this department of his profession he was unrivalled, and *sola sicca secum spatiatur ardua.*—O'Regan.

* The following may be taken as a specimen of the ludicrous phraseology to which he sometimes resorted:—A witness having sworn that as he was returning, at a late hour, from a supper party, he was assaulted by Mr. Curran's client, the counsel, in his cross-examination, asked him—"if the number of eggs that composed his supper was not more than that of the graces and equal to that of the muses?—if he did not usually drink a little coarse wine at dinner, by way of foundation to keep the claret out of the wet? if he did not swallow a squib after dinner, by way of Latin for his goose? and if, after his foundation of white wine, with a superstructure of three pints of claret, a stratum of nine eggs, a pint of porter, and a supra-cargo of three pints of Geneva punch, his judgment was not a little under the *yoke?*"—C. [In the case Massy *v.* the Marquis of Headford, Mr. Curran had described the "noble" defendant, as *a hoary adulterer.* In the cross-examination of one of the witnesses, he found it difficult to prove his age. At last the witness admitted, that the Marquis was gray. "You will admit," said Curran, quoting a well known adage, "that *he was gray before he was good.*"—M.]

and with a tone of indifference as to the answer, or in a manner implying that it had been already admitted, some vital question, to which, in all probability, the desired reply would be given before the perjurer had time to recollect whether he had previously asserted or denied the fact. So unexpected and surprising were his discoveries of a person's character and morals, from external indications so slight as to be imperceptible to others, that the lower orders of his countrymen had an almost superstitious reverence for his abilities, as if he were gifted with a supernatural power of "looking through the deeds of men." From the prevalence of this opinion, his name was the proverbial terror of the Irish informer. Even those wretches who, in "drudging for a pardon," or a reward, had so steeled their conscience against remorse and shame, that they could hear unmoved the deep buzz of smothered execrations with which the multitude announced their approach, and even glory in their indifference to the "sound of public scorn," had not the nerves to sustain his torturing development of their unrighteous lives. They were not only abashed and confounded by that art, which he so consummately possessed, of involving them in prevarication, by confronting them with themselves, but they have been actually seen, as if under a momentary shock of virtuous panic, to plunge from off the public table, and fly to shelter from his upbraiding presence, leaving the rescued victims to reward by their blessings their advocate and saviour.

It will not be necessary to dwell at any length upon Mr. Curran's character as a lawyer. He was never profoundly read; but his mind had firmly seized all the leading principles of the English code, more particularly those of constitutional law; and he was always considered by the members of his own profession to have displayed eminent skill in his logical application of them. In the earlier part of his carreer his reasoning powers were admitted to have been of the first order, until the splendour of his eloquence gave rise to the unfounded notion, that where there was so much imagination the faculty of reason must have been deficient. But some of his published arguments amply refute this opinion.

His judicial history contains little requiring particular notice. Upon the bench he religiously respected those privileges which at the bar he had so strenuously supported. If he fell into any error upon this point, it was that his abhorrence of favouritism often led him to be over scrupulous in granting any indulgence, where the counsel claiming it happened to be one of his personal friends.

With regard to his general reading, much of it may be collected from his speeches. The frequency of classical and scriptural allusions, and of expressions borrowed from the English poets, sufficiently point out the writings with which he was most familiar. He was never deeply versed in general history; he had, however, studied with attention and success that portion of it (the great constitutional epochs in the history of Great Britain and Ireland) which it was peculiarly incumbent on him, as a lawyer and a senator, to know. The enthusiasm with which, in a passage already cited, he has described the scientific and literary genius of Scotland, proves the impression made upon him by the noble productions of that intellectual people. His early knowledge of the French language has been mentioned. He continued to cultivate it during the rest of his life; and though his study of it was only occasional and desultory, and his residence in France never exceeded a few weeks at a time, he spoke and wrote it with unusual correctness. It may be added, as a peculiarity of his taste, that he used to express himself to be more sensible of the beauties of that language than of his own. Among the French serious writers he always preferred Rousseau. He understood Italian sufficiently well to comprehend the popular poetry of modern Italy; but Italian literature was never one of his favourite pursuits.

After having stated so much in commendation of Mr. Curran's intellectual superiority; it may seem like the spirit of boundless eulogium to go on; but who, that ever knew him, could dismiss his life without dwelling for a moment upon his colloquial and convivial powers? As a companion, he was, in his own country, confessedly without a rival. In speaking of the charms of his conversation, it would be exceeding the truth to assert, as has sometimes been done, that the creations of his careless hours were often more vivid and felicitous than his more studied public efforts; yet is it no small praise to be justified in saying, that they were equal, or nearly equal; that few who approached him, attracted by his general reputation, ever left him without having their admiration confirmed, if not increased, by the vigour and originality of his ordinary conversation.* According to the testimony of those who had enjoyed his society at an earlier period, some of its attractions had latterly disappeared. The survivors of the "Monks of St. Patrick," are those who best can tell what Mr. Curran was at the festive board. It was in that season of youth and hope, when exalted by the spirit of their classic and patriotic meetings, and surrounded by "those admired and respected, and beloved companions," that his mind surrendered itself to every emotion of social enthusiasm, throwing off in exhaustless profusion every thought that could touch the fancy or the heart. No laboured description can now convey an adequate notion of those

* It was in conversation when he was properly in his own climate; when in high tone, and harmonised by fit accompaniments, that he "discoursed most excellent music." Often happiest when his subject was gravest, or when letters, men, taste, past, or passing events were touched. On these topics he entered with a curious felicity, so as to swell the listener's mind to participate in the proud consciousness of human superiority, of which he could be scarcely apprised till he heard him. And whether he courted the mournful muse, or were his even the sallies of gaiety and mirth, such was the *sombre* of his pencil, or such the playfulness and airiness of his imagery; and so surprising were the rapid transitions to the most exquisite comedy, that days and nights passed thus with him were truly in his own phrase (on some other occasion) "the refections of the gods." His quotations, though frequent, were never pedantic: he melted down the classic sentiment, and it became more pure, and you felt the allusion or illustration in all the freshness of its original force. It was on these occasions his soul resembled a finely-toned instrument, which a rude or clumsy touch flung into disorder: it was the harp which played to the zephyr, and whose wildest were its sweetest notes!"—O'REGAN.

effusions. The graver parts, had they been preserved, would have been found to resemble many admired passages in his printed speeches; but the lighter and most frequent sallies, deriving their charm from minute and evanescent combinations of characters and circumstances, have necessarily perished with the occasions for which alone they were intended.

Numerous specimens of his wit have been preserved, from which its style, rather than its extent, may be collected. It may be generally observed of his wit, that it delighted, not so much from the naked merit of any single effort, as from the incessancy and unexpectedness of its combinations. It also possessed one quality, which is above all value, that of never inflicting an undeserved wound. In all those cases where the words might seem to intend a personal reflection, he never failed to neutralise the poison by a playful ironical manner which testified his own belief of what he was asserting. It would be difficult to produce an equal number of pointed sayings, in which the spirits consist so little in particular of general satire; neither do they appear, like the humorous sallies of many celebrated wits, to have been dictated by any peculiar set of speculative opinions. The sceptic, the misanthrope, the voluptuary, and all, in short, who habitually look at the business of life through the medium of their particular doctrines, are perpetually betraying in their mirth some open or lurking application to their favorite tenets: the instances of their wit, if accurately examined, may be resolved into illustrations of their system. Thus the humour of Voltaire is for ever reminding us of his impiety; that of Swift, of his splenetic contempt of human folly , but almost all of Mr. Curran's lively sayings were suggested at the moment by the immediate circumstances and persons, or verbal associations; they are in general insulated and individual, ending where they began, and not referrible to any previous systematic view of human affairs.*

*An entire collection of the *bons mots* attributed to Mr. Curran would fill many pages. The following are selected as a few specimens. In all of them it will be seen how much

Mr. Horne Tooke, after having passed an evening in the company of Mr. Curran and the late Mr. Sheridan, whom he had, upon that occasion, for the first time met together, was asked his opinion of the wit of each. He replied, "that Sheridan's was like steel highly polished, and sharpened for display and use; that

less the essence depends upon the satire than upon the fanciful combination of words or images.

Mr. Curran was engaged in a legal argument—behind him stood his colleague, a gentleman whose person was remarkably tall and slender, and who had originally designed to take orders. The judge observing that the case under discussion involved a question of ecclesiastical law—"Then," said Mr. Curran, "I can refer your lordship to a high authority behind me, who was once intended for the *church*, though (*in a whisper to a friend beside him*) in my opinion he was fitter for the *steeple*."

An officer of one of the courts, named Halfpenny, having frequently interrupted Mr. Curran, the judge peremptorily ordered him to be silent, and sit down. "I thank your lordship," said the counsel, "for having at length *nailed that rap to the counter*."

"I can't tell you, Curran," observed an Irish nobleman, who had voted for the Union, "how frightful our old House of Commons appears to me." "Ah! my lord," replied the other, "it is only natural for murderers to be afraid of ghosts."

A deceased judge had a defect in one of his limbs, from which, when he walked, one foot described almost a circle round the other. Mr. Curran being asked how his lordship still contrived to walk so fast, answered—"Don't you see that one leg goes before like a tipstaff, and clears the way for the other?"

Mr. Curran, cross-examining a horse-jockey's servant, asked his master's age. "I never put my hand in his mouth to try," answered the witness. The laugh was against the counsel, till he retorted—"You did perfectly right, friend, for your master is said to be a *great bite*."

A miniature painter, upon his cross-examination by Mr. Curran, was made to confess that he had carried his improper freedoms with a particular lady so far as to attempt to put his arm round her waist. "Then, sir," said the counsel, "I suppose you took that waist (*waste*) for a *common*."

"No man," said a wealthy, but a weak-headed barrister, "should be admitted to the bar who has not an independent landed property." "May I ask, sir," said Mr. Curran, "how many acres make a *wise-acre*?"

"Would you not have known this boy to be my son, from his resemblance to me?" asked a gentleman. Mr. Curran answered—"Yes, sir; the maker's name is stamped upon the *blade*."

Mr. Curran was asked what an Irish gentleman, just arrived in England, could mean by perpetually putting out his tongue? Answered—"I suppose he's trying to *catch the English accent*."

At a public dinner he was defending his countrymen against the imputation of being a naturally vicious race. "Many of our faults, for instance (said he), arise from our too free use of the circulating medium (*pointing to the wine*) but I never heard of an Irishman being *born drunk*."

Curran's was a mine of virgin gold, incessantly crumbling away from its own richness."

The celebrated Madame De Stael, who during her last residence in England, was surrounded by persons the most distinguished for talent, frequently observed that she had been most struck by the originality and variety of Mr. Curran's colloquial powers. This was in 1813, when his health and spirits were in a state of depression, which rendered the effort to support his part in such company a painful exertion.*

Among his papers there are a few sheets covered with thoughts loosely thrown together, from which a few extracts may convey some idea of the more striking passages of his conversation.

"England has been industriously taught to believe, that whatever degrades or tortures this devoted country is essentially good for her; and that if some supernatural spirit (a Popish imp to be sure) were to take advantage of some dark night, and in the morning the Irish peasant should awake in astonishment to find his cottage with its roof thatched, and its floor dried, and clothes and food miraculously supplied for his children, I can scarcely doubt that when certain intelligence of so disaffecting a visitor had arrived in Britain, a solemn fast and humiliation would be proclaimed by our orthodox rulers to expiate whatever of our crimes had drawn down so heavy a punishment, and to atone for the offence, for example, of abolishing the slave trade, and to show our contrition by giving it a five years' reprieve, that so it might recover itself and live for ever, to the satisfaction of a merciful God, and the true glory of his holy religion."

"(*Bourbons : freedom of the press*)—Perhaps exile is the

* Alluding in a private letter to one of those parties, he says, "I dined yesterday with a society of wits at Madame de Stael's; Sheridan, other great names, &c. I find that even sugar may cloy. Perhaps there is no society in which less bona-fide cordiality reigns. In truth where can you look to find so much false money as among coiners by trade? Believe me I have passed much pleasanter evenings at Whitehall. (A country-place in the vicinity of Dublin.)—C.

bitterest ingredient of captivity. The Jew felt it so, when he wept by the waters of Babylon. If adversity ever becomes a teacher, surely her school ought to be found in exile."

"(*Christianity.*)—The first ages were hypocrisy and imposture. These soon excited their natural enemy, free thinking. Religion could have been no party in the conflict. She was neither a sophist nor a poet; she had little dealing with rhetoric or metaphysics; but at last, when Hypocrisy and Atheism have made peace, she may come round again."

"(*Lord* ——.)—These small folks are as much afraid of the press, as Robinson Crusoe's man Friday was of the musquet, when he 'prayed massa gun don't go off and kill poor wild man.'"

"(*How holds Ireland.*)—The upper orders gone and the remains following. The people agriculturists."

"(*Agriculture.*)—The mother and nurse of a military population. Ireland has been forced to this. It was thought that she was sunk under the arbitrary tyranny of British monopoly. Let the proud Briton regale himself in the wholesome air of mines and workshops, and become ossified in the strengthening attitudes of monotonous labour, while the degraded Irishman draws health and number, and fierceness, and force, and becomes too nimble to be caught by his crippled owner, who hobbles after him and threatens him with his crutch."

"(*Irish administration.*)—I should much sooner presume to speak out against the solid substance of an English ministry, than venture on a whisper against their shadows in Ireland.

"I know the seeming moderation of these men, but I fear it is like the moderation of the drunkard who glories in the sobriety of the morning; who mistakes exhaustion for contrition, and is vain of reformation that stole upon him while he slept.

"To inflame the public mind on a point of theology, was to divert them from the great point of national oppression on which the country could not but be unanimous, and to turn it to one on which England would be against us.

"I don't hesitate to say, that a good government would in a week have Ireland tranquil.

"Putting out the law will never do; but here the insurrection act was clearly a topic in argument, not a measure of necessity.

"In all countries revolutions have been produced by the abuses of power. If you would mark the process of force look to '98.

"The tyrant may say to the slave, you are bound in conscience to submit—the slave may put the question to his conscience, and receive a very different answer.

"Obedience is founded on allegiance and protection; but if an idea is held out that a nation, containing at least two-thirds of the military population of the empire, is to remain upon their knees in hope of the interval when cruelty and folly may work themselves to rest, and humanity and justice awaken—I say, forbid it the living God! that victim man should not make his elections between danger and degradation, and make a struggle for that freedom, without which the worship of his name has no value."

Mr. Curran's manners were remarkably simple and unassuming. In his youth, before his value was sufficiently ascertained to procure him uniform respect, he occasionally exhibited before his superiors in rank some signs of that pride with which men of genius are disposed to assert their dignity; he never indulged however in this feeling to an offensive degree. The early and long continued habit of his mind, was to underrate his own talents and importance. It was only where he imagined that some slight was intended, that he showed a consciousness of his claims; but the occasions of exciting his vanity or indignation on this point entirely ceasing as his character became known, the feeling itself was soon extinguished.

In his daily intercourse, he scrupulously avoided an ordinary failing of superior men, that of impressing upon less gifted persons a sense of their inferiority. In this department of the business of life, he eminently possessed (to use a favourite expression of his own) that nice *tact*, which taught him to accommodate his style and sentiments to the various characters and capacities of those with whom he conversed. However humble their rank or pretensions, he listened with good humour to all they had to offer, and was never betrayed into a ridicule of those little demonstrations of vanity and self-love, which they who mix in the world have to encounter every moment.

In his political relations, he was not vindictive. The prominent and decided part which he took in public affairs necessarily involved him in many enmities, which the condition of the times, and the nature of the question at issue, inflamed into the highest state of exasperation; but as soon as the first fever of passion and indignation had subsided, he evinced a more forgiving disposition than he found among his opponents.* In his later years, he spoke of the injuries which he had sustained from Lord Clare and many others, with a degree of moderation which could scarcely have been expected from a person of his quick and ardent temperament.†

* He was in principle a Whig. His passions, his habits, his friendships, and his education, made him so. He did not obsequiously follow any individual model; nor did he on all occasions pursue the measures of his party. He had an abstract idea of what love of country should inspire; to this he sometimes referred his actions. If there was any one person among those with whom he acted, to whom he would submit his judgment in cases of doubt or of difficulty, so highly did he venerate Mr. Fox, that his authority would alone be very likely to have decided him.—O'REGAN.

† A few years before his death, Mr. Curran strolled one day into the Poet's Corner in Westminster Abbey. As he contemplated the monuments, he became deeply affected by the spectacle of mortality on every side, and for the moment dismissing every harsher feeling, gave up his mind to the solemn reflections which the scene was calculated to inspire. "The holy influence of the spot (to adopt the words of an illustrious countryman of his in relating this circumstance) had so subdued him, that he began to weep." While he was in this softened mood, he observed at a little distance his old antagonist, Doctor Duigenan. Mr. Curran, considering that they were both to be soon beyond the possibility of further contention, and that no place could be more suited for the exchange of mutual forgiveness, approached, and affectionately offered him his hand. "I shall never take Mr. Curran's hand," replied the doctor, and abruptly turned away.—C.

Mr. Curran's person was short, slender, and ungraceful, resembling rather the form of a youth not yet fully developed, than the compact stature of a man.* His face was as devoid of beauty as his frame. His complexion was of that deep muddy tinge by which Dean Swift's is said to have been distinguished. He had a dark, glistening, intellectual eye, high arched, and thickly covered brows, strong, uncurled, jet-black hair, which lay flat upon his forehead and temples. When his thoughts were unoccupied (which was rare) his features were not particularly expressive; but the moment he became animated, there was a rush of mind into his countenance which dilated every fibre, and impressed upon it a character of peculiar energy and genius.

[Mr. Phillips thus glances at his appearance in 1805;

"Mark well that slight short figure with restless gait, and swaying motion, and speaking gesture—he with the uplifted face, protruded under lip, and eyes like living diamonds. See how the young men cluster round him. Observe the spell-bound gaze—hark to the ringing laughter. That is Curran—the unique, the wondrous, the inimitable Curran—who spake as poets in their inspiration wrote, and squandered wit with Rabelais profusion. Curran, whose words, merry or mournful as his country's music, commanded tears or laughter† at his bidding. Curran, in evil days, erect amid the

* O'Regan says "Mr. Curran was in person rather under the middle stature; his frame wiry, yet muscular; and, though the countenance was not prepossessing, yet it was redeemed by the eye, which was full of fire and energy; and might be likeued to that of Coriolanus, *which could have pierced a corslet.* He often said it would cost him half an hour more to get at the heart of his hearer, than it would a handsome man. He was always pleasant on the subject of defect of beauty; and, when in Parliament, turned it very happily against another member. One of the messengers brought in an unsealed note from the door of the House, hastily written, and not addressed to any person. Mr. Curran looked at the back of the paper, and observed that it was not for him and asked why he had handed it to him? The messenger answered, by saying, the gentleman who had given it to him was at the door; that he pointed at Mr. Curran, and desired him to give it to the ugliest gentleman in the House: he directly pointed to the other side, and desired him to give it Mr.——, for it was for him it was intended."

† I never met a person who possessed this wonderful faculty before. Lord Brougham one day, in my presence, asked the late Dr. Birkbeck, who knew Curran, whether my

groveling, pure amid the tainted; in public life, the most consistent of patriots; in private, the most social, exquisite, enchanting of companions."]

His voice was not naturally powerful or musical; but he managed it so skilfully, that he gave full expression to every feeling and passion which it had to convey. Its unrivalled excellency lay in communicating solemn and pathetic sentiments. In private and serious conversation, it was remarkable for a certain plaintive sincerity of tone, which incessantly reminded those who knew him of the melancholy that predominated in his constitution. His delivery, both in public and private, was slow, and his articulation uncommonly distinct. He was scrupulous in his choice of words, and often paused to search for the most expressive. His powers of language and delivery were the result of assiduous industry and observation. There was nothing, however minute, connected with the subject, which he deemed beneath his attention.*

It is perhaps time to close this account; yet as many might feel disappointed at the omission of those minuter traits which render the individual still more peculiar and distinct, and bring him into a kind of personal acquaintance with those who never saw him, some passing notice shall be taken of the more striking

estimate of him was not exaggerated. "All I can say," was the answer, "is, that for the five weeks he and I lodged together in Paris during the peace of Amiens, there were not five consecutive minutes within which he could not make me *both laugh and cry!*" Ten years later, Lord Byron says of him, "I have met Curran at Holland House. He beats every body. His imagination is beyond human, and his humor (it is difficult to define what is wit) perfect. He has fifty faces, and twice as many voices, when he mimics. *I never met his equal.*" Again: "Curran! Curran's the man who struck me most. Such imagination! There never was any thing like it. He was wonderful even to me who had seen many remarkable men of the time. The riches of his Irish imagination were exhaustless. *I have heard that man speak more poetry than I have ever seen written, though I saw him seldom, and but occasionally.*"

* He sometimes mispronounced the word "tribunal," throwing the accent upon the first syllable. When reminded of the error, he alleged in his excuse, that, having once heard the word so pronounced by Lord Moira, whom he considered a model of classical pronunciation, he adopted his method; and, though subsequently aware of the incorrectness, unconsciously repeated it.—C.

features of this subordinate class, which separated Mr. Curran from other men.

One of his great peculiarities was, that, in the most trivial things, he was peculiar. He did not sit in his chair like other persons: he was perpetually changing his position, throwing himself into attitudes of thinking, and betraying, by the most incessant play of shifting expressions on his countenance, that there was something within which was impatient of repose. It was the same when he walked or rode. Long before his features could be discerned, his friends recognized him from afar by the back of his hand firmly compressed upon the hip, his head raised towards the sky, and momentarily turning round, as if searching for objects of observation; or, if he was in conversation, by the earnest waving of his body, and the fervour of his gesticulation. These were the external signs of that latent impulse which was the source of his genius. One of the most extraordinary circumstances in his constitution was the length of time to which this impulse could continue to act with undiminished force. He used to assure his intimates, that, long after the body's exhaustion had incapacitated him for farther exertion, he felt a consciousness that the vigour of his mind was unimpaired. Even his capacity of dispensing with bodily rest, considering the apparent delicacy of his frame, was surprising. During the more active period of his life, he frequently sacrificed a night's rest with impunity. After passing the day in his professional occupations, and one half of the night in the House of Commons, and the other in the convivial meetings of the leaders of his party, he re-appeared on the succeeding morning in the courts, as fresh for the ensuing labours of the day as if he had spent the interval in renovating sleep. There were, in his more ordinary habits, many similar indications that his frame was, as it were, overcharged with life. In his conversation his fancy generally became more brilliant as the night advanced. He retired to bed with reluctance; and his friends often remarked, that he was seldom so eloquent and fascinating as after he had risen from his chair, momentarily about to depart, but still lingering and delighting them—"indulgens animo, pes tardus erat." In his own house, after his guests had retired to their chambers, he seized any excuse for following one of them, and renewing the conversation for another hour; and the person thus intruded upon seldom considered himself the least fortunate of the party. It appears from all this, that Mr. Curran was not much addicted to sleep. One reason why his frame required so little may have been that his sleep was generally most profound, and uninterrupted by dreams. The latter circumstance he often regretted, for he was inclined to think that the throng of fantastic ideas which present themselves in dreams might, if carefully attended to, have supplied him with new sources of poetic imagery.

In his diet he was constitutionally temperate: he ate little, and was extremely indifferent regarding the quality of his fare. For the greater part of his life he was subject to a debility of the stomach, which, though it could scarcely be called a disease, was yet so permanent as to be the source of the utmost inconvenience. Whenever dinner was delayed beyond the expected time,* the irritation of his stomach became so intolerable, that he was frequently obliged to retire altogether from the company. From his attachment to the pleasures of convivial society, he was supposed to have been addicted to wine; but the fact was that a very small quantity excited him; and, whenever he drank to any excess (as was sometimes the case in large companies) it was rather mechanically and from inattention than from choice. When left to his natural propensities, he was almost as temperate in this respect as in his food. At his own table he was hospitable and unceremonious. In every transaction of common life, he dis-

* He insisted, at home and abroad, on dining at five o'clock. On the contrary, Toler (Lord Norbury) liked to dine late. One day, Mr. Toler was going to take his ride, and meeting Mr. Curran walking towards his house to dine, passingly said, "Do not forget, Curran, you dine with me to-day;" "I rather fear, my friend," replied Mr. Curran, "it is you who may forget it."—M.

liked and despised the affectation of state. His maxim was, that the festive board should be a little republic, where the host, having previously provided whatever was necessary for the general interest, should appear with no greater privileges or responsibilities than a guest.

From the same distaste to show, he was always remarkable for the plainness, and even negligence, of his external dress; but he paid the most scrupulous attention to personal cleanliness. His regular custom was to plunge every morning when he rose into cold water. It may be generally added, that in all his ordinary habits, in his house, his equipage, his style of living, of travelling, &c.—the same republican simplicity prevailed. During the two or three last years of his life, he might often be seen, on the road between London and Cheltenham, seated outside one of the public coaches, and engaged in familiar conversation with the other passengers.

His constitutional tendency to melancholy has been already noticed; yet, in the familiar intercourse of daily life, the prominent characteristic of his mind was its incessant playfulness—a quality which rendered his society peculiarly acceptable among females and young persons. He took great delight in conversing with little children, whom he generally contrived to lead into the most exquisitely comical dialogues. He was fond of giving ludicrous appellations to the places and persons around him. His friend Mr. Hudson the dentist's house was built in "the Tuscan order"—a celebrated snuff-manufacturer's country-seat was "Sneeze-town"—the libraries at watering-places were "slopshops of literature." He called a commander of yeomanry (who dealt largely in flour) "Marshal Sacks"—a lawyer, of a corpulent frame, "Grotius"—another, who had a habit of swelling out his cheeks, "Puffendorf." He often humorously remonstrated with a friend, who was of a very tall stature, and with whom, as one of his "very longest acquaintances," he used that freedom, "upon his want of decorum in going about and peeping down the chimnies, to see what his neighbours were to have for dinner." This list might be extended to a greater length than would be necessary or suitable.

In speaking of Mr. Curran's literary habits, it should have been mentioned that he was, for the greater part of his life, an ardent reader of novels.* In his earlier years, it was his regular custom to have one under his pillow, with which he commenced and closed the reading of the day. His sensibility to the interest of such works was so excessive, as to be scarcely credible by those who never saw him sobbing, almost to suffocation, over the pathetic details of Richardson,† or in more extravagant paroxysms of laughter at the ludicrous descriptions of Cervantes. There was a kind of infantile earnestness in his preference of anything of this sort which struck his fancy; for days it would usurp his thoughts and conversation. When the translation of the Sorrows of Werter first appeared, he was for ever repeating and praising some favourite passages,‡ and calling upon every friend that chanced to visit him to join in the eulogy, with all the impatience of a child to display a new toy to his companions.

Such were his excellencies, or his harmless peculiarities, and the office of enumerating them has been easy and attractive. But biography, if the fidelity to truth which it demands be too rigidly exacted, may become a harsh task, converting a friend, or one nearer than a friend, unto the ungracious character of an accuser. Every lover of genius would wish that this account of Mr. Curran's life might here have closed without rendering it liable to the charge of having suppressed any circumstance which it would not have

* So was O'Connell, all his life.—M.

† Particularly the will of Clarissa Harlowe, which he considered a masterpiece of pathos—C.

‡ Among them was the following, from one of Werter's letters—"When in the fine evenings of the summer you walk towards the mountains, think of me; recollect the time you have so often seen me come up from the valley; raise your eyes to the churchyard that contains my grave, and, by the light of the departing sun, see how the evening breeze waves the high grass which grows over me."—C.

been to the interest of his name to have disclosed. But the question will be asked, has this been a faithful picture?—Have no shades been designedly omitted?—Has delicacy or flattery concealed no defects, without which the resemblance cannot be true? To such inquiries it is answered, that the estimable qualities, which have formed the preceding description, have not been invented or exaggerated; and if the person, who has assumed the duty of collecting them, has abstained from a rigorous detail of any infirmities of temper or conduct, it is because a feeling more sacred and more justifiable than delicacy or flattery has taught him, and should teach others, to regard them with tenderness and regret. In thus abstaining from a cruel and unprofitable analysis of failings, to which the most gifted are often the most prone, no deception is intended. It is due to that public to whom Mr. Curran's merits have been here submitted as deserving their approbation, to admit with candour that some particulars have been withheld which they would not have approved; but it is also due to his memory to declare, that in balancing the conflicting elements of his character, what was virtuous and amiable will be found to have largely preponderated. He was not perfect; but his imperfections have a peculiar claim upon our forbearance, when we reflect that they sprung from the same source as his genius, and may be considered as almost the inevitable condition upon which that order of genius can be held. Their source was in his imagination. The same ardour and sensibility which rendered him so eloquent an advocate of others, impelled him to take too impassioned and irritating views of questions that personally related to himself. The mistakes of conduct into which this impetuosity of temperament betrayed him cannot be defended by this or by any other explanation of their origin, yet it is much to be able to say that they were almost exclusively confined to a single relation, and that those who in consequence suffered most, but who, from their intimate connexion with him, knew him best, saw so many redeeming qualities in his nature, that they uniformly considered any exclusion, from his regard no so much in the light of an injustice, as of a personal misfortune.

There was a time when such considerations would have failed to appease his numerous accusers, who, under the vulgar pretext of moral indignation, were relentlessly taking vengeance on his public virtues by assiduous and exaggerated statements of private errors, which, had he been one of the enemies of his country, they would have been the first to screen or justify. But it is hoped, that he was not deceiving himself when he anticipated that the term of their hostility would expire as soon as he should be removed beyond its reach. "The charity of the survivors (to use his own expressions) looks at the failings of the dead through an inverted glass; and slander calls off the pack from a chase in which, when there can be no pain, there can be no sport; nor will memory weigh their merits with a niggard steadiness of hand." But even should this have been a delusive expectation—should the grave which now covers him prove an unrespected barrier against the assaults of political hatred, there will not be wanting many of more generous minds, who loved and admired him, to rally round his memory from the grateful conviction that his titles to his country's esteem stand in defiance of every imperfection, of which his most implacable revilers can accuse him. As long as Ireland retains any sensibility to public worth, it will not be forgotten, that (whatever waywardness he may have shown towards some, and those a very few) she had, in every vicissitude, the unpurchased and most unmeasured benefit of his affections and his virtues. This is his claim and his protection; that having by his talents raised himself from an humble condition to a station of high trust and innumerable temptations, he held himself erect in servile times, and has left an example of political honour, upon which the most scrutinizing malice cannot detect a stain. Nor will it be deemed an inconsiderable merit to have thus, without fortune or connexions, forced his way into a situation of such responsibility. "He that seeketh to be eminent amongst able men (said the ablest of men) hath a great task." * This task Mr. Curran fulfilled. In the generous struggle for distinction, he was surrounded, not by a race of puny competitors, whom accident or wealth had lifted above their sphere, but by men of surpassing vigour, in whose ranks none but athletic minds could be enrolled. Flood, Yelverton, Daly, Burgh, Perry, Forbes, Ponsonby, and, to crown the list, their leader and solitary survivor, Henry Grattan,†—these, all of them great names, and worthy of their country's lasting pride, were the objects of his honourable emulation, and to have been rewarded by their approbation, and admitted an associate of their labours, is in itself an evidence of his value, which neither praises can increase, nor envy take away.

* Bacon's Essays.

† Henry Grattan died (soon after the above was written) on June 4, 1820. He was interred in Westminster Abbey, next to Fox.—M.

APPENDIX.

ANECDOTES OF CURRAN AND HIS FRIENDS.

When Mr. Curran was in Trinity College, Dublin, he was summoned by the Board of Senior Fellows (the moral and literary censors of the University) and stood before them in all that may be conceived lachrymose in feature, penitent in exterior, yet internally unmoved. After a long lecture, delivered in Hebrew, and explained into Greek, the accusation amounted in plain English to this, that he "kept idle women in his chambers," and concluded according to the form of the statute and good morals. He saw he had no way to escape but by the exercise of his wit, and solemnly assured them that the accusation was utterly unfounded, as he never in his life kept any woman *idle* in his rooms.

Bills of indictment had been sent up to a Grand Jury, in the finding of which Mr. Curran was interested. After delay and much hesitation, one of the Grand Jurors came into court to explain to the Judge the grounds and reasons why it was ignored. Mr. Curran, very much vexed by the stupidity of this person, said, "You, Sir, can have no objection to write upon the back of the bill, *ignoramus*, for self and fellow jurors; it will then be a *true* bill."

When the habeas corpus suspension act passed, some time before the year 1798, some person arguing for the propriety and necessity of that law, had thrown out doctrines and opinions unfavourable to the freedom of the constitution; he, whose countenance and doctrines were by no means agreeable to his hearers, was opposed by one of them, who said, "Were you incarcerated for six months under this law you so much éxtol, I should be glad to see how you would *look*." On which Mr. Curran observed, "Perhaps he would not look a *bit the worse*."

A member of the last Irish parliament, who had held one of the highest law offices under the crown, all on a sudden came over to that party who opposed the Union, voted against that measure, and lost his office, not without much regret. Some person speaking of his conduct on this occasion, extolled it highly, and observed, that he had made great sacrifices for his country's good, and had proved himself a sincere patriot. "Sincere! no," said Mr. Curran, "he is a *sorry* patriot."

A learned serjeant, whose promotion to the bench was daily expected, happened to be rather tedious in the statement of a case on trial before one of the chief judges, who, anxious for compression, observed to the serjeant, that when he came to administer justice, he would then know the value of time. A gentleman well known for his humour, and not having much esteem for the judge, in relating the matter, gave quite another turn to it by omitting the word administer; "When you come *to justice* you will *then* know the value of time."

Whenever any barrister is promoted, it is a rule on circuit that he shall send to the bar mess, at least a dozen of claret, to drink his health. A gentleman, not very much distinguished for ability, was recently appointed to one of the county chairs, and his claret was announced in these words: "This is Mr. ——'s health, and may he live long to administer justice, as I am sure he will, *indifferently!*"

A barrister whom Mr. Curran very much esteemed for many amiable qualities, among others, for a fine temper and good nature, dining with him, was asked to be helped to green gooseberries and cream; he said he liked them very much, but feared, if he ate of them, he might be called, as Dr. Goldsmith was, a *gooseberry fool.* Mr. Curran said, "Take the gooseberries, my friend, and the milk of human kindness which so abundantly flows round your heart, will soon make a *fool* of them."

During Lord Westmoreland's administration, when a number of new corps were raised in Ireland (and given as jobs and political favours,) it was observed that when inspected there, the establishment of each regiment was nominally reported to be complete at embarkation for England, but when landed at the other side, many of them had not a quarter of their numbers. "No wonder," said Mr. Curran, "for after being *mustered*, they are afraid of being *peppered*, and off they fly, not wishing to pay for the *roast*."

Mr. Joseph Atkinson and Mr. Curran went on a visit to Scotland, where they passed a day with the family of Lord Boyle: Lady Charlotte Boyle, the sister of Lord Hopetown, asked Mr. Curran what he thought of Edinburgh? "I think, Madam," said he, "speaking of the Ancient and New Town, it is like an old gentleman married to a blooming young bride; he venerably loves and protects her, whilst she graces his side by her beauty and elegant attractions."

A person observing how many new houses were erecting in Dublin, said, "*What will they all end in?*" Mr. Curran replied, "they must end in *smoke.*"

On Mr. Curran's visit into Scotland, he heard that the priest of the temple of Hymen at Gretna Green no longer forged the chains of wedlock; that he was not now a *blacksmith*, but a tobacconist. Mr. Curran said, "*So much the better, for he will make the happy couple give* quid *for* quo."

Mr. Egan the lawyer, when chairman of Kilmainham, had entertained expectations that he would be thence promoted to a seat on the bench; he was perceived by Mr. Curran to have paid great attention to some beautiful woman; and his principles not being exactly of the *Joseph* character, he was jocosely charged by Mr. Curran as to the motives. Egan, fearing that his immorality might become an impediment to his advancement, Lord Manners being at the head of the law department, said, "I am free to confess I am not restrained by *morals*, but by *Manners*." "You should rather have said," observed Mr. Curran, "that your *bad* manners are restrained by his *good* morals."

Of some attorney, whose character for litigation fame dealt severely with, Mr. Curran observed, that every one's hand was raised against him, and his against every one. And he thought him like a rat which had got under the chairs, where every one made a blow at him, but no one could hit him.

Some time after the Union, Mr. Curran was walking by the Parliament House with a certain member, a friend of his, who had supported that measure; this gentleman observed that he never passed that house without the deepest melancholy and regret. "I do not wonder at it," said Mr. Curran, "I never knew a man who had committed murder, who was not haunted by the ghost of the murdered whenever he came to the spot at which the foul deed was done."

In Ireland they have a good-natured, familiar, open manner of friendly intercourse, which enters frequently into the most serious and solemn affairs. A gentleman of the age of thirty, about four feet high, and quite a boy in appearance, for want of accommodation in a very crowded court, in the county of Kerry, got into the jury-box. He was very much beloved, and being too low to peep over the box, perched himself on the brawny shoulders of one of the jurors. In the progress of the trial it was observed, that there were thirteen persons in the box. This created some confusion, and it was objected, that it would be a ground to set aside the verdict. Mr. Curran said that, considering the difficulty of the question, the jurors were right in putting as many heads together as they could ; but be that as it may, the verdict would not be endangered, for it would be secured by the maxim of the law, which says, "*de minimis non curat lex.*"

Of some learned serjeant, who had given a confused, elaborate, and tedious explanation of some point of law, he observed, that whenever that grave counsellor endeavoured to unfold a principle of law he put him in mind of a fool whom he once saw struggling for a whole day to open an oyster with a rolling pin.

He said of a busy, bustling, garrulous lawyer, that he always thought him like a counsellor in a play, where all was stage-trick, bustle, or scene-shifting.

In cross-examining an old clergyman whose evasions of truth were disgraceful to him, Mr. Curran closed with this question, "Doctor, when you last put your spectacles in the Bible, give me leave to ask you, did you close it on that passage which says '*Thou shalt not bear false witness against thy neighbour?*' "

He told an anecdote of an Irish tenant in Kerry, who came to pay his rent of £500, and the lady of the house perceiving he had a propensity to play, she being very ugly, of a musty, dingy countenance, with a bad squint, and who never looked straightly at any object but a pack of cards, or the money set on the game, she prevailed on him, however, to play, till he had lost all his money, and she still continued to encourage him, relying on his honour now that his money was lost. At length, fixing his eyes fiercely on her, he excused himself, declaring in a decided tone, that he would play no more with her ladyship, for that she had the devils' *look* [luck] and her *own.*

Such was the effect of Mr. Curran's pleasantry, that even on ordinary occasions, servants in attending on the table often became suspended, like the bucket in the well, and frequently started as if from a reverie, when called upon for the ordinary attendance. Sometimes a wine glass could not be had, or if asked for, a knife or fork was presented in its place; their faces turned away, you heard nothing but the breaks of a suppressed laughter. He had a favourite black servant who lived with him for many years, and to whom, for his great fidelity, Mr. Curran was very much attached. This poor fellow was observed for a few days before his departure, to have been oppressed with gloom and sadness, the cause of which was not directly enquired into. One morning, whilst in this state, he came up anxiously to his master, and with apparent regret and an air of much dejection requested to be discharged. Mr. Curran told him he was very much concerned to lose the services of so faithful a person, that he had a strong regard for him; and on enquiring into the reason of his desire to leave him, the black replied, "it is impossible for me to remain longer with you, massa." "Why, my good fellow, we will see all care taken of you." "No massa, I cannot live longer with you, I am losing my health with you, you make me laugh too much."

A brother barrister of his, remarkable for having a perpetuity in dirty shirts, was drily asked in the presence of Mr. Curran, "Pray, my dear Bob, how do you get so many dirty shirts?" Mr. Curran replied for him, "I can easily account for it; his laundress lives at Holyhead, and there are nine packets always due." This gentleman wishing to travel to Cork during the rebellion, but apprehensive he should be known by the rebels, was advised to proceed *incog.*, which he said was easily effected, for by disguising himself in a clean shirt, no one would know him.

Of the same gentleman, who was a sordid miser, it was told Mr. Curran that he had set out from Cork to Dublin, with one shirt, and one guinea. "Yes," said Mr. Curran, "and I will answer for it, he will change neither of them till he returns."

Going to dine in the country with the late Judge Fletcher, he had arrived early enough to take a walk in the garden; Mr. Fletcher's country seat is separated from a public road by a stone wall, which having fallen in during a severe winter, the gardens were thereby left open to the dust of the road: it was now the month of April, and Mr. Fletcher was observing on the rows of brocoli, which he said were very backward, and scarcely to be seen, though they had been carefully *drilled.* On which Mr. Curran observed, "It is very true, but consider, they have been much exposed to the dust, and look as if they had been after a *long march.*" This sally it is said to have cost the judge more than he calculated upon, as he immediately raised the wall six feet higher.

Lord Avonmore supported the measure of the Union, it is supposed, as the result of his judgement; Mr. Curran opposed it. It was said, in gratitude for this, the lord obtained from the crown an office of considerable emolument.* When the draught of the patent was sent to him for his approbation, he called into his study a few of his friends, among the rest, Mr. Curran, to see if all was right. The wording ran in the usual form; "To all to whom these letters patent shall come, greeting, &c &c. we of the *united* kingdom of Great Britain and *Ireland*, king, &c. &c.;" Mr. Curran, when the reader came to this part, exclaimed, "Stop Stop!" "My God!" said Lord Avonmore impatiently, "why stop?" "Why? because," said Mr. Curran, "it sets out the *consideration* too early in the deed."

Mr. Curran made occasional visits into France, where he met with many of those most celebrated for genius and letters; among others he became acquainted with the Abbé Sicard, and returned him thanks in the name of human nature for the good he had done to mankind. He was also well known to Madame De Staël, and his account of her accords with what has long before been known to the public. He conversed with her, and though her face was by no means prepossessing, he describes her as having the power of *talking herself into a beauty.*

A barrister entered one of the Four Courts, Dublin, with his wig so much awry as to cause a general titter. Seeing Curran smile, he said, "Do you see any thing ridiculous in my wig?" "No," replied Curran, "nothing but the head."

* At the Union, Lord Avonmore (who voted for it), was elevated in the peerage from the rank of Baron to that of Viscount, and received a patent (probably the document above named) appointing him Principal Registrar of the Irish Court of Chancery, with a salary of 4199*l.* and succession to his son, by whom it is received to this hour. By this Lord Avonmore was Chief Baron of the Exchequer and a clerk in the Chancellor's Court. It is curious to find his lordship so invariably praised, by Irish writers, for his *patriotism.* As plain Barry Yelverton, briefless (and nearly shirtless) he was a "patriot," for many years,—as a judge, peer, and unionist what was he?—M.

A lawyer, a friend of Mr. Curran, who had devoted much more of his time to the study of Hoyle than of Hale, a notable gambler, but a person of eccentric and lively turn of mind, got entangled with Mr. Curran one day after dinner, and losing a little ground on the score of temper, sharply observed, that he had too much spirit to allow any person to go too far with him, and passionately added, "No man shall trifle with me with impunity;" to which Mr. Curran replied, "*Play* with you, Roderick, you mean."

Mr. Curran one day riding by the country seat of one of the judges, was struck by a group of lovely children whom he perceived playing in the avenue ; he stopped to inquire to whom all these fine children belonged ; he was answered by the nurse, who had a beautiful infant in her arms, that they were the children of Judge ———. "Pray, my good woman, how many of them has he?" "There are twelve playing about inside, and this in my arms is the thirteenth." "Then," said Mr. Curran, "the judge has a full jury, and may proceed to trial whenever he chooses, and the young one will make an excellent *crier*."

Mr. Egan, the lawyer, was a person of very large stature and of great thews and sinews : on going into a bath, he exultingly struck his breast, all over matted with hair, and exclaimed, "Curran, did you ever see so fine a *chest*?" "*Trunk*, you mean," said Mr. Curran.

Egan, in addressing a jury, having exhausted every ordinary epithet of abuse, he stopped for a word, and then added, "this *naufrageous* ruffian." When afterwards asked by his friends the meaning of the word, he confessed he did not know, but said "he thought it sounded well.'

Mr. Curran happening to cross-examine one of those persons known in Ireland by the insignificant description of half gentlemen, found it necessary to ask a question as to his knowledge of the Irish tongue, which though perfectly familiar to him, the witness affected not to understand, whilst he, at the same time, spoke extremely bad English : "I see, sir, how it is, you are more ashamed of knowing your own language, than of not knowing any other."

A lady having shewed him her fan, with the map of *England* upon it, he said, "Madam, it should be the *map of the world*, for it puts all our hearts in a flutter like yourself."

A gentleman who was too desirous of attracting the attention of those about him to the style and fashion of his dress, and one time, to the shape of a pair of half boots, which he had that day drawn on, appealed to Mr. Curran, among others, for his opinion, who said, "He observed but one fault,—they shewed too much of the *calf.*"

A gentleman, whose father had been a wealthy and respectable shoemaker of the city of Dublin, and who had indulged many persons with credit, had lately died, and left, with other property, his account books to his son, who was a person of great vivacity and good humour; an old debtor of the father, in bandying wit with the son, annoyed him with the piquancy of his raillery, the son observed, that he was paying off in an odd coin, demanded payment of the debt, and said, if it was further delayed, he would ***sue*** him: the other asked in what capacity would he *sue?* "As *sole executor*," said Mr. Curran.

Mr. Curran made frequent excursions to England, "*to distract*," as he said, and there he enjoyed the society of many friends, Lords Moira, Carleton, and a long catalogue of persons eminent for rank and talents. Burke and Sheridan, though known to him, he appears never to have set so high a value upon as other men did. Of Burke, he used to say, that "his mind was like an over-decorated chapel, filled with gauds and shews, and badly assorted ornaments." Of Dr. Johnson, that "he was a superstitious and brutish bigot, and that, with the exception of his Dictionary, he had done more injury to the English language than even Gibbon himself."

Of John Horne Tooke he thought in the words of Mr. Grattan, that no man was to be found of more acuteness, or of more undaunted resolution. "Methinks," said Mr. Grattan, "if Mr. John Horne Tooke purposed to drink his glass of wine, and that the bolts of heaven had rent asunder the earth beneath his feet, Mr. J. H. Tooke would still drink his glass of wine." Mr. Tooke, in once asking a countryman of Mr. Curran's, what opinion the Irish entertained of his wit compared with that of Mr. Sheridan; on being answered, that his own countrymen conceived no other man living possessed it in equal brilliancy, richness, and variety, the philosopher of England observed, "I know both these gentlemen, and I know them well, both in public and in private; Sheridan is laboured and polished, you always see the marks of the chisel and hatchet about him; Curran is a rich and glittering ore, which is raised from the mine without effort, and in the most exuberant profusion."

It was once observed in Mr. Curran's company, that the late Mr. Fox had no relish for broad humour. "I am not sure," said Mr. Curran, "that Fox disliked humour; sometimes, when the hoyden raillery of my animal spirits has ruffled the plumage of my good manners, when my mirth has turned dancing-master to my veneration, and made it perhaps a little too supple, I have sported playfully in the presence of this slumbering lion, and now and then he condescended to dandle the child. He laughed inwardly. It was not easy to say what Fox would call a *mot*, but when said, I thought I saw a smile rippling over the *fine Atlantic of his countenance*."

Mr. Curran had occasion to hire a servant; and wishing to procure a person of good character and respectable appearance, he requested a friend to look out for such. The friend was a wag, and had very lately dismissed his own servant, who happened to be the reverse of what Mr. Curran wished for. The friend had two objects to gratify; one to amuse himself with Mr. Curran, the other, to humble the presumptuous expectations of an arrogant, dishonest, and conceited fellow, whom, on account of his vanity, &c., he had discharged. The candidate was shown up one morning to Mr. Curran; his appearance was much in his favour. He was dressed in the best fashion of a Bond-street beau. Mr. Curran was for a moment under a mistake; observing him unfolding some papers, and conceiving him to be no less than some gallant defendant in a *crim. con.* action, and that he came to retain him, he requested him to take a chair, and asked him if he had had breakfast. The other answered by producing his discharges. Mr. Curran perceiving his error, proceeded to business; and asked him, after the production of his credentials, "what wages he would expect?" to which he answered, "My last wages at Sir Thomas ——— were 100*l*. a year, and two suits of coloured clothes." Mr. Curran inwardly started, and observed, "You, sir, to be sure, are highly noticed by those with whom you have lived; and, from your appearance, and the strong recommendations you have got, even the value you set upon yourself cannot be considered too high; and, if all other matters could be understood, possibly no difference may arise on this head: but, as my occasions demand particular and punctilious attention to hours, I would be glad to know what time you would wish to devote to yourself." "Why, sir, from one to five o'clock, as I generally ride out each day." "But if you get these hours, would you be quite exact in your return?" "Certainly, sir." "What do you generally drink after dinner?" "Why, sir, my last allowance was one bottle of wine a day." "Are you quite certain that a moderate portion of wine would have no injurious effect?" "Oh! certainly not, sir," with a smile. "Pray, sir, am I to understand you, that you keep your own horses, or am I to keep them for you?" "Why, sir, out of such small wages, it would be quite impossible that I could keep my own horses." "Well, sir," said Mr. Curran, "I think I now pretty well understand you: let me see, between wine, wages, clothes, horses, keeping, &c. &c., your service may stand me about 350*l.* a year." "Why, something thereabout, sir." Wearied with this creature's impudent, arrogant expectations, he ended, by saying, "My good friend, there remains but one point of difference between us, which you may easily adjust; it entirely rests with you: suppose we were to change sides; for on these terms, I assure you, I should anxiously desire to become your very *humble servant!*"

There were two gentlemen of the Irish bar, one a northern, the other a southern: they were tall as poplars: of them he said, "One is the north pole, the other the south pole." One of them being seen in London walking with Mr. Curran, some person asked him who that extraordinary man was, that so much resembled Lismahago, and what was his business to London? Mr. Curran replied, "that though he was one of his *longest* acquaintance, yet he did not precisely know what his business to London was, except, perhaps, to peep down the chimneys of the Londoners, to see what they had for dinner." One of those gentlemen had, by the length of his legs, so annoyed an English lady who sat opposite to him in a public coach, that, when he proposed to some of the company to take a walk for a short stage, on his going out he observed, "I think it will be of great use to me to *stretch* my legs." "Good God! (the lady remarked,) sir, if you do, there will be no enduring you, they are so long already."

Mr. Mahaffy, (who long presided in the Admirality Court, as deputy for Sir Jonah Barrington, the Judge) a very tall gentleman, was retained by Archdeacon Verscoyle in a cause which was instituted to try his right to a certain church. In one of the stages of the trial, the Archdeacon despondingly asked Mr. Curran (who was of counsel for him,) his opinion as to the event of the suit. Mr. Curran gave him every hope; and, pointing to Mr. Mahaffy, observed, "My dear Archdeacon, as you have *retained* the spire, the church can be in no danger."

Of some person who voted for the Union, and owed his elevation to his vote, he observed, "that he was the foulest bird that ever perched upon the ruins of a broken constitution."

From one of those Greek isles recently reillumed by the vigorous and fascinating poetry of the most original writer of this century, a beautiful Smyrnese lady, perhaps sister to the Bride of Abydos, lately arrived in Dublin. To the repose and softness of her eye, the finely turned oval of her face, there were added a languishment of air, and a richness of dress, peculiar to those delicious climates, from which time has not despoiled them of every thing by despoiling them of freedom. Such were her charms, that she was followed in the public assemblies and in the streets, by crowds of admirers. Walking in one of the squares, she was perceived by a friend of Mr. Curran, who instantly exclaimed, "Oh! there is the beautiful woman from Smyrna, I must leave you for a moment to see her." Shortly after returning, he found Mr. Curran, who said, "Well my friend, what say you, *Quid tibi visa Chios, quid Smyrna?*"

He was engaged on behalf of a plain tradesman, a citizen of Dublin. who had been ill-treated, where insult was added to injury, and where the man was horse-whipped, beaten down, and falsely imprisoned. He complained through Mr. Curran to a court of justice, and a jury listened to his tale of woe and of sufferings, which wanted not the colouring of imagination; it was most affectingly told by his counsel: he used no ornaments to dress out the victim which had already suffered so much. His appeals were deeply affecting, because natural. He gave up to the jury the case of an innocent and oppressed man in terms which were directed to the heart,—the jury and the audience were touched: but the client, who heard all, was so overwhelmed that he burst forth from a silence he had before been noticed for, into a sudden exclamation, accompanied with tears: "Oh! my Lord, all the counsellor has told you is every word of it true, but till this moment I never knew I had been half so cruelly ill-treated."

A hot fool, plunged into distress, was playing at billiards, and having wagered his only guinea on the success of the game, became tremulously anxious on the last stroke of the ball; perceiving the clock giving notice to strike *one*, as he hoped, and fearing some distraction, he paused for a moment; another and another succeeded, till the clock went insensibly on to twelve. Thus suspended, his irritation increased, he played and lost, and in his rage seizing the ball, drove it at the clock with such fury and force that he broke it in pieces: the owner sought compensation and obtained it. This being related in the presence of Mr. Curran, he observed "That the damage should be very small as the *clock struck first.*"

An Englishman, visiting Dublin for the first, sat next Mr. Grattan at a civic feast, and found him as dull—as the place and occasion required. He was much disappointed; and seeking an occasion to meet Mr. Curran a few days after at dinner, not apprised of the unbroken intimacy and friendship which politically and privately ever subsisted between those gentlemen, indiscreetly observed, that Mr. Grattan, appeared to possess nothing striking in conversation, and to have exhibited nothing of those extraordinary powers for which he was so celebrated. Mr. Curran started, and replied, "Surely, sir, you cannot expect that the sun will be always found in its meridian: permit me, however, to ask you where you had the good fortune to have met this gentleman." On being answered, at a city feast; "Oh, yes: it is very true: I comprehend it perfectly. *Yet,* take my word for it, my good sir, he is still a sweet bird, *though he never sings but in his own climate.*"

Shortly after the establishment of our colony at Botany Bay, when the population was fast increasing, Mr. Curran in one of his speeches upon a criminal trial, observed, "that should the colony thrive, and become a regular civil government, what a pleasant thing it would be to have the laws administered by judges reprieved at the gallows; by justices who had picked pockets; by counsellors who had pleaded at the bar for their lives; by lawyers who had set the law at defiance; to see house-breakers appointed to protect the public property; highwaymen entrusted with the public money; rioters invested with commissions of the peace, and shop-lifters to regulate the markets. Such, however, said he, were the original people of Rome; and such the foundation of the states of America."

A beautiful young woman of the name of Serjeant, whose father was an officer of a yeomanry corps in Dublin, happened to pass Mr. Curran in the street; struck by her beauty, he inquired of a friend who she was, and being answered, that she was the lovely Miss Serjeant whom he had seen ten years before at Cheltenham—"What, not married yet? then I suppose her father will make her a *permanent* Serjeant."

Mr. Hoare's countenance was grave and solemn, with an expression like one of those statues of the Brutus head: he seldom smiled; and if he smiled, he smiled in such a sort as seemed to have rebuked the spirit that could smile at all. Mr. Curran once observing a beam of joy to enliven his face, remarked, "Whenever I see smiles on Hoare's countenance, I think they are like tin clasps on an oaken coffin."

A gentleman of one of the southern counties in Ireland well known for a certain determination of mind, and unaccommodating strength of resolution, was perceived to be very active on some trial in which Mr. Curran was engaged; it was proposed to refer the case to the arbitration of this gentleman, as he was reputed to be an honest man: on the other side an objection was raised, founded on the known sternness of his character; and it was also remarked, that his *iron* leg was the softest part about him; "Oh, surely," said Mr. Curran, "that must be *irony*."

The printed speech of some young barrister* had been laid before Mr. Curran, and his opinion asked after he had carefully perused it. "Why," said he, "there is much more of flower than figure in it—more of fancy than design: it is like (as I suspect the mind of the author to be) a tree in full blossom—shake it, and you have them on the ground in a minute, and it would take a season to reproduce them."

An eminent member of Parliament, a leader of the opposition, being in the company of Mr. Curran, had heard him copiously and vehemently descant on the numerous grievances under which he represented Ireland to be labouring. This gentleman, became very urgent in his solicitations to get materials for some good speeches from such a source, rather imprudently requested of Mr. Curran to supply him with a list of these grievances, accompanied by such observations and details as he would wish to make upon them. Mr. Curran suspecting that there was full as much of personal interest as of patriotism in the request, declined gratifying it. Some friend asked him, in a few days after, why he did not comply with the earnest desire of the person alluded to. "No," said Mr. Curran, "I have no notion whatever, at my time of life, nor indeed at any, *to turn hodman to any political architect.*"

A barrister of the name of *Going* had, among other pleasantries, a favourite story, which he so agreeably exaggerated every time he told it, that at length it became too monstrous for belief. He was charged with this in presence of Mr. Curran, who observed, that the story was not the worse for being enlarged, that it was an excellent story, and had the merit of proceeding like Fame—"*Nam vires acquirit eundo,*" *i. e.*, "it gathers strength by *going*."

* Charles Phillips, his future biographer.—M.

Speaking of the supineness of Government, while the fire of rebellion was not yet extinguished, but raked over, he observed they were like the silly sea-boy, who thought that during the time he slept, the ship ceased to move.

In Parliament, on the debate of an important question, involving some of the deepest interests of his country; perceiving the House to be very thinly attended, he rose, and after many arguments and observations, he at length demanded in a commanding tone of voice of the Speaker—"Where are the members? have they not been summoned? It seems then," said he, "they are not forthcoming; perhaps at this very moment, they may be found chained in couples in the kennel, or under the management of the ministers' secretary."

Enthusiastically fond of music, he perceived at a rehearsal, one of those Roderigos or foolish gentlemen, who haunt concerts and oratorios, busy and bustling, ordering and disordering everything! vexed with the popinjay, he observed to a friend—"Mark that fellow, he is like the fool who blows the bellows for the organist, and because he does so, he thinks it is himself who performs the instrument."

Speaking of the profession of the law, he compared the hope of success to the gamut of the musicians; he said one should gather his strength and begin with the low notes; and this he illustrated by saying, "It reminded him of a cunning barber, who began his trade by shaving a beggar, in the hope that one day or other he would rise to shave a duchess."

Walking one evening in autumn, in Saint James's Park, accompanied by Mr. Charles Phillips, celebrated equally for his eloquence as for his poetry, there suddenly came on a violent tempest, which rived the gnarled oak, and shook the leaves, and strewed them over the walks, as thick as those in Vallombroso, which Mr. Curran remarking, said, "My dear friend, observe here; we are desired by philosophy to take lessons from Nature; yet how foolishly does she seem to act on the present occasion; she flings away her blessings and her decorations; she is at this moment very busy in stripping those defenceless trees, at the approach of winter and of cold, at that very season when they most want covering."

THE END.

INDEX.

www.ingramcontent.com/pod-product-compliance
Lightning Source LLC
LaVergne TN
LVHW021257110826
845150LV00003B/415